LIVING WITH REALITY

Also by Beth Maynard Green

Books
God's Little Aphorisms
Memoirs of the New Age: A Book of Stories, Prayers & Fables
Sacred Union: The Healing of God
The Autobiography of Mary Magdalene

Original Music
A Souls' Journey Through Darkness and Light
In the Mist
The Gift of Peace

Founder
The Stream spiritual community and nonprofit educational corporation
www.thestream.org

The Spiritual Activist Movement
www.spiritualactivism.org

Co-Founder
Center for Healing & Higher Consciousness
www.healingandhigherconsciousness.com

Reality for a Change
Transformative Processes for Business
www.realityforachange.net

Programs & Services
Consciousness Boot Camp
www.consciousnessbootcamp.org

LifeForce: The Inner Workout
www.lifeforceworkout.com

Workshops on Sex & Spirituality and Other Topics
Psycho-Intuitive Counseling, Consulting & Training

Other Places to Read Beth's Writings
Beth's blogs and articles also appear in many venues, including:
The Huffington Post
*Science and Spirituality—A Conversation Between Twenty-eight Leading
Scientists and Renowned Spiritual Leaders,* edited by Profs. Ervin Laszlo and
Kingsley Dennis

LIVING WITH REALITY

WHO WE ARE, WHAT WE COULD BE, HOW WE GET THERE

BETH MAYNARD GREEN

iUniverse, Inc.
Bloomington

Living with Reality
Who We Are, What We Could Be, How We Get There

iUniverse books may be ordered through booksellers or by contacting:

iUniverse
1663 Liberty Drive
Bloomington, IN 47403
www.iuniverse.com
1-800-Authors (1-800-288-4677)

Because of the dynamic nature of the Internet, any web addresses or links contained in this book may have changed since publication and may no longer be valid. The views expressed in this work are solely those of the author and do not necessarily reflect the views of the publisher, and the publisher hereby disclaims any responsibility for them.

Any people depicted in stock imagery provided by Thinkstock are models, and such images are being used for illustrative purposes only.
Certain stock imagery © Thinkstock.

ISBN: 978-1-4502-5654-4 (sc)
ISBN: 978-1-4502-5655-1 (hc)
ISBN: 978-1-4502-5656-8 (ebk)

Library of Congress Control Number: 2011918454

Printed in the United States of America

iUniverse rev. date: 10/31/2011

CONTENTS

PREFACE

Who We Are & What We Could Be

Life is a struggle. Insects, animals, vegetables, microbes all struggle to survive, and so do we. In such a world, fear and pain are inevitable; injury, old age, and death are universal; loss and insecurity are the lot of every species that has the capacity to feel. This is reality. Can we change it? Yes and no. The fundamentals of existence are what they are. We may not like it, but it is so. But what we can change is the consciousness we bring to the daily struggle. We can either continue to experience needless pain, or we can co-create the world we all want.

As children, many of us dreamed of a better world. We were acutely aware of needless pain. We observed that while some wasted food, others went hungry. We witnessed individuals striking out at one another, each overwhelmed by his or her feelings of despair and helplessness and often unconscious of the pain they caused. We saw people lost in depression or compulsive eating, gambling, alcohol, drugs, ambition or rage. We were shocked by unfairness, violence and domination. We felt cheated when others got more than we, but we felt uncomfortable when we were given more than others. We were horrified by war. Over time, we saw ourselves becoming angry and rebellious, or passive and weak. We felt self-conscious and confused. If we are honest, we saw ourselves developing the kinds of negative behaviors we disliked in others.

As children, we asked, "Why do people do these things?" As adults, we ask, "Why do I?" As children, we dreamed of a better world. For many of us adults, the dream has died.

I have never stopped dreaming, and I have never stopped wondering why. And I have never stopped trying to find a way to help. Until my mid-thirties, I was a social activist, trying to make the revolution from the outside. In 1978, I had a spiritual awakening and realized that our fundamental problem is human consciousness and that we will never transform our world unless we confront ourselves honestly and find a way to change.

In 2002, I was scheduled for a speaking engagement where I was to talk about a multi-addiction recovery program that I had designed for The Stream, a nonprofit spiritual organization I founded in 1983.[1] The night before the talk, I woke up at about 2 a.m., and literally out of "nowhere," I heard these words: "Beth, get a piece of paper and write this down." I grabbed a pen and an envelope, and these were the words I wrote: Living with Reality: Five Platforms for Becoming Ourselves. Then I wrote: Becoming Oneness, Becoming Co-Creative, Becoming Mutually Supportive, Becoming Accountable, Becoming Becoming.

I had no idea what I had just done or why. But the next day, when I went to speak, I did not talk about the multi-addiction recovery program The Stream had been practicing for years. Instead I spoke about Living with Reality and the five platforms for becoming ourselves. Within days, I was guided to expand the five platforms to nine, including Becoming Differentiated, Self-Aware, Integrated and Not-Knowing, and soon after, I was off and running, writing this book.

It has taken nine more years to complete the writing of *Living with Reality*, because it has taken that long to develop the living practice of these platforms, including the tools and techniques that transform us. Theory is not enough. We need to know that these principles work, and they do. Our Stream community lives by these practices and teaches them to others. We are not perfect, but we are conscious, accountable and growing. And, yes, we are all much happier.

Because I have seen real and permanent results from using this program, I feel confident to offer it to you through *Living with Reality*. If we live the platforms in this book, if we practice the tools, techniques and perspectives offered here, we will change our lives and our world. While not a replacement for all other teachings, programs and practices, *Living with Reality* is a fundamental manual for living, the manual that was unavailable to us when we were born, and it is a stepping stone to the

---

[1]   For more information about The Stream, see Appendix.

new era we all crave, a time when all being lives from a place of Oneness, accountability and mutual support.

God[2] is dreaming. And I think God is dreaming a better world for us. Let's dream, too. But let's not only dream; let's take action. Let's learn to live with reality in a state of consciousness and grace.

---

[2]   You do not need to believe in "God" to benefit from this book, but it helps if you can connect to the reality of higher dimensions of consciousness. There are many different names for this: God, The Source, higher consciousness, divine intelligence, the Great Spirit, Oneness consciousness, a higher power. Use whatever name works for you. I alternate names depending on the context and the aspect of the universal intelligence I am referencing.

ACKNOWLEDGEMENTS

It is difficult to acknowledge all those who have helped me with this book. First, there is The Stream, my spiritual community. While the overall contents of the book came from my inner guidance, the tools, techniques and practices were developed in response to the needs of Stream members, who called upon me to explain and sketch out broad concepts and ideas. Thanks to them, what I thought was going to be a short work turned into a detailed textbook for developing higher consciousness. In addition, many of the tools magically emerged during workshops with Streamers and other participants, and all this material became incorporated into the ever-expanding manuscript. Perhaps most importantly, my faith in the practices described in this book comes from observing myself and fellow community members bringing these ideas to life. Streamers have studied and applied these teaching over a period of years and have given me encouragement and feedback all the way through. So, to my friends and fellow Streamers, I say "Thank you."

Regarding copyediting, I realize that there are still many gaps. I received copyediting and proof reading support from Christine Benton, Helen Chang, Linda Stewart and Ann Brennan. But having been written over a period of 9 years and having been produced on many different computers using different versions of computer programs, the completed manuscript was extremely inconsistent, and trying to fix all those inconsistencies has proved rather daunting. So while the above-named heroes tried to impose some order on the chaos, I have not been able to bring this manuscript to the level of editing and consistency I would have liked. I am, however, satisfied with the contents—or rather, as satisfied as I can be, realizing that there is always a better way to say something. Rewriting and revising a book of this length is quite a project; yet I rewrote and revised it many times. And while I know it could be improved much more, it doesn't feel right to do so. Amazingly, fixing spacing and formatting issues has been an even tougher job, due to computer idiosyncrasies, and Ann and Christine worked numerous hours to correct these. Many are still there, and I'm sure there are occasional proofreading errors as well. Now I have to make a choice: Try to perfect the book, or accept its imperfections and hope that it helps people. My choice is to release the work in a flawed state in the hopes that it can be useful, rather than perfect. How incredibly appropriate, since the theme of this book is living with reality!

On a personal note, I would also like to acknowledge Christopher Minor, who was a tremendous support in the early days when the first chapters were emerging. He read every word and cheered me on. Christine Benton took on that role later in the project, reading the pages that were flying out at 2 AM. And now I have the support of James Maynard Green, as well, who has been helping me with the love that makes everything better, especially the pain of sore muscles, strained eyes, exhaustion and the feeling that the project would never come to completion.

Finally, and ultimately, I want to acknowledge higher consciousness for allowing me to be a channel for wisdom I don't have and clarity I can't muster, in order for me to support people I may never meet. In some ways, writing this book was blood, sweat and tears, to use a cliché. In others ways, the book wrote itself. In fact, at an earlier house where I was working on this manuscript, a statue of the Buddha sat in my fireplace, and I was reassured by that calm presence. It helped me become increasingly neutral about myself and human nature and emboldened me to say what many did not want to hear. If there is any wisdom in this book, I attribute it to the wisdom of Buddha, God and other sources of higher consciousness who have cut through our self-deception and helped alleviate needless suffering on this planet. Thank you.

INTRODUCTION

Ego, Instinct & Evolution: Are We Ready to Change?

If suffering were sufficient motivation for change, humanity would have transformed a long time ago.

Have you ever found yourself compelled to behave in a way that you knew would hurt yourself or others, but you just couldn't stop yourself? Eaten the wrong thing? Married or slept with the wrong person? Said something that you knew would be shaming and/or counterproductive? Avoided a conversation long overdue? Did you feel baffled by your action at the time? Did you kick yourself later? Or did you go into denial and blame someone else for the negative outcome?

You and I have created needless pain, and so has everyone else. Sometimes we are the only ones to suffer the consequences; sometimes we hurt a lot of other people along the way. Sometimes our actions are individual, such as buying the widescreen TV when our bank account is empty; sometimes our actions are collective, such as when the auto industry focused on SUVs and gas-guzzling vehicles in the face of global warming. Sometimes we create pain through our actions, such as driving when drunk; sometimes we inflict harm through our words, such as demeaning someone who is already vulnerable.

Many of us are aware that we create needless pain, and we're trying to do something about it. The popularity of personal counseling, twelve-step programs, self-help books, and other healing modalities points to our desire for self-transformation. Through our experience, we have learned a lot about what works. For example, we know we need to:

- Acknowledge that much of our suffering is self-created
- Embrace a positive vision of what is possible
- Utilize tools and techniques that enable us to fulfill that potential
- Support ourselves and one another so that we can accomplish together what we can't face alone

But if we have the tools, motivation, and support, why are we still so often stuck in our old destructive and self-destructive patterns? Why are we still addictive, reactive, and focused on short-term gain, rather than long-term sustainability? Why are we alienated from ourselves, depressed, anxious, and stressed? Why do we continue to overeat? Why do so many women still wear uncomfortable clothes? Why do so many men still drink beer instead of talk about their feelings? Why do we continue to compete rather than cooperate, worry about how we look more than how we feel, demonize one another rather than acknowledge our similarities, and fight reality, rather than learn to relax into the process of living? In other words, why do we all still do stupid things?

And we human beings all do them—one or one hundred destructive and self-destructive behaviors. When we're not in denial of these destructive behaviors, we often busily blame one another for it. When we're not blaming one another, we tend to blame ourselves.

One thing is clear: If so many of us are stuck in the old patterns, the problem cannot be rooted in our individual psyche. It must be rooted in the way we are designed as human beings. For example, if only a few people were compulsive eaters or anorexic, we could assume that those individuals had unusual physiological or emotional characteristics that affected their eating. But we know that is not the case, because millions of people have food disorders. Similarly, if the only addiction we had was food disorders, we could assume that human beings had a particular physiological or emotional tendency to be compulsive about food. But we know that is not the case; we can be and are addicted to many substances. And if our only negative behaviors were related to addictions to substances, we could conclude that human beings have a tendency to become addicted to certain chemicals, such as those found in alcohol, drugs, or food. But we know this is also not the case; we are equally addicted to behaviors, such as gambling, overwork, thrill-seeking, and escapism. We also compulsively shop, worry, self-sabotage, abuse, criticize, and act out sexually.

Individually and collectively, we human beings suffer from the compulsion to behave in ways that often hurt us and others, and these ingrained behaviors are difficult to break. Part of the difficulty, of course, is that we are patterned physiologically—either through genetic inheritance or repetition. But even when we are able to overcome the physiological addiction, we are still patterned psychologically. And when we try to change, we meet our own resistance—the tendency to cling to the same behavior over and over regardless of the negative result. What's worse, we often deny that our actions are causing those negative results, which is evident when talking to couples where each party blames the other for their misery.

We should not shame ourselves about this tendency to stay stuck in destructive behavior. It is clearly a human phenomenon. But we do want to change it. To change, first we have to confront our denial of our dysfunction. Then, once we get past our denial, we have to face our shame. Once we have released our shame, we can commit to transformation.

So the bottom line is: If we could finally admit the sorry state of human consciousness, including our own, we could look into the psyche of humanity in order to understand why we resist self-awareness and positive change, individually as well as collectively, and we could then use our understanding of the human psyche in order to develop strategies to overcome that resistance and really support us to transform.

Living with Reality provides a comprehensive, compassionate, step-by-step roadmap to the human psyche and its reprogramming and transformation. But before opening the map, we need to understand and overcome our resistance to using it. Let's confront that resistance now.

Why Do We Resist Self-Awareness and Change?

First, let's acknowledge our resistance to change. We can use reading this book as an example. Listen to some of the ways people express resistance to this book:

- "Very interesting, but what you're saying doesn't apply to me. What I really wish is that my husband would read it."
- "Don't you think this book is a little negative?"
- "It's too much work."

- "Do you really expect me to look at everything I do, think, and say? What for? I'm not hurting anyone."
- "I've already changed. I don't need to look at myself anymore."
- "Are you asking me to be a saint?"
- "Great book. Of course, I read only the first 20 pages, but I'll get back to it when the kids are in school again, summer vacation is over, my mother has gone home, I've finished my MBA, I've gotten adjusted to my new job . . ."
- "I live in the real world. Nobody in the real world can do what you suggest."

Who says these words? The woman who finds herself helplessly inhaling ice cream, even though she's promised herself to eat healthy, and then diets herself sick in order to fit some image of how she should look. The executive who convinces himself it's normal to drink a cocktail every night to recover from stress; the worker who does the same with a beer. The couple that fights over everything, resents each other, and stays together "for the children." The guy who gambles himself into crime; the girl who lets herself be abused by men. The mom who is dominated by her kids' demands; the father who works overtime to get away from his family. The woman who keeps staring in the mirror dreading wrinkles. People whose lifestyles give them diabetes, strokes, and high blood pressure. The society that has consumed itself into ecological disaster; the societies that still live like cavemen fighting over resources, notwithstanding the fact that our clubs are now cluster bombs and nuclear weapons. In other words, the people who come up with a million excuses are us. And we are the ones who suffer, yet find all kinds of reasons to continue living and thinking in the same old painful ways, always hoping that something outside ourselves will change, so we don't have to change ourselves.

Why do we resist self-awareness and change? Why do we resist the help that could free us from our painful behavior? Throughout this volume, I address specific obstacles to our stepping into different paradigms of existence. But here I would like to address our resistance to help itself, namely:

- We fear we'll discover things about ourselves that cause us to feel shame.
- We fear we'll feel even more shame if we try to change and can't.

- We fear we'll end up alone if we break out, change, and become different from our fellows.
- We are afraid to empower higher wisdom, because it is outside the ego's control.

As I will demonstrate in this chapter, all this resistance stems from one fact: Our destructive patterns were developed to ensure our survival. And so, when these patterns are exposed and challenged, our survival feels threatened. Yes, it's strange but true. We are hurting ourselves because of unconscious, deeply programmed patterns of behavior based on the survival instinct, and yet we are afraid to disturb these patterns because we associate them with our continued existence—even in the face of suffering, even though we are killing ourselves and one another, even though they don't work.

Once we grasp that we are up against our survival instinct, we can have compassion for ourselves and others, and we can start the process of overcoming our resistance. So let's begin by comprehending the link between our fear of change and the survival instinct, and to do so, we need to go back to creation, way back to the beginning of time.

For those of you who like myths, you will enjoy this section. For those who don't relate to myths, please consider the following a metaphor for what occurred, not a description of actual events. This next section may seem abstract or theoretical to some of you, but soon you will see how everything fits together.

The Myth of Creation

In the beginning, there was the Oneness—the amorphous whole, formless and without distinctions. Everything was peaceful, because everything was one. There was no difference between energy and matter or heaven and earth. There were no colors, sounds, hatred, love, events, objects, or forces. There was nothing, because if everything is one, there is no contrast, and when there is no contrast, nothing exists.

Let's see how this works. If everything were the same shade of blue, all we would see is blue. We couldn't see the shapes of the animals, the sky, or the forest, because each would blend into the other. Contrast is essential to all existence. Without up, there's no down. Without left, there's no right. Without life, there's no death.

In perfect Oneness, there's no experience, because there is no one to experience the experience, and there is no experience to be experienced. And there is no suffering, because there is no one to suffer and nothing to be suffered. Sounds great, doesn't it?

Or does it? Pretty dull.

In any case, great or not, the universe changed, and we evolved out of the Oneness. Why and how?

I like to say that The Source did it, and by The Source, I mean the energy behind existence. Some folks think in terms of "God." Others refer to The Great Spirit, the universal consciousness, or some other formulation. For the purposes of this book, it doesn't matter which you prefer.

Back to our story and the reason that the universe evolved from the Oneness: As I mentioned earlier, I like to say The Source did it. One day he[3] decided to explode himself into a myriad of fragments, and from that time until the present, the process of fragmentation has continued to evolve. And why would The Source fragment the Oneness? Because she was bored. She wanted to experience herself as real, but couldn't feel real in the Oneness, because when there is only Oneness, there is no contrast; without conflict, there's no creativity; and without challenge, there's no evolution.

You could say this idea is inconsistent with the rest of our story, because if there were only Oneness, there could have been no Source to be dissatisfied or bored. And you would have a point. We could change the story and avoid the whole question by claiming that evolution itself was programmed into the Oneness; that at some point the Oneness was destined to fragment into distinct parts. But that doesn't work either. If there were nothing but Oneness, who or what programmed the Oneness to evolve? Meaning that we've eliminated one inconsistency, but created another.

So, if you ask me, we should say that The Source did it, because myths are lovely and they aren't logical. And more important, they're not supposed to be logical. They are supposed to make sense not to our minds, but to the knowing that resides deep inside us where our collective memory lies. And for those who can't feel that knowing and who seek proof, think of this as a metaphor for the Big Bang theory, or suspend disbelief, relax and have fun.

---

3   The Source has no gender, of course; so I have chosen to alternate the male and female pronouns to denote it.

Now back to our myth. The Source was bored with the Oneness and wanted to feel himself as real, so he had to create the world. With that in mind she fragmented the Oneness into a myriad of ever-evolving unique manifestations of the whole: insects and stars, particles and waves, thoughts and emotions, rocks, trees, star dust, atoms, quarks, and, yes, humans. Each fragment is a form of consciousness, each form representing one manifestation of the Oneness, each an aspect of the whole. In other words, the Oneness was the whole before the Spiritual Big Bang, and what we see now are the fragments created by that event.

So with the fragmentation of the Oneness, there was a world, and with the world, there was experience. That was the first step of evolution from the amorphous whole.

Pretty heady stuff. But on some level, we all know that we come from the same source, are made of the same stuff and are One. We sense that there once was a time when we felt the peace and comfort of that Oneness, and we long for that Oneness again. We see that longing in action, as we gather together in couples and families; in sororities and fraternities; in religious, political, business, work, sports, and social organizations and movements; as we gather together for spiritual experience.[4]

But though we know that we are One, we don't seem to feel or behave that way. My hangnail hurts me more than your broken leg, because I experience myself as separate, because simultaneously with the creation of the world, the ego was born, and we lost our sense of connection to the whole.

Uh-Oh. Not the Ego!

What is the ego? The ego is the awareness of individual existence, awareness of the separation from Oneness that arises at the same moment that the whole fragments into distinct parts. This even applies to God. The moment the whole fragmented into distinct parts, the moment "God" was differentiated from non-God and the heavens were seen as distinct from the earth, separation was born, and so was the ego, because as soon as something has individual existence, distinct from the whole, it has awareness of that existence, and it has ego. It doesn't matter if the thing is a person, an animal, an "object," a thought or a collective of persons, animals, objects, or thoughts. Everything has ego. Even the ego

---

4   We discuss this concept fully in Part Two, Platform One: Becoming Oneness.

has ego, meaning that the ego is conscious of its own existence separate from everything else. Ego is a natural outcome of evolution. Through the process of creation and fragmentation, everything developed ego, because without awareness of ourselves as individuals, we would be back in the amorphous blob, and there would be no experience and no evolution.

What Does the Ego Have to Do with Instinct?

The ego's job is to ensure the survival of the fragment, and what enables it to do its job are instinct and learning. Instinct is comprised of genetically programmed patterns for survival that are ingrained in us at the moment of existence; learning occurs through observation and experience.

Let's look at some examples. When the baby exits from the womb, it finds itself separated from the Oneness. Without ego, the baby would not feel the need to survive as a separate individual, and it wouldn't eat, or cry or do anything else that is necessary for its survival.

The baby's ego has actually begun developing even before birth. We see it instinctively struggling for its separate existence as it fights its way out of the womb, oblivious to the mother's health or the doctor's schedule. It has one drive: to take care of "me," be born and survive. Once out of the womb, the reality of separation becomes even more apparent to the infant, and its need to fight for its life grows accordingly. Now it has to fight for air and food because its needs are no longer provided for, and so it does just that: fight for its needs. Aware that it is now separate from the womb, the ego knows how to fight for those needs because it has been programmed with the instinct to cry and suck.

Without some level of awareness of separateness, there would be no drive to exist, and without survival instincts, we wouldn't cry. Similarly, every aspect of the Oneness—every thought, being, and object—fights for its survival. Anything that has no instinct for survival dies without reproducing and so does not continue to exist in our world. This is natural. It's the way we were designed.

But does this natural pattern work optimally? The infant is, in fact, not separate. It is born into a family, a community, a world. It is an individual, but it is dependent on its parents, siblings, and caretakers who also have needs. These are the needs of the whole. If the mother is exhausted by the baby's continual demands, she could weaken and die. If the siblings are ignored by the exhausted mother, they could become even more demanding and pull away the mom's attention, which could undermine the infant's care. If the father is rejected by the mom because she's focused on the child, he might get angry and abandon the family or harm the child in rage.

We can see that even in the case of an infant, the fact that the ego focuses on its own narrow needs actually jeopardizes its own existence. In reality, the survival of the infant is dependent not only on its own wellbeing, but the wellbeing of all around it, the highest good of all. Mom has to be well enough to care for it, but, of course, the infant does not have the ability to integrate this information and act accordingly. Driven by its own ego-need for survival and using its instinctive mechanisms, the baby cries and demands, unaware of the negative impact it is already having on the world around it, the negative impact it is already having on the whole, including itself.[5] Dominated by ego and instinct, the infant has no sense of the Oneness from which it came. Just born, it has already forgotten that we are One. Of course this is not the baby's fault; what it is doing is natural. It just isn't most effective.

Programs Based on Genes and Experience

Once the human infant is born, it fights for its life and survives, and it does so because it has ego. If it doesn't fight for its life, it dies. In the infant, the fight for survival seems pretty straightforward. It cries, breathes, eats, and eliminates. All of this is instinctive. But there's more to survival than those four skills, and this becomes the ego's challenge. How can the ego ensure our survival, given our genetic programming and our environment?

We begin, of course, with our genetic programming. Some of us are born with more aggressive natures than others; some are born with chemical imbalances that impede learning; some have weak bodies; some have great intelligence; and so on. Given our genetic programming, however, the ego needs to discover how to capitalize upon our strengths and weaknesses in order to ensure our existence, and the way to best capitalize on these characteristics depends on our environment. What will best work for us under the circumstances in which we live? How well the ego succeeds in manipulating our particular environment determines whether or not we survive and how

---

5   There is a full discussion of the concept of the highest good of all in Platform Four: Becoming Mutually Supportive.

well we're cared for.[6] The successful strategies become internalized to such a degree that we begin to think the survival strategies are us.

Let's go back to the infant. After a while, the mother may get fed up and want to rest, but the baby is hungry. If the baby has a truly aggressive nature, it'll cry its brains out until the guilt-ridden mom drags herself out of bed and feeds it. If she continues to respond to the baby's assertiveness, the child is well on its way to becoming demanding.

Suppose the baby learns that its mother doesn't respond to assertiveness. Maybe crying makes her angry, but "good baby" flatters her ego. As soon as the baby discovers that gurgling and smiling works better than crying and demanding, and as soon as it's capable of that much self-control, the child is on its way to becoming "good." Still asserting its needs, the baby's assertiveness is now cloaked by acting "nice."

Some babies discover that no matter what they do, nothing works. Mom will come when she comes. Now the baby is on its way to becoming passive. If the baby is fundamentally assertive in nature, it may be seething with resentment. If the baby is genetically predisposed to being unassertive, it can become disempowered and depressed.

The baby's programming is being affected by the interaction between its genetic predisposition and the environment in which it lives. Of course, a million factors actually impact that programming. We may discover early on that Mom resents Dad, so rejecting Dad is a smart way to go. Or we realize that Mom will never care about us as much as she does the first-born son, so we scramble for someone else to be our ally—Dad, Grandma, the nanny, or an older sibling. Or we learn that Mom feels responsible for our weaknesses, so we develop ways to turn weakness to our advantage by feeding her guilt through always looking helpless. Always "thinking," learning, and experimenting, we are becoming a series of programmed responses.

But underneath all of these responses are our egos, instinctively attempting to ensure our survival, leading us to develop the strategies that

---

6   There are some unfortunate folks whose genetic programming is very strong (people who are extremely disabled physically or mentally, for example) and/or whose parents aren't programmed to care for them or don't have the resources. If these people are unable to manipulate the people around them to care for them, they will be dumped onto the streets or into institutions, if available, or they don't survive at all.

will be with us all our lives. Of course, the smart ego is always aware of the other egos around it, but its awareness is not focused on the wellbeing of others. On the contrary, it evaluates those other egos primarily in terms of how they factor into *our* scenario; for example, how "we" can get what "we" want out of "them" in the face of the realities we confront.

I am not suggesting that children have no compassion. Of course, they do. They still have ties to the Oneness, which reveals itself in the sweetest ways. But fundamentally driven by the sense of separation and the instinct to perpetuate themselves as discrete beings, children learn what we adults have already internalized: We have to fight for our survival, either directly or through manipulation, and experience will show us how.

Why Self-Awareness Can Seem Like a Threat to Our Survival

From this brief discussion, we already understand that confronting our primary patterns of behavior threatens us on a deep level. Our egos have learned how to keep us alive through developing patterns that work in the moment, and even though these patterns ultimately turn out to be destructive and self-destructive, their genesis is so early on and so deeply instinctive, questioning them feels like a threat to our very survival. And because these patterns are developed at such a young age, before we are capable of higher levels of consciousness, they are very infantile or childish.

Let me give an example. Suppose we have an alcoholic man who is drinking himself to death. He knows it. His family knows it. His boss knows it. Why doesn't he stop? Let's say he drinks for two reasons: one is that he has a genetic tendency; the other is that he uses alcohol to suppress his feelings. Why does he continue to suppress his feelings with alcohol, even though it's killing him? How can this possibly be an example of his ego promoting his survival?

If we dig deeply enough, we discover that our guy's father was a raging alcoholic and his mother was depressed. Let's say he realized from birth that Dad was never going to take care of him and that he would have to rely completely on Mom. But we know that a depressed mom doesn't want to take care of anyone. As a child, how was our guy going to get someone to meet his needs? If he's not genetically geared to be aggressive and to care for himself, he had to get someone else to do it. Through trial and error, he discovered that Mom responded well to attention and that she was most likely to care for him if he listened to her, comforted her, sided with her, and acted as her confidante. He was now gearing himself to be a satellite to the mom who focuses on herself. If his ego gave him the survival strategy of making Mom feel good about herself so that she would care for him, he would have learned to suppress his feelings, consciously or unconsciously blocking himself from telling her he's angry that she's staying with Dad, or that she's passive, or neglectful, or bitchy.

If this son's ego has given him the strategy of protecting Mom's image of herself as a great mom, he can't even tell her that the kid next door is beating him up in the schoolyard because if he did, she might feel she's a bad mother who is somehow not protecting him. Depending on Mom's attitude, he may not even be able to express that he is angry at the abusive Dad, because if he expressed his anger, he might be forcing her to choose between her husband and her son. If she's afraid to face life alone, she'll feel that her survival would be threatened by leaving Dad, but staying with him makes her a bad mother. So the son decides it's better not to bring it up.

Remember, the child's ego has trained him to maintain his mother's self-image so that she will feel good about herself and take care of him. So he's blocked from telling Mom how he feels. Plus, the boy certainly can't express his anger to Dad, because Dad's too big and too scary. The same scenario would exist if the roles were reversed and the mom were the abusive or neglectful parent.

How is our young man being programmed? He has learned to suppress his feelings, and he has learned well. But his anxiety and rage are eating him up, so he starts searching for a way to comfort himself. Because he has a genetic predisposition for alcohol, he gravitates to drink. His ego has taught him to act sweet, to placate, and be caring, and not to yell, complain, or share his pain. His ego developed this program as a strategy for survival, but the pattern turns into a strategy for self-destruction because in the long run, his drinking is killing him and so is the suppression of his feelings.

To add to the man's problems, his ego feels obliged to defend the self-destructive pattern of suppressing himself, and it will do so with every tool in its arsenal. So it's hard to intervene. Maybe you are a close friend. You realize that the man needs to express himself, and you try to interrupt the program of self-suppression. You may be surprised at his resistance, until you understand that your support is stirring up the old fear that Mom won't take care of him if he expresses himself honestly. Feeling threatened, his ego may try to kill you off by pulling him away from your relationship or discounting your suggestions. The irony is that this man's killing himself to try to keep himself alive, yet your efforts to keep him alive feel to him like a threat to his survival.[7]

An Exercise in Self-Awareness

Let's take a moment to self-examine, so you can see how this pattern applies to you.

1. What were the circumstances of your birth?
2. Who was the person your survival depended on?
3. What strategy did you develop to ensure that person's care for you?
4. Was this strategy reinforced during your early life, or did you have to adjust it?
5. How do you play out this survival strategy in your life today?
6. Can you feel the survival fear under this behavior?

If you are able to complete this exercise, you may find that your drive to please, work hard, self-express, intimidate, look good, dominate, attract sexual partners, over-spend or use food, drugs, or alcohol has a deep source within your psyche. No wonder it's so hard to change negative behavior, even when it's destructive.

It's an Ego-Eat-Ego World

Now that we have a general idea of how we are designed, we can better understand the people around us and our relationship to them. All of us have egos that instinctively develop programs and patterns to ensure our survival. This means that just like us, others are also operating out of programs inspired by their survival instincts. Sometimes our programs reinforce one another; sometimes they conflict. But if we are to survive on this planet, we have to make sure we have the resources we need, and to do that, we need to convince others that what they need for their own survival is *us*.

---

[7] A detailed discussion of the obstacles to self-awareness will come later in Platform Five: Becoming Self-Aware.

In other words, we learn to play into other people's egos by convincing them that their survival is somehow dependent on us. And unless we develop other ways to ensure our survival, we are left with a powerful unconscious pattern of constantly focusing on the manipulation of other people's egos to get them to need us. What starts with our families quickly spreads to our peers, employers, friends, lovers, and even our children. Now that's a job of a lifetime!

How do we manipulate each other's egos to believe they need us to survive? If you think about it, the process begins before we are even born. Human beings are programmed to bear and raise children. Remember that everything has ego, including collectives, which means that the collective of humanity also has an ego. Just as the individual's ego has the job of continuing its existence as a separate entity, the ego of humanity has one purpose, which is to ensure the survival of the species. And just as our individual survival is initially orchestrated by instinct, so is our species' survival.

The instinct to reproduce is deeply ingrained in the collective human ego, because obviously if we did not reproduce, we would not survive as a species. The instinct of the collective ego motivates individuals to have children to ensure the survival of the species, even when the existence of those children conflicts with the wellbeing of the parent as an individual. The man or woman who craves to have a child isn't aware that his or her behavior is motivated by the collective ego. She is thinking, "Oh how cute kids are". Or he wants someone to carry on the family name, genes, or business. Or he craves someone who "will always love him" and deludes himself into thinking that because his children are dependent on him, they will always be there for him. Whatever motives individuals have, however, human beings are driven by the instinct to reproduce the species.[8]

Our personal instinct for survival is linked to our collective survival instinct, which is also served by having children, whether or not it's truly in anyone's highest good. Our individual survival depends on our ability to fit in with a group. This goes back to our earliest days. We can only imagine how terrifying it once was to walk the earth, with the elements battering us

---

[8] I am not suggesting that there aren't people who actually like children and enjoy being in their company. I am suggesting that the overwhelming drive to have children is based on the collective ego's need to reproduce the species; if it were not, we would be making more conscious decisions about whether or not to reproduce and when.

about and large, dangerous animals hunting us for food. Staying with the tribe was clearly a matter of life or death.[9] This reality has not changed, and we are still driven by a need to be in a collective that increases our chances of survival, whether that collective be a family, community, political party, labor union, or anything else. I will discuss this subject further later in this book.

It should not surprise us, therefore, that we humans instinctively seek ways to stay in the good graces of our community, which requires us to adapt to the dominant culture, even when doing so creates pain for us and people we love. Up until the current era, for example, our culture has predominantly equated the value of a woman with her reproduction. So it should not be surprising that many women feel unconsciously pressured into giving birth even when they have no affinity for children. Add religious and family pressure to the mix, and you can see that people are not so free in their decisions to give birth as they may believe.

Of course, we have other survival-based drives to reproduce. Throughout history, in various cultures including ours, having children ensured the existence of sufficient labor to keep a farm going. In non-agricultural families, raising devoted children has also been an attempt to ensure our futures by guaranteeing that we would not have to face old age alone. For those of us in the industrialized world, th se factors are becoming less and less relevant, as we have abandoned lal or-intensive farming and families break up and scatter around the wc rld. In the face of new realities, we have created institutions to ensure our future survival, such as senior living facilities and Social Security. Nevertheless, the hope that children will secure our futures still motivates many of our behaviors.

Clearly we have a myriad of reasons for having children other than a true desire to relate to a child. Some of us truly enjoy children and have the material circumstances to support our offspring comfortably. In this section I am merely focusing on the fact that our individual and collective survival instinct drives us to have children, regardless of whether or not doing so threatens our individual survival, including our economic and emotional wellbeing.

Whether for unconscious motives or because of a true desire to relate to a child, let's say we have children. When the new infant is born, reality hits,

---

[9]   We see this in animals as well. When a lone wolf or coyote is thrown out of the group, its survival becomes much more precarious.

and perhaps neither parent is truly ready to deal with the baby's insistent demands. Perhaps there are already too many children in the family, or Dad feels pushed away by the preoccupied mom, or Mom realizes that she is happier employed outside the home. Or perhaps both parents truly want the child, but the strain is much greater than they had anticipated. Or perhaps the parents are generally happy with the child but have moments of exhaustion and resentment. Or the child has colic, Mom has postpartum depression or the primary wage earner loses his or her job.

The baby immediately senses it is a burden and becomes scared. It unconsciously thinks, "If I am helpless and totally dependent, or if I am a burden, will anyone care for me?" From that point on, the child's ego looks for reasons for the family to channel its human and material resources to it, so the child will survive. The ego needs to convince the child and everyone else that the baby is worth caring for, despite the strain on the family, despite the parents' fatigue, despite the siblings' jealousy, despite the fact that it can do very little to make up for what others need to sacrifice to keep it alive.

Since the ego's job is to protect the child's existence, the child must continue to find a way to manipulate its environment so that someone continues caring for it. What the ego quickly discovers is that the best way to do that is to create the belief that the child is essential to the existence of others. In other words, the baby's ego needs to convince other people's egos that their egos need the baby for their survival. And as the child grows up, it continues to develop or refine its strategy to ensure its importance.

The specific strategy the child's ego chooses is once more contingent upon its genetic qualities and the ego needs of others in the family. It will try to be perceived as essential to whomever seems the most likely to provide it with care—among parents, siblings or workers at an institution. The baby can become Dad's pal and ally, Momma's little helper, or a source of pride for the family's ego, succeeding in school or at sports or music. If there is no room for the child to excel, it can try to look less needy than it actually is (this ploy usually convinces the child more than anyone else). It might develop a personality based on self-sacrifice and self-effacement. In this case, the way the child proves its value is by demonstrating how few resources it requires. If one of the child's parents values his or herself as extremely giving, the child may make itself look extremely needy, so that the parent can feel very generous. Or, the child can demand resources by looking bad, so that its mother's value in the world is threatened. Once the child looks like it's a problem, the mother will rush to provide resources to fix her son or daughter so that the mother's image in society is protected. Or the child can engender compassion based on someone's guilt, knowing the person can't live in good conscience without helping the child. The child can also combine these strategies or use completely different other strategies as well.

No matter what strategy the child adopts, it still knows that it is a burden. We are all burdens when we are young, and we all sense that unconsciously. Even in families where the child is wanted, there are moments when the exhausted and stressed parent feels overwhelmed. So no matter the value of the child on an emotional, spiritual, or even physical level (Mommy's little helper again), the child is a disproportionate consumer of attention and resources and it will feel the insecurity of that, especially in a family where it is not wanted or where physical, emotional, or material resources are already stretched thin.

The ego works overtime to make us feel secure by convincing us and the universe that we are more valuable than someone else, more valuable than sister, brother, mother, father, any and everybody. This is the reason we are desperately and constantly trying to prove how wonderful, smart, charming, pretty, helpful, useful, strong, attentive, talented, and understanding we are. Or alternatively we try to convince others how desperately needy we are, so that the people around us can feel how wonderful, smart, charming, pretty, helpful, useful, strong, attentive, talented, and understanding *they* are. We do this so they will take care of us, because we give them the feeling that they are indispensable, which feeds right into their survival instinct, because we are now the proof of their value. This is the beginning of shame, because we know on some level, it is a lie.

Here are some questions to help you discover what strategies your ego decided to take on:

1. What circumstances in my family caused me to feel like a burden?
2. Who did I think would care for me?
3. How have I manipulated them to do it?
4. Can I see myself doing that now with others?

What Does Shame Have to Do with It?

Shame is the experience of feeling worthless as a human being. If we are worthless, we are expendable. If we are expendable, we fear we will lose the resources we need to stay alive. In other words, shame is inextricably connected to the fear of death, which is why we feel like dying when we experience it.

Being a true threat to our survival, shame becomes the emotion that we most fear and dread. Some of us handle the fear of shame by becoming defiant ("You think I'm bad? I'll show you bad."). Some become compliant, others defensive. Some just hide, so that no one will see us doing anything at all—that way, we can't be criticized or shamed for anything! Whatever our specific coping mechanism, the fear of shame drives us.

The Shame of Existence

Shame starts early, as we've already seen, because we are consuming a lot of resources and are not able to compensate the family. Then as we grow older, that shame is reinforced. Let's take a fairly universal example. If Mom wants me to be smart and I come home with a bad report card, her disapproval of me creates shame; that is, I feel worthless and so my survival instinct is triggered. Maybe this is the last straw. I'm afraid that Mom, who is already struggling to pay the mortgage, will finally decide that I am too much of a burden and not worth the trouble to give me what I need. This fear is probably mostly in my head, because Mommy would feel too much shame to starve me to death, but she might withdraw love, goodies, and approval, which feels very threatening to a child.

Adopted children have this experience in spades, but so do all children, especially the kids of sick parents, poor parents, blaming parents, parents with many children, and dysfunctional parents, among others. In some families, the fear of being a burden is exacerbated by abusive parenting. The father or mother who beats the child is constantly reinforcing the child's belief that it has no value. Not only does that child fear for its life on a physical level, it is being shamed for its existence on a psychic level. It has received the message that it should not exist.

On some level, we all feel shame for existing. If we have been treated exceptionally well by our parents, we feel the shame of having taken more resources than our siblings and often more than our parents themselves. If we have also been born into a privileged family in society, we have the additional shame of comparing the resources spent on us with resources consumed by ordinary people or children of the poor. Some of us respond to this shame by becoming very altruistic, trying to hide how much we are consuming. Some of us become defiant, pretending that we believe that we have a right to everything we've received. Some pretend it isn't true, that we really haven't been given much.

Ironically, whether we are spoiled or abused, whether we brag or shrink, whether we are givers or takers, we share a common shame and a common fear: The insecurity that someone, society, God, will discover that we are pigs, taking more than our share just for our own measly existence, and we will be punished or, worse, abandoned.

And everyone around us has the same fear. They too are functioning out of the survival-based ego instinct to ensure their survival, and their interactions with us are based on the same motivations as ours are with them. They, too, are feeling the shame of their existence, and they, too, are trying to prove their worth.

Now we are in the battle of the egos. Each one of us has to prove that we are better than the other, number one, the most useful, least selfish, most beautiful, most intelligent, most steady, most loyal, most capable of taking the family into material comfort and wellbeing, most able to bring social status or social value, most willing and able to take care of the elderly, the best parents, the best something . . .

And we bring this survival-based ego competitiveness into our most intimate relationships, where we try to convince our partners that they can't live without us, while feeling desperately insecure because we fear that we can't live without them.

Here's an exercise to help you determine how your survival-based ego competes:

1. Can I identify the feeling of shame, of having no value?
2. Can I admit that I took more than I gave as a child?
3. How have I tried to prove my value?
4. With whom am I still competing to have more value?

The Shame of Having an Ego

Now that we have discussed the shame of existence, let's talk about the shame of having an ego. Even though everything that exists has ego, we feel shame about having one. Let's see how this shame can develop. Let's say little Johnny has a toy that baby Sarah wants to play with. Being in the ego-based universe focused on herself, she wants to grab it. When she grabs the toy, her mother says, "Be Nice. That toy belongs to Johnny and you have

19

to ask for it politely." What has Sarah learned? That "My mother doesn't like it when I grab"—even though that behavior is a natural, ego-based response. Generally speaking, the mother will be using an inflection which suggests shame as well as disapproval, because shame is the most common mechanism parents use to get their children to behave the way they want.

So through such experiences, what we have learned is that it is shameful to have ego. It is dangerous to be natural and show that we are selfish, even though we *are* selfish, because selfishness is a part of our ingrained survival instinct. In other words, our survival is threatened by showing that we're fighting for our survival. If we are selfish with our siblings, parents, grandparents, or other kids, we will be shamed, unless we can convincingly justify our selfishness through some extraordinary need or some extraordinary talent or usefulness. And even if we've established our right to resources because of our gifts, needs, or value to Mom or Dad, we know that we're on thin ice.

Surrounded by others who are also run by their egos, resentment festers underneath all who are sacrificing for us, because our family members, too, are motivated by their egos and instinct for their own survival. They are sacrificing for us as children, because our need for them feeds into some need of theirs to appear sacrificing. Or they sacrifice for us, because they find their value through the development of our gifts, or they experience their value through fulfilling the role of "great provider." Or they are forced to accept our gobbling up resources because their approval by others is contingent on their acquiescence to our needs, which makes them look like good parents.

This situation, however, never feels completely safe. Children know intuitively that at any point, sacrificing caretakers can change their minds and take the support away. It could be that suddenly Mom loses her job, another sibling becomes ill, Grandma moves in, or the child fails to perform. And so the child has to keep working hard to prove his or her value.

No matter how much we as children justify or act smug about our position in the family, we have to hide our egos or there may be a backlash. We may act innocent, as though we don't notice that we are taking a disproportionate chunk of the family resources. We may act grateful and stroke the egos of our parents. We may act entitled, hoping to bluff our way into the continuation of good fortune. Growing up, we may drive ourselves mercilessly in order to justify the family's investment. But whatever else we do, we don't want to look selfish.

As children, we may have intimidated or manipulated our families into putting our needs first, often despite the seething resentment of other siblings or one or both of our parents. But when we leave the nest, we are in store for a rude awakening. Now we are surrounded by others who are equally dominated by their egos but who have no historic relationship with us. We are now compelled to be on the lookout for ways to manipulate a whole other universe of folks with whom we hope to play the same games that have kept us alive at home. If we can't, we need to quickly strategize alternatives. For example, if we dominated at home by looking super-talented, what do we do when we find ourselves in the larger world where we are not? We have to find some edge. Or, desperately seeking security, we look for a partner in life, a person to whom we can become indispensable, so that we can relax into the knowing that there is at least one other person in the world who cares about our survival. Of course, our partner is doing the same thing, and clashes ensue.

But so afraid are we of showing our egos, we are constantly striving to get our needs met without looking like we are. Here's a number of games we play to hide our egos. We pretend our self-centered actions were motivated on behalf of others. For example, we rationalize being greedy by saying we did it for the sake of our children, the company, or the nation. Or we cloak our self-interest behind some seemingly noble cause, such as when we grabbed up the land from the Native Americans because of Manifest Destiny. Or we pretend we didn't know that we were hurting anyone when we took actions that damaged others. Or we justify that we cut corners at the school construction site, because we were just following the company's directives, or we were forced to act by the foreman under threat of losing our jobs. We blame others, shame others, anything to avoid the shame that we are in our egos or acted thoughtlessly on our own behalf. This is because we fear that our egos will be obvious, which will cause us to feel shame, which returns us to our childhood feeling of worthlessness, which causes us to feel that we have no value, which will retrigger in us the fear one more time that we are dependent and will not survive.

What's worse is we believe that we *have* to continue this selfish, self-centered behavior—even though we feel we have to hide it—because we live in an ego-driven world. We fear that if we don't manipulate others, others will manipulate and dominate us. We'll be eaten alive. We'll die. Help!

Self-Awareness Threatens Our Survival

Why is it threatening for us to be aware of all this ego-based behavior? Because we are afraid we will feel shame, the shame that we are selfish, grabbing for ourselves at the expense of others, worthless and not worth supporting. We're afraid we'll discover that we did something wrong, hurtful, stupid, unworthy, and the world will no longer want to support us. We're afraid we'll be abandoned, thrown out of the tribe, snubbed, or judged.

What's worse, it's all true. We are selfish and we are often wrong.

No wonder we want to avoid self-awareness! It is dangerous to our health!

We discuss Becoming Self-Aware further in Platform Five. For the moment, however, let's ask ourselves a few questions about our attitude toward our own egos.

1. How do I feel when someone accuses me of being in my ego?
2. How was my selfishness viewed in my family?
3. What was the attitude toward the selfishness of other family members?
4. How do I try to hide my ego now?

The Ego Twice Born

Since I have said that the ego is natural, I bet you're wondering if I'm suggesting that the solution to the world's problems is to just admit we are selfish and continue to be shortsighted and self-destructive until we have destroyed the world and ourselves. Not at all. Because what I have been describing is the ego as we have known it, the ego once born, the ego that developed patterns of behavior based on infantile consciousness overlaying the survival instinct. I like to refer to this as the lizard brain. Aren't we capable of more than that? Yes, we are. But in order to realize that potential, the ego needs to grow up and be born a second time.

What Do I Mean by the Ego Twice Born?

Let's summarize what we know. The ego is a natural result of the process of evolution. As each discrete entity comes into existence, it is immediately gifted with an ego whose purpose is to ensure its continued existence. Armed with instinct, the ego learns how to manipulate the world in order to ensure our survival, even at the expense of others. This, in turn, leads to the shame of existence, a condition seeded at birth and reinforced through our childhood experience of consuming more than we produce. The shame of existence is further reinforced by our experience of being shamed for the existence of our ego, e.g. being considered selfish, self-centered, or inconsiderate.

Compelled to continue to consume resources while trying to hide or justify that reality and driven to convince others that our existence is essential so that we will continue to be supported and survive, we act out of a seemingly desperate need to constantly prove our value to ourselves and everyone else. This requires us to diminish and demean others. Now our ego is working overtime, attempting to grab what we can for ourselves and continually justifying that behavior through more and more elaborate mechanisms, including hiding that we need anything at all.

This is the ego once born, fighting for our wellbeing in an infantile and instinctive way. Programmed from infancy, acting on instinct, motivated by short-term survival needs and hiding our shame, each one of us attempts to manipulate the universe to meet our own individual needs and each of us is driven to justify doing so. This is the ego at its worst. This is what happens when the ego is once-born. What makes matters worse is that because our egos are associated with our survival, we fear confronting our egotistic behavior, no matter how destructive it is. We fear letting that behavior go, lest any change threaten our survival. And we especially fear even considering the question of the common good, because to consider the common good might threaten us.

We can see how well it has worked for us to be dominated by ego: Couples shame and blame each other, corporate executives line their pockets while pension funds are decimated, desperate souls rob the poor, and clever souls rob the collective. All this leads to crime, abuse, addiction, and climate catastrophe. Meanwhile, each one of us endures a private hell of shame and fear, terrified that we will lose whatever edge we have managed to develop in order to protect ourselves, whether that edge is based on financial, sexual, physical, or political power, or based on the guilt, admiration, or dependency we've fostered in others. And left unchecked, we will continue to focus on our ego-based agendas, no matter the cost to ourselves and to those around us.

Again, because we are programmed for survival, we are afraid to look at these realities. We're afraid of change, which we believe will fracture the very survival mechanisms we have so painstakingly developed, and we're afraid of feeling shame, which in and of itself feels like a threat to our survival because it causes us to feel worthless and therefore not entitled to support.

Later in this book, we will explore together the many ways in which our sense of separateness has hurt us. But for now, what is important is to recognize that our sense of separateness—resulting from our egos—is natural and instinctive; it is not shameful. Having recognized this reality, however, there is another, deeper reality that we can now address.

The ego as we know it is natural and necessary, but it is immature and damaging. Just as we would not allow a child to raise itself with no socialization, we must not allow our egos to raise themselves without the intervention of our higher consciousness. As children, we are not bad, we are just immature. So it is with the ego; it is not in itself bad, but it is immature. And just as immature children do harmful destructive things to themselves and others, immature egos do harmful and destructive things to us all.

The purpose of this book is to take us back to school, to reprogram our egos to choose behaviors and attitudes that are supportive not to our individual survival, but to our collective and individual thriving. We need to teach the ego to say "Yes" to the highest good, "Yes" to the collective, and "Yes" to The Source. To do this, we need to confront the domination of our lizard brain, the instinctive part of us that always grabs for "me" first, without realizing that protecting me jeopardizes *we*, which ultimately kills us all.

You may wonder if this reprogramming is any different from the programming we received from our parents, who socialized us by telling us to be nice and to not grab the toy from Johnny. Yes, this is different. We are not suggesting that we cover up our survival instinct with patterns aimed to manipulate the goodwill of others. We are suggesting that we support our survival instinct by shifting the locus of our consciousness from the lizard brain to our higher selves and that we reprogram our egos so that they become our true friends—friends of our inner beings, friends of our collective self, and friends of the Oneness.

Can this be done? Yes, once we understand that our egos are in a stage of development. As we have seen, our egos develop at such a young age, they are inevitably associated with the unconscious, infantile, lizard, survival-oriented mind. Our conscious minds develop only later. What if we were able to connect our ego with our higher consciousness? What if we were able to use our higher consciousness in order to pattern ourselves anew? What if we could release ourselves from the pain and fear that drive us to make unconscious, painful, and self-destructive choices? What if we didn't have to fight our egos in order to force ourselves to respond in a more sane and long-sighted way, because our egos automatically geared us in those directions? What if we didn't have to hide who we were, because we actually were becoming different?

How can we do this? By developing the capacity to experience ourselves as individuals in the context of Oneness, instead of only as separate selves. By developing the capacity to hold the paradox within us, the paradox of existence, which is that we are both distinct individuals and unique manifestations of the whole, integrally connected and ultimately One. By developing the capacity to connect to higher consciousness and thrive!

Remember our definition of the ego? The ego is the consciousness of individual existence, consciousness of the separation from Oneness that arises at the same moment as the whole fragments into distinct parts. In other words, as soon as something has individual existence, it has ego. Acting according to its purpose, the ego focuses on its separateness from the whole. We see this behavior in children whose egos are developing. As they progress past infancy, they become more and more insistent on being them "selves." And so they should. It is in the evolutionary process of the naturally evolving child to hit the "terrible twos" and say, "No." We see even more of this as the child reaches adolescence.[10] The game of the adolescent ego is, "I pretend that I'm different, separate, and independent." None of this is actually true, because we are not yet terribly competent, but we feel the need for this fiction in order to convince ourselves we can be independent in a scary world.

The immature ego—the ego once born—is stuck in the stage of separation: "No, me, I." It is still two years old, at best adolescent. It asserts its "self" through separation and fights for itself at any cost. The ego twice born has matured beyond "No, me, I." Instead, it speaks the language of "Yes, we and us." It remembers the Oneness.

The twice-born ego remembers: "I truly am well only when connected to all. I truly am functional only in a functional whole. I truly am happy only when I exist in the context of Oneness. I truly am self-realized only

---

[10]   This phenomenon is further developed in Platform Two: Becoming Differentiated.

when I say 'yes.' Yes to reality, yes to evolution, yes to the universe, yes to the true nature of myself—which is to be part of the collective consciousness in the process of evolution—yes to the universal consciousness that fills, feeds and inspires me."

The immature ego was programmed into us from the beginning of time. The potential for it to become twice born is programmed into us as well. Its emergence is part of evolution, but the realization of that evolutionary step requires us to do our part. Although we often behave unconsciously, we are a conscious aspect of the Oneness, and with that come the responsibility and possibility for us to cooperate in the process of evolution itself. Our job in the process of evolution is to acknowledge the way we are and its negative consequences, to wake up to our potential, to intend to change, no matter the obstacles, and to develop and utilize powerful tools to move ourselves to the next stage of development. Once we have evolved to the next stage, new processes will be set in motion that will bring us to yet higher levels of evolution, levels that we cannot envision now.

Why do I believe that this is the time for the next evolutionary step? Because we have many of the preconditions for our evolution. Here are some contributing factors:

- Material resources that allow us to go beyond the focus on minimal survival
- The maturity of the collective consciousness, which includes sufficient experience of the negative consequences of our ego-based behavior and sufficient time for self-awareness
- Well-known processes for self-reflection
- Inspiration from above
- The influx of beneficial energies onto our Earth.

We can see how many of these factors exist in our time. We have achieved hitherto unimaginable levels of material abundance and technological advancement, which have allowed us much more time for self-cultivation and reflection and enabled us to develop mass education and mass communication. This in turn has created the opportunity for large numbers of people to experience the many modalities for self-awareness, including self-help programs and therapy. We have had long experience of the negative consequences of our immature ego-based behavior. We have had and continue to have many wonderful spiritual teachers who are promoting ancient wisdom throughout the planet. And we have an abundant influx of beneficial energies from above—pure and intense vibrational energies that are penetrating our planet through a variety of practices, including yoga, qi gong, LifeForce,[11] meditation, martial arts, and just plain opening our hearts.

I believe that our time has come, that the potential for our egos to be twice born can now be awakened and is in fact already awakening. There now exists the possibility of transforming consciousness on this planet, not just for the few enlightened ones, but increasingly for all of us, which is the only way a true shift in human consciousness can take place. This kind of change does not happen all at once. First one by one, then hundreds by hundreds, then thousands by thousands, people support themselves and one another to overcome the domination of instinct in order to achieve freedom and happiness.

This book is dedicated to the ego twice born. The platforms in Section Two will offer a step-by-step process that will enable us to live from a place of Oneness, where we identify with the whole, instead of the fragment, where our egos say "Yes," instead of "No." But before we can move to the platforms, we need to look more deeply at the way we are, which is the purpose of Section One of this book. But before we can proceed to be born again, our once-born egos need one big reassurance.

I Am Meant to Exist

We all suffer from the shame of existence, which has reinforced our need to compete to prove our value, which has set ego against ego. What if we had no shame of existence? How much more relaxed and mutually supportive we would be.

Let us release the shame of existence by simply acknowledging that we were meant to exist. No longer locked into justifying our existence, we can admit that we have ego and that we consume to survive. No longer needing to keep proving our individual value, we can focus on supporting one another to be wise, to do well and to thrive.

---

[11]   LifeForce: The Inner Workout is a unique mind-body spirit program that I offer daily on the Internet. It's quick and easy to do, it fills us with beneficial energy and it's free unless you choose to subscribe. You can find it at www. lifeforceworkout.com.

Let's begin that process by trying a simple exercise. Take a deep breath and say the following lines out loud, taking another deep breath between sentences:

I am meant to exist.

I am meant to receive all the resources that are destined for me.

If I do not receive the resources destined for me, those resources will not fulfill their potential, and neither will I.

And if I do not fulfill my potential, neither will we.

And if we do not fulfill our potential, neither will you.

Changing Our Perspective Supports the Ego's Evolution

Now that we have said these lines, let us examine this exercise more deeply. Is this process the same as the ego justifying its existence? No, and it doesn't feel the same. Our immature egos force us to fight for our own survival, which leads us to the shame of existence. Our shame of existence forces our egos to continually try to prove something about ourselves to justify our consumption of resources. Our self justification requires us to reinforce our different-ness. And that's what we've historically been doing—proving our specialness to justify our existence, all to ensure our survival. And that has forced our egos to separate even more from one another.

For the ego to be twice born, the ego itself needs to identify our wellbeing with the wellbeing of the whole, which requires us to focus on our similarities instead of our differences. By asserting our right to exist, we can drop the shame of existence. We find that there's nothing to prove. We no longer have to demonstrate that we are different. We can begin to identify with the Oneness and support the wellbeing of the whole. And we can support the ego to evolve.

Of course, I don't mean that there are no distinctions among us and that we won't need to point those out when appropriate. For example, when we are in a political discussion, we need to acknowledge that different perspectives and policies may lead to different results, and some candidates are more suited for a job than others. But pointing out distinctions and considering the consequences of different paths is a very different process from demonizing one another and attempting to gain an advantage at someone else's expense. When the ego evolves, the intent of pointing out distinctions is to support the wellbeing of the whole, instead of to establish the superiority of ourselves.

But is that natural? Yes, in a sense it is the most natural thing for us to do, because in fact we are not distinct beings who can survive without one another. We are unique manifestations of the Oneness who forgot that we are One. And it is natural to think in these terms, because in fact we know we cannot exist and thrive in a sick home, community, nation, or world. If we don't remember our Oneness, we will self-destruct as a species on this planet. Remembering our Oneness does not in fact threaten our survival; what threatens our survival is forgetting.

The Ego Remembers: We Are Meant to Exist Because We Are Part of the Whole

The ego twice born remembers that we are part of the whole, and each of us has a purpose in the evolution of that whole. The twice-born ego remembers that we are here to fulfill the purpose of the whole, and for each of us to fulfill our purpose, we need the resources to fulfill that destiny. Which means that accepting the resources destined for us is not selfish; it is necessary for the collective evolution.

Now let us repeat the exercise that we did a few minutes ago. Take a deep breath before starting and another deep breath between each sentence.

> *I am meant to exist.*
> *I am meant to receive all the resources that are destined for me.*
> *If I do not receive the resources destined for me, those resources will not fulfill their potential, and neither will I.*
> *And if I do not fulfill my potential, neither will we.*
> *And if we do not fulfill our potential, neither will you.*

There is no shame of existence when we reframe our view of ourselves. Through our old perspective we see ourselves as individuals who are good, bad, selfish, stupid, hungry, lonely, frightened, self-confident, kind, something. Through the prism of the immature ego, I am just I. Programmed with a survival instinct, I have to continue my existence, and so I have to consume, even though I may feel guilty about it.

Seen through our new perspective, I am no longer just I. I am a part of everything. I have a job in the collective, which is to be a unique manifestation of the whole and to evolve as part of the evolution of all. I need the resources to fulfill that destiny. There are particular resources—material, spiritual, educational, and emotional—that are destined for me, to enable me to fulfill my potential as part of the whole, so that I can help the whole to evolve. The more consciously I take on fulfilling my part in the evolution of the whole, the more relaxed I am about consuming the resources destined for me. (This becomes much clearer when we reach Platform Nine: Becoming Becoming.)

Many people ask the question: "What's my purpose?" Here's my reply. "In fact, I have no individual purpose, apart from being part of the whole." To claim an individual purpose would be like asserting the individual purpose of an ant, whose function cannot be separated from the existence of the colony. My purpose is simply to be part of our purpose, and within our collective purpose, I have a job, which is to accept being myself, work with the challenges I have been given and transform according to the needs of our collective evolution.[12]

We are all parts of the evolution of consciousness itself. Many of us marveled to see an African-American man and a Caucasian woman running in the 2008 U.S. Democratic presidential primary. Both candidates had specific qualities that uniquely qualified them for their place in history. Yet neither of them could have done what they did without thousands of years of human evolution, hundreds of years of political evolution, and scores of years of civil rights struggle. Along with the two candidates, thousands of people dead and alive co-created the moment of these historic campaigns, and these campaigns are just a moment in the process of the evolution of consciousness itself.

So it is with each one of us. Each of us lives a day-to-day life which may seem insignificant, and yet is a part of the evolution of human consciousness. We are part of the resistance to change; we are part of overcoming that resistance; we are part of both. We are part of humanity experiencing the negative consequences of poor choices; we are part of humanity experiencing the positive consequences of more conscious choices; we are part of both. We are part of humanity grappling with the domination of our egos, or failing to do so, and experiencing the results.

---

[12] Of course, if we look at the microcosm, we can say that, "My purpose is to raise children or make automobile parts or drive a taxi in New York City." But on a deeper level, what is the purpose of any of that? Even being a "spiritual teacher" has no purpose outside the context of the evolution of consciousness, which goes beyond the particular teacher.

I may have no awareness of my place in history, and I may feel no conscious connection to evolution, but this doesn't matter. The ant does what it is programmed to achieve. And so do we. Whether we know it or not, each one of us represents an aspect of consciousness trying to work out a small part of evolution. But when we do become aware of this reality, we can shift the focus of our consciousness from the individual self to the whole, we can become conscious co-creators of evolution and we can gladly embrace the resources destined for us.[13]

What are the resources destined for us? Experiences, things, vibrational energies that we need for us to be who we are meant to be, which encompasses all of us, including our weaknesses and strengths; experiences, things, vibrational energies that we need for our growth, however jagged that growth may appear to ourselves or others. We may be meant to be drug addicts who are given a chance to get clean and support others to do the same. We may be meant to be drug addicts who reject that chance and who die an early death, which in turn supports others to make better choices. We may be meant to be sports heroes who are deified and then crucified for being human and who can then use their experience to enlighten us all. We may be meant to be physically sick or mentally ill, and we may become examples of self-acceptance and generosity of spirit despite our own difficulties. We may be meant to be the wealthy one who gives away her property to care for others, or we may be meant to be the wealthy one who squanders her fortune on vanity and dissipation. We may be meant to appear unexceptional, and yet show the power of the human spirit when connected to the divine.

To do these jobs, we need resources. Resources can look like talents, love, attention, spiritual energies or luck. Resources can also look like challenges, pain, consequences and lack. Resources can look like too much money, which causes a sense of uselessness; or too little money, which causes us to confront our fear and our sense of worth.

---

[13] The importance of feeling a part of something larger than ourselves is very evident in our desire to volunteer for important causes or join larger social or political movements. Those of us who lived through times of collective protest, the '60s, for example, were exhilarated by the opportunity to be part of something larger than ourselves. What we don't realize is that we are always a part of something larger than ourselves.

When we reach the end of our program, Platform Nine: Becoming Becoming, we will more deeply understand the role we play in the universe and the opportunity we are given to participate in the evolution of consciousness. But for now, let's acknowledge that in order for us to be who we are meant to be, we need resources, and these resources are destined for us.

When I accept my right to exist and I embrace the resources destined for me, my ego can relax. And I can allow those same resources to flow through me to wherever they might be destined next. Released from the need to prove anything about myself, I don't have to own the biggest house or car. I don't have to have the best job or be seen as the most powerful person. I can see myself as an instrument of divine consciousness, and I can differentiate between the resources that I truly need and the resources that I can pass on to others. No longer feeling competitive and alone, I don't feel dominated by fear and therefore don't need to consume in order to alleviate that fear. Nor do I need to consume to prove my value, or to express my defiance to cover the shame for having too much. I can take in the resources that are truly meant for me and reallocate those that are meant to pass through me to help others, and I will do so not out of a sense of self-sacrifice and shame, but out of a feeling of relaxation and rightness of the action.

And We Can Be a Blessing

Whatever resources are destined for us can be used for our growth and the evolution of all. They become beneficial energies that are fully utilized for the highest good of all. With this in mind, let us repeat once more the exercise that we did a few minutes ago, with some important changes in wording. One more time, take a deep breath before starting the exercise and between each sentence.

> *I am meant to exist.*
> *I embrace all the beneficial energies that are destined for me.*
> *If I do not embrace the beneficial energies destined for me, those energies will not fulfill their potential, and neither will I.*
> *And if I do not fulfill my potential, neither will we.*
> *And if we do not fulfill our potential, neither will you.*

Once we have internalized that we no longer have to justify our existence, once we begin to see the value of our existence as part of the whole, we can see the purpose of the beneficial energies destined for us, which is to help one another, as well as ourselves. Every child represents countless hours of labor performed by parents, older siblings, teachers, and others who have shaped that being. Are those assets wasted? Not at all. It has been said that "To whom much is given, much is required."

But let us reformulate this statement and say, "To whom much is given, much can be received." Those of us who have been given much help and many opportunities can offer much to others. Those of us who have struggled with deprivation can offer lessons in grace and allowance. Those of us who fail can offer valuable lessons in self-destruction. All of us can turn all of our experiences into the fertilizer of new life and new awareness. All of us can contribute to the evolution of consciousness.

If we use our blessings to bless others, then those blessings have truly fulfilled their potential. And then we are truly blessed.

Turning Ourselves Around

From the perspective of the whole, we finally comprehend who we are. We are not individual beings with individual problems. We are unique manifestations of the whole in the process of evolution. Our problems are collective, and so are the solutions. And the solution to our collective ego problem begins with the awareness that we are creating needless pain because we are stuck in the immature ego that remembers that it is separate but forgets that it is also One. And with that awareness, we can collectively flip the switch to remembering.

Ultimately, we have to flip the switch collectively. It is extremely difficult to shift an individual, because we are not individual; we are not separate from the whole. Yet, we face a paradox: I am totally responsible for the unique manifestation that I am. And yet, at the same time, I am part of the Oneness and, therefore, can't completely control myself, because I cannot control the whole of which I am a part. I am responsible for my individual consciousness; yet I am extremely influenced by the attitudes, behavior, and feelings of others.

This is the challenge: In the face of the impossibility of personal salvation, I need to continue to do my part. Whether or not my family stops drinking, for example, I need to take the steps necessary to keep myself clear physically, mentally, and emotionally.

And here's another paradox: Insignificant as I may seem, I am also responsible for the whole. Because I am not separate, not only do I have to take responsibility for the unique manifestation that I am, I have to take my full responsibility for the Oneness. Yes, on some level, I am responsible for you, because I am you, because we are all part of the whole.

And here's the final paradox: We are each responsible for the whole, but we can ultimately only succeed by taking that responsibility collectively, with each one of us stepping up to the plate, one by one, then ten by ten, then thousands by thousands.

To change our world and to change myself, we collectively have to say, "Enough!" to the domination of the old dysfunctional patterns. We have to say, "Enough!" to the infant within us that rants and raves when we don't get our own way. We have to say, "Enough!" to the immature ego that dominates almost every thought, feeling and action we have. We have to say, "Enough!" to the lizard brain, which is the first to get activated and the last to relax. We have to say, "Enough!" collectively, and the collective starts with me.

The good news is the collective nature of who we are can also be a benefit to us as individuals. The more others join the movement for transformation, the easier it will be for each of us, because it is much simpler to practice principles of mutual support in a context where others are doing the same. It is easier to be gracious when others are gracious to us. It is easier to be accountable when others are willing to be accountable, too. It is easier for our egos to be twice born when we are dealing with other egos that have the same commitment.

What Will Bring Us to Say "Enough"?

I started this introduction by saying that if suffering were sufficient motivation for change, humanity would have transformed a long time ago. That is true. Suffering alone will not change us. What we need is the courage to face and overcome our survival instinct, as it expresses itself in infantile and unconscious ways, so that we are no longer driven by fear that self-awareness and change will threaten our survival, so that we embrace self-awareness and change, and so that we can collectively move toward the vision of who we could be: Thriving individuals in a thriving world. In other words, we have to face the fear of death in order to live, and we have to overcome the domination of the ego as we have known it.

Earlier in this chapter, we enumerated some of the prerequisites for such an evolutionary change, prerequisites which we already have, namely:

- Material resources so that we can go beyond the focus on minimal survival
- Maturity of the collective consciousness, which includes sufficient experience of the negative consequences of our ego-based behavior and sufficient time for self-awareness
- Technologies for self reflection
- Inspiration from above
- The influx of beneficial energies onto our Earth
- To succeed in playing our role in evolution, we need to develop five more elements, namely:
- **Self-Awareness**—the process of identifying the attitudes and behaviors that contribute to the misery of ourselves and others
- **Compassion**—understanding the survival-based motivations that keep these behaviors in place
- **Intention**—the focus on overcoming our inner resistance, so we can alter patterns that have been with us for a long time, patterns that are so close to us, we often can't see them
- **Support**—new paradigms, tools, and techniques to help us change and a collective of like-minded folks who support us to make the transformations we can't achieve alone.
- **Higher Consciousness**—the ability to access the vibrational energies that will help us transform.

If we have been programmed unconsciously to think, feel and behave in ways that are destroying us, we must take responsibility to redo that programming. *Living with Reality* can help us do that. But will we use this tool? Will we overcome the domination of the ego as we've known it, or will this book join the other spiritual volumes that sit on our nightstand and make us feel guilty? Will we overcome, or will we capitulate?

The answer is in our hands; and the answer is the next step of evolution. We can do this. Our collective experience and our collective suffering are not for naught. If the ego was born once, it can be born twice, the first time as a "no" and the second time as a "yes"—yes to Oneness, yes to existence, yes to evolution.

If we are to survive as a species, we have to evolve. When we become conscious co-creators of that evolution, we realize that there is help. Deep within us already exists a template for who we can be. All we need do is connect the intention to become ourselves with the powerful forces of the universe that can bring that intention into manifestation. In order to do so, we need to let go of reliance on our human identity, agendas and limited vision and become instruments of the divine consciousness of which we are a part.

Yes!

Living with Reality

SECTION I

The Human Condition
Who We Are

CHAPTER 1

What Is Reality,
And Why Is It So Hard to Live With?

Reality is what is—what we see and what we don't see. It is objective. It is not an illusion. There is a spectrum of colors, whether we can see them or not. The tree falls in the forest, whether we hear it or not. The climate is changing, whether we acknowledge it or not. And people are driven by inner drives and demons, whether they are aware of them or not.

In addition, there is another realm of reality that most people cannot see or even sense or measure. While many refer to that reality as the spiritual realm, it is no more or less spiritual than the color blue. This reality is the spectrum of vibrational energies that have not yet been measured, but which impact matter and can alter our emotional state. For those of us who have worked with these realms, they are as real as peanut butter.

All this seems relatively simple and straightforward. Reality exists. Let's expand our understanding of it. Let's live with it. If this is so straightforward, why do I need to devote an entire book to the topic? Because we don't see or don't want to deal with reality, and there are several reasons why.

1. Our perceptions are limited, individually and collectively, to what we can see.
2. We each live in our own subjective world.
3. Our egos have designed behaviors to cope with our subjective experience.
4. Reality gets in the way of our wants, desires and plans.

Let's look at these one at a time.

OUR PERCEPTIONS ARE LIMITED, INDIVIDUALLY AND COLLECTIVELY, TO WHAT WE CAN SEE

Our perceptions are limited by at least four factors:

- Our built-in physical capacities
- The limitations of the instruments we have designed to go beyond our own capacities
- Our willingness to see
- The partialness of our perspective

Our Built-In Physical Capacities

Let's look at light waves, as an example. With the naked eye, we can see only a certain spectrum of color because of the limitations of our physical capacities. But today we are well aware that there are infrared and ultraviolet rays that we can't perceive with our eyes, but which have an effect on us. When we look at a person, we can't see his or her genes, but much of that person's life has been influenced, if not pre-determined, by his or her genetic makeup, something we can't see with our unassisted eyes.

While our senses cannot see everything, we can often detect the effect of things that we cannot directly perceive. For example, long before we started understanding heredity, people would comment that, "The apple doesn't fall too far from the tree." We noticed similarities within families, though we couldn't distinguish between characteristics that were inherited and those that were caused by environmental influences. To a large degree, we still can't. We saw the effect of gravity long before we could measure it. And, speaking of apples, we knew the apple would fall from the tree long before we knew why.

We have become used to the idea that there's much in the material world that we cannot see and that we need instruments or theories to begin to grapple with them. We are also beginning to realize that people, too, have motivations of which we may not be aware. You meet Mary. She's wearing a blue dress. Why? You think she's wearing the dress because she likes it, if you think about it at all. You have no idea of her unseen motivations. For example, maybe Mary feels insecure and misses her mom. Her mother loved blue, and wearing the dress reminds Mary of her. Or maybe Mary thinks George will like the dress and be attracted to her. Or maybe she doesn't feel feminine and hopes that a dress will change the way she feels about herself. Or maybe Mary really wanted to wear jeans that day, but all her comfortable clothes were sitting in the laundry basket, because she was up half the night eating popcorn and watching Clint Eastwood movies. Or maybe Mary hates blue, but she's broke and the dress was on sale.

People are tremendously complex. Few of us have a clue as to what goes on behind the façade of appearances, and yet these motivations fuel our behavior and the behavior of everyone around us. This is as true on a collective level as it is on an individual level. We may go to war because we're collectively feeling impotent about some circumstances in our lives, not because war is actually called for.

Few people will now deny the existence of the psychological and sociological realms, whether or not we truly understand them. But many still deny the existence of the spiritual realms. Sometimes we can see the effect of a reality even though we can't see the cause. As I mentioned before, we can see the effect of the earth's gravitational field, even though we can't see the field itself with our naked senses. We see the infection, though we can't see the germs. And we experience the impact of all kinds of unseen vibrational energies, whether or not we even acknowledge their existence. It would be wise to learn more about them.

The Limitations of the Instruments & Methodologies We Have Designed to Go Beyond Our Own Capacities

Today our ability to understand is greatly expanded by new instruments. There was a time when we couldn't even imagine a sub-atomic level of existence, much less the vast expanses of the universe. Over the past centuries, however, we have come to realize that there are realms of existence that we cannot perceive without tools, and so we have aggressively sought more sophisticated instruments and understanding. But our tools and instruments are still limited. The instruments themselves may lack the power or sensitivity to reveal what is there, and/or we may lack the knowledge or sophistication to correctly interpret what information they bring.

The same is true of human psychology and social behavior. We are beginning to comprehend what motivates us, but we are still blinded by self-interest, as well as limitations in our thinking and in our perceptive capacities. Most of us cannot see deeply enough into the psyche to recognize the subtle and historic causes of our behavior, and if we have no experience with this level of inquiry, we won't even ask the right questions or try to design the means to answer them. (See Platform Five: Becoming Self-Aware.) In addition, we are still misunderstanding the mind-body-spirit connection, and few of us even take into consideration the collective consciousness within our families and communities, going back generations, much less the impact of energies that are unseen and unperceivable.

As an intuitive, I am well aware of our collective blindness to that which motivates our reactivity and responses. And as an intuitive, I am a more sensitive instrument for perception than most other people. But even though I am able to see more than most, I am still well aware of my own limitations. How much more limited are those who don't acknowledge the existence of these realms of reality and who don't work toward understanding them?

Since people are often frightened or reluctant to acknowledge the unknown, we often deny the existence of that which we don't or can't see. But rather than limit ourselves, let us open our minds to all realms. Let us acknowledge that we are still limited by our perceptions and instruments of perception, and let us become more sensitive ourselves while developing more sensitive instruments as well. We would gain more understanding if we explored the unknown, rather than insisting that if we can't see something, it must not exist.

Our Willingness to See

We've admitted our limitations and designed instruments and modalities to compensate for our limited capacities, and we will continue to do so. But even with better tools, our vision can still be limited by what we want to see. Even scientists can hit blind spots when ego gets involved and the scientist doesn't want to acknowledge something that threatens her status. Blind spots are common when it comes to understanding history and human behavior, too. For example, we may not want to recognize in ourselves behaviors that cause us to feel shame, such as a sexual obsession with children or other actions or thoughts that we consider reprehensible or perverted. We also tend to ignore reality when it frightens us or would cause upheaval in our lives, such as was the case when German Jews denied the implications of the growth of Nazism in Germany before World War II.

Our willingness to see reality is also a function of our attachment to patterns of behavior, the familiarity of which gives us a false sense of safety and security. We may not want to see that they are not working or are even destructive. We could be blind to a personal pattern, such as the inability to be open and honest in an intimate relationship; we could be similarly unwilling to see a collective pattern, such as a failed foreign policy in which we continue to invest.

What are we willing to question? What are we willing to see?

And what are we willing to see about the reality beyond our current vision of what is? In much of Western society, we are not very open to examining the mostly unchartered spiritual domains. This closed-mindedness may be because we already have a spiritual belief system to which we are attached or because we refuse to consider having any at all. Let's quickly look at both behaviors.

Some of us already have pat answers about spirituality, and having pat answers give us a sense of safety in the world. This is my religion or belief, and my beliefs explain the way things are, how to cope, and how to be. I don't want to consider anything different, even if my current beliefs seem to be creating needless fear, pain, or shame, and even if they have effects opposite to that which was originally intended. Are we willing to question our beliefs in the light of what we see? Are we willing to see anything that conflicts with what we believe? (I discuss all this further in Platforms Eight and Nine: Becoming Not-Knowing and Becoming Becoming.)

Some of us reject the unseen realms altogether. Sometimes this rigid view has been caused by our reaction to having had earlier disappointments with spiritual belief systems. If a system seemed not to have worked for us, we might have tossed out the whole realm. Rather than question the specific beliefs, we may have denied the reality of higher consciousness itself. The ego contributes to this reaction. Let's say I prayed. I asked God to save my mom or get me a pony, but God did not give me what I wanted.

I am now angry because my prayers failed to harness the universal forces for my goals. My conclusion: There is no higher intelligence in the universe.

Sometimes we reject the possibility of the existence of realms beyond ordinary consciousness because we know we cannot control them, and that reality makes us feel uncomfortable. The ego is at work here again. The unseen energies feel vast and are not in our ego's control, so maybe we can just pretend they don't exist.

The Partialness of Our Perspective

We have been discussing the difficulty of knowing reality, because of our limited perceptions. Before leaving this topic, let's acknowledge something else that we also know: that we can each see only a piece of a puzzle, and we often refuse to be cognizant of that. There's an old story about three blind men touching an elephant. One touches her trunk, another her side, and another her tail. Each one describes what he perceives. If each is stuck in the belief that his perception is the truth, each will have a very distorted picture of an elephant. If the three trust one another and share information, they will be able to transcend their own limitations.

Our egos tend to get very attached to our perspective. If I am a welfare recipient, a welfare worker or a taxpayer, I am likely to have a different perspective on welfare. Only when we all come together and share information do we begin to be able to describe reality.

Here are some questions to help you expand your perspective of reality.

1. Do I believe in only that which I have personally seen or experienced?
2. Have I had an experience where I believed in only my own perceptions, only to discover that I was wrong?
3. In what areas of life am I closed to questioning?
4. Do I believe there are realms beyond my perception?
5. Do I have fixed beliefs about them?
6. Why?
7. Have I been in a situation where I felt attached to my own perspective?
8. Did I ever come to realize that my perspective was narrow?

WE EACH EXIST IN OUR OWN SUBJECTIVE WORLD

We have now discussed how our perceptions are limited and how limited perceptions influence our ability to be in and, therefore, live with reality. Now we're going to discuss an even more fundamental limitation. Human beings don't live in reality at all. We live in our heads, in our emotions, in what we experience. We were built that way. We are sentient beings. We feel.

Let me say that again. We do not live in reality. We live in our reactions and feelings on the physical, emotional, and psychic levels. Because we are sentient and sensitive, we can easily become uncomfortable. When we are uncomfortable, we suffer. And when we suffer, we tend to focus on trying to alter our feeling state, so that we can stop suffering. The result of this simple reality is that human beings focus on fixing our reactions and feelings instead of addressing reality itself.

Let's say you fall off the roof. What are you experiencing? Your immediate experience is the physical sensation of falling and the emotional fear that you will hurt yourself. Yikes! What's going to happen? Your next experience is the hideous physical pain of having hurt yourself and all the emotional worries that come along with the fall, worries such as: How badly hurt am I? Who will come rescue me? Will I be able to work after the fall? Will I be permanently disabled? Can I afford the hospital bills? The third experience typically is some psychological interpretation of the event and who is at fault. I feel embarrassed for having fallen. I feel stupid for having been on the roof when I wasn't competent to be there. I feel angry with the person who asked me to work on the roof. I feel annoyed with myself that my pride caused me to climb on the roof when I knew better. I feel ashamed that I couldn't afford to hire someone else to fix the roof. And so on.

Our bodies are busily trying to cope with the reality of what has occurred, but our brains are experiencing pain on both the physical and emotional levels. Why?

Because we are sentient beings. We are designed that way. We feel. We experience the physical world through our five senses, and we experience life through our feelings. Many of us are locked into the delusion that we are rational and realistic, and that rationality is what motivates us. But this is not the case. We are always moved by some motivation that has to do with changing or maintaining a feeling state. If I feel good, I want to continue feeling good. If I feel bad, I want to escape or change the bad feeling, unless feeling bad somehow makes me feel good. Even rational behavior is motivated by a desire to feel something positive. I may want to look rational because looking rational makes me appear different or better than somebody else, while looking irrational might humiliate me or make me feel vulnerable to others. For example, looking rational might give me and/or others the impression that I am in control of the universe, even though I'm not, and appearing to be in control makes me feel good.

Even when we are actually being objective, we are being motivated by feelings. I know that a certain behavior will cause me pain, so I stop myself from pursuing that behavior. I look like I'm being motivated by rationality, but I'm still really trying to avoid pain. I'm still experiencing life through a feeling state.

If we're busy experiencing life through our feelings, everything is complicated. Let's go back to our example of falling off the leaking roof. Let's say that I believe that if the house had been better built or maintained, the roof wouldn't have leaked. Now watch all the feelings that might plague me. Why am I living in a poorly built house? Did I make a foolish choice? Am I too poor to rent or buy a better place? Why am I too poor? Am I a failure at earning a living? Isn't it my boss's fault for not giving me the raise that would have gotten me a better house? The house inspector should have noticed this weakness in the roof, and I should have known that the inspector was doing a lousy job checking out the house. Who recommended that inspector anyway? The roof is leaking, but what I'm feeling is shame and anger.

If I have a life partner, the leaking roof might bring up other negative feelings. I'm angry with my partner because he or she has not been aggressive enough in earning more money, or because he or she didn't notice the problem with the roof before, or can't fix it. My anger at my partner can be a camouflage of more shame about myself. Why am I stuck with a loser as a partner? Is it because I'm not smart or sexy or something enough to have attracted someone who would make enough money so that we could live in a better house, where the roof wouldn't leak? Or if I'm single, I could think: God damn it! Why do I have to do everything? Why don't I have a partner? What's wrong with me?

Lots of feelings, lots of drama, but what the heck does any of this have to do with the roof? The roof is leaking, but what am I experiencing? Shame and anger. And those emotions cloud my judgment and drive me into emotionally based decision-making.

Let's take another example. Bruce and I are up for the same promotion, and Bruce gets it. I know that if Bruce does a lousy job, we may lose customers, the business could falter, and I could lose my job. So the first thing I might experience could be anxiety about my financial security if Bruce fails. But beyond that, I might feel shame that the boss thought better of Bruce than of me; hope that Bruce will fail, along with embarrassment that I hope that Bruce will fail; anxiety that someone will notice that I hope that Bruce will fail; anger at my girlfriend for saying out loud that she hopes that Bruce will fail or anger at my girlfriend that she genuinely thinks that Bruce will do a better job; panic that I will never get a promotion and will never have enough money to live the way I want; resentment that my father didn't support me to get the education that might have helped me get the promotion; anger at myself for wasting time when I was in school instead of studying; despair about my innate abilities and my chance for self-improvement; happiness for Bruce because I know he's got three children to support; irritation that I have to now take orders from Bruce. Egad. I feel so many things—most of them negative. This is the reality that I experience.

If we confuse our feelings with reality, we may miss reality altogether. Reality may be that you did nothing hurtful. Nevertheless, I may accuse you of hurting me, because I feel hurt. Reality may be that our son wants a trip to Las Vegas for graduation. Yet I decide that our son needs a big graduation party, because I am feeling unimportant and want a way to impress my friends. Reality may be that we need to reduce greenhouse gas emissions. But I may continue spewing pollution into the air, because the technologies that pollute may bring my company greater profit. If I want to feel like a hero at home, supporting my family at the level they desire, I may ignore the needs of the planet. All of these behaviors are based on my feelings, not on the realities of the situation. Yet not only do I take irrational actions, I will have unshakable dedication to the proposition that I am behaving in a way that is realistic.

The pattern of experiencing reality through our feelings starts at the beginning of our existence. When we are infants, reality is "I'm hungry. I'm cold. I'm wet." Suppose we're hungry. We cry, we get fed, and we get comfortable. That's reality, because that's all we can see or feel.

But, of course, reality is also what we don't see. Some of these realities directly impact us. While mom is feeding me, dad is in the next room furious that mom is paying too much attention to me; he's puffing on a cigarette and throwing carcinogens into the air I breathe. Mom feels unsupported and is thinking negative thoughts about him while she's feeding me, and I absorb that negativity with the milk. My older brother is jealous and is sending hateful thoughts to me when he passes by my room. My sister is getting a good grade on her report card; I feel her competitiveness as she runs into the room to show off to Mom. Grandma is depressed and watching television, and there's noise in the house that disturbs me. Other more far-flung realities affect me as well. There's a war going on, which is absorbing a tremendous number of resources, human and material, so there's less money for roads, which means dad's commute is harder than it could be, which makes him angry, which brings more tension into my world. My doctor's nurse's husband is in that war and she's worried, so she is less attentive to me. And so on. I am being impacted by all these events. My immediate reality is the feeling that "I'm hungry. I'm cold. I'm wet." But I'm also being impacted by other realities.

Many other realities impact me as a baby, as well, though those influences are even harder to see. While I may be one of the lucky children who get cared for, there are many other children who are hungry, cold, and wet, and for them there is no comfort. At the same time that I am trapped in my crib, there are beautiful sunsets happening somewhere, and someone stands in awe. While I am focused on the tension in my own house, there's a kind person in Ireland who has just smiled at a child. The planets are in their orbits, and there's an order in the universe. Every one of us is a part of the collective consciousness, which we explore in Platform One: Becoming Oneness, and each one of us is impacted by that collective. But until I bring that reality to my consciousness, what is my reality? Only that "I'm hungry. I'm cold. I'm wet."

When we are adults, our perception of reality expands and the stimuli to our feelings become more diverse. But we are still experiencing reality through the prism of our feelings. Instead of just being hungry, cold, and wet, I'm worried about money, the leak in the toilet, what to make for dinner. I am happy about my raise. I am sad about my best friend's divorce. I am striving to advance at work. I'm desperate for a job. I'm proud of my children. I'm alone. I'm anxious about my health, my upcoming party, climate change. I'm feeling unsafe. I don't want my daughter to sleep with that bum. My parents are getting old, and I'm not sure how to help them without becoming even more exhausted than I already am. I'm upset about what he/she/they did, or said, or even implied. I have gas. Where the hell did I put my keys? When will I ever find someone to love me?

Isn't this the reality that we live with every day? Our feelings, our anxieties, our wants, needs, and desires? The world according to "I?" At some point we may become aware of the expanded reality. For example, if we have seen television programs about hunger in America, now hunger is also in our awareness, even if we are not hungry ourselves. But in what way is that hunger in our awareness? Are we seeing hunger? Or are we experiencing our feeling of upset, compassion, outrage, helplessness, or numbness about that hunger?

We experience life through the prism of our senses and feelings. That is a reality about ourselves we have to face and live with. Once armed with this knowledge, we can make a greater effort to see past our feelings and attempt to identify what is real. And we can work with our feelings so that they don't overwhelm us. But transcending our immediate feelings can be difficult, because the strength of our feelings creates a sense of urgency to fix them. For example, if I'm hungry, I want to satisfy that hunger *now*. If I'm lonely, I want to feel loved *now*. If I'm anxious about something, I want to relieve that anxiety *now*. Whatever my discomfort, I feel the desperate need to fix it now. And my ego tries to figure out how.

Detaching from our feelings and acting for the highest good of all, including ourselves, is even more difficult because we are deluged by feelings about our individual "me." This is because our egos interpret everything as being about "me," because awareness of "me" is the job of the ego. As we view the universe through our individual prisms of "me," we have a lot of feelings to fix. The individual "I" might believe that Daddy left Mommy because of me. The boss is looking disgruntled because of me. My boyfriend is in a bad mood and isn't taking care of me. He's not attracted to me. What will the recession mean for me? The ego will guide our interpretation of experiences in such a way that the interpretation always somehow ends up being about me, either for the positive or the negative. Which means that I am overwhelmed by feelings about myself, even when the reality doesn't actually relate to me.

These questions may help you distinguish between your feelings and reality:

1. Can I identify the difference between my feelings and reality?

2. Can I acknowledge experiences where I felt something was real and then later realized that I was wrong?

3. When something bad happens, what kinds of thoughts and feelings do I have?

4. How difficult is it for me to focus on the problem itself?

5. Can I think of situations where I have believed or interpreted something as being about me, even though it wasn't?

All of this leads us to our next point.

OUR EGOS HAVE DESIGNED BEHAVIORS TO COPE WITH OUR SUBJECTIVE EXPERIENCE

Once we have an uncomfortable feeling about something, our egos busily go about fixing the feelings, instead of the problem. In other words, when presented with a "problem," we rarely address the problem itself; we seek a way to alter our feelings, and we try to alter those feelings fast.

Let's have compassion for ourselves about this. Reality is about what is, not about how we feel. Yet we experience life through our feelings and our senses, and thus we are naturally motivated to fix the way we feel. If I feel tense, I will want to feel relaxed, even if the fix hurts my body or my mind. If I feel vulnerable, I want to feel safe, even if the safety is an illusion. On the other hand, I may have cancer, but if I'm not yet feeling the symptoms, I won't think about my health. Yet if I have a pimple and it hurts, I am motivated to take action.

Because of the urgency of our feelings, physical and emotional, the ego becomes a slave of our subjective experience. As a result, it finds itself focusing on protecting us from feelings, rather than facts. If I feel good on cocaine, it's hard to stop taking it, even though the feeling of wellbeing is going to be short lived. If I feel good about appearing to be rational, I might like to play the role of the problem solver, even when the problem is way out of my league.

The ego has the job of caring for us, and it therefore has the job of coping with our feelings. Let's use our baby example again to see how it learns. Why does the baby cry when it needs its diaper changed? Let's say I'm the baby. I don't cry because I have peed in my pants; I cry because I'm uncomfortable. In this case I'm uncomfortable because I'm wet. As a baby, I'm not aware of the connection between wet and the discomfort. All I know is that I am uncomfortable, so I instinctively cry. Now that I have cried, someone has come and changed my diaper. I am now comfortable again. My ego, whose job it is to be aware of my needs and me, has learned a valuable coping skill: When I'm uncomfortable, I cry, and sometimes someone comes and changes my feeling state.

Driven by our discomfort, we try to fix our feelings, but focusing on altering our feeling state can get us in serious trouble. Let's look at our roof situation again. Let's say the roof is leaking and needs repair. But let's also say that I feel that my value is tied up in being handy. I'm facing a leaking roof, but more importantly I have to feel valuable. If I don't fix the roof, I'll feel ashamed. To add to the mess, I may also feel embarrassed that I haven't fixed the leak already. Now what is reality? The reality is that last year, I had an accident that impacted my balance, so I shouldn't try to stand on the roof. But my need to feel valuable and my desire to cover up my embarrassment for not having already done so compel me to climb onto that roof. I go onto the roof and fall. Now I really feel stupid, and I may even break my neck in the bargain.

The existence of a real problem does not guarantee that we will address it. Whether or not we address the problem directly depends on factors such as how difficult the problem appears to be and whether or not addressing the problem will create even more uncomfortable feelings.

If it is easy to fix the problem, we may strive to fix our feelings by fixing the problem. For example, if the reality is that I am experiencing water leaking on my head and the anxiety caused by water ruining my carpet, I can fix my discomfort by fixing the leak. But if fixing the problem is not easy, we tend to focus more on just fixing the feeling. If I can't fix the leak myself but don't have the money to hire a plumber, I will try to fix the feelings caused by the leak by a) escaping into the television and drinking a beer and b) deflecting the shame onto somebody else, by doing something such as complaining about the baby crying while I'm escaping into television and drinking a beer. If I am the wife and feel helpless because my husband is not fixing the leak, but I don't have the money or the nerve to call a handyman, I will fix my feeling of helplessness by yelling at my husband and complaining to my mother. Nothing is being done about the roof.

Even if the problem is fixable, I may not fix the problem, if the fix appears to be too difficult. I am still being driven by my feelings. In this case, my feelings of fear and/or helplessness over my own behavior drive my actions. For example, if I have a food-related illness, such as high cholesterol, I might prefer to pop a pill rather than address the overeating and the emotional issues causing me to overeat. Maybe I believe that I can't control my eating, that I just don't have the strength. In the process, I barely want to consider that the impact of the medication and the impact of my continued overeating will, in the long run, cause me much greater difficulties than confronting my addiction ever could.

Looking for the quick fix may also be a way of avoiding more uncomfortable feelings. Let's say we feel unhappy in a relationship. Self-examination might lead us to understand why. We might ask questions, such as: Why does my partner's behavior make me feel uncomfortable? What is my part in the strife? Do I need to leave? Questioning our own behavior might trigger feelings of shame, if we believe we are at fault. And considering leaving might trigger fear, if we have to consider living alone. These feelings are uncomfortable.

So instead of dealing with the realities of our relationships, we are more likely to try to force the other person to change, so that we can get comfortable without having to do anything that might be difficult or threatening to us. Or we might seek escape through other pleasurable experiences. In other words, we don't want to have to face uncomfortable feelings in the process of solving our problem, so we seek ways to change our feelings without addressing the problems at all.

Trying to Fix Our Feelings Can Have Serious Long-Term Effects

When we focus on fixing our feelings, instead of dealing with reality, we find a quick fix but create needless pain—sometimes for the rest of our lives. Let's pick an example to discuss in depth. It's an example we've all seen if we haven't done it ourselves.

Let's say you're a teenage girl, and you're coming to the time in life when you have to face the world. You're feeling very insecure, but resent your parents' authority. You're longing to change the way you feel; you want to feel loved, safe, and valuable. You want to feel like a woman, but you don't feel equipped to be on your own. You don't want to live with your parents, but you're extremely insecure about yourself. You also have raging hormones.

What is the real problem? You are young, immature, have raging hormones and lack self-confidence and self-worth. Some ways to fix the problem would be to understand why you're lacking in self-worth and deal with those underlying issues. You could develop your skills, so you have more value and therefore more confidence. You could find a way to channel your sex drive without getting in trouble. You could work on your inner self: quit smoking pot and stop hanging out with boys. You could build in yourself qualities that you value. Then you would be fixing the problem.

But what do we typically do? We try to change the way we feel about ourselves without changing the reality of who we are. Let's go back to our teenage girl who's longing to feel safe, loved and valued. If you are she, you may see another way out of your problems: starting a family of your own. If you can get married and pregnant, you will have the symbols of all you want to be. You have value, because a man wants you and because you're a mother. You will be loved, because you've got your husband and child. And you will feel safe because you won't be alone. You also have an outlet for your raging hormones. Perfect. Now here's a guy, Tommy, who can help you attain it all. He's the fix. And he's the fix, not because you relate to him well, but because he has a compatible fantasy. He also has raging hormones, feels insecure and wants to look like a man. He thinks that a family is the answer: Marriage and baby are symbols of manhood.

So your problem is solved. Tommy is "it," the answer, the means for you to be married and become a mom. Both of you are immature, and neither of you is ready for marriage or parenting. You don't know enough about life or each other to be sure you are making the right choice, and you lack the tools to face the challenges of relationship and parenting. But you ignore all these realities, because you don't want reality to get in the way of your pursuit of the desired symbols. Underneath the excitement, you're really scared of your choice, because on some level, you sense this is a big mistake. But you want the status of marriage, and you don't want to hear otherwise. So the solution to the underlying sense of anxiety is to keep focusing on symbols: the wedding, the apartment, the dishes. Now you're floating in a dream state. Your family and friends may warn you you're being foolish, or, on the other hand, they may get caught up in the fantasy, too.

Done. Now the wedding is over, and real life begins. Of course, Tommy doesn't fix your insecurities about yourself. He can't. You have to learn about life, build your strength, and develop yourself. Marriage hasn't changed your need to pursue your own development; in fact marriage makes your need for maturity even more urgent. What makes the situation worse, of course, is that Tommy isn't ready for marriage and responsibility either. He's been kidding himself, too, pumping himself up and playing at looking like a man, rather than being a man. Now that reality hits, Tommy starts to experience you as a drag. You want him home, and you want him to look like the husband you had in your mind. He wants to hang out with his friends. He wants to have beer with the guys. He doesn't want to have to go to work every day. He feels unprepared and inadequate, which are the opposite experiences he intended when he chose to marry. Things get worse because, in the meantime, you've gotten pregnant. Oh, wow, morning sickness and an angry relationship. The baby comes and you're desperate, because now Tommy has left.

Wouldn't it have been better to face reality to start with?

What If We Have Numerous Feeling States & Opposing Fixes?

Take John. He's gone into his father's business, and he has two feeling states to deal with. One is that he is insecure and doesn't think anyone would pay him as much as dad. The other is that he is angry that his father is still ordering him around. The fix for his insecurity is to stay with the job. The fix for the anger is to leave. If he is motivated by his feeling state, which fix does he choose? Or does he first focus on his insecurity by staying on the job and then later get overwhelmed by his anger and stomp off the job?

So far, I've been focusing on changing a feeling we don't like. The same idea also holds true when we try to maintain a feeling we do like. We do foolish things. I feel comfortable in your arms, so I try to create the illusion of a relationship, just to ensure that I continue to feel that comfort. I like the feeling of cuddling an infant, so I try to keep my daughter dependent and childlike to maintain that feeling. I enjoyed the experience when people laughed at something I said. Now I try to be funny all the time, so that I can continue to experience that high. Of course, there's nothing wrong with being funny; but when it becomes compulsive, driven from the need to escape insecurity, it becomes a problem.

Here are some questions to distinguish between problems and feelings:

1. Can I identify feelings that I have trouble tolerating?
2. How have I tried to fix those feelings?
3. Can I identify a reality that's making me feel uncomfortable?
4. How am I trying to fix those feelings?
5. Can I identify a situation where I am torn between two feeling states and opposing fixes?
6. Which am I choosing?
7. What feelings do I try to maintain and in what way?
8. What price have I paid for trying to alter or maintain my feelings instead of living with reality?

REALITY GETS IN THE WAY OF OUR WANTS, DESIRES & PLANS

Here is the bottom line. Who wants to deal with reality? I want to feel the way I want to feel. If I feel like a bird when I dance on my toes, I will ignore the condition of my feet. If I want to feel important, I will puff myself up. If I want to buy a house in Cape Cod, I will ignore our finances. If I want to be president, I will pretend I'm the best candidate. If I want to live two more weeks, I will demand the government spend fifty thousand dollars on heroic and ultimately useless procedures, even though millions of children have no primary care. If I want to continue the lifestyle I have, I will reject the notion that my behavior is threatening the survival of the human species.

If we experience life through the prism of our feelings, we will constantly be looking for a way to feel better, safe and comfortable. To hell with reality. Now we're beginning to understand our egos. The ego's job is to protect *me*. I feel uncomfortable or pained or afraid of pain. The job of the ego is to find a way to cope with that pain. The ego could think long-term sustainability, but it generally doesn't, because in our anxiety to alter our feeling state, we demand that our egos find a solution that will instantly change our state. Now we understand why the ego focuses on short-term gain and goals. Our egos want quick fixes that give us the fastest relief from discomfort or anxiety.

Our short-term solutions often backfire and cause more pain. If we continue dancing on our toes, ultimately our feet will pay the price. If we buy the house in Cape Cod, we may go bankrupt. If we puff ourselves up, we will suffer the stress and fear of being exposed as a fraud. Does that mean we should never dance on our toes, buy the house, or puff ourselves up? We can do what we like, but we need to be in reality about the consequences or possible consequences of the choices we make.

We can now understand why our egos focus on me-based goals. The fulfillment of such goals provides us with the immediate fixes. Even though hundreds or thousands of people may suffer when we cut corners on the construction of a building site, we recklessly pursue the feeling of success that comes with higher earnings. My ego does not think in terms of the highest good of all; it wants to help *me* feel good now.

Driven by the need to alter or maintain our feeling state, we avoid awareness, sometimes with devastating effect. Maybe I know that I am in the wrong intimate relationship, but I don't want to leave, because I can't face the economic dislocation, loneliness, insecurity or disruption to my social life. So I stay and regret my decision for the rest of my life. And so do all others involved who carry the feelings of guilt and responsibility for my miserable relationship.

What can we do? We are sentient beings, and we are focused on our feelings. How can we deal with reality in a way that does not create needless fear and pain? If we think back to the discussion on "Ego, Instinct & Evolution," we remember the ego twice born. This is what we can do: support that evolution. We can realize the price that we pay for our foolishness. We can start associating our wellbeing with long-term instead of short-term goals. We can retrain ourselves to focus on the joy of contributing to "we-based" goals, rather than "me-based" ones. We can start focusing on the unseen realms of higher consciousness, which bring us greater wisdom and peace. We can reprogram our egos to adopt more enlightened behaviors.

We can continue to be normal human beings with a focus on altering and maintaining our feelings, but in a way that supports our highest good. We can bring higher consciousness to our normal instinctive behavior, so that we can intervene in the patterns that cause needless fear and pain.

How we do all this is the practice of *Living with Reality*. But before we can get to this program, we need to discuss our primary sources of discomfort: the pain and fear that drive us.

CHAPTER 2

The Human Condition:
The Pain & Fear that Drive Us

We have now acknowledged that, as humans, our experience of reality is based on our senses and feelings. We've acknowledged that our egos have the task of altering or maintaining those feelings, according to whether we find those particular sensations pleasurable or not. In this chapter, I would like to briefly address two of the feelings that most often drive us to attempt to alter our feeling state: pain, and its cousin, fear.

PAIN

Life is wonderful and exciting. It is also difficult and painful. This is reality. As we have already begun to see, much of our pain is self-created, as in the example of the teenage girl in our last chapter. But much of our pain is simply the result of the way life is.

We humans are beset with many sources of pain. Take the physical world. Many of us have to endure pain on the job—standing at a machine, stooping over a hoe, carrying lumber, or typing all day. Then there's the pain of headaches and other stress-related conditions incurred from work or life situations where we suffer a lot of pressure. There's suffering caused by violence from other humans, sometimes even those we know and are close to. There is illness and injury, childbirth and dental work, and although the suffering can be mitigated by good medical care, ultimately there is increasing physical pain as we age.

We also endure emotional pain, loss, and betrayal. A beloved child, pet or friend is gone, and we feel loneliness and grief. A trusted or much-needed parent neglects us, and we feel powerless and in despair. A love partner goes through an emotional crisis and suddenly becomes abusive or emotionally unavailable. These pains are situational. Other emotional pain is not situational. Some of us are born with chemical imbalances that gear us toward mood swings or depression.

As we have been observing so far in our book, we also suffer a great deal of needless pain. In Chapter One, we saw that we create a lot of needless pain in the process of fixing our feelings. Further in this chapter we will discuss the pain of disconnection. But for now, let's take a moment to look at the second most impactful emotion that we feel: fear.

FEAR

Once we have experienced that pain is possible, even likely, we develop the habit of fear. Why are we fearful? Because we anticipate pain. Imagine us back in the cave days. We're sitting around a fire, enjoying a hot meal. Great. How long does that last? How long is it before a wild animal threatens our existence, or a neighboring clan picks a fight, possibly because our own clan threatened them at some time in the past? We could be maimed or killed. Our children could die of exposure or starvation. Our husband or wife could be injured and die. Life is short and precarious.

How different are our lives today? We have insurance policies, doctors, Social Security, seniority, laws. Are we secure? One minute, we're sitting around the living room table, enjoying a hot meal, and there's a knock at the door. A drunk driver has killed our son. Our job has been exported to Mexico, and now our credit card bills can't be paid. Our spouse has a mid-life crisis, and we find ourselves alone. We injure ourselves standing on a ladder changing a light bulb. The IRS audits us, and the news isn't good. We buy a car and have an accident on the way home from the dealership. We lose love. We lose our health. We get old and lose our independence. Now life is long and precarious.

Nothing can truly eliminate the insecurities of life, and nothing can eliminate the pain of loss. We attribute all power to God; maybe God can fix it. We hope that God will be on our side, if we are good. We think we have the ultimate fix; we "behave" for God, and we begin to feel secure. But then our child dies of leukemia. Why?

No wonder we carry fear within us. Humanity carries memories of war, illness, natural disasters, and human cruelty: the everyday uncertainties of life. Life is raw. Security is fleeting. Peace is hard to maintain.

Much of our fear today is exacerbated by our feeling alone. At one time, we organized ourselves into clans, tribes, small communities, and extended families in order to collectively minimize our difficulties and reduce our fear. To a degree, this strategy worked. To an extent, we were able to support each other through difficult times and even through the everyday stresses of growing food, hunting, and raising children. We may have shared our disasters. But no, the disasters themselves never ceased.

Such communal living gave us some security, but it exacted a price as well. Living in communities has its own tyranny. Sometimes the group, and often just a few members of the group, decides what is right and wrong, what will be rewarded and what punished, and what we should think or do. Many of us don't like feeling dominated and rebel against the authority of the group. Given the choice, many of us have chosen freedom. Unless we were Native Americans or slaves, we or our ancestors left the known world for the New World. Many of us have travelled across the country or the world to strike out on our own. And when given a chance, we left our collective living situations, such as the apartment buildings with their community laundry rooms, and found ourselves in our own individual homes, standing alone at the washer and dryer. We have struck out on our own, so that we could in fact express our individuality. The result has been more freedom; the result has been more fear.

In the face of the continuing uncertainty of life on Earth today, for many of us, our social network is pretty slim. We may choose, for example, to move away from our parents to gain our freedom when we're young. But where are the grandparents and aunts and uncles when we have kids and need free babysitters? We may choose to live in single-family households, but where's the help, when we sprain our ankle?

The desire to find a balance between the individual and the community is a ceaseless evolutionary process, which we will discuss in the first four platforms of our program. But let us be frank: most of us don't particularly trust each other in the larger community, especially when the community is seen as global and therefore out of our control, different, foreign, or inscrutable. Focusing on those with whom we feel more aligned and safe, focusing on those who we have some reason to believe will protect us in some way, we tend to pursue our own interests or the interests of those close to us through ties of family, race, nationality, and social class. Few of us focus on the needs and interests of others. Even if we wanted to consider the needs of the whole, of the group, who decides what those needs are and how we would meet them? (We discuss this in depth in Platform Four: Becoming Mutually Supportive.) And just as we are not concerned about the wider community, others are not that concerned about us. It's frightening world.

Later we will find out that the ego plays a part in this as well. It feeds off "them" and "us" and encourages fear and self-protection. But now, at this point, let's just consider a few questions:

1. Have I tended to be with a group or go off on my own?
2. Why did I make that choice?
3. What price have I paid for my choice?
4. Do I feel secure?
5. Whom do I trust?
6. Whom do I care about?

Looking at the broader society, the United States, the West and even much of the developing world have embraced a social and economic system based on individualism and self-interest, and in the process, we have lost community. Now we turn more and more to objects and financial schemes to give us the feeling of security once provided by the tribe. To a degree, these things may help, but how much? Every object needs to be maintained, fed, and supported. Plus the more things we have, the more headaches we have as well. We used to have to worry about the weather and our health. Now we have to worry about our investments, too. We're still in fear.

Even advances in the field of health have not made us secure. We are definitely living longer, but look at the new fears we have to face: years of incapacity, dependence and loneliness, as we lose our friends, spouses, family and freedom. As much as we have tried to find ways to protect our health, we are constantly discovering new things to worry about. We realize now that we have poisoned our air, food, and water. We see now that we're damaging ourselves through substances such as alcohol, drugs, sugar, tobacco and caffeine. Not that long ago, we were ignorant or in denial of the negative effects of these behaviors and substances. What are we going to discover tomorrow?

We also find that while medical treatment can help, it can also be dangerous. Our hospitals are complex, and we can't rely on a harried staff to take the best care of us. We're overmedicated. We take drugs whose side effects don't become known for years. We create new resistant strains of bacteria. We can easily pick up infections in the hospital. Even immunizations are now seen as a mixed blessing. Where's the safety?

Every advance that we have created to deal with our insecurities has its down side. We're busy, stressed, and trying desperately not to make mistakes. We don't want our kids to fall behind, and we sure don't want to be blamed if they do, so we run them around town, bringing them to a million activities, until sometimes they are way overstressed—and so are we. We try to keep up with all the technological advances, and we still haven't figured out how to use the last set. We spend, we consume, we insure. Yet there is no security. A terrorist bomb can drop from the sky. A deranged teen can kill the child we have so painstakingly raised. A recession can destroy the value of our home.

We ceaselessly seek ways of dealing with fear and anxiety. We escape into movies or other forms of entertainment to run from our feelings, or we stress ourselves out trying even harder to create the illusion of control.

But we can't. There are always new things to worry about. So much for security.

Didn't we determine in "Ego, Instinct & Evolution" that the ego has taken on the job of protecting us? With all these anxieties, real and created, no wonder the ego is in high gear all the time!

Let's ask ourselves a few more questions at this point.

1. What means have I chosen to make myself feel secure?
2. Have they worked?
3. Did they create their own problems and insecurities?

63

Having acknowledged the reality of life's fears, what can we really do about them? We can learn to look at them realistically, and we can learn to identify which are real and which are programmed.

Let's say we're back in the cave. Three times when we were between the ages of 10 and 12, a saber-toothed tiger came to our cave and took away a friend. Each time that happened at dusk. Now the tigers have died off. But every day at dusk, I feel uneasy. Now I'm programmed.

Obviously the same phenomenon happens in each of our lives. We have a series of experiences that create associations, especially when our families reinforce them. "Oh no," says Mom. "It's dusk. I wonder if the saber-toothed tiger is coming."

In addition to noticing how many of our fears are programmed, we can see how fixing one fear can create another. Yes, we're late for a business appointment, but do we need to have stomach cramps and drive like maniacs, which creates the additional fear that we will get in a wreck? Don't we have more to fear from our reckless speeding than we have to fear from being late? Will we really lose our jobs? And if so, is that worth our lives?

What can we do about our needless fear and pain? A lot. Practicing this program will help us change our programming and free ourselves from the compulsion to fix our feelings, which will free us from creating fixes which, in turn, create more fear and pain. Practicing this program will help us connect to the universal energies that support us to feel whole and calm. But before delving into our program, we have two more subjects to discuss: first, the needless pain and fear caused by our separation from ourselves, one another and the process of living, and second, the addictions we use to try to alter our feelings.

CHAPTER 3

The Fear and Pain of Disconnection

We have now recognized that we do not live with reality; we live within a feeling state that we attempt to either alter or maintain. We have acknowledged the fear and pain that drive us and discussed some of their real and self-created causes. Now we will examine a very large component of our fear and pain: our disconnection from ourselves, from one another and from the process of living. The impact of this disconnection is so important that I am devoting a separate chapter to it.

WHY DO WE FEEL DISCONNECTED?

We feel disconnected first and foremost because we see ourselves from the perspective of the ego, meaning we think of ourselves as distinct and separate, which, in itself, causes us to feel alone and afraid. Then in order to overcome the fear and pain of an existence dominated by ego consciousness, we try to cope by artificially creating the feeling of connection, which, in turn, leads us into a great deal of dysfunctional and destructive behavior. This point is so important, I will reiterate it: In order to overcome the fear and pain caused by our experiencing ourselves as separate, we try to artificially create the feeling of connection, and this causes enormous harm to us and everyone else.

Of course, the real solution to the fear and pain of disconnection is to overcome the domination of the ego as we know it, thereby overcoming the pain of separation. It is, in fact, the experience of many people that when we viscerally feel part of the Oneness, we aren't dominated by the fear and pain that drives us into self-destructive behaviors. This is the state of consciousness we begin to practice more regularly when we reach the end of this book, and many of us have had glimpses of it already.[14]

However, at this point in our collective history, most of us remain stuck in the ego-based universe and are subject to the terrible consequences of that fact.

DISCONNECTION FROM OURSELVES

Most of us are not truly connected to ourselves, and that causes us pain. Disconnected from ourselves and unable to identify our true needs, we cannot truly care for ourselves, and that reality also causes us great pain. Why aren't we connected to ourselves?

Generally speaking, we are not encouraged to know ourselves, because if we did, it might threaten the social order as we know it. Every society seeks to impose its norms on the individual, and that's very understandable.

---

[14] I call living from a place of Oneness "living vertically." When we live vertically, we feel filled by the universe, guided, abundant and happy. When feel separate from the universe, on the other hand, we feel insecure, alienated and alone, hungry, afraid and empty. Naturally, we are desperate to change this feeling state. Our desperation severely impacts our relationships, because we relate "horizontally" to one another, meaning that we are turning to one another to resolve our inner tension. We seek out relationships for what they can give us: to fill us up, puff up our egos, meet our needs and compensate for our weaknesses or lacks. Being horizontal distorts our relationships and causes us to try to manipulate one another for our own needs. Shifting into vertical relationships is touched upon at the end of this book, and living vertically is the starting point of the New Era. I will address it in a future work, but fortunately every step in our program, starting with Becoming Oneness, Platform One, moves us toward it.

Supposing I just "feel" like driving on the left side of the road. Perhaps doing so more closely matches my physical strengths and vision. Well, regardless of my individual nature, here in the United States, we all have to drive on the right side of the road, because if we didn't, we would crash into one another on an even more regular basis than we already do.

Social norms are a way of directing traffic, the flow of resources. All societies divide their resources in very specific ways, and that division of resources is reinforced by our social structure and norms. Social norms regulate the flow of everything we deem valuable: money, prestige, land, power, and even love. And because they are collective, these social norms seem "normal." Let's take a family. Dad may be an abusive alcoholic, but we may have a social norm in our family that he sits at the head of the table and gets to bully everyone around. Why? Because he brings home the money. So Mom takes the abuse and teaches you to take abuse, too. You are internalizing the family's social norm: He or she who brings home the money has special dispensation to behave badly. Social norms can also be societal. In some societies, slaves were supposed to shut up; executives are supposed to want to work 60 hours a week; Mexicans are supposed to be satisfied laboring for minimum wage; children are supposed to go to college; and women are supposed to want to have children and to like making their husbands feel good.

What we're allowed to think and do is highly controlled, in order to keep the social order in place. Indeed, the purpose of socialization is to teach us how to fit into our place. And so, having learned how to be, whether we are supposed to command or obey or to serve or be served, having learned where to defer, where to dominate, what to believe, what to reward, and what to do to be rewarded, most of us are living up to some concept of who we are or think we should be. This complex mix of beliefs and socialization is so ingrained, it seems natural.

Our self-protective egos work in tandem with our socialization. We know that our survival could be threatened if we don't go along with the norms of society, and so we do—unless we get into a group that prides itself on rebellion. Even so, the principle remains. If in our group, the social norm is rebellion, we will follow the group, even when we feel uncomfortable or even when doing so endangers us.

The fact that our roles are normal and socially defined does not make them fit us as human beings or meet our true needs. To challenge them would certainly stir things up. What would happen if we all decided to get in touch with ourselves and dump our social roles on the same day? There might be chaos: dinners unmade, garbage left on the street, children uncared for, and nobody to drive the bus. People would loot and grab private property; there would be no order. That's scary. Chaos is frightening to everyone, not just to those who have the most to lose. Let's ask ourselves some questions regarding our social norms:

1. Where do I fit in the social order, whether that is with family and friends, the community, the nation, or the world?
2. Where did I learn that?
3. What would happen if I connected to myself?
4. What am I afraid I would do?
5. What do I fear others would do, if they connected to all the aspects of themselves?

Who created the social order? We did, over time. Those on top have used whatever means necessary to maintain their power, means ranging from education, conditioning, and rewards, to threats, ostracism, and physical force. But whether we are on the bottom or the top, it is our mutual agreement to maintain that order that keeps it alive. Even a king could not sustain his crown if his army deserted and his subjects refused to follow his commands. So it is our collective fear of chaos and the vested interests of large groups of people that maintain the status quo. Those of us who threaten that order threaten our collective security, which threatens our collective ego, and naturally we punish, marginalize, or shame those who question the "system," whether that system be the family, the school, or the balance of power in the world.

So does that mean that we shouldn't get in touch with ourselves, because it might threaten our collective or individual security? And is it true that the only possible outcome of connecting with ourselves would be anarchy, chaos, and collective mayhem? Would we all "turn on, tune in, and drop out," as the hippies were encouraged to do in the 1960s? Would we all think only of ourselves and ignore the needs of others, dump our responsibilities and become violent and out of control? "Yeah, man, I kill frogs in my spare time, but, like, it's me!"

Is it true that getting in touch with ourselves could be dangerous and destructive? Not at all. Not if we begin to understand reality. Not if we realize the limitations of our ego-based perceptions. Not if we practice the processes represented by *Living with Reality*.

Connecting to ourselves is not what creates problems. What causes our problems is not connecting to the whole. We do not perceive ourselves as a part of and responsible for the collective, and that is the problem. We believe that connecting to ourselves would cause chaos, because the self we think we will connect to is the ego self, the "me" self, the self disconnected from the whole. I want, I must have, I have to get, I, I, I, I, I. It's the two year old with no socialization. In that context, of course getting in touch with ourselves and doing whatever we feel like could lead to havoc. But were we to connect to our true selves, the opposite would occur, because the true self's needs are not addressed by grabbing, having, getting, or puffing itself up. It comes from harmonizing with the Oneness, and that true self we need to come to know and become.

In Platforms One and Four: Becoming Oneness and Becoming Mutually Supportive, we set the stage for self-realization. It's not about "I'll do it my way"; it's about who I am, who you are, and how we can co-create a reality that supports the highest good of all. These platforms enable us to understand our role within the whole, and our wellbeing as part of the collective wellbeing. We learn that discovering ourselves is for the good of the whole.

Without a concept of mutual support, and without true self-knowledge, we're afraid to support the individual to become totally self-realized, because we're afraid we would be creating a bunch of spoiled ego-driven individuals. So instead we suppress one another and ourselves, and cause needless pain in the process.

Ask yourself:

1. What comes to mind when you think of people getting in touch with themselves?
2. Think about people from other countries and cultures as well as your own.
3. What do you think they might do?
4. How do you feel about that?

It is not just society, our parents, teachers, the police, bosses, and the powers that be that fear our self-expression. So do we. Where would it lead us? What if I discovered that I hate my job and don't want to work more than four hours a day? Would I quit, and what would I do for income? What if I went back to my adolescent dream of writing the great American novel? Would I dump my responsibilities, stop paying my taxes, and leave my kids to wander around the neighborhood begging for dinner? What if I told my clients I was sick of their problems and didn't want to hear them whining anymore? Would they walk out on me, leaving me with a mortgage, a car payment, and a room full of empty chairs? What if I admitted that my husband gets on my nerves, doesn't smell good, and is an arrogant fool? Would I leave? If I let myself feel all these feelings, would I smash my life as I know it and destroy the safety net I have so painstakingly erected? Hell no. I'd much rather forget those nagging feelings that I'm not doing the right thing for myself. I'll just have another beer, another anti-depressant, another piece of chocolate, and just forget about it. Again, this is a misunderstanding of what our true selves would do, which would be to act for the highest good of all, including ourselves, even though it might rock the boat. Wow, but we'd really have to know ourselves in order to do that.

Again, ask yourself:

1. What feelings of mine am I afraid of?
2. What am I afraid I might do?

Why else are we not connected to ourselves? Because we're afraid of ourselves, and the fear of ourselves is largely associated with our inner critic. Consider this. When we look at our destructive behaviors, we automatically look at ourselves with shame and disgust. Why? Because most of us have been taught through shame and blame, and so we adopt that same attitude toward ourselves when we observe our negative behaviors, which makes us self-critical and judgmental. So why would we WANT to connect with ourselves, if we think the self is going to be bashing us for our mistakes or weaknesses? And because we see ourselves from the perspective of that inner critic, why would we want to look at ourselves honestly, when what we think we will see is that we're stupid, selfish, naïve, inadequate, weak, addicted, pushy, not pushy enough, too much, too little, or just too? Fearing the inner critic, we tend to unconsciously lie to ourselves in order to avoid looking honestly at our motives and behaviors; we go into denial just to avoid our own harsh self-judgment.

So far, we're noticing that fear has been keeping us from connecting to ourselves. And if we need any more reasons to fear that connection, we have another big one. We might alienate others. I want to be a pianist, but Dad wants me to be a lawyer. If I follow my inner needs, there goes his love, my inheritance, my seat at the table. More fear and insecurity. I want to sleep in on Sunday mornings, but my wife thinks I should be in church. If I do what I feel is right, she'll be mad. I'm a kid, and I want to eat at 10 am and play at noon, but the teachers all say that I need to play at 10 am and eat at noon. Why are they all yelling at me?

In addition, it's not easy to see ourselves clearly, even when that's our intention. By practicing Platform Five: Becoming Self-Aware, we can delve into our innermost realms and come to peace without shame or fear of what we'll see. By practicing Platforms Eight and Nine: Becoming Not-Knowing and Becoming Becoming, we develop the center that allows us to take the risk of being who we are. By developing self-compassion, as we teach throughout our book, we free ourselves to fully engage in our natural curiosity about ourselves, no longer fearing the judge within.

All these practices are based on Oneness, a completely different way of experiencing life and ourselves, as we will soon see. So hang in there until we get into our program. We will come to be honest with our own best friends: ourselves.

Questions for introspection:

1. Do I tend to be self-critical?
2. What are my judgments about myself?
3. Whose critical voice am I hearing in my head? (For example, the voice of a parent, sibling, old teacher or former spouse?)
4. Who am I afraid I'll alienate?
5. Why?

What is the Impact of Not Connecting with Ourselves?

With inner and outer pressures keeping us from connecting to ourselves, we feel lost. We have no integrity and no center. Without a center, we feel as though we are floating in space, desperately needing an anchor, something to connect to. Now here's a feeling that's uncomfortable, a feeling that our ego has to fix. So we'll fix it by finding an anchor, and what can that anchor be? Anchors can be internal or external. Here are some internal anchors that many of us have used: Some of us attach to our minds or to mental obsessions, some surrender totally to our emotions, some overly focus on our bodies, some try to escape through our spirits, some focus on some ambition. It may look like we're connected to ourselves, but we're not. We are connected only to fragments of ourselves, and a fragment of me is not me. The fragment gives me a sense of identity, but it deprives me of my self-connection.

Typically the fragment of ourselves that we habitually focus on is usually the one that has been most rewarded. Dad encourages my mind; I think I'll study more. My peers encourage my sexuality; I will become more flirtatious. The church encourages my selflessness; I'll want to give more. Mom gives me extra chocolate pudding when I put my toys away; I think I'll be a good boy again. My boyfriend tells me he loves me every time we have sex, even if I don't want to; I think I'll become a sexy lady. The boss gave me a promotion for ratting on my friends; I think I'll take on the role of the boss's eyes and ears.

When we try to anchor ourselves in some fragment of ourselves, we just become more disconnected from the whole of us. But what makes things even more complicated is that the fragments of ourselves can themselves be in conflict. Here are two examples: our minds may want to work when our bodies want to rest; our heart may want to leap toward a relationship while our brain says put on the brakes. In addition, any given aspect of us can be fragmented. Our emotions may want us to approach love because of our need; at the same time our emotions may want us to avoid love, because of our fear of disappointment. Our minds may want security and at the same time may long for challenge.

Whenever I connect to a fragment of myself, I'm in trouble. I am a teacher, a wife, a manager, a cop, a nice person, a thief, a peacemaker, a spiritual being. Connecting to that fragment gives me a sense of identity and sometimes a sense of purpose. But it robs me of the totality of myself and forces me to give up the parts of me that don't fit. How can I get angry, when I'm a spiritual teacher? How can I want to get a job, when I'm a mom?

And what of external anchors? We try to anchor ourselves to jobs, money, food, objects, anything, or everything that gives us a sense of location, a sense of security, a sense of relationship to something. We also try to anchor to other people, which we explore more in the next section. We look for external anchors because we are not connected to ourselves, but being dependent on external anchors is risky and in itself causes needless fear that we also have to fix.

By practicing Platform Six: Becoming Integrated, we find that we no longer have to be fragmented, and we connect to the being that we are, and so, wow, there goes a lot of needless fear. But right now let's look at where we are.

1. What fragments of myself do I tend to attach to?
2. Do I tend to connect to one aspect of me more than another?
3. Do I tend to anchor myself more to my body, mind or spirit?
4. Why have I chosen to connect to that aspect of myself?
5. What parts of me do I give up to maintain those identities?
6. What anchors outside myself do I look for?

What is the needless pain caused by being disconnected from ourselves? We pursue what we don't need, because we don't know what we do need, or if we do know what we need, we don't know how to get it. We look to other people and things, when we need to look to ourselves. We are conflicted, without center, and confused. We lack self-acceptance, integration, self-awareness, and self-love. This is painful, but not the inevitable pain of life. This is the pain of disconnection from ourselves.

We have briefly discussed the pain of disconnection from ourselves, but before closing this section, I would like to share one important point about the value of being connected with who we really are. Ultimately, the most important thing we have in life is our self-respect, and self-respect comes from a sense of integrity. What is integrity, if not wholeness? We feel integrity when we know that we are willing to do what we consider right, no matter the consequences. We feel integrity when we know that we are true to our higher selves, not to the ego-based, self-centered, scared, protective self, but that inner self that is connected to higher consciousness. We cannot respect ourselves, if what we do is not worthy of our respect. We cannot deeply love ourselves, unless we feel worthy of our own love. And while we must always find self-compassion, no matter how badly we might behave or how severely we might betray ourselves, true self-love comes from integrity, from Oneness with ourselves. It is the energy of connection with ourselves that permeates our being.

Yes, self-honesty brings pain, and pain is a feeling state that we usually want to avoid. But the pain of self-honesty is temporary. If we can face that we have damaged our bodies, minds, or spirits out of our weakness and fear, out of our need to "belong" in a superficial way, to "please" or to avoid trouble, and if we have damaged others for the same reasons, we can practice Platform Seven and Become Accountable. Then we can begin to feel free.

As we learn throughout our program, let's start with reality. We are all weak in one or many ways. That doesn't make us defective. It makes us human. By facing our weaknesses, we can deal with them, either by finding ways to strengthen ourselves or by getting the support to compensate for those flaws. Denial of our weaknesses leaves us with no weapons to fight our own needless pain. Facing the truth about ourselves with compassion and objectivity, even when it feels humiliating, and learning to live more and more in integrity, these are the gifts that we need to give ourselves.

Integrity is the key to self-respect, and self-knowledge is the key to integrity. We cannot be true to ourselves if we do not know ourselves, if we are not connected with ourselves. Connection with ourselves is, therefore, the cornerstone of self-knowledge, self-love, and wellbeing. The lack of it brings only needless pain. Ask yourself:

1. Do I really know myself?
2. Do I know my needs?
3. What are my weaknesses?
4. How do I feel about them?
5. Do I try to hide them?
6. Am I in integrity with myself?
7. Am I willing to pay the price?
8. What is the price of my lack of integrity?

DISCONNECTION FROM OTHERS

We've already discussed that we feel disconnected from ourselves. Disconnected from ourselves, we feel empty, uncentered and confused, and so we seek to anchor ourselves to something, and that includes other people. But we don't feel truly connected to others either.

In our introduction, "Ego, Instinct & Evolution," we discussed how ego is the awareness of our individual existence, and while ego is a natural result of our experience, perceiving reality from the perspective of the ego automatically causes us pain, because it causes us to feel alone.

The only way to overcome the pain of alienation and aloneness is by Becoming Oneness, the capacity to think, act and feel in a way that includes the whole. But even those of us who have absorbed this concept have difficulty knowing how to live from this paradigm. And so because we don't feel our Oneness, we try to link together by creating emotional, social, legal and obligatory bonds in the effort to fit together like a bunch of fragments into a giant puzzle. But we aren't a bunch of fragments to be linked together; we are individual manifestations of Oneness. So we try to bond to one another, but it doesn't work; it doesn't feel like Oneness.

To summarize thus far, we long for Oneness but few of us experience that state in any consistent way. And just as disconnection from ourselves causes us to try to create artificial bonds with others, disconnection from others causes us to do the same. The attempt to create artificial bonds only creates further problems. Let's look at some of them.

To anchor ourselves in others is to give up our freedom and our integrity, because maintaining others as our anchor can become more important than having ourselves. This again creates needless fear and pain, because now, not only are we feeling afraid and alone, we're also feeling fear of being dominated by those in whom we are trying to anchor ourselves. And that can lead us to feel enslaved or cause us to pull away.

Without a strong center in ourselves, we are unable to maintain our autonomy while feeling close, so it's impossible to relate to others in a healthy way. Terrified of losing control over our lives and ourselves, we become reluctant to be intimate. We're afraid of having love, and at the same time, we're afraid of losing it. The worst fear is that the love will be lost, and we will have no vote.

Let's look at this closer. In order to keep our love object—whether it be a parent, friend, or mate—we find ourselves giving up important aspects of ourselves. Giving ourselves away makes us more disconnected from ourselves, which renders us more empty and thus more desperate to anchor ourselves in other people. And when we can no longer tolerate the loss of ourselves, we create rigid boundaries, giving ourselves the illusion of power by drawing imaginary lines around our vulnerability. Or we make demands on our beloved, so that we can fool ourselves that we have regained control over ourselves by establishing control over them. We have acted in similar ways when we've tried to connect with clients, bosses or others on whom we feel dependent.

While we have turned to others as a substitute for being connected to ourselves, have we been successful in feeling connected? No. How can we feel connected to anyone else when we aren't connected to ourselves? It's like having the cable connected to the electric socket, but we forgot to plug the other side of the cable into the computer. We are connected to others, but even more lost in ourselves.

All this pain and dysfunction, yet we keep trying to connect to others. Being alone is for humans a fundamentally unnatural and unsatisfying experience. It doesn't honor the reality of the connection that exists among us all; nor does it honor that we are fundamentally pack animals; nor does it satisfy the human need for love. While there may be a few people who are genuinely happy alone, most solitary souls are not truly fulfilled. They are just too scared of intimacy to try to connect, and they choose the pain of aloneness over the pain of unhealthy connection. Even those of us who deny our need for closeness often exhibit behaviors that show we are seeking community: we go to parties, flee to work, watch television, hang out at bars, attend football games, cling to families with dysfunctional relationships, read books, search the Internet, or have lunch, friends, or sex. These pseudo-relationships may give the appearance of connection, but do these experiences satisfy our need for Oneness?

And who would have taught us to have healthy relationships, where we feel our individuality in the context of Oneness? Our parents were often absent, frazzled, needy, controlling, smothering, molesting, abusive, or addicted themselves. Experience is the greatest teacher, and few of us had parents who knew how to have healthy relationships with us or anyone else. As children, we found ourselves making bargains for their love and/ or pretending we didn't need their love and going numb. Either way, we became disconnected from ourselves and others.

And what has society taught us about love and romance? We've learned that "he" or "she" is the answer to everything: our need for love, security, companionship, handyman services, domestic help, sex, and intellectual compatibility. Oh, and haven't you heard? Romance will end loneliness.

Not so. Our greatest loneliness is caused by our disconnection from ourselves. No partner can meet that need. In addition, no partner can fulfill and meet all our fantasies and expectations. And yet, astonishingly, this illusion persists.

Of course, reality ultimately interferes with our romantic notions. Then we have two choices. We can try to avoid disappointment by continuously seeking the perfect mate, or we can try to avoid disappointment by giving up on wanting to feel connected to a partner at all, either by choosing not to enter into intimate relationships or by openly settling for security rather than love.

Why does the romantic notion persist? In the first blush of love, our partner is still a fantasy, and all our dreams will be fulfilled. Often we're willing to give ourselves up totally to have this fantasy. We lose ourselves, and then we blame that loss on our partner. "They" are trying to control "us." As we get to know our mates, we feel disappointed with the inadequacy of both our partner and the connection we've created. Of course, this is also their fault. We then try to control our partner in the hopes that if we could get them to do x, y, or z, they would be perfect for us. Then they would be able to be there for us in the way that we want. Then we wouldn't be alone. Then we would be able to feel connected.

Our partners feel the same way toward us. Each of us is still fragmented in ourselves and unable to connect fully to ourselves or each other; each of us feels shame, self-doubt, anger and fear, and each is crippled in our ability to fully love ourselves or each other; each of us feels incomplete and has difficulty feeling our differentiation once in a relationship; each of us has little trust and few internal resources to deal with our disappointments; each of us suffers from a lack of internal balance and integration; each of us feels frustrated in our craving to connect; and each of us blames the other. Blaming is easy, because in fact our partners are inadequate in one or a hundred ways. Quickly we lose our fantasies about each other and ourselves, and we end up angry and still starving for connection.

Angry and disappointed, we seek another mate. When we've become totally disappointed with intimate relationships, we're back to seeking something else to fill the need for connection: food, sex, work, something to distract us from this fundamental pain. Even though we long for intimacy, we can't trust other humans, so we go to our "safe" partner—some familiar substance or behavior that we can rely on. One more time, we look for an anchor in things, food, anything we can seem to control. Gee, I wonder why I've gained 25 pounds since I got married.

None of this means that love is not important. Of course it is. And love does exist. In fact, some people have truly mastered the art of relationship, but that requires two individuals who are connected to themselves and higher consciousness, and that's not the reality of most of us at this time in history. Sadly, though, the romantic ideal continues to dominate our thinking, followed by disgust with our real-life mates. Fantasy meets a hard death.

Our disconnection from others expresses itself in many ways. As we will discuss at length in Platform One: Becoming Oneness, we are raised in a them/us universe, and we're afraid of one another. And just as society does not encourage us to connect to ourselves, it doesn't really encourage us to see our Oneness with others. In fact, living from a place of Oneness may be seen as a threat to our social norms, values and behaviors. Yeah, I'm a citizen of the world until and unless my family is competing with your family to buy a house, our nation wants to keep the better jobs here, we are in a basketball tournament with the school in the next town, or our government decides we need somebody else's oil. Oneness is great for church on Sunday, but not for the way we run our everyday lives.

In fact, if we break the social agreement to connect to "us" instead of "them," we risk antagonizing our own group. There's the not-too-subtle reminder not to forget who's supposed to come first: your mate, children, friends, family, race, religion, nation, species. Aren't you patriotic? Loyal? Devoted? How can you betray "us"? Step out of line, and you're in danger of being ostracized and alone in a scary world.

Sometimes we try to relieve the pain of disconnection by turning to God. We create a God that is all-loving and all-powerful, who will help us deal with our fears, as well as our loneliness, and we decide that God is the connection that's supposed to solve all our need for Oneness. But does it? Not when it blocks our relationship with ourselves.

And it can. Just as we learn an idealized vision of romantic love, we are taught a particular concept of God and spirituality. This concept has usually been taught to us by the social group of which we are a part. We don't always stick with our original spiritual belief system. Some of us give up our family's beliefs and exchange them for another set, but all belief systems are human creations. Differing groups in different societies and times have differing concepts, but each is held up as real and absolute, and we're then expected to feel in synch with that particular spiritual orientation, regardless of our true feelings and experience. If we don't feel, think, and act in accordance with these socially determined concepts, there must be something wrong with us. Forget the fact that all religion has been filtered through human understanding, which makes it no different from any other part of the socially determined norms.

None of this means that spirituality is not important. Of course it is. In fact, it can be critical to a happy life and is ultimately essential for transformation. But spirituality can alienate us from ourselves when we lie to ourselves. I believe that I'm supposed to feel gratitude, when I feel resentful. I'm supposed to never have adulterous feelings or thoughts, when I'm feeling empty and dissatisfied with my relationship. I'm supposed to feel love for God, when I'm pissed as hell. If we can't admit those realities, we are cut off from ourselves.

Spiritual belief systems can turn us against ourselves in other ways. I may think that my misfortunes are caused by me, by my bad thoughts, by my weak intention, by God's punishment, by my bad karma. Talk about a recipe for self-condemnation! Plus spiritual belief systems can also be full of confusing and contradictory precepts. I'm supposed to love my neighbor, while marching off to war.

When our connection to the universal energies is real and is grounded in our deep connection to ourselves and the Oneness, it is the ingredient that allows us to live with reality and thrive. It is the ingredient that fuels transformation. It is calm, neutral and pure consciousness. But when spirituality is used as an escape, it is like any other addiction.

How do we use spirituality as an escape? By using it addictively to temporarily change our feeling state. When we use spirituality to temporarily change our feelings, we cut off connection to reality in order to achieve a spiritual high. Hooked on the spiritual high, we begin to think that reality is the enemy because it interrupts the high. When the high is over, we're left feeling strangely empty, because we don't want to reconnect to our bodies and our lives.

Escaping into spirituality may give us moments of bliss, may give us a feeling of connection to the whole. But if we are using spirituality to escape, the moments don't last, and then we feel devastated when reality strikes, like a terrorist attack on the heart of the city.

Where else do we anchor ourselves? Some of us try to use intimacy itself—addictively trying to connect to anybody at every moment. Some of us try to lose ourselves in social groups, movements, sororities, support systems, counter cultures, even *Living with Reality*, if used incorrectly.

While each of these experiences has value, there can be a price. Once again, I may find myself fearing to connect with myself, because connecting with myself might lead me to question or disagree with the prevailing belief system or the group through which I want to dissolve my aloneness. If I connect to myself and higher consciousness, I might have to speak or act against the group, which would leave me once more stuck with myself, alone, scared and in pain.

Connecting with others in these traditional ways never fills the void, because it never brings us the feeling of Oneness and connection we need with ourselves, the universe and each other. Instead, desperate and unsatisfied, we always long for something more or something else. By practicing Platforms Two: Becoming Differentiated and Nine: Becoming Becoming, we discover that we can connect to one another and the universe without losing ourselves.

1. How have I tried to become one with others?
2. What did I expect?
3. Have I been disappointed?
4. Have I tried again?
5. Whom have I blamed?
6. How else have I tried to lose myself?
7. Have I tried to fit myself into a spiritual or religious belief system?
8. Have I blamed myself if I didn't?

DISCONNECTION FROM THE PROCESS OF LIVING

As we said in our preface, life is a struggle, and it's a tough one at that. The struggle is not going my way. It hurts. I have to fight when I don't want to. I have to accept what I can't tolerate. The people around me are not meeting my needs. Every time something good comes my way, it's taken away. And so on and so on.

Okay, life is tough. Becoming Oneness allows us to co-create and flow with it. When disconnected from Oneness, we are struck with the ego-based response of either fight or flight. Some of us are told to give in: that we should surrender to what is. You're black; sit in the back of the bus. You're a woman; repress your needs for the benefit of others. You're a guy; break your back on the assembly line in exchange for a few drinks Saturday night. You can't fight city hall. Accept your lot; that's the way it is.

As we said before, all of us are taught to acquiesce to our role so as to protect the social order, whether that be the order in the family, our subculture, the community, or the world. Refusal can be dangerous to our health, physical or emotional. In fact, refusal can make us the enemy, to be punished or banished, and this can be a threat to our very survival. The demand that we acquiesce is as true for rebels as it is for conservatives. Even if I'm with a band of rebels, I need to acquiesce to the rules and beliefs of the group in order to belong. If gays are discriminated against, I need to either merge with society and pretend I'm not gay, or blend into gay society to have a group with which to be safe.

The ego, determined to protect our safety, becomes the enforcer. We internalize that we must acquiesce to what is expected in the context of whatever group or subgroup with which we have identified our safety.

Of course, it's natural that we are taught to follow certain rules, and we have to follow them, if we want to function within a certain context. If I want to live in the United States, I have to pay taxes; if I want to live in my father's house, I can't sleep with my boyfriend in the living room. There's nothing intrinsically wrong with following rules, as long as we do so as a conscious choice and it's right. I agree to pay my bills, leash my dog, and desist from breaking into my neighbor's house. Why? Because we believe those actions are for the highest good of all, as we learn in Platform Four: Becoming Mutually Supportive.

But to acquiesce unconsciously, just because we've been taught to do so, or just because we are afraid, means that we are following along without examination or choice. To acquiesce through unconscious decision disconnects us from ourselves and from the process of living. It is antithetical to joy and self-expression. It's depressing and keeps us feeling suppressed and unfulfilled.

But, you protest, haven't you been saying that life is tough, and you have to be in reality? To live with reality, don't we HAVE to go along with the program? No. Life is a process of co-creation, not acquiescence. Reality is not fixed. It's a never-ending process of becoming, which we co-create with the universe in a subtle dance of intention and allowance (Platform Three: Becoming Co-Creative). In fact, we co-create, whether we know it or not, because even when we're acquiescing, our acquiescence itself is part of that co-creation. It was only our collective agreement to maintain segregation that allowed it to continue.

Life is a process of evolution, and meeting challenges is part of participating in the evolutionary process itself. If we throw in the towel, we're not meeting the challenges with our whole hearts and our energy, and we're not doing our part in the co-creative process. We are not partnering with life itself.

So if acquiescing to "the way it is" is antithetical to partnering with life, what else can we do? In our ego-based world, we can see only one other option and, in fact, are encouraged to take it. It's to fight, and it looks like our never-ending striving for control. Instead of acquiescing to life, we are taught that we should conquer it. Or to be more precise, we should acquiesce to the group we belong to, whether it be the family, the social group, sect, or community, in order to conquer life itself.

Now how the heck are we going to do that?

Over time, we've used a numerous strategies to attempt to control reality to satisfy our ego's agenda. Let's start with our religious or spiritual belief systems. In many systems, we posit the concept of the omnipotent God, who has the power to make everything all right, which usually means that everything will go our way. God can smite our enemies, save my child, get me that job. So if God controls the universe, how do we control God? Sacrifice three goats, bring offerings to the volcano, think right, pray in a certain way, fast, bend in a particular direction, flagellate ourselves, have positive thoughts, feel differently, whatever, and the gods will be propitiated.

By controlling God or the gods, we are ensuring our desired outcome. Neat trick, if you can pull it off, but, of course, we can't. So now we have a choice. We can get mad at God for not doing what we asked, which could be dangerous, because God could punish us. We can think we did something wrong or did "it" the wrong way. Or we can search for more sophisticated methods to control the universe, including mastering spiritual laws or techniques. All of this is painful. It is based on satisfying our ego agendas and turns us against ourselves.

Obviously, spiritual and religious belief systems can be a great comfort to us and can bring us into higher realms of consciousness. But being human, we want not only to connect with God, but to use God to control life, because, as we have already discussed in Chapter One, we are already seeking to maintain or change our feeling state, and we need God to fix the uncomfortable feeling of being without control in a scary universe.

When we try to use spirituality to make life something other than what it is, we are fighting the process of living itself. And if we have tried to control the universe and failed, now we have to deal with the rawness of reality, plus our shock, shame, anger, and fear about the failure of our spirituality. We have the shock that our spirituality and positive attitudes couldn't prevent us from getting cancer, make our boss have a change of heart, attract the perfect guy, or otherwise achieve our goals. We have the shame that we must have done something wrong, or we would have succeeded. We have the guilt that we're pissed at the gods for screwing us, and we shouldn't feel that way. And add to all this, we have the fear that God is going to know that we're angry or in doubt of him or our beliefs, and what's the punishment for that?

Well, then, let's try another way to control life, either instead of spirituality or in addition to it. And here it is: with the advent of science, psychology, political science, and economics, we have a new God: Us. Yes, the job of controlling life and the universe now falls to us. Our knowledge is supposed to bring us control, happiness and security. We'll control every microbe known to man, and we will be well. We'll figure ourselves out, and we will be well. We'll be positive, and we will be well. We will achieve political dominance, financial security, the perfect body weight, and we will be well. We will have achieved dominance over life.

The desire to dominate life is rooted in the fact that we are sentient beings, as we established in Chapter One, and it's very difficult to tolerate the pain, fear and discomfort intrinsic to life. Because pain and fear are inevitable, the process of living is the enemy, and like any enemy, it must be defeated. Just look at a few examples of our perceived need to control life. We have to live forever and look forever young. We need to tame nature and obliterate all threats. We have to eliminate fear with faith, and pain with pills. We have to do something to make life less real.

Of course, it's natural that we would all like to extend our lives and feel better, more secure, and more comfortable. It's natural that we would like to make life better for not only ourselves, but everyone. To some of us, in fact, reality seems so horrendous, we feel that we need to either fix it or die. Genocide, rape, torture, emotional and physical abuse, poverty, sickness, degradation, and pain, these aspects of reality seem totally unacceptable, and we just have to fix them! Or we'll kill ourselves.

Sometimes we acknowledge our own powerlessness, but then assign the power to someone else. Our husband, our mother, or a politician—they have the power. They can fix life for us and for everyone. When they don't fix it, we blame them.

But no matter how we try, we can't stop life from being life. We fix one problem and create a new one. Or we try to create social change, but the collective consciousness slows it down or stops it altogether.

As natural as it is to want to change life, the fantasy that we can actually solve all our problems or create a perfect life only creates more stress and pain. Control is not real, so it becomes an unreachable goal. It's antithetical to reality, which is that life is a process of evolution with constant challenges. It creates shame, because we think we ***should*** conquer life and, if we don't, there must be something wrong with us.

Our perceived need to dominate life feeds our determination to learn and know everything, because knowledge is power, and we can use that power to fix everything. We can eliminate illness by creating medicines. We can eliminate insecurity by analyzing the economy. We can eliminate crime by putting enough people in jail. We can eliminate addiction by making drugs illegal. We can legislate behavior, enforce beliefs, and solve all our problems.

Of course, striving for knowledge is a wonderful human quality. It keeps us growing. But striving for knowledge and understanding is not the same as striving for control. Knowledge brings us into harmony with what is and teaches us how to work optimally with reality. Control is an effort to impose our will on something much greater than we are.

This is at the root of our disconnection from the process of living: the belief that we can and should control life to eliminate the fear and pain that drive us. What makes it worse is that, because we believe, or want to believe, that knowledge, or God, or material power, or the mental, spiritual, or physical will eliminate the inevitable pain and fear of life, we are reluctant to admit that we are still in fear and often out of control, despite our best efforts. And we believe that having no control means either that we have done something wrong, that we did not get "it" right, or that there is no way to get it right and that we need a new paradigm. Pretty threatening.

Which leads us to pretend that we are on the right track, but just haven't gotten there yet. Of course, we can conquer reality; we can succeed in creating the lives we want. We just have to try harder, learn more, and keep going.

What's the alternative, we ask? If we admit we still feel alone, alienated and afraid, some enemy might sense our weakness and "get" us. If we acknowledge our fear, we might feel overwhelmed by its intensity. If we disclose that we're irrational, crazy, dominated by patterns of behavior that are destructive and self-destructive, someone will surely shame us or tell us it's our fault, that we did or thought something wrong, because we SHOULDN'T FEEL THAT WAY, because we shouldn't be that way, because we have God, or we had good parents, or we live in a great community or a great nation.

Let me be clear about this. Of course, we need to learn, and of course we need to make efforts to solve our problems. But when we go from addressing our problems to "having to solve them", we go from being co-creators with the universe to being in a delusional state, where we refuse to face whatever facts fly in the face of our burning need to succeed, to force, to fix.

To relax into the process of living, we need to move from acquiescence or domination into partnership and co-creation. We need to practice Platform Eight: Becoming Not-Knowing, to understand that we don't and can't know, and that life, which we are trying to know, is not a knowable thing but a process of becoming. And we need to see that there's nothing wrong with any of it, our mistakes, our foolishness, and our inability to live with reality itself, that we were designed this way and that we are offered an opportunity to embrace who we are and become a part of the evolution of consciousness itself.

Because, as we discover in Platform Nine: Becoming Becoming, ultimately life is a process of growth fueled by challenges, and the elimination of those challenges is antithetical to the process of becoming becoming. And the process of becoming is not about trying to *be* someone or something, which is pre-defined. It's about connecting to the higher consciousness that allows us to lose our focus on ourselves and thus to reach our potential in the Oneness, nurtured by the beneficial energies that are there for us all.

Is it possible to come into a deeper place of relaxation, even in the face of life's fears and pains? Absolutely. Yes, by living life from Oneness consciousness, which is the basis of our program, *Living with Reality*. But before proceeding to learn how to do so, let's ask ourselves:

1. How do I feel about life?
2. Where do I acquiesce?
3. Why?
4. How much energy do I put into controlling life?
5. Do I believe anything will give me control?
6. How has my desire to control manifested itself in my spiritual beliefs?
7. How has it manifested itself in my view of physical and social science?
8. How have I blamed myself for not knowing and not controlling?
9. How would I feel if I gave up trying?

CHAPTER 4

Changing Our State
Addictions & Fantasy

What we experience as reality are our subjective feelings, and our subjective experience is that we feel alone and separate, even though in reality we are not. This subjective experience of aloneness is a natural result of having ego, the consciousness of individual existence. In addition, we have developed patterns of disconnection from ourselves, one another and the process of living itself, all of which cause us to suffer needless pain and fear. Faced with these difficult emotions, we feel desperately uncomfortable, and we seek to alter those feelings by escaping reality. Addictions are patterns of behavior that we develop in order to escape the fear and pain of our experience of reality. Altering our feeling state is what addictions are for, and that includes the addiction to fantasy itself.

Most of us don't have the skills and inner stability to live with reality, and we are too scared, too unsupported, too rigid, too reactive, too fragile, too something-or-other to calmly face all the pains and fears that beset us. Instead we find ourselves trying to change our state by resorting to food, alcohol, drugs, television, sex, love, fantasy, work, shopping, exercise, obsessing, over-thinking, rage, timidity, manipulation, gambling, control, even spirituality, something, anything to give us a momentary escape from our pain or to give us a temporary illusion of being able to control that which seems to be threatening us.

When repeated, these behaviors become addictions of body, mind, and spirit: patterns and internal programs that we have developed to alleviate discomfort, but which are self-perpetuating because they cause more fear and pain, which causes us to strive more to alter our feelings and moods, which causes us to reach for more fixes, more addictive behaviors, more efforts to escape. Resorting to these behaviors doesn't help. Instead, it backfires.

Why do we become addicted to certain substances or behaviors? Of course there are physiological components: nicotine, methamphetamine, caffeine, sugar and other substances are physiologically addictive, and they create the cravings they are meant to satisfy. And it's not just substances. Behaviors also create chemical reactions in our bodies. Notice what you experience in your body when you feel cherished, or angry, or powerful, and notice whether those feelings could be addictive as well.

But why do we start to use addictive substances and behaviors when we know better, and why do we continue when we see the destructive path where they lead? An addictive substance or pattern may have altered our feeling state once, or we may have seen it seem to work for other people, so we try it. Longing to immediately relieve ourselves of an uncomfortable feeling, physical or emotional, we are compelled to act despite common sense.

And yet, as we shall soon see, giving in to the addictive substances or behavior actually ultimately creates more pain and fear. And so we turn to the addiction again to relieve our pain and fear. The addictive behavior once again creates more pain and fear, and so to relieve ourselves, we turn once again to the addictive behavior. *In other words, addictions are habitual behaviors that we develop to deal with our pain and fear, but which cause more pain and fear and the need to turn to the addiction again.*

Many of us think we have no addictive behaviors, but that's untrue. All humans are stuck in some pattern of behavior—even if it's just worrying, obsessing, complaining, or pretending that everything is all right—behaviors that keep us from dealing with reality and which create needless pain and anxiety for ourselves.

Let's look at some simple examples of how addictive habits of body, mind, or spirit self-perpetuate and how they worsen the very problem they are meant to alleviate. As we read through these, let's ask ourselves if we practice these behaviors.

Overeating and Anxiety

I feel alone and anxious, unable to deal with the unpredictability of life, so I reach for the bag of chips to relieve my anxiety. Maybe my mother offered me food or a pacifier as a child. Or maybe I didn't have enough to eat at some time in my life, and I thought my anxiety would be relieved if I had more. In any case, I eat, and in that moment I feel relief. But I have to keep eating to keep relieving my anxiety. After a while, I notice that my body feels stuffed, uncomfortable, out of balance. This experience causes me anxiety. Perhaps I'm also starting to gain weight. I feel anxious about that as well. I don't want people to see me. I hide. I try to hide how much I'm eating. Maybe now I'm purging or vomiting, trying to get rid of the evidence of my "weakness," of my compulsive eating. I have now created a tremendous amount of anxiety trying to deal with my anxiety. Where are the cookies?

Alcohol and Loneliness

I feel alone with my problems—I'm lonely, powerless or frustrated in my life, I'm stressed, misunderstood, unappreciated. I deserve a drink, so I reach for the bottle. Ah, what a relief! I go to places where people are drinking, so I won't feel alone, and where we can find a common bond and not be judged. Or I find myself spending more and more time in my own company, trying to hide my drinking from others. People start criticizing or avoiding me. Now the only people who want to be around me are others who drink too much. We can hide our drinking with each other. I feel ashamed and disgusted with myself, powerless over myself, embarrassed to be with most other people, and most important, I can't even stand myself. I've created the very aloneness I meant to cure. Let me have another drink.

Rage and Lack of Control

I feel frustrated and misunderstood. Nobody seems to appreciate my good intentions. I feel disconnected and alone. No matter how I try, I can't seem to influence my surroundings. I have to prove myself to others. If I can just get them to do things my way, they'll see how valuable I am, and they'll want to connect to me. Wow, this isn't working. Despite my efforts to impress them, they don't seem to be listening. I still feel impotent, and my needs are not being met. I'm scared I'll be abused. I can't trust anyone. Nobody's listening to me. I start to rage. Perhaps a parent of mine used to rage and intimidate me, so I learned that rage equals power. I think if I rage enough, I can intimidate others. I can get people to do things my way. That will make me feel safe. The more I rage, the more people fear me. Although their actions may be controlled by me, they look at me with disgust and anger. I know they hate me. I am not feeling loved and valued. They don't understand me. I rage some more. Maybe if I can scream loud enough, someone will hear me. Why are they all going away?

Sex and Lack of Validation

I desperately need to feel loved and validated. I need to experience that validation immediately. I offer myself sexually to a stranger. He or she wants me. It feels good. We have sex. I can feel that we are disconnected. He reaches for the telephone to go on with his day. She smokes a cigarette and shows me the door. He wants to call me next week, when he's horny. She wants me out of there before her husband comes home. I feel used and ashamed. I desperately need to feel loved and validated. I turn to masturbation. I can give myself pleasure while not being vulnerable to rejection. I feel engaged for the moment, but when it's over, I feel empty. I'm still alone. I must have validation immediately. I offer myself sexually . . .

Work and Insecurity

I need to prove my worth. I work endless hours so that everyone knows that I'm indispensable. I make everyone around me overwork as well, or I communicate the message that my overworking makes me better, a martyr. I come home wanting to be praised for my devotion to earning money. Everyone in the family is stressed and tired, because I haven't participated in family responsibilities. I feel resentful. Can't they see my contribution? If I work harder, someone will see my value . . .

Co-Dependence and Fear of Loss of Love

Growing up in my family, I learned that making others need me was the way to keep people's love. I try to take care of everything and everyone. I show them that I can do everything better. I know what's best for my husband, my child, my friends. No matter how wonderful I am, they feel controlled. They resent me. They start to pull away. If only I could let them see how incredibly wonderful and helpful I am, they couldn't leave me. I think I'll try harder to take care of their needs.

Placating God and Fear

I know I can't control my life, but I hope someone can. I have been trained to believe that God is the perfect father, who has all control. If I can only find a way to placate God, maybe he will protect me. I try everything to please God. I pray, meditate, say the right things, suppress my rage. Just when I think I've got everything under control, something happens that upsets me. I'm afraid to blame God, so it must be my fault. If I could fix myself or change something in my behavior or thinking, maybe then God would protect me, and nothing bad would happen to me or my loved ones again. I must try harder to fix myself and to figure out what God wants from me.

Higher and Higher

I feel stressed by life's demands. I need relief. I'll take anything to make me high: drugs, sugar, loud music, over-exercise, spirituality. I'll do anything to get out of my body and away from life. Wow, I'm on the moon. Uh oh. I'm coming down, down, down. Everything is still waiting for me when I get back. Now all the "undones" are multiplied. I feel stressed. Got to get high.

We can use anything addictively. It is not the substance or the behavior that is the addiction. The addiction is the self-perpetuating use of the substance or behavior that creates more pain in the process of trying to relieve pain. And we all do it, because we are human and are sentient beings who lack the training and the wherewithal to live with our feelings and to face reality. Who among us is not caught up in some or many addictive behaviors?

Now let us ask ourselves these questions:

1. Which of these addictive behaviors have I tended to practice?
2. Can I see how they were self-perpetuating?
3. What other addictive behaviors or thought patterns have I engaged in?
4. Don't they also have a tendency to perpetuate themselves?
5. Does it scare me to think of giving them up?

Addiction to Fantasy

Let's spend some extra time on one addiction: fantasy. Indirectly, we have been talking about fantasy throughout this book. When we attempt to alter our feelings through the pursuit of symbols, we are in fantasy, such as was the case with our teenage girl who got married and pregnant out of the fantasy that these symbols would fix her problems. We are in fantasy when we think that yelling at someone will change their nature. We are in fantasy when we think our problems go away when we pretend they don't exist, like the person who hides the bills in the drawer and is shocked when the car is repossessed. We are in fantasy when we think we feel empowered by looking at naked women at a peep show.

Those of us who prefer to live in fantasy have a good point on occasion. If you were being tortured, wouldn't you want to be able to leave your body and pretend you were in a garden or in the arms of a loved one? In this case, isn't fantasy the approach the psyche chooses to survive?

The truth is that fantasy can be valuable. It can keep us going when reality would break our spirits and destroy our minds. It can keep us going until we can face the truth. But what if we lose sight of reality and make fantasy more real than reality itself? What if fantasy becomes a habit? What happens when we have to face the consequences that are down the road? What happens when we can no longer distinguish reality, or if we can't recognize that the fantasy is no longer needed, such as when we are in situations where we are no longer a helpless victim or powerless child? What if we forget that fantasy is a coping mechanism, not a way of life?

Here's what happens if we live in fantasy, rather than reality. Let's go back to our extreme case of torture. If I am being tortured and I disconnect my consciousness from my body for the moment, I can temporarily escape the pain. But if I stay disconnected, I'm apt to miss the opportunity to escape the torturous situation even when I have choices. If I'm not in reality, I won't notice that the prison gate has been left open. Or I may walk into other tortuous situations, because I am now too disconnected and too numb to know what I'm feeling.

The same is true on the emotional plane. If I was raised in an abusive family and I escaped through fantasy, fantasizing may have kept me alive until I could get help to deal with my emotions. But if I pack my bags and move into fantasy, I won't be connected to my pain, and this could render me impotent. I am likely, for example, to tolerate relationships that are abusive. Not only am I likely to stick with the abusive relationship, I may make myself so oblivious to my pain that I won't think to confront the person who is hurting me. As a result, I may be losing the chance to actually do something about the problem.

At the same time, if I am in fantasy about myself, I won't be able to see reality at all. I won't be able to distinguish between a relationship where I am really being abused and one that is filled with the normal conflicts and difficulties that arise among people. I will see abuse everywhere.

Being disconnected from reality can also endanger us on the physical plane. I may be out of my body and not realize when I'm cold or in danger or when I'm working too hard. Then what? I may have initially disconnected from my body because I was being hurt by circumstances outside of my control, but now I am tolerating or creating circumstances that I could control. Now I am hurting myself.

Living in fantasy may temporarily make us feel better, because it disconnects us from painful realities, but ultimately it disempowers us. We cannot move forward and affect our lives if we are using fantasy to escape. And so, like any habitual behavior, living in fantasy may have been a perfect coping mechanism for some given moment, but when it becomes a habitual mode of behavior, it defeats its own purpose.

Another pitfall of living in fantasy is that we reject that which has value because it doesn't live up to our fantasies. I want a guy who is wealthy, charming, considerate, sensitive, strong, healthy, powerful, levelheaded, perfect and devoted to me. Good luck!

If I am not in reality, I will believe that such a man exists and/or insist that my real partner live up to those ideals. Not only do I hurt my real partner, negating the essence of him, because he doesn't live up to my fantasy, but I also deprive myself of a real relationship, the relationship that is possible with this real man or with another.

Not being in reality robs us of life. If I am gay and I try to be straight, I will miss the opportunity of experiencing my gayness. If I am flat-chested and insist on being voluptuous, I am likely to hate my body. If I am disabled and want to be "normal," I abandon the life I can have for the life I can't. If I have ADHD children and I want them to "sit still," I'll most likely shame them and shame myself.

The worst kind of fantasy is fantasy about ourselves, who and what we really are. Self-delusion blocks us from admitting our faults and weaknesses, seeing our part in our pain and doing anything to really change our circumstances or ourselves. It causes us to blame others for our feelings and seek to change everything but us. It keeps us in ignorance and perpetuates the fear that anyone or anything can suddenly smash our fantasy bubble. And it prevents us from seeing our true gifts and the value of the lives we have.

So, in summary, refusing to be in reality causes us two negative results:

- We become powerless in our lives because we are disconnected from ourselves and can't act in our best interests.
- We miss out on the lives we could have, losing the opportunity to experience what is possible, while we're fantasizing about what we wish we had.

Let me clarify a few more points. Fantasy and hope are different. Fantasy puts us out of reality. It prevents us from seeing what is and working with it. Hope, on the other hand, is a spirit of optimism for reality itself. It keeps us connected to what is, while simultaneously helping us to continue stretching toward the future.

Similarly, fantasy and dreams are different. Fantasy disparages what is and blocks us from taking action toward attainable goals. Dreams begin with what is and help motivate us past our fears, so that we can aim for the highest level of development of which we are able.

It's not always easy to tell a dream from a fantasy. If I'm in a wheelchair, it's a fantasy to strive to become a long-distance runner. But I can surely dream of winning the wheelchair race. Or can I? Do I have upper body strength and stamina? Can I develop those qualities, or am I in fantasy?

When I have hope and dreams, they lead me to reach for my fullest potential, without needing to set up some fantasy end goal. If I'm weak, I can nevertheless dream of strengthening myself, even if winning the race would be a fantasy. That dream leads me to work hard and grow. I may not achieve the "win"—that depends not only on my own capacities and ability to work hard, but also on the strengths and weaknesses of my opponents, which I cannot affect.

But I can stretch toward my potential. Stretching should not be confused with striving. When we strive, we create an objective and try to reach it, whether it is attainable or not. The goal is external, driven by some ego agenda to prove something or look some particular way. When we stretch, on the other hand, we start with who we are and what we have, and we challenge ourselves to become more.

If fantasy is so damaging, why are we so prone to it? For many of us, fantasy is a reflection of how powerless we truly feel. We feel trapped, inadequate, and unable to move forward. We don't see our own strengths and our capacity to change our situation by either changing our circumstances or changing ourselves. And for some of us, we're afraid that if we landed in reality, we couldn't bear it. Perhaps we fear we would even kill ourselves.

Yes, we are back to our original premise. We are sentient beings who experience reality through our senses. Fantasy is the ultimate way of changing our experience without changing ourselves or addressing our circumstances.

When I understand the downside of fantasy, I choose reality, with all its fears and pains, pitfalls, and pathos. I choose reality, because in it, I can live fully. I choose reality, because there's plenty of magic in it, just as it is. I choose reality, because, ultimately, that's all that there is.

But if I'm committed to choosing reality, that doesn't mean I know how to cope with it. In fact, sometimes I don't even know what it is.

Living with reality, that's the purpose of our program and the journey of a lifetime. If it were easy, we wouldn't have so much therapy and so many self-help books and spiritual paths. If it were not valuable, we wouldn't choose to live.

Let's now ask ourselves some questions about the role of fantasy in our lives:

1. What role has fantasy played in my life, past and present?
2. What do I tend to fantasize about?
3. What have I been trying to escape?
4. Was I feeling powerless over something?

5. What kinds of fantasies have I had, and how were they ways of coping with powerlessness?
6. Am I willing to look at people and see who they are, or do I tend to fantasize about them?
7. Am I willing to look at myself and see who I am, or do I tend to fantasize about myself?
8. How do I know the difference between reality and fantasy?
9. Has fantasy become a way of life?
10. How has fantasy impacted my ability to act?
11. Do I tend to strive toward some external goal, and has it caused me stress?
12. Have I learned to stretch myself instead, challenging myself toward my potential?
13. Do I still have hope?
14. Do I still have dreams?
15. Do my dreams move me through my fears?
16. Do I work toward them realistically?
17. Am I ready to give up fantasy? Why?

CHAPTER 5

Who We Are & What We Could Be

Life is full of fear and pain, we are always trying to change our feeling state, we are prone to addictions, our addictions backfire, plus we have the old ego constantly reminding us that we're alone and blocking our self-awareness and ability to change. So is there an answer? Yes, yes, yes. Yes we can learn to live with reality. First, we can learn what reality actually is. Then, we can learn to cope in more productive ways. Finally, we can thrive.

During the first section of this book, we've been taking the first step. We have been talking about reality and about who we are. Now let's take a minute to talk about who we could be.

We are what we see and what we don't see. We have the capacity to learn. We can practice Becoming Oneness, Differentiated, Co-Creative, Self-Aware, Integrated, Accountable and Not-Knowing, and we can experience Becoming Becoming. We can become more happy, relaxed and inspired. We can become ourselves.

And it all starts with this: Shifting our relationship with ourselves, with one another, and with life itself—shifting from fear and alienation to partnership and connection. These shifts bring us into a greater state of relaxation, through which we can face life with energy, determination, humor, and grace. And shifting these relationships allows us to finally become infused with the higher vibrational energy that can completely transform us.

Okay, life is scary and painful. We can all agree. But it can be a heck of a lot better than it is now. It's not a mystery how to change our world: we change ourselves. Once we understand the sources of needless fear and pain, we know how to do it:

- We face reality and stop focusing on fixing our feelings.
- We overcome the domination of our ego-based view that we are alone, and support ourselves to identify with something larger than ourselves.
- We feel compassion for ourselves and others.
- We co-create a mutually supportive world and gain real feelings of security from that experience.
- We heal the disconnection from ourselves, one another and the process of living.
- We reprogram ourselves to want the experience of those things that are for our highest good and for the highest good of all being.
- We develop self-respect and self-love.
- We actually feel better and don't need to alter our state.
- We see into the essence of life and embrace the adventure that is before us.

We know what we have been. Now let's dream God's dream for us. Suppose we could face the reality of who we are, be totally honest about ourselves, our flaws and our strengths, and understand that our suffering, struggles and victories have meaning beyond our lives and are actually contributing to the forward movement of the universe? Suppose we could actually feel calm, full and inspired? Suppose we could feel connected to the life force of the planet, the heartbeat of consciousness, the dreams of God? Suppose we could be in the mind of the divine intelligence that brought us into being?

Suppose we could? What could life be?

Much more than we can imagine. Let's do it.

CHAPTER 6

How to Get There
Learning to Live with Reality:
An Outline of Our Program

ARE WE READY?

1. Do we understand that we have to learn to live with reality, even if we don't like it and wish it to change?
2. Are we ready to stop the endless effort t Our Egos Have Designed Behaviors to Cope with Our
3. Subjective Experience o escape or alter our feelings and accept that we may have to feel discomfort in the process?
4. Have we made the commitment to connect with ourselves, one another, and the process of living itself, no matter our fears, conditioning, and the apparent cost?

5. Are we willing to be scrupulously honest and to see ourselves and everything else with whatever objectivity and clarity we are capable?

If we are, we're ready for our program. Let's start with the platforms. What are they?

1. THE NINE PLATFORMS OF LIVING WITH REALITY:

    1. **Becoming Oneness**
        The Essence of Who We Are

    2. **Becoming Differentiated**
        Individuation in the Context of Oneness

    3. **Becoming Co-Creative**
        How We Relate to the Universe

    4. **Becoming Mutually Supportive**
        Living Oneness

    5. **Becoming Self-Aware**
        The First Step toward Self-Mastery

    6. **Becoming Integrated**
        Gaining More Command over Ourselves

    7. **Becoming Accountable**
        Awareness, Amends, and Transformation

    8. **Becoming Not-Knowing**
        Becoming Available to Higher Consciousness

    9. **Becoming Becoming**
        Relaxing into the Process of Living

2. HOW THE PROGRAM WORKS

In the next section of our book, each platform is described in detail, and exercises, tools and techniques are offered all along the way. But very briefly, here's how the program works.

PARTNERING WITH OTHERS

Platform One: Becoming Oneness

First, we internalize the reality that we are one, aspects of a greater whole. This helps us to relax.

Platform Two: Becoming Differentiated

Then we learn how to individuate without losing our connection.

Platform Three: Becoming Co-Creative

Following that, we learn to comprehend co-creation and how our individual and collective intentions help shape all reality.

Platform Four: Becoming Mutually Supportive

We begin to identify our interests with the highest good of all, and we become mutually supportive, co-creating a world in which we can all thrive.

PARTNERING WITH OURSELVES

Platform Five: Becoming Self-Aware

Knowing our destructive behavior is not our "fault," we let go of shame and look realistically and compassionately at the stimulus, reaction, and response patterns that we have unconsciously practiced.

Platform Six: Becoming Integrated

As we become aware of our reactivity, we find ways of overcoming it by releasing the charge around our fears and needs. By releasing them, they no longer dominate us, and we become more relaxed. We also come to understand our egos and how their domination has hurt us, as well.

Platform Seven: Becoming Accountable

As integrated, self-aware beings, we acknowledge our impact on ourselves and one another, and we learn how to make amends. We also learn the Seven Dirty Secrets of the Dark Side, through which we come to understand the role that negative energy plays on our planet. We start to become able to truly regulate the flow of our own energy.

PARTNERING WITH THE PROCESS OF LIVING ITSELF

Platform Eight: Becoming Not-Knowing

We let go of the obsessive need to "know," or at least pretend that we do. We become increasingly empty of agendas and imperatives, relax, and become more open to growth and evolution.

Platform Nine: Becoming Becoming

Life is not external to us. It is the moment-by-moment opportunity to transform as individuals and as a collective. With a deeper understanding of life, we can relax into the process of living and become conscious partners of evolution itself. We surrender to higher consciousness and become truly ourselves.

Wow. Is it that simple? Yes and no. We have the rest of the book to learn how to make these changes and the rest of our lives to practice them.

SECTION II

The Platforms
What We Could Be & How to
Get There

A FEW REMINDERS BEFORE WE START

The Nine Platforms of *Living with Reality* are processes that we can use in order to evolve. Each platform offers a perspective, an alternate way of thinking, feeling, being and dealing with reality. Each platform supports us to become more of who we are.

Reality is complex, and so are we, but in each platform I have tried to offer some essential understanding and many tools and processes that can support our growth. Of course, the true learning is in the practice and the sharing.

You'll notice that there is no set format that all chapters follow. Each platform is explained according to the need and to the best of my ability. Regardless of the form, in all of the chapters, there is an explanation of the platform itself, plus why we need it, what blocks us from practicing it, and why we would want to adopt it as a practice. In addition, I've outlined specific habits, tools and techniques to help us live it.

The nine platforms are presented in logical order, yet it's best to practice them simultaneously. I suggest that you read the book through and then go back to study, work and live the program step by step, answering all the exercise questions the best you can. By considering each platform in sequence, you are more likely to develop a thorough grasp of the approach and to develop deep positive habits. But do use the platforms in any way that is most appropriate to you.

Let's not judge ourselves by how "perfectly" we apply these practices. There is no destination, no point of arrival. We are human and evolving. The platforms are not rulers by which to measure ourselves; they are platforms to support us, guidelines meant to bring us back on course.

Let's remember, too, to always have compassion for ourselves. Everything in life is based on cause and effect. Let us try to understand the cause of our behaviors, as well as to acknowledge their effects.

One final reminder: Our platforms are meant to support us individually and collectively. In the spirit of our program, we encourage you to join with others, either formally or informally, to study the book together, so that we can live the reality of mutual support.

PART 1

Partnering with Others
The First Four Platforms

PLATFORM ONE

Becoming Oneness
The Essence of Who We Are

WHAT IS BECOMING ONENESS?

There is no platform more important than Platform One. It provides the foundation for all the others. Why? Because Becoming Oneness is the realization of who we are in the universe. Everything stems from that.

In our introduction, "Ego, Instinct & Evolution," we talked about the genesis of all differentiated existence, which was the fragmentation of consciousness and the evolution and role of the ego. In Section One: What We Are, I discussed the needless fear and pain associated with our incessant drive to alter our feeling state and to compensate for our sense of separation. Now I would like to discuss the answer to our needless fear and pain, starting with Becoming Oneness.

What do I mean by Oneness? Aren't we discrete individuals? Your foot hurts, mine doesn't. Isn't that obvious? Well, like many things about reality, the answer is yes and no. We are individuals. That's only common sense. But at the same time, we're not separate, and believing we are separate causes needless fear and pain.

We humans are not a collection of individuals. We are individual manifestations of the Oneness.

What does that mean? On the surface, we are all separate and different. So from that point of view, when we come together, we create a collection of individuals, just like cars in a parking lot are a collection of cars, or stamps gathered together are a collection of stamps. Seems obvious.

But let's turn this idea on its head. Let's start with the simple example of cars. Let's think of "cars" as a category. Then every car in that category is an example, or manifestation of the category "car." Now we can see that the vehicle is primarily a car and secondarily a Chevy or a Mercedes Benz.

Now let's look at humans. If we think of "humanity" as a category, then each one of us is an example, or manifestation of the category "humanity." We are humans first and only secondarily Mary, Jean, or Jo; black or white; Christian or Muslim.

Let's take this thought one step further. Suppose we were to look at the Earth compared to the rest of the solar system. Everything on the Earth would have certain similar qualities, as compared to what we would find on Mars, for example. Things as different as skyscrapers and ants would still be examples of Earth-reality, as opposed to Mars-reality. So each thing would be an example of life on Earth, or a manifestation of "Earth" consciousness.

Suppose we really stepped back and stretched our minds. Lots of people believe that there is a God, or a universal consciousness, or an overall design or order in the universe. From that perspective, then, we could say that everything that exists—every thing, thought, process, emotion—everything that exists past, present, and future is an example of, or a manifestation of, that universal consciousness.

Just as every known thing on the physical plane is made up of the same elements—subatomic particles and empty space—so everything in existence has underlying patterns that show it all to be of one creation. Together, we are a universe, and each one of us is a manifestation of the creative force behind that universe. From this perspective, we can see that just as a Mercedes and a Chevy have more that unites them than that divides them, we can see that all existence has more that unites than divides it.

Some people see this as a spiritual or religious reality. God created the universe in his image. We are all creations or manifestations of God. We are, therefore, all aspects of God, reflections of God, just like a painting is a reflection of its creator. Others express this reality in scientific terms. $E=mc^2$. Energy is matter; matter is energy. Energy and matter must be of the same essence, or they could not be converted into one another. Energy and matter are one.

If we accept this simple idea, then we must conclude that we are primarily one consciousness and secondarily individual manifestations of that consciousness. That means that I am not just a separate, distinct individual—even though I tend to experience myself that way. I am actually a part of a much bigger reality, a manifestation of universal consciousness.

Sounds pretty heady, and who cares anyway? But hold on a minute. In fact this is a most crucial understanding, because it means that we are, by nature, essentially one. And when we don't feel at-one, we suffer the pain of disconnection and fragmentation.

This isn't just theory; it's our experience. Don't we really know, intuitively, that we are one? When you suffer, don't I feel your suffering? When an animal cries, doesn't it evoke deep sadness in me? If I walk into a room of people who are angry, don't I feel their anger? When everyone around me is tense, don't I have a tendency to get tense myself?

Let's look at this in another way. Haven't you ever had a hunch that someone was going to call you, and five minutes later the phone rang? Haven't you ever had a bad feeling about something "for no reason," and sure enough, something awful occurred? Haven't you ever spoken some words at the same moment as your spouse? Haven't you ever known what someone was thinking or feeling, without them speaking, sometimes without your even being in the same room with them? Haven't you heard of people who knew the moment of their loved one's death, sometimes even when the death was totally unexpected? Haven't you ever been in distress and suddenly felt calm, somehow "knowing" that everything would be all right? So many examples that point in one direction—that we are connected to each other and the divine by an invisible chord or strand of energy; that we are not as separate as we seem.

Finally, we show our essential Oneness through our emotions. Don't we long for connection? At the time of our conception, we are connected to our mother. Birth is an interruption of that connection, and it is necessary in order for us to evolve. But don't we long to feel that Oneness again? Isn't sexual or spiritual union an attempt to feel at-one with another? Don't we enjoy identifying as fans of the same football team, or citizens of a town, or members of a class, or as women, intellectuals, or regular guys? Don't even those of us who like to think of ourselves as "different" enjoy characterizing ourselves as "rebels," which puts us in a group? Aren't we constantly seeking to fit in with something or somebody?

Connection and unity are essential to us, because they are essentially who we are. And yet, we've been brought up to see ourselves as separate. We learn to compete, to compare, and to contrast. Leading lives of great separation and conflict is the cause of our deepest fear and pain, which, in turn, leads to so much of our addictive behavior as we try to alter our feeling state.

WHAT ARE SOME OF THE BLOCKS TO BECOMING ONENESS?

It is not our fault that we focus on our separateness. As we learned in "Ego, Instinct & Evolution," our egos are constantly looking for an edge, so that we can get what we need to survive. We see then that the tendency toward fragmentation is inherited with the birth of our egos. In addition, our sense of separation is a result of programming. We actually learn to live from that paradigm, because that is what we are taught. If that programming is not challenged, we continue those old behaviors without even noticing, because they seem so familiar. Challenging this paradigm is the purpose of Platform One.

At a later point in our book, we begin to experience Oneness on a different level, where we experience ourselves at-one with the infinite, which automatically allows us to feel our Oneness with everything else. That sense of Oneness is less about how we think and more how we feel. But that's another stage of Becoming Oneness, better left to later in our program.

In this section, I would like to focus on the ways fragmentation and disconnection are learned and reinforced through our everyday lives, and I'd like to discuss what we can do about it.

Society teaches us to identify with certain subgroups, which are always posited in contrast to others. For example, if I am taught to identify as a woman, that identity exists only in contrast to something else, such as being a man. If I am taught to see myself as white, that's in contrast to being black. If I'm taught to identify as Christian, that's in contrast to Jewish, Muslim, Hindu, and every other faith. If I'm taught that I'm smart, that's in contrast to being stupid. And if I'm taught to identify with my family, that's in contrast to being a part of yours.

Of course, we want to belong to someone or something. That's natural, especially in light of the precariousness of life and our fundamental nature as Oneness. Yet the way we learn to identify with one group is to not be part of another. So ironically, our desire to connect to something or someone is simultaneous with the sense of being different from others.

The "them" and "us" syndrome prevails within "us" as well. For instance, in relation to the world, "them" and "us" could look like my family vs. the rest of the universe. But within my family, "them" and "us" could be mom and me vs. dad and Joey. Or it could be my family vs. the rich, snobby aunt, or vs. the pathetic drunk cousins, or the noisy neighbors. Or at work it could be the typing pool vs. the engineers. Very quickly and deeply, we are ingrained with layers and layers of "them" and "us" scenarios.

The them/us context is grounded in fear and the need to stick together. My little group, clan, family, race, nation, will protect me against your group, clan, family, race, nation. In a world where people tend to focus on good guys and bad guys, on people like us vs. people who are different, consciously or unconsciously, it's natural that we feel that I really need "us" to protect me from "them." And of course in the process I forfeit membership in the human race.

There is always a "them." Am I exaggerating? Consider this. Most of us tend to protect the interests of people above "wild" animals or insects. If it comes down to a choice between my life and microbes, the bacteria will die! Suddenly I'm a member of the human race, but not a part of the web of life. Forget that Oneness stuff.

How else are we fragmented? In an uncertain universe, competition is a deep-rooted instinct. Animals compete for food and territory; humans compete for domination over one another and everything else in the universe; even ideas compete. If I don't try to dominate you, I fear you'll dominate me. I can try to dominate directly, or, if I feel unable, I may try to manipulate instead. Women and children, who have been historically deprived of positions of power in the world and often even basic human rights, have commonly attempted to wield power through manipulating those who have the power to wield. Often children manipulate women who manipulate men. None of us is above manipulation. And who among us doesn't try to manipulate God?

Beyond domination, we have many other forms of competition. At school, there are a limited number of scholarships to "good" schools. If you get the last one, I don't, so we have to compete. Not everyone can become the star pitcher on the major-league baseball teams, so we have to compete. A company has only one president, so we have to compete.

Even with our loved ones, we tend to compete. I think my idea is better than yours. You think yours is better than mine. And the kids know that theirs are better than both of ours put together.

Competition is deep within us, fed by our ego's continuous need to prove our value, and it is constant, even when it's subtle. Consider the constant comparisons that go on in our heads. These, too, are a form of competition. When I meet you, I measure you against others as well as myself. Are you better or worse? Richer or poorer? Smarter or less intelligent? Shorter or taller? More or less powerful? I'm always comparing myself to you, judging you and myself, and separating myself from you. How can I experience our Oneness, when I'm always looking for our differences?

Judgment is another block to Oneness. When we live in a universe full of judgment, it's hard to admit to having qualities that are met with disapproval, so we separate from those whose characteristics are not admired by us or others. This obviously alienates us from "them." At the same time, we tend to project our negative qualities onto others to make ourselves look better. Now we are not only alienated from them, but we are alienated from ourselves, as we refuse to look at ourselves with self-honesty.

What do I mean about projecting our negative judgments? We may, for example, characterize some other group, race, or individual as mean, selfish, corrupt or lazy. If I think those qualities are "bad," I will simultaneously pretend that "we" are not. If you want evidence of this phenomenon, listen to the debates and arguments at the dinner table and on the TV screen during any election season! What we do with groups, we also do with individuals. We are quick to point out that someone else is a thief, a child molester, judgmental or a racist, but we rarely make such announcements about ourselves. In fact, we don't even seem to notice the ways that we are the same or similar. We're happy to point out that some other person is needy, clingy, and manipulative, but we do it with a tone of voice that clearly implies that they are unlike us. We don't want to admit that we are one with these people, because that would imply that we might be like "them." Excuse me? While you may be like "them," that's just not true for me. I don't like those qualities, and I don't want to admit that I have them, too.

So we can see that racism and other forms of bigotry are often a phenomenon of projection, projecting onto others what we dislike about ourselves. Refusal to see negative traits in ourselves is especially likely with those qualities that are socially condemned, illegal, or otherwise subject to punishment. I tend to pretend I don't have these traits, and I righteously judge you or even punish you if you do, demonstrating to you, me, and the universe that we are not alike. A perfect example of this phenomenon was the self-righteous way the United States Congress dealt with the sexual addiction of one of our recent presidents, as well as the public shock whenever we discover that other politicians or sainted public figures are doing the same things we and our neighbors do all the time. I guess none of us is ever unfaithful, stretches the truth on our income taxes or exploits our power in any way. While it may be true that we don't do these things in exactly the same way as the one we judge, we can usually find some way we do them, if we are honest with ourselves. Here's our pattern, and the bottom line is: If I disapprove of you, I am not you, and I will lie to myself and everyone else to maintain that illusion. All of this blocks Becoming Oneness.

There are many ways that we deny our Oneness with those we judge. Here are some: Sometimes I identify with you in secret while condemning you in public. Wow, I'm molesting my daughter, too, but I'm going to call for you to go to jail for molesting yours. I am pretending we are not one.

On the other hand, I may admit identification with people whose behavior is socially condemned, illegal, or subject to punishment, but I pretend that this condemned behavior makes me superior to others. I'm now judging and separating from those who do not behave in these condemned ways. "Yeah, I admit that, like you, I smoke dope. But, hey buddy, you and I both know that we are hip, as opposed to the guys who don't get high."

Or we bond with the condemned group and justify our behavior toward those we hurt, which separates us from the victim. "Yeah, I beat my wife, just like you beat yours. Sure, people tell us we're wrong. But we know that force is the only way to control 'them'." Now I'm bonding with "you," but I'm still fragmenting, and I'm using our bond to justify myself.

And, finally, we may combine several ways of separating, such as when we bond with the condemned and simultaneously use that bond to prove our superiority to others. "Yes, we are both child molesters, but only you and I know that we are the real lovers of children." Now I'm bonding with you, disconnecting from the pain of the children we are molesting, and simultaneously asserting our superiority over those who are judging us. I'm also using you to disconnect from myself and from my own revulsion at what I'm doing. I'm still not in the Oneness.

Oneness is our deepest desire. Without the experience of love and connection, we feel alone, frazzled, and more prone to fear. But in our ego-based universe, our habitual ways of feeling and thinking make it hard to feel at-one.

The blocks to Becoming Oneness are dramatically played out in intimate relationships, because intimacy creates fear of dependency. We have such a great need for connection, we fear that need will drive us toward behaviors and attitudes causing us to lose ourselves, and once we lose ourselves, we blame the other person for doing something to us. Being angry with them allows us to separate ourselves from them, so that we don't feel so dominated. Yes, we need to feel Oneness, but then we get scared and separate.

What are some of the other blocks to Oneness in intimate relationships? If we judge ourselves as weak because we need our partner, we can also judge our partner as weak, simply because they need us, too. In other words, we despise the "beloved" for needing us as much as we need them, because we judge need as "needy." Seeing their "neediness" makes us separate from them. Ironically, sometimes we're afraid to acknowledge our partner's need for us, because their need for us makes them look weak in our eyes, and we need them to be "strong." So if we want our partners to be strong to compensate for our weaknesses, we have to pretend that they don't need us even though they do, even while we're complaining that they don't!

We can also exhibit contradictory behaviors simultaneously. We may bash our partner for being weaker than we want to admit we are, yet simultaneously pretend that they are stronger than we are when we want them to make us feel safe in the face of our weakness. Here's an example: I constantly complain about John's insensitivity, which I consider a weakness, but I want him to take care of business if and when I don't want to, using the excuse that John is tougher than I am, more able to take care of himself and us. Even though I call him weak, I want John to face the landlord, the mouse, the I.R.S., or the business world. Or we can separate from our partner by ignoring our similarities and exaggerating their strengths. For instance, I can claim that Mary is more patient and understanding than I am, and even though the kids would get on anyone's nerves and she really needs a rest, I know she has the capacity to deal with the children better than I. So I'll just let her.

We create separation by not seeing that John and Mary are just like us—scared, vulnerable, tired, unsure as to how to proceed and needing support—because we want them to compensate for our weaknesses, and then we separate from them again when they fail to live up to our fantasies. All of these behaviors block Oneness.

How do we shift our thinking and behavior, so that we experience more Oneness and less fragmentation? That is the purpose of Platform One. It offers us concrete ways to remember our Oneness and to develop the deep feeling of connection we so passionately crave.

Before we move on, let's quickly recap. Becoming Oneness appears contrary to our immediate perception of reality, but, in truth, we are one, each of us a manifestation of the collective. We all know this intuitively, and we've all experienced it. But we don't feel it in everyday life, and we don't act from that awareness. Why? First, because we are born with ego, which is the awareness of individual existence, which we discussed at length in this book's introduction. Second, because we are programmed to respond to everyday situations in habitual ways. Here's a summary of some we've discussed, plus a few more. As we observe this summary, we realize that they are a series of habits, seven habits that get in the way of Becoming Oneness:

1. We experience ourselves as separate and are dominated by the ego's instinct and training to protect our "selves." Therefore, we bond with those whom we think will protect us and fragment from the "others."
2. We fear domination, so we respond by trying to dominate.
3. We're trained to compete.
4. When we see qualities in others that we dislike, we don't want to acknowledge those qualities in ourselves. We may not see other people's good qualities in ourselves, either.
5. We act out behavior that is hurtful toward others, and we have to disconnect from those we hurt in order to deny our impact.

6. We desperately need intimacy, but intimacy can lead to the loss of self, if we are not able to Become Differentiated (see Platform Two). We either give in to the need for intimacy and suffer from the loss of ourselves, or we struggle to find ways to disconnect from that need and lose the chance for connection.

7. We are seeking the perfect father, mate, boss, friend, or God to make us feel loved and safe all the time. We expect ourselves to be perfect, too. When this fantasy is not fulfilled, we feel angry and become alienated from ourselves and each other.

Living from a place of fragmentation and disconnection is a habit, a deeply ingrained habit, which we need to face. Becoming Oneness is a habit we need to acquire.

HOW DO WE BECOME ONENESS?

Thus far in our book, we've acknowledged that fragmentation and disconnection lie at the root of the needless fear and pain that drive our destructive and self-destructive habits of body, mind, and spirit, and so connection and Oneness must lie at the root of our recovery. Becoming Oneness, instead of living in a consciousness of fragmentation, is the platform upon which our recovery and our evolution are built.

From our understanding of the ego and the obstacles we've just discussed, Becoming Oneness certainly seems to go against the grain. What can we do?

To begin with, we recognize that we are one. That is the truth. To live that truth is a process that we can learn. Fragmentation is only one aspect of our consciousness. While it's based on the realities of life—we feel alone and scared and we need to protect ourselves—it's not the only reality. We have had glimpses of the feeling of Oneness. We love it, and we long for it.

The desire to bond, identify and connect is deeper than the habit of fragmentation. But Oneness needs to be understood, acknowledged, nurtured and given expression in everyday life. It's not enough to go to a spiritual service once a week and experience Oneness. It's not enough to have fleeting moments of ecstasy. Becoming Oneness is a day-to-day practice of consciously choosing to look and act from that understanding. We will soon learn in Platform Two: Becoming Differentiated, that

Oneness is not the same as merging, and we will learn in Platform Nine: Becoming Becoming, to stay connected always to ourselves and higher consciousness. These will help.

But at this stage of our understanding and development, there are already many steps we can take. If we are to break the habit of fragmentation, we will have to work very hard to change our thinking. But how do we do that? We've already made a list of seven of our habits of fragmentation. Each one of these can be replaced, if we but try.

Let's look at them one at a time.

HABIT ONE

Negative Habit One

We experience ourselves as separate and are dominated by the ego's instinct and training to protect our "selves." We bond with those we think will protect us and fragment from the "others."

Let's replace this habit with another. Let's put forward the first positive habit.

Positive Habit One

We experience ourselves as one. As such, there is no "them" and "us." Everyone is real, of equal value and equally connected to me.

Let's examine the two approaches. Let's begin with the habit of fragmentation. Undeniably, we experience ourselves as separate. If the weather is cold, and there is one sweater and no other source of heat, one of us will be cold; if we share the sweater, both of us will be cold. That's life. That's our experience. From that experience and from our training, we learn to protect our "selves," as though we really were separate.

Suppose we started with the realization that although I seem to "win" when I get the sweater, I really don't win at all. If you are cold and miserable, you will be angry, or feel depressed or defeated, and that will impact me, too. If I want to connect with you and have fun, we may both be blocked from that experience if you're cold. With you feeling uncomfortable, you might be withdrawn. Suddenly, I'm alone. Is that what I want? In addition, on some level, I intuitively feel your pain as well as mine. I can pretend that I don't, but that's not true. So if you're cold, I resonate with your pain. Sometimes it is still right for me to get the sweater, but that would have to be determined by practicing Platform Four: Becoming Mutually Supportive.

Protecting our "selves" is self-defeating. My favorite example has to do with a lake in the Northern part of the United States. The city where I lived had a large working class section downtown. The wealthy lived in the far-away suburbs. In total disregard of the needs of the "others" (in this case, the workers), the industrialists allowed wholesale pollution of the city—so much so that the river, which was running through the city, burned. Generally speaking, the owners of industry didn't care about the state of the environment or the living conditions of the workers. They lived by the lake, not by the river. They were not impacted. Finally, the city became so polluted that the lake became polluted too. Now the owners of industry became concerned about pollution. A little too late did they realize there is no "them" and "us."

We live in the same universe, and we cannot pollute our air without choking ourselves. So the first step in Becoming Oneness is to remember that we are not "selves" that can be separated. We cannot bond with our kind and forget everyone else.

Let's now look at the relevance of our first positive habit, which is to realize that there is no them and us, and to acknowledge that we are all real. Returning to the example of the industrialists and the burning river, if the industrialists had realized we were one, they would have noticed that their actions support only the short-term interests of their own class and that they had relegated workers to the category "them," those whose needs were less important. If they embraced our first positive habit, they would have called upon themselves to see everyone as real and having equally important needs, and they would have cleaned up the pollution for the workers, before the pollution ever reached them! In fact, they would have realized that the earth has rights and needs, too, and the pollution would never have reached that proportion to begin with.

Let's look at ourselves in the same light. Because we live in a nation dependent on oil resources, we can easily forget that the foreign lands that produce the oil are inhabited by human beings. When we pursue only "our" interests, we ignore the needs of others; in fact, our needs feel threatened, when "they" try to take control over their own lives. The trick is to get beyond the "them/us" universe." Can we look beyond narrow self-interest and see those people as real? Can we acknowledge their history, their needs and their pain? Can we see that just as the Islamic fundamentalists think we are "them," we think *they* are "them?" The truth is that we are all "us" and all "them." But that's hard to remember when we feel threatened.

Practicing this habit makes us reconsider our relationship with all kinds of people who we regard as "them." It makes us look at the way we treat our bosses, our employees, even our life partners and children. It makes us look at the way we treat other species, prisoners, anyone who is not "us."

Positive Habit One is based on a very deep understanding of the reality of Oneness. It is based on the understanding that I cannot be happy in a world where others are cold, hungry or oppressed. I cannot be happy in a world where others are raped emotionally or physically. I cannot be the one happy person in a world of misery.

When we ignored the problems of the black community, the cities burned and drug addiction moved to the suburbs. We cannot run away from each other's unhappiness. We share the same mental/emotional environment. The princess in the ivory tower was a lonely being. And the white minority in South Africa was a frightened group, indeed.

Each day, let us practice Habit One of the First Platform of Becoming Oneness. We experience ourselves as one. As such, there is no "them" and "us." Everyone is real, of equal value and equally connected to me.

Every day, let's look at how much we were or were not able to practice this habit. Let us do an inventory of our own behavior and attitudes. Let us ask ourselves:

1. Who did I bond with today? Who was "us"?
2. Who did I make less important, less valuable or worthy? Who were "they?"
3. Did I see everyone in this situation as equally real, equally connected to me?
4. Did I at least ask the question: What can be done for the common good?
5. Can I reconsider any of my decisions, thoughts and behaviors based on this inventory?
6. Should I make amends?
7. Can I do something different?

We may not always be able to come up with new and different solutions, because we cannot create a new universe by ourselves, but we can start thinking differently, and soon our behaviors will automatically change, as well.

HABIT TWO

Negative Habit Two

We fear domination and respond by trying to dominate.

Let's replace this habit with another:

Positive Habit Two

We realize that all of us feel powerless and fear our needs won't be met. We let go of trying to control each other, as we learn to practice cooperation instead.

As we have already discussed, we live in an unpredictable world, and we are powerless over much of what happens to us, including natural, health and economic upheavals. In addition, in an ego-based reality, everyone is fighting for his or her survival or advantage; so our perception is that we need to dominate or face domination. All of these factors create in us the feeling of being constantly threatened, and so, always seeking to fix our feeling state, we continually attempt to shift our feeling from fear to control. This is the purpose of attempting to dominate.

We may, in fact, experience ourselves as dominated by strong forces, whether they be drought or tornadoes, raging parents or recessions. We even seem dominated by our own thoughts, cravings and emotions. In return, we try to dominate life, the earth and each other. To some degree, this is a reasonable response to life's perils. The attempt to control nature or at least to control the impact of nature has led to farming, housing, electricity and hurricane warnings. The effort to lessen the impact of more powerful forces has led to our scientific progress and our way of life. We have hardly been totally successful in controlling life, and the price has been high—we keep creating problems with every problem we solve (as in new resistant strains of bacteria)—but we have had some success.

We've also attempted to dominate social forces—manipulate people and the economy. These human sciences have been perhaps even less effective than the natural sciences, but we keep trying.

Our dominating approach has led to many unwanted outcomes, however, such as the extinction or near-extinction of many species and the poisoning of our environment, and many are calling upon us to have a more cooperative relationship with the earth itself. Organic farming, solar power and the study of ecosystems exemplify our realization that we are part of a greater system, a greater whole, and that we need to become respectful participants rather than domination wannabes. But it is natural to desire to dominate our physical, emotional and spiritual environment.

In this chapter, we do not address our desire to dominate life itself. Shifting that relationship is explored in Platform Nine: Becoming Becoming. Our purpose in practicing Positive Habit Two is to end the domination dance with one another. Please note, however, that our desire to dominate one another is connected to our inability to dominate life and larger social forces. We feel so helpless in light of all that we cannot control, including our workplaces and world, that we feel the need to alter that feeling by dominating members of our own families, the guy in the supermarket, our dogs, children or anyone else where we think we have a chance of success.

In addition, we try to dominate each other because we are tremendously impacted by each other's choices and behaviors. If I am married to a woman with a shopping addiction, for example, her spending will tremendously impact our financial security, and so it is natural that I would try to find a way to control her as a means of controlling the damage. I will lecture her, take away her credit cards, send her to a twelve-step program, or do whatever else I can to try to impact her, so that she will change.

I am, in fact, being impacted by her behavior, but I am being impacted even more by my reaction to her behavior. I only see, however that she is dominating me, and when I try to control her behavior, she, of course, feels dominated by me, too. And so, she has to fight back. She lets me know that she doesn't have a shopping addiction; or that my addictions are worse; or that all her friends do it. Feeling helpless over herself, afraid that she may not be able to stop her addictive behavior, she may try to ignore my interventions or attack me for trying. Or she may find ways to appeal to me emotionally, so that I don't take her money away. Now we have come full circle. I feel controlled by her; she feels controlled by me. And none of us seems to have any control.

Fear for our material or emotional survival tends to make us tense and self-protective. We usually drag out whatever survival strategy we learned as children, although sometimes we call on a new, improved approach that we may have adopted through experience or study. But none of us can actually control the forces of the universe. And ultimately, we cannot even control one another, and we have trouble controlling ourselves, too.

While the habit of domination is, of course, based largely on how helpless we feel, its root cause is separation. In a world of seemingly separate entities, we believe or perceive our needs to be different, often opposing, and, therefore, we don't trust others to care about our needs or even to actively consider them. In other words, we feel unsafe with one another. This is not only belief or perception. Our experience has often led us to believe that other people do not feel their Oneness with us, and simultaneously we don't feel our Oneness with them. Marion feels tense, and she wants to change her feelings by retiring from her job. She lobbies for retirement so that she can take care of the grandchildren, and she ignores the fact that all the financial stress will fall on me. I feel tense, too, and believe that my joining the local golf club will fix it, so I start lobbying that "we" need me to join the club, because I will gain important business contacts. We both feel that the other one is selfish, we both believe our need is reasonable and correct, we feel too threatened to even consider each other's needs and the highest good, and we desperately attempt to ensure that our needs dominate.

Domination is a habit that we've learned in order to deal with our fear. A girl grows up in a family where the father beats his wife. What does she learn? That you beat or get beaten: you dominate or you will be dominated. What can she do? Be aggressive, be submissive, or try to make herself look so tough that no one will even try to mess with her. A boy grows up in a neighborhood where bullies torment kids in the schoolyard. What does he learn? To be fearful of domination. What can he do? Become a bully, too, or find ways of avoiding confrontation.

We grow up in families where the mom is overstressed and takes it out on the kid, so we learn to be self-protective in the face of someone who seems angry. How can we protect ourselves? Either placate authority or eventually get strong enough to fight back and beat it. We grow up in a world where big companies buy out little ones, so we learn that he who has money can eat up the competition; we must dominate or be dominated. What can we do? Feel powerless in the face of a greater power, or fight back.

Dominate or be dominated. Those of us who cannot or will not dominate openly often find other ways of protecting our perceived interests. We can manipulate, for example. Manipulation is the art of compelling a more powerful force to do what you want; it is the victory of cunning over power, and it's something most of us learn very young.

As we discussed in our introduction, "Ego, Instinct & Evolution, we realize early that we cannot always win through sheer force. We discover, for example, that when Mom or Dad really doesn't want us to do or have something, the answer is no—unless we can find a way to change his or her mind. Perhaps crying works, or guilt, or some other type of threat to the parents' self-esteem. Some of us learn to please and flatter. But all of us learn some way or ways to manipulate those who appear to have power. And often if we learn to manipulate one parent, we may be able to use that parent to dominate the other.

Is there another way? Let's look some examples of domination and manipulation. A boy grows up in a family where the family dog is put in the backyard every night, despite its cries to stay inside where there's love and warmth. The boy protests that he wants his friend. What does the boy learn? That someone will win in any conflict, and the one who wins is the one with more power. What can he do? Try to be the one with more power. He may not have the power to force his parents to change their minds, but he can rant and rave to get his way. He can cry. If he uses these techniques and his parents are susceptible to guilt, he may win, which means he's well on his way to learning the art of manipulation. If they're not susceptible, he gets even stronger messages about his powerlessness, and he either internalizes that he is and always will be powerless, or he will be convinced the he needs to learn better ways to dominate as soon as he can.

There are bullies everywhere—in the boardroom and in the bedroom—and we learn to acquiesce or dominate through force or manipulation. You may laugh, but this is life.

Here's an adult example. You and I are in a relationship, and we're decorating our first house. I like green, and you prefer blue. You have a tendency to get very agitated when I put forward my views. What do I learn? That if I stand up for my wants with you, you're likely to get mad. What can I do? Have a big blowup, just give in, or decorate the house when you're not home. Or I can find a way to manipulate you into accepting what I want. Which of these patterns I choose is probably as much determined by my own history as it is by how well any of them work with you.

125

But what happened to Oneness? How can it be practiced in a world of conflicting interests? It can, when we realize that we are essentially one and that we do not benefit by the defeat of another. So let's try Positive Habit Two: We realize that all of us feel powerless and fear our needs won't be met. We let go of trying to control each other, as we learn to practice cooperation instead.

How would this work in the examples we just gave? Let's start with the little boy whose family puts the dog in the backyard. We can easily imagine the family resolving the issue with good communication and mutual concern. First of all, there can be a discussion among all family members. Who wants the dog in, and who out, and why? What is for the highest good? Maybe the boy just lost his best friend who moved to Alaska, and he really needs the comfort of the dog being inside. Maybe the parents realize that this is important to the boy. Or suppose we find out that Mom is upset because the dog lies on the couch at night, and she doesn't want the couch dirty. Perhaps the couch could be covered. Maybe the dog can sleep in the boy's room. Maybe the boy will take responsibility for the dog, and that will be good for both of them.

Or maybe the boy finds out that the mom is allergic to dogs and is keeping the dog just to make him happy. Then the boy realizes that his mom is actually being extremely generous, and so he talks to the dog. He and the dog want so much to be together, but he becomes reconciled to the idea that the dog will be all right sleeping outside. Maybe he'll hang out in a tent from time to time. Or perhaps he'll realize that the mom can't have him in the house and the dog is too miserable outside, and he'll agree it's better to give up the dog to a family that can have him in the house.

This kind of process requires time, investment of energy, willingness to be completely honest and a belief in Oneness. We acknowledge that every one of us is afraid our needs will not be met; yet in the face of that fear and belief, we try cooperation anyway. We start with the belief that if we truly communicate and there is no manipulation or domination, we will find an answer that is for the highest good of all (which we discuss at length in Platform Four: Becoming Mutually Supportive.) If this process occurs, what has the boy learned? That people can care about each other's needs and support each other, even when it causes some hardship to one or more of them. He is beginning to learn the concept of mutual support, rather than competition of needs. He is coming to understand that it is possible to live without attempting to dominate one another. He is transforming, not only his own consciousness but human consciousness too. He is learning to practice Positive Habit Two. But, of course, all parties have to be willing to play.

What about the example of the relationship where I love green and you blue, the one where you get agitated when I put forward my desires? How can we become Oneness in this situation? If you get agitated when I say I want green, I could let go of being defensive and try to practice compassion. What's really bothering you? What is the issue that's really triggering you? I can express the truth that I can't be happy if you're miserable. At the same time, you could look at your own behavior. Why are you so agitated? Can you let go of your fear that your needs won't be considered, so that we can talk? Can we consider other colors or different colors in different rooms? Can you believe that I'm not trying to manipulate you?

Becoming Oneness means that we start with the assumption that we are one, and, if we do, we all gain as a result. Trusting our Oneness, we can relax, because we know others will consider our needs. We feel more open, because we are not constantly protecting ourselves from others. We all become amazingly smarter and more creative, because we are not tied in the knots of anxiety and defensiveness. We feel better about ourselves, because we are seeing ourselves practicing attitudes of love and generosity.

From this vantage point, practicing Positive Habit Two seems an obvious choice for dealing with conflict. But if it's so obvious, why do we have to work so hard to remember to do it? Because we have that visceral fear that we will be dominated and that our needs will not be met. Because we're tied up in our ego's perception of the world. Because our fear and perceptions blind us to the realities of the situation. And because it's hard to practice cooperation when others do not.

We do not yet live in a world where everyone is committed to Becoming Oneness. Even with the best of intentions, it's hard to practice Habit Two. Life continues to be unpredictable, and I feel the desperate need to control "something." With everyone else acting out of the domination or manipulation paradigm, it's even harder to practice cooperation. Bullies continually create in us a need to deal with domination issues, one way or another, and we are constantly responding to others' attempts to control us, if we are not actually covertly also trying to control them.

Nevertheless, we can commit to practicing Positive Habit Two. Let's go back to the example of the guy with the wife who has a shopping addiction. Can't he behave in a way other than domination? Can he practice Positive Habit Two? Absolutely. He can practice Becoming Oneness. He can be in a neutral frame of mind when he sits down to talk with his wife, which requires him to release his need to dominate her and trust that both he and she have the same desire, which is for both of them to be well. He can believe that on some level, she knows she's out of control and hurting herself and everyone. He can acknowledge that there is a need she is trying to fulfill, albeit in a self-destructive way. He can listen to her actively and try to understand what is happening for her. He can acknowledge his own addictive behaviors. He can offer to help. If he does, she will experience him differently. She may or may not change her behavior, but if he practices this habit, his change will impact the quality of the relationship and the possibility that she will seek help. If he needs to take actions, such as cutting up her credit cards, at some level she will know why and feel relieved. Finally, he will feel differently about himself and will have grown.

Of course, if she can't practice Positive Habit Two as well, his best efforts may yield limited results, and he may have to live with the situation or get a divorce. We do not control the universe. Without you changing, I cannot entirely change my world. Yet, we need to shift our own attitude. And we need to trust.

We need to trust that, since we are one, if we want Oneness, so does everybody else. We have to trust that we would love to live in a universe where cooperative folks help co-create more productive and happy solutions for our collective problems. We know that dedicated people are already working on this habit, and it seems an uphill battle. But should we give up? Hardly. The buck always stops here. We can't wait around for others to create a universe safe for us; I need to try to create a universe safe for you and for us.

Why? First, because domination hurts the dominator as much as the dominated. Dominating creates in us a sense of false power and perpetuates the sense of separation. We may feel "in control," but we never feel loved. Similarly, allowing ourselves to be dominated creates in us feelings of shame and resentment, and no one who is dominated ever feels loved.

Second, because cooperation releases tension. I don't want to live in constant fear and to experience life as a constant power struggle. If I dominate, I have to remain constantly hyper-vigilant, trying to protect my position, whether it be in the family, at work or in the world. If I'm dominated, I will always seek revenge overtly or covertly, and I may even try to undermine the dominator, so that I can never be dominated again. A perfect example is the battered wife who one day picks up a gun and ends the batterer's domination forever.

And third, cooperation brings better results. All of us experience life as uncontrollable, we all feel uncomfortable with that powerlessness, and we all automatically try to dominate each other, even if it's by letting someone else take control, which forces them to take on all the responsibility. When we surrender to this reality, we understand that the only way to deal with the collective anxiety caused by our collective powerlessness is to stop trying to alter our feelings through the illusion of domination and address reality through working cooperatively to solve our collective problems!

We can do this. Cooperation is an instinct, no less than is domination. When we have a natural disaster, such as a hurricane, we remember this instinct and neighbors help neighbors. Of course, some also will exploit these crises for their own advantage, such as when a company unscrupulously destroys the competition during a recession, a family member asserts his or her authority in a crisis, or a governmental agency takes inordinate power during a time of fear, such as starting a war or carrying out a terrorist attack.

It should not surprise us that people return to such default behaviors. Ego, instinct and evolution. We need to experience Oneness in order to start behaving sanely.

There is a divine irony here. We feel compelled to dominate each other as an emotional response to feeling our powerlessness over life. Yet the more we practice Habit Two, the more we come together to meet our mutual needs, the less uncontrollable life itself becomes. No, we cannot stop the natural disasters, but we can come together to mitigate their effects. Sometimes we can even devise new and better ways of either preventing or coping with those disasters that do occur. Social Security and Unemployment Insurance are examples of cooperative ways of coping with the uncontrollable. While they are not perfect, they do demonstrate the possibility of mutual support in the face of life's traumas.

So at the end of every day, we can ask ourselves how well we practiced Habit Two.

1. Did I feel powerless today, and how did I respond?
2. Did I try to control life or others?
3. Did I get caught up in my own fear of being dominated?

4. Did I acknowledge that others have the same fear?
5. Did I try to bully, placate or manipulate?
6. Did I listen to all sides and consider everyone's needs?
7. Did I practice cooperation?

As I watch myself falling on my face on a regular basis, I can laugh at myself—which is perhaps the key to practicing this habit, just as it is the key to practicing them all!

HABIT THREE

Negative Habit Three

We are trained to compete.

Let's replace this habit with:

Positive Habit Three

We support each other's success and wellbeing.

In "Ego, Instinct & Evolution," we discussed the genesis of competition, which is the ego's effort to create a sense of value for ourselves so that we can be supported. Earlier in this platform, we discussed briefly the fear that underlies competition. The fear is scarcity—scarcity of love, money, success, attention. There are two applicants and one job. There are five professors, but only one head of the Chemistry Department. There's one dad, but three children and a mom are vying for his attention, and vying not only with each other, but with his job, the football game, and the bottle of beer. If looking cute is valued, I'll compete to be the cutest. If being smart is valued, I'll compete to be the smartest. If being "good" is valued, I'll try my hardest to be good.

Not only do we experience our own fear of scarcity, we experience each other's fear, as well. If I start conversing with someone who's competing with me to look smarter, I start to feel uncomfortable. I might withdraw or compete back. It is highly challenging to avoid the impact of their competitiveness, because in fact we are engaged in a relationship, which is defined by both of us. Even if I withdraw and refuse to compete, I'm still being impacted by the competition: I'm withdrawing.

Competition is rewarded and encouraged in sports, school, and our economy. At the same time, competition may be criticized within the family. Whether it is rewarded or criticized, however, it continues. Even when we attempt not to compete because our family doesn't approve of competition, we are competing with competitive family members to look less competitive and, therefore, to gain favor.

In a world where our very economic system encourages and rewards competition, in a world where loved ones are exhausted or stressed and lack the resources to satisfy all of the needs of all of us, competition feels inevitable.

Inevitable or not, what is the cost of competition? We feel angry with the one who wins, so the winner loses love. We feel disappointed with ourselves when we lose, so the loser loses self-love. If we win, we may feel ashamed of our competitiveness, so the winner may lose again. We may see the loser being protected, so we resent the loser. We may all talk about team spirit, but the kid who blows the last chance at bat is a sad Little Leaguer at the end of the day.

Beyond the emotional costs of competition, we have economic and social costs. Two companies fight for a contract. The lowest bid wins. But perhaps the quality of the work is as low as the bid. Maybe as a result of being built by the lowest bidder, the bridge collapses or the school starts to decay. Or competition forces out the local artisan, whose work is superior, but whose prices are higher. Or companies seeking a larger share of the economic pie drop prices in the short run so that they can drive out their competitors, which will, in turn, allow them to raise prices later. Or in their competitive need to keep prices low, companies will shut down plants, put people out of work and send factories to areas of underpaid workers. Or they indiscriminately rape the earth in order to generate the cheapest possible resources to undercut the competition.

Competition is deep and personal. It is based on a fear of failure, a fear of not winning, or a fear that we will not meet expectations. As we already have discussed, all of these fears trigger the survival instinct.

Now what about Becoming Oneness in regard to competition? Positive Habit Three tells us to support each other's success and wellbeing. How do I do that? How do I go against the grain of competition? First, I need to remember that I am really one with the people I resent. Since we all live in the same universe, since we all impact each other, I am actually positively impacted by the success of others. Just as I am distressed by the stress of others, I can be uplifted by others' joy. But just tell that to my little ego. I have to remind myself that people who are feeling content within themselves tend to be more loving and less competitive toward everyone, including me. If people around me are having their needs met, they can afford to be more generous toward everyone, including me. If there is joy in the air, I will feel happier.

Oh boy, this is a hard one to swallow.

So let's look at some specifics. Until I started practicing Positive Habit Three, I felt competitive with other counselors, authors and even with myself. Let's look at how this can change.

Competing with Other Healers: If I am practicing Positive Habit Three, I realize that the counselors I resent are me, aspects of my own consciousness. That means that they are me doing a different part of the same work. I also realize that the help other counselors give to people also helps the world become a more conscious and loving place, and if the world is a more conscious and loving place, it will be a better place for me. Finally, other counselors might be supporting people to reach a level of consciousness where they are then available to work with me, just as I might be helping clients move to a level where they can be further helped by someone else.

Other Authors Being More Successful: Authors who have popular ideas are filling a need, and I can rejoice that the people who are getting helped have more wellbeing and are, therefore, more loving toward us all. If others are getting accolades for ideas that I have also been teaching without reward, I can remember that our having the same ideas is an indication that we are, in fact, a collective consciousness. There are no unique ideas anyway. Ideas don't belong to "me." We are all part of the collective that generates and supports evolution.

Competition with Myself: Finally I can remember that I don't need to compete with myself, because I am a person who is becoming, and I don't need to push myself to grow.

Most importantly, I can realize that I am part of a whole, that each one of us has a part to play, and that I need only to play my own. This is concretely true. When I started doing intuitive work back in 1980, I was considered an oddball. Today, there are many doing this kind of work.

When I feel scared that I'm not good enough, I fear that "they" are going to take away "my" business. When I'm feeling sane and am Becoming Oneness, I remember that the popularity of the intuitive process is actually creating more acceptance of me. In other words, the work of others makes the world safer for me.

Through all these practices, we are retraining our egos to realize that the best way for me to take care of myself is supporting the wellbeing and success of others. At first, it feels awkward and unnatural. But after a while, this way of thinking becomes automatic and self-evident.

On some level, competition is an idea, not a necessity. If we see the universe as a whole, we see that every part of the universe has a role to play, and only through each one of us fulfilling our own part do we have a functioning whole. I may want the status of doctor, but if you would make a better physician, please get the job; because I'd rather have a competent you attending to my ills than an incompetent me! I may feel competitive about your beauty and strength, but please become the ballerina. I would love to have the pleasure of watching you perform in a manner I could accomplish only in my dreams. And if you have greater stamina, please become the cleaning person. I would rather have a powerful person clean my house than have a dirty home.

Much easier said than done, especially in a world where doctors out-earn cleaning women by . . . well, you know the answer to that as well as I. So how can I say so blithely that if I'm best suited for cleaning, I'd be happy to give up the chance to be a plastic surgeon?

Of course, it would be a lot easier not to compete if incomes were not so vastly different. It would be a heck of a lot easier to give up the Beverly Hills medical practice if the cleaning job paid much better. Nevertheless, I know in my gut that I am a happier woman when I live in trust that there is a place for me, and that I only need to fill it. I know that I am happier when I am doing what I am suited for and not worrying about how it looks or even how much it pays.

Even though our world is very uneven in its rewards, I can do a lot to work on my own competitiveness. Years ago, I was upset with myself because I had not figured something out in a group counseling session and someone else had come up with the answer. There was a slight financial fear associated with this. Suppose people decided that I wasn't that great a counselor, that I wasn't needed. Perhaps they wouldn't want to pay me for my work, or even want my help.

Sure there was a material fear. But mostly it was my pride that was bruised. That evening, as I was getting down on myself for not having had "the answer," God said to me, "Beth, if I had meant for you to know everything, I wouldn't have had to create other people, would I?" An unforgettable lesson and an unforgettable message.

In Platform Four, Becoming Mutually Supportive, we come to understand the concept of the highest good of all, and we begin to see how important it is for each one of us to do what we are meant to do, to start trusting that there are other ways of organizing society other than through competition. But for now, let's simply say this:

In fact, when I really support other people to do well, I feel good. I am helping the world to become a better place for all of us, including me. At the same time, when I am not competing with you, I am also releasing myself to find my own place, the place I belong. In the depth of my being, I want to do what I am suited for, not what my ego thinks will look best on a resume or in my own mind. If we all did that, we could actually begin to feel the bliss of taking responsibility for our part within a universe where others do the same. Wow, what a concept! Living in a highly functioning universe, where we all fulfill our potential. Wouldn't that be a better place to live?

Let's acknowledge the truth: that when I support others to reach their own potential, I am supporting the existence of a universe that hums. I am allowing others to give their gift, and I allow myself to give mine. When I contribute to others' failure, I am co-creating a universe where nothing works well. I may get the momentary satisfaction of "winning", but I gain nothing in the long run. To be a fully functioning part of a fully functioning group is a far more joyful experience than being the absolute authority in a dysfunctional household.

So how do I contribute to that universe that hums? I become Oneness by practicing Habit Three to the best of my ability. And how do I do that? One way is to bless those with whom I feel competitive. Even when I don't feel like doing it, I can practice this habit. In the end, you, I and everyone else will discover that supporting the success and wellbeing of others will become a wonderful, rewarding, and productive habit.

As I mentioned earlier, we will discuss this in much greater depth when we come to Platform Four: Becoming Mutually Supportive, where I offer practices to help us make this shift. Working towards that, we can begin now. At the end of every day, we can ask ourselves: How well did I practice Positive Habit Three?

1. Was I competitive today and with whom?
2. Why?
3. Did I emotionally and spiritually support the wellbeing of others?
4. Did I open my heart to allow myself to be in my place and allow others to be in theirs?

HABIT FOUR

Negative Habit Four

We see qualities in others that we dislike, and we don't want to acknowledge those qualities in ourselves. We may not see good qualities in ourselves, either.

Let's replace this with:

Positive Habit Four

When we see a quality in others that we dislike, we say, "I am that." When we see in others qualities that we like, we say, "I am that," too.

I love this habit because it goes so against the grain!

In the past few days, I met a man who was trying to sell me a house for far more than it was worth. He had certainly wasted my time! Then I met a man who was trying to buy my motor home for much less than it was worth. The nerve! Each of these men was living in fantasy, and each was totally self-centered, thinking only of himself.

I want to be indignant and say that I'm not like those two men. But here I am trying to practice Positive Habit Four. Okay, I am that. But how could I be? I'll tell you how, and I'll be very specific. Because I want to find some distressed seller who will let me have their house for less than it's worth, and I want some distressed buyer who is willing to buy my motor home for more than it's worth. Like the two men I criticized, I'm in fantasy, and I'm thinking only of myself. Pretty amusing!

We are definitely habituated to seeing the differences between us and those we criticize, because we want to be accepted or admired. Let's look at an important example. In our introduction, "Ego, Instinct & Evolution," I talked about how our egos have to hide our egos. If our mother used to criticize others for being selfish, for example, we'd go to any lengths not to be seen as such. But we are selfish. In fact, aren't we all selfish? Don't we all live within our own skins? I have often admitted that my hangnail hurts me more than your broken leg does. That's because the frayed nerves of my hangnail are attached to *my* brain, not yours. It's true, of course, that we are one, and it's true that when I allow myself to feel our Oneness, I can experience your pain (in fact, sometimes when I'm actually channeling another's feelings, I feel them as acutely as if they were my own), yet in my ordinary consciousness, I am not aware of my connection to you, and I experience my pain more acutely than I experience yours, or at least I believe I do!

Is it surprising, then, that there is a natural tendency to be selfish and to want relief from my own distress? Do I want to cause you pain in the process? No. But while I don't intend to cause you pain, I do want to get out of my own. Do I sometimes go blind to the pain that I'm causing you in the process? Of course, because if I acknowledged it, I might not be able to act in my "self interest." And if I saw the impact of my behavior on the whole, on society, I might not be able to act in my "self interest" either. And why would I want to know anything that would get in the way of me relieving myself of distress, which we know is the underlying motive for all our behavior?

Selfishness is easy and natural. On the other hand, it takes a conscious effort to learn awareness of other people and their pain and needs. Good parenting encourages us to do that. If I hit Mommy, and she doesn't cry, I think I can act without consequences. When Mommy shows me it hurts and discusses my behavior, I am more likely to develop the habit of awareness of my impact on others. This helps me to deal with my natural self-centeredness. I don't eliminate it, but I expand myself to be greater than that selfishness.

But what if I'm really stressed? Amazing how that survival instinct takes over in me and in most of us. Me, myself, and I. I'm hungry. I need money. I'm tired. I'm scared. Whatever happened to you and us? A good example of this is people who want every type of expensive treatment to keep them alive two days longer, when those resources could be used for others who could have a full life. Yes, the instinct to survive is strong.

Focusing on self is natural enough, but how can I admit that about myself? I heard Mommy speaking judgmentally about people she considered selfish. I heard spiritual people denouncing selfishness. Because of these experiences, I don't regard the instinct to care for myself as a natural instinct that I need to work with and transcend. I think of it as a quality that must be condemned and obliterated. At the very least it has to be hidden.

So, when I see selfishness in others, I self-righteously condemn them. The persons who are selfish are "them," as opposed to me. Phew, I'm safe. I'm describing "them," not "me." But am I?

Developing the habit of acknowledging, "I am that" takes a tremendous amount of self-discipline and honesty. And it requires us to accept our human qualities. If I accept that survival is an instinct, and focusing on my needs is natural, I can accept that I am selfish. I can have compassion for myself and use my reason. Is it reasonable for me to ask for x or y? Am I scamming or hurting others in the process? Can I find a greater part of me that can go beyond this instinct? When I transcend instinct, I am using my consciousness, calling on the totality of me, so that I can withstand the domination of my ego. In so doing, there is no need for me to judge myself, only to become conscious.

Selfishness is only one example of qualities that I wish to pretend I don't have. Let's each of us take a long moment to think of qualities we condemn in others. After we do that, let's ask ourselves how we have behaved in essentially the same ways in our own lives. And let's ask ourselves what has led us to believe that these qualities are so bad that we feel we have to disown them?

I led a workshop once, where I asked people to identify a group or race that they judged harshly. The purpose of this was to see how we play out on a global level the habit of projecting negativity on others. One woman identified that she disliked Mexicans, because they had too many children that they didn't want and couldn't take care of. After deep probing, we discovered that this very woman had had a child when she was quite young. It was during World Word II, and with her husband was gone, she felt incapable of caring for the child. Naturally, on some level she didn't really want the baby, because she didn't have the resources to care for it.

Ultimately this son became mentally ill and was diagnosed as schizophrenic. The woman always blamed herself, unconsciously believing that the child had become ill because she didn't want him. To heal, she needed to come to peace about her decision to have that child and about her limited capacity to care for him. At the workshop, she talked to him telepathically, made amends for having given birth to him with so much ambivalence, and realized that he, too, had made the decision to be born and that he was glad for his life. Her vehement dislike of Mexicans was now seen for what it was—a projection of her own self-hatred.

There are so many qualities we project onto others. Blacks are sexy; Arabs violent; Mexicans lazy; Whites are prejudiced. The list goes on. If we could only contain "them," disempower, imprison, or even kill "them," these qualities would be obliterated from the earth. But would they?

Are we afraid of our sexuality, our violence, our laziness, our prejudice? Have these qualities plagued us or dominated us? Can we not find a way to own them as ours and integrate them into us (more on this in Platform Six: Becoming Integrated). Isn't the first step toward integration to own that these qualities are ours?

Just as we project onto others the qualities we dislike, we often project onto others qualities we would like to have, but don't recognize in ourselves. For example, I may see you as successful; her as saintly; them as impactful; whereas I may (consciously or unconsciously) consider myself a failure, a bad person, or impotent. I may be full of self-judgment, comparing myself negatively to others, not acknowledging where I might in fact also be successful or kind.

We especially tend to miss our Oneness when we don't have the hated or admired quality to as great a degree as someone else. Oh yes, I'm selfish, but she's more selfish. Oh yes, I'm out of control of my emotions, but he's worse. Oh yes, I'm intelligent, but not as intelligent as they are. One more time we find a way to assert that we are different.

But this assertion is a trick of the mind. We don't have to have the qualities to the same degree, in order for this practice of Becoming Oneness to be real. The point of this habit is to realize that the essence of who we are is the same, and distinguishing between their worse behavior and our less bad behavior is just another way of avoiding that reality.

Disowning the negative and the positive are two sides of the same coin, which is the inability to acknowledge the totality of who we are. If I deny the totality of who I am by projecting negative qualities onto others, I am likely to deny the totality of who I am by projecting positive qualities onto others as well. Or I am likely to project them onto God, who many of us believe is the only perfect being in the universe.

We are complex, evolving beings, and we have the full spectrum of qualities within us. If we don't acknowledge that reality, we fragment the universe into you and me, them and us, God and human. If we are to practice the platform of Oneness, we are going to need to see ourselves in our totality and identify how you, they, and God have all the spectrum of qualities that also exist within us. Which qualities we emphasize and feed depends on us (this subject is covered in the next chapter). But it is a given that we have them.

In an ego-based universe, distinctions are necessary for us to prove we are worthy of existence, but having accepted that we deserve to exist, we can take another important step in Becoming Oneness. Let's start practicing positive Habit Four.

Tool: I Am That

When confronted by conduct that annoys, angers or perhaps even horrifies you, before responding with judgment, take a minute to connect to your self-honesty. Ask yourself how you do the same thing that is angering you to the other. Be scrupulously honest. While you may not do the behavior in exactly the same way, I bet if you look deep in your heart, you will see that you are more like that other person that you would care to acknowledge. Once you have grasped how you are like the other person, smile or laugh. Say to yourself, or share out loud, if possible, "I am that. I do that too." You can use the "I am that" tool in other ways, also. When someone is sharing with you something painful about their life, look for the way you relate to that experience, and tell them that you've experienced that also. If someone admits some part of themselves they judge negatively, see if you can't relate, and tell them "I am that, too." Do this, and it will revolutionize you and your relationships.

How do I practice this habit? Bite the bullet, and at the end of every day, ask myself:

1. Who did I judge today either as good or bad?
2. What were the qualities that I was judging?
3. Why did I think they were good or bad?
4. How am I like that?

HABIT FIVE

Negative Habit Five

We act out behavior that others might perceive as hurtful. In order to do so, we feel compelled to disconnect from them.

Let's change this to:

Positive Habit Five

We acknowledge that sometimes we have to cause others pain. Before we do so, however, we examine our motives to the best of our ability. Once we decide to make the intervention—whether it is a verbal confrontation or an action—we stay connected to them through the process.

Sometimes we have to do or say things that hurt others, meaning it will make them feel pain. Even if something is ultimately for their good, they may experience the intervention as uncomfortable.

Here are some examples. We have a small company, and our employee has a drinking problem. We have to talk to him about it, and if the employee refuses to take action, we need to fire him. Even though the employee has a need to be called to consciousness about his drinking, he will experience pain. The employee will feel scared and angry and may even lose his job, which could cause distress to his entire family. We have a child who stole a toy from a friend. We need to explain to her why this action is damaging to her and others. The child will feel hurt. She will feel ashamed and criticized. She may feel astonished that other children can have things that she can't. She'll feel hurt by our criticism and hurt to know that she can't have something. We have a spouse who is hitting our child. The spouse's behavior needs to be confronted, and in the worst instance, he or she needs to leave the home. Our mate will feel hurt by this confrontation and action. He or she will feel the pain of shame and may even face the loss of home, family, and security.

When is it "right" to take action, even if it causes another pain? Sometimes the course is clear. We know something is for the person's good or is necessary. Sometimes it's muddy. How do we know that what we're doing is right? Regardless of how certain we are, taking these actions most often will create in the other person the perception of pain (I say perception, because it is the person's bad behavior being surfaced to awareness that is actually causing them pain, not our intervention), and their perception of pain will cause pain for us.

Why? Because we are one, and ultimately we feel each other's pain. Because the confrontation might cause the loss of the relationship. Because we don't like to be disliked, and the person we are confronting might get angry with us. How do we manage to act anyway? Habitually, we do it by practicing Negative Habit Five—we disconnect. Let's look at the impact of this habit, and let's consider another way.

First, let's look at how we disconnect. The easiest way to disconnect from another's pain is to get angry with the person we have to "hurt." Yes, the easiest way to detach from the pain we are causing is to detach from the person, and the easiest way to detach from the person is to become angry and blame them. That person is a no-good-son-of-a bitch, or a lazy woman, or a selfish bastard, or whatever we come up with. They are bad and don't deserve compassion.

Being angry with them serves an additional purpose. It supports them to get angry at us in return, and if they are angry at us, it's easy for us to get angrier and more detached from them. Here I was trying to help them, and they got angry. Screw them! Or I knew they were hopeless. Let me get rid of them as quickly as possible.

When we are disconnecting from someone who might perceive our action as hurtful, even if it is "for their own good," we tend to practice Negative Habit Four, as well; that is, we focus on how we are different from them—more responsible, more kind, more honest, more something. There may, of course, be some difference between them and us in our behavior, but the essence of their behavior is something we can always identify with. I may not have come drunk to the job, but I may have been distracted by some emotional problem. I may not have stolen a toy from a friend, but I have wanted things for myself that I couldn't have. I may not have beaten my child, but I may have been unkind or emotionally cruel.

Remembering that there is no "them" and "us" reminds us to practice Positive Habit Five—to stay connected when delivering a message that might hurt the pride or cause fear to the other person. And to stay connected, we need to remember our Oneness, to remind ourselves how we are like the person we are confronting.

Starting from the perspective of how alike we are, we find ourselves feeling and speaking differently in the confrontation. If we come from a place of identification, rather than separation, we are more likely to find ways of communicating that are compassionate, as opposed to judgmental. We may find ourselves identifying even as we speak, talking about how we understand the other and tend to do the same kind thing. Sometimes we just *feel* more understanding, because in fact, we do understand, because, in fact, we are really very similar, because, in fact, we are one.

The person we are confronting may still be defensive and may still feel hurt, but, on some level, he or she will pick up the difference in our attitude. Even though he or she might still maintain their denial and attack us, that person will receive more impact from the intervention. Even if we can't see the difference in them, most importantly, we will experience a difference in us, because we will have been coming from our acknowledgment of Oneness, and this will change *us*.

When we're stuck in Negative Habit Five—practicing our tendency to disconnect from those whom we are punishing, criticizing, or alerting to some negative behavior—we inevitably hurt ourselves. We experience the pain of disconnection, and we are likely to experience shame, if our disconnection leads us to become abusive. It's easy to become abusive when disconnected. The other person is not real to us, because we're wrapped up in ourselves, explaining to ourselves over and over exactly why we need to confront the other person. When we're lost in our heads, instead of relaxing into the knowledge that the intervention is necessary and focusing on loving the other person, we ruminate on the legitimacy of our perspective and blind ourselves to their feelings. Under these circumstances, we are more likely to treat our employee with contempt, hit the child or shame our spouse and throw in their face their out-of-control behavior.

Why do we tend to fall into Negative Habit Five? Because we're scared that we will feel paralyzed by connecting to the being or thing whose pain we are triggering. The fear is: If I feel my employee's pain—not just the pain I seem to be causing, but the pain that's causing him to drink—I will not be able to fire him. If I feel my child's pain, I won't be able to discipline her. If I feel my spouse's pain, I won't be able to throw him/her out. In addition, we might feel insecure about the intervention and bully ourselves to go forward. We're disconnected from ourselves, too.

The pattern of disconnecting from those we are afraid we would hurt applies to many areas of life. If I have to kill to eat, cut down trees to build a house, "beat out" another to get a job, I feel that I have to disconnect from the animal, tree, and other applicant, so I can justify, or not experience, the pain I cause. In order to kill animals, I hire others to slaughter them. Not only do I disconnect from the animal, I disconnect from the people I hire to do the killing and never examine the slaughterhouse and see how it's done. Out of sight; out of mind. I want to believe I can't feel the animals' pain because I disconnect from my action. How do I cut down the trees? I pretend that they are not living, as well as close my eyes to the neighbors, other species, and planet that might need those trees. I simply focus on the house I'm building and don't allow myself to think of the consequences of my actions. How do I let myself "beat out" another to get a job? I try to numb myself to the pain of the applicant who loses the job. I can tell myself I need the job more, or I am just plain better qualified than he or she, or I just don't even think about it.

When we disconnect from others, we fragment not only from them, but from ourselves. We know we are one. We know that when we are connected to ourselves in the deepest sense, we are connected to each other, including the person, being or species we feel we are hurting. In order to deny that pain, we deny our connection to those persons, beings or species. We are, thereby, denying our connection to our deepest selves.

Cruelty, abusive behavior, denial, and disconnection from self, these are some of the costs of Negative Habit Five. How can we practice Positive Habit Five? First we need to acknowledge that sometimes we have to take action that causes another pain. Going back to the question of when to do this, we start by asking ourselves about our motives. Why are we taking this action? Do we really need to confront the child, the employee, or the spouse? Do we need to cut the tree or kill the animal or compete for the job? Are we supporting everyone's highest level of consciousness, to the best of our ability? Are we acting for the highest good of all?

Sometimes we know, or at least we believe we know. When we confront the employee, child, or spouse, we hope that we are supporting them to move in a better direction for themselves. We know we are doing no one a favor by letting them continue to drink or abuse a child; if we do, we are just enabling them to go down that painful path forever.

Okay, but what about the tree or the animal or the other applicant? How can we say we are supporting them? Consider these possibilities. When we get the job instead of the other guy, the competing applicant may benefit, because he/she may not be qualified for the job and getting the job would have led to a sense of failure. But what about the tree or the animal? We can say that the animal is fulfilling its purpose by being consumed, or that there may be too many trees in an area. Now perhaps we're moving closer and closer into rationalization. Maybe sometimes we have to acknowledge we are simply choosing our survival over the survival of others. Even if this is the case, we don't have to disconnect from them. We can be respectful and grateful.

There is a further way to check in on the rightness of our action, which is to ask for higher guidance, but we'll discuss this later in the book when we get to Platform Four: Becoming Mutually Supportive. At this later point, we will learn how to truly inquire into the question: What is for the highest good of all, including me?

At this point, however, we can still say this: The more honest we are with ourselves, the less likely we are to cause others pain, because the less likely we are to be motivated by impulses such as jealousy or revenge. And the more connected we feel to others, the more likely our behavior will actually support their consciousness. On the other hand, to speak honestly, sometimes we take actions just because we have the power to protect our interests over the interests of another—like killing germs or rats or even stopping a gang from taking over our neighborhood.

Even with the best of intentions, the truth is that we don't always know when it's right for us to take an action that hurts another. We can only search our hearts to know our motives and get support from people whose fairness we trust. Am I trying to support the other person's consciousness and support the whole, for example, the company or the family? Or am I really being controlling, unrealistic, or unfair? Am I actually being motivated by anger? Am I getting revenge for something altogether unrelated, something that person may have said or done to me, and now I have a chance to get back at them? If, after searching our hearts and getting support from people whose fairness we trust, we believe that we have reason to speak to the person or to take action, then what?

If we feel that we need to cause pain to another, let us do it while practicing Positive Habit Five, which is to stay connected. Positive Habit Five requires us to remember we are one even in the face of taking these actions. It asks us to stay connected to the animal we kill, the tree we cut down, the spouse we kick out of the house, and the applicant we beat out. Now that's not easy. That means we need to feel our love for them, how we are like them and how much pain they are in—not just the pain of the confrontation, but the pain that motivates their negative behavior to start with.

And if the other person reacts angrily, we can have compassion, because I am that. I have felt anger or shame when confronted, too, especially when I know that the person confronting me is right.

It's not easy to practice Positive Habit Five, but we can keep it in our consciousness. Let's accept the fact that sometimes our actions trigger pain in others. Before taking those actions, let's examine our motives to the best of our ability. And once we decide to take an action—verbal or otherwise—let's stay connected to the other person through the process.

Let's embark on our practice of Positive Habit Five by first becoming aware of our own actions in the past and the present. How have we treated those we felt we had to hurt? What were our motives? How did we disconnect from them? How are we behaving today?

Every day we can ask ourselves these questions:

1. Did I feel I had to say or do something today that would make another uncomfortable or would cause them pain?
2. Did I do it, or did I run from it?
3. What were my motives? Were they along the lines of supporting them or protecting someone or something that needed protection? Was I acting out some other agenda? Or was it a mix?
4. Did I stay connected to them, when I spoke or acted?
5. If not, what excuse did I use?
6. Did I remember that I am that?
7. How could I do this differently in the future?

HABIT SIX

Negative Habit Six

We desperately need intimacy, but intimacy can lead to the loss of self, if we are not able to Become Differentiated (see Platform Two). We either give in to the need for intimacy and suffer from the loss of ourselves, or we struggle to find ways to disconnect from that need and lose the chance for connection.

Let's change this to:

Positive Habit Six

We acknowledge our need for intimacy, and we acknowledge our fear of losing ourselves. At the same time, we connect to the totality of ourselves and trust that by connecting to that totality, we can afford to take the risk. We have compassion for ourselves and others, and instead of losing ourselves in relationships, we learn through them. We stay connected to our higher consciousness.

This is another tough one. Connection with others is both our greatest desire and our greatest fear, and both the fear and desire for intimacy cause us to develop all kinds of self-destructive behavior. Basically, we either get overly attached, or we get too scared to connect at all, or we tend to do both in a dizzying pendulum swing.

It's not our fault. Our experiences have made us really gun-shy. It is, in fact, very difficult to be in a relationship without losing ourselves, and that's reality. We lose ourselves because we fear the loss of love or friendship—our loved one can leave or die. And because we fear rejection, the loved one can disapprove of us. These fears are reality-based. People do leave us, and they do reject us. And it does hurt. So we tend to do whatever it takes to stay connected. We adopt beliefs that are not ours, habits that we dislike, drink with the alcoholic, have sex when we don't want to, watch movies we hate, and adopt personality traits that feel foreign.

This is to be expected. The need for emotional and material connection is profound. We are by nature social creatures, and as we have already established, we are in fact one. To be cut off from that feeling of Oneness is painful.

We have already discussed this subject in Chapter 3, when we discussed the pain of disconnection, but let's just review some points. Let's look at this from the material and emotional perspectives. First the material: It is, in fact, virtually impossible to live in this world in total isolation. Even those of us who pride ourselves on independence are ultimately dependent on the guys in the supermarket, the U.S. mail, the workers in Bangladesh, and the people fixing the road. So physical independence is obviously an illusion.

Emotionally we're dependent as well, starting with our parents. Their smiles, their frowns, their praise and their beatings deeply impacted us, our sense of safety and wellbeing, our sense of value and pride. As a result, we either twisted ourselves to meet their expectations, convincing ourselves that their standards and values were right, or we felt oppressed by their demands and expectations and rebelled, often pretending we didn't need them at all. Parents are hostages, too. If the baby cries, Mom feels like a failure, and when our children don't imitate us, we feel affronted, as though our value were in question.

The need for material and emotional connection, of course, goes way beyond the parent/child relationship. The need for connection causes us to look for love and companionship in many ways. We go to restaurants and football games, seek mates, cling to family, adopt pets, join clubs, hang out with friends. In fact our reliance on each other never ceases. We all need validation, love and closeness with something or somebody.

Who are we without each other? Who will reflect back to us that we are valuable, desirable, lovable?

Our reliance on others comes with a price. When we're in school, we may find ourselves trying to please a certain teacher; or we might try to bond with other kids by not bonding with our teachers at all. When we experience first love, we often blind ourselves to our lover's flaws or liabilities, as we fantasize about how wonderful our lives are going to be. We may suddenly find ourselves dressing or talking differently, and we may cut off old friends who get in the way of our new passion. When we're already in a relationship, we are often desperate to maintain this extremely crucial emotional and economic unit, especially when we have children, and we may suppress our anger, repress our creativity, or attempt to fit into our mate's expectations. When we've been in a community for a long time, we may be afraid to leave, because we fear the loss of our social and material connections.

Before going forward with this discussion, let's take a look at how these observations apply to us. Let's examine some of our key relationships, past and present: parents, friends, teachers, associates, bosses, lovers, and mates.

1. How have we felt hostage to each of these people?
2. How have we tried to make ourselves acceptable to them?
3. Have we allowed ourselves to be abused?
4. What's been the result of these behaviors on our lives and our self-esteem?

Acknowledging how we have lost ourselves in relationships is good. Not only does it allow us to be honest with ourselves, it also allows us to understand others, as well, because, guess what? The people to whom we have been hostage have been hostage to us, too. Let's take a moment to do another inventory.

1. Who has been hostage to us?
2. How have they tried to make themselves acceptable to us?
3. How have they let us abuse them?
4. What's been the result of these behaviors on their lives and self-esteem?

We've been talking about how we abandon ourselves to be in relationships. But there is an additional, subtler way that we lose ourselves in relationships, and that is the impact of another's thoughts and feelings on our own. Let's look at that now.

Earlier, when discussing this platform, we described how much we have in common and how connected we are. Those of us who are conscious of these connections can easily be aware of the unconscious impact we have on each other. But whether or not we are aware of this impact, its effects are real.

Let's look at some examples. Have you ever been in a really good mood and then walked into a room of people and suddenly felt tense? Why are you tense? Are you nervous about the situation because you don't know anyone? Or are you feeling tense because everyone else in the room is feeling tense, and you're picking up on their feelings?

Have you ever been feeling happy and suddenly felt sad, without knowing why, only to later find out that a painful experience has just happened to a loved one? Have you ever felt loving toward a person and then found yourself getting impatient, way more than you can explain?

Why do these things happen? How do these things happen? Once again, we start with the reality that we are connected. Although we are rarely conscious of this connection, we regularly feel each other's feelings and often have each other's thoughts. Yet we don't know that those thoughts or feelings did not generate with us. In addition, we are impacted by each other's thoughts and feelings in much more obvious ways. People tend to automatically adopt core ideas, beliefs, and behaviors from family, friends, or community, and we think these ideas, beliefs, and behaviors are our own. This is another way that we lose ourselves.

How do we avoid the phenomenon of losing ourselves? First, let's look at some negative strategies we have habitually used to avoid being hostage to others or at least to look like we're not. Which of these have you tried?

1. Run away from intimate relationships, claiming that we don't need them or that we "can't" find anyone.
2. Pretend that our partner or friend needs us more than we need them.
3. Create ways of looking tough.
4. Develop compensating behaviors to lessen the impact of the lack of intimacy. For example, the use of food, drugs, work, sex, television, busyness, achievement, friends, money or fantasy to fill up the hole that the lack of love leaves behind.
5. Try to reduce the power of others, so that they look more weak and dependent than we do.
6. Try to be the dominant partner in order to hide our vulnerability from ourselves.

What positive alternatives do we have? How can we connect to others without losing ourselves? As I mentioned before, ultimately, we need to live in a universe where our primary connection is to ourselves and The Source, but let's look at what we can do now.

We can practice Positive Habit Six: We acknowledge our need for intimacy, and we acknowledge our fear of losing ourselves. At the same time, we connect to the totality of ourselves and trust that by connecting to that totality, we can afford to take the risk of connecting to others, as well.

We have compassion for ourselves and others, which allows us to be less reactive and more objective. Instead of losing ourselves in relationships, we experience them and learn through them. We stay connected to our higher consciousness.

How do we do these things? The first step is to admit our needs and our fears. In this way, we are being honest with ourselves and others, so we can deal with what is. In addition, just the admission of the truth can help us experience our Oneness. We know from Positive Habit Four that *I am that*. But if I am that, you must be that, too. So acknowledging how I am feeling and considering our Oneness, I can consider the possibility that no matter how you may act, I am no more a hostage to you than you are to me. If we are one, I cannot be the only insecure, needy person on the planet; and you cannot be the only person who is not needy and insecure! Voila! We are each other.

How does this allow more intimacy? If others don't look so big, I don't have to feel so small. And if I don't feel so small, I don't have to puff myself up to make myself look even bigger, different, better, less vulnerable than you. I can let you see who I am, and I can see who you are, and we can see how alike we are. The result is more Oneness and more connection. Similarly, once I understand you're vulnerable, too, I become less afraid of my own vulnerability. I can take risks in this relationship, because I know you're a hostage, too.

We are each other. Knowing that fact creates intimacy and gives me the courage to go toward the intimacy we all seek.

Acknowledging our vulnerability to each other also reduces shame. Suppose I have lost myself in relationships before. Perhaps I have betrayed my values or let myself be abused. Should I feel ashamed of that and beat myself up? Should I hide that from you, which reduces our intimacy? Should I let that shame keep me from trying again? Obviously not. The tendency to lose ourselves in relationships is part of the reality of being human, and I can accept it. Now that I know that we are the same, I can also pretty much figure that you have lost yourself in relationships, too.

Now here's a surprising statement. I can actually be glad that I have lost myself in a relationship, that I have hurt myself for love. Having had this experience demonstrates that at least I haven't been so scared that I denied my needs and ran away from relationships altogether! (Of course, ideally, I can learn from these experiences and not repeat them. We discuss this more in Platform Two: Becoming Differentiated, which is coming later.)

Earlier I mentioned that we pick up each other's thoughts and feelings and that this is another way of losing ourselves. I may get angry with you, only to find out that it's your anger at yourself! I may feel anxious, only to discover that it's your anxiety.

What can I do about this? Just as acknowledging our neediness is the first step toward overcoming it, acknowledging how impacted we are by each other is the first step toward dealing with that impact. If I have an unexplainable mood, or if I suddenly feel angry with you, I can always stop and ask myself: Are these my feelings, and if not, whose could they be? In fact, if I feel angry with you, I can ask you whether or not you feel angry with yourself. If I am feeling anxious around you, I can ask you whether you're feeling anxious, as well.

Will we always get an accurate answer? No. Many people have no idea what they're feeling and may not be able to answer us honestly, even when they want to. What's important, however, is the asking. Let's not assume that our thoughts and feelings are always our own. We are not separate islands. The rain falls on all of us equally, and sometimes I need to question myself closely to determine whether the feelings are just in my space, in which case I'm watering the garden, or there's a storm in my space. Just acknowledging that the feelings may not be mine can help me to differentiate from them and begin to connect to myself again.

The first step toward practicing Positive Habit Six, then, is acknowledging our needs and fears. Let's take the second step: realizing that we are greater than our needs. Yes, I am vulnerable to you. Yes, I need your love, but I am also greater than that need and that vulnerability. I have other qualities—intelligence, common sense, self-love—and I have other resources to meet my need for love, even if these other resources can't meet the need entirely.

Is this beginning to sound like I'm pretending again that I don't need you? Not at all. I admit I need you. I admit that I feel a hole when you're gone. I admit that nothing can take the place of your love. But once I admit these realities, I don't have to run away from them, hide them or be dominated by them. I can affirm them, and at the same time I can affirm other parts of me, as well.

I feel lonely when you are gone, *and* I can feel the love of others. I feel rejected when you don't want me, *and* I can want myself. I desperately want you to approve of me, *and* I have to be true to myself or else I will lose my own approval.

We do not succeed in living a balanced life by denying our vulnerabilities. We succeed by acknowledging them without being overwhelmed or dominated by them. We give our vulnerabilities their space, their place, and their voice. We can let the desperate need for love and connection cry out and get our attention. We can love ourselves for those vulnerabilities and needs. And, once they have voice, we can become the parent to our vulnerabilities. We can offer them the strength of the rest of ourselves, the totality of ourselves. And ultimately, we can find a connection to ourselves and higher consciousness that truly reduces those vulnerabilities.

We are needy, but that is not all of who we are. We are also strong, caring, and self-aware. We are fearful, but that is not all of who we are. We are also courageous, wise, and far-sighted. We are the totality of who we are, not a fragment. (More about this, by the way, in Platform Six: Becoming Integrated, where we begin to liberate ourselves from the domination of any of our needs.)

The third step toward practicing this habit is to develop compassion. This is especially important when we are feeling abused. How does this work? If I am in a relationship with you, and you are becoming abusive, shouldn't I leave? What does it mean to develop compassion?

Here's a paradox. The more I feel compassion for you, the less I am dominated by you. When I observe you being abusive toward me, my fight or flight reaction is to either shut down and shrink inside myself (flight) or to counter-attack (fight). If I can get beyond my immediate fear response and call on my intelligence and common sense, I can look at you with compassion. I can think about what's happening that's causing you to get so abusive toward me. I can stand my ground and ask, "What's going on for you?" And I can decide on the course of action best for me.

When we feel compassion for the abuser, we are connecting to our own POWER. Instead of feeling small and victimized, we feel bigger, calm, detached, the observer of the interaction, and that makes us feel much more in command of ourselves.

I am not suggesting that we stay in relationships that are physically or emotionally abusive, because that's destructive to us and the other person. Allowing people to abuse us hurts them, because people who are abusive need their behavior confronted, if they are ever to come to awareness and deal with themselves; and allowing people to abuse us keeps them unconsciously in the shame of their abusiveness, whether they deny their shame or not. At the same time, allowing people to abuse us hurts us, because it reinforces our negative feelings about ourselves, which further prevents us from feeling self-love, and diverts us from relationships that support our wellbeing.

But life is often not so black and white. In reality, most people are abusive from time to time—and yes, that is true even of us. What is abusiveness? It's using someone's vulnerability against him/her. The batterer exploits our physical vulnerability, and the emotional abuser exploits our emotional vulnerability. For example, teasing someone about something painful to them, continually pointing out someone's defects, cavalierly threatening to leave someone who loves you desperately, asking someone to alter themselves physically or emotionally just to satisfy your needs, all these are acts of abuse that we all tend to engage in from time to time. So if everyone left a relationship because of some abuse, there wouldn't be many relationships left.

Abusiveness is based on fear, fear of pain. I feel threatened in some way and so I abuse you to give myself the illusion of power, and I can get away with it, because I exploit your insecurities and vulnerabilities. Let's look at four examples of our abusiveness: shaming you, wanting you to look better than you do, screaming at you because of behavior you can't help and withdrawing when you've done something of which I disapprove.

- Shaming You: I feel ashamed of myself, and therefore I deflect that shame by shaming you. You put up with it because I can exploit the shame that I know you already feel about yourself, whether or not you deny that you feel this shame.
- Wanting You to Look Better: I feel insecure and want you to look better than you do. I try to get you to improve your appearance or status in the world, because your appearing more beautiful or successful is an attempt to compensate for my insecurity. You go along with it, because I can exploit your insecurity about your looks or performance, and I can exploit your insecurity about my desire for you.
- Screaming at You for Behavior You Can't Control: I feel threatened by the possible consequences of your uncontrollable behavior, and I scream at you to try to substitute my control for your lack of control. You accept my screaming, because I can exploit your shame over your behavior.

- Withdrawing When You Have Done Something of Which I Disapprove: Your behavior makes my life feel out of control, so I punish you by withdrawing. You don't leave, because I can exploit your need for me.

We, the abuser, feel threatened, and we think we need to attack to establish some illusion of power. Sometimes our perceptions are based on our fear of a real consequence. Sometimes our perceptions are based on our history and have no relationship to reality at all. For example, suppose my husband takes drugs and may run off the side of the road. I freak out and get abusive. If my husband has a tendency toward being an addict, this fear has a basis in fact. If he doesn't, but my father had a tendency toward drug addictions, my fear has a basis in history. Whether our fear is irrational or not, it exists. We react, we can become abusive and our partners do the same.

Since we are all abusive from time to time, we can either wait for the perfect relationship where neither of us is ever triggered into being abusive, or we can work on the relationship we have. If a relationship is worth maintaining, we are going to have to accept that there may be occasional fear-based behavior from our partners and from us.

In the case of physical abuse, we need to evaluate the danger of hanging in there. In any case, abusive partners must be confronted immediately with the consequences of their behavior. We may have to call the police or leave the relationship, and we certainly need to insist on the person seeking immediate help. We should do the same for ourselves when we see ourselves as being physically abusive.

At the same time, we need to try to understand what's happening to ourselves and our partners, when we act out. Although abuse is never acceptable, it can be understood. What was the dynamic between us that contributed to this behavior? Did I provoke physical abuse by my emotional abuse? Did I exploit the person's vulnerability (for example, he/she can't express verbally and is at a disadvantage in a verbal dispute)? Did I create a situation in which my partner felt the need to choose between feeling shamed and getting physically violent? (Of course, the person could always walk away, but that's very difficult for someone who already feels inadequate, and the capacity to do this needs to be learned and nourished.) Could I be an abuser, too? Or is my partner reacting totally out of his or her history, and my behavior was not a trigger at all?

Emotional abuse between adults can be handled similarly. I need to inform my partner that abuse is not acceptable, and at the same time I have to look at my own abusiveness. Nothing is gained by judging another. We may end up feeling self-righteous, but when we do, what have we learned about ourselves or anyone else?

Compassion is the capacity to understand that if we were in the same situation, we could easily respond the same way. It is the ability to say *I am that*, or I could easily be. It often starts with asking questions.

Compassion allows us to ask why another person behaved in a way that caused us pain. Compassion reminds us that all negative behavior is based on pain or fear. Compassion is not one-sided. We certainly need to feel compassion for our own pain, and we need to not sacrifice ourselves for or to another. But with compassion, once having experienced and acknowledged our pain, we can go beyond it, feel for another, and then make choices as to our responses.

Compassion doesn't require us to stay in an abusive relationship, but it does allow us to practice Oneness, even if we leave. Compassion allows us to learn from painful experiences, it helps us to learn something about ourselves and something about others, and hopefully it helps open a door for "abusers" to confront themselves and their own demons.

Once we start to practice compassion and realize that our partner is behaving abusively out of fear or pain, once we understand that we behave abusively out of fear or pain as well, we see the pathway toward taking care of ourselves in a relationship. And that pathway is to go beyond fight-or-flight reactions.

Doing this requires us to experience ourselves as large, rather than small. When we feel the victim, we feel small—smaller than the "perpetrator," even when we cover up our feelings of smallness with anger and judgment. On the other hand, when we feel compassion and begin to understand ourselves and one another, we feel large; strengthened, rather than weakened; expanded rather than contracted; more whole, rather than less. Compassion makes us feel big. Reaction makes us feel small.

So how do we practice compassion in fact? When our partner is unkind, let's first try to ask, "What's going on for you?" If we are the unkind one, let us ask ourselves the same question. Partners worth having will use the opportunity to explore their reactions. Partners who will not walk through that door to greater self-discovery are probably not going to be our partners for the long run.

Step four toward practicing Positive Habit Six is learning through the relationship, rather than losing myself in it. We stay connected to higher consciousness. Wow, how do I do that?

Actually this step is just the summation of all the others. If I acknowledge my needs and vulnerabilities, if I connect to the totality of me, if I look honestly and compassionately at myself and my loved one, I will be growing, learning about myself and others, discovering my needs, and dancing with the universe. Somebody said that relationships are the crucible through which we come to know ourselves. Were they ever right! Staying connected to higher consciousness allows me to release myself from the domination of my own reactivity, and this allows me to become more and more myself. But much more about that in the platforms that follow.

So at the end of each day, let's ask ourselves a series of questions about our relationships:

1. To whom do I feel a hostage emotionally or physically?
2. How is that impacting my feelings and behavior?
3. Am I feeling someone else's feelings or my own?
4. Am I losing myself or denying my needs?
5. Can I acknowledge and accept my neediness?
6. Do I acknowledge and accept the neediness of others?
7. Do I know that there's more to me than my needs and vulnerabilities?
8. What other qualities do I have?
9. If I am losing myself, do I need to leave this relationship, or do I just need to find the balance between my needs and my other qualities?
10. Am I looking at others with compassion?
11. Do I see their behavior as being based on their own needs and fears?
12. What's my part?
13. What am I learning about myself here?
14. In what ways am I finding myself?

There's a lot to this habit, and I will offer much more information in Platforms Two, Six and Nine: Becoming Differentiated, Integrated and Becoming Becoming. But, in the meantime, as difficult as it is, if we don't practice Habit Six, we'll find ourselves reacting and flipping back and forth between losing ourselves and running away from intimacy.

The ego has trained us to separate and look for reasons to withdraw from or use one another. We can retrain ourselves to understand one another and find new ways to connect. Whether in a romantic relationship, a friendship or any other relationship, without being able to deal with the challenges of intimacy, we can't become Oneness, and we'll be doomed to the isolation and fear that impoverish our lives and make reality much harder to bear.

HABIT SEVEN

Negative Habit Seven

We are seeking the perfect father, mate, boss, friend, or God to make us feel loved and safe all the time. We expect ourselves to be perfect, too. When this fantasy is not fulfilled, we feel angry and become alienated from ourselves and each other.

Let's change this to:

Positive Habit Seven

We let go of the fantasy of the perfect parent, mate, boss, friend, God, or self and embrace a relationship with an evolving parent, mate, boss, friend, God, or self. We let go of the idea of perfection in life and refocus on evolution.

To conclude this brief discussion of Platform One: Becoming Oneness, we discuss one of our most pervasive fear responses. We look to each other to make ourselves feel safe. Whether it is our Higher Power, partner, child, boss, friend, or other, someone has to make us feel loved and provide for us the sense of security we crave.

Is this ever a step away from living with reality! As we have already discussed, there are always threats to our physical, emotional, and spiritual wellbeing. No one and nothing can always make us safe within ourselves and within this world, not even ourselves, at least not until we can reach a level of consciousness where we are beyond the instinctual ego reaction that focuses on survival.

As children, we hope our parents will always act loving and make us safe, but we discover this is not reality. Let's start with love. Can our parents always love us? What happens when Mom has three other kids to attend to and is short-tempered, or when she feels helpless and angry because her boss is pressuring her to work more, and her anger spills out against us? What happens when Dad has had a miserable day at the factory and wants to get lost in front of the TV, or when he's afraid of losing his job and resents the children he loves? Or what happens when our parents feel angry because they are disappointed with each other, when they are shut down and resentful and take it out on us? Or what happens when our parents' struggle with reality turns them to drugs, overwork, compulsive eating, gambling, drinking, or some other addictive behavior that takes them away from us?

What happens when we add to our parents' stress? We're cranky and tired. We're sick. We're having trouble in school. We're struggling to accept their divorce. We are jealous and want Mom or Dad to ourselves. We are competitive and throw frogs in the new baby's crib. How easily can our parents love us now?

Human beings are limited, and so is their capacity to express, feel, and practice love. That's hard to accept when we're so dependent on our parents' care. So we either pretend our parents are perfect, or we get mad that they're not.

Then there's the issue of safety. At first, we think our parents are God and can do anything. Then we find out they can't protect us from the local bullies, the pain of rejection by other kids, illness and our second grade teacher. What a shock it is that even our parents can't ensure our safety. And sometimes it's worse: one parent might not be able to protect us from the other or even protect us from their negative selves.

What happens when we find out that even God can't protect us from all pain and fear of life on this planet; when we can't feel loved and secure in our world and in our lives?

When we attribute to anyone or anything the ability to make us always feel loved and safe, we are setting ourselves up for disappointment, and we project the cause of that disappointment onto the one who failed us. We are then angry with them and lose once more the feeling of Oneness.

Perfectionism also causes us to lose the feeling of Oneness with ourselves. We expect more from ourselves than we can deliver. We can't be all-loving or all-powerful. We can't protect ourselves from every fall. We can't always be the best, the smartest, the fastest, or the wisest. And we can't always love.

If we expect perfection, we judge ourselves, and if we judge ourselves, we are standing outside and separate from ourselves. Now we are alienated not only from others and reality, we're alienated from ourselves.

Let's look at the alternative, Positive Habit Seven. We let go of the fantasy of the perfect parent, mate, boss, friend, God, or self and embrace a relationship with an evolving parent, mate, boss, friend, God or self. We let go of the idea of perfection in life and refocus on evolution.

This is a hugely important step toward living with reality, one that we will discuss again in Platform Nine: Becoming Becoming, but for now let's discuss this point briefly.

If there is no perfect person, God, or self, then what are we? We are beings in the process of evolution, beings that are working to find and co-create a new reality. We are bound to stumble and fall. That's part of the process of learning.

Referring to earthquakes as a metaphor, God once told me that it is through the earth's "faults" that it evolves. The same is, of course, true for us. As we discussed in "Ego, Instinct & Evolution," without instability there is no change, only stagnation. Without challenges, there would be no evolution. With perfection, there could be no growth.

It is a painful part of reality that no one can protect us or always make us feel loved, but it is a wonderful part of reality that we can change and evolve. The two go together.

When we practice Positive Habit Seven, we feel our pain, feel our anger, and feel our insecurity. At the same time, we embrace the reality of imperfection. Now we are catapulted into a new level of understanding of Oneness.

When I am practicing Oneness, I can and must forgive your inability to perfectly love and protect me. Every failure you exhibit, I exhibit too. Any inability of yours to love or protect is mine as well. Every action against me that causes me to feel pain is an action I am capable of as well.

Let me be more specific. When I was young, I was outraged by the corruption of people who protected their own interests at the expense of others. I saw them as bad and causing great pain. As I have lived, I have found myself acting in similar ways. At first, I cringed when I had this realization, but now I laugh. Every foolish act of mine connects me to some foolish act of yours, and I feel our Oneness. Every deceitful act of mine connects me to some deceitful act of yours, and I feel our Oneness. Every unkind, corrupt, self-serving act of mine connects me to some unkind, corrupt, self-serving act of yours, and I feel our Oneness.

I have forgiven all those who have failed to love or protect me, as I have seen myself in their moccasins as well. I embrace a universe where we are all learning and experiencing, where we can co-create a new reality. I embrace our Oneness.

Finally, regarding wanting the perfect outcome, there is one more point. Perfect for whom?

If I get the job, that might feel perfect for me, but how perfect is that for you? If my child performs perfectly by my standards, perhaps my child is not truly expressing herself. If it's a perfectly sunny day, perhaps the plants are thirsting for water. If the wolf fails to kill the buffalo, the buffalo breathes a sigh of relief and thanks the universe for the perfect outcome, but what about the wolf and its hunger?

When we practice Oneness, we come to understand that perfection is subjective and, therefore, impossible. By connecting to the whole, we give up on the idea of perfection and surrender to reality.

So at the end of each day, let's ask ourselves the following questions about wanting life to be perfect:

1. What fears did I experience today?
2. Who or what did I hope would rescue me?
3. Did they?
4. How did I react when they did or didn't?
5. Who do I want to be always loving toward me, and how do I react when they're not?
6. Am I willing to allow others to be who they are, not who I want them to be?
7. How do I expect myself to be perfect?
8. Am I willing to see myself as flawed and evolving?
9. How do I feel about that? Am I willing to laugh at and with myself?
10. Am I willing to see others the same way?
11. Does that make me feel closer to them, or am I consumed by anger?
12. Can I acknowledge my fear and pain? Can I accept them, without feeling the need to fix it all?

13. Can I see all of us working together, winging it in an evolving universe? Do I see our Oneness?

The ego has a view that we need to prove something about ourselves in order for us to survive. It drives us to appear to be what we are not. Once more, let us support our ego by retraining it and us to live with reality.

We have finished our discussion of the seven habits of separation and seven habits of Becoming Oneness. Now I would like to offer you a very easy-to-remember tool to help you live a life of Oneness every day of your life. The tool sums up much of Becoming Oneness in a simple, direct and usable way.

Remember, Becoming Oneness is a choice. It's a decision we make in the face of our habit or desire to separate. So when you notice yourself veering toward separation, make another choice. Remember our tool: I am that.

Tool: I Am That

When confronted by conduct that annoys, angers or perhaps even horrifies you, before responding with judgment, take a minute to connect to your self-honesty. Ask yourself how you do the same thing that is angering you to the other. Be scrupulously honest. While you may not do the behavior in exactly the same way, I bet if you look deep in your heart, you will see that you are more like that other person that you would care to acknowledge. Once you have grasped how you are like the other person, smile or laugh. Say to yourself, or share out loud, if possible, "I am that. I do that too." You can use the "I am that" tool in other ways, also. When someone is sharing with you something painful about their life, look for the way you relate to that experience, and tell them that you've experienced that also. If someone admits some part of themselves they judge negatively, see if you can't relate, and tell them "I am that, too." Do this, and it will revolutionize you and your relationships.

PLATFORM ONE: BECOMING ONENESS
SOME FINAL COMMENTS

We have spent a lot of time on Platform One, because it is the foundation of our program. It directly addresses the feeling of aloneness and alienation that is our deepest pain and that causes us to feel the greatest fear.

Yet as much space as we've allotted for Platform One, the seven habits discussed barely scratch the surface. Please do not feel limited by what is written here. I invite you to work with these habits and add your own. Look at your own process of fragmentation and come up with new habits of Oneness.

Now, in preparation for moving on to Platform Two: Becoming Differentiated, I would like to make a few points. First, going beyond the feeling of fragmentation isn't easy. Separating from others is a bad habit, and Becoming Oneness is a habit we have yet to develop. Separation is the perspective of the ego, and the ego is a natural result of our very existence. So let's practice Becoming Oneness with the utmost compassion for ourselves and one another.

Second, Becoming Oneness is a process we are embarking on, not a destination where we need to arrive. Many of us have had this awareness for years; some of us have just arrived at this consciousness. However long we work with this platform, we will always be journeying on this road. It will always be a daily, step-by-step process of calling ourselves to awareness and asking ourselves to think and act in ways that seem directly opposite to instinct and training.

Third, on some level, none of us will be able to totally practice Oneness until we all do. Why? Because ultimately, we are really one, aspects of a larger consciousness, and if we aren't all practicing Becoming Oneness, none of us can. We need to not judge ourselves harshly as we struggle with this process. At the same time, because we are all one, the more we practice Oneness, the more we are impacting the consciousness of all, including ourselves, which means that we need to support each other to practice Oneness, if we wish to more completely practice Oneness ourselves.

Having said that Platform One is the foundation of our program, let's say what Platform One is not. It's not the panacea we've been looking for. It's not the solution to all relationship problems. It will not remove all our pains and fears. It's the beginning point of our program, not the end.

In a sense, Becoming Oneness is the touchstone of a new identity of self.

- Becoming Oneness reminds us that we are one in the face of all the "realities" that tell us we're not.
- Becoming Oneness gives us guidance toward overcoming the source of our deepest pain, which is feeling our disconnection from ourselves and each other. It gives us compassion for ourselves, even as we desperately try to hide the pain of disconnection and to hide from the pain of disconnection.
- Becoming Oneness offers us a way to understand and deal with our fear. Fear is harder to face when we're alone, and Becoming Oneness helps us to move toward connection. Learning how to connect to others naturally brings us into a feeling of community, and community helps us feel comforted and more courageous in the face of our fear.
- Becoming Oneness helps us actually move toward more love and connection. Once we see that we are all the same and equal, equally in need of love and connection, we realize that everyone is as vulnerable as we are—even those who look less vulnerable. Once we see each other's vulnerability, we realize that we need not feel intimidated by others. This allows us to go toward the love and intimacy, the sharing and the honesty, that we have always desired, and it allows others to do the same with us.

As I mentioned before, Becoming Oneness doesn't solve all our relationship problems. In fact, dealing with the challenges of relationships will be the thread that weaves through our entire program. But it is the foundation without which we can't go far.

In this platform, I have not addressed the most compelling practice of Becoming Oneness, which is Becoming Becoming, a practice of feeling Oneness with higher consciousness and becoming filled with those vibrational energies that change our lives. But this topic is for another day, after we have completed many other practices.

So, now that we have laid the foundation of Oneness, let's continue on our journey through the rest of the nine platforms, and let's see where *Living with Reality* takes us next.

PLATFORM TWO

Becoming Differentiated
Individuation in the Context of Oneness

WHAT IS DIFFERENTIATION?

Introduction

In the last platform we talked about the need to become Oneness in the face of our tendency to separate. Now we are going to talk about the need to individuate in the face of our tendency to merge, and we're going to learn to do it through differentiating, instead of separating.

Individuation is the process of taking responsibility for ourselves and our consciousness. You could call it becoming your own person. To differentiate, which is to individuate without separating, we:

1. Call ourselves to consciousness moment by moment about the behaviors and attitudes that hurt us and others.

2. Commit ourselves to choosing a different path, which promotes all to reach their potential.
3. Confront the urge to merge with the people around us, as well as the negative attitudes or behaviors that are our own habits.
4. Acknowledge that we are like the people we wish to differentiate from; that we carry the energies, attitudes and behaviors that we may not like.
5. Connect to our higher consciousness to recognize what behaviors or attitudes we prefer to energize.
6. Find the divine or human support to choose those behaviors and attitudes.

Differentiation is exciting, sometimes difficult, but essential for us to become healthy human beings in a healthy society.

Let's look at some easily recognizable challenges: If I'm at the water cooler at work, and a bunch of co-workers are complaining about the boss, whom I may also dislike, how do I stay calm and centered and look objectively at the issue they are discussing, rather than leaping automatically to their side? If I'm with a group of guys who are bashing women, how do I encourage the men to look at their flaws, instead? If I know in my heart that my child shouldn't eat sugar, how do I stand up to the other moms, who offer cupcakes at their parties? In fact, how do I stand up to my child, who wants cupcakes, and to my husband, who is himself bribing the kid with candy? If I am in a crabby mood, how do I shift into gratitude and appreciation? How do I stand up to my own addictive tendencies? How do I tell my friends that I'm tired of pretending that we're having meaningful relationships, when we're not? How do I oppose a popular war? Or support an unpopular cause? In these situations, do we take the apparently easy road and merge, or do we differentiate and face the consequences?

Merging: Its Definition, Cause and Harmful Effects

Very simply, merging is losing ourselves in something. Feeling alone and afraid, we desperately turn to people, groups, roles, food, drugs, illusions, whatever we can, in order to make us feel safe. We merge in the effort to escape the experience of the ego-based universe, but it doesn't work.

Why do we merge? As I have mentioned before, we crave Oneness[15], the feeling of being part of something larger than ourselves, and we crave Oneness, because Oneness is essential to who we are. This craving is a reflection of the unity of consciousness that existed before we fragmented into the ego-based universe. (See Ego, Instinct & Evolution.) Having fragmented into seemingly separate individuals, we still feel the desire to be one. In fact, without that feeling, we suffer from the pain of fear and loneliness. If we could experience ourselves as individuals in the context of Oneness, if we could find ourselves in the whole, we could overcome the fear and pain of disconnection, and we wouldn't need this book. But our egos haven't evolved enough for us to achieve this state of consciousness, at least not on a continuous basis. We still seem stuck in the "me" universe.

So merging is what we substitute for Oneness. Most of us don't know how to feel connected in any other way, and we don't even believe anything else is possible. In fact, if you have never experienced Oneness, you could easily confuse it with merging, but the two states of consciousness are distinctly different. Let's see how.

The Difference between Merging & Oneness

Through both merging and Oneness, we experience ourselves as part of something greater than ourselves. But here's the difference:

Merging:

- We start with experiencing ourselves as separate, so we feel fundamentally alone.
- We merge in order to alter the feelings of fear and pain that accompany the feeling of aloneness.
- We sell ourselves out, manipulate, or create artificial, temporary fixes in order to feel as though we are connected to something, in order to alter the fear and pain of separation.

---

[15] We have gained some tools for Becoming Oneness in Platform One, and that is a step. But true Oneness requires us to go even beyond the cognitive experience of seeing our relationship to one another. Oneness is an energetic experience and a state of consciousness achieved more when we have reached the end of our program and the platform Becoming Becoming.

Oneness:

- We feel connected to ourselves and the universe.
- We don't feel separate, so there's no overwhelming fear or pain to alter.
- We automatically and naturally feel more calm and filled.[16]
- We are free to be our true selves.

In merging, we lose ourselves. In Oneness, we find ourselves.

Let's look at some common examples of merging:

- Feeling safe in someone's arms—those of your mom, or dad, or a lover.
- Blending into a group—a spiritual service, a therapy group, a twelve-step meeting, a pajama party, or a great concert.
- Getting high and feeling in a haze, just for the moment losing the sense of your own defined edges.

When we're merging, we feel connected, wonderfully warm and loved, accepted, and without boundaries. These experiences, while different from one another, all help us to let go of our sense of separation and temporarily bring us into something akin to Oneness. Sometimes we are actually experiencing Oneness, but that's the exception; usually we are just merging with each other or the experience.

So what's wrong with merging? Merging is an attempt to escape from the needless fear and pain caused by our bad habits, programming and the domination of our egos. But it has two major drawbacks. Because it's not based on our actual transformation, it does not free us from needless fear and pain, and so it can't be permanent. Reality will intervene, and then we will need to merge again. The temporary nature of the relief is the reason that merging is so addictive. We need the stimulus again and again. And

---

[16] In the first section of this book, I referred to horizontal and vertical relationships. Here again I am referring to the same phenomenon using different words. When we are horizontal, we merge. When we are vertical, we feel connected to ourselves and the Oneness, and we can relax into being ourselves.

second, merging would be limiting, even if we could keep it going. If we merge with others, we can't be truly ourselves.

Let's discuss how merging is temporary and addictive. While the experience of merging may feel great in the moment and may be tough to release (can't we just hang with the lover, the crowd, the Dalai Lama, a joint, something, forever?), but then that darned reality seems to intrude again. The alarm goes off, and it's off to work; he goes his way, I go mine. The spiritual service is over, and I'm still the angry woman I was before I came, or it's back home to the bickering family. The football game has ended, and the parking lot empties. The jazz club closes, and I leave with the makings of a hangover. The pot high wears off, and we realize we've trashed ourselves. Back into "reality." It's out of the womb with you and into the cold cruel world. Drat!

Life's needs intervene. Reality will force us to let go of the high and go out to earn a living, embrace different experiences, and take on our individual responsibilities. The feeling of warmth and safety may cover up the fundamental feelings of pain and fear that we talked about as the root of much of our destructive behavior, but because we have not yet internalized our connection to the universe, we are dependent on the occasion to give us the feeling. Because we can't continue the circumstance that elicits the feeling, we are thrust back into reality. Merging can be addictive, if we feel desperate to get that feeling back. No matter how much we want to hang out in bed, clinging to a lover's embrace, we have to let go or we'd starve, pee in the bed, neglect our bills, or just plain get bored.

The other problem with merging is that ultimately we don't want it. Even though it feels good in the moment, it is too limiting. If we could remain merged, we could not have the complex society we want, nor would we retain the possibility of self-realization that we also long for. We would feel stifled.

Let's look deeper at some of the limitations of merging. First, it blocks self-realization, and here are some simple examples: Maybe you want to lie in bed, and I want to go to the beach. Maybe you enjoy the excitement of the stock market, and I want to be an intuitive counselor. Maybe you like rock and roll, and I like Beethoven. Maybe you feel connected to Christianity, and I to Buddhism. If we merge with one another, we cannot individuate. We would have to do the same thing, feel the same thing, and think the same thing all the time. We would live like Siamese twins. After a while, we wouldn't even know what we felt or thought, and we'd hate each other for confining us. Ugh.

Merging also blocks the functioning of society. If George stays glued to his girlfriend all day, he can't drive the bus that gets me to the beach, pull that aching tooth of mine, build my house, answer my computer questions or pick those nectarines! If Marianne stays high, she can't get my medical records transferred to my new doctor, represent me in court, teach my children Spanish, sew my clothing or fix my auto transmission.

Merging doesn't work. We need to individuate. But no, I don't want to go back to "me," again. Not "me," the isolated, competitive, judgmental, scared, and alone, ego-based "me" again! Nope. We haven't gone through the process of Becoming Oneness only to go back to being isolated me's, but we can't stay merged either.

There is another way. It's individuation in the context of Oneness, and that is the definition of differentiation. Individuation is the process of becoming an individual. Differentiation is the process of becoming individuated while still staying connected to the collective. In other words, it is a process that begins to transcend the domination of the ego, because it allows us to feel ourselves as individuals and yet not separate. Now that's something worth fighting for.

The Value of Individuation

Before going on let's take a brief look at the purpose of individuation. How does individuation support the individual and the collective?

We said earlier that we are really one, all aspects of a collective consciousness, all parts of the whole. But does that mean that we are not also different? A sedan and a pickup truck are both vehicles, are both made of essentially the same stuff—metal, glass, motor, etc. But they are also different. They have different qualities and purposes.

Fulfilling our individual potential helps society fulfill its potential. We couldn't carry our families comfortably in a two-seat pickup, and we can't haul lumber in a Mercedes-Benz. If we look at this simple fact, we realize that having two types of vehicles serves the good of the individual and the good of the whole: the truck gets to fulfill its destiny, and so society can haul lumber.

Obviously and similarly, we get to fulfill ourselves in different ways, even though we have different temperaments and capacities, and by so doing, we support the collective. If everyone were the same, we would be in a heck of a pickle. If everyone were a soprano, there would be no bass and, therefore, no chorus. If everyone were a doctor, there would be no food on the table, and we'd all starve and die anyway! If we were all women, there would be no babies. Again these examples are simple and obvious.

Individuation also supports evolution. If no one opposed me or had a different view, I would always think I was right. Well, what's wrong with that? I am right, am I not? Well, maybe not. Or, perhaps to put it another way, it's not about "right"; it's about perspective. Perhaps each of us brings a point of view that's necessary for the good of the whole. Merging would block us from bringing forward those points of view. We would be too focused on pleasing.

All perspectives have a function. When I walk into a room, I think I see the room. Yet what I see is determined by my height, my vision, my capacity to observe and my prior experiences. Having you share your perspective helps me realize the limitation of my viewpoint and supports me in understanding the bigger picture.

I had an amusing experience with this long ago. At one time, I had a husband who stood 6' 4", and I stand less than 5' 2". One day, he sat me on his shoulders and carried me around. Suddenly I began to see my home from his perspective. What an experience! I saw an entirely different view, almost a different room. One shock was that the top of the refrigerator was dirty. Wow! I had never even thought of the top of the refrigerator. A different perspective; a broader view of reality.

We are naturally all attached to our own perspective, but without the perspective of others, we would not be challenged, and without challenge, there is no evolution. Even people we despise have perspectives that we need to integrate into our understanding, if we can get out of judgment. And there is no possibility of a healthy society when all voices are not heard, which we have learned from our historic experience of shutting out the perspectives of women, blacks, children, stockbrokers, welfare mothers, or other minorities.

This all sounds simple and obvious, but it's tough to accept in fact. When my view is opposed, I feel myself bristle, and it takes all my self-discipline to ask myself, "What piece of the puzzle do you represent?" It's also tough to acknowledge another's perspective when those opposing me are "foreign"—people of other nations, religions, or ethnic groups:

strangers from strange lands. Hey, of what value are they? Aren't some of them just weird?

Not really. People and societies are individuated from one another, but not different. Having practiced the process of Becoming Oneness, I now know that we are all connected, all one. If I try to understand you, for example, I will find that underneath all our differences are simple, relatable qualities. No matter how strange you seem, you, too, are trying to deal with your pain and fear, and it's our egos that make us think otherwise.

Realizing that we are fundamentally the same helps me to approach you in a way that lets me see you. By assuming that you are like me and I am like you, I will focus on understanding your history, beliefs, and hopes. And guess what? At first you may seem strange to me, but after learning about you, I find that I can understand you after all. I can see from your perspective. Once I see from your perspective, I see that you have a piece of the whole puzzle. Once we all see the whole puzzle, we can approach questions and issues in different ways. New solutions and directions present themselves. We can evolve.

To summarize: Individuated people and groups have different roles to play in our collective evolution, and together, we make up the whole. If everyone merged with us, we would lose the richness of the whole. Does this mean that everything that exists should continue to exist in the same form? No. In fact, that's part of the evolutionary process itself. While you can understand my perspective, you may point out to me that my behavior is hurtful or self-defeating. Wow, I need to change, to evolve, and perhaps you need to evolve, too. But each one of us has or has had a value in the overall scheme of things. Our individuation has contributed to the whole, and our impact on one another may support us both to evolve.

It's not always easy to see the value of individuation. Sometimes it's nearly impossible. Who can see the value of the rebellious child, the unfaithful spouse, or the fascist movement? We have, in fact, developed the negative habits of separating and criticizing others who are different from us. How can we turn that around? We'll discuss that in the next section. But now, let's take a moment to look at some of our habitual ways of thinking and reacting, and let's see if we can develop some new habits.

1. Whose opinions do I think are wrong?
2. What groups do I think are crazy or just weird?
3. Why?

4. Can I understand that other person's or group's perspective?
5. What value does that perspective bring?
6. How is that perspective a piece of the whole?

Seeing the Value of Others' Individuation

Up until now I've been talking about appreciating how individuation supports the collective. But it is equally true that individuation supports the individual, as well.

We're a group of friends in the fourth grade. We dress the same, eat the same, talk the same. We want to keep the group together, and we get upset when one of us starts to move away physically, emotionally, or philosophically. We find fault with that person. We make him or her wrong.

But that person needs to individuate, just as we do. Without individuation, that person cannot become him—or herself. Here's an example. We're in a gang based on defiance of authority. Perhaps one of our members suddenly wants to go to college and become a school principal. Without taking the freedom to individuate from the gang's mentality, that friend will not be able to go through the process of learning required for him to achieve that goal, and our buddy will not be comfortable with later taking on the authority role of educator, which the gang had derided. If our friend stays in the gang and hangs out on the corner, he has lost the possibility of realizing himself as an educator, and our neighborhood is deprived of a much-needed school principal. We will pressure him to stay like the rest of us. Our fear of his individuation can cost us all.

Whether we are talking about friends, family members, or members of clubs, organizations, businesses, or social groups, we need people to continue to individuate from us and from one another. If we try to make our friends act or think like us, we prevent them from evolving and offering their gifts to society. If they try to keep us like them, they prevent us from doing the same.

Well, you can say, what about those who break from the crowd and move in a "bad" direction? What about our friend who became a drug addict or gambler? Easy to find fault, isn't it? But how sure are we about that person's path? How do we know that becoming a drug addict or gambler isn't part of his or her evolution?

Ultimately, if we are honest, we will find that we subtly or not-so-subtly pressure others not to change because we feel threatened when they individuate in ways that seem to take them away from us—especially when we are extremely connected to or dependent on them. We've been married twenty years, and suddenly you decide to become a Hare Krishna. Or you're my son, and you decide to become an Alaskan fisherman. Or you're my best friend, and we've been single together, and you decide to get married. I am threatened. You are changing, and I'm going to lose you! I don't want you to individuate, if it moves you further from me—or even if I just think it will! Whatever rationalizations justify our clicking our tongues and shaking our heads, it is our discomfort and insecurity that block us from seeing the value of others' individuating.

It may be habitual for us to feel threatened by the individuation of others, but with some consciousness, we can change that. So let's ask ourselves a few questions.

1. With whom have I felt bonded?
2. How are they changing?
3. How does that change threaten me?
4. How do I try to stop them from changing?
5. How do I rationalize my trying to stop them?
6. How can I see their change as a support to me?
7. Does their change give me permission to change as well?

We have examined some of the fears of others individuating, but what about our fears of our own individuation? What could they be, and how could they get in the way?

SOME OF THE BLOCKS TO OUR OWN INDIVIDUATION

First Block: Insecurity

We are insecure about our own individuating, too. I sit with my friends at lunch. They're all wearing sophisticated clothes and makeup. This morning, I decide to express my sexuality in a blatant way. I show up in a tight mini and with bright red lipstick on my heavily made-up face. How am I going to feel? Scared of rejection, of course. I'm breaking the collective rules.

I've been in a conventional marriage twenty years, and it is I who feels the need to become a Hare Krishna, or a Republican, for that matter.

Or I decide that I need to experience free love or to go back to school and become a lawyer. Don't I fear that I will be met by opposition? Don't I have a legitimate suspicion that others will disapprove of my individuation, because it will take me away from my husband, or—to be more accurate—it will change me from the person I used to be in that relationship?

I fear my own individuation, because people might leave or reject me. It may very well cut me off from whatever love and security I have managed to garner for myself. This threatens the ego's sense of self-protection. Individuation doesn't seem like a good idea now! Will I individuate or will I merge?

Merging is not only a phenomenon we experience with people. We can also merge with a role, an idea, a movement. If we merge with any of these, we could fear becoming ourselves because to do so might threaten our relationship with our role or place in the world, or some identity which has given us a sense of safety or value.

The fear of individuation is very powerful, and so is the urge to merge. Where could the power of this urge come from? How did it develop? We've talked about the general reason, the ego-based universe with its fear and pain, but let's consider this phenomenon in more specific detail, so that we can find clues about ourselves and our own patterns.

Let's start with a familiar example. Let's say that my childhood was very insecure. Perhaps my parents fought a lot. Or perhaps my mom or dad was alcoholic or mentally ill. Despite their best intentions, my parents could not teach me the skills of navigating successfully through a difficult world or of coping with life's traumas without resorting to violence or addictions.

What did I learn about caring for myself? Very little. As I grow through adolescence, I *feel* extremely vulnerable, because I *am* extremely vulnerable. I lack coping skills, and I know it. How might I try to create the feeling of safety? I might behave in one of two modes. One would be to look tough on the outside to hide my vulnerability and lack of coping skills. Yes, inside I feel weak and clingy, but I want you to think I am strong and competent, so you won't think I am easy prey. I pretend that I am tough. I'm going to go it alone. Alone, maybe, but individuated? Not at all. Individuation would require that I be in the process of becoming myself. Acting tough is a role I create for both your consumption and mine, a role I merge with in order to feel safe, a role which I fear to let go of.

Suppose, on the other hand, I am willing to look clingy, even though it makes me look weak, because I'm more afraid of being alone than looking pathetic. How would that get in the way of individuating? I will seek someone to take care of me. I might even exaggerate my appearance of weakness, so that I can attract someone, anyone, to cling to, to make the world seem safe for me. It would then become extremely challenging for me to individuate in relation to that person or that role. Wouldn't I want my "savior" to see me in a way that elicits his or her loyalty, so that they would be willing to care for me? Wouldn't I want them to think I'm needier than they? Wouldn't I want them to think that I have tastes, values, and opinions that are similar to theirs? Wouldn't I want them to think that I admire them, even if I don't? Am I willing to individuate, to express myself, if any of these ties are threatened? Would I be willing to individuate myself if it contradicts the illusion of the person *they* want me to be?

Whether merging with a role or a person, merging is a reflection of my being dominated by my feeling of vulnerability. I'm trying to fix how I feel, regardless of the consequences, and I do it by merging rather than individuating.

There are many other early childhood experiences that could lead me to try either to look tough and independent (merging with a role and an image of myself) or become dependent (merging with who you need me to be). Suppose my parents lost all their money very suddenly, and as a consequence I lost my home, my friends, and my lifestyle in a quick moment. Or perhaps my sister was kidnapped or died of leukemia. I probably got no help with my feelings. Again, I could spend my life trying to look invulnerable or looking for someone or something to save me from the sudden disaster I know is around the corner. Or I could do both at once by looking tough while secretly seeking someone to save me.

Less dramatic realities cause us to experience the feeling of vulnerability that we try to fix by merging. As a child, I lost my parents' attention when another child came along. How am I going to ensure love without merging with someone to hook them into loving me? Or perhaps as an adult, I become ill and feel desperately in need of someone to help me. I take on characteristics that I think will make others more likely to care for me. Or I may have children and fear that I can't support them myself. Unconsciously I try to please my spouse, rather than become myself.

Or suppose I just love and need my parents, and I feel compelled to please them? Or suppose I give up on my parents ever loving or nurturing me, and I seek a group of peers to hang out with, to feel safe with, to merge with?

Every one of these situations, though natural, leads us to an emotional or psychological block to individuation. In fact, our lack of individuation can become so habitual, we don't even notice that it's there. But if we are honest with ourselves, we can see where insecurity may have blocked us from becoming ourselves. Let's ask ourselves some questions about the insecurities that may have blocked us from individuation.

1. What in my childhood experience would have led me to feel insecure about my ability to care for myself?
2. Did that make me act tough or weak?
3. Did I turn to peers or authority figures to bond with?
4. How do I look for safety now?
5. Do I turn to a group or an individual?
6. How have I tried to merge with them?
7. What values and attitudes of theirs have I adopted?
8. How have I tried to please them?
9. Am I willing to face the fear of their loss?

A Second Block: Fear of Pain

I see the pain of the folks living around me, and I want to be different from them so as to avoid their pain. But what will happen if I do? Will I "fail"? And can I face the potential pain of that?

What is failure, if I'm trying not to replicate the pain of others? Perhaps I won't really turn out different, after all that huffing and puffing and those brave statements. I hated my dad's alcoholism, and I don't drink, but I smoke pot instead. Or perhaps I will lead a different lifestyle, but I'm even more miserable than the folks I left behind. I've made the money, but I still feel insecure. Or perhaps I will end up alone and repudiated by others, because I've gone off on some limb and alienated everybody.

I could be afraid to try, afraid to individuate and look different from the crowd, afraid that I will end up even worse off than they and humiliated to boot. That would be painful, so I continue to put my dreams away and replicate the lives I see. I continue to merge with those around me.

Now let's look at this phenomenon in a different way. Suppose I don't feel good about who I am and where I come from. Suppose I look at my dad, who's drinking and slaving in a factory all of his life. Now suppose I bravely proclaim, "I am not him!"

Hey, that's individuation, isn't it? In one sense, yes. I am declaring that I am different from him. I am trying to become myself.

But how do I try to become myself? Perhaps, I look across town and see another guy's dad. He's a lawyer. He has property, money, and prestige. I model myself after him. I'm not going to be like my poor, overworked, miserable beer-drinking father. I'm going to be like this really cool dad. (Of course, I don't realize that he too is overworked and, while he's not drinking beer, he's drinking martinis or snorting cocaine, but hey, don't ruin the image.) I'm going to be a lawyer, too. I'm going to get to the "right" side of town. Now, hmmm, am I becoming myself, or am I going to work my butt off to become somebody else, someone other than Dad but someone who still isn't me? Yup, ironically I'm both separating and merging: separating from my dad and merging with some fantasy guy. Either way, I'm trying to avoid pain, and I'm still not individuating.

Or we can try the instant fix. I come from a family where my parents yelled, screamed, and divorced. I start smoking dope at 13 and sleeping with boys at the same age. I see myself slipping into a life of misery. I'm already half-way there. I'm doing "my own thing," but am I individuating?

Hey, look at the cool girl at school. She's a cheerleader, popular, dating the captain of the football team. Suppose I could date a football player, too. Could I feel really cool, as well? Could I be instantly swept into a better life, far away from the pain of my bickering parents? Am I individuating, or am I again just merging with a fantasy, a fantasy that I think I can achieve right now?

In our efforts to get away from pain, we try to find ways of living that will ensure us protection against it. We merge with those around us who we believe have no pain. We get nose jobs and tummy tucks to mimic people who we believe lead charmed lives. We dream about being movie stars and singers. We strive to have 2.3 kids and be the president of the PTA. Whomever we believe has escaped the pain of life, we will imitate. But instead of individuating, instead of becoming who we are, we struggle to become someone other than who we fear we are destined to be, so that we may, instead, lead the charmed life.

Of course, we haven't a clue as to the reality of most other peoples' lives. We can't look into their hearts and minds. We don't want to consider the possibility that pain is within everyone and within every lifestyle. No, because if we did, we'd have to give up fantasy and learn to live with reality.

But if we did that, then we could truly individuate and become ourselves.

Wow! The fear of pain is a powerful force, and it leads us into habitual patterns of merging with fantasy. The ego tries to protect me from pain by blocking me from being myself. And yet, in the end, most of us discover that we are fundamentally the same as the people we're trying not to be, and there is no fantasy life. Yup, after all is said and done, I'm more like my mother than I ever imagined. Merging with a fantasy is useless and self-destructive. There is no avoidance of pain, just the opportunity to make the pain a part of our evolution.

Let's take a moment now to take a look at some of our blocks to our own individuation. Let's acknowledge our fear of pain.

1. How did I feel about my parents' lives?
2. Did I think they were happy?
3. Did I want to be like them?
4. Did I take chances to be different?
5. Who did I want to be when I was growing up?
6. Why?
7. Did I think their lives were less painful?
8. Did I imitate them?
9. Did I succeed in becoming like them?
10. Has my life become less painful?
11. Do I still believe pain can be avoided?

Another Block to Individuation:
The Impact of Others' Consciousness

We've talked about psychological or emotional blocks to individuation. Now let's talk about another, more subtle block. Because we are, in fact, connected, it is very difficult for us to get away from each other's thoughts and feelings. We feel each other, because on some level, we are each other. This makes it difficult to know whose thoughts we are thinking—ours or those of someone else. Yes, it is hard to individuate our own mental and feeling state.

People who are very psychic or "sensitive" may come to understand this reality; but, whoever we are, it is a fact for all of us. Let's take the extreme. If I'm very intuitive, it's easy for me to know what others are feeling and thinking. I feel very ill on the day a friend was taken to the hospital, even though I didn't know about the occurrence until later. I may suddenly panic, because there's been a bombing somewhere, and I feel that fear without being aware of the circumstance. Or I may awaken in the middle of the night, feeling my partner's pain and can't let go of it until we've talked.

What a gift! What a curse! Being highly intuitive allows us to help people by tuning into their unconscious feelings, which could be useful if we intend to help them. We are a living example of our Oneness, which demonstrates the lie of separation. On the other hand, those of us who are extremely intuitive may feel confused about what we feel, and, worse, we have a need for everyone to clear their feelings and deal with their pain so that we can stop feeling their pain as ours. Individuation becomes urgent.

Whether or not we are extremely sensitive or intuitive, all of us are impacted by the thoughts and feelings of those around us, because we are one. So even though we tend to see ourselves as separate and apart, our energy fields don't work that way. On a deep level, we are connected, and we can't help but be impacted by one another's state of being.

This psychic connection has powerful implications. At any given moment, do I know whose feelings I am having? Do I feel anger, because I am angry with you? Or am I feeling anger because I am picking up the anger you feel toward yourself? Am I ashamed of my father, because I am embarrassed by his behavior? Or am I picking up his shame and reflecting it back to him? Am I wanting to leave you, because I have lost passion for you, or because you feel unworthy and are expecting me to leave? How do I know?

Do you think this confusion of feelings doesn't happen to you? Guess again.

We feel one another's anxiety when we go to a party. We feel the tension of the couple that are getting divorced. We can be overwhelmed by the excitement of being with a crowd at a football game. We have felt nervous entering the office, only to later discover that the company is in financial trouble.

Do we need more proof? What could induce perfectly nice people to lynch someone? Or put other human beings in gas chambers? Or drop napalm on children? Some will say that these behaviors are the result of people's repressed anger, and that's true. But why does everyone's repressed anger come out in that same moment and in that extreme form? Because people pick up on the collective energy, and we have to make a conscious effort to differentiate.

It's been called "the mob." It's mass consciousness. It's the impact we have on each other's thoughts and feelings. It can be dangerous and out of control, or it can be uplifted and energizing.

Is it important to become individuated? Absolutely. It's essential. I cannot be responsible for myself unless I make my own decisions. I cannot make my own decisions without knowing my own mind—which thoughts are yours and which are mine. I cannot know my own mind without being able to individuate, detaching from the energy of the collective consciousness.

How do I individuate in the face of the collective consciousness? First, let me say that most of us are unaware of this problem. We assume that what we think consists of our own thoughts alone. Sometimes we just buy into those thoughts and let them guide us. But, instinctively, when we feel uncomfortable with the energy of others, we tend to separate. I have to leave him. I have to leave her. I have to go to the mountaintop and be by myself.

While this may work, it also may not. When a collective energy is really strong, it's hard to escape even on a mountaintop. And sometimes we carry the residue of someone else's consciousness wherever we go.

How many of us have tried to break from our parents' values and behaviors, only to find ourselves hooked into the same behavior when we're under stress? Patterning is strong; so is the residue of a consciousness that has permeated our own. Frustrating, isn't it?

Throughout this book, I will return again and again to the problem of differentiating from other people's energy, but for now, let's start with awareness. Individuation has value. Losing ourselves to others' consciousness is habitual. Let's call on our own consciousness to make ourselves aware of this process and to develop the habit of awareness.

At this point, let's stop and ask ourselves a few more questions. Let's examine how the consciousness of others blocks our individuation.

1. Looking at some folks I know, how do they feel about themselves? Angry, ashamed, proud?
2. Do I share those feelings about them?
3. Are those feelings really mine, or am I caught up in theirs?
4. How do I know?
5. As a child, did I share my parents' or peers' perspectives, and why?

6. What collectives do I belong to now? Men, women, Americans, Chileans, Republicans, socialists?
7. What are the thoughts and feelings of the collectives of which I am a part?
8. Do I get caught up in their intentions and energy?
9. Can I honestly say that I know?

But wait, Beth, one more time, aren't we hitting that paradox? I thought you said we are one, one collective. If we are connected, how can we individuate? Are you now advocating separation? And if we do separate, aren't we back to denying our Oneness?

Absolutely not. I am suggesting that there is another way. We don't have to separate at all; but we must differentiate. But before going on to discuss that issue, let's summarize a few points we've already discussed about the value of individuation.

- Despite our tendency to see ourselves as separate, we feel compelled to merge. Merging directly, though temporarily, alleviates the pain and fear that drive us.
- Merging can, however, be destructive. It can lead us to squelch gifts that could bring us richer lives and that could empower us to enrich the lives of others, as well. And it can lead us to thoughts, feelings, attitudes, and actions that are painful to us and contrary to our nature.
- Merging also blocks the functioning and evolution of society.
- Individuation has value, but it is blocked in many ways.
- We fear others individuating, because it can seem to threaten our safety.
- We fear our own individuation for the same reason.
- We are impacted by thoughts and feelings of which we are not even aware.
- We can become aware of these blocks and fears.
- We can confront the habit of merging.

We have been talking a lot about the blocks to individuating from other people and collective energies. But before going on, we need to refer to one more challenge, which is the overwhelming power and familiarity of our own emotional responses from which we also need to differentiate.

How do we choose to be different? If we are dominated by familiar negative patterns within us, we might as well be merged with a gang. We have lost our chance to be free and develop our potential.

Instead of discussing this topic in this section, where we are exploring individuation, we will return to it just a little later in this chapter, where we explore differentiation. The reason will be clear as you see how differentiation is really an inside, as well as an outside job.[17]

DIFFERENTIATION INSTEAD OF SEPARATION

As we have said, differentiation is the process of individuation in the context of Oneness. Let's review what we said in the beginning of this chapter. Individuation is the process of taking responsibility for ourselves and our consciousness. You could call it becoming your own person. To differentiate, which is to individuate without separating, we:

- Call ourselves to consciousness moment by moment about the behaviors and attitudes that hurt us and others.
- Commit ourselves to choosing a different path, which promotes all to reach their potential.
- Confront the urge to merge with the people around us or with the negative attitudes or behaviors that are our own habits.
- Acknowledge that we are like the people we wish to differentiate from; that we carry the energies, attitudes and behaviors that we may not like.
- Connect to our higher consciousness to recognize what behaviors or attitudes we prefer to energize.
- Find the divine or human support to choose those behaviors and attitudes.

By this time, we know both that we need to stop unconsciously merging out of habit and the desire for safety; and that we don't need to separate from others in the process. We can acknowledge that we contain within us the totality of all consciousness, because we are one, but that we

---

[17] And stay tuned with me as we later explore Platform Five: Becoming Self-Aware and Platform Six: Becoming Integrated, where we become much more capable of the self-command required for true differentiation.

choose the aspects of consciousness we wish to energize within ourselves and within the collective.

Many of us have heard the following Native American story. The grandfather tells the child that there are two wolves raging within his heart: the wolf of anger and the wolf of compassion. The child asks which wolf will win. The grandfather replies, "Whichever one I feed." That is the essence of differentiation. We choose the aspect of us and, by extension, the aspect of the collective, that we wish to feed at any given moment.

The Habit of Separation

Habitually, when I don't want to merge, I separate. In my effort to become truly myself, I reject you, it or them. It is not accidental that we tend to separate before we learn to differentiate. It seems to be part of our human DNA or at least our programming, and we see it in children. Let's take a brief look at some of the characteristics of individuating through separation.

Individuation through Separation

- Separation is a part of an important developmental step.
- It is based on "I": I exist outside of "you" and the collective.
- It tells me that I am different from you, whether that makes me better or worse.
- It's based on insecurity.
- It is based on ego.
- It is based on "no."

Separation seems to be a necessary and normal process of evolution. In order to develop a healthy self, the child must see itself as individuated from its parents and sibling. As a two-year old, we learn the word "no." We also learn the word "mine." Why does the child need to say "no" and "mine"? Because that's how the child establishes its identity. "No" is the easiest way the child can distinguish itself from others, especially those with more power. Why is the energy so vociferous? Because the child is first discovering his or her individual identity, and it feels insecure about it. Feeling its security threatened by the necessary individuation, the child has to puff itself up in order to give itself the courage to follow through. Without this stage, we could not become individuals.

We go through a similar but even more threatening process in adolescence. I know that I'm preparing to go out into the world as an independent being, and I have to convince myself that I can do it, that I'm capable, even though I'm scared. In addition, I can feel insecure as I find that my feelings and views may differ from my parents. Am I really right? Even if I am, are they going to support me to be different? Are they going to support me if I *am* different? What will I do if they don't? What if I'm really alone?

How do I overcome the fear of individuating from my parents? I make myself believe that I feel less insecure than I do. Or I make them "wrong" and me "right", so that righteous indignation propels me forward. Boy, my parents are losers. I'm going to be better than they are. Or I try to override my fear with the appearance of bravado: "Back off! I know what I'm doing." See, I'm separate, different, tougher, smarter, right.

The terrible twos and adolescence are brave and necessary transitions. They are also done in a childish unconscious or semi-conscious way, which is, of course, natural. Nobody teaches us that there is another way to individuate, and few people actually know that there is. But what happens when we come to believe that we actually *are* separate and when the illusion of separation becomes our normal consciousness and our habitual way of being and thinking? Then we move into deeper and deeper levels of isolation and fragmentation. When we do, there is nothing to prevent the domination of the ego.

This is what has tended to happen to most of us, as we already discussed in Platform One. We see ourselves as separate. We try to distinguish ourselves from people who exhibit qualities we don't like in ourselves. We puff ourselves up in righteous indignation and proclaim to ourselves and to the world that we are not "them," not like them at all! (Is there a little insecurity lurking here?) We also compete, judge, and blame. We feel alone.

Using separation to define ourselves may be an understandable practice, but it is destructive. Separation is the illusion; the reality is that we are one. And, therefore, not feeling our Oneness is the core of our pain as human beings. If we are to live with reality, if we are to face the pain and fear that plague us without ending up in self-destructive addictive behaviors, we need to find ways of living that bring us feelings of love and safety, even in the face of the inevitable realities of life. So from a personal perspective, we need to find another way to individuate, one that does not require separation, and that way of individuation is differentiation.

There is another reason we need to move beyond separation consciousness. Survival requires us to find a new path: a way to distinguish ourselves without separating. Humanity is facing problems that could lead to self-annihilation, including war, weapons of mass destruction, epidemics, economic polarization, addiction and climate change. We cannot meet these terrible challenges as isolated, fragments battling one another. We must collectively solve our collective problems, and separation won't bring us closer to that goal.

So does that mean we should all merge into one blob? On the contrary, we have seen that individuation has value. In fact, individuation is part of our Oneness and is essential for our very survival.

There is another way: differentiation as opposed to separation. We've looked at separation. Now let's look at differentiation.

Individuating through Differentiation

- Differentiation in the context of Oneness is our next evolutionary step.
- It is based on Oneness: I am like you. I am you. We all have the same aspects. We are part of the same whole. But I choose the aspect of myself and us that I wish to energize.
- It supports us to evolve as individuals and as a collective.
- It comes from choice, rather than insecurity.
- It connects us to higher consciousness.
- It is based on "yes."

When we become differentiated, we start with "we" and continue with a "yes" to that which we choose.[18] Now we can return to the question of differentiating not only from other people and their energies, but also from energies and patterns within ourselves. We realize that when we differentiate from anything outside us, we are also differentiating from that which is within us and vice versa, because we are differentiating from the consciousness we don't wish to energize, and it doesn't matter

---

[18] Please recall "Ego, Instinct & Evolution," where we discussed the ego twice born, first as a "no" and then as a "yes."

185

whether that consciousness is manifested within us or outside of us in the collective.

Let's reiterate some of the ways we carry all consciousness. We, each of us, have within us all the different aspects of the collective consciousness because we are one. We all are loving, hateful, corrupt, ashamed, proud, generous, stingy, fearful, courageous, sad, and so on. If we are having a disagreement, I am capable of being loving or hateful. Which do I choose? Whichever I choose is not about you—not about merging with or separating from you. It's about choice, my choice. I may choose to energize the aspect of me that is loving or the aspect of me that is hateful. In the process, I energize within the collective consciousness that aspect that is loving or that which is hateful. When I choose the aspect of me or the aspect of the collective that I wish to energize, I am Becoming Differentiated. And to do so, I connect to the aspect of the collective that supports me to make my choice.

Let's start with an important example that we will be exploring in depth over this chapter. I said earlier that if you are angry with yourself, I will probably pick up on that anger and be angry with you, too, because we are connected. If I don't differentiate from your anger, I become your anger. I lose myself, my own feelings and emotions, and am caught up in your feelings toward yourself. I am caught up in the energy of anger itself. I am not me—the totality of my thoughts, feelings, and emotions. I am dominated by the fragmented energy of anger itself.

Can I make another choice? Only part of me is anger. The rest of me is reason, common sense, compassion, pain and so on. If I were able to observe the anger for a moment, I could notice that there is anger in the field, and I could ask myself the question: Am I angry? If so, why? Perhaps upon reflection, I realize that while I am angry because of your behavior, your behavior is merely a reflection of your own pain. Perhaps I realize that I am not angry at all, that I feel sad for you, but that you are angry with yourself, and my anger with you is only feeding your anger with yourself.

Would I then feel angry? Not necessarily. If I realize that it is you who is angry with yourself, I may not feel the anger at all. Or if I also feel anger toward you, I may experience compassion, as well. In the process, I have differentiated from your anger.

Here's another form of differentiation from your anger toward yourself. As we will discuss in much greater depth in Platform Six: Becoming

Integrated, anger is a marvelous quality of consciousness that brings my attention to the possibility that something is wrong, or threatening, or out of harmony. It is information. I may not automatically express my anger at you, even if your behavior needs to be confronted. But I may feel dependent upon you and so be afraid to feel or express my anger. Becoming Differentiated requires me to detach from my dependence on you and allows me to express my anger, if I need to. Able to express my anger about the situation, instead of being dominated by my fear of losing you, I am more likely to release my anger after noticing it and then go to a place of compassion, understanding and calm.

Does this mean, by the way, that I should tolerate bad behavior? Sometimes yes, because it may be temporary, something we can discuss and resolve, or it may be part of your journey that you are addressing. There are no perfect people, and we all behave destructively at times.

And sometimes no, I should not tolerate bad behavior, because your abuse may be too dangerous or destructive. It may be habitual, and you are not addressing it. It might endanger the wellbeing of others dependent on you, and I need to take action. It might be a reflection that we are in the wrong relationship.

The same is true with another person's self-abuse, such as substance abuse or gambling. Your self-abuse may be too painful for me to live with. I might not be willing or able to watch your self-destruction, and I may refuse to enable it. Or your self-abuse might express itself in your continual ranting and raving at me (You are expressing your anger toward yourself by expressing anger toward me.) Or your self-abuse might be coming out as self-sabotage, or diving into addictions, or other negative habits of thought that I can choose not to tolerate or support.

Becoming Differentiated is the first step in deciding how to handle difficult situations. I may realize that I have to leave you, but my action won't be caused by my having gotten caught up in your self-hatred. I will leave because it's what feels right to me or, even better, because I am practicing Platform Four and realize that leaving is for the highest good of all! In these cases, I will be acting out of the totality of my being, including my connection to divine consciousness. My leaving will not be coming from a "no" to you, but a "yes" to myself and to life.

One note here. Many people justify running away from difficult challenges by claiming they are abused, when they are actually co-creators of a painful relationship abusive to both parties. Until and unless we clean up our part in a relationship, unless we can differentiate from our own painful reactivity, it will be difficult to be sure whether we are releasing a situation that needs to be released or running from a pattern that needs to be confronted.

Now let's look at differentiation on a bigger scale. Facing the power of the collective energy, I need to be very conscious of differentiating from it. If I can be impacted by an individual's fear, pain or anger, I'm even more likely to be drawn into the collective energy without even realizing it. When a collective feels threatened, it can become very defensive or even violent. It can become very prejudiced and judgmental. It can become self-congratulatory and smug. The collective's feelings will tap into my feelings, and my feelings will tap into its.

This happened with the 2001 bombing of the World Trade Center in New York. With the collective feeding on its own fear, a perfectly peaceful person might have fallen into the escalating frenzy. With so much fear in the collective energy field, people feel fear. Then those folks may have unconsciously sought to merge with the larger collective, in order not to feel alone with their own fear. Here is the irony: Some people sought safety by merging with the collective fear, in order to feel part of something larger than themselves, even though merging with the fearful collective created more feelings of fear. Or people may have felt overcome by the collective fear and experienced emotions that weren't even their own. Either way, those people lost connection to the whole of themselves, and they merged with the energy of fear itself. That's how fear turns to collective irrationality.

Very understandable.

But if I can step out of the collective energy of fear, I can connect to the totality of myself instead. Then I can connect to other aspects of myself, aspects such as accountability, understanding, compassion, and reason. Going back to the World Trade Center example, I can ask myself the questions: How am I like the terrorists? What is the cause of their behavior? What are they trying to tell us? Can I address their concerns? Is our violence the most useful response? What is the appropriate degree of violence that I believe is necessary in this situation? What is the energy I want to support?

I may conclude that the only appropriate response is the War on Terrorism, or I may not. Whatever my choice, however, let it be based on my thoughts and evaluations, on my higher consciousness, not on the mass consciousness of which I can so easily be a part. And let the choice be based on the totality of me, not just the fragment of me called fear.

Being influenced by the energy of others is habitual and easy precisely because we are one, because we all carry the same energies within us. If I am in a crowd that's feeling anger, that anger will tap into mine. If I'm in a group that's feeling bliss, that bliss can easily tap into mine, as well. That's why we turn to each other for support. We are looking for a collective energy to impact our own, a collective energy that will support the aspect of us that we want to bring forward. Which energy we choose defines our state of consciousness and often our lives.

The corollary is also true. Because we are connected, I can impact the collective consciousness with my own. I can add to the fear and hatred in our collective consciousness, or I can support the peace.

Clearly, we must be very careful about our choices, and I'll discuss this point in more detail further on. But first, let's consider the definition of differentiation.

Differentiation is the process of individuation in the context of Oneness. We acknowledge that we contain within us the totality of all consciousness, but we choose which aspects of consciousness to energize within ourselves and within the collective. We say "yes" to that which we want to be.

Earlier in this chapter, I talked about three blocks to individuation: insecurity, avoidance of pain, and the Oneness of our energy. How does becoming differentiated apply to each of these?

Let's talk about insecurity. Insecurity makes us want to merge with what someone else wants us to be. We hook into their consciousness. If we differentiate, we acknowledge that whatever others want us to be is also a part of us, and we acknowledge the pull to please them for our own sense of safety. But instead of merging, we energize whatever aspects of ourselves we choose—aspects we value. By so doing, we also energize those aspects of consciousness in the collective, as well.

Here's an example. I'm living with a woman whom I support financially. She wants me to be the breadwinner, and I work hard to satisfy her. Why? I feel very insecure within myself. When I come home with the money, she looks at me as though I were her hero. Wow! I am getting to look strong and competent to myself, but I'm doing it without really asking whether or not being the breadwinner is what I want to do. I am merging with her. In fact, we are colluding to create me as the breadwinner. If I am willing to break from this collusion and take the risk of her rejection, I may choose to energize other aspects of myself, which is to become more truly myself.

When I start to individuate, my first instinct, of course, is to separate—to blame her. She has done this to me. She made me be the breadwinner. With consciousness, I realize that I have taken on the role. I was trying to merge with what she wanted me to be. And I probably was also merging with my father, who was a very protective, larger-than-life guy I admired. I wanted to be him. Now I realize that it's my desire to appear like a hero that has driven me, as well as my own desire to be wanted by my wife.

These elements are me, part of me. But are they the only parts? No, they are parts out of balance with other parts of me that need expression. Let's look at some of them. Would I like to be protected, as well? Do I need to express my feelings of humility and powerlessness? Would I prefer a different line of work, one that brings in less money? If I were Becoming Differentiated, if I could face my fear of being rejected by her or Dad, I could ask what other parts of me I would want to energize, and I would find the support to do it.

My wife is probably experiencing separation and merging, as well. She instinctively knows that I have a need to appear the hero, and she is merging with my desire to look big by letting me play the role. In addition, she never felt protected as a child, and having me support her gives her the feeling that finally someone will make her feel safe. She runs this pattern and hardly asks herself whether she is suppressing her own autonomy in order to keep me supporting her.

Is this really who she is? If she could acknowledge that feeling protected is only one of her needs but not her only need, she could choose to energize the aspect of her that also wants autonomy. She doesn't need to pretend she doesn't need or want protection. She doesn't have to separate by blaming me for "making her dependent." She doesn't have to accuse me of having suppressed the qualities in her that threaten me. She can see that suppressing those qualities has been her choice, our collective choice, and she can choose to break from our collective collusion that keeps her in this role. Now that she is differentiating, she supports the collective consciousness to do the same.

This is precisely what happened with the women's movement, for example. As individual women differentiated from the collective consciousness, they created the energy of a new collective consciousness that allowed more and more women to make the same choice! As is understandable, given human habits and history, in the beginning many women felt the need to separate from men in order to take the step. Women blamed men for their plight. But ultimately women had to face their own desire to merge and stop projecting it on men.

Now let's look at the avoidance of pain. How does Becoming Differentiated operate around my wanting to avoid pain? What does that have to do with the "we"?

In the earlier section, I described how rebelling against one role could lead me to merge with another. If I were to become differentiated instead, I would have to choose which aspects of me that I want to energize, not for the purpose of rebellion, but for the sole purpose of becoming myself. And, of course, that means I would have to face the possibility that my own choices may create pain for me.

Recall that in an earlier example, I wanted to become a lawyer because I didn't want to be the beer-drinking factory slave my father was. What if I were Becoming Oneness and Differentiated? Then I would realize that we are all one and that, therefore, we all have pain to deal with. I would look at the lawyer quite differently. I wouldn't be able to fantasize that becoming a lawyer would relieve me of the necessity to deal with pain. I could question choosing law as a career based on whether or not I wanted to embrace the experience of being a lawyer, not avoiding pain.

I would look more realistically at my friend's father, the lawyer. What is his life really about? He, like me, is insecure. He may have been under-nurtured or smothered as a child. He probably has problems relating to his wife and children. They're angry that he's gone from the house too much. He goes to meetings at night and sometimes he works long hours. He gets heartburn. He drinks too much.

Not the fantasy I thought it was. No, he's not a factory worker with a factory worker's pay. But if I were Becoming Oneness and Differentiated, I would realize that, in fact, on many levels he's no different from my father. He rages, he escapes, and he's dissatisfied with his life.

To make an honest evaluation, I would have to admit that the choice of becoming a lawyer could very easily bring its own pains, and I would have to admit that whatever my profession, income, and social status, I will have the pain and fears of every human. Oh no! That means there's no escape. There is no special class of divine beings free of human pain.

Back to me and individuating myself. Individuating in my family might entail becoming a lawyer or not. But it would not be motivated by trying to be different from my father or the same as someone else. I would be looking at myself and asking myself the pertinent questions. Do I want to be a lawyer? Why? Do I like to be adversarial? Would I rather be a mediator? Would I have to conform to the values and attitudes of a big firm, or could I take the risk of being on my own? Do I want to defend or prosecute people? Am I looking for money or social justice? Do I enjoy detailed contracts and legal documents? Can I handle the frustration? Can I handle the pressure?

Who do I want to be? What are my gifts? My deficits? Knowing there is no way to avoid the universality of human pain, my choice will now be based on whether or not being a lawyer is a good fit for me and whether or not doing legal work would support me to grow.

What about our third block to differentiation—the fact that we are impacted by each other's consciousness? Earlier I gave the example of me trying to separate from your self-hatred by separating from you. Sometimes that's necessary, and sometimes it works.

But how do we practice Oneness and differentiation instead? By becoming aware of how I am like you, it or them, while simultaneously choosing other aspects of the totality of myself.

When I choose to differentiate from your self-hatred, for example, I am not pretending that I have no self-hatred or anger in myself. I acknowledge those parts of me and then choose to become more than that anger. I also recognize that I am getting swept up in your self-hatred and that I may or may not be angry at you at all, that my perceived anger at you is entirely a reflection of yours. I call on the totality of me, and I relax and choose compassion, neutrality and understanding, which are the aspects of me that I prefer to empower.

By differentiating myself from your anger—as opposed to separating from you—I am strengthening the collective. When I choose to energize compassion, for example, I am energizing the energy of compassion itself. I am energizing your compassion for yourself, and I am energizing compassion within the collective. Because we are one. We are each other.

The same is true with collective fear. When I differentiate from the collective fear, I don't deny that fear is part of me as well. Rather I acknowledge the part of me that is fear, and I choose to energize other aspects of myself and the collective, such as calmness, reason and love.

I am not *separating* from the "bad you." I am **connecting** to the aspects of you, me, and the collective that I want to energize! I go from the "no" to the "yes."

Again we can see the difference between separation and differentiation. Separation says that I am not like the rest of the collective. Becoming Differentiated is a process whereby we say that we are part of the collective fear, and we want to energize another aspect of ourselves and the collective.

Why would I want to differentiate from these energies? Partly because I am becoming aware of their negative impact (and we discuss this in great depth in Platform Seven, when we talk about the Dark Side.) But on a more visceral level, I choose to differentiate because of how I feel. If I want to feel more love in my life, I can't lose myself in your self-hatred. Though I feel the impact of the collective fear, I want to feel peace, so I choose to support the energy of peace in myself.

Differentiating from fear and anger does not mean that I am never fearful or angry. It simply means that I allow those energies when appropriate, learn what they have to tell me (see Platform Six: Becoming Integrated), and move on to the state of consciousness I choose to empower.

Sounds easy, but the opposite is the case. Developing the habit of differentiation is incredibly hard, and we will discuss this in the next section. But before going on to discuss how to differentiate, let's summarize a few points.

Differentiation is the opposite of separation. Separation starts with I—I am not like you. Differentiation starts with we—we are each other. And because we are each other, I and we have the totality of our emotions, thoughts, and feelings within us. Coming from a place of whole, I do not have to get lost in your energy or the energy of the collective. I can choose to support the aspects of us that I wish to energize.

Let's take a moment now to examine our own behavior regarding differentiation and separation.

1. Do I tend to differentiate or to separate?
2. Have I ever tried to stay connected to another, while trying to stop merging? What happened?
3. Have I ever tried to fantasize about another's life?

4. Have I wanted to be that person?
5. Have I gotten honest about their reality?
6. Have I gotten caught up in another's feelings?
7. Have I tried to separate from them in order to separate from the feeling?
8. Do I do the same with the collective? Do I try to separate from others by blaming or getting angry at, for example, the government? The masses? Other classes?
9. How else do I try to separate, rather than differentiate?

HOW DO WE BECOME DIFFERENTIATED?

We've talked about why we tend to merge, why we need individuation, and what habitual ways of thinking and feeling might block that. We've also touched on how differentiation is different from separation as a means of individuating. And we've seen how differentiation embraces Oneness and how it is part of becoming ourselves.

But how do we do it? Let's repeat one more time our brief outline of differentiation:

Individuation is the process of taking responsibility for ourselves and our consciousness. You could call it becoming your own person. To differentiate, which is to individuate without separating, we:

- Call ourselves to consciousness moment by moment about the behaviors and attitudes that hurt us and others.
- Commit ourselves to choosing a different path, which promotes all to reach their potential.
- Confront the urge to merge with the people around us or the negative attitudes or behaviors that are our own habits.
- Acknowledge that we are like the people we wish to differentiate from; that we carry the energies, attitudes and behaviors that we may not like.
- Connect to our higher consciousness to recognize what behaviors or attitudes we prefer to energize.
- Find the divine or human support to choose those behaviors and attitudes.

1. Call ourselves to consciousness moment by moment about the behaviors and attitudes that hurt us and others.

If we are to become differentiated, we are going to have to develop a lot of awareness about our attitudes and actions. Let's say I hang out every night with a bunch of friends who drink after work. I accept this behavior as normal. If I am going to become differentiated, I have to be willing to question whether or not spending my time in that manner is actually for the highest good of anyone, especially me. If my friends and I have been drinking together for years, of course, questioning my behavior could feel threatening. If I determine that I should stop, will we still be close if I stop drinking with them? Do we have another basis of friendship? What will I do, if I have no friends? Am I actually addicted and using my friends as a cover for drinking? Am I willing to confront that addiction?

In the face of all these fears, I still have to ask myself some questions: Is alcohol hurting my body and/or disabling my consciousness? Am I squandering my time? Am I avoiding something in my life? Am I secretly bored with the whole situation? If the answer is yes to any of these questions, then I have to go on to step two, which is to make a commitment to change.

Drinking with friends is only one example. Let's look at some others. Am I dressing in a way that is hurting my body, such as in wearing high-heeled shoes, in order to fit in? Am I indulging in gossip, which has no purpose other than to make all of "us" feel superior to "them?" Am I letting my wife dominate me, because I'm afraid to risk confrontation? Am I going to the family reunion, just because it's expected? Do I get submissive when my boyfriend is angry? Do I hate my wife when she's in a negative mood? Do I really believe in everything that I am doing, or am I just going along?

2. Commit ourselves to choosing a different path, which promotes all to reach their potential.

Once I have called myself to consciousness, and I realize that my behavior and attitudes are due to merging, what am I going to do? My husband comes home in an angry mood. He starts picking on me and the children, and I want to bite his head off. I know he's in pain. He is being pushed around by his boss, and he hates himself for not standing up to her. I can buy into his self-hatred and get angry too. This will make me upset, he will feel worse, and so will the kids. Is this what I want? Is my behavior supporting us all to reach our potential? Am I willing to commit to changing, even if I don't know how?

I see myself focused on providing my children with every lesson available on the planet, in order to merge with the in-crowd in my neighborhood. Am I exhausting myself running them around? Are they feeling stressed by all this pressure and activity? Have my wife and I taken on extra jobs to pay for it all? Is that depriving the kids of their parents? Is fitting in with the group supporting our family? Am I willing to choose a different way of relating to our family, friends and neighbors, even if it makes us look like we are less than everyone else, even if our kids feel embarrassed?

I've just met a guy, and I'm pretending that I agree with a lot of what he says. Is this the right way to develop a relationship? If not, can I commit to behaving differently, even if it scares him away?

If we are to differentiate, we must commit to changing ourselves, regardless of our fears.

3. Confront the urge to merge with the people around us or the negative attitudes or behaviors that are our own habits.

I realize that I have to change, and I've sort-of made the commitment, but it feels scary and uncomfortable. So I postpone, avoid or claim I "can't" do anything about my behavior and/or the situation now, yet, or any time soon. If I am going to differentiate, I have to confront my behavior and stop giving myself excuses. I may not be able to change yet, but I can stop justifying my habitual merging. Here are some things I can do to confront myself.

- To start with, I can practice self-examination (discussed in detail in Platform Five: Becoming Self-Aware, which we discuss later in the book). For example, I can ask myself: Why am I so invested in being accepted by the group or individual with whom I am merging?

- I can openly acknowledge merging with addictive substances and behaviors, which are dragging me down, and stop pretending that it's okay to be living on sugar and caffeine or to be shopping compulsively.
- I can admit that I am indulging in anger and using someone else's anger as a rationalization.

Confronting our merging is a step beyond making the commitment to change. We go into action by questioning our habitual patterns and standing up to our own inertia. We look into the mirror, stop giving ourselves excuses and begin to deal with the fears that arise around change. And we do all this while being compassionate with ourselves, realizing we are still at the beginning of this transformational program.

Instead of looking for justifications for bad behaviors, we start looking for ways to change.

4. Acknowledge that we are like the people from whom we wish to differentiate; that we carry the energies, attitudes and behaviors that we may not like.

Here's where we focus on differentiation vs. separation. Even though I am going to stop hanging out with my friends in the bars, I can tell these co-workers that I may still have the urge to drink and that I understand why we have all been doing it. Even though I want to stop blowing up when my husband is angry, I can admit to him that I feel anger, too, that I am not a pretend saint with no out-of-control emotions. I can share with my co-workers that I no longer am going to gossip, not because I'm holier-than-thou, but because I can feel that gossip is cruel and makes me sick. I am still that, like others, but I choose a different path.

5. Connect to our higher consciousness to recognize what behaviors or attitudes we prefer to energize.

In the moment that I am merged with somebody, something or some feeling, it is hard for me to conceive that anything else is possible, but of course it is. My anger wants to justify itself, my dependency wants me to stay glued to the other person or group, my self-justification tells me I'm okay, and my experience tells me that I am not capable of being different, so I should throw in the towel.

But there is another voice, and it's the voice of higher consciousness that will tell me something radically different. It tells me to believe myself capable of being more, better, free, self-expressed. What would that look like? Remember, we don't want to be saying "no" to what we don't want. We want to say "yes" to what we do want.

To access that other voice, I go into the most peaceful, quiet state of mind I can, then I look at the options. How am I being, and how would I like to be?

Let's go back to gossip, for example. Let's say I have always felt uncomfortable about gossip. It makes me feel ashamed of myself and embarrassed when I bump into the person I'm gossiping about. At the same time I want to belong to the group. Now what? If I give myself the chance, if I check in with my self-honesty and higher consciousness, I realize that I detest this behavior, and I don't want to sell out my soul. I may notice that I can actually identify with the person I'm slandering. I can see their flaws and identify with their pain. Wow, I recognize that I can break with the crowd and go toward the "outcast" with love and compassion. Maybe I notice that I actually envy the person about whom we're gossiping, and so does everybody else. I realize I can confront my group and tell them that I admire the person we're mocking. I can even approach the outcast person with humility, perhaps even asking them for advice about how they achieved the qualities I envy. I can stop energizing anger, viciousness and envy, while choosing to energize love, compassion, admiration and humility.

I see my wife beating the children. I have been acquiescing so as not to upset her and cause a fight. I can choose courage and caring for the wellbeing of my children.

I see my best friend eating herself to death. I don't confront her, because I don't want to antagonize her, and she's my only friend. I don't want to embarrass her, and, by the way, I don't want her to snap back at me about my constant dieting. Nevertheless, with courage, I can choose to energize self-honesty, rather than collusion. I can risk the friendship for the truths that both of us need to face.

Wow, I get it. I see what I can do differently. I can differentiate, not only from my friends, but from the qualities and characteristics that we have been collectively supporting.

6. Find the divine or human support to choose those behaviors and attitudes.

I know what's possible. I have recognized my habitual way of thinking or behaving and realize I have a choice. I am ready to confront myself and see alternatives. But, yikes, how do I break the habit? How do I deal with my shaky legs when I confront my boss, my husband, my next-door neighbor? How do I stop engaging in angry yelling matches with my wife? How do I stop letting my kids run my life?

We need the will and the determination to make changes and to differentiate. And we also need support, support, support.

Here's why. One: As we discussed in our introduction, "Ego, Instinct & Evolution," from birth, we developed survival strategies, and merging is definitely a big one. So it's hard to confront our own habitual behaviors, because they run deep and bring up the fears of survival. Two: Habits become ingrained and, as we know, are difficult to break. They become the automatic default behaviors that run us. Three: All consciousness is collective, because we are one. When I am fighting my own bad habits, I am dealing with similar habits that are carried throughout the universe. When I am confronting my food addiction, my tendency to merge, rage, acquiesce, or walk blindly down the alley that goes nowhere, I am confronting that same tendency in the collective, because we are one. Four: I have been doing this behavior so long, if I confront it, I might have to acknowledge all the needless pain I have caused to myself and others. Without a lot of self-compassion, I could fall into deep shame.

Add to this the power of the collective consciousness. If I'm having trouble confronting my own habitual merging, how difficult is it to break a pattern that is almost universal? Look around you. Aren't the people around you also merging with groups, individuals and energies that they allow to dominate them?

Once again, let's acknowledge that what we feel are the feelings of more than ourselves, and every step we make to differentiate from negativity is a step that has to overcome the inertia of personal habit and the collective consciousness. How can we do that without the support of a power greater than ourselves?

That is the essence of support: Greater truth coming from a power beyond ourselves, whether that is the power of God or a group of conscious people, or sometimes even music, tai chi or an inspirational movie or book. If I can find a support group that shares my vision of what is possible, great. For instance, if I want to stop drinking, I can go to Alcoholics Anonymous, or if I want to work on my marriage, I can befriend a group of folks who focus on their own behavior, rather than blame their spouse.

If I cannot find a group to help me, or if I'm standing in the kitchen in a helpless rage, noticing myself acting like a total fool and there's no help around, I can always turn to divine support. Even those of you who do not believe in a god can simply raise your consciousness and reach out for help. It can look like taking a long breath or focusing on the top of your head as you reach upward, trusting in that moment that the ramblings of your mind do not define the highest level of consciousness available to you on the planet. And as soon as you can, reach out for support to people who will not feed into your anger and reactivity, but who will help you look at why you're reacting in the moment.

As we get further into this book, you will develop a much deeper understanding of how to access higher consciousness and how to become imbued with the energies that can help us, but for now, let's just do the best we can to stop merging with that which is harming us or others.

Tool: Shifting our Energy

Here are some ways we can shift our energy. If we're caught up in emotion or behavior that is destructive, let's:

- Give ourselves a time-out, just as if we were a child, in order to interrupt the energy.
- Lift our consciousness upward and reach for a higher understanding.
- Take a walk.
- Call a friend.
- Turn on music that energizes a different aspect of ourselves.
- Pray.
- Ask ourselves why we are reacting.
- Try to offer the energy we want to receive.

I'd like to talk about the tool of "trying to offer the energy we want to receive" for a moment. If we are feeling resentful because we feel unloved, and we choose to differentiate from that resentment, we can offer love to someone else. In the moment that we are giving love to another, we are immersed in the energy of love, and that will change our state. If we feel misunderstood, we can strive to understand someone else, thereby energizing the energy of understanding.

When Do I Need to Leave?

We've talked about leaving relationships when there is abuse. Let's speak a little more about when to leave and when not to leave. We would all love to get away from negative feelings, and relationships often bring up bad feelings, especially about ourselves. Here's an example. You are behaving in a reprehensible way, and I can't do anything about it. That makes me feel helpless. I hate feeling helpless, which fills me with rage. Now I feel embarrassed by my rage, foolish for being with you and stupid in front of my friends for loving a jerk. In order to stop all these negative feelings about myself, I feel that I need to leave you.

Maybe you are behaving badly, but maybe I am, too. Will leaving solve the problem of my behavior? We want to think that the other person is carrying all the nastiness, anger or resentment, and if we leave, all will be well. But when we differentiate, we realize that we, too, are carrying those energies, and so we commit to being different.

Sometimes I can't differentiate. Even though I realize that these energies are within me and are taking me over, I may need to separate from the person or situation that is triggering me. I just can't connect to any other aspect of myself in the face of this person's anger, self-hatred, and destructive behavior. There are times when that's true in an absolute sense, and sometimes that's true only because I am still immature.

There's no reason to stay in a wrong relationship because staying is just another form of merging. Some relationships are based on mutual need or convenience and don't have the substance of shared values and mutual respect that will sustain them. Some people are incapable of working on a relationship and cannot be true partners. But we are often more responsible for the relationship's negativity than we realize, and we need to confront our own behavior and attitudes, too.

If we keep finding ourselves leaving relationship after relationship, we may discover that we have a lot to learn by sticking it out. Even if I am being impacted by your energy, your insecurity, anxiety or self-contempt, I may be able to learn to differentiate from it. Everyone has negative feelings and problems to address, so I can't leave everyone who has them, thinking that a perfect partner is out there. Unless I address my own weakness, which is the foundation of my being overwhelmed by the energies and consciousness of others, I will spend my life running away from people, feelings or anything that seems bigger than I am. Unless I deal with the negative energies within me, I'll have to keep running from myself, as well!

Developing the Habit of Differentiation

We see now that we can and need to differentiate from other people, groups and consciousness that can easily dominate us, whether that consciousness is a group phenomenon or just the feelings of the person in the room, and we are learning to do it.

By working toward Becoming Differentiated, we are developing new awarenesses and practicing new habits. But this platform is only part of the process of becoming ourselves, and we need to learn more about other platforms in order to have additional tools that will enable us practice this habit more successfully. We need to become more self-aware, for instance, through practicing Platform Five. And we need Platform Six: Becoming Integrated, to develop a greater wholeness, so that we are less dominated by those energies that don't support us. When we study Platform Seven: Becoming Accountable, we learn to more successfully deal with negative energies. And when we reach Platform Nine: Becoming Becoming, we are more in alignment with the higher energies that help us withstand the urge to merge or separate.

As we embark on the lifetime challenge of differentiation, let us be gentle with ourselves. As I mentioned earlier, Becoming Differentiated is extremely challenging to do by ourselves. We are not separate individuals, and so it's difficult to always hold the energy of peace in the face of the collective fear, the energy of compassion in the face of the collective self-justification, or the energy of love in the face of all the collective anger. And if I am in relationship with a person who denies his or her own feelings, I may never realize that the energies I am feeling are not even my own.

But I can try, and I can get help and connect to higher consciousness. To stand alone is to be weak. To stand together is to be strong.

Simultaneously, while I need support, I am also responsible for doing my part to differentiate and to add to the energy of differentiation on the planet. Whether I know it or not, whether I can feel it or see it or not, every choice I make influences and impacts the whole, no less than every choice made by the whole influences and impacts me. Hallelujah, that means I can also be a force for the good.

And here's more good news: The more that I energize the aspects of consciousness that are beneficial, the more you will be able to do the same for yourself. And the more you do the same, the stronger that energy in the collective that will come back and support me! So, in the same way that the collective consciousness can devastate me, it can also support me. In the same way that my consciousness can add to the negativity infecting our planet, my consciousness can also support the higher consciousness of our planet. When I support peace, peace supports me.

Ultimately, Becoming Differentiated, choosing the aspects of consciousness that I want to energize, is a process of the collective consciousness itself. Looked at in another way, we can say that when I choose peace, it is the collective consciousness that is choosing peace through me. When I choose hate, it is the collective consciousness that is choosing hate through me. When I choose peace, the collective is creating an energy of peace that can then allow others to choose peace as well. When I choose hate, the collective is creating an energy of hatred that can then allow others to choose hatred as well.

I know who I want to be, and I think you do, too. We may not always be that person, but my individual efforts will help to support us all. And the same is true for you.

FINAL THOUGHTS
CHOOSING OUR SUPPORT: THE KEY TO DIFFERENTIATION

By now it should be clear that the key to differentiation is the nature of the groups, collectives, and consciousness that we choose to feed. If we don't want to slip, we don't go into slippery places, as is said in Alcoholics Anonymous. If you don't want to be a gang member, go to school, and hang out with kids who are striving for education. If you don't want to smoke dope, stick with people who don't. If you want to be conscious, find people who value consciousness.

Differentiation requires us to have the support of higher consciousness, and even going toward that higher consciousness may require us to differentiate from those who want us to stay stuck in the old ways. Many of us have friends, spouses, or social groups that are not supporting the consciousness we espouse. We have bonds of loyalty, history, and comfort with these people, but they may not be the right ones to help us become who we can be. Should we stay in those relationships, leave them or just change the way we relate? Making the right choice can threaten our security.

The right choice may threaten us in another way: people who support our consciousness may not support our feelings. People who only support our feelings are just merging with us, adding energy to our rationalizations and self-justifications. If we are to grow, we need to differentiate from those whose support causes us to stay stuck in our habitual unconsciousness.

We may not know many people who have developed self-knowledge and self-awareness, so we have to make a special effort to find them, but such people exist, and we need to seek out, embrace, and support those who will call us to accountability and higher consciousness. This can be scary. Such people will see us as we are, call us on our own self-justifications and not let us get away with our own stories. Are we up for it?

Here are some final questions to ask ourselves about differentiation.

1. Do I choose my relationships carefully?
2. Am I aware of the impact my friends and I have on one another?
3. Am I aware of the impact that my spouse and I have on one another?
4. Do my friends and mate tend to support my consciousness or my feelings?
5. Am I afraid of people who can really see and support me?
6. Am I willing to turn to a source of higher consciousness?

Differentiation is possible. Differentiation is essential. Differentiation is a process. It takes vigilance, self-honesty, and support. Let's commit to it.

PLATFORM THREE

Becoming Co-Creative
How We Relate to the Universe

We co-create reality with the universe in a subtle dance of intention and allowance. Co-creation is the way the universe operates. Outcomes are the result of the intersection of all intention, including our own. If we consciously choose co-creation, we can overcome our own limitations and experience richer lives and more fulfilling outcomes.

WHAT IS BECOMING CO-CREATIVE?

Introduction

Co-creation is the way it is. Whether we like it or not, no matter how big or powerful we think we are, none of us has domination over the universe, and we'd better learn to work with that reality. At the same time, co-creation is a powerful tool, the wave of the future and the hallmark of healthy society and empowered living. So let's learn how co-creation operates, get our egos out of the way and start using this powerful tool to help co-create a better world.

In our first two platforms we have been trying to understand who we are in relation to the whole. Becoming Oneness is the process of recognizing that we are aspects of the collective, part of the whole. Becoming Differentiated tells us that we need to individuate and that in order to do so, we choose which aspects of ourselves and the collective we wish to energize.

Platform Three is the process of seeing our relationship to one another and to life itself. How do we, differentiated individuals, relate to the collective of which we are a part? How do we relate to the forces of the universe, including forces other than people? And how can we support better outcomes, which are for the highest good of all?

The Value of Co-Creation

Before describing the process of co-creation, I would like to address why we would want to be co-creative and why we don't.

What can we really do alone? There is no baby without a sperm and an egg, the community who helps it be birthed and the many workers who create the clothing and food that sustain the mother and child alike. So much for "I" had a baby.

There is no choir without many voices. Even a soloist cannot reach her potential without an instrument or an accompanist, a composer, a record company or, at the very least, an audience. Brilliant ideas need to be heard and applied. Scientific breakthroughs cannot be achieved without computers or pencils and someone to listen and apply them. Readers wouldn't know about this book without the internet, or the radio or the word-of-mouth of other people. Even when people say, "my" company, they are referring to the efforts of many people. If there are no employees, there must at least be buyers, vendors and lots of others in the mix. And can "my" family exist without other members?

So the truth is that we are always in the process of co-creation, but our egos have a problem with this reality, because egos want credit for something! The ego might not want me to co-create even with my spouse or lover, because I want to keep him or her in a less powerful position. The ego even drives some of us to compete with our own children, just to feel better about ourselves.

Additionally, Becoming Co-Creative can conflict with the ego's perceived job of ensuring our survival. As we have already discussed many times, our very existence seems contingent on our recognized value, so Becoming Co-Creative might appear to threaten our value and therefore our survival. How often have we noticed ourselves subtly or not-so-subtly letting others know that we had some thought or idea first, that our contribution to the mix was really important or that "it" couldn't have been done without us? Not only do we crave appreciation for our value, but that need becomes even more acute when raises or promotions are at stake.

Let's get real about the world as it is now. If we are all co-creating, how do we distribute the rewards? Who should get the bigger piece of the pie? How does acknowledging co-creation ensure that my children get sent to the best schools and pad my retirement account?

Oops, co-creation is not looking so good right now. But it gets worse.

Co-creation really sounds grand in the abstract, but in the concrete, it can be very frustrating. We find some people difficult, pushy or lazy, or we judge them as just plain stupid, especially when they disagree with us. Some people think these negative attributes apply to us. We are particularly annoyed when we're sure that our ideas and assessments are right, and other people are standing in the way.

And then there's the urge to dominate, which we have already discussed in Platform One. Whose ideas are going to win? His or mine? Who is going to get her way?

Of course, we see that all the fears of co-creation come from ego-based consciousness, but they feel and are very real in that context. If we are to shift the way we work together, we are going to have to practice Oneness and differentiation, which we have started to do. We will also find great tools in our next chapter on Platform Four: Becoming Mutually Supportive.

But in the meantime, let's acknowledge this: We all have some resistance to co-creation. But having admitted this fact, let's have compassion for ourselves and one another, laugh, and keep on plugging. After a while, we'll really comprehend the reality:

- No matter how independent we think we are, we are always co-creating with the universe.

- The more we understand co-creation, the more successfully we can work with it.
- Out of conscious co-creation can come solutions that transcend the limitations of our capacities and imaginations.
- Co-creation with the universe itself is the key to our survival and evolution.

Now, with a sense of humor and self-compassion let's ask ourselves:

1. With whom do I resist co-creation?
2. Why?
3. Do I want to look good?
4. Do I want to get ahead?
5. Am I afraid of being dominated by others?
6. Am I ready to consider another way?

Once we understand that we are going to be co-creating anyway, why don't we jump into the chapter? Let's first take a look at some of the ways co-creation occurs in the universe.

But I Thought We Created Reality!

Some people have gotten caught up in the belief that we create reality. That is a partial truth. Let's go back to our car analogy. Let's say we're all in different cars and trucks driving down the freeway. The whole is all the cars, plus the asphalt, the signs, the air, the birds, the buildings in the distance, the construction workers on the side of the road, and so on.

Since we're driving the car, we like to think we're in control of where we're going and how long it might take us to get there. But, of course, that's only a partial truth. If we're hit by another car, we may end up in the hospital. The number of cars on the road and the degree of congestion may impact our timetable. A dog might wander into the road, and we swerve to avoid her. Somebody drops an old sofa off the back of a dilapidated pickup truck, and the road is blocked. The exit sign fell down in the last storm and it hasn't been replaced, and, because I'm unfamiliar with the road, I miss the exit. We are one of a maze of forces of which we are only a part.

We don't like this reality. We want to be in control of our drive. Some of us get great big trucks in the hopes that we can intimidate others. Some of us pick small sports cars so we can get around others. Some of us pick comfy sedans so that we can be comfortable while we're putting up with others. But no matter what we do, we are part of the flow.

Do we create reality? No. Are we total victims of circumstance? Also no. We, along with all the other cars, dogs, birds, and construction workers, are co-creating the reality of all the experiences that everyone is having on the road, including us. To us, others are factors in our trip. To other people, we are a factor in their trip. We impact them, and they impact us. Together we co-create the whole. That's the way life is, like it or not.

Our intentions are important. We do have an impact on our trip, and here are some of the ways. Did we dawdle getting dressed before we left? Did we leave enough time to program our navigation system? Are we good drivers? Are we sober and clear-headed? Do we keep our car in good condition? Do we have the right directions? Do we have a bunch of stops to make along the way? Have we thought through the timing?

Our intentions impact the trip, but other factors impact us as well, and we can't control them. Ultimately we have to allow the freeway ride to be what it is, and that's life.

Unintentional Co-Creation

The co-creation we have been describing is unintentional. When I left the house, I didn't plan on the dog straying onto the road and the unexpected is what we experience most of the time. A great metaphor for unintentional co-creation is a vehicle accident. We have an accident and what happens? Cars of equal weight that collide head on will generally stop each other. Cars that intersect at an angle will generally change each other's course. A car that rear-ends another will send that hit car careening forward with more speed than the driver intended. In life, as in accidents, we want to accomplish something. But most of us find that there are people, institutions, and other circumstances that will stop us, change our direction, or catapult us forward.

This is unintentional co-creation. We intend to achieve a certain goal. But the universe is full of other forces moving along their paths. Those forces could be individual people, social or economic forces, animals, weather, and even microbes. We can collide, intersect, side-swipe, or rear-end each other, and that impacts all of us.

Intentional Co-Creation

I see a goal, a need, a possibility, and I know that I can't achieve it alone. I realize that I need to co-create with the universe. The goal could be as simple as getting the house cleaned on Sunday morning or as complex as cleaning up the earth's oceans. If I co-create consciously, I look for resources to support the project. Who should I work with? How will we work together? Can I allow that my own ideas may change or that my wisdom or abilities may be challenged? Am I willing to allow others to look or be smarter? Do I realize that I cannot control the outcome?

In some ways, intentional co-creation looks like the car accident we used as a metaphor for unintentional co-creation. We still collide and intersect, side-swipe or rear-end each other. But when we bring together these forces intentionally, we have chosen some of the players with wisdom and awareness. I know that I'm going to butt heads with Mary, but because she is such a smart businesswoman, I should consider her input. My operations manager is a stubborn human being, but he is worth fighting with, because of the value he brings. I think my fellow congress people are corrupt, but I can't get this bill through without them, and I believe in the legislative process.

Even when co-creating intentionally, I am still not in control of the process, but I have made a conscious decision that co-creation is necessary, and I am willing to face myself and all the frustrations inherent in the process. We can't do great things if we don't delve into the process of co-creation. Even though there may be times when we need to differentiate from everyone else and pursue an unpopular idea, at some point we have to work with others to bring that idea into its full potential.

Let's ask ourselves a few preliminary questions about our participation in co-creation.

1. Where do I see myself co-creating?
2. Am I doing it intentionally or unintentionally?

The Process of Co-Creation

Whether intentional or unintentional, co-creation follows the same process, and Becoming Co-Creative is the way we adjust to the realities of that process. Let me present it now:

We co-create reality with the universe in a subtle dance of intention and allowance. Co-creation is the way the universe operates. Outcomes are the result of the intersection of all intention, including our own. If we consciously choose co-creation, we can overcome our own limitations and experience richer lives and more fulfilling outcomes.

Co-creation is the process of intention and allowance, instead of domination and submission. Easy to say; not so easy to do.

BLOCKS TO BECOMING CO-CREATIVE

Having come this far with me through this book, you will not be surprised to learn that the blocks to becoming co-creative are fear and pain, because fear and pain lead us to domination and submission, rather than the intention and allowance required for co-creation.

Let's look at this a little closer. As we discussed at length in Platform One, fear and the fear of pain lead us to the fear of domination, and the fear of domination leads us to the habit of trying to dominate others. If I let you have anything to say about anything, you might dominate me. So let me be in control. Co-creation is not on the agenda. I may realize that I'm trying to dominate, or I might do it so automatically that I am not even aware of my behavior.

Submission is a way of merging with other people's thoughts, feelings, values, and agendas, and it prevents co-creation, as well. Submission, too, is caused by the fear of pain. If I submit to others' will, I hope to placate them and protect myself from their potential hostile reactions.

Just as co-creation can be intentional or unintentional, the lack of co-creation can be intentional or unintentional, too. I know I'm afraid of my father, so I knowingly refuse to speak and give up on co-creating a different family life. On the other hand, if I fear your withdrawal from me, I may trade my contribution for your approval, and I may do it without even being aware of it. Or if I'm insecure, I might always assume I'm wrong and submit without examining the relative value of our ideas.

Both domination and submission are painful. When we practice the habit of domination, we feel guilty. We know that we have run roughshod over others, and we feel compelled to keep justifying ourselves. We also feel fear. When will the dominated rebel? When we dominate, we also lose the opportunity to learn from others. As already indicated in Platform Two,

211

the individuation of views and perspectives allows us all to learn. And, finally, when we dominate, we lose love, because we create resentment in others. Domination always leaves us feeling alone.

The habit of submission is also painful. When we submit, we feel shame, because we know we have betrayed ourselves. We also hurt everyone else, because we deprive everyone of our perspective, both the dominator and the rest of the collective. In addition, we deprive the dominator of our love, because no matter how we behave on the outside, we feel resentful and unloving toward those we allow to dominate or abuse us.

Some of you might be thinking you already live from a place of co-creation. "Co-creating with the universe is easy. All it takes is trust, and I don't mind trusting the universe. After all, we are talking about some benevolent higher power—not some nasty little person who could in fact hurt me or withdraw their love."

Hmmm. You trust the universe, because it won't hurt you? Perhaps we're not talking about the same universe! The universe I'm talking about is the totality of all that exists past, present, and future. Some people call this totality God.

"Well, I trust God."

But maybe not. Maybe not when you realize that the God we're describing is everything, and that would include your ex-husband, second-grade teacher, and stingy landlord. How much do you trust them?

"Hmmm, maybe I need to draw the line here."

In our hearts, most of us can acknowledge that we don't, in fact, entirely trust the universe. If we felt complete trust, we wouldn't experience fear, and we wouldn't feel the need to compel the universe to conform to our wishes and desires. And don't we all try to compel the universe to conform to our wishes and desires? Aren't we always trying to figure out how to get our way? I do.

Sometimes our intention to dominate the universe can look greedy and self-serving. I want you to give me your money, that job, the biggest piece of cake. That kind of domination is easy to spot. Sometimes our intention to dominate the universe can look virtuous and self-sacrificing. All I want is for everyone to get along in peace and harmony. I'm asking for nothing for myself, but I'm still trying to call the shots. That kind of domination even seems justified.

And sometimes our intention to dominate the universe can look like submission, which is a form of manipulation. If I submit to you, then you will do or not do x, y, and z. If I'm good, then God, my parents, my teachers, friends, or bosses will love me, reward me, get out of my way, ultimately do what I want.

Whether our attempt to dominate is disguised, obvious, or justified, every one of these wants—whether pious or not—puts us in conflict with some other energy or force in the universe. Even if we are submissive and manipulate those directly around us, there are still other forces who won't want to do x, y, or z, no matter how "good" we think we've been. Whether or not we're obvious about being greedy or self-serving, there are always other forces that want the biggest piece of cake, too. And no matter how noble our intentions to achieve peace and harmony, there will always be those who can justify war and strife.

How do we deal with the rest of the universe—the rest that may not go along with our agenda? The guy who wants the same parking spot, or who flips us off, or who beats up our kid or who puts a suicide bomb in our restaurant parking lot?

Many people tell us that we must accept what is, and there is truth to that. We can't fight everything or change everything, because we are, in fact, parts of a collective (oh darn, that collective again). Another truth about the value of acceptance is that when we start by accepting "what is," we can take steps to change what we dislike. When we deny what is, we can't take its measure and see what, in fact, we can do to impact it. When we accept what is, we can examine it and see what we can do.

But acceptance is only a part of the process. Lack of acceptance can turn into resignation in the face of superior odds, and resignation makes us sick. Here's resignation: "Give up. That's the way the world is. It's always been this way." In and of themselves, these statements are blind. "Give up" encourages us to give in to situations that may, in fact, be permeable. "That's the way the world is" ignores that things are not only "this way;" they are also "that way." What do I mean?

Here are two examples. People who say that the world is unkind are ignoring all the kindness that does exist. People who say that George is a jerk don't acknowledge all the ways George isn't a jerk and all of George's potential not to be a jerk.

When people urge us to resign ourselves to what is perceived as reality, they have defined the universe in a particular way. This is the world. But is it? Their definition of the universe is only what they see, what they choose to see or what they have been taught to see. Seeing the world as "this" or "that" is a habit. Have I looked at the world lately? Do I really know how the world is?

Those who urge us to accept what is may be justifying themselves—their comfort, privilege, or habitual behaviors. Or they may be simply justifying their fear. They may say, "What's the point in trying to fight this? It's always been this way." But what they actually mean may be, "I don't want to have to try to fight this, and I can justify my not fighting by saying the cause is hopeless."

When I was a young woman, I fought for disarmament and against the Vietnam War, among other social causes. When I started to work for these causes, they seemed hopeless. Those who wanted disarmament were considered whacko, and those against the Vietnam War were traitors. Now, lots of people want disarmament, and few would justify the war. Who can say how the world "is"?

Similarly, people who insist that a particular illness is hopeless may be wrong. Perhaps in their experience, there is no recovery. But their perspective is based only on their experience. Perhaps they don't know what can be overcome and what cannot. Perhaps by refusing to accept that an illness is incurable, someone can find a remedy.

While some people promote the pole of acceptance, others promote the other extreme: You can do it. You create your own reality. There's truth to this point as well. As we have heard before, we can't win the Lotto if we don't buy a ticket. If we don't apply for a job, we won't get one, unless Aunt Dorothy's third cousin calls us up as a favor to Grandma. And if we don't ask the girl we love to the dance, she may end up sitting at home or jitterbugging with some other frog.

People who don't follow their dreams won't achieve them. But most people who do follow their dreams won't achieve them either.

What? Blasphemous, but true. Let's look at this more deeply.

First, even those people who succeed in achieving their "dreams" may discover that their dreams realized are a lot different from their dreams dreamed. I may dream that this book will reach a huge audience and that it makes me rich and famous. But supposing it did? I would be dealing with the unexpected repercussions of that dream. A lot of people might actually call upon me to do things that I may not have the energy for. If I were exposed to a larger audience, I might encounter a wealth of criticism and hostility that would be devastating. Being rich might be nice, but I would have to learn how to handle large sums of money or rely on others to handle my finances. Being famous could destroy the pleasures of everyday life, where anonymity allows me the freedom to go anywhere and be any way I choose without being noticed.

Being outwardly successful could also make me more cautious. Before my success, I had nothing to lose, and so I was totally real and courageous. Now that I am successful, I could lose my audience, reputation, and big income. Oh my God, should I say x, y, or z and alienate all those people who have just found so much of value in what I have to say (yup, a little ego could creep in there)? Furthermore, people might start besieging me to read their books and endorse their work. How would I look if I refused? Might I suddenly become a victim of my own self-image? Was that my dream?

Beyond these unintended side-effects of the dream realized, there is a glaring reality: for every person who becomes rich and famous writing a book, there are hundreds, probably thousands, who don't. Follow my dream? If my dream is to write a book, I can probably manage it. If my dream is to write a book that becomes "successful" in the sense of public acceptance, my chances become slimmer. If my dream is to impact human consciousness, then my chances are really slim.

Am I saying don't follow your dream? No, of course not. My dream is to be healthy, and despite decades of illness, I work on my health. I eat well and take care of myself. I look at the psychological and emotional issues that could be getting in my way. I try every reasonable and sometimes unreasonable healing modality that comes along. Do I need to do this? Yes, because if I don't, then I am not giving myself a chance to get well. Yes, because anything health-affirming that I do for my body, mind, and spirit is actually going to support my body to deal with its ills, and anyway those choices make me healthier on every level. Yes, because I ain't dead yet, and you never know when the miracle could be around the corner.

But if I follow the dream and *expect* the **result** of becoming a healthy person, I could become bitter and disappointed. Why? Because my body may never be capable of going beyond a certain level of functioning. Or because no one yet has the knowledge to cure me. Or that knowledge exists, but I have no access to it. We have all heard of the people who defied the doctors and learned how to walk despite some dreadful accident. But what about all the people who tried and couldn't overcome their paralysis? Were they defective? Was it their fault? Did they not try hard enough?

No, because we alone do not create reality. We co-create reality with the universe. My thoughts and intentions are only one piece in any puzzle, including the puzzle of our lives. I can be the best me I can be, but if I live alone on a deserted island, I won't get that guy I long for. Or if we live in a country whose population of young men has been decimated by war, not every young woman will find her mate. Or if I live in the desert, I can't create a stream to run by my house—though I may be able to design a fake one. If my sperm count is too low, I won't be able to procreate my own children. And if I want to end war, I can't make that happen until the mass consciousness chooses peace.

Submission and domination; resignation and creation of our own reality—these are poles of the continuum of reality. To get habitually caught in either pole is a reaction to feelings of impotence. When we submit, we have accepted feeling impotent, and we try to make peace with it. When we try to dominate, we reject the feeling of impotence and try to hype ourselves into believing that we *are* the power. Being stuck in the habit of living from either pole can lead to unnecessary pain.

Let's look at some of the unnecessary pain associated with resignation. If I am stuck in the habit of submission, I can believe that an abusive husband can't be stopped or left, and so I tell myself that I might as well stay. That leaves me in the pain of an abusive marriage. Or I may tell myself that one stingy boss will only be replaced by another, so why should I look for another job? Or that I haven't succeeded in finding a house in my budget, so why look? Or that I've tried to quit drinking before, so why try again? Or that people won't like me, so why try again to make friends?

Defeated before getting out of the barn, we draw the picture of our future by picturing our past.

But many people who have believed that they could "make it happen" have also suffered from the results of living out of that habitual paradigm. When they find they can't "make it happen," they turn against themselves. Untold women who have read books on getting the right guy have been devastated when they couldn't or didn't. Either they got no guy, or they discovered that the guy they got was a drug addict, workaholic, emotionally unavailable, moody, irresponsible, or something that made him not the dream that they had imagined. Because of their belief that they could "make it happen," they believed it was their fault. It never dawned on them that "perfect" men don't exist in a society racked with pain. Or if they do exist, they are few and far between.

Similarly, men who have strained to be the absolute best at work have become frustrated and angry when they were passed over for promotion.

They can go into self-doubt, as well. Did they not get that promotion because they didn't try hard enough, or was it because they didn't believe enough or weren't assertive enough? Stuck in the paradigm that they create their own reality, they may ignore the obvious: The boss was pressured by his silent partner to bring in his second cousin. Or the company needed characteristics that our hero simply didn't have.

Intend! Believe! Visualize! At our final game of the little league season, I didn't hit that baseball out of the stadium. I must have been self-sabotaging. I didn't believe in myself. It couldn't be simply because the opposing pitcher was too good for me and in fact was destined to become a major league baseball player.

Attempts to give orders to the universe will not work. I may ask for what I want and there are times when I should ask for what I want. I need to intend, believe, and maybe even visualize, because these actions energize my intention. But my intention remains my intention, and it's not the only factor at play.

Acceptance is sometimes appropriate. Thinking positively can be helpful. But being stuck in one pole and one paradigm is not being in reality and is the cause of needless pain.

Here I'd like to clarify the use of the word acceptance. I am using the word acceptance at this point, because it is easily understood. A bit further in this chapter, I will explain why I don't use the word acceptance for co-creation; instead I use the word allowance. But for these introductory remarks, I'm using the word "acceptance," as it is most generally understood.

Before going on to talk about the process of Becoming Co-Creative, let's look at ourselves for a moment. Which habitual patterns do I tend to practice?

The Habit of Seeing Ourselves as Either Powerful or Powerless

1. Do I tend to submit or dominate?
2. In what kinds of circumstances do I tend to submit? In what kinds do I try to dominate? Is my submission another form of domination?
3. When I try to submit or dominate, do I get resentful?

4. What is my agenda with people I know? My agenda with work? My agenda with my family?
5. Do I expect my agendas to be achieved?
6. What have I dreamed about in the past?
7. Did I achieve those dreams?
8. Did they turn out to be what I dreamed they would be?
9. Do I tend to over-emphasize acceptance?
10. Do I think that I can create my own reality?
11. Is it true that I can?
12. Do I tend to blame myself when my dreams have not come true? Do I tend to blame others?

Changing Our Paradigm

How are we going to avoid getting stuck in either pole? How do we develop a paradigm that works, one that brings us into alignment with life without simultaneously making us feel or behave as though we were powerless?

First, we need to understand the nature of the universe and the nature of ourselves. In Platform One, we discussed that we are one. Let's look at the implication of this concept in terms of co-creation.

Becoming Oneness tells me that I am not an isolated self. I am part of the universe. If I am not really a single, isolated self, there is no isolated "I" to create my own reality. I am part of the whole that creates reality. Therefore, I cannot be all-powerful.

At the same time, I am not powerless. If we are really one, then I am a part of the collective. As a part of the collective, I have an effect on the whole. I can influence that collective, and I may even have a major impact on the outcome. But that impact may not be just as I had intended.

With our understanding of Platform One: Becoming Oneness, I am inextricably bound to the collective. That makes me neither powerful nor powerless; or more accurately, it makes me both! Doesn't this, in fact, coincide with our real life experience? Don't I have an influence over the course of events? Doesn't my action or non-action have an impact? Of course. Do I have control over the impact? No.

We co-create with the universe in a subtle dance of intention and allowance. And just what are intention and allowance?

Intention and Allowance

Here's how it works. At the end of Platform Two, we realized that we differentiate ourselves from others by energizing the aspects of the collective consciousness that we choose to support. I choose, for example, to energize either war or peace. This is my intention. What I intend will impact the collective, but how much and in what way? That is not in my hands. That depends on the collective intention of the rest of the universe. My ability to understand and work with this reality is my allowance.

Let's look at intention and allowance more closely. But first, let's remind ourselves of the definition of Platform Three: Becoming Co-Creative:

We co-create reality with the universe in a subtle dance of intention and allowance. Co-creation is the way the universe operates. Outcomes are the result of the intersection of all intention, including our own. If we consciously choose co-creation, we can overcome our own limitations and experience richer lives and more fulfilling outcomes.

Now let's get a better sense of each element: intention, allowance, and co-creation.

What Is Intention?

Intention is the process of focusing our energy on a desired outcome or direction. It is an attempt to impact the universe in such a way as to meet our individual or collective needs for survival, self-expression and wellbeing. Individuals intend, and collectives intend. Everything intends.

What Is Allowance?

Allowance is the process of relaxing around reality. It requires us to take a breath and let go of the struggle to impose our will. It facilitates us to examine how the universe has responded to our intention. It leads to new intention. It can lead to the reinforcement of our original intention or to a shift in direction. It leads to our growth. And it always begins with a pause and a willingness to see and hear.

What Is Co-Creation?

What occurs in life is the result of the collective intention. Co-creation is the way the universe works. It is the result of the intersection of the intentions of all involved. To practice co-creation is to be in harmony with this process. We begin with the acknowledgement that we all have intentions, and that we need to accept that everyone's intentions will intersect. We intend and allow. Once we are impacted by the response of the universe, we intend and allow again.

Before proceeding, I would like to explain why I use the word allowance, rather than acceptance. Acceptance can simply mean taking in. For example, I accept your invitation, your love, your donation. Allowance does not necessarily mean that I am taking something in, only that I am allowing that it is. I may not take in your criticism, but I allow it. I may not take in your anger, but I allow it. Allowance contributes to our being in a more neutral place about harmful realities. I cannot fight all the abuse on the planet. I may do my best to help change it, but I must allow it, while it exists. Otherwise I am caught in impotent rage.

Intention, allowance, co-creation. Let's see how this works. Here's a simple example. My child has a failing grade, and I think it's unfair. The teacher won't listen to me, so I go to the principal. My intention is to get the teacher to pass my child. I talk to the principal. I'm clear and impassioned. But what will be the result? My impact will depend on the intention of the principal. Is the principal willing to listen, or does she already have a fixed perception of my child and the teacher? Is she intending to be open-minded, or is she being impacted by insecurity about her job and an unwillingness to conflict with the staff? Isn't the outcome also impacted by the totality of my intention? Am I there only to talk and argue my point, because my ego is at stake, or do I want to help my child? If I want to help my child, do I intend to listen in order to discover if there's something to learn from the principal? And what about the intention of the child? Does his performance demonstrate an intention to work hard or to slough off? Does my child's intention bolster my argument with the teacher or undermine it? We can see that the results will depend on the interweaving of the intentions of the child, the principal and me.

The teacher will factor in as well. If the principal sides with me, she may talk to the teacher. If the teacher's intention is to be open to whatever is right, the teacher may see my point of view and pass my child, or fail my child but give her more attention, or pass my child but be even more resentful or negative toward her. All of the intentions of the rest of us can be blocked or deflected by that of the teacher.

Although this may not have been the intention of our communication, I may have impacted the principal. She may align more with the teacher, she may be swayed by me, or she may have a subtle doubt planted in her mind about her staff member in relation to my child. At the same time, talking to the principal will impact me. Once I talk to her, I may walk out angry and reinforced in some negative belief about the teacher. Or I may walk out feeling relieved and supported, or with a new perspective on my child.

How do I know what will transpire? How do I know what the result of my intention will be? How do I know what will be the result of the intersection of all our intentions? When I connect to any part of the collective, I am exercising my will. I am intending, but I am not determining the outcome. That depends on many other factors. That's where allowance comes in.

Co-creation is bringing what I have to the table with whatever intention I have, and working with, or allowing, the result, which is dependent on the intention of others. Co-creation also teaches me that everything is impacted in the process. When I connect to the collective, my views may change or be reinforced. When I connect to the collective, my direction may be shifted. When I connect to the collective, my goals may be reshaped. When I connect to the collective, the collective might shift as well.

The example of the principal and the parent involves individuals. Now let's look at an example that deals with collectives themselves. I wrote a book called *Sacred Union: The Healing of God*.[19] If I had not made the effort to write the book and get it published, it never would have reached anyone. It would not have reached the collective. But my relationship with the collective actually began even before then. I was, in fact, connecting to a collective consciousness when I wrote the book, the collective that carries a similar belief system. My ideas are not "mine," because I am not separate. They are a co-creation with a collective that I may not even know exists.

Having written the book, I now present it to the public. But how much impact will this book have? That depends on the collective again.

---

[19]   Green, Beth. *Sacred Union: The Healing of God.* Idyllwild, Rising Mountain Press, 2002.

If no one wants to read the book, it will be left on a shelf collecting dust. If some of the collective resonate with its ideas, those people will read it and carry the message. If a lot of the collective resonate with the book's ideas, the book will have a great impact. But what impact? I may intend the book to bring people into a new paradigm of higher consciousness and spirituality. But I cannot control that. Some may shift into a new paradigm. Some may momentarily vibrate with the ideas and then promptly forget them, although the ideas may or may not surface another day. Some may read the book, hate its premise and be confirmed in their old ideas. And some may read the book and incorporate the ideas into a new synthesis that goes beyond both my and their original thoughts.

And, of course, it's even more complicated than that. If somewhere in the collective there is a group or member of the collective that thinks they can benefit from this book, either spiritually or financially, they will bring more energy into the promotion of the book. My intention is now joined by theirs. Does that make a difference? You bet it does. Ultimately readers will determine the book's success. But with financial and spiritual backing, and perhaps with the cleverness and manipulation of advertising, the book might be introduced to a much larger collective right off the bat. With only my own resources—including only my intention—being brought to bear, the book may never get past the resistance to its message. With more intention behind it, perhaps it might have a greater impact. Is that all in my control? No, the outcome will be impacted by the intentions and motives of many others.

Will I rant and rave if it's not a "success"? Will I spend my life relentlessly arguing against a universe that is not responding positively to my attempts to express myself? Will I see myself as the world's victim, if nobody agrees with my own estimation of its value? Will I stop writing? Will I resent the co-creative process of the universe?

Or will I practice allowance? Will I start with the natural momentary ranting and raving, followed by a deep breath? Will I then consider the possibility that the book is not as great as I think it is? Will I realize that lots of people write valuable books that don't "go anywhere"? That what is happening to me is also happening to everyone, meaning that we are all part of a universe that is in the process of co-creation? Will I intend and allow and find ways to make myself comfortable with the realities of life? Will I brush myself off, learn whatever I can, and bring my energy into the next moment of life? The next book? Or the next walk in the woods? Will I support others to do the same?

Practicing Co-Creation allows me first to intend and then to allow. To not intend is to give up; to not allow is to bang my head against a wall! To co-create is to be part of the fabric of evolution. To refuse to co-create is to surrender to the ego's vision that I am right, that my limited vision is all-knowing and that I should be in control of the universe!

To summarize some general points about co-creation: I am not separate from the universe that I am intending to impact. First, my own ideas are impacted by what is already thought and felt in the universe. I am not a separate "I" that is intending. Then I offer my ideas to the collective consciousness, which will embrace, reject, or modify them. Not only is the collective to a large or small degree impacted by me; I am impacted by it. We are all impacting and co-creating the movement of life. Through the intersection of our collective intentions, the universe evolves and I am a part of it.

One more point before we discuss how to practice Becoming Co-Creative. Some will ask: When our intentions are thwarted, isn't it always for our own good? Is there a higher benevolent consciousness that leads us through our many trials to a better end?

Some people carry a belief in a totally benevolent universe. I have a different view, which is that everything is evolutionary, as opposed to benevolent. I have already discussed this issue in depth in the book I mentioned earlier, *Sacred Union: The Healing of God,* and it is not necessary to discuss these points here.[20]

But I need to make some comment on the question, as it relates to co-creation and intention and allowance. Many times I have struggled and struggled to "make something happen", yet it didn't. Whatever loss I experienced caused me great grief at the time. Later, however, something more marvelous occurred, and when I looked back on my thwarted intention, I thought: "Wow, I'm so grateful that I didn't succeed in getting that job, that guy, or whatever experience I thought I wanted. The universe brought me into a much better experience, and I see that the universe really took care of me."

---

[20]   Green, Beth. *Sacred Union: The Healing of God.* Idyllwild, Rising Mountain Press, 2002.

Yet at other times, I look back at thwarted intentions—mine and others'—and find the results very painful. I've seen battered women trying to escape a stalking husband, only to be killed. I've seen children who desperately pray for their parents' kindness and love, but never get it. I cannot say that I believe all outcomes are beneficial.

But if I cannot say that all outcomes are beneficial, I can say that I can find benefit in any outcome! There is a larger consciousness of which I am a part. I can be a positive, cooperative part of it and embrace the process. Or I can kick and scream and try to control it all the way to the grave. If I accept this reality, I can use everything that happens to me for my own good and for my own growth. I can support you to do the same.

In that sense, I am co-creating the benevolent universe that we all want.

As a child, I thought I was the center of the universe. Most days, I still do. But I know better. God once told me, "Beth, I am not part of your mission. You are part of my plan." Whether or not you have a belief in God, the point is still well taken. The evolution of the universe is not part of my mission. I am part of the evolution of the universe. I might as well find a way to enjoy the ride.

HOW WE BECOME CO-CREATIVE

Developing the Habit of Co-Creation: Understanding the Dynamics of Intention and Allowance

Let's summarize where we've come. To develop the habit of Becoming Co-Creative, we start by realizing that we don't control the universe and that co-creation is, in fact, the way the universe functions. We all experience intention and allowance. The second step is to come into alignment with this process, to accept and work with this reality, to get comfortable with it.

Following are examples of the dynamic of co-creation. See if you have experienced similar situations, and ask yourself how you reacted to them.

The Universe Impacting Me More than I Impact It

We can have an intention, and the universe may respond by changing us! Here's an example some of you may identify with. I want a mate with certain characteristics. I make my mental or written list. Where did that intention come from? Whose idea of a mate am I carrying? Does my intention come purely from me, or is it impacted by societal values, family views, rebellion, fantasy? Does my mother want me to catch a certain kind of guy? Am I going to follow her view or rebel against it? Am I not already being impacted by the collective and its intentions?

Suppose I have a clear idea of my mate—whether or not that idea has come purely from "me." Now I prepare myself to attract such a mate. I work on my blocks, fears, and expectations. I call out to the collective to bring me my mate. I look, pray, search the internet, go to dances, make affirmations, whatever seems best to me. Who will the universe provide?

What are the characteristics of the men in my society? What does the pool look like? Are they struggling with identity issues, just as women are? Are they struggling with addictions, because we all are? What options does the universe have? Aren't my chances once again impacted, if not determined, by the state of consciousness of the collective?

The universe presents options not to my liking. These men do not fit my shopping list. How do I respond? Do I rant and rave and blame men? Do I shrug my shoulders and go home to write poetry? Do I keep trying, taking the approach that trying is the only way to have any chance at all?

If I practice allowance, I take a breath and look at my options. I may stay single, or I may choose to relate to one of these men. If I do choose one of these men, I get into a relationship that will be challenging. I may not like the man's behavior and the relationship we develop. It might make me uncomfortable. In fact, I may not like the way I'm behaving either.

If I am practicing allowance, I embrace the lessons of the relationship. My fantasy man is really going to make me feel good. But this guy is a challenge to me, because our relationship does not go smoothly, and I don't like who I am in relation to him. Now I have to look at myself. If I try to learn something from this experience, I realize that the greatest outcome of this relationship is that I am learning about myself, learning even more than I had wanted to see about myself! And, to my surprise, I may even find in this relationship a deeper connection and love than I expected.

Why? Because in the process of dealing with a real man, I may have to see the real woman within me. I may even see how we are one. I may develop compassion for both of us and work on growing together.

All of these experiences change me. None of this is what I had intended, but this is what I need to allow. In this case, not only is the universe co-creating my mate; it is actually co-creating me!

Let's ask ourselves some questions about intention and allowance within the context of relationships.

1. Have I ever had a relationship that was far from my fantasy or my shopping list?
2. Did I grow from this relationship? How?
3. Can I think of other experiences where I was offered options different from those that I intended? If I took them, did they support me to change in positive ways?
4. Have I continued to make wish lists of things I want?
5. How do I perceive those lists now?

The Strength of My Intention as Only One Factor

You would think that a strong intention would lead to the desired outcome more so than a weak intention. Not always.

If I make an offer on a house, and I am passionate about the place, I will probably make a very strong offer. The likelihood is that the seller will sell it to me. But if the seller receives a better offer at the same time as mine, he or she will sell it to the other people. No house for me. It may be that the other buyers had a stronger intention, but perhaps not. Perhaps they simply had more money, or they have cash, or there may be some other factor that has nothing to do with the relative strength of our intentions. Regardless of the strength of my intention, if the intentions of the seller and new buyer are more in sync, that deal will go through. If, on the other hand, I am ambivalent and make a weak offer, the seller might sell to me anyway, simply because mine was the only offer in months. In this case, my wobbly intention is bolstered by the intention of the seller, and we have a deal.

In one case, I had strong intention, but the outcome was not favorable. In the other case, I had weak intention, but the outcome was favorable to me, if you consider it favorable to get a house about which you are ambivalent!

If I practice allowance, I may be saddened by the loss of a house I want, but I will accept that this is the response of the universe, because my intention was in conflict with the intention of the seller. He wanted more money or cash, or whatever else the other buyer offered. If I don't practice the platform of allowance, I could easily become enraged, feel cheated, or blame myself!

How have I responded to thwarted intentions?

1. Have I ever made a 100 percent commitment to something that did not come through?
2. How did I feel?
3. Did I end up with something better? Or not?
4. Did I try to rationalize away my feelings?
5. Did I ever get something I felt ambivalent about?
6. How did I feel?
7. What did I learn from these experiences?

Co-Creation as the Way of History

We just looked at an example where my intention is either blocked or bolstered by the intention of another individual.

The same principle applies on a grander scale. Those who are successful in their intentions are usually those who find themselves going where the collective—or a large part of it—is already going. If my book resonates with the conscious or unconscious longing of the collective for change, it will certainly succeed. If it resonates with the conscious or unconscious longing of only a tiny part of the collective, then I need to redefine success for myself.

Nowhere is the co-creative process more clear than with the dynamic of leadership. A leader appears to be leading, when actually the leader and "led" are co-creating. No leader can choose him or herself—the collective tends to choose or accept leaders who articulate what they are already thinking, feeling, or longing for, even when those thoughts or feelings are not in their conscious awareness.

Martin Luther King was a great leader, but if there were not enough people who supported his consciousness, he would have been considered a crackpot or become an unknown hero. His ability to lead was contingent upon the consciousness of Southern Blacks, who were willing to stand up against segregation. And Southern Blacks were not the only members of the collective to impact the outcome. It was also impacted by the intentions of Southern Whites who wanted to defend their way of life, as well as by Southern Whites who had an economic or philosophical interest in change. It was impacted by the support of Northern liberals, young radicals, and a federal government that felt compelled to stand up for Civil Rights. It was impacted by the entire collective that put that federal government in office, and it was impacted by many other forces as well. Each of these groups was a collective within the larger collective, and the intention of each group impacted the results.

Similarly, those who promoted Nazism in Germany were a collective that needed a leader who imbued a sense of superiority in order to offset feelings of defeat after World War I. Even if his followers were unaware of that need, it nonetheless primed them for what Hitler had to say. If not, Hitler would have been strutting around in his own house and would have become the laughingstock of a collective whose intention was different from his own. In addition, Hitler's rise was impacted by other collectives as well: collectives such as arms dealers, industrialists, fascistic energies throughout Europe, the German military, the Jewish community, all of whom had intentions of different types and whose relative power impacted the outcome. And then, of course, Hitler was able to realize his intentions only to a point. Once he rose to power on the wave of the collective consciousness, his ability to realize his dreams of an empire was crimped by the intentions of larger collectives whose intentions conflicted with his.

Does that mean that the collective has all the power? Yes. And, of course, no, because we are part of the collective that has all the power. The collective may intend to lynch a man, but one voice may speak up and appeal to the aspect of that collective's consciousness that does not want to see him lynched. By speaking, by differentiating ourselves from the mass consciousness, we can call to the surface in the mass consciousness another thought, another feeling, a different longing.

How do we practice allowance in the face of these collective energies? First, we acknowledge how difficult it is to move large numbers of people. We ask ourselves if our intention is to be a leader at any cost or to represent a philosophy that we truly believe in, but which may not find much resonance in the collective. We ask ourselves strategic questions as to where we begin with our campaign. We accept the difficulty of the road.

If we don't understand co-creation, we can make needless mistakes. We can expect our Volkswagen to stop a Mack truck. We may misunderstand how to fight for our own cause. We might try to fight harder, when we need to try to find allies. We may fail to strategize and evaluate what we need to do.

If we do not understand the co-creation between leaders and groups, we will not understand history or even our current times. We can become enraged and blame an individual for the acts that could only have been created by the collective, or at least a collective within the collective. (This is what we see when people claim that World War II was Hitler's "fault.") If we do not understand co-creation, we misunderstand life. This will contribute to our feelings of frustration and prevent us from accomplishing even what we could.

Let's ask ourselves some questions here about leadership.

1. Have I ever tried to offer leadership?
2. What supported it? What opposed it?
3. Did I understand the dynamic at the time?
4. Did I develop new strategies for gathering support?
5. Do I tend to blame an individual for happenings that could only be caused by the collective movement of consciousness?

The Results of My Intention Being Different from What I Intended

I am your mother, and I know that you need friends. I suggest (intend) that you join the Boy Scouts. You refuse. I feel rejected and hurt. You come back with another idea. You want to join the wrestling team. (Your intention.) You don't care about making friends, but you would like to wrestle, and you see this as a great opportunity to put forward your idea. I am distraught. I don't like wrestling. I think it's dangerous. But that's what you want. Do I allow you to wrestle?

How do I practice allowance in this case? First, I take that breath, rather than react to your opposition. Then we talk. From there, many outcomes can emerge.

Perhaps I see that your heart is set on wrestling. Because my ultimate intention is for you to have friends, I accept your choice. I realize that my intending you to have friends allowed you to express your intention to wrestle, which may very well bring you into a new career choice or open the door to friends. I am intending the Boy Scouts; you are intending wrestling. Out of our interaction comes something neither of us may have expected.

On the other hand, I can refuse to let you join the wrestling team. I feel that as your mother, I don't have to allow you to co-create with me. Perhaps it's my controlling nature; perhaps I'm simply concerned about your wellbeing. Your response may be that you submit to joining the Boy

Scouts, or you may refuse and just sulk. In these cases, you will not feel like a co-creator, and I will not experience the outcome as a happy one either. If I am going to hold firm, I may get the result I wanted in terms of keeping you off the wrestling team, but I am not realizing my intention. I did not intend for you to be angry or resentful. Whether I like it or not, if I am to hold firm, I have to allow you to be angry with me.

Of course, I can always hope for a different outcome and work toward it. I still hold firm to my rejection of the wrestling team as an option, but we continue talking. As a result, you come to see my point about wrestling and you acknowledge your need for friends. Maybe you don't want to join the Boy Scouts, but you come up with another idea. I agree. We come to a meeting of the minds. We both feel like co-creators of this decision. More important, perhaps, we both feel good about our relationship. This is the result of a powerful joint intention, which is to maintain a good relationship. We have, therefore, co-created both the result and the relationship.

Which of these outcomes will occur? How much leverage do I have over you? How much leverage do you have over me? How well do we communicate and understand each other? How important is our relationship to us? How the universe works this out has a great deal to do with both of our intentions, our relationship to each other, and our characters and personalities.

Results are hard to predict. I may get you to join the Boy Scouts. Out of that decision, you may gain friends, or you may not. You may thank me for it later, or you may resent me forever. Or you may fight my intervention, join the wrestling team despite my objections, make lots of friends and convince me you're okay. Or you may break your neck. Now you feel ashamed and lose your confidence in your ability to make good choices. You feel shame and start smoking pot. Intention and allowance. I made a difference in your life, but not exactly as I had intended.

Let's look at some experiences we have had where our original intentions were not fulfilled.

1. Can I identify a situation where I intended something and the result was entirely something else?
2. When dealing with other people, do I tend to focus on the outcome or the relationship?
3. Do I tend to get stuck on one idea of the "right" outcome, or do I tend to be co-creative?

The Defeat of My Intention Seen as Positive

I want to be president of the school board. I have a lot of good ideas, and I want to share them. I work hard, campaign hard, and intend hard. I lose.

In the process, I unintentionally discover qualities in myself. I may see that I am more hardworking and dedicated than I had realized. I feel good about that.

Or I may see that I am more competitive and ego driven than I had admitted. I feel less good about that. Perhaps during the campaign, I saw myself attacking others. Perhaps my negative claims were just a little exaggerated. Perhaps I saw myself promising things I wasn't sure that I could or wanted to deliver. Perhaps I saw myself driving my body into the ground.

The campaign is over, and I get to reflect. By allowing myself to accept the defeat and to learn about myself, I might actually go through a whole metamorphosis. Perhaps I now see that winning would have hurt me because it would have supported aspects of me that I do not choose to energize! Perhaps I go through a period of introspection and give up politics. Or perhaps I go through a period of introspection and decide to come to the next election with a clearer intention of how I want to do the campaign, rather than a stronger intention of winning.

Following are some questions to help us see ourselves more clearly.

1. Have I ever felt defeated?
2. Did I learn useful things about myself?
3. Did I drop my original intention, or did I return to the fray with new attitudes?

Allowance as a Way of Seeing Myself on Deeper Levels and Staying Connected to Others

What happens when we're defeated, and we still think we're right? What happens when we feel passionate about this defeat? How do we not disconnect from the collective? How do we not fall back into the pain of separation? We do it through allowance. We breathe; we accept what is, without getting caught up in anger and separation. We look for another way.

When our intention is thwarted it's so easy to become angry and blaming. Here's one example. Let's go back to the Vietnam War. I was part of the movement that opposed the war for many years before the movement of history ended it. I felt angry toward my country and my government. That anger alienated me from everyone except others in the anti-war movement.

If I had been practicing allowance, I would have stopped screaming, and I would have started asking myself some questions. Was I feeling and behaving just like the people I opposed? Wasn't I, just like our government, trying to impose my will on others? Why was I doing that? Why was our country? What was motivating me, the American people, and all other parties? How could I begin to listen? How could I help others to understand my view? Was I willing to understand theirs? Was I more invested in my anger than my effectiveness? Was there a way to impact the collective? If so, what was it?

Instead of taking these actions, I separated totally from the people I opposed. My separation was not only poisonous to my soul; it also made me less effective. The more I felt outside the collective, the more strident I felt, and the more poorly I was able to communicate. The louder I scream, the less you can hear me.

Let's look at an example on a more individual level. Let's say I am married to you, a practicing alcoholic. I see you killing yourself and destroying your family. I beseech you to stop drinking, but to no avail. You continue. I end up feeling bitter and alone.

I emotionally separate from you. I tell myself that I am not you, not like you at all. I don't look for ways to relate to your behavior. I don't self-examine to see how I am also addicted. I don't acknowledge that the manner in which I'm trying to force you to stop drinking is as addictive as your drinking. I scream at you, rage at you, and show you contempt.

I am no longer practicing Oneness. Rather, I have separated from you. This makes me sick, because it causes me to lie about myself, about my own addictiveness, and it alienates me from the essential Oneness of all being. It also makes me less effective, because it causes me to talk at you, rather than with you.

Can I practice Becoming Co-Creative and use this as a moment for self-examination? I want to leave you. Am I motivated to leave, because that is for the highest good of all? Or am I driven to leave because I'm angry that you're out of my control? Is your drinking the real problem, or am I using it to avoid dealing with something going on in myself? Can I release you without anger and blame? Can I grow through this experience?

Think of an example where you feel angry about a goal being defeated. Now ask yourself:

1. If I have unsuccessfully fought for a cause, do I separate from those who I blame for the defeat?
2. How am I like the collective that defeated me?
3. If I feel thwarted by an individual's choices, how am I also like them?
4. What did I learn about myself in the process?
5. Can I practice Oneness in the face of my despair?
6. What does it take?

Allowance as a Way of Seeing the Gift

I write an article, and I think it's awesome. I show it to others, hoping for a resounding "yes." What I hear is a resounding "no." If I struggle against the universe, I will think everyone who has read the article is misguided. If I open myself to allowance, if I open my heart and mind, I may see the gift in the "no." What is the message? That the timing of the article is wrong? That the article has good points but is poorly presented? That my ideas are not well thought out? That my ideas are well thought out and well presented, but not presented in a way that can touch my audience? Have I separated from my audience in the writing? Have I created obstacles through my own attitudes and words? Have I missed something that I need to know?

Only by taking the breath of allowance, only by introspection and a willingness to hear the collective can I learn the message in the "no." I will never abandon what I think is right. But if I'm willing, the "no" of the universe might support me to reconsider how I'm approaching my material and my audience.

If I find a useful message in the "no," I will continue to work on my article. Through this allowance, the article is improved. I present it again. Perhaps now, I hear a "yes." Perhaps not. In either case, I have learned about myself, thought through my material on a deeper level, and produced something of greater value. I can feel better about what I have done.

The gift of allowance is that I don't fight the message of the universe; I learn from it. Let's take a moment to examine ourselves in this regard.

1. Do I tend to be resistant to criticism or opposition?
2. Do I capitulate, or do I go away mad?

3. Do I self-examine?
4. Have I learned to integrate the information and use it?

Allowance as a Way of Supporting Evolution

My political party has an agenda. We're all intending a certain outcome. We're sure we're right. The other guys have a different agenda. They're all intending a certain outcome. They're sure they're right. Other folks are involved and will be affected. Whether or not they are organized, they're all intending a certain outcome or many different outcomes, and each one thinks he or she is right.

Democracy is supposed to be a manifestation of Becoming Co-Creative, intention and allowance. The debate and give-and-take among all perspectives is meant to bring forward a better result. At first, we balk when our views are not completely adopted by others. But by practicing allowance, we begin to realize that we are not entirely right. We may be right in certain respects, but we've missed something, because, as we saw in Platform Two, we may actually be bringing forward only a piece of the puzzle.

If we are committed to the collective good, and if we are able to listen and communicate, we may actually come up with an alternative that none of us predicted. By allowing ourselves to be impacted by one another, we will be supporting the evolution of our collective and our ideas.

I wish this process always worked flawlessly for the highest good of all. In reality, some forces are so overpowering that many important voices are never heard, especially those who are weak or disorganized. But whether for the good or evil, whether or not we reach the highest level of which we are capable, none of us in politics is so powerful that we don't have to come together and co-create a reality that none of us may actually have intended! Like it or not, evolution has occurred!

Perhaps the universe has an intention, and it is only revealed through the clash of our own fragmented intentions! How have I participated in such experiences? Let's look at these questions.

1. Have I been engaged in causes, large or small?
2. Was I open to learn from others' viewpoints?
3. Was I willing to acknowledge that they might also be right?
4. Were we all able to come together and create something better?

Intention as Its Own Reward

Sometimes no matter what I do, I can't make a difference. Instead of beating myself up for my failed effort, I can feel good that I made any effort at all. Besides, we never know when our efforts may bear fruit much later. In regard to surrendering results, let's ask ourselves:

1. Do I see the value in my own efforts?
2. Do I judge myself by the quality of the results or by the quality of my effort?
3. Do I offer others the same support for their efforts?

Allowance as a Way of Clarifying Our Intention

Up to this point, we have been talking about our intentions as though they were perfectly clear to us. But we are not that simple. Much of what we intend is not even in our conscious awareness. What is our intention in any given situation? Is it what we consciously think, or is it what we unconsciously feel or believe?

Those who believe we create our own reality have often accurately pointed out that we may say and believe that we intend "x," while we are actually intending "y." We may fail to achieve a goal, because in fact we are unconsciously programmed to defeat ourselves. Or we may fail to achieve a goal, because we have a stronger unconscious motive to achieve an opposite goal.

It is true that we may be subtly sabotaging ourselves because of unconscious programming. On one level, for example, we may want to become healthy. On another level, we may not be ready to give up some real or imagined advantage of being ill.

Let's look at the example of relationships. Suppose, for example, I say I want a relationship, but I am terribly afraid. I may constantly pick unavailable women, or I may end relationships before they have a chance to work out. Or perhaps I want a relationship, but I'm afraid of letting go of my father, so I unconsciously pick men who will leave me. In these cases, our intention may be totally unconscious and not what we think at all! Or at the very least our intention may be partially unconscious, with the conflict unknown to us.

At times, then, the defeat of our conscious intention is really a reflection of the strength of our unconscious intention. Allowance in this case is the process of stopping, breathing and self-examining. In this case, our inability to achieve a certain goal can be used as an indicator that leads us to ask ourselves the question: Am I really in conflict with myself? The answer may be yes, and then I can start the process of healing. On the other hand, the answer may be no. Then allowance is the process of accepting the pain of reality. We may not have self-sabotaged at all.

Let's take a look at relationships, for example. Not every "failed" romance is a reflection of our unconscious intention to avoid relationships. Sometimes an ended romance is just the logical outcome of the interaction of two people. Here are some situations where that might occur. Sometimes a relationship has great value, but only within a limited period of time. The relationship may have helped me heal from the death of a spouse; or it may have helped me restore self-esteem; or it may have taught me that I have a long way to go in terms of my capacity to be loving or forgiving.

Sometimes a relationship needs to end because the partners need to become differentiated, and our differentiation is leading us to true incompatibility. Or perhaps we need to let go of a relationship that is not truly fulfilling, because there is a greater adventure ahead. Or perhaps a relationship needs to end because one of us is willing to become self-aware, while the other partner does not feel drawn to the path of growth and becomes a drain on our energy.

Through these examples of "failed" relationships, we see that sometimes a relationship ends because our intention is weak or self-contradictory. Yet sometimes it ends because we are continuing to evolve. And we can learn. Did we, for instance, self-sabotage when we chose this partner? Were we just lonely and afraid to look too closely at whether or not it was right for us? Did we compromise in the hopes the relationship would work out, and it didn't? Was it a good choice for the moment? Allowance stops the knee-jerk reaction of just fleeing or feeling bad because a relationship has ended. Allowance, instead, encourages self-awareness and inquiry.

If we see the same pattern occurring over and over in our relationships, we need to ask ourselves why. Is it because of unconscious programming or not? Do we pick unavailable men because of our unconscious intention to sabotage a relationship, or because most men have been socialized to be emotionally unavailable and, therefore, truly available men are not easy to find? Are we choosing men who need rescuing, because we're trying to rescue our dads, whom we couldn't rescue when we were children? Or are we finding men who need rescuing, because so many of us feel a need to be rescued? Are we choosing short-term relationships because we're afraid of commitment? Or are we moving quickly through relationships because we are working out our relationship issues, and being with many partners supports us in learning the lessons we need?

Whether we are self-sabotaging or not, whether we are being dominated by inner conflicts and programs or not, we need to be in allowance. Regardless of the degree that we are being impacted by unconscious programming, we are always in the process of life's learning. If we can be in allowance of our own confusions and conflicts, we can free ourselves from the fear of our judgments. Freed from the fear of our own judgments, we can look more deeply into ourselves and learn. Allowance promotes consciousness, and consciousness of our inner conflicts can help us move much more expeditiously through our own learning process.

If we can examine the events that occur in our lives and if we are open-minded, we can use seeming defeats to learn about our own intentions. Was our intention defeated because of an unconscious fear or block? Or did we need to have this experience for another reason?

Let's look briefly at another common example. Earlier in this section, we mentioned health. Let's take a little deeper look at this question. I may be ill and continue to try different remedies. Nothing works. Is this the result of unconscious programming or not? It is easy and fashionable to blame someone for their own illness. Sometimes there is blame. The person is drinking or self-abusing in some way. The person doesn't make any effort to get well. The person has an unconscious need to be sick.

But, again, the existence of a pattern of illness does not necessarily prove the existence of an unconscious self-sabotage. Perhaps the person is drinking contaminated water and doesn't know it. Perhaps the person has been impacted by the release of radiation into the atmosphere. Perhaps the person was treated by damaging drug therapy in the past. Perhaps the person was born physically weak. Perhaps the person's illness will be treated successfully in 100 years, but the cure is not now available.

Some people will tell you that they have cured themselves and you should be able to, also. Is it because they had a stronger intention? Perhaps. But perhaps they have a fundamentally stronger constitution and immune system. Do you know? Do they?

As I mentioned in Platform Two, whenever we face other people's pain, there is a natural tendency to blame them. Why? Because if we can make it their fault, then we can insure ourselves against the pain by telling ourselves that we could do something different.

We have the same difficulty accepting our powerlessness over our own pain. Only scrupulous self-honesty will help us continually come back to the clarification of our true intentions: Am I contributing to my difficulty? Am I truly powerless? What can I do to improve, if not eliminate, the problem? Is my intention clear, but the solution out of reach?

To summarize: If we keep having the same experience over and over, we can see that there is some pattern being repeated here. But we can't assume why. If we stay out of judgment, we can look at that reality and ask ourselves what we are learning about ourselves and our subconscious patterns through this experience. Let's ask ourselves some questions now.

1. When things don't work out as I intended, do I always assume that I am wrong in some way or self-sabotaging? Or do I tend to blame something outside myself?
2. When I look at patterns that keep repeating in my life, do I ask myself if there is an unconscious intention underneath? Do I assume yes or no?
3. What problems do I tend to experience over and over? Relationships, health, jobs, money?
4. Am I willing to look realistically at all the factors and see which I might be contributing to?
5. Am I willing to look realistically at all the factors and accept that there may be some beyond my control?
6. Am I willing to acknowledge that I don't always know?

Practicing Intention and Allowance within Ourselves

Suppose we do find unconscious intentions dominating our behavior? Do we support ourselves or beat ourselves up?

Just as we have to intend and allow with the rest of the universe, we need to practice intention and allowance with ourselves. I may intend to make a change within myself, but how successful I am is determined by the myriad of conflicting intentions that are contained within me. Just as I am only one factor in the universe of forces that impact the outcome of my intentions, my conscious intention is only one factor in the universe of internal forces that impact me. The outcome will be determined again by the relative strength of all these intentions and how they intersect with one another.

Remember the car analogy. Cars of equal weight will stop one another if they collide. Cars that intersect at an angle will probably change each other's course. A car that rear-ends another sends that car careening forward with more speed than intended. If these cars represent different energies, forces, and intentions within me, the outcome will depend on their relative strength and direction. Am I totally conflicted with myself? Or am I just sideswiping myself?

Here's an example. I may absolutely intend to stop over-eating, only to find that potato chip in my hand five minutes later. Many forces in my unconscious have impacted that action. If I am practicing allowance, I will attempt to understand myself, rather than to beat myself up. I will attempt to identify the pains and fears under my behavior. I will acknowledge the complexity of my intentions. I will try to identify them and try to deal with them. And finally, I will try to differentiate from my addictiveness by getting the support to increase the relative power of my conscious intention. Let's look at some of our own ways of dealing with our own mixed intentions.

1. Do I acknowledge that my intentions can be mixed?
2. Do I try to understand myself and my many intentions?
3. Do I try to deal with them in a way that is self-compassionate?
4. Can I allow that I will occasionally slip?
5. Do I go into self-hatred and thereby sabotage any movement toward improvement?
6. Do I give up?
7. Do I gently bring myself back to my conscious intention?
8. Do I look for new ways to support myself?
9. Do I move toward the collective that supports me to change in positive ways?

Co-Creation with Forces other than Human

We have all experienced nonhuman forces that impact us as well. The farmer watches the rain, the forest service watches the lightening, the fisherman watches the size of the catch, the car skids over the cliff on the ice, the auto worker's arm gets caught in a press, the coyotes devour my cat, the asteroid threatens the earth, computers crash, and we all stand helpless as epidemics and economic instability rage over our world.

How helpless we all feel in the face of nonhuman forces. With humans, at least, we believe we can have some impact. With nonhuman forces, we have little.

Yet the principle of intention and allowance doesn't change. In this context you could say that everything in the universe has intention. The car that rolls over the cliff is intending to go straight while we intended it to take the curve; the clouds are intending to dump rain; the germs are intending to flourish; the asteroid is intending to continue along its path; and death is intending to consume the life of its prey.

Our intentions will clash and/or intersect with all of these. The results are often painful. But just as with other experiences, we need to practice allowance. We breathe, we acknowledge the power of the forces we face, we do what we can, and we adjust to the outcome. Having allowed the unwanted experience, we intend again. Here are some of our intentions: We try to design better tires or machine presses; we try to better predict weather; we try to understand the economy better; and we try to improve our medical care to negotiate with death. These are reasonable responses, and each has value, as long as we don't expect that our intention will now dominate. We must always remember intention and allowance.

If we don't accept intention and allowance, the tragedy is two-fold: first, the acute tragedy of our powerlessness to stop a painful event; second, the chronic tragedy of our crushed spirits and bitter souls.

If we surrender in resignation to the forces of the universe, we die inside. If we fight to impose our will, we crush ourselves. If we intend, then allow, then intend again, we find our direction through the pain.

The One Intention Whose Realization I Can Guarantee

Anything I do in life—any victory or defeat—can be a learning experience. Perhaps, then, the only intention whose realization I can guarantee is that I will learn.

I may not be able to control what I learn—because that depends on the experiences the universe throws at me and my capacity to integrate the lessons—but I can guarantee that I will learn something! If I am not careful, I may learn some destructive lessons, such as:

- I tried and failed, so I should give up.
- I worked hard to win over others and was defeated, so I conclude that everyone rejects me.
- I tried but didn't get sufficient support. That must mean that everyone else is stupid, selfish, or just on the wrong path.
- I tried and failed, so I must be a failure.

On the other hand I may learn some important, positive lessons, such as:

- I am a part of the universe of intentions, and what happens to me and on the planet does not revolve around me, my thoughts, and my intentions.
- The universe can give me direction, if I'm willing to listen.
- While I cannot control the outcome, I can lend my energy to co-creating something I want, and I can feel good about myself in the process.

Before concluding the discussion of Platform Three, let's ask ourselves a few more questions to help us clarify our own tendencies.

1. As I have gone through these different examples of intention and allowance, what have I learned about myself?
2. Am I more likely to overdo intention or allowance?
3. How do I tend to react when my intention is thwarted?
4. Where have I practiced this platform today?
5. Am I willing to learn from the universe's response, even when it's painful?

A FEW FINAL THOUGHTS ON INTENTION & ALLOWANCE

Learning to Become Co-Creative requires an incredible degree of humility and self-discipline. To keep expressing our intentions, to keep working toward goals and at the same time, to keep learning from the universe requires us to understand and accept our connection to the ALL. It requires the humility of being teachable. And it challenges us daily to remember that those who thwart us are "us" as well, because we are an aspect of the collective that defeated "us."

Practicing Becoming Co-Creative brings many gifts. It allows us to look forward to defeats almost as much as victories, because of the lessons we may learn. It allows us to hold on to our faith in the face of adversity. Faith in what? Faith that I may not create my life exactly as I intend, but that with a mature adaptation to life's curveballs, I can be a student of life until the day I die. I can learn. I can grow. I can evolve.

Practicing Becoming Co-Creative brings us other benefits, as well. It brings us the realization that failure to realize our intention is not a statement of our weakness; it is part of the process of living. It relieves us of the need to prove our power or our rightness, because we aren't that powerful, and we're certainly not "right." It releases our energy, because we're not constantly butting up against the universe in a futile effort to get our way. It relieves us of the shame of not getting our way and relieves us of the fear of failure, and relieved of that burden, we experience less pain when our hearts' desires are thwarted.

Sometimes I see the wisdom of the collective, the wisdom of the universe, and I feel at peace about the process of intention and allowance. I realize that by bringing my own views and intentions into play, we as a collective are able to create a fuller and more productive movement of energy. In those moments, I'm glad that I am not the emperor of the universe.

Sometimes I do not see the wisdom of the collective, the wisdom of the universe. I believe we are being self-destructive, and I see needless suffering. In those cases, I feel grief.

Whichever I feel, however, I know that intention and allowance are how I relate to the universe. I can't change it, and I'd better make the best of it!

Join me in practicing the process of Becoming Co-Creative. If we all were consciously dancing the dance of intention and allowance, there would be more harmony among us all. There would be less ego-butting and less blame. If many were consciously dancing the dance of intention and allowance, it would be easier for any one of us to practice it, because, as we have learned in Becoming Differentiated, as more of us practice any platform, there is more energy supporting the practice of it, and the more energy that supports the practice of a platform, the easier it is for any one of us to do the same.

Yes, we impact our lives and our universe, but not exactly as we intend. We live in a wildly complex universe. Every animal, vegetable and mineral, every human, every thought and idea, every group, nation and philosophy adds to the mix of what will occur.

So what about our fear and pain? Would Becoming Co-Creative end their sway? No. We earlier discussed how the responses of submission and domination create needless pain for us. But we should also acknowledge that allowance can be painful as well. In the moment we are faced with the husband who won't get sober, the child we can't save, the loneliness of not being invited to the dance, the loss of our farm, we feel pain. The pain of that loss makes it difficult for us to move into allowance.

But now we have realized that the allowance of pain is an important part of our wellbeing. No matter what occurs, we take a breath and look at what there is to do or learn. We are ready to reconsider, rethink and revamp. We have avoided needless pain, and now we are ready to grow.

Domination and submission are habits. Practicing intention and allowance can become a habit, too.

How Do We Become More Consciously Co-Creative?

Now that we have described the way the universe co-creates, I would like to add a few comments on how we become more conscious co-creators with the universe, how we become more intentional about being co-creative.

1. Embrace the experience of intention and allowance.
2. Confront our ego's need for credit and reward.
3. Acknowledge that life's problems are greater than our limited consciousness.
4. Realize the value of what others bring.
5. Join with others to accomplish that which we cannot achieve ourselves.

Announcing My Intention to Become Co-Creative

I want you. I need you. I cannot become myself without you, without the challenges you bring, without the resources you offer, without the wisdom you embody. Even this book is a co-creation. As I mentioned much earlier in this book, I started writing Living with Reality in 2002, but it has taken me years to complete it. The depth of understanding that it offers comes from my working with people to comprehend and transform human behavior, and the tools that are contained come out of the workshops where The Source offered me techniques to help people understand and utilize these simple ideas. Without needing to explain these concepts to others, I would not have gained the understanding myself.

Furthermore, as I rewrite this book in 2011, I realize that what I can say has changed, because the collective has moved forward since 2002. What others can hear influences what can be said, and all the work you and I have done on ourselves, and all the work accomplished through the efforts of other counselors, teachers, writers and communicators, all this collective work has co-created a different world through which I discover greater wisdom and find greater expression, and I hope the same is happening for you.

Finally, I would like to acknowledge that I have been influenced by the ideas and thoughts of millions of people I have never met and never heard, because we are one. I am being influenced and fed by the beautiful music that is inspiring me right now. And I am and continue to be a channel of the consciousness that is moment by moment still evolving in the universe.

There was a time when I believed that I was important and hoped that I could make a contribution to our world. Today I realize that "I" am really a co-creation of all the forces that have come together, intentionally and unintentionally, to co-create "me," and that includes my own gifts, will and nature, and so much more.

Let us all take a moment to reach up to the universe that co-creates not only our lives and our experiences, but also our very beings. And let us give thanks.

PLATFORM FOUR

Becoming Mutually Supportive
Living Oneness

WHAT IS MUTUAL SUPPORT?

Mutual support is the process of relying upon higher consciousness to guide our actions for the highest good of all, including us. It is the key to our own personal wellbeing, as well as a living experience of Oneness and community. As such, it creates in us feelings of real safety and relaxation and is the essential ingredient in the co-creation of a new society.

We make an infinite number of choices every day, choices as to what to eat and drink, choices about our attitudes and behaviors at home and at work, choices about our health and our relationships. How do we typically make these choices?

Most frequently, we make them unconsciously. Even when we believe that we are choosing, we are more often than not being driven by our fears or programming, as we will understand even more clearly when we discuss Platform Five: Becoming Self-Aware and Platform Six: Becoming Integrated. In addition, in our relationships with one another, we are often driven by ego to protect ourselves at whatever cost.

Becoming Mutually Supportive is a radical departure from unconscious and ego-based decision-making. We look at every choice we make and understand it in the context of the highest good of all, which must include ourselves. Becoming Mutually Supportive can be practiced by ourselves or in a group, but it always includes the orientation of higher consciousness, which supports us to be neutral, aware and guided by an intelligence that transcends our limited perspective. When we practice mutual support as a community, everyone in it feels safe, because we all know that everyone else is looking after our highest good, as well as theirs. Wow!

How Do We Typically View Support?

What could be simpler? I help you. You help me. Everybody helps everybody, and everyone is better off. Is that Mutual Support? No.

First of all, let's address the first question: What is support? I want to get across the room, but I don't have the use of my legs. A wheelchair enables me to move, despite my disability. That's support. I'm an athlete and a great runner. I'm trying to run the fastest mile. An experienced coach helps train me, so that I can dash to the finish line. That's support. I'm on my last journey, the one toward death. A loved one sits at my side and helps me walk into the light. That's support. I am living life in my habitual way. Someone challenges me and in the process reveals my weakness. I am able to recognize that weakness and overcome it. That's support.

So let's look at one way of defining support. Support is whatever enables me to accomplish my goal. Support enables me to do what I cannot do alone, without help. In other words, support is what enables me to go beyond my own limitations to achieve something.

Here are some questions to ask ourselves about support:

1. How have I been supported in my life?
2. What limitations did that support help me to transcend?
3. Did I achieve my goal?

Well that part is simple. Or is it? Let's look at an example that demonstrates how complex it may be to determine what is support. Suppose I want to drink myself to death, but I'm too ill to go to the liquor store. You bring me a bottle. Is that support? That is the question.

Let's review the above definition of support: ***Support is whatever enables me to accomplish my goal. Support enables me to do what I cannot do alone, without help. In other words, support is what enables me to go beyond my own limitations to achieve something.***

By this definition, your bringing me the bottle of alcohol is support. First, it will enable me to kill myself, which is my goal. In addition, it is enabling me to go beyond my own limitations, in this case, the limitation being that I'm too ill from drinking to get the drink that will kill me. So, sure, getting me a bottle of liquor is support. It is enabling me to accomplish my goal.

But wait a minute. Is this support? My wife might disagree. She might say that true support would be to deny me a drink and drag me to a meeting of Alcoholics Anonymous. She says I can be helped to get sober. Even though I am not articulating that goal, she claims that denying me the drink is helping prolong my life and supporting me, because once I come to my senses, I will embrace my higher goal, which is my life and my recovery.

But is that a valid point? My goal is to drink myself to death. That being the case, bringing me the bottle is the only valid support. Her goal is to have a husband and a father for the kids. So bringing me to the A.A. meeting is supporting her, not me. Each one of us is asking for support for ourselves. People with conflicting goals want conflicting support. That's still pretty simple.

But, wait a minute, she says. It's still not that simple. I say I want to drink myself to death, but do I? She doesn't think so. She thinks I'm depressed and discouraged at the moment, and it's just a passing feeling that I want to kill myself with drink. She thinks I really want to get well, but I am too impaired at the moment to know what I want. If this is the case, bringing me the bottle would not support me. What would support me would be helping me overcome my limitations of faith and imagination, which could support me to achieve my true goal of wellness.

And I could go deeper. Is it all of me or a fragment of me that wants to die? Am I unconsciously begging for help? Or am I in so much inner hell that death is the only answer? How can people make that decision for me?

Oh yes, living with reality. How complex it is. How do I know what truly will support you, what truly will support me? It's tricky, isn't it?

So before we move on, let's consider a few questions.

1. Who have I tried to support in my life?
2. What goals of theirs was I supporting?
3. How did I try to support them?
4. Did they agree with my view of what would support them?
5. What was the outcome?
6. How have people tried to support me in my life?
7. Have I been in agreement, or did I feel they were pursuing an agenda?
8. Which aspects of me were they supporting?
9. How did I react?
10. What was the outcome?
11. Who has the right and ability to decide what my goals should be?
12. Who can determine what support I need to achieve which goals?
13. Can the fulfillment of a goal actually block the fulfillment of my potential?

Now that we see the ambiguity of support, we need to redefine what support means, and that's just what we are going to do as we get into Platform Four: Becoming Mutually Supportive.

Definition of Mutual Support

Mutual support is a culture of wholeness, whereby the individual supports the highest good of the whole and the whole supports the highest good of the individual. Through supporting the whole, our own needs are met. We acknowledge that we are one and cannot be well at one another's expense, and we also acknowledge that we need not sacrifice, because the good of the whole always includes ourselves. We determine the highest good of all by transcending our ego-based fears and connecting to our higher consciousness, individually and collectively.

What do I mean by a culture of wholeness? How is this approach different from our usual vision of support?

Individuals Helping Individuals versus Mutual Support

Mutual support is not defined as individuals supporting one another, which is essentially doing favors or bartering help. Mutual support is individuals supporting the whole, which supports the individual. Mutual support is based on Oneness, which is covered in Platform One. I support you, because we are all part of the same whole, the same collective, and so by supporting you, I am supporting the collective that supports me. I am, essentially, supporting myself.

Helping one another can be very important for people's survival, but it is not mutual support. When we practice mutual support, we may actually act in the same way as we do when we are simply helping one another, but we choose those actions from a different consciousness, from the consciousness of Oneness.

Here's an example of doing a favor. Harry needs help mowing the lawn, so I get out there and give him a hand. I like Harry. I know he has a bad back. I want to do Harry a favor, and it makes me feel good about myself.

All of these actions are good and supportive. I may be helping Harry because I'm a good guy, or I may be helping Harry because I hope someday when I'm in trouble Harry may help me. But regardless of why I help Harry, I have not broken out of the "I" universe. It is the "I," me, helping the "I," Harry. Helping Harry is a favor I am doing for him, and it creates in Harry a feeling of "owing" something to me.

What if I were practicing mutual support? Then I would help Harry because he and I are part of the collective neighborhood, and I know that my fate is tied up with that of my neighbors. I would be keeping up property values, or creating an environment that I enjoy. With the consciousness of mutual support, I am not doing a favor for Harry. He owes me nothing. I am acting on behalf of all of us, including me, and I hope that Harry will support the whole in his own way.

We've looked at favors. Next let's look at bartering needs. I will type your paper, if you fix my plumbing. I love you, if you love me back. Bartering needs has been extremely important for our survival. If we didn't barter needs, we would all be left to our own devices and our own limitations of time, energy, and talents. But again, we are not leaving the "I" universe. The "I" me is helping you, because the "I" you is helping me.

When I barter, I expect something of equal value in return from you. When I don't receive it, I feel cheated. In a universe of mutual support, I would type your paper to support the whole, and I would know that someone else in the universe would fix my plumbing when I needed it. Bartering creates expectations and stress among people. Mutual support does not. Sounds great, doesn't it? But it requires a collective practice. If we don't all practice mutual support, I will become depleted, because the whole is not supporting me. If the universe doesn't take care of my plumbing, there is no mutual support.

Is mutual support possible? Yes. Sometimes mutual support happens "accidentally." For example, I may type my brother's term paper, and my sister might fix my plumbing. I may receive love from my father and thus have love to give to my little sister. If everyone in the system contributes what he or she can, mutual support exists. Yet Becoming Mutually Supportive means that we are bringing this process to a higher level. When we consciously choose to practice mutual support within the context of world that consciously practices mutual support, we all gain clarity of purpose, quit keeping count of what we do for one another and experience consistent feelings of safety and wellbeing.

So let's summarize: Doing favors and bartering needs are both based on the consciousness of separation. Mutual support, on the other hand, is based on Oneness. It is the process of each one of us supporting the whole, which in turn supports each one of us.

Before we go on to further differentiate mutual support from other states of consciousness, let's look at a few questions.

1. Do I tend to do favors for other people?
2. How does that make me feel about myself and them?
3. Do I think of my actions as being about supporting the whole?
4. What do I barter? What do I do for my emotional partner or spouse, children, friends, bosses and community, and what do I expect in return?
5. How does that impact our relationship?
6. What has been the result?

We've just differentiated between individuals helping individuals and the practice of mutual support, and we've seen that the difference refers to our consciousness. Another way of highlighting the consciousness around mutual support is to see the difference between mutual support and interdependence. And that's what we'll do next.

What Is Interdependence?

When I go to the supermarket, I buy an apple. I pay you, the grocer, for having brought the apple to me. You are meeting my need for the apple, and I'm meeting your need for money. This is interdependence. We both need and depend on each other. We don't take these actions by conscious choice; we do them out of need, and we do them unconsciously.

If we look at this same example at a deeper level, we, of course, see that the interdependence involved in this exchange is much broader than the grocer and me. The grocer buys the apples from a distributor in Washington. The apple was shipped in a truck made in Detroit. The truck is made of steel from Ohio and uses oil from Saudi Arabia. The oil is taken from the ground through machinery built by people who wear clothes sewn in Bangladesh. And so on and so on. When I buy the apple that meets my needs, I am sending financial resources to all these people, and I am being supported by their labor. The web is wide and international.

Our interdependence is real and profound. We may not think about it, but when the thread is broken or when the impact is negative, we suddenly become very aware. If there is a virus in Hong Kong, what is it to me? Maybe life or death. If the medical establishment in Hong Kong cannot contain the virus, many Chinese will be impacted. A stranger from Hong Kong can bring the virus with her on an airplane, the man next to her can become a carrier, and that man can be standing next to me in that same supermarket line where I bought the apple. I realize that I am dependent on the medical profession of Hong Kong to protect me from what could be a deadly disease. Another example of the impact of our interdependence: If there is a strike of dockworkers who would normally deliver my favorite apples, I may simply not get those apples, or I may have to pay an inflated price.

In a family, interdependence is also profound. If Mom doesn't go to work, there may be a tremendous drop in our income, which means I can't afford the gym shoes or maybe even the apples. If Dad becomes ill, Mom may have to work outside the home and suddenly my life is dramatically altered, as I find myself cared for by strangers, or I may be locked in the house after school until my older brother gets home.

And speaking about older brothers, if my older brother makes Dad mad, he may be in a dark mood all day, or if I become ill, precious family resources will have to be siphoned to me, and my brother will lose his chance to take the special lessons he wants or to be driven to basketball practice by my now overstressed mother. And if Mom feels neglected by Dad, she may start drinking, and whatever happened to my mom, my best friend?

Now if Grandma, who has been taking care of us, needs us to take care of her . . . Well, we could go on and on. The family is a constantly fluctuating web of interdependence, and so is the world. That makes us terribly vulnerable to one another, and there is nothing we can do about it.

Some of us claim that we are independent. Nothing could be further from the truth.

Interdependence Is Unavoidable

To some degree we can choose on whom we rely, but our ability to choose is very limited. Let's take the example of a woman who doesn't want to be dependent on men. She may choose not to depend on a husband, but she may very well end up hiring a plumber, who may be a man! Even if she does the plumbing herself, our independent woman is relying on the folks at the hardware store and all the folks they rely on, many of whom are men.

I might prefer to rely on a plumber than a husband. I may prefer to rely on a woman plumber than a male plumber. But that woman plumber exists within the web of interdependence as well. She may be driving a car manufactured by great number of male workers. In addition to which, the president of the United States may be a man and may decide to launch a war that affects the price of the steel and aluminum that go into the plumber's tools.

As long as the universe is populated by men, I will always be interdependent with men; unless I'm on a deserted island, I will be interdependent with other human beings. Even being on a deserted island does not end my interdependence. I'm probably using tools and clothing created by others in the past. I continue to be dependent on the plants, animals, and fish, not to speak of the weather, which is being impacted by global warming, which is impacted by other humans many hundreds or thousands of miles away!

So is this a problem? Most definitely. Because where there is interdependence, there is danger. If I am dependent upon you for validation and love, you have power over me and vice versa. If I am dependent on the refuse company to pick up the neighborhood garbage, that company has the power to create disease as well as discomfort. And if I am dependent on a handyman to fix a broken stairway, I may be stranded.

Each being on whom we depend has flashpoints of vulnerability in their capacity to do what we wish and expect. My lover may be in a bad mood or full of self-hatred and, therefore, incapable of giving me validation and love. The garbage company may be stingy with its workers and cause a strike. My handyman may be drunk or too busy to come.

I hate my vulnerability to you, but I am stuck with it. I want my lover to be perpetually emotionally available. I want my garbage collection company to be the cheapest in the area. And by the way, while I want them to be the cheapest, at the same time, I don't want them to have labor problems due to their workers being underpaid (amazing, aren't we?). I want my handyman to be sober and reliable, which could, of course, lead him to be busy, but, of course, not too busy for me!

I want to control my interdependence, but can I? One way I try to control interdependence is to control those on whom I am interdependent, and one way to do that is through their dependence on me! If my lover is not forthcoming with love and validation, I can punish him by withdrawing my own love and validation. He will then hopefully realize that he needs me so much that he has to overcome his own feelings and needs and focus on mine! I can threaten the garbage company to replace it with a competitor. I can tip my handyman or try to make him feel a personal bond with me, so that he will go out of his way to meet my needs before anyone else's.

I must get my own needs met. That's the perspective of the ego. And, if I can, I will manipulate, threaten, cajole, anything to get my needs met *first*. I don't habitually consider the needs of the persons I'm dependent on or the needs of others who might be dependent on them. I am more concerned about my husband's ability to take care of my needs than I am about whether or not his caring for me will cause him to overburden his secretary. I am typically more concerned that the handyman fixes my plumbing than the neighbor's. I don't habitually check first to see if those on whom I am dependent have the emotional or physical capacity to meet my needs. I grab first and check later. And, of course, they do the same to me.

Sometimes, in a moment of enlightened self-interest, I will recall that others cannot meet my needs unless their own needs are met. So I will give my nanny a raise, or compliment my wife, or give my employees a decent health care package. Sometimes consciously and often unconsciously, I recognize that in an interdependent world, all must be cared for on some level. I may even love the people on whom I am interdependent and truly care about them and their suffering.

But as long as I live in the "I" universe, I will be on the hunt for ways of taking care of myself, and I will only secondarily at best be concerned for the needs of others. And generally speaking, others are approaching me in the same way. If the people who make my shoes go on strike, the furor might bring to my attention that they are earning 20 cents an hour. Suddenly shocked, I may demand that they be given raises. But until they go on strike, I rarely question how I was able to get those great shoes at such a cheap price, and then I complain when the prices go up.

This is interdependence. It's the reality of the way we live. It's all of us "I's" trying to live together. But it's not mutual support.

Next we will discuss mutual support and how it differs from interdependence, but before we do, let's stop and ask ourselves a few questions:

1. Name a few people or groups where I personally feel my interdependence.
2. How does that interdependence make me feel?
3. How do I try to control those relationships?
4. Can I think of examples of me thinking of my needs first?
5. Who does the same to me?
6. What is the impact of these behaviors on myself and others?
7. Can I imagine us being more supportive to one another?

Mutual Support versus Interdependence

Earlier in this platform, we discussed the difference between individuals helping one another and mutual support. We saw that it was a difference of consciousness. In this section, we are going to talk about the difference between interdependence and mutual support, and we will see that it is a difference of consciousness, as well.

We have acknowledged that interdependence is a reality, whether we are conscious of it or not. It is an objective fact. But it is not mutual support, which is an attitude, an intention, an action that begins with Oneness consciousness.

Let's go back to our example of the apple. We've already discussed the myriad of people who have come together to provide me with that apple. That's an objective fact. That is interdependence. How could I shift my interdependence into the consciousness of mutual support?

Here's interdependence: The apple appears on the supermarket shelf, and I am not responsible in any way for the people who got it there. I am interdependent with them, but not focused on supporting them. I am thinking only of myself—of how I can get the cheapest price. I will be uninterested in the living conditions of the worker in Bangladesh that made the pants of the person who built the machinery that was used to extract the oil that ran the truck that delivered the apple from Washington.

Here's mutual support: I live in a culture of wholeness. I realize our Oneness, and I wish to practice mutual support. I recognize that I need to be concerned about the living conditions of the worker in Bangladesh or any other Third World nation. Why?

First, of course, because we are one on a spiritual plane, and your pain is my pain, as we have already discussed. Second, because our world is in fact one. Your poverty causes diseases that will reach my shore. Your poverty causes you to be willing to destroy your forests, which destroys the quality of my air. Your poverty causes you to seek to immigrate to my country, where you may compete for my job. Your poverty causes you to be angry and to feel exploited and may cause you to support terrorists who may threaten my safe little haven. And, finally, your poverty makes you a lousy market for our goods and services, which means less money in our society, which means less money for people to come to me as an intuitive counselor.

Let's look at an example closer to home. My wife and I share our home with live-in help to take care of our children. We are interdependent, because the nanny takes care of the kids, which allows us to work and make the money that keeps the family going. My wife and I may unconsciously push the nanny to the brink, hoping she'll do as much as possible, so that we can get time for ourselves or so we can work outside the home as much as possible. If our nanny does not have medical care, a social life, love, and appreciation, she may sicken or at the very least be secretly resentful of the kids. But even though I'm aware of our interdependence, I won't be worrying about our nanny's state of being until and unless she starts to break down, in which case I may try to fix or replace her, or if I have a tendency toward guilt, I may compensate her with a higher wage.

If I am in the universe of mutual support, on the other hand, I will realize from the start that we are a functioning whole and that we must all be well and happy for any of us to be well and happy. I will support the nanny to find her limits, connect to her own needs, and get them met, even though that might mean more strain on my wife and me. In the long run, I realize that we will all be better off if the nanny is thriving. In fact, if she meets some great guy, I encourage her to move on with her life, knowing that we can't be happy at her expense and trusting that the universe will provide another solution.

Once I enter the universe of mutual support, I realize that if I do not help co-create a world where Bangladeshi workers get good pay, if I don't support my employees to get their needs met, too, if I do not support the life of other species, if I do not help co-create a world that is healthy, wealthy, and wise, I am sowing the seeds of my destruction. The growth of anti-Americanism and terrorism attest to this reality. The destruction of the land and the seas attest to this reality. The increasing addictiveness and despair at home attest to this reality.

We are reaping the harvest of separation and disinterest in the collective needs of our planet and ourselves. Mutual support is a conscious choice that will bring us a harvest of goodwill and a better-functioning world.

Let's take a moment to ask ourselves some questions about our consciousness regarding mutual support.

1. Can I see my interdependence on others?
2. Is my instinct to grab more for me?
3. Do I see my impact on others who are interdependent with me?

4. Do I feel that I want to support others?
5. Do I think in terms of supporting the whole?
6. Do others in my universe share the same view?
7. Do I feel supported by them?

Our "Good" vs. the Highest Good

Now that we understand the differences between mutual support and relationships, such as bartering and interdependence, there's one more distinction we need to make in order to embark on Becoming Mutually Supportive, and that is the concept of the highest good of all.

The highest good is that which supports our evolution. It is not necessarily that which is comfortable, nor is it that which puffs up our ego. It may be challenging, it may be difficult, it may even be something we fear or loathe. But if it supports us to evolve, it is for our highest good.

Let's look at an example from the beginning of this chapter. We had the severely ill alcoholic asking someone to bring him a bottle of liquor, because he was too weak to go himself, and we asked what represented support in this case. To the alcoholic, the answer is clear. He's thirsting for a drink, or, worse, he's going through alcohol withdrawal and his body is in trauma. To his alcoholically impaired mind, support would look like a friend bringing him a bottle of scotch.

But would it be for the highest good of all? The alcoholic's highest good would be served by getting sober, because sobriety would support his evolution as a human being, as well as the highest good of his family, who need him to become a responsible participant. Perhaps getting him a drink in the short term would be supportive, if it could stop him from shaking long enough to get to a meeting of Alcoholics Anonymous or to reduce his symptoms while on the way to the hospital. His short-term good is to get drunk; his highest good, and the highest good of all, is for him to get sober.

Our highest good is that which supports us to grow past our limitations, and the highest good of all supports the collective to do the same. Let's touch on a few examples. What about a child who wants her parents to fight her battles for her? Does it support her evolution and the wellbeing of the whole family for Mom to respond to her daughter's pleas? Wouldn't Mom's stepping in reinforce her daughter's insecurities about her own capacities? Wouldn't it feed Mom's ego need to be needed? Wouldn't it be for the highest good of all for Mom to confront her own urge to merge, and instead teach the child how to fight for herself?

What about a woman who is intimidated by confrontation and who, therefore, believes that a man who never argues is just what she needs? Is it? Perhaps the woman's highest good would be better served if her husband stood up to her, which would help her overcome her fear of confrontation? Maybe he could encourage her to go into therapy, so she could stop being run by fear and the need to control him. Wouldn't it also be for his highest good to stop pandering to his wife's fear and become a differentiated being, who can express himself?

Let's look at some other examples of making choices based on the highest good. Very early in our book, we talked about there being one sweater and two people. What do we do? If I am extremely self-centered, it might be for my highest good to give you the sweater and be cold myself, because I need to confront my insistence that the world serve me. If I am extremely self-effacing, on the other hand, and have a tendency to give up my needs in order to be loved, it might be for my highest good to ask for the sweater for myself, as long as I either have a greater need for physical warmth than you or if our needs are equal.

A Word on the Highest Good of All

I will discuss this concept further in the chapter, but I'd like to say a few words about it here. We are one. If any part of us is damaged, we are all damaged. We may have to cut off our foot to save our body, but our entire being suffers the loss.

The same is true of our world. Whether we are discussing the highest good of a person, a couple, a group, people we don't know or the world, the principle is the same. We are one and we none of us thrive if the whole is not thriving, but our fears and egos block us from this simple reality.

So just as we need to make decisions based on an awareness of our higher needs, the highest good of all requires us to make decisions based on the higher needs of the whole. Let's not be daunted by this thought. As we proceed in this book, we will learn how to determine what is for the highest good of all, but for now, let's recognize that our highest good is often not the most comfortable choice and trust that in the Oneness, we are all served.

To summarize this section: If we are to practice mutual support, we must commit to do that which is for the highest good of all, even though it might be challenging. So to fulfill this commitment, we are going to have to confront our fears and self-protectiveness and become aware of the needs of others.

Let's examine some of our feelings around this commitment.

1. What kinds of outcomes do I feel attached to?
2. Am I willing to consider that they are not for my highest good?
3. Am I afraid to know what is for the highest good of all?
4. Do I believe that it won't include me?

While practicing mutual support may be an obvious necessity, it doesn't seem to come naturally. It is not a habit. Rather, it seems more natural to practice self-interest, and it's more natural to give into what our egos prescribe. That's because working from the consciousness of short-term self-interest is a habit based on fear, conditioning and ego. I will be discussing this fear, conditioning and ego later in this chapter, but before I do, let's take another short journey. Let's look more deeply at why we would want to practice mutual support. Are we really better off supporting the whole, rather than merely focusing only on ourselves?

WHY WOULD WE WANT TO PRACTICE MUTUAL SUPPORT?

Most of us are taught to take care of "number one," ourselves, in any given situation. This is habitual. But this turns out to be a painful way to live. You're the only rich child in a poor neighborhood; you're the spoiled child in a family of ten; you're the best-paid programmer in your company. How do these experiences feel?

If we plumb the depths of our souls, we have to admit that these experiences feel painful. Being the only rich child in a poor neighborhood causes you to be isolated and alone. You are likely to be taunted and the object of envy. You can pretend to feel great about it, but secretly you yearn to be with the other kids. Being the spoiled child in the family may feel powerful. Yeah, Daddy likes me better. Ha ha. But secretly you feel isolated. Your siblings resent you and don't include you in their play. You have to turn to Daddy for all your love, because no one else loves you.

This makes you even more vulnerable to Daddy's love and approval. What starts out looking like an advantage turns out to be a liability.

You're the best-paid programmer in your company. Boy, that's great. Or is it? You feel isolated and maybe even guilty. The other programmers don't ask you to lunch. They talk about you behind your back. You glide into work in your Mercedes, but the guy you depend on to help you do your job is stuck on the freeway because his car has broken down. You're not benefiting by his poverty. Sometimes you wonder why you are better paid. You tell yourself that you're better. Sometimes that's true, but maybe you're just being rewarded for being better looking or for being politically more astute or for sucking up to the boss. You're in conflict. You want to belong to the group, but you don't want to give up your advantages.

None of these experiences feels good. We think that being favored will make us feel better, but it doesn't. On a deep level, it disrupts our sense of belonging and destroys the harmony of the group, which is what gives us true contentment. Being the favorite is not what it's cracked up to be.

What about mutual support? How does that feel? Let's envision some groups where mutual support is working, where the whole collective is functioning at its highest level. How would you feel if:

- You join a company where everyone is doing his or her job. Your new boss assigns you a mentor to help you get oriented. You're well trained and confident. You know what to do, you have plenty of support, and all your fellow employees are competent, as well. The reports you need are on your desk in plenty of time, office supplies are on hand, the people you depend on do their jobs, and you do yours. At break time, you can relax and chat with friends, because you are confident about the functioning of the whole. People who depend on you are thrilled with your performance. You find yourself doing a great job. Wow.
- You get to the train station. Everybody is working efficiently. The ticket seller smiles as she sells you a ticket. The coffee shop fills you up with sandwiches for the trip. Everything is fresh, healthy and tasty. The train comes on time. There are seats for everyone, and the view from the window is great. Wow, wow!
- There's a potluck for Thanksgiving dinner. Grandma's job is to spoil the children. All the dishes are hot and on time. The table is set by Joey and June, and the ice cubes are sitting in the

bucket. Everyone is focusing on relating to one another, because all the prep work has been done effectively. Right after dinner, the cleanup crew whisks away the dishes, so everyone else can relax. Wow, wow, wow!

Fantasy? Or possibility?

A well-functioning whole. What makes it possible? Mutual support. Everyone doing his or her job and supporting everyone else to do the same. Doing that which is for the highest good of all. Everyone working together toward the goal. Everyone supporting the whole, and the whole supporting everyone.

We are trained to compete, and we think that what will make us happy is being "the best," special, singled out, the one with the highest status or best-paying job, the "favorite." In fact, the opposite is the case. We are far more nurtured by being in a functional whole where everyone can thrive.

Before going on, let us remember some of our own experiences.

1.   Where in my life have I wanted to be the best, the favorite?
2.   Did I succeed?
3.   How did I feel toward others in the group?
4.   How did they feel toward me?
5.   How well did the group function?
6.   How happy was I?
7.   Have I ever been part of a well-functioning whole?
8.   How did I see myself in the group?
9.   How did I feel about myself?
10. How did I feel about others?

Do We Need to Be Perfect for Mutual Support to Work?

On the contrary. Normal, flawed human beings can co-create a well-functioning whole, if we allow ourselves to be honest about who we are, what we have to offer and what weaknesses we face. It's our refusal to be honest with and about ourselves that prevents us from working harmoniously within the whole.

Let's look at an example. Suppose we have three men: one is blind, one has Attention Deficit Disorder (ADD), and one has a bad back. We're trying to run a train. If the blind man drives the train, the guy with ADD tries to organize the schedule, and the one with the bad back is the porter, what have you got? A disorganized schedule, a train that stops at the wrong place, and luggage that never reaches its destination. The consumers of the service are miserable, and the employees are miserable as well. Each is angry with the other for not doing his or her job, and all are ashamed of themselves because of their own lack of success.

Why would all these mismatches happen? In a world dominated by ego consciousness, people get placed in the wrong spot for them because of many factors. Let's look at some:

- My family or society esteems certain work, and so I try to get into those professions to win their approval.
- My family is very success-oriented, so I have to push myself to reach the "top," even if I am not suited for those positions.
- I am very money—or status-oriented, and I never ask myself what I want.
- My family or I have connections that get me into a job that I could not otherwise gain.
- I cheat.
- I have the money to buy my way into a position.
- I don't care what I win, just as long as I win.
- I think that certain professions, marriages, social clubs or schools have more status than others, so I do everything and anything I can to get into them.
- I really want to be with you, but you aren't hip, slick, or cool. I force myself to be with others who, I imagine, give me more esteem.

These are all ego-based motives. None of them is remotely connected to our soul's happiness or our ability to thrive. None of them addresses the question of what is for the highest good of all. If we understood our Oneness, these factors would have no power.

So now let's go back to our example of the blind man, the man with ADD, and the man with the bad back. We were making the point that you don't have to be perfect to co-create a functional whole. But in our misguided, competitive universe, each man was in the wrong position, and nothing was working well. But if we learned to be mutually supportive, if we cut out ego-based competition, if we started with the concept that we are all better off as a part a well-functioning whole, how could this be different?

We know that the blind man wouldn't be great at driving the train or carrying luggage. But he might be great at scheduling. Doing the schedule in Braille, with a fabulous internal sense of organization and with the help of technology that could translate Braille into written letters, he could whip the crew into shape. The guy with a bad back wouldn't be good at carrying luggage, and maybe he's not the kind of guy who could sit at a desk all day either. But he might be great at conducting the train. He could be helped by having a supportive seat made for him, and he could stand up and walk around at each stop, so as to give his back a break. And our friend with ADD might be awful at scheduling and get distracted while conducting the train, but he's got more energy than God and would be super at carrying luggage for people. With no need to maintain long-term attention, with his outgoing, friendly temperament, and with his requirement for constant stimulation, the demands of many short-term assignments with lots of interaction would make him the friendliest guy at the station.

Here we would have a well-functioning whole that supports us all. The train conductor knows that the blind man is doing the schedule. He would feel confident that the schedule is right. This would make him more confident that he will not encounter something dangerous and unexpected on the tracks. He also knows that the porter is doing his job and that all the luggage is in the right place. This also lets him relax more into his job. The porter knows that the schedule works and that the conductor will get the train where it belongs on time, so that he can just focus on his job. And the scheduler knows that the conductor will follow the schedule and that the porter will make sure that the luggage will end up where it belongs. Each member of the team feels supported by the functioning of the rest of the team. Everyone is good at his own job. There's no competition, just cooperation. Everyone is more relaxed and feels better about himself.

What is required for us to have this happy ending? Mutual support. It's the realization that I am best off in a well-functioning whole, where each of us does our part, which contributes to the whole, and where the good functioning of the whole contributes to each of us. I actually want you to do your best. You want the same for me. I can call on you to help me. You can call on me to help you. We are not competing with one another. We are supporting one another. We are supporting the whole, and we are supporting the highest good of all.

To practice Platform Four: Becoming Mutually Supportive, we start with Platform One: Becoming Oneness, where we overcome the ego-based separation and competition. We continue with Platform Two: Becoming Differentiated, where each of us embraces our uniqueness. We comprehend Platform Three: Becoming Co-Creative, knowing that we need to co-create our universe together. And we continue with Platform Four: Becoming Mutually Supportive, where we start manifesting a new world by supporting one another and the whole, rather than grabbing blindly for ourselves.

Does this mean that we ignore our own needs? No, we discover them. Does this mean that we don't rise to the top? No, we rise to our greatest potential, which is the real top. Does that mean we get swallowed up by the collective? No, we find ourselves in it.

Mutual support. It's critical. In a world where good land is turning into desert, where our resources are being depleted, where violence is rampant, where greed and consumption run amuck, where our stress level is out of sight, where "me" is the measure of all good, we have come to emotional bankruptcy and possible global destruction.

So now let's take a look at some questions about our attitudes toward mutual support.

1. When I make choices, do I ask myself what's for the highest good of all? Do I even ask myself if I am choosing what I truly want?
2. What has influenced me to choose relationship partners? friends? schools? jobs?
3. Have I tended to find myself in the right place?
4. Am I in the right place now?
5. What groups or collectives do I belong to?
6. Is everyone in each collective functioning at his or her highest level? Are we all in the right place?
7. If not, why not?
8. Do we support one another to do our best, or do we compete?
9. In the past and present, have I received all the preparation I've needed?
10. Do I feel comfortable asking for help?
11. Do I offer to help others?

12. How does the failure of others affect my ego? How does it affect my level of stress?
13. How could these groups function better?
14. When am I at my happiest in these groups?

Bottom line: Most of us in our society aren't happy. We feel rushed, stressed, frustrated with ourselves and with one another. We see great dysfunction in our government, businesses, and world. With all the technological advances, with all the resources we have, with all the avenues for competition, we are not functioning in a well-functioning universe. We need a new paradigm of what will make us happy, what will make us successful, what will make us thrive, what is for the highest good of all. That new paradigm is mutual support.

Why would we want to practice mutual support? Because it allows all of us to live together in a well-functioning whole, where I am able to function better as well.

Some questions to ponder:

1. Do I feel excited by the idea of mutual support?
2. Do I feel threatened?
3. Why?
4. Do I agree that we don't live in a well-functioning universe?
5. Do I think that a better-functioning universe is possible?
6. Do I think I would have a place in it?
7. Who are the people I am dependent on?

OBSTACLES TO MUTUAL SUPPORT

The major obstacles to mutual support are, of course, fear, conditioning and ego. Let's examine some of these.

Fears that Are Obstacles to Mutual Support
What About Me?

Without early training, without continual self-monitoring, outside of a mutually supportive universe, supporting the good of the whole is a difficult platform to practice. If I put my energies into supporting the whole, into supporting you, then what will happen to me?

Survival fears can grip us. If I support you to get the job I want, even if it's for the highest good of all, how will I pay the rent? If I let go of a man, a job, a relationship that isn't for my highest good, will something replace it? If I support you to move forward in your life and to let go of our relationship, where will that leave me? Who will help me? If I help you in order to reduce your stress, will you adjust your behavior to help relieve mine, or will I just be working double? If I care about the whole, will the universe care about me as well? If I stop over-consuming, overpopulating, and polluting, will others do the same, and will there be any improvement in our world, or will I just be making a futile protest?

Will I survive? Will I survive? Will I survive?

This is a limiting question, a question based on fear. The question that few of us ask is: Will I thrive? The struggle for survival is what we know—each of us fighting for our crumb, our slice of the pie, often regardless of the consequences to one another or ourselves. And if I let go of my fundamental survival mechanisms, will the universe and I really thrive?

The answers to these questions depend on how much all of us practice mutual support. Will we all loosen our grip on what we think keeps us alive? Will we all let go of things and relationships that no longer fill our needs, so that those things and people can move to where they belong? Will we allow others to let us go, too? Can we support the evolution of the individual and the whole?

Even if I am willing to take the first step, can I practice mutual support in a world that does not do the same, or in a relationship where my partner is too unwilling or too dysfunctional to practice mutual support, as well? If I am in a marriage that no longer works for either of us, can we both let go with love, and can we support one another to move forward? Or will you be angry with me for letting you go and wreak havoc on me, if you can? If I step aside from a position that no longer suits me, will someone else step in? If I help you when you're in need, will you or anyone else do the same for me?

Few of us have grown up in a universe of trust, where we feel confident that we will all truly care for one another. This creates and continues to reinforce our survival fears. So now, let's take a look at a few questions related to our fears.

1. Am I afraid to support others?
2. Have I ever realized that something I wanted wasn't right for me?

3. Was I able to support someone else to have it instead?
4. What was the result?
5. What do I believe I need to do to survive?

Fear of Looking Selfish:
Self-Sacrifice as an Obstacle to Mutual Support

Even if there are others to support me, will I allow myself to be supported? Mutual support must include me in order for it to be mutual, but many of us either have no idea of what we need, or we aren't capable of asking for it.

The inability to acknowledge or receive what I need is an obstacle to mutual support. How ironic. Even though we live in a culture based on self-interest, many of us have gotten into self-sacrifice. Why? Here are a few possible reasons.

- We think that self-sacrifice will be rewarded by love, which is a primary need. Example: I give everything to my children, so that they will love me and stay with me forever. Fact: if I keep something for myself, my children won't need to feel responsible for me and might love me more and resent me less.
- We have a lot of spiritual books that make us feel that we *should* sacrifice ourselves for the purpose of spiritual growth. Example: Jesus sacrificed for us, so I should do the same. Fact: trying to look spiritual is a foolish, ego-based behavior, which is designed to make us look a certain way, regardless of the truth and regardless of the consequences to ourselves and others.
- We were never taught by our families to care for ourselves, and we can't switch gears. Example: We were trained or even coerced into sacrificing our own needs for a sick younger sister or a mentally unstable mother or to appease a raging father. We continue this behavior long after it's necessary. Fact: While this behavior looks noble and self-sacrificing, it is destructive, because it causes us to not self-care, which will ultimately make us ill or emotionally empty. We become another member of the family in need.
- We want others to take care of us, and we make ourselves needy and vulnerable to guilt them into sacrificing for us. Example: I don't want to learn how to drive, because I like to make my

husband prove he loves me by driving me around. In this case, my lack of self-care causes my husband to resent me for pulling on him, and this reduces the love I actually receive, unless he has an equal need for me to be weak, so he can look the hero, which keeps us both sick and makes our relationship unhealthy and dysfunctional. I don't care for myself in order to keep myself weak. Fact: this makes us all weaker.

- We don't know what we need and are afraid to take responsibility for identifying our needs. Example: Where do you want to eat dinner tonight? I don't know. You decide. Fact: I may look sweet, but I am actually placing all the responsibility on my partner, which isn't sweet at all.

- We know that support would challenge us into higher functioning, but we're afraid. Example: I am offered a scholarship to go to college, but I decide not to go, ostensibly for the good of the children, but really because I'm afraid I might not succeed. This deprives my family, me, and society of a higher functioning member—me. Not fulfilling myself may cause me anger and resentment later in life, when I regret my choice and blame my children. It will cause my children anger, because they feel my resentment. And it will cause me to despise myself, because I know that I was just plain afraid and hiding behind my family. Fact: I pretend to be sacrificing, but I'm depriving everyone of the benefit of my gifts and making others responsible for my pain.

- We know that support would cause us to change, and we're afraid of the consequences. Example: I am offered the same scholarship, and I decide not to take it, this time because I'm afraid I'll threaten the relationship with my husband. In this case, too, I say that I am staying home for the good of the children. Ultimately, this will cause me to resent my husband and children, again with devastating effect. Fact: I pretend to be supporting others through my choices, but I am motivated by fear and will ultimately emotionally leave them anyway.

I am not saying that we should never sacrifice ourselves, when it is for the highest good of all, including me. But I am saying that habitual self-sacrifice has nothing to do with Mutual Support. And when we feel called to sacrifice ourselves for the highest good of all, we know that somehow that highest good includes us, so it is not a sacrifice.

Let's consider some questions about self-sacrifice.

1. Do I see myself as self-sacrificing?
2. Do I identify with any of the above scenarios? If so, which ones?
3. Did I believe that I was really sacrificing myself for some higher good?
4. Can I see those choices differently now?
5. Were they truly for the highest good of all?

We cannot have a mutually supportive universe if any of us is excluded, and that requires us to identify our needs and take responsibility for them in the context of the whole. But many of us are afraid of looking selfish: in fact, some of us see selfishness as a sin.

What Is Selfishness?

Selfishness is the result of not practicing Platform One: Becoming Oneness. It's the process of seeing only ourselves and of seeing our interests as separate. It is not a sin, but it is destructive to ourselves and others, because it doesn't lead to happiness or fulfillment. It leads to isolation and fear.

So is it selfish to identify our needs and receive support? No. The opposite is the case. The only way any of us is going to thrive is for all of us in the collective to thrive, and that must include us. Not caring for ourselves creates pain and loss for everyone.

If I don't care for my health, for example, I am more likely to break down, which creates a drag on all of us. If I am so distraught that I turn to prescription drugs, I could possibly kill you in an auto accident, make a mistake in the operating room, or make an accounting error. If I break down physically, I will need society's resources to provide my healthcare. If I am mentally down, my children will need everyone else to provide for their emotional and sometimes physical needs. In fact, I may become abusive, and others may have to protect my children from me!

We have an obligation to see to our own thriving! We are not sinful for wanting to care for ourselves. Our lack of self-care is the real problem.

Self-Care or Self-Indulgence?

Isn't it self-indulgent to want things, love, rest, a new car, nice clothes? No. It is not indulgent to want things and relationships. It could be safer and more exciting to have a new car. It could be part of the evolution of our self-expression to have new clothes. We all need love, and we desperately need rest and relaxation. Wanting things and relationships becomes self-indulgence only when we become blind to the needs of the whole or when it is a substitute for self-care.

- Self-care becomes self-indulgence when it is at the expense of others. I want that new car, even though mine still works and yours is falling apart. I want new clothes, even though my closet is full and yours is empty. If I were truly caring for myself in these cases, I would know that I will feel guilty and alienated if I go only after my own needs. Self-care would in these cases actually result in my letting go of my wants for the good of all.

- Self-care becomes self-indulgence when it is a misguided attempt to satisfy a deeper need. When I lack something I truly need, I am likely to indulge myself with things I do not need to order to compensate for the lack. If I stuff myself with ice cream in front of the television, for example, I am probably lacking in love and self-esteem. I am indulging myself with what I don't need in order to compensate myself for what do I need, but believe I cannot have or don't know how to get. If I were truly caring for myself, I would identify my true need and try to meet it, even if that meant changing myself.

Self-Care or Self-Interest?

So what differentiates self-care from self-interest? Self-interest is based on a narrow perception of self. It is ego based, whereas self-care is part of Mutual Support. Self-interest is based on me, me, me. But self-care in the context of Mutual Support encourages true care of self, the true self, not the ego self.

I would like to become a surgeon. Why? Because I have an ego need to live in a big house and have a maid? Or because I know that being a surgeon is my gift and it would support everyone, including me, to do this work? Do I need a big house and a maid? Maybe. If I'm working 12-hour days and need to be relaxed for work, I might, in fact need physical comforts and a maid for the highest good of all. On the other hand, if my patients don't have the money to support my having a rich lifestyle, I may determine it to be for the highest good of all to forgo luxuries that might make my life easier so as to be able to treat my poorer patients. I can acknowledge that I have other needs, but realize that under the circumstances of my community, it's not for the highest good of all, including me, to focus on their satisfaction.

If I want the house, the new car, the nanny, the promotion, the vacation, the karate lessons, and I see only my need, then I am living out of the paradigm of self-interest. If I have those same desires, acknowledge those desires, yet am willing to recognize how they fit in with the needs of the whole, I am living out of the paradigm of Oneness, and I can still practice mutual support.

In addition, the very same desires may, in fact, be a reflection of practicing mutual support to start with, meaning when those desires arise from the Oneness. In that case, it is important that I meet the need for the house, the new car, the nanny, the promotion, etc, because having access to these resources will support my ability to serve on a higher level. Without a new car, I am always breaking down on the road and pulling on others' time to rescue me. In this case, my motivation is not the ego-based "I;" it is the practice of mutual support. Similarly, the willingness to forgo certain needs may be based on a lack of self-care or the unwillingness to take on the responsibilities that accompany the satisfaction of those needs, as in when we are afraid to get the new car, because we lack the self-discipline to care for it or are unwilling to use it to drive others, if driving others would be for the highest good of all.

To summarize, then, self-care is not self-interest, and it is not selfish. Self-interest starts and ends with "I" and exists outside the context of Oneness. It denies the true self, the inner self, and sacrifices all to the ego. Self-care encompasses "I" and "we" and is essential to a thriving world.

How do we relate to the issue of selfishness versus self-care? Let's see.

1. Do I feel comfortable asking for help?
2. Do I feel comfortable asking for what I need?
3. Am I afraid that someone will think I'm selfish?
4. After this discussion, do I think I'm selfish?

5. Why?
6. When I consider my needs, am I practicing self-care or self-indulgence?
7. Do I feel clear about the difference between self-care and self-interest?
8. Do I feel embarrassed to care for myself? Why?
9. Do I avoid self-care, because I am avoiding some growth or responsibility?

Conditioning: What Are We Taught in Our Society?

We've talked a little about the fears that are obstacles to the practice of mutual support. What about the conditioning? We have already touched somewhat on conditioning when we discussed the fear of looking selfish and our tendency toward self-sacrifice. But we have not yet discussed the conditioning that gets in the way of the principle of mutual support, itself.

The Principles Practiced in Our World

On what principle do we base our world? That's fairly obvious—the principle of self-interest. We have been taught that if we all pursue our own self-interest, the invisible hand will somehow balance everything out for the best of all possible worlds.

Of course, reality is that unbridled self-interest cannot be allowed and isn't allowed, even in the United States, which is probably its greatest proponent. Laws are supposed to represent the collective good, and there are laws against theft, extortion, monopoly, pollution, etc. Obviously even in the land of self-interest, there is an acknowledgement that there is a common good that must be served.

Have we become a little leery of unbridled self-interest? Absolutely. We are inundated with reports of the corporate accounting scandals, revelations of adulterations in the food industry, laxity in safety for school busses and airlines, oil spills, and nursing home abuses. These kinds of news stories keep reminding us that unbridled self-interest can lead to disaster and even death. And exposés often have led to regulations, such as anti-trust laws, food and drug regulations, and inspections.

But these incursions of regulation and law are supposed to reign in excesses in self-interest. They do not challenge the underlying paradigm, which is that each human is and must be out for him—or herself.

Even though we find ourselves lonely and afraid, we cling to individualism. We have tried to create pockets of mutual support through mechanisms such as Social Security, unemployment insurance, and the insurance industry. But, again, these mechanisms exist within the context of individualism. They were created to save capitalism and individualism, not to challenge it.

Here let's ask ourselves a few quick questions about our social paradigm.

1. Have I ever been upset with the way we run society based on self-interest?
2. Have I or my family members ever been hurt by unbridled self-interest?
3. Have I been embarrassed or ashamed by the unbridled self-interest of my family?
4. How did I respond?

Why Do We Continue to Rely on Individualism and Separation?

While our society may be based on me, myself, and I, few of us are totally comfortable with that consciousness, because it supports us to be fragmented, alone, and afraid. But if that's true, why do we cling to the theoretical belief in individualism?

The first reason, of course, is that this is what we are taught. Secondly, we have inertia. We have social, economic, and political structures already in place, which makes it hard to change. Third, within these structures are people who have a vested interest in maintaining them.

But there are deeper reasons, too. Let's look very briefly at two of them: Failed efforts to make fundamental changes and our collective rebellion against domination.

A Reason We Rely on Individualism: Failed Efforts to Co-Create a World Based on a Different Paradigm

Let's look at two efforts to co-create a new world: socialism and communism. The socialist model is: From each according to his ability, to each according to his work. The communist model is: From each according to his ability, to each according to his need. These models were based on a concern and a belief. The concern was for human suffering, and the models were an attempt to alleviate gross exploitation. The belief was that if people had

273

the same interests and were not divided by class or income, they would come together in mutual self-interest and create a better world for all.

Of course, as a practical matter, these models didn't pan out. In general, social revolutions have led less to mutual support and more to state control. The state ended up owning and controlling everything and it, in turn, became the vehicle through which individuals could pursue their own self-interest again! Not the original plan. And since self-interest was still a huge motivating factor, when members of the society had no self-interest to work harder, often people slacked off and got lost in mediocrity and lack of motivation.

Has it been different in other societies or in the distant past? Are there or were there ever societies practicing real communitarianism? Probably. Perhaps in tribal societies, there was less competition. In small intentional communities, the same may be true. Certainly when we were in the more primitive time of evolution, when small tribes wandered the earth, we must have been acutely aware of our dependence on one another. If five of us were hunting and one of us was ill, the impact on the hunt could have been lethal. We knew how much we needed each one of us to be strong. We must have been more aware of our interdependence and the need for mutual support.

But how much did we practice mutual support? Perhaps we still simultaneously wanted to be the "best" hunter? We know that in many societies, the competition within the tribe or group was also strong, and social structures were put into place to protect the group as a whole from the overwhelming competition of some of its members. We also know that even when there was true cohesiveness within the tribe or group, competition and lack of mutual support was common between and among groups. These rivalries often created the condition for invading armies to defeat original inhabitants.

In addition, our collective experience of tightly knit societies has often been suffocating. Keeping people in their place has been a hallmark of many, if not most societies, especially when nonconformity could threaten or could be seen to threaten survival. People were stoned or thrown out of the group as a way of ensuring obedience to societal norms over which individuals felt they had no control.

Whatever our dreams and whatever our past, one thing is clear: Mutual support is not generally practiced on the earth today, and the emphasis on individualism has been growing throughout our world, at least up until now. These days, more and more people are questioning these paradigms. But up to this point, whether or not there have been some wonderful exceptions on earth, generally speaking, human beings have been ruled by the energy of domination, domination based on money, power, sex, generation, connections, you name it. And few of us have grown up with much hope for anything different. Looking out for number one has become almost a religion. What else could we expect when our consciousness is still dominated by ego?

Let's take a look at some of our own experiences.

1. Did I ever try to create a more communitarian society?
2. Did I ever try to practice mutual support?
3. What was the result?
4. How have those experiences impacted me?

Another Reason We Rely on Individualism: Rebellion Against Being Dominated

I don't like to be told what to do. Neither do you. For most of us, experience tells us that the best way to avoid being dominated is to be the dominator or to be on our own.

Earlier in our book, we talked about our historical tendency to try to escape the control of the tribe, family or narrow community. In our families, we have been dominated by our elders, and sometimes later by our spouses. Leaving home or divorce has seemed like the only answer. In school, we have been dominated by clubs and cliques, and at work by bosses or supervisors.

We hate the domination, so we get out of our home-towns, or we try to start our own businesses. It feels sometimes like the only way to be ourselves is to bolt from the group; instead of trying to find new ways of relating to members of that group or developing new ways for all members of the group to relate to one another.

The decline of the collective in favor of individualism can be seen and understood clearly by looking at the fragmentation of families within our own society. The downside of the extended family, for example, is the lack of freedom to differentiate. Simply put, I can't stand my mother-in-law trying to tell me what to do, so we move to Florida.

If we track immigrant families who came to the United States, for example, we can see the power of the collective: families that were able to move members from total impoverishment to power and prestige, families that were able to lift up new generations through schooling and higher incomes. Yet what happened to those families? Many members felt stifled by the need to conform to family norms and demands, and when they had the opportunity, they moved geographically away or broke away from the family culture, yearning either to belong to the greater community—U.S. culture—or just simply to belong to themselves.

We see extensive evidence of the rebellion against the authoritarianism of the group and the difficulty in finding true mutual support. People vote with their feet, and the number of people who abandon apartment living for houses, who leave the old neighborhood for new ones, who splinter from the club and who start a new club, demonstrates that we tend to feel stifled by groups that don't have principles and practices of mutual support, and when given the chance, we're just "out of there."

So clearly one of the obstacles to mutual support is our experience. We have tended to move toward individualism when given the opportunity, because we hate being dominated by one another. As we have become more affluent and individualism has become more possible, we've grabbed the chance. In order to move into mutual support, we need to examine these experiences and develop attitudes and mechanisms that allow for differentiation and where we, in fact, support one another to become ourselves, not to become mere tools of the group.

We cannot create mutual support. We can only co-create it. If we are dealing with others who are not willing to examine their own tendencies toward domination, our experiences will tend to be negative. Once again, let's look at some of our personal experiences.

1. Was I ever a part of an extended family?
2. What were the good and bad points for me?
3. Did all members try to respect the individuality of one another?
4. How do I feel when someone or some group tries to tell me what to do?
5. Have I given up on working with groups, or am I still trying?

What Are We Taught in Our Families?

Now let's take a brief look at what we're taught in our families.

Generally speaking, families teach individualism, as well, even when we try not to.

Let's look at an example of how we try to teach our children not to be "selfish." As we described in our introduction, "Ego, Instinct & Evolution," Johnny has a toy. It's Johnny's toy. Don't steal Johnny's toy.

Very good, as far as it goes. Mommy wants me to realize that if I steal Johnny's toy, Johnny is likely to get resentful. He will either try to bully me back, in which case I may be crushed, or he will be crushed by me, in which case I learn to dominate. Neither of these outcomes results in mutual support, however. When our mothers tell us not to steal Johnny's toy, we're learning not to bully, which means no to domination, but the paradigm of competition and domination may not yet have been challenged.

Some of us did learn mutual support within our families. We may have had parents who taught us to share. I get my needs met. You get your needs met. We're all happier, and we get not only the toys, but the love of one another. What a beautiful concept. Too bad this concept has such a small environment of teaching.

Because even if our parents are enlightened enough to teach us about mutual support when it comes to Johnny and me, what are they teaching us about our relationship to the rest of the world? Are they teaching us competition in relation to other kids or families? Are they teaching us self-interest in relation to others?

Let's say Mom has taught me not to steal toys from friends. That's important. But now let's say that Mom feels insecure in her world and it's extremely important to her that we live in a big house with fancy furniture in order to make her feel successful in front of her mother and friends. Suppose that means that Dad has to work harder and for longer hours. That makes Dad at the very least tired and unavailable to me. Perhaps he becomes angry and resentful.

What have I learned about mutual support in this situation? Nothing.

Suppose Dad has a need to feel important. Suppose that means that when he comes home, he wants to be served by Mom, even though she's tired, or he wants to be served by his kids, whether or not they need to be doing something else for themselves. Suppose that means that he likes to go hang out with the guys at night and doesn't come home till late. That leaves Mom overstressed and resentful.

Have I learned mutual support? No.

When I go to school, I'm told that I shouldn't steal other kids' lunches, but I need to compete for the highest grades to get into the best schools. Me, myself, and I. There might even be a fear that if I help other kids achieve at their highest level, they may get better grades and get into the better schools. That will ruin "my" life, and that will never do.

Am I learning about mutual support? Again, no.

Just as children need to learn to share, we need to learn to support one another. We need to see our mother saying to Dad, "I would love to live in a nicer house. I've always felt insecure and that would make me feel great in front of my family. But it's more important to have you home, Jim, and that's where my real comfort and security lie." We need to hear Dad say, "Man, I've worked my ass off today, and I sure would love to have you make me dinner, but I see that you're tired, too, and it's more important to me that you feel well and rested so that we can spend some quality time together. Let's make dinner together and then hang out in the hot tub."

We need to hear our parents tell us that getting into the "best school" and getting the "best" job is not the most important thing in life. As we have discussed in Platform One: Becoming Oneness, and earlier in this platform, Platform Four, we need to be taught that a well-functioning society has well-functioning members. This means literally that if someone else gets the job and does a better job than we would have, that's to our benefit. It's best to have the people with the most talent for a job doing that job, whether that job is performing heart surgery or cleaning houses. Each job has a value to society, and all people have natural gifts and proclivities. Some people like detailed work; some can't do it. Some have wild imaginations and need lots of freedom; others need structure. Some can work in short but intense spurts. Some like a regular flow. Some have mechanical gifts. Some have gifts of the heart.

If we all do what we are best at doing, our society will function best. Obvious? Perhaps, but it is still something we need to be taught.

Recently I have had a series of medical bills. The billing departments sent the bills to the wrong insurance company, and the insurance companies processed each bill incorrectly. My energy has been spent doing and redoing bill after bill after bill. Why is that? Mostly because of the poor system and overstressed people involved. Yes, people. People who are stressed, people who are not educated to do their jobs, people who are resentful of their companies, people who live in a culture of "do as little as possible for the greatest reward" will not do a good job. Does that impact me? You bet. Instead of writing this book, I'm spending hour after hour dealing with the insurance company, the doctor's offices, etc., etc.

My personal "I" life is impacted by the personal "I" life of every person I come in contact with. But I don't spend my nights lying awake worrying about the stress level of the workers at Anthem Blue Cross. I only think about it when I have to keep redoing my bills. Even when confronted with the result of the disorganization and the dysfunctional workers, my first reaction is anger. I do not ask the question: What is happening with the people and systems of all these companies that is causing nothing to work smoothly or well?

We need to confront our conditioning. We have to intervene with ourselves in order to think differently. We need to be trained to think of ourselves as part of a vast system whose functionality directly impacts us.

So let's think about some of the conditioning we received in our families.

1. What did I learn about mutual support from watching my parents interact?
2. How did they treat me?
3. Did we tend to be supportive or try to dominate one another?
4. How did I react?
5. Have I tended to try to dominate, or have I abandoned being in groups altogether?
6. Did anyone ever teach me to be concerned for the wellbeing of others? Of those close to me? Of strangers?

Social Rewards Discouraging the Practice of Mutual Support

There is no question that inequality of social rewards creates the conditions that discourage mutual support. Social rewards can come in many forms, such as money, status, or prestige. How can I want to be doing what's right for me and everyone else, when the rewards are so different for different positions? How can I want you to have the classy girl, the job, the home by the lake, when I am going to be deprived of money, status, or comfort?

The cost of making choices based on social rewards is high. Of course, the men and women who become psychiatrists because they want the money will be lousy psychiatrists and will probably never be satisfied by the money. But who is anxious to let go of a $250,000 a year job to pick strawberries for a few cents a pound? Or to become a carpenter? Or a nurse? Some men or women may feel the need to be home with their children full time; yet if they don't have independent incomes, through jobs or inheritance, they can feel the sting of their partners' words: "I earn the money. I am supporting you and the kids." Such people may not want to stay home full time, even though it might be best for them and their families. A young boy may feel really attracted to teaching high school, but he may feel afraid that prospective wives may see him as a loser, so he becomes a computer programmer instead. A loss to everyone. A young woman might want to marry a really sweet guy, but he might not be seen as powerful in society, and another wrong marriage is consummated.

We need to design a social system that rewards people who support the whole rather than those who grab for themselves. But in order to do so, we have to confront the disparity of rewards that drive people to grab at the best for themselves, even if it means the dysfunction of the whole. The first step is to realize the cost of the system we now support.

Let's look now at some of the impacts of social rewards on us.

1. What choices have I made based on social rewards?
2. What did my parents do?
3. Did I ever feel pressured by my parents to make choices based on social or economic rewards?
4. Did I feel pressured by my peers? Or by myself?
5. Have I regretted these decisions?

Earlier I said that the obstacles to mutual support were fear, conditioning and ego. We've discussed fears and conditioning, and we have seen that ego has lurked under them all. Seeing ourselves as separate is the source of the fears and behaviors that keep us locked in dysfunctional patterns of mutual relating. But before moving on, I'd like to discuss one more obstacle to mutual support.

The Confusion of Belonging to Several Collectives

It is confusing for us to determine what is for the highest good of all, especially in the face of belonging to more than one collective. Which group's highest interest am I supposed to be considering? Let's say Jack belongs to three primary collectives: his family, his Marijuana Anonymous (MA) meeting, and his job. Let's say his wife unexpectedly goes into labor and rushes to the hospital to give birth to a child. Should her husband also rush to be with her? Well, obviously, yes. But perhaps not.

Suppose the husband works at a job that is critical to his clients or coworkers, and suppose he's not prepared with a backup person because the birth is premature. What is for the highest good of all in that situation? Should he rush to the hospital and leave his clients or coworkers high and dry? Should he stay at work until he finds a replacement?

The husband is a member of Marijuana Anonymous. Suppose he has promised to bring a guy struggling to get clean to a meeting that night. The addict's life is at stake. Does he run to pick the guy up, drop him off, and then go to the hospital? Does he try to find someone else to pick up the guy? Does he forget the newcomer in a mad dash to the hospital?

Suppose the husband has very little sobriety. Perhaps he needs to go to a Marijuana Anonymous meeting just to stay clean. If he goes to the hospital and doesn't go to a meeting to deal with his fears, he may look like a hero in the short run, but he may not really be supporting the whole. He may show up in the hospital, but get stoned afterward and start back down the road of drug addiction. This could cause him to lose his ability to either support his family financially or take care of his wife or baby. In that case, his going to a meeting would have looked selfish but would really have been for the highest good of all.

On the other hand, perhaps the man is using the M.A. meeting as a way of avoiding his responsibilities as a husband. Then it is for the highest good of all for him to go to the hospital and ask his sponsor to meet him there. Yes, he can find a way to meet his own needs while working toward the highest good of all. In that way, not only does he support the collective of his family, he is also supporting the collective of Marijuana Anonymous by not surrendering to his addiction or irresponsibility.

Later in this platform, I'll discuss how we determine what is for the highest good of all. But let's be honest. Life is complex, and we may not always be sure of our choices, but when we are asking the question, "What is for the highest good of all?", and we are open to the answer, we will find one. I will discuss this further in the next section, but in the meantime let's consider:

1. What different collectives do I belong to?

2. Do their interests conflict or seem to?
3. Can I think of a situation where I got confused about what was for everyone's highest good?
4. How did I respond?
5. Did my choice in fact serve the highest good of all, or was I caught in fear-based behavior?

One more point before leaving the discussion of the confusion that can arise when we belong to different collectives. It is easy to see that we might feel conflicted, if we feel pulled by loyalty to any one group. But loyalty is never the same as the highest good of all, including me. In fact, it's truly the opposite.

Loyalty is a form of merging, which is based on ego. Loyalty requires us to act in a way that meets the expectations of others, rather than consider what is for the highest good of all and acting on that basis. When we truly begin to understand mutual support, we realize that whatever we do needs to be geared toward supporting the highest good of all, and that includes everyone and everything, even if it conflicts with the groups to whom we feel loyal, identified and safe. When we take this step, we are beginning to enter into a universal consciousness where we are not loyal to anyone, but are connected to the divine consciousness that guides our lives, if we let it. We will understand this much better when we get to Platform Nine: Becoming Becoming.

So now that we've talked about what is mutual support, why we would want it, and some of the factors that block us developing this approach, let's talk about how to practice it.

HOW DO WE BECOME MUTUALLY SUPPORTIVE?

Mutual support is a culture of wholeness, whereby the individual supports the highest good of the whole and the whole supports the highest good of the individual. Through supporting the whole, our own needs are met. We acknowledge that we are one and cannot be well at one another's expense, and we also acknowledge that we need not sacrifice, because the good of the whole always includes ourselves. We determine the highest good of all by transcending our ego-based fears and connecting to our higher consciousness, individually and collectively.

How Do We Practice Mutual Support?

As children, most of us dreamed of a world where we all cared for one another and for the earth, where the lion sat down with the lamb, and we could all fulfill our potential. But over the years, most of us have lost that dream. Competition and scarcity, cruelty and unconsciousness have left us scrambling for our own needs. If we were not going to be left out or left behind, we had to fight for ourselves. Me me me. Or even us us us, but only the specific us: my family, friends, community and group.

And who can blame us? Whether it was fighting for our parents' attention, for acceptance by other kids, for the favor of our teachers, for a job, for the "desirable" date, or the top place on the *New York Times* Bestseller's list, we were in the "me" universe. As women, we had to protect ourselves from being raped, as men from being beaten up, as workers from being exploited, as employers from being ripped off, as old people from being warehoused, as disabled from being ignored. Where's the space for us to care for one another? Who can even think about the whole of the universe, including other nations, species and galaxies? Who is worrying about the highest good, when we're focused on survival?

To choose mutual support is to step into the unknown. We have to be willing to give up the tried and true "me" universe for the unknown "we" universe. And yet is the experience totally unknown? Haven't we already had glimpses?

Have you ever been in a group of people—with friends or family, with your spouse, lover, or child, in a 12-step meeting or with co-workers who were trying to get something done as a team—and in such an environment for a moment you felt safe and at-one? Have you ever had the experience of not having to "do" anything to be loved? Or where your contribution felt like enough? Do you remember the feeling of wellbeing, the momentary suspension of fear, anxiety, and aloneness? Do you remember the feeling that you are okay as you are, and so is everybody else? The feeling that you can, indeed, for that moment, relax into being just a member of the group, of the larger whole, because everyone supports everyone and that includes you? The feeling that you do not have to fight for a place, because you have a place? That despite our individual weaknesses, together, we are enough? Do you remember that feeling? Do you remember the hum?

That is the feeling of mutual support, and if you can remember that feeling, and if you were touched by it, then you have had a glimpse of what is possible, and you know that mutual support is worth working toward. And how do we work for it? By becoming aware of the option and choosing it. We might start checking in with just ourselves or with us and a friend or lover and consider issues that only affect the few of us. Then we might extend our understanding to our community, nation and finally the globe and beyond. When we get to the point of truly connecting to the Oneness, we can finally relax into the hum with the whole universe. So let's get started.

Before going on to discuss how, let's remind ourselves:

1. When have I felt mutual support?
2. When have I been conscious of offering it?
3. How did I feel?
4. Is it worth working toward?
5. Can I imagine having that feeling with the entire universe?

Practicing mutual support is not complicated, but it is difficult because:

- It requires us to challenge the habits of acting from fear and functioning from the consciousness of the "me" universe.
- It requires us to trust that if we practice mutual support, we will not be stranded as the only ones supporting the good of the whole; that there are others already doing the same; and that, together, we can and will influence the rest of the universe to join us.
- We have to be willing to let go of agendas and ask the universe to guide us as to what is for the highest good of all.

Can we fulfill these requirements? Yes.

How Do We Take the First Step?

The first step is to start differentiating from fear, ours and everyone else's. Oh my God, can I actually relax into the belief that there is a highest good of all and it, by definition, must include me? That I don't have to fight for myself?

To differentiate from our fear, we need human and divine support. We can always turn to God, The Source, our Higher Power, however we experience higher consciousness. And we can turn to those who practice mutual support themselves.

Despite my fear, I can alter my actions through conscious choice. Sometimes my fear is so great, I want to convince myself that my "me me" actions are right and reasonable. Yet in my heart, I feel sickened. I would like to behave otherwise, but I feel paralyzed. What allows me to alter my actions? Acknowledging that I feel fear and at the same time calling on the collective that will support me to be mutually supportive. With support, I may not yet be able to stop feeling the fear, but I can choose not to let it dominate me. Then it's not so hard.

There's nothing like the love and support of others to reduce my fear to manageable proportions. When I differentiate from the fear and call on the universe to support other aspects of myself, I feel more relaxed, I can be more objective and think more straight. Then I realize that I am capable of inquiring as to what is for the highest good of all.

I may also need my hand held when I take the actions that support the whole. That's a very appropriate use of support, as well. If I ask a friend, a mentor, or a counselor to help me take an action that stands in the face of my fear, asking for their help is actually practicing mutual support. Their support of me is supporting me to do what is for the highest good of all. It is, therefore, in their highest good as well.

Can I Practice Mutual Support in a World that Doesn't?

Part of facing our fear requires that we believe that we can practice mutual support in a universe that is still hanging back. It is true that, ultimately, we need to live in a mutually supportive universe in order to be totally mutually supportive, but each one of us can and needs to take the first step. By so doing, we are impacting the whole world to move in that direction.

Mutual support, like other good things, is infectious. Let's say I am going for that job interview with the attitude that what should happen is for the highest good of all. If I ask friends, family and others to support me in this attitude, some may shake their heads and think I'm crazy. But all will be affected. They'll hear my reasoning, and they will be moved by my vision of a world where everyone is in the right place. What's more, I will be beaming and relaxed when I go to the interview. That will impact every other applicant in the room, helping lift their spirits as well. And it will bring relief and relaxation to the interviewer, who is very much on the spot, experiencing the pressure of making the right choice and aware of the pain she will cause the applicants who are rejected.

We spark change through our own transformation. Let's say I acted compassionately toward an ex-boyfriend who cheated on me. How did my friends react? Did they think I was stupid or feel inspired? The part of them that is scared will be challenged, and the part of them that wants global change will be ignited. Regardless of their reactions, I know that I am part of the Oneness and thus realize that every time I choose to step beyond the ego paradigm, I am sending ripples through the universe.

Look at those around us who are already acting with this consciousness. Their examples strengthen us, and we are becoming a growing collective consciousness that supports us all.

Before going on with this discussion, let's ask some questions about the ways I've dealt with my fears of Becoming Mutually Supportive.

1. Think of an example where I felt afraid.
2. How clear was my thinking?
3. Did I get support?
4. Did my thinking change?
5. What actions did I take?
6. Have I ever or frequently practiced mutual support?
7. Was I supported by others?
8. Did I impact them?
9. Who do I know who practices mutual support?
10. How do their actions and attitudes impact me?

Now let's get into action.

Mutual Support in Action

Mutual support is a culture of wholeness, whereby the individual supports the highest good of the whole and the whole supports the highest good of the individual. We acknowledge that through supporting the highest good of all, we create a healthy whole that supports us all. We acknowledge that we are one and cannot be well at one another's expense. And we also acknowledge that we need not

sacrifice, because the good of the whole always includes the good of ourselves.

So, how do we Become Mutually Supportive? Get support to practice the following simple habit. This is a tool you can use in every moment of your life, when you are wondering whether you should eat salad for lunch, go to the movies with Fred, take the new job, or have a baby.

When confronted with a choice, a situation or a challenge, take a breath. Let go of your agenda for the outcome of any situation. Experience yourself becoming as neutral as possible. Feel yourself connecting to higher consciousness, and, if possible, and ask the question: Would it be for the highest good of all, including me, for me to do "x?"

If you feel particularly challenged, gather a group of people to support you in asking the question, people who would be willing to be neutral and let go of their agendas. Direct them to ask the question at the same time that you do. They could ask, "Would it be for the highest good of all, including me (in this case, the "me" refers to the friend who is supporting you and joining you in the question, because your highest good will be for their highest good as well), for [your name] to do "x?" So let's say, for example, that you are trying to decide whether or not to join the armed forces. You ask, "Would it be for the highest good of all, including me, for me to join the armed forces?" Your friends would say, "Would it be for the highest good of all, including me, for Linda to join the armed forces?"

In the silence following the asking, an answer will come. If you don't all get the same answer, or the answer seems unclear, discuss the fears and factors that could be impacting any of you that are present. Perhaps one of the women in the group is attracted to you and doesn't want you to go. Perhaps you're afraid that your mother thinks it unseemly for women to serve. Perhaps you really don't believe in violence and are thinking of joining the armed forces for security purposes. The discussion can help bring out these issues, so that they can be at least acknowledged before asking the question.

When you are with a group of people who are trying to make a collective decision, whether it is where to go on vacation, to whether or not to start a new business or a war, you do the same practice.

Whenever we gather a group, what we are seeking is an intuitive consensus, which I will explain in a moment. But first, trust. Remember that intending to do that which is for the highest good of all changes everything, and asking the question opens us to new possibilities.

THE MUTUAL SUPPORT TOOL

The mutual support tool is powerful. It promotes all of us to be more in inquiry. It enables us to see undercurrents, such as lack of clarity and tension, which we have not acknowledged. It trains us to connect to higher consciousness. And ultimately it allows us to make decisions from a place of intuitive consensus. Let's, therefore, review this tool and break it down step by step.

∽

The Mutual Support Tool: Asking for That Which Is for the Highest Good of All

When confronted with the need to make a decision, from the simple to the most complex, whether the decision involves only one or all those present, do the following:

1. Calm your minds.
2. Let go of agendas and prejudices toward a certain outcome.
3. Feel yourselves lifting up for a higher consciousness.
4. Ask the question: Is it for the highest good of all, including me to do "x."
5. If you are asking for guidance for one member of the group, as opposed to asking for guidance for the collective decisions, the other members ask: Is it for the highest good of all, including me, for [the person in question] to do "x."
6. If you are unsure of the answer, or if members of the group get different answers, discuss the issues involved.
7. After the discussion, ask if it's for the highest good of all to ask again in that moment.
8. If yes, re-ask the question. You may get a completely different answer this time.
9. If you're not ready to ask again, have more discussion.

10. If you can't come to an intuitive consensus, let go of the question for the moment and come back to it when you have more information or more objectivity.

The Spirit in Which We Ask the Question

Before, during, and after we ask the question, what will support the highest good of all is keeping ourselves open. For those with a spiritual orientation, that might look like prayer: ***God, help me do that which is for the highest good of all.*** Or, ***God, let what occurs be for the highest good of all.*** For those of us who do not relate to the concept of God, we can say the same prayer, but address it to the universe, or we can sit in quiet meditation and put out the intention that what we do and what transpires be for the highest good of all.

Whatever the form of the expression of our intention, the intending in itself will make a huge difference. Our intention to support the highest good automatically shifts our feeling about a situation, influences the questions we ask and the answers we hear. If we are intending to support ourselves in the narrowest sense, we will hear answers that lead us to take actions dominated by our egos. When we intend to support the highest good of all, we become neutral about our own narrowly-defined interests, and we are more likely to hear answers that truly promote the highest good.

What Do We Do If There's No Consensus?

Let's say the two of us are planning on painting the bedroom, and we are trying to get an intuitive consensus on the color. We use our mutual support tool, but you keep getting that the room should be blue and I keep getting that it should be green. What do we do?

We talk about the issue in depth. Why might you be wanting the room to be painted blue? Could it be that your mother loved blue and you're still merging with her? Why might I want it to be green? Could it be that I feel anxious in a room of any other color and have no faith that our relationship can create the experience of calm and nurturance that I am seeking through the color?

Once we have discussed and revealed to ourselves and to one another what might be impairing our objectivity, we ask higher consciousness again. Perhaps we'll get that the room should be painted pink. Or perhaps it should be blue, because that color will support our highest good, because blue will impact our consciousness to make our relationship more calm. There is no way of anticipating what the answer should be. We need to let go of our beliefs and agendas in order to be guided by higher consciousness.

Let's look at how this works with a larger group. Let's say we have a small company with a team of five key employees and we are discussing alternatives for a new path at our property. After discussing the pros and cons of all the choices, we ultimately have to make a decision. This is the moment when we can use the tool of mutual support. When we ask what is for the highest good, four of us get that we should use cement and one gets that we should use decomposed granite. Is the person wrong who reports that their sense is that we should use decomposed granite? Not necessarily. All we know at this point is that we don't have an answer, because we are not getting the same answer. If we let go of agendas, become neutral and connect to higher consciousness, we should all sense or hear the same answer. Why aren't we?

Our lack of consensus could be higher consciousness signaling to us that we need more discussion at the moment, or it could be signaling to us that we are not ready to make this decision, because we need more information. Or it could be opening us to the possibility that there's a third alternative we never considered. The fact that four of us get one answer and one gets another says nothing about the outcome. The only thing we know for sure is that we haven't been able to get to the right answer, the one that is for the highest good, because if we had, we would all get the same one.

When we receive different signals from our higher consciousness, instead of making someone wrong or outvoting them, we trust that there's a reason that we're not getting clear. Perhaps we are actually all scared about the cost of the project, and we haven't acknowledged that yet. Or perhaps we don't even want to stay together as a group, and we shouldn't be installing a path at all, or that we should be installing the path in order to sell the property and dissolve. Once we are clear on all of that, we can ask the question again, and we might get answers that differ dramatically from those we sensed the first time we asked.

This is how we attempt to transcend our egos, connect to higher consciousness and be guided to do that which is for the highest good of all.

Being human, even with intuitive consensus, we could all be wrong. We might all be influenced by ego, fear, competition or the need to merge, but at least we are intending to do the right thing and that is an important step.

Practicing mutual support is not simple. The obstacles are great. For example, we can be blocked by:

1. Our own fear.
2. The fears of others within our group.
3. The fears in the collective consciousness.
4. Our lack of experience connecting to higher consciousness.
5. The stresses, foods or other substances that impair our ability to connect to higher consciousness.
6. Our lack of patience with the process and unwillingness to go through the demanding task of discussing the factors that could be blocking our clarity and consensus.

Obstacles or not, we make the effort. The more we do so, the more adept we will become at practicing Platform Four. When we feel blocked, the more we are willing to be honest about our agendas and fears, the more likely that we will be able to clear them and return to ask for guidance again. The more we cultivate relationships with people who use the mutual support tool, the more confident we can be that we are with a group of people equally dedicated to confronting our egos and doing that which is for the highest good of all and, ultimately, the more natural this process will seem. The more natural this process becomes, the less willing we will be to make decisions based on ego, because we will have learned that connecting to higher consciousness in mutual support gives us the greatest sense of serenity possible for us on earth.

When we have connected to our higher consciousness and made a choice, we feel much more comfortable about our decisions. Even if the outcome feels painful, we know that we have done the right thing.

Let's take a look now at some common examples where we can use our mutual support tool:

1. Is it for the highest good of all, including me, to eat coffee and donuts for breakfast? Grin.
2. Is it for the highest good of all, including me, for us to buy the house on the corner?

3. Or, more precisely, is it for the highest good of all, including me, for us to make an offer on the house on the corner? (We can't really know the outcome of our action.)

4. Is it for the highest good of all, including me, to buy a toy for my child?

5. Is it for the highest good of all, including me, to try to get pregnant?

6. Is it for the highest good of all, including me, to buy a new car this year?

7. Is it for the highest good of all, including me, for me to change jobs or hire a particular job applicant?

8. Is it for the highest good of all, including me, to embark on a sexual relationship with someone?

Nothing in life is trivial; and nothing should be beyond higher consciousness. Our wellbeing is based on the decisions we make moment by moment. Our health or lack of it is impacted not only by genes and accidents, but by the daily decisions we make. Our futures are molded not only by external circumstances but by the moment-by-moment choices we make. So to lead the most relaxed, healthy and mutually supportive life, we need to get into the habit of asking for guidance from higher consciousness about everything. When we have trained ourselves to ask about little things, we can rely on that habit when confronting the big stuff.

Try using this tool. Don't expect to always do it well or perfectly. In time, with a lot of honesty and self-discipline, your life will change.

Before ending this chapter, let's look at a challenging example of Becoming Mutually Supportive and see how it can work in practice.

Mutual Support in Action: A Challenging Example

I have a severely autistic son, and I don't know whether or not to keep him at home. I feel conflicted as to whether keeping him in the home is helping him or enabling him to stay sick. How do I decide what action to take?

If I am not motivated by the good of the whole, what would be motivating me? Ultimately, it's what I perceive to be my own interest. Without conscious intervention, narrow self-interest is my default mode, because it's what I've been taught and what I've practiced. The fact that

I am in narrow self-interest may not be immediately evident, because self-interest can look many different ways.

In the example of the autistic son, what could be the result of not consulting higher consciousness? I might decide for him to stay home and be cared for by my family. Looks selfless. But maybe I am being motivated by guilt, and my self-interest will encourage me to assuage my guilt. Why might I feel guilty? There may be autism on my side of the family, or I may feel that I was a neglectful father. In either case, I may think his condition is my fault, so I want to relieve my guilt. Whatever my conscious motivations toward my son, I may in fact be motivated by a desire to reverse my bad feelings about myself. So now I want to be a hero and demand that we keep him at home. This is narrow self-interest masquerading as selflessness.

Oddly enough, that same self-interest might lead to an opposite behavior. I may feel so guilty that I consider institutionalizing him so that I don't need to face my shame. Regardless of which of these choices I take, my motive is self-interest, not mutual support. I am not looking at the highest good of all. I am reacting out of a need to assuage my guilt.

So, suppose I'm willing to go beyond my narrow self-interest and ask what is for the highest good of all, now what? We use our mutual support tool, but first I get honest with myself. I acknowledge that he is part of several collectives, including our family, and our community. Who will be impacted by our decision? Would keeping him at home support a younger sister who might be frightened by him? Can we address her fears? Would it drain the mother, who is trying to care for him, herself, and everyone else? Could he be a danger to himself? Will that support the whole? Will the guilt for disrupting the family create in him more shame and despair? Will that ultimately make him sicker? Will putting him in an institution remove him from his only sense of security? What does he need?

Asking myself these questions is, of course, only the beginning. I then need to discuss all these issues with everyone involved—with my daughter, wife, sometimes even friends and neighbors. We can get professional help, as well. Can we discuss things openly with him? If not, can we connect to him emotionally, intuitively, telepathically? Can we hear his voice? If not, what does his behavior tell us? What do his eyes say?

When I speak to each of these people, I need to try to posit the questions in such a way that they, too, ask what's for the greatest good of all. If I ask my wife if she's willing to make the sacrifice to care for our son, for example, she may say yes, because that's what she thinks she needs to do in order to look like a good person in her own eyes. But if I ask her if she thinks it's for the highest good of our family, including her, and if I can help her see the ramifications of each choice, she is more likely to be more objective as well, to consider what her emotional and physical resources are and to see what impact his staying with us would have on her and the rest of us.

After we have all been honest, we need to use our mutual support tool, willing to be guided to do that which is for the highest good of all, including me, him and all concerned. Whatever we ultimately decide, I will feel calm, knowing that I have thoroughly and honestly considered all the implications and connected to the highest level of consciousness I am able.

At this point, let's look at some of our own challenges.

1. What are some of the challenges I face?
2. Have I asked myself what is for the highest good of all?
3. Who have I left out of the equation?
4. Have I consulted with others?
5. Who have I left out of the consultation?
6. If I'm not practicing this habit, what has gotten in the way?
7. Has my view changed in the process of asking and discussing?
8. Have I changed?
9. Did I get neutral, let go of my agenda and ask for the guidance of higher consciousness?

Be willing to keep changing course as situations evolve.

Whatever decisions we make will be tentative, as we allow situations to evolve. (More on this in Platforms Eight and Nine: Becoming Not-Knowing and Becoming Becoming.) We keep our autistic son in our home, because we feel it to be for the highest good of all, and then we see that our daughter is becoming traumatized. That's hurting him, too. So we change course. Or we institutionalize our son and then see that he's regressing and we all miss him. It's causing our daughter guilt. We check in again, and now we all feel guided to move in a different direction.

We keep revisiting our decisions, and we continue to ask the same questions, over and over. What is for the highest good of all? How can I support that? How can we?

Through the process of living and experiencing, we change, and so must our actions. But our ultimate intention does not change. Being clear that our intention is the highest good of all allows us to be grounded in a platform of integrity, and at the same time, enables us to allow life to evolve. Through our experience, we continually learn what is for the highest good of all, moment by moment. There is something else to keep in mind, as well: Not only does our perception keep changing, the highest good itself may keep changing, as the people and circumstances around us evolve. Staying open allows us to continually connect to our higher consciousness.

When we proceed to Platform Eight: Becoming Not-Knowing and Platform Nine: Becoming Becoming, we will be much more adept at connecting to our higher consciousness, but we can start now with our tool of mutual support.

Before proceeding to our final comments, let's ask ourselves:

1. When in the past days have I prayed or intended the highest good of all?
2. When and why haven't I?
3. Can I do it now?
4. What have I discovered?
5. Has my view changed regarding what is for the best?
6. Is it only my view that has changed, or has the reality changed as well?
7. Have I been disappointed and frustrated by what seemed like limited options?
8. Have new options continued to emerge?

SOME FINAL COMMENTS ON BECOMING MUTUALLY SUPPORTIVE

If we are to thrive in a thriving universe, all of us need to be included in the process of co-creation. No one can be left out, and all need to reach our highest potential. As we saw in our earlier example at the train station, each one of us in synergy with others can create a functional train system.

If we are competitive and pursue what our egos believe is best for us, we will be cheating ourselves of the benefits of truly following guidance from an intelligence greater than our own, an intelligence that is not dominated by the ego. When we let go of being dominated by the ego's viewpoint, we discover that we are more, much more than we think. (We discuss this thoroughly in Platform Six: Becoming Integrated and Platform Seven: Becoming Accountable.)

If we organize our society and our world in a mutually supportive way, we can co-create something wonderful, something beyond our imagination. At the same time, we will enable each one of us as an individual to reach our highest potential.

Becoming Mutually Supportive challenges us to grow, day by day, decision by decision. It challenges us to confront our fears, self-protectiveness and self-limiting concepts. But living in a mutually supportive universe requires not only a shift in paradigm from the "me" consciousness; it also requires patience, tolerance, and love. Oh yes, if we are isolated beings, we don't have to put up with one another's weaknesses. We don't have to put up with the neighbor's boombox, the clerk's forgetfulness, the salesman's incompetence, the lawyer's arrogance, and our spouse's inadequacies. But while we don't have to put up with one another's weaknesses, neither do we benefit from one another's strengths. We are limited to what we can manifest alone, and that isn't much.

When we live from a consciousness of mutual support, we realize that our highest good is not always the easiest, most comfortable way. It may be the most challenging way, but it is the way that supports all of us to reach our highest potential as spiritual beings.

There are no real giants. When we're young, we look to our parents to be God-like, omnipotent, omniscient, and omnipresent. We don't see our worth, because we don't see their need for us. But as we develop, we come to realize that big people aren't big, that we are all wonderful, limited, capable, and incompetent, and that our ability to work together for the highest good is what makes us great, as individuals and as a society.

We must turn our hearts to mutual support, despite the many difficulties of clashing egos and bitter disappointments. We must turn our hearts to mutual support, not only for the sake of the whole, but for our own sakes as well. When I lose the belief that true mutual support is possible, when I stay stuck in the "I" universe, I become self-centered, lonely, and tied up in knots. When I forget the true meaning of mutual support and that it includes me, then I become self-sacrificing, and then I become used up, lacking in resources, and I have little left to give. To the degree that I stay connected to my vision of the highest good of all, I feel more connected to everyone and actually feel less fear and pain in my life, which allows me to more fully become myself.

How Can I Stay Connected to This Vision?

- By having faith.
- By recognizing the experience when I have it—the hum that we all feel when we are acting in mutual support.
- By remembering that I have felt it.
- By continuing to commit to the practice on a daily basis.
- And by asking for support to practice Platform Four, so that my own fears don't block my and our potential.

Mutual support is a critical part of our program, and we will discuss it again in different contexts as we continue with this book. But to conclude this chapter, I would like to say, personally, that I need to offer mutual support, and I ask you to do the same. Because it is only through your support of me and the whole that I can be my best self and that I can do my best work with this book, which, in turn, I can offer to you. It's through my support of you and the whole that you and I will co-create a world where we want to live and where we all can thrive.

PART 2

Partnering with Ourselves
The Second Three Platforms

A Few Comments to Introduce Our Next Section

Our first four platforms were devoted to changing our relationship to one another. We acknowledged and began to experience our Oneness through practicing Platform One. Then we were able to work on Platforms Two, Three and Four, through which we became differentiated, co-creative and mutually supportive. Through these efforts, we moved from separation and competition to partnership and cooperation.

Now that we are in a more realistic and mutually supportive relationship to the universe, we need to look squarely at our relationship to ourselves. Are we really partnering with ourselves, or are we justifying and rationalizing behaviors that are destructive to us and others? Are we ready to stop focusing on changing the world and start focusing on changing ourselves?

Increasing self-mastery is the job of Section Two of Living with Reality. In this part, we will discuss three platforms: Becoming Self-Aware, Becoming Integrated and Becoming Accountable. These platforms will:

- Bring clarity to our own attitudes and behaviors.
- Release us from being driven by unconscious programs.
- Enable us to confront the domination of our egos.
- Teach us how to recognize our true accountability and make amends when we are hurtful.
- Enlighten us as to how to best deal with negativity within ourselves and others.

Through the process of practicing these programs, we come to like and respect ourselves more and more, and we become our own best friend. Then we'll be ready to go on to our last two platforms, which teach us how to partner with life itself.

PLATFORM FIVE

Becoming Self-Aware
The First Step toward Self-Mastery

WHAT IS BECOMING SELF-AWARE?

Introduction

So far, all the platforms have called upon us to have some command over ourselves and our behaviors. But what will aid us in developing that self-command? Becoming Self-Aware is a first step.

More than we might think, we resist self-awareness. Many of us believe that life happens to us and that we are compelled to respond the way we do. We tend to want to blame our behaviors and discomfort on everybody and everything else. When we do see our flaws, we often feel baffled by them and unable to change the way we react. If we feel comfortable, we want life to stay the same. If we feel uncomfortable, we want the world to change. Self-awareness brings us back to ourselves. What am I feeling? Why? What impact am I having on others? What can I do about it?

Platform Five is our opportunity to focus on our inner selves, so that we can understand what stimulates our reactions and responses and so that we can learn to intervene with them. Understanding stimulus, reaction and response is the core tool of this platform, but before we delve into it, let's face some truths about ourselves.

- We have been destined by genes, environment, experience, ego and conditioning to react and respond to specific stimuli in specific ways.
- We believe these reactions and responses are natural and inevitable.
- Stuck in self-justification, we exist as a constellation of conditioned responses.
- Self-awareness allows us to question these responses and embark on a path of choice through which we can become ourselves.

Becoming Self-Aware is going to challenge us to the core, but it is also the first step toward freedom. Before we can be free, we need to understand how and why we are not. So let's start with a discussion of cause and effect.

Cause and Effect

All action is comprised of cause and effect. If a meteor careens toward the earth, there is some cause that propelled it. We may not know the many occurrences that led to this event, but we can all see the crater!

Human behavior is no different. Let's look at one example. If I raise my voice when people don't do what I want, there is a cause. What could be some possible causes?

- chemicals automatically released in my body that cause me to feel agitated
- thoughts and feelings that cause the body to produce more of those chemicals
- experiences that automatically cause those thoughts and feelings
- drugs, alcohol or other substances that I have deliberately ingested

- a personal history that leads me to believe that raising my voice will bring me control of the situation
- habit

And so on. My yelling is an effect; there are many possible causes.

Whatever the cause, my yelling then becomes the cause of other effects. Let's look at some possible effects of me raising my voice. First, there is the effect on me. I might feel even more upset and agitated and maybe even falsely powerful. My child might cower and then steal money from my purse. My mate might feel criticized and start self-justifying, resenting me and/or hiding his or her behaviors. My employee might worry about her job and grumble to her fellow workers, who end up withholding effort from the company. All of these are effects of me having raised my voice, effects of the thoughts, emotions and chemicals released in my body because I have become angry about something.

Sometimes it's hard to see the cause of a behavior, even when it's our own. I may not realize that I am yelling at someone because I feel jittery from not having eaten lunch, or because the perpetrator of the offending behavior reminds me of my mother, or because I'm losing my job and I'm scared about losing my security. With other people, we may be even less likely to see the cause of their behavior, because we lack important pieces of information. My neighbor raises his voice when he comes over to discuss the way my car seems to be encroaching on his driveway. I think he's a jerk. I don't know that the reason he's raising his voice is because he doesn't believe he'll be heard, and he doesn't believe he'll be heard because he was abused as a child.

The true cause of our reactions may be hard to discern, but what makes us even less likely to be self-aware is that we often don't even question our behaviors. They seem natural. If I'm shaming someone, my reactivity might be so habitual that I don't even consider that my shaming is due to something within me. I assume it's caused by the other person's behavior. Even when I do want to be self-aware, I still might not be able to see the underlying causes of my shaming words, or I'm too carried away by my emotions to be able to see anything about myself. Sometimes we don't have the intention to look at the causes of our behavior, because we like acting out. I like the adrenalin rush of raging, and I simply have no desire to stop.

While causes are usually harder to spot than effects, we are often reluctant to look at the effects of our behaviors, as well, especially when our actions could be seen as the cause of a negative outcome. We don't want to admit that we have caused damage to ourselves or to others, because we might feel shame or have to change. If we don't examine and understand cause and effect, however, we are powerless to see what's going on within and around us, and we are powerless to change. We are lost in the world of shadows.

The World of Shadows

Most of us are lost in the cave of shadows. Because we resist understanding cause and effect, the world is a place where things seem to happen and where the source of these "happenings" is either hidden from view or is someone else's fault. We see the shadows, which are the effects of choices, ours and others', but the real actors and sources are hidden, especially when one of those causes or actors is me.

Denial of cause, denial of effect and denial of accountability may seem the easier way, but any form of denial actually makes the universe a very frightening place. If we don't understand the causes of reality, we cannot intervene. The cave of shadows is unpredictable, totally outside our control, and so our attachment to stay there keeps us in an unpredictable, uncontrollable universe. Conversely, self-awareness and accountability make the world a less frightening place. If we bring more light into the cave, we begin to see that there are actual objects casting these sometimes frightening images. Light on objects is the cause; shadows are the effect. We then realize that we exist in a world where what we are experiencing are the effects of causes that are knowable, and that these causes are themselves the effects of other causes.

If we could see everything that is simultaneously occurring and if we could follow the trail backward generation after generation, we could find the cause of everything in the universe. Our limitations of knowledge and perception may prevent us from actually ever being able to find the cause of the cause of the cause, but just acknowledging the existence of cause and effect helps us by turning our attention to understanding, instead of just reacting. When faced with negative consequences—the shadows we dislike—we can now seek to comprehend the causes. And once we have some comprehension of the causes, we can try to act appropriately, perhaps addressing the causes, rather than reacting to the effects, which are merely the shadows that frighten or disturb us.

Typically, however, we fight the shadows. Let's look at one example. Let's say we are afraid of the violence endemic to our world. The violence is the effect, but what is the cause? We can fight the shadows by incarcerating everyone who commits acts of violence. This will lead us to lock up vast numbers of people, who then become more violent. Our behavior will cause the very effect we did not intend. The alternative, of course, is to comprehend the causes of the violence and attempt to do something about them. We may not be completely successful, because we don't know enough about the causes of violence and how to alter them, but we will be on the path to real change. Dealing with causes requires thought, patience and awareness, whereas it only takes reactivity to fight effects. Reactivity is easy; thought, patience and awareness take effort.

While there is much in life that is frightening and outside our control and knowledge, focusing on cause and effect makes life more comprehensible and, therefore, less frightening. Here's another example. I'm feeling emotional pain. I discover the cause is my husband's withdrawal. Once I understand I am reacting to his withdrawal, I can talk to him and try to comprehend the source of his withdrawal. If there's anything I can do to impact the source of his withdrawal, I attempt to do it, if it's for the highest good of all, including me. If I cannot do anything about it, I can refocus from his behavior and focus completely on my own reactions instead. Now I can help myself. Why is my husband's withdrawal causing me so much pain? Because I am afraid to face life alone. Why am I afraid to face life alone? Because in the past I have felt insecure about my capacity to support myself emotionally or financially. Can I do something now to increase my capacities? Get help? Go to school? Have I already gained the capacity to support myself, but I just haven't yet acknowledged that it is so? True empowerment and less emotional pain. That is a great benefit of leaving the cave of shadows.

Sounds good, doesn't it? Let's all start looking at cause and effect, and we'll be happier and more relaxed. But, wait, it's not so easy, because in order to see life clearly, we have to be willing to see ourselves clearly, and for that we have to see everything else clearly. And to see everything clearly requires that we give up our denial—a lot of illusions about ourselves, others and our world. We have to give up our attachment to control—the demand that reality fit our preconceptions, needs and desires. And we have to relinquish our fantasies—the right to believe whatever we want to believe, regardless of its relation to reality. Gosh, give up our denial, control and fantasy? Not so easy after all.

Let's pause for a few questions about our relationship to cause and effect.

1. Do I feel overwhelmed by the complexity of life?
2. Do I feel like I'm surrounded by events I don't understand?
3. Do I take an objective look at their causes?
4. Do I believe I can? Where am I willing to give up denial?
5. Where am I not?
6. Where am I willing to give up insistence on control?
7. Where am I not?
8. Where am I willing to give up my fantasy that life will change to suit my desires?
9. Where am I not?

Who? Me?

We don't want to look at cause and effect because if we saw ourselves more clearly, we would realize that we would have to stop trying to change others, which we can rarely accomplish anyway, and start focusing on changing ourselves, which sometimes seems even more difficult! This does not mean that we shouldn't intervene with one another. Of course we should. Telling one another the truth is not a contradiction to becoming self-aware. But before we can successfully intervene with another, we need to see ourselves more objectively. If we are more in command of ourselves and our accountability, our interventions are more likely to be correct and for the highest good of all.

So all intervention with others starts with self-awareness, and as I become more self-aware, I observe that I am the major actor in my play. So if I want to change my life, I need to become more aware of my impact on myself, others and life itself. I am the cause of much of my pain and the pain of those around me. But the good news, then, is that no matter the difficulty or situation, there's always something I must and can do to change my experience of it.

Perhaps I might have to face how my behavior is directly creating the undesired effect. Or I might have to simply remove myself, even though that could threaten my security, which would force me to deal with my fears. Or I might have to admit that a painful situation cannot be changed, because I cannot impact its cause, and I can't get out of it. And so to be relieved of frustration and pain, I need to change my reaction: move into allowance (see Platform Three: Becoming Co-Creative) and release the need for things to be different (see Platform Six: Becoming Integrated).

Release the need for things to be different? Tell that to the woman being raped by an invading army. Tell that to the man being dragged to jail for a crime he didn't commit. Tell that to me, when my teeth hurt and I don't have the money to go to the dentist. Yet even in these cases, we will find that our reactions to these terrible circumstances are causing much of our pain, and those reactions can be changed! I can refuse to feel shamed for having been raped; I can embrace my jail time to learn something about myself; and I can stop eating sugar to deal with my frustrations for lacking of dental insurance and refocus my time and energy on finding free dental care or working more to earn extra money. At the very least, I can confront the anger and rage within me, which in turn makes me bitter and impermeable to all the comfort and love that is still available in the universe.

Squarely facing cause and effect both compels and enables me to observe life's reality, the reality of myself and everything else, and that can be a chilling experience. I might have to be in allowance of what feels terrible or unimaginable. For example, suppose reality is that my lover feels stifled by me and is convinced he has to leave or that the housing bubble has burst, the value of my home has crashed and I have lost my life savings. Becoming Self-Aware allows me to focus on my reactions and responses to these dreaded realities, which gives me relief even if I can't change the realities themselves. In addition, when I develop increasing command over myself, I become more capable of actually impacting the realities that trouble me, because I can think more clearly.

Without self-awareness, I can get locked into destructive or limiting reaction responses, and I can use my experiences to justify them. If I am raped, for example, I may become traumatized. But if I use the rape as a justification to stay traumatized, I can continue fearing or hating every other man I ever meet, and I can blame the rapist. This helps no one, least of all me. If I were practicing self-awareness, I would refocus from blame to healing, and I would have a chance for a more fulfilling life. But to do so, I would have to delve into the depths of the question: What exactly was the nature of the trauma? Why do I feel so traumatized? What can I release so that I can heal?

What makes healing so challenging is that our own parts in the co-creation of the situation/experience are unclear, so the exact nature of the trauma is clouded. I may see the apparent cause of my reaction: that I've been raped, unjustly imprisoned or stuck with a toothache. That part is clear. But what else is influencing the way I feel? Do I feel guilty because the night I was raped, I shouldn't have been out alone? Did I lack dental care because I lost my job through my inattention to detail? Was I unjustly imprisoned, but do I feel guilty about other infractions I committed, where I wasn't caught? All of these feelings and doubts about myself are causes contributing to my reactions of upset or anger over the traumatic event, but I can't heal these feelings because I don't know they are impacting me, because I am not focusing on my part, but am blaming circumstances. If I don't deal with these feelings, I will have a hard time letting go of the pain triggered by the negative events.

One of the most common experiences of this nature is the all-too-common child molest. Many of us were molested as children, and the impact lingers, often more than we realize. But frequently we can't heal because we are not allowing ourselves to examine where we, too, felt at fault in some way. We may have been flirting with the adult, we may have enjoyed the attention, or we might have refused to tell on the other person, because of our own fears or shame. All these are hidden causes of the trauma following the molestation.

Even when I make a sincere effort to look at my own part, I often find that I am blind or that my understanding and vision are severely limited. Like most of us, I automatically believe that my responses are reasonable, rational and in fact the ONLY way to respond in a given situation. Of course, I was angry, HE. Of course, I felt hurt, SHE. Of course I was critical, THEY. Of course, I was traumatized, IT. We are invested in our responses, and we see few or no alternatives.

When we get further into this chapter and start to reveal the stimulus-reaction-response pattern, we discover that we hardly ever HAVE to respond the way we do, but for most of us, the causes of our responses are hidden to us and we proceed on automatic. Back in the cave of shadows, we see effects—our emotions and behaviors—but don't see their true causes. We assume that we are reasonable and compelled to respond as we do, and we collect people around us who will bolster our position. If we want to clearly see cause and effect, if we want to illuminate our caves, we have to shine the light on ourselves. When we do, we discover that the shadows on the wall are our responses, whose causes are often hidden from us.

If we can face the fact that our responses are caused by something within ourselves, we can probe our deepest fear, the fear of ourselves, the fear that our patterns of feelings and behaviors can never be changed or controlled. Many of us fear either that we will never comprehend ourselves, or, if we do, that we cannot change. Insecure about our own capacity to change, we desperately need everything and everyone else to change instead. Isn't it damaging to reinforce the belief that others can change, but we can't?

Becoming Self-Aware is a huge step toward confronting the fear of our own irrationality and self-destructiveness. We CAN learn to understand ourselves. We can move past the frightening cave of our own unconscious minds, and we can find the passageway into a happier, more relaxed way of being. But in order to do so, we have to confront ourselves and our rationalizations and stories; we have to confront our attachment to the universe according to us. Let's take a moment for self-awareness right here.

1. Do I focus on what is happening to me or on how I'm reacting?
2. Do I want things around me to change, or do I want to change myself?
3. Do I think I can?

Surrendering the Universe According to Us

To face reality, we have to be willing to surrender our version of reality. When I was a little girl, I had the conscious thought that I was the only person who was real. I thought that everyone and everything existed for me and in relation to me. Pretty funny, huh? Yet how much have I really changed in this regard? Don't I still see the universe through the lens of how everything and everyone affects me? Don't you? I want. I need. I have to have. And so you must do, say, be this for ME. From this ego-centered perspective, can I truly see myself and my part? Can I be truly self-aware if I'm wedded to this world view?

No. The more ego-centered we are, the less we know ourselves. Dedicated to maintaining the world from the "I" perspective, I have to continue to rationalize my reactions, behaviors and perspectives. I have to continue to deny reality.

The woman who has the emotional need to control her son's life will continually find or create stories to prove that he is not able to handle himself in the world, and she will be blind to the ways she undermines him. The man who is driven to have an affair in order to feel young will justify his actions by pointing to the fact that his wife doesn't understand him, while simultaneously ensuring that she can't.

The more entrenched we are in our stories, the less objective we are. Because we are invested in justifying our stance in life (e.g., self-pity, anger, self-righteousness, superiority, greediness, cowardice, competitiveness) and because we are dedicated to defending our positions (I want to do this, and I don't really care what anyone else feels or needs), we become deaf to any information that conflicts with our intention to justify and defend, and we make ourselves blind to the impact of our behavior on ourselves and everything around us. We actually resist becoming aware and self-aware because we might have to confront that we are rationalizing, and we would have to change.

I, I, I. I want, I need, I have to have. And therefore, you, he, they, she. I want to marry that guy, and I don't really care whether or not he really prefers another person or even whether or not he and I would make good partners. I want that ring, and I can't look past the wedding day. I'll pretend that I'm pregnant and will make his life miserable if we don't marry. I want to have sex with that girl, and I don't really care that she's underage, ambivalent or too immature to make an informed decision. I'll get her drunk and I'll succeed.

Do I really want to face that I'm trying to manipulate the world and life for some idea I have of what should happen? Am I ready to confront my stories, justifications and rationalizations, my self-centeredness, my willingness to coerce and manipulate others for my perceived benefit? Am I willing to honestly ask myself whether my reactions and behaviors hurt or help others or even myself? I want a promotion and I don't care whether or not I am truly the best person for the job. We want that profit, and we don't care how much we are truly undermining the company or the eco-system by raping the land and squeezing the employees. We refuse to stop, think and become aware of our behavior and its potential impact. Here are some questions to help us see how this applies to us:

1. Can I think of situations where I was so intent on a certain outcome, I blinded myself to whether or not something was possible or desirable in the long run?

2. Did I really consider the consequences to myself and others?
3. What were the outcomes to myself and others?
4. Did I feel guilty?
5. Do I regret those "successes?"

But Does It Make Us Happy?

Resisting self-awareness does not make us happy. It keeps us stuck. So even while it feels hard, sometimes even threatening, to give up our self-justification, self-awareness is necessary for our happiness and it's necessary for our individual and collective survival.

Let's start with happiness. When we are driven by unconscious motivations and drives, we are stuck in the cave of shadows. We believe that the causes of our pain and fear are external, and therefore we are their victims. He did this. They did that. She did the other thing. And life did it all! Ignorant of our own part in any negative situation, we feel helpless to affect those problems. This makes us unhappy.

Ultimately we dislike ourselves. Let's take manipulation as an example. Underneath our denial, most of us know when we have been manipulative, and we secretly blame ourselves for poor outcomes. I blame Tom for our lousy marriage, but deep inside I know I manipulated him into it, and I really blame myself. I blame the boss for not giving me enough support after my promotion, but deep inside, I know that I wasn't cut out for the job. Whether or not I admit it, I know that I had a part in the poor outcome. I feel deeply unhappy with myself, yet because of my denial, I am no closer to understanding myself and changing. So now I dislike myself not only for my behavior but for my inability to change.

Living in the cave of shadows, we disrespect ourselves, because we know that we have behaved badly, and we won't admit it. If we get honest with ourselves, we realize that we often hold ourselves in contempt for behaving in ways we don't like and wouldn't condone in others. This sometimes unconscious self-contempt drives us even more to rationalize our behavior, which drives us deeper into the cave of shadows.

Lost in the cave of shadows, in a world we cannot understand, whether we blame ourselves or others, we are filled with inexplicable anxiety, because we can't fathom why our lives are so painful or why we are out of control of ourselves. Full of fear and pain, we continue to do things that hurt us and those around us. We are not the masters of ourselves, the captains of our ship. We are awash in a sea of unconsciousness that restricts our choices and limits our self-realization. We create needless fear and pain for ourselves and for others. And it's their fault, or our fault, or God's fault. We're still in the cave. We're doomed to be unhappy. Wow, that's a big price to pay for the lack of self-awareness.

And What About Survival?

The resistance to self-awareness often threatens our very survival. To be well, I need a healthy body, mind and spirit. Yet I don't want to see what I'm doing to my body with the food I eat, the drugs I take and the anger or self-pity that poison me every day. I don't want to recognize what I'm doing to my family by my violence, manipulation and refusal to act in a way that is for the highest good of all. I don't want to witness the impact of my compulsive spending or gambling on my wife, who earns all the money. I don't want to acknowledge its impact on my children's future and even on my own retirement. I don't want to admit how shame and guilt are poisoning my mind and making me sick.

Our denial is not just individual, it is also collective. We as collectives—men or women, gays or straights, Americans or Africans, workers, students or farmers, Christians, Jews or Muslims—can blame others and reject self-awareness and accountability. And we all pay the price. We Americans, for example, have wanted to believe that we could continue focusing on short-term financial gain and ignore our impact on ecology. Now we and the rest of the world are paying the price of global warming and a degraded environment for us and all those who follow us. Others have done the same, and economies like the Chinese have chosen to follow our example, ignoring the lessons in favor of short-term gain, and again, the whole world has to pay.

Is denial worth the price? Or, more importantly, is the price of unconsciousness high enough for us to choose a different way: the way of awareness and self-awareness?

In order for us to be willing to look at things as they are, we must be willing to overcome our resistance to seeing ourselves and our part. Self-awareness does not solve all our problems, but it is a huge turning point for those of us who want to co-create a mutually supportive world in which we all thrive. Just as the first four platforms help us change our relationship to our world, Platform Five: Becoming Self-Aware, supports us to partner with ourselves. It opens the doors to integration, accountability, not-knowing and becoming. Self-awareness opens the door of a new life. Denial shuts that door. While it's not easy, self-awareness is imperative.

Before going on, let's take a look at our relationship to self-awareness.

1. Where have I most resisted self-awareness?
2. What has been the cost to me?
3. What has been the cost to others?
4. Where has my family, class, gender group, religious community or nation most resisted self-awareness?
5. What has been the cost to us and to others?

What Is Self-Awareness?

There are two aspects of self-awareness. The first is the process of becoming objective about our reactions and responses, and that's what we will primarily address in this chapter. The second is the process of becoming aware of the self underneath our programmed self, which is the work of our whole program. Becoming Self-Aware allows us to bridge those two aspects of self-awareness, because seeing our behavior helps us to differentiate from it, which enables that true self to emerge.

Becoming Self-Aware is the ability to see ourselves objectively; to notice our reactions and responses, realize their causes, and acknowledge the impact of these reactions and behaviors on ourselves and others. Self-awareness allows us to trace the relationship between the way we feel and what we do; and then trace the relationship between what we do and the outcome of those choices. As we begin to differentiate from our behavior, our true self emerges.

As usual, our platforms sound simple. We're going to watch ourselves and become conscious of everything we're doing and why we're doing it, and we are going to examine our impact on ourselves and others. It may sound simple, but in fact self-awareness is not simple at all. It requires us to become conscious of everything we do, think, eat, feel, say, intend and ignore.

To be truly self-aware, we are going to have to make the unconscious conscious. What are we doing every moment? Why? What's the effect? Is this what we want, and is there an alternative?

315

Why do we need to do all this work? Because we need to take fundamental steps toward altering our programmed behavior, and self-awareness can facilitate that transformation. Self-awareness is a doorway to consciously co-creating a better world by consciously responding, rather than unconsciously reacting. Once we go through this doorway, we can come to the next space, which is where our inner selves guide us, where we no longer need to make mental decisions about everything we do. In a state of self-awareness and alignment, we are relaxed and observant, freed from the constant mind chatter created by the fear within us, and from that place, we are spontaneous, guided and more relaxed. But more about that in Platform Nine: Becoming Becoming.

In the meantime, before we can come to that level of being, we need to do the work of Becoming Self-Aware. Those who try to skip this step often try to fool themselves into believing that they are more evolved and self-mastered than they are. So let us acknowledge our current level of development and focus now on the need for self-awareness and for a profound understanding of cause and effect.

Summarizing Self-Awareness as a Key to Our Wellbeing, Survival and Partnership with Ourselves

Self-awareness is the key to our growth as individuals and our survival as a species. Without self-awareness, we can't track our own behavior and its impact. If we can't track our behavior and its impact, we can't change anything about ourselves or our world. And if we don't change ourselves and the way we impact our world, we will not thrive; we may not even survive.

If we acknowledge climate change, for example, but don't see our part in global warming, we will be helpless to do anything to help ourselves and preserve all that we love about our planet. If I see that my family can't pay its bills, but don't recognize that my spending is destroying our finances, I won't be able to make the changes crucial to restoring them. If I notice that my wife is distant, but don't realize that my belligerence is driving her away, I won't commit to achieving inner peace and take the steps necessary to re-establish faith in our potential.

In addition, self-awareness holds the key to a new partnership with ourselves. Naturally, we are alienated from ourselves, if we don't want to know ourselves for fear that knowing ourselves would feel too shameful or painful; naturally we are alienated from ourselves if we do not trust ourselves, because we are out of control. Becoming Self-Aware, Integrated and Accountable ends our alienation from ourselves, because we now feel free to look at ourselves and support ourselves to be better. We become partners with ourselves.[21]

What does that partnership look like? We develop trust in ourselves, because we have now experienced that we can see ourselves clearly and can change, that we don't need to be at the mercy of our unconscious motives. We develop self-love because we behave in ways we respect and earn our own regard. And we feel more confident in our lives, because we realize that we are not simply victims in a world we cannot understand or control; we can and do have an impact. In addition, practicing the three platforms of Becoming Self-Aware, Integrated and Accountable makes us much better friends, partners, lovers, employees, teachers, parents and so on. With self-awareness, we recognize when we're hurting others, and we can stop. This, in turn, brings us admiration and love from those around us. While admiration and love may not be our primary motivation, which is to take responsibility for ourselves, they are wonderful byproducts that can be enjoyed.

With all these motivations for self-awareness, you would think we would be begging for information about ourselves, our motives and our impact. But all too often the opposite is the case. In our introductory chapter, "Ego, Instinct & Evolution: Are We Ready to Change?", we discussed the underlying fear of self-awareness and change based on our ego and its relationship to the survival instinct. Please review this section, if you need to. In the following section, I would like to discuss in detail some of the specific obstacles to self-awareness.

---

[21]   Once we have taken this step we can embrace the other two platforms shifting our relationship to ourselves. Platform Six: Becoming Integrated will help us achieve balance, and Platform Seven: Becoming Accountable will allow for restitution, amends and restoration of trust. Taken together these three platforms make us partners with ourselves.

THE OBSTACLES TO SELF-AWARENESS

Fear of Shame

The biggest block to self-awareness is simple. We don't want to know ourselves, because we're afraid of what we'll find out. We're afraid that our motives will sound "bad". Oh, no, we really are greedy, selfish, stupid, mean, something undesirable, and we will feel shame.

Shame is one of the most toxic emotions we can experience. It is the kind of emotion that makes us want to fall through the floor, disappear, curl up and die. Guilt tells us we did something wrong. Shame says that there's something wrong with US. We are intrinsically bad, wrong, defective, unlovable, evil, worthless, dirty, less than a worm. As you'll recall from our introduction, feeling worthless stimulates our shame of existence and the fear that we will not be cared for and die. Shame stimulates the fear of death, which of course is intimately connected to our lizard brain, our survival instinct as it overlays our ego.

At the same time that shame is the most toxic emotion we can experience, shame or the fear of it is one of our more prevalent emotions. Why?

In Section I of our book, we discussed the fear and pain that drive us. We are afraid of out-of-control behaviors, both our own and that of others, and we use shame to try to stop these behaviors. Bluntly put, in a world based on fear of one another and ourselves, shame is a powerful weapon. When shame doesn't work, we resort to laws, and laws are backed by the ultimate form of control, which is, of course, force.

How is shame a tool for social control? I spoke much earlier in this book about the ways that we structure society in order to distribute our collective resources. In order for these structures to remain in place, we need a collective agreement to maintain them. For example, if everyone burned their money tomorrow morning, the economic system would be in chaos.

How do we get people to agree to follow the designated social agreements? One way is education and conditioning, and that's critical. Parents, teachers, therapists, clergy and the media all have a hand in our programming. Another form of social control is the threat of coercion. Parents can beat or ground us, teachers can fail us, supervisors can have us fired, and social workers can take our children away. Ultimately if conditioning and relatively mild coercion don't work, we authorize our police to incarcerate or otherwise institutionalize those who don't cooperate.

Shame is the moral handmaiden of education and conditioning. If you don't agree to "the way things are done," you're bad, a deviant, morally unfit, something really shameful. Of course, some parents are brutal and beat their kids. But most use the weapon of shame, the everyday enforcer of social norms, either as their primary tool of control or in conjunction with punishment or physical abuse.

Are these enforcers always "wrong" in what they teach? No. But is shame the best teacher? Not if we want healthy people, who can look at themselves wisely, objectively and with self-compassion.

Good, bad or indifferent, shame is a common form of social control. It's handy, everywhere, inexpensive and easy to use. Compare it to relying on force alone. Think of how expensive and inefficient it would be to have to police everyone with force. That was part of the inefficiency of slavery. Offering incentives, such as money, and threatening shame and social ostracism are much more effective than force alone.

Shame is a handy and free first line of defense against "bad" behavior. We try to shame thieves, adulterers, molesters, abusers, liars, cheats, the violent, the angry, cross-dressers, sexual deviants, drug pushers and whoever might be considered a threat to our wellbeing. We may even use shame to prevent behavior that threatens only our point of view or our self-image. If you disagree with our going to war, you're a coward and a traitor. If you're my child and insist upon being gay, you're an embarrassment to me.

Is shame necessary for our functioning? No. Consciousness would be a better foundation for us to build a healthy society. When we shame someone, we want them to feel bad about themselves, and we hope that the toxic feeling of shame will prevent them from ever acting in that shameful way again. We are actively trying to make them feel small and disempowered. We are trying to create in them a sense of fear, fear that they will have to experience the devastating feeling of shame again, fear that they will become ostracized from the group and not survive. On the other hand, when we seek to increase people's consciousness, we are hoping to make them aware of the negative consequences of their behavior to themselves and others, and we attempt to empower them to make better choices. We hope they feel good enough about themselves and life to support the highest good of all. Our purpose is to make them larger by empowering them to differentiate from the negative energies within and around them.

Generally speaking, we haven't developed our collective consciousness to the point where we have healthy ways of teaching and learning. So at this point in history, we tend to resort to shame in our desperate effort to make the world safe for ourselves.

So how does the fear of shame block self-awareness? It stops us from wanting to know ourselves deeply. As we have already discussed, most of us have been taught through shame, and we're afraid to feel it again if we are found out to be "wrong" or "bad." Look at our conditioning. Shame on you for having hit your sister, taken Johnny's toy, ignored your mother, lusted after your father, failed the test, cheated, stolen the candy, not wanted to visit your grandparents, talked back to your father, masturbated, cut class, or peed in the bed. "You should feel ashamed of yourself young lady or young man." Oh, wow, I did something bad, and I am bad. Nobody will want me, and I will die.

Few of us grew up in environments where people understood one another's destructive behavior, knew how to support one another or even asked the question, "Why? Why were you driven to choose that behavior?" Shame was used to control our behavior, and we shame ourselves and one another for the same purpose. The worst of it is that shame hasn't really driven out the parts of us that are "bad"; at best, it's driven those parts underground. So we have constantly recurring shame, because we know we're still bad, even when we're acting "properly," because we know that the shameful parts of us have just gotten shoved under the bed.

With this history, naturally, we experience a relatively constant underlying fear that we're going to feel shame. Even if we weren't personally heavily shamed, we may have seen someone else being shamed, and we fear becoming the target. Your brother is a bad seed. Your mother is a whore. Your father is a worthless bum. The neighbors are trash. "Loose" girls are sluts. Gosh, I don't want to be seen like that!

Some of us carry an extraordinary load of shame. We may have gotten it from our families. Your mom neglected you, so you must be unlovable. Your Dad abused you, so you must be really worthless. Your parents blamed you for their arguments, their poverty, their illnesses, their lack of freedom, so you should not have been born. Your family made unreasonable demands on you, so you always feel like a failure.

And some of us carry a huge load of shame from our religious upbringing. You had impure thoughts, so you are shameful. You crave sex, hate your parents, want to curse God, question the social order. Shame on you. Shame on you. Shame on you.

Some people have grown up with so much shame that they can't face even one more drop. They are convinced that they are unworthy, that they are not deserving of the support of the collective upon which they depend, and so they either implode into self-hatred or become very defiant.

We can also receive a huge load of shame from our society. Here are some examples of how we as a society can shame people.

- When we feel ashamed of ourselves, we shame the victim. For example, we justify slavery by demeaning our slaves. We justify exploitative wages by thinking of our workers as inferior, violent, not like us, stupid, lazy or subhuman.
- When we feel ashamed of our inability to help people, we blame the people we can't help. If we don't know how to help a child learn and gain self-control, we treat the child as stupid or willful. If we don't know how to help sexual abusers recover, we try to shame them into good behavior.
- When we simply don't know what else to do, we shame people, so that we can lock them up, ship them out, or somehow try to make them go away. We've done this with the mentally ill, with prisoners and sometimes with our own family members. (We may in fact have to take some of these actions, but we don't have to justify them with shame.)
- When we feel threatened by others, we shame them. People of the wrong color or the wrong nationality, people who are gay, people who are disabled or deformed or disadvantaged can seem to threaten us, so we try to make them feel inferior or even negate their humanity.

People who are socially condemned are socially shamed. This again creates toxic levels of shame.

Again, once we're carrying a toxic load of shame, we can't tolerate another drop. So we become afraid to be wrong, which means we have always to prove that we are right. How can we be self-aware, if our agenda is to be "right?"

Even those of us who have not been heavily shamed have had a big enough taste of shame to create fear. Fear of shame turns into fear of awareness. I can't possibly look clearly at myself because I might realize that I have done something WRONG, that I am BAD, and I just can't face that. Without a healthy dose of self-compassion, self-awareness can feel lethal. (Much more about this in Platform Seven: Becoming Accountable.)

Now let's look at some questions that help us identify our relationship to shame.

1. Was I shamed by my family?
2. What for?
3. Did I see someone else being shamed?
4. Was I shamed by my religion?
5. Was I shamed by society?
6. What for?
7. Am I in a group that is shamed by society?
8. What about me feels shameful?
9. Do I feel that I carry toxic levels of shame?
10. How do I feel about being "wrong?"
11. Can I connect to the fear of being shamed?
12. Who do I shame?
13. What's my fear of them?
14. Do I practice self-compassion?
15. Does that help?

Fear of Shame; Fear of Death

One more point about our fear of shame. Behind that fear is a fear of death. Yes, we're back to the survival instinct that formed the programmed self. If I am shameful, I may be tossed out of society and have to face life alone, and whether I live in caveperson society or New York City, being outside the circle of human support can mean death. If I live in tribal society, that may be death by the elements, starvation or vulnerability to wild animals. If I live in modern society, I won't have any of the supportive connections of my social class, family, school, professional organization, union, gender support groups or political association—whatever helps make me safe in a world of economic and physical vulnerability.

What can be more frightening than having to face all of life's difficulties by ourselves? So I'd better not be discovered as being "anathema," shunned by my peers. Shameful behavior can get me thrown out of the "club," it can lose me a job, it can get me reviled, or it can get me imprisoned with a bunch of people whose level of violence can threaten my very existence. Wow, if I admitted I flirted with Mimi's husband, my friends would shun me. If I gave into my desire to be a cross-dresser, my medical patients would run from me. I cannot face that I am or might be something that could be seen as shameful, and that I might be thrown out in the cold. Whether on a physical or social level, shame can send me to a symbolic Siberia, where I have to face the brutal elements of life on my own.

Let's look at our own experience with shame and its dangers.

1. Have I ever been tossed out of a group where I felt safe?
2. Why?
3. Has my fear of being out on my own caused me to change my behavior?
4. How do I feel about that?

Fear of Looking at Our Weakness

Many of us are afraid to look at our weaknesses. Perhaps we had a father who humiliated us when we cried or who beat us when we failed. Perhaps we were laughed at in the schoolyard because we were awkward or failed at sports. Perhaps we live in a neighborhood where bullies prey on the weak, or perhaps we exist in a world where large corporations wipe out smaller competitors. These experiences teach us to hide our weaknesses.

Perhaps our moms always had us dressed perfectly, kept an immaculate house, and were presidents of the PTA. How can we live up to that? Or perhaps they weren't perfect at all; perhaps our moms were mentally ill, slovenly and spent every afternoon watching the soaps. We can't be weak like they were.

In addition to our personal experiences, we live in a society that creates images of heroism or power that we are supposed to match, such as the image of the soldier who has no fear, or the man who is super-sexed, or the competent career woman, or the long-suffering martyr mom.

Not only is weakness humiliating, it can be dangerous or at least seen as such. The mom gets beaten by the dad, the younger children by the older, the Honda gets creamed by the Hummer, and the small nation with fewer resources gets pushed around by the super powers.

If weakness is both humiliating and dangerous, we fear it within ourselves and do our best not to be identified with it. We admire movie stars, powerful business leaders, athletes, tough guys, people who seem powerful in themselves and in the world. We want to be cheerleaders, captains of the football teams, geniuses, movie stars, generals, something or somebody that looks powerful to us.

This fear of weakness does not only apply to men. While women are supposed to look weaker than their husbands, they're supposed to be strong in other ways. A popular image is the girl who is confident, popular, capable, not too needy, sexy and smart, and yet who surrenders to the power of the more powerful male. Another popular image is the tough woman who single-handedly raises four children on the washer woman's wage and sends them all to college, or the wonder woman who can hold down a job and hold her family together, or the compassionate ever-nurturing mom who can care for all the people in her family without ever becoming angry, frustrated or mean. Women fear being seen as weak and needy, and at the same time fear being seen as too strong or threatening to men.

Good heavens, how can we be self-aware when what we may discover within ourselves is a shameful weakness, a dangerous weakness, or a weakness that, if discovered, could lead not only to shame, but something worse? If you know my vulnerability, you can dominate me, manipulate me, take advantage of me.

Granted there are family members who seem to dominate through their weakness, such as a sick person who grabs all the attention. But such a person is not weak except in their body. Their mental strength helps them find other people's vulnerabilities to exploit. Mom has migraines, makes us all feel guilty for causing them, and makes us all tiptoe around her. She is not dominating through her weakness, but through our weakness, which is our guilt.

Let's consider some of our attitudes toward weakness.

1. Who in my family did I consider weak?
2. Were they really?
3. How were they treated?
4. Who do I think is weak in society?
5. How are they treated?

6. Do I see my own weaknesses?
7. When I look at them, do I feel afraid?

Fear of Punishment

If the fear of shame and weaknesses were not enough, we have the fear of punishment. Punishment can be physical or emotional. If I admit wrongdoing, I may be beaten, abused or ostracized. If I admit that I cheated at school, I may be failed. If I spill something on the carpet, Mom may scream at me, give me the look of disappointment or hit me with a belt.

What does this have to do with self-awareness? In a household where there is fear, we learn to avoid accountability and to blame others. I didn't do it. Johnny did. We often don't even realize that we have become afraid to be truthful, even when there is nothing more to fear. Lying to ourselves comes just a step behind.

And let's add one more dimension. If we blame others in order to avoid punishment, we feel ashamed of ourselves and cut off from the people we allowed to take the blame. Yeah, I let Dad beat Jose. I now feel guilty toward Jose and have to justify my behavior by convincing myself it's really his fault. Or I admit it's not his fault, but now I feel like avoiding him in order to avoid feeling my shame. In addition, while I'm blaming Jose, I may not even want to admit to myself that I'm lying to Dad, because I feel ashamed of my cowardice. So now I'm lying to myself even more.

We can become so afraid of punishment that we either put on a tough guy image, so we don't look weak, or we create a persona of the good girl or boy. Now I can't even ask myself how I feel or what I want. I need to act only in ways that support my persona. What happened to self-awareness?

Let's ask ourselves some questions about our possible fear of punishment.

1. What was the form of punishment in my family?
2. What behaviors were punished?
3. Who was punished more, my siblings or me?
4. How did that make me feel?
5. Did I learn to blame others?
6. How did I feel about myself?
7. How did I feel toward the ones I blamed?
8. Did lying, blaming and avoiding responsibility become a habit?

9. Am I still afraid of punishment?
10. Did I try to create the image of good boy or girl? Why?
11. Did I try to look tough? Why?
12. Did I squelch myself in the process?

Fear of Blame

In the last section, we discussed how we adopted the behavior of blaming others in order to avoid punishment and ensure our survival. But there are other sources of blaming behavior that can come out of our experience and conditioning. If we live in a household where we see our parents blaming one another and not taking accountability for their own part, we learn the habit of blame. Blaming others seems natural. In addition, we have learned to expect to be blamed, so we blame first.

Self-awareness and self-honesty can seem dangerous, and so we can't acknowledge that most situations are co-created. Instead, we seek to find "the" person to blame and we try really hard to ensure that it is not us. Again, we can't be honest with ourselves, because we have to deny whatever part we have played in a given situation, afraid to face the shame, blame or punishment.

And so, we can feel gripped with fear when the question of accountability arises, and that fear keeps us blind. This can happen even if, in the current situation, there is nothing to fear! Let's now look at some of our own relationship to blame.

1. Was there a lot of blaming going on in my family?
2. Was there someone who took most of the blame?
3. Am I afraid to be seen as someone to blame?
4. Does that make me afraid to acknowledge my part, when things go wrong?
5. Who do I tend to blame?

Fear of Accountability

The truth about me may scare me. Good heavens, if I look at myself honestly, I may discover that I'm doing things that are damaging to myself or to others. How can I live with that reality? Would I feel compelled to make amends to those I'm hurting? Would I have to change myself or my behavior? Can I?

First, am I willing to pay the price of accountability, when the price may cost me money or some advantage, real or imagined? Let's say when I look at my business practices objectively, I discover that I am exploiting my employees. Now what? Do I just calmly acknowledge my exploitation and continue to do it? Do I increase their wages or improve working conditions? Will that impact my profit and my ability to send my children to college? Will I have to give up my trips abroad or my wife's facials? What about my business? Will I be able to compete with the store across town, where conditions are even worse and the pay lower? Should I give my employees back wages? Oh, no, let's just forget it.

Second, am I capable of making the required changes? Let's say I realize that I am domineering toward my life partner. I want him/her to do it my way. We go on vacation where I want, or we eat according to my standards, or we have sex when I want. Am I willing to give those things up? Or let's say I'm overindulging my children because I am substituting things for time, or because I want to be loved but am obsessed with money or can't relate? Am I willing to change this behavior and meet their real needs for me? Can I? What about their need for loving discipline? Am I willing to be disliked and resented, if it's for their good? Or let's say I realize that I'm compulsively gambling away my family's savings. I don't want to face this reality, because I fear I can't stop.

Fear of accountability can lead to fear of self-awareness. If I don't look at myself, if I don't face what I'm doing, I won't feel the pain that I'm creating, and I won't have to change.

Let's ask ourselves a few questions to examine our potential of accountability.

1. Are there areas in my life I don't want to look at?
2. Can I think of some relationships that I already know are not healthy?
3. Am I scared to look at them?
4. What am I afraid I would lose?
5. Can I think of some behaviors of mine that I already know are destructive or self-destructive?
6. Am I afraid I can't stop them?
7. Do I want to?

Fear that Significant Others May Feel Threatened

Not only can we be afraid to be self-aware, others might be afraid of our self-awareness, as well, and we may be afraid of the consequences of their reactions. Let's say my partner and I have been parenting in a particular way, and now I realize our parenting is damaging. Perhaps my partner is not ready to make the change. Or let's say my wife and I have been drinking buddies for 20 years, and suddenly I want to stop. Or let's say I decide that I have been co-creating an abusive relationship, and I want it to change. Or let's say I realize that I'm destroying my health by working in a factory emitting heavy fumes, or that I'm hurting my own body by working too many hours as a doctor, and I shift into more health-conscious behavior. How much would my family want me to realize the damage I'm doing to myself, if they had to pay for the change in my lifestyle?

Or supposing I realize that our collective patterns of consumption are causing spiritual decay to ourselves and are depleting our collective resources. And let's say I've decided to do something about it? How many groups—employers, employees, ad agencies, stores, distributors, banks—are going to feel threatened by my new awareness? Let's take a look at our own possible fears of other people's reactions to our self-awareness.

1. Are there patterns in my personal life that I'm afraid to address because I'm afraid of upsetting a spouse, friend, child, or other loved one?
2. Have I already tried to make changes that seem healthy?
3. Were the people around me threatened?
4. Have I ever tried to address social issues?
5. Who did it threaten?
6. How did I respond to their reactions?

Self-Awareness Is Not Taught

As children, most of us focus on ourselves, on getting our "needs" met in rather primitive and unconscious ways. For example, if I am craving attention, I may jump up and down and say "Look at me. Look at me." The child is not consciously thinking that it needs attention, but it is acting out of some visceral need. Our parents typically respond in one of two ways: They either feed the behavior by giving us the attention and calling it cute, or they feed our shame by making us feel that these needs are bad.

Neither of these responses teaches self-awareness. The parents who feed the child's endless need for attention teach the child that they are entitled to attention-on-demand, and the child never questions his or her behavior. The parents who shame the child for needing attention teach the child that their needs are bad and need to be hidden.

Does either of these responses help the child understand his behavior and motives? Does either response help the child find healthier ways of meeting her needs? Fast forward. Now we're adults, and we are fundamentally the same. If our pattern was to be indulged, we won't feel loved if we're not indulged. So if my husband's attention is absorbed by work or golf or anything but me, I feel shocked and surprised. If our pattern was to be shamed for our needing attention, we may fear to ask our partner for the relating we need and just simmer with resentment, or we may be driven toward constant attention in order to compensate for unmet needs from the past. Where in this behavior is self-awareness? Most of the time, we don't even know we're struggling with issues of attention. We only know that we're grumpy when George is out with the boys.

In some ways, becoming adults makes self-awareness more difficult. We are so conditioned, we can't see enough outside ourselves to realize we're in a pattern, or we're so embarrassed by the childishness of our behavior and motivations, we won't admit them. For example, suppose I feel driven to run for president of the PTA, even though it will take time away from my own family. Maybe this is an admirable activity, and maybe it is for the highest good of all. But perhaps it's really motivated by a need for attention. I may think that the need for attention is childish, and so I hide my motivation even from myself. I create elaborate rationalizations for my behavior. I convince myself that I am only concerned about my children's welfare, even though I'm neglecting them in order to run for office.

It would be elucidating and in some ways amusing to make a list of all our actions throughout the day and to try to determine the motivation behind each. So let's take a moment to examine our behaviors over the past day or so.

1. How have I behaved?
2. What was I seeking?

3. Do I feel comfortable admitting my motive?
4. Did I exhibit similar behavior as a child?
5. Was it rewarded?
6. Was it shamed?
7. Do I tend to insist on getting my unconscious needs met?
8. Or have I sent my needs underground?

Who is going to teach us self-awareness? Not the people around us who are not aware themselves. They are reacting and responding to us out of their own needs and cannot help us clearly see ourselves. Their perceptions of us are generally based on their own unconscious agendas.

Let's go back to a much earlier example: Mary, jumping up and down in front of the camera, saying "Look at me." Maybe Mom is embarrassed by Mary's obvious neediness, and maybe Mom is embarrassed because she is a sex addict focusing on her attractiveness, and she has neglected her child. Perhaps Mary's constant craving for attention reveals Mary's neglect. Feeling exposed, Mom's reaction to Mary's acting act might be to shame the child for exposing Mom's negligence to the whole world. Or maybe Mom is so desperate for attention herself that she gets vicarious pleasure out of everybody watching her daughter, so she encourages Mary to jump up and down. In fact, she takes her to Hollywood and offers her as the next child star. Or maybe Mom is not a sex addict but feels guilty because she spends too much time at work, so she indulges Mary's acting out to get herself off the hook about her absence.

How can an unconscious parent teach her child consciousness? The same can be true of teachers, social workers, religious leaders, all the people who are instrumental in our mental formation. If I am a therapist and my client is not getting better, am I willing to point that out to the client? Do I think that would make me look bad? For example, suppose my client claims that he is being victimized at work. Is he? Do I tend to reinforce the client's belief in his rightness, rather than to confront his behavior and where he might be at fault? If so, has my unwillingness to confront him supported him to stay dysfunctional? On the other hand, is the client refusing to get honest with himself or try other suggestions? Does his lack of progress necessarily indicate my failure as a therapist? Is my fear of confronting these questions getting in the way of my confronting him and thereby supporting him to be more self-aware?

We hope that people in positions of influence are sufficiently detached from self-interest to be honest, but how many of us are so clear that we are free of agendas? Let's look at how well we were taught self-awareness.

1. Who taught me self-awareness?
2. Were they self-aware?
3. What agendas might they have had?

Lack of Perspective; Lack of Higher Consciousness

To add to all these obstacles to self-awareness, we need to add another really big one. We don't have the capacity to see ourselves objectively when we lack perspective, and most of us lack the higher consciousness that would give us that perspective. Reality is complex. Shame and blame are the deadly duo. We're driven by unconscious fears and motivations. And we are impacted by forces we can't see. How many of us have the skills and perspective to see past all this?

Self-awareness requires higher consciousness, perspective, a vantage point from which we can actually look at ourselves and everything that surrounds us. If I am an ant, I can't see from the perspective of an eagle. I may be able to see my immediate surroundings, but I can't see the bigger picture. And when I'm stuck in me, how well can I see ME? How do I get beyond my own narrow perspective?

We as humans tend to see everything from our ant-like perspective. Most of us become aware only when we feel a sensation, whether that be pleasure, pain, heat, desire or some other physical or emotional feeling. Now "aware," we decide that what feels good is "right" and want to feel it again, or we decide something is "wrong," because it has caused us discomfort, and we try to fix it.

Some of us barely feel our own feelings. Some of us are aware of our sensations or emotions. Few of us see what immediately caused those feelings. And even fewer see the big picture of cause and effect that led to it, especially if it was an action of ours that caused it. If I have that ant-like perspective, I may feel wet when I accidentally walk into a puddle, but I may not see that it was my route that got me there.

Blindness to My Part

Here are some examples. I feel the pain of a marriage, and I become aware of my unhappiness. I immediately think that this must be my spouse's fault, because I don't see the many steps I took that helped co-create the condition of our relationship. I don't notice that I have been hurtful to my spouse. If I could acknowledge that I am hurtful, I might discover that my behavior stems from the fact that I don't want to be in the relationship. Perhaps I married the guy out of fear of being on my own. But now that we are married, I can't stand the life we are co-creating. Instead of taking accountability for the poor decision that I made and acknowledging that I have co-created a painful relationship, I get stuck in the feeling that I am disappointed with HIM, that he has changed and this has caused me to feel distant. He feels my distance and pulls away from me. What am I aware of? That he is distant from me. What am I not aware of? That I am distant from him.

Let's look at another example. I feel angry, because I'm poor. I have three kids and a husband who drinks. My awareness focuses on my feelings of anger. He's a God-damned son of a bitch. They are brats. The landlord is a pig. And my feet hurt. Do I acknowledge that I have three kids because I had sex unconsciously? Do I recognize that I unconsciously had sex because I wanted to get pregnant? Do I see that I wanted to get pregnant because I wanted to stay home with kids, because I was afraid of failing in the workplace? Do I admit that I was afraid of failing in the workplace because I did poorly in school? Do I see that I did poorly in school because I have undiagnosed dyslexia? Do I acknowledge that it's difficult for one salary to support our household? Do I understand that my husband resents me because I am not earning money? And so on and so on.

My awareness starts late, when I'm experiencing the negative consequences, rather than early, when my steps are already leading me into the trap. Once in the painful situation I've co-created, I want to avoid feeling shame, too, so I will certainly blame someone or something else. This can lead to endless rationalization and self-justification. If I am a bit more honest, I may see my "fault," but this leads me to becoming angry at myself. I am not seeing the long trail of cause and effect, which includes the reasons that I have behaved foolishly. Whether I'm in denial or self-blame, I'm feeling compassion for no one. In fact, when I'm filled with shame, anger or self-loathing, I am less likely to think clearly and make good future decisions.

Rationalization and self-loathing block self-awareness. To see clearly, instead of blaming others or myself, I need perspective so that I can identify the fears, the programming and the cultural determinants that went into my choices.

In American culture, we often confuse our feelings with objective reality. I feel abused; therefore it must be so. It is my "truth," and I can always create a circle of friends to reinforce my view. In fact, emotions are just one source of information that we need to integrate in order to be self-aware. Only with dual consciousness, which I will discuss later, can we use our inner awareness and combine it with higher consciousness, so that we can become increasingly self-aware.

Let's pause for some questions about our level of awareness.

1. What am I most aware of? My feelings? Conditions?
2. Who or what do I blame?
3. Do I see myself as having taken steps that led to these conditions?
4. Do I think I could have done any better?
5. Do I go into shame, denial or blame?

Blindness to the Culture

Okay, so it's hard to see myself when I'm in myself. Let's add to that the difficulty of seeing myself in the context of the whole. Even if I want to be honest with myself, do I have the capacity to rise into a much higher, more objective place and see all the influences that create my condition: not only my personal characteristics, but my culture and family, our time in history, the multiple sources of my reality?

We are the sum of all our conditions, and that includes forces that we did not create and may not even see. First, we have to deal with the impact of others' consciousness. I am born into a family with a certain perspective. I automatically adapt to their view. Being in that family limits my ability to see my family's beliefs as merely beliefs, not as truths. Children brought up in Christianity tend toward Christian beliefs, not Native American spirituality. Without noticing it, we adopt values, paradigms and thought structures that make it difficult to see ourselves clearly, because each value, paradigm and thought structure is seen as "true" in its own cultural context. Infidelity is bad; incest is evil; marriage is desirable; thin is better than fat; soft hair is better than frizzy; and so on. Some behaviors may, in fact, be more beneficial than others, but the value of a behavior needs to be determined through evaluating experience, not through prejudice and programming. Social programming blocks the process of evaluation, because it doesn't allow us to ask the questions.

It is easy for negativity to dominate when it is supported by our culture and when we can't detach enough from our social programming to look at ourselves clearly. Suppose we live in a culture where militarism is a given and a value. How easily can we differentiate from that energy and look at militarism as fear-driven and maladaptive? Or suppose we live in a culture where earning money is emphasized more than any other aspect of us. How easily can we disconnect from that influence and nurture our wholeness? Or suppose we grew up in a drinking culture. Are we even aware of the power of that collective consciousness as we try to stand on our own and choose whether or not to drink? How well can we even see the subtle and not so subtle influences of our programming and the many negative forces around us?

Negative energy is anything that blocks the realization of our potential, and it is everywhere.[22] Collective fear, pain, hate and self-abuse to a great extent run our world. But we are not conscious of negative energy because it seems normal. Listen to our media and notice how many programs are devoted to humiliating, exposing and criticizing people. Turn on the television, and watch the advertising that encourages us to feel insecure about our looks, our weight, our breath or our social status. See the images that feed addictive spending, drinking, eating, dieting and ambition.

And observe what else we consider normal. Look at the children already jockeying for power and the teenagers already grasping for ways to escape their pain with drugs and sex. Addictive behaviors, fear, hate, greed and compulsion are considered normal. We are not trained to see behind the veil of our behavior, individual or collective. We don't see the negative energies that influence our decisions, and we don't even acknowledge they exist. We fear to see the power of negativity that runs rife on our planet, and we don't know how to confront it when we see it.

Let's ask ourselves a few questions about our programming.

---

22   We discuss negative energy in depth in Platform Seven: Becoming Accountable.

1. What have I been programmed to see as positive?
2. What have I programmed to see as negative?
3. Are they?
4. What do I consider to be a negative energy?
5. How does it block my potential and the potential of others?
6. What groups carry these energies?
7. How powerful do they seem?
8. Do I think of them as normal?

Fear of Feeling Impotent

What's the use of looking at what is? I can't change it anyway. Now that's a great excuse not to look at ourselves, and it has no validity.

First, let's listen to the excuses. Sure I'm in a bad marriage, job, whatever. I made my bed, and I'll have to lie in it. Sure I'm a gambler, but I went to a couple of Gamblers Anonymous meetings, and it just didn't work. Sure I gave myself diabetes through my compulsive eating, but there's no point dwelling on it; nothing I can do about it now. Hand me another donut.

While sometimes it is true that we cannot change our external condition, we can work toward changing our inner experience of it. When we come into our last platform, Becoming Becoming, we learn to embrace all experience as an opportunity for learning and growth. We don't deny that some, perhaps many life experiences are painful. But pain in and of itself does not make an experience bad or not worth having. It can be birthing ground for evolution.

If we become self-aware, aware of the cause-and-effect nature of reality, we can become more compassionate toward ourselves. Since self-hatred is one of our most toxic feelings, having understanding and compassion toward ourselves in itself reduces our pain. This means that even if we cannot change our circumstances through awareness, we might be able to change our reactions and responses. We are no longer impotent.

In addition, coming to self-awareness allows us to share our experience with others, gives meaning to our lives and turns shit into fertilizer. Anyone who has been to a twelve-step meeting can appreciate the value that sharing our pain and self-honesty can bring to others. And finally, self-awareness can help us avoid making the same painful choices again and again.

Let's pause again to consider how confident we are in our ability to change.

1. What conditions of mine am I afraid to confront?
2. Do I fear that I can't change them?
3. Can I?
4. Can I examine my reaction to my own behaviors?
5. Can I learn how to avoid repeating these behaviors?
6. Can I share my awareness with others?

A Final Word Regarding the Obstacles to Self-Awareness

We can see that we have our work cut out for us. The obstacles to self-awareness are great. To be in reality, we need to see cause and effect, and we need perspective, self-honesty and self-compassion. We need knowledge, courage, effort and help. And we need to get past the rationalizations and subterfuges of the ego and the programmed self, and we need to connect to and support the being that's underneath.

Even if we just recognize the difficulty of true self-awareness, we have taken a step toward freedom, because most of us are trapped in the belief that our view of reality is true and therefore immutable. We can't see anything differently, because our view is already true, right and complete. We can't change anything, because we are blameless. We can't connect to our real selves, because we have come to identify with the programmed self as us, and we aren't even looking to connect with anything else. Self-awareness contradicts all this.

We, the collective of humanity, are not very experienced at self-awareness. Even if we try really hard, it's difficult to achieve a perspective that permits the objectivity, self-compassion and neutrality that we need to be self-aware. Developing that capacity is discussed in the section on How to Become Self-Aware. But for now, let's just recognize that self-awareness is amazingly difficult, even with the best of intentions. We need to give ourselves gold stars just for trying.

WHY WOULD I WANT TO BECOME SELF-AWARE?

If self-awareness is so difficult and challenging, especially to our egos, as we discussed in the introduction to this book, why bother? The reasons are powerful.

Let's use our common sense. Imagine you were in a battle. Wouldn't you want to know exactly the weaknesses and strengths of your troops, and wouldn't you want to learn whatever you could about the opposition? Of course. Sure, sometimes we win by dumb luck, but more often than not, what helps us to win is information, analysis, and good strategy.

That's what we need to live better and feel better. We need information: the factors that undermine our wellbeing; analysis: the causes and essential nature of these factors; and good strategy: how we can change or eliminate these factors. Self-awareness provides the information and analysis; Platform Six: Becoming Integrated and the rest of this book provide the good strategy.

Information gives us the clues to strategy. If you see that you're driving your wife away, you can go to counseling. If you see that your drinking is ruining your life, you can go to Alcoholics Anonymous. If you see that overwork is ruining your health, you can start taking time for regeneration. If you see that you are consistently angry with your children, you can stop blaming them for being children and find a way to enjoy your family. If all of us see that our collective polluting is destroying the earth, we can start putting long-term goals ahead of short-term ones.

Good information and strategy can help us to eliminate needless fear and pain. Earlier in this book we stressed that life is a struggle and that fear and pain are inevitable. But we've also stressed that most of our fear and pain is needless. Self-awareness helps us avoid the needless pain, ours and others', because armed with information, we can begin to strategize a happier way to live.

While our initial motivation to become self-aware may be the desire to see what it is that is hurting us and others so that we can be empowered to change, we quickly discover that our self-awareness is the greatest gift we can bring to others as well. Going back to our earlier examples: The man who stops drinking can have true relationships with his wife and family. The woman who stops overworking has energy to offer her loved ones. The parent who starts enjoying his or her children brings joy to the whole family. And when we start caring for the earth, we all benefit. Self-awareness brings us into the realization of the impact of our behavior on others, so that we can take accountability for our behavior and stop inflicting needless pain on them. (More on this in Platform Seven: Becoming Accountable.)

Becoming Self-Aware is not only important to us as individuals, it's essential to us as human society. Imagine a time when all of us could stop blaming one another and begin to look at our part. Free from our tendency to justify our reactivity, we would be able to admit that we, in fact, are causing hurt to one another. That step alone would relieve everyone of needless pain. We would not feel secret shame about ourselves, while covering it up, and those impacted by our negative behavior would not feel constantly discounted or blamed. If we could take further steps to act on our awareness, we would be able to solve many more of our problems.

When we are blind to our behavior, its causes and effects, we don't have the essential tool for regulating our behavior. Who me? I didn't do anything. But if we are willing to be honest, self-aware, aware of others' needs as well, and if we are able to regulate our own behavior for the highest good of all, we can help eliminate needless fear and pain.

And having changed our behavior, guess what? We might still get killed by the guy next to us who is driving on cocaine.

To Make Real Change, We Need Collective Self-Awareness

Reality is that if we are to change our lives and our world, self-awareness needs to be collective. Let's look at our example of driving. If nobody were driving on cocaine or otherwise impaired by physical or inner stress, nobody would be in a hurry, and everybody would be driving in a more relaxed and stress-free way. The trip would be a lot more pleasant.

If I'm the only sober driver on the freeway, I'm still in danger. My sobriety helps me regardless of the impairment of others, because it allows me to make better choices in my driving. For example, when the guy next to me is swerving, I can try to get out of his way, call the police and/or drive defensively. And of course my self-awareness can help me reduce my reactivity to the fact that the guy next to me is high on cocaine. If I'm angry and reactive, I will drive worse than if I can stay calm and try to avoid a crash.

But no matter how self-aware I am, I cannot control that the guy is on cocaine and might drive right into me, despite my best efforts. And no matter how self-aware I am, if most everyone on the freeway is impaired either by drugs, alcohol, emotional upset, lateness or sleep deprivation, no matter what I do, it's going to be a dangerous ride.

Only the collective consciousness, the collective self-awareness and the collective freedom from reactivity will allow us to reach a place where we are co-creating a collective universe in which we are all safe, relaxed, well and supportive of one another. Taking our freeway example, if we can simultaneously and collectively reduce our driving, stagger our trips to work, care for our minds and bodies so that we are more capable of making safe choices, create highways that are all beautiful and build emission-free cars, our driving experience would become entirely different. Just so, if everyone in the universe woke up on the same day with a sudden dose of self-awareness, able to recognize and correct our impact on ourselves and one another, kids would go to school without the fear of bullying; people wouldn't thoughtlessly dump trash in streams; employers would create work environments that nurtured their employees; and we would eliminate racism, sexism, classism, denigration of gays, fat people, the disabled and so on overnight. There would be no more war, because we wouldn't be busy grabbing at the earth's resources; we would be striving to understand rather than demonize one another; and intimate relationships would be much more loving and supportive. Yes, we would have problems, but we would face them with awareness. This all could happen if the collective became committed to self awareness.

But in the meantime, while we are supporting the collective to become collectively self-aware, Becoming Self-Aware ourselves is a huge step toward freedom from needless pain.

Self-Awareness Also Helps Free Me from Needless Fear

Thus far we have been talking about eliminating needless pain. But as we discussed in Platform One, the self-centered me also lives in a universe of needless fear, the fear of being dominated, discarded, and killed physically, socially or psychologically, regardless of the realities. I am afraid of everything and everyone, I need to control everything and everyone, and I am under constant stress, as I try to achieve just that goal.

If I can be self-aware and see reality, I can refocus my energies on real problems instead of imagined ones. I can actually protect myself better by comprehending where I am truly weak and taking steps to either strengthen myself or compensate for that weakness. I can stop my knee-jerk reactions to others' negative behavior, investigate what is truly happening to them and even try to help them feel better or more secure. I can come out of the world of shadows and start impacting reality. Needless fear begins to vanish, and I can actually face my problems and those of others.

As discussed in the introduction to our book, our ego-based programmed self lives in needless fear because we are always afraid that someone or something will reveal that we are weak, greedy, afraid, wrong, or something else we perceive as negative. So life becomes a frightening series of threats to our illusions about ourselves. If, on the other hand, I embrace self-awareness, I don't suffer the needless fear of exposure, because exposure only reveals to me the truths that I already know and offers me a way out. Instead of dreading exposure, I embrace it.

Yes, I see myself, my fears and my motives and they are transparent to me; yes, I can understand where those fears and motives come from; yes, I can have compassion for myself while I'm trying to shift myself; yes, I can laugh at my foibles, and I can laugh at everyone else's, too. Because I live in the world of cause and effect, I understand these foibles and try to support myself to change, instead of living in self-condemnation, which keeps me forever entrapped. Self-discovery becomes fun, a life-long enterprise with no endpoint.

We have so many needless fears, such as the fears of not looking good to others or meeting some standard that has nothing to do with us. When we are self-aware, we see these needless fears for what they are and can release them and the grip that they have on us.

The Self-Aware Me Has More Fun

Not only does the self-aware me have less needless fear and pain, it has more fun. The self-aware me is always laughing at me and others, deeply appreciating the humor of human behavior. Truly self-aware, I can see what I'm doing and why. I can see what you're doing and why. I can observe the silly dances and patterns between us. I can see all of us trying desperately to control one another or get something from one another. And I can relax through it all, because I am not invested in winning the game because I am aware that it is a game.

Self-awareness allows me to become more relaxed for several reasons. First, I have become more the observer and not the defender or the denier, so I'm not stressed out trying to figure out how to hide what I'm doing. And second, I don't feel so driven to change the unchangeable. For example, if I am unhappy or uncomfortable because YOU are doing something annoying, I can be very frustrated because you won't change. The un-self-aware me insists that I have just GOT to get you to stop in order for me to get comfortable, and how likely is that to happen? The self-aware me realizes what's bothering me and why, feels much more capable of changing my state of mind by shifting myself, and focuses on myself instead of you. I release my frustration that I can't change YOU and in so doing let go of the imperative that you change. How relaxing is that?

Concluding Why We Would Want to Be Self-Aware

This concludes our brief discussion of why we would want to be self-aware. We've discovered that while many of us believe we want to be self-aware, there is a lot of fear and resistance, and there are many obstacles to self-awareness. Yet staying unaware only keeps us powerless, lost in the cave of shadows. There was a time in human history when we didn't know that germs cause disease in a vulnerable host. Doctors would not wash their hands between procedures and so disease spread. Staying unconscious about ourselves is like going back to that degree of ignorance. Why would we want to?

Furthermore, think of the relief we feel when we learn to embrace self-awareness. Our first act of Becoming Self-Aware was acknowledging our resistance to it, and that alone might have made me feel ashamed. But now that our resistance is revealed, we can see that such resistance is common, in fact endemic to human society. Suddenly I don't feel so dumb about mine. In fact, I can feel compassion for myself. All or almost all of us have some resistance to self-awareness. The obstacles are intense, and it's pretty normal to resist the pain, shame, embarrassment and challenge of seeing ourselves clearly.

Oh, sure Becoming Self-Aware is difficult. But now that I know that it's difficult, I can have compassion for myself and figure out ways to make it less painful. We can become Self-Aware in groups[23], so that we feel less alone with our problems and more normal about having them; we can laugh a lot; get tools to deal with our problems, so we don't feel hopeless; keep focusing on the benefits.

---

[23] Mutual support groups help enormously with our tendency to judge ourselves. If you study this book with a group, you'll find yourself laughing frequently about how alike we are.

Wow. Self-awareness is not so bad after all. In fact using self-awareness to examine my resistance to self-awareness has allowed me to make self-awareness a way to make Becoming Self-Aware a lot more fun.

Finally, think of the freedom we would all experience if we did not need to hide our motives from others or ourselves, if we were not afraid to be busted, if we could observe rather than judge ourselves and the people around us, and if we had a true sense of the ridiculous. Think of how much more powerfully we could intervene with life and with ourselves, if we could understand ourselves better. And think of how much more successfully we could meet our needs if we could get past our programmed behavior and connect to our true selves. And if we became collectively self-aware, think of how different this planet would be.

Our wellbeing deepens as we go on to Platforms Six and Seven: Becoming Integrated and Becoming Accountable, as we become freed up from our self-destructive behavior. But Becoming Self-Aware alone, and having the willingness and ability to see ourselves clearly and without judgment, relieves us of amazing amounts of needless fear and pain and allows us to move into a state of mind where we can allow, relax and be happier.

And guess what? We might even discover some wonderful things about ourselves, too! Self-awareness is not just about seeing the negative. It's about seeing what is. Maybe we will see that in many ways, we are pretty terrific. We've lived through a lot, survived a lot and learned a lot. Despite everything, we still care, and we're still ready to grow. I am incredible!

Let's ask ourselves a couple of questions about that.

1. What can I see that's really good about myself?
2. How often do I notice that?

HOW TO BECOME SELF-AWARE

Let's review our definition of self-awareness.

Becoming Self-Aware is the ability to see ourselves objectively; to notice our reactions and responses, realize their causes, and acknowledge the impact of these reactions and behaviors on ourselves and others. Self-awareness allows us to trace the relationship between the way we feel and what we do; and then trace the relationship between what

we do and the outcome of those choices. As we begin to differentiate from our behavior, our true self emerges.

If you recall our book's introduction, our egos are born when we come into existence and their job is to ensure our survival. They develop strategies to do just that and those strategies come to be identified with ourselves. When we develop the ability to objectively see our responses and reactions, we are actually becoming aware not so much of ourselves, but of the programs that we have developed to ensure our survival. In a sense, then, the person of whom we are becoming aware is not ourselves in an intrinsic sense; rather it is a set of reactions and responses that we have identified with and which have become self-perpetuating, like a machine run amuck.

When we think of it that way, we can see how much needless pain we have experienced about ourselves. Even when we have been foolish or destructive, who is the "we" that is being foolish and destructive? It's not really us; it's just a set of patterns and programs. What then is there to be ashamed of?

And it gets better. There is another us, a self under the programs. This relates to the second level of self-awareness, which is becoming aware of the self that underlies the programming itself. This self refers to our potential self, the self we could still be if we would strip away the programs and all the fears and feelings of worthlessness that drive our ego-based behavior. And this is the self we are going to become as we advance through this book.

But in this platform, let's focus on the first level of awareness: the task of becoming increasingly aware of our programmed behaviors, so we can support ourselves to release them.

As we proceed with this self-examination, let's remember to have compassion, compassion, compassion for ourselves. Remember that we are investigating a set of programs that were set in motion at infancy, stimulated by the lizard brain and designed by our egos to ensure our survival.

Stimulus, Reaction, Response: The Programmed Self

As we said earlier, the ego-based self is a set of programs set in motion at a young age to ensure our survival. Driven by the lizard brain, it combines instinct, genetic characteristics and conditioning. How do these programs come into existence? Through a process called stimulus-reaction-response. The circumstance is the stimulus. Then the ego takes over. The ego evaluates the stimulus and the threat it poses to our survival and wellbeing. This becomes the basis of our reaction, and our behavior is the response.

Let's look at a simple example. Mommy has a new baby and is not paying much attention to me. That's the stimulus. I feel left out, which makes me feel that my survival is threatened. Fear is the reaction. I jump up and down and scream to grab the attention. That's my response.

Pretty obvious. I may not be conscious that I'm feeling threatened. I may not know why I'm jumping up and down. I may not even be aware that I'm being stimulated by the new baby. But when examined, the links are obvious.

My purpose is to bring mommy's attention to me in order to restore my power in the family. I am not thinking about mom's need to get more rest. I am not thinking of the new baby's need to feel secure in its new life. I am not even aware of my own true needs. Because I instinctively feel that what I need is attention, I ignore my true needs for a mom who is happy and rested and a baby brother who is secure and positive, both of which would create more joy and more relaxation in the home, which would release more energy for me. No, my lizard brain joins forces with my ego to create an experience of fear (reaction) when attention is withdrawn from me, and the ego creates a response of me demanding attention, which makes everybody feel tense and threatened, which makes Mom exhausted and frustrated. It's a strategy that actually meets nobody's needs. But I'm too immature to understand this.

As we get older, this pattern is either reinforced, refined or replaced. Let's look at a case where it's reinforced. Supposing Mom gives me attention, negative or positive, for jumping up and down. She drops the baby and runs to me, coddling and cuddling me, or yelling and berating me. Since my aim was to get attention away from the baby and get it redirected toward me, I have succeeded and am well on the road to a habitual reaction-response pattern when I encounter the stimulus of a loss of attention. After a while I have become defined in my eyes and in the eyes of the world as the child who jumps up and down when attention is withdrawn and when it feels threatened. That behavior, that pattern is becoming me.

As adults, we may laugh at this obvious and childish behavior, but we will likely continue this pattern in a refined form. Let's say that now it's my husband who's distracted by work (stimulus). I feel abandoned and unloved, and my position is threatened (reaction). Now for the adult response: Instead of jumping up and down physically, I find a way to attract attention. For example, I may start complaining about my husband's weight, which upsets him, because it's an area where he feels very vulnerable. He may not be happy with me; but I've got his attention. Oh, yeah, positive or negative, the attention comes to me.

Sometimes it's hard to track my response to the reaction and stimulus. For example, I may suddenly become very emotional over some small thing that went wrong, or I may start criticizing my best friend for some real or imagined slight. I'm still jumping up and down trying to get attention, even though I may not be directly asking for that attention from my husband, and even though I may not even realize that I'm responding to my husband's withdrawal of attention.

When I observe myself responding in an exaggerated way to a slight problem in my life or to my friend's behavior, I am confused. I know that something has to explain my emotionality or anger or criticalness. But if I am not self-aware, what do I see? I see that some random thing went wrong and THAT'S why I'm upset. The kid spilled the milk. Or my friend said something bitchy. I think I know why I'm upset and, unaware of the true nature of my reaction-response, I justify my reactivity.

If I'm semi-conscious, I may look for a reason for my "overreaction," and I may realize that I'm having a reaction-response pattern that is being stimulated by my husband's behavior. But because I still lack self-awareness, I think that the stimulus (the behavior triggering me) is my husband's "neglect." In other words, I'm blaming him for my reaction and response by claiming to myself and all within reach that my husband is neglecting ME, and of course I'm upset.

With my inner reaction-response program running on autopilot, I lack the objectivity to evaluate whether or not my husband is in fact neglecting me. In fact, I don't consider that he might be neglecting himself. I'm too busy reacting, and I don't question my reaction, because I probably think it is natural and justified because my reaction is something that comes easily to me, because it started 30 years before, when my survival felt threatened by the birth of my baby sister. Now in full-blown reaction and justification, I may even embellish my interpretation further: he is neglecting me because he's a louse, I've gotten fat or there's another woman in his life. I don't think to inquire as to what's going on with him that he feels compelled to overwork, because I'm focusing on myself. I complain that he's neglecting me, when I'm actually neglecting him.

Sometimes through a lot of self-examination, I realize that I have this particular stimulus-reaction-response pattern to George's overwork, and I realize that I might be over-reacting. But does this stop the pattern? Not always. On the contrary, now armed with the knowledge of the cause of this pattern, I often proceed to use this knowledge to beat up everyone in sight.

"George, you're neglecting me and that's really upsetting me. You know how sensitive I am to abandonment issues ever since I was as a child when my sister Lucie was born."

Blackmail does not represent Becoming Self-Aware. This is a form of pseudo-self-awareness, where we use information about ourselves in order to manipulate and control the behavior of others. We still haven't shifted to self-awareness, which focuses on us becoming objective about our behavior, so that we can use the knowledge to change ourselves. Ironically, I am still using jumping up and down to get attention, this time through my emotionality.

In fact, in all probability, by this time I have used emotionality so often to get attention that I don't even see the stimulus, much less the reaction anymore. I simply see my response—my emotionality, and it seems perfectly reasonable to me. "George, you know how sensitive I am. And therefore you need to pay more attention to me."

And George? What about George? Why is he overworking? Who knows? Who cares? It's all about ME!! Let's ask ourselves some questions to see how this might apply to us.

1. Am I angry with someone for something they are doing to me?
2. What are they actually doing?
3. Are they doing it to me?
4. Do I care, or do I want to stay in my reaction?

Deflecting the Focus

Let's take a moment to look at a different facet of this pattern. Let's say I'm upset about George overworking, but I don't want to antagonize him. Let's say George makes more money than I and his work offers me greater social status than I could achieve myself. My survival seems contingent upon George's supporting me. Not wanting to mess with my survival, I don't want to focus my reaction on George. Instead, I refocus my anger on my best friend, Linda. Let's say that Linda works for the same company as I, and she has gotten a sale that I think I should have gotten. All overwrought and looking for something to lay it on, I turn my upset toward Linda and accuse her of conniving to cheat me out of the sale.

We know that I'm already feeling threatened about George's overwork, that I am actually being triggered because George's work is stealing his attention, just as the second child stole mom's attention. But now could I not also be having a simultaneous stimulus-reaction-response to Linda's sale, as well? Here's how this could go. Linda got the sale because she's smarter than I am. This is just like my experience with my sister 20 years ago. She was smarter than I and that threatened my feeling of value in the family. Since my reaction-response pattern to the loss of attention was to get upset and jump up and down way back when she was born, I continued the same attention-seeking pattern as I grew older. My sister was more successful in school, so I had to find some other way to deflect attention back to myself. I might stay out all night, or I accuse my sister of cheating at cards or flirting with my boyfriend. I grabbed attention again. Now as an adult, I am experiencing the same kind of stimulus, the success of a "sibling," and I'm reacting with the same feeling of threat, and I'm responding similarly by jumping up and down in a negative way by accusing Linda of doing something underhanded to beat me to the sale.

So now two things are going on: 1) I feel threatened by George's overwork and deflect my upset to Linda because I am afraid to confront my relationship with George and the security it gives me. 2) I am also going through the same trio of reactivity around Linda's success. So actually my value feels threatened by both of them, and getting angry at Linda is a perfect response. What a mess.

If I could connect to myself and break the programs, I might discover that I don't have to act out my habitual reaction-responses. I might find that I enjoy George's absence because I have more time for myself. I might find it relaxes me to see Linda succeed. She's just gone through a divorce and is desperate for money, and if she does well, I won't be so worried about her. And, besides, I mentored Linda, and her success is partially a tribute to me. If I could connect to myself, I might discover these things.

If I were in a different state of mind, I would either not care about these stimuli, or I would find their positive sides for me.

But when I'm caught in the negative programming, I don't see reality. I just react. And what's worse, if confronted with the question as to why I am having such a big reaction to Linda's sale or George's weight, I will be bound and determined to justify both. Of course, I am annoyed with Linda or George; "they" . . . I don't recognize that I am reacting to George's absence and my baby sister's birth. Look at how alienated from reality I have become. I am having a reaction-response to stimuli that are invisible to me, and I feel compelled to justify myself.

Secretly, I am feeling uncomfortable with my reactions. I know something is going on with me, because I can feel the upset and anxiety that are driving me. But blind to my part, I am reduced to blaming others or circumstances, and I never get any peace or relief from that.

In fact, if I am challenged about my reactions, I now have a new stimulus that causes another chain reaction. Being confronted about my reactions appears to make me feel guilty, stupid or embarrassed. In fact, nothing is "making" me feel guilty or embarrassed; some stimulus is just causing these feelings to surface. But I don't know that. I think that what are making me feel bad are you and your questions. Now the new stimulus is you asking me questions, the reaction is guilt and shame, and the response is me justifying myself more and making you wrong. Ah, what a tangled web we weave.

Without self-awareness, I am digging myself deeper and deeper into habitual behaviors that I have to rationalize. Our original trio of George's absence, my feeling threatened and my attention-seeking irritability have triggered in me the same stimulus-reaction-response, the same rationalizations, and the same no self-awareness that I had as a child. Since I have engaged in this trio thousands of times, it is only becoming more habitual and more ingrained in me. The habit is becoming ME, the programmed me.

Let's consider some questions to see how these points might apply to us.

1. Can I identify some experience I'm having that is upsetting me?
2. Am I dealing with it directly?
3. Am I deflecting to something else which feels less threatening?

Confronting the Pattern of Stimulus-Reaction-Response

We've already established that when we reject self-awareness, we become attached to our reactions and responses and justify them without thought. When we develop the habit of self-awareness, we notice our reactions and responses, and we question them. Our purpose is not to shame ourselves, but to free ourselves from programs that are encroaching upon our freedom.

For example, let's say one day I notice that I am snapping a lot at the people around me. I notice I'm snapping at my kids, too. Instead of accepting my rationalization that I am irritable because the kids are acting out, I turn my focus to myself and to my reactions. I notice that I'm irritated at the kids because I am irritable. I have gone from believing my response is justified to noticing that it is caused by a reaction, my irritability. Then I question my reaction, instead of justifying myself by saying that I am reacting irritably because Linda, because George, because the kids, because whatever; I pay attention to the nagging feeling of insecurity that's under my reactivity, and then I trace those nagging feelings back to George's overwork.

Once I have tracked my anxiety to George's overwork, then I can go into even deeper self-awareness. Why am I triggered by George overworking? What is being triggered in me? Am I truly threatened by George's absence? Is his love being withdrawn? Is his health being threatened? What is the source of his absence? Is he replacing me with another woman, or is he actually working very hard in order to create a nest egg for me, for us? If I look even further into myself, I may realize that I'm unconsciously remembering feeling threatened at two years old when the new baby was born. Wow, so this isn't about the kids' behavior, nor is it about George's overwork. It's about an old pattern of stimulus—reaction-response, and that pattern is getting in the way of my happiness and the happiness of everyone else. Now I can intervene with myself.

Now we're back to cause and effect. Once I realize that there is a stimulus that is triggering a reaction that triggers a response, then I realize that much of my behavior is the effect of stimuli that are triggering me, even though I don't recognize them, and that what I feel is a reaction to something that may or may not even be occurring. And once I notice that I am reacting and responding without making conscious choices, I realize "I" am not acting at all. It's my programs that are reacting and determining my responses. Instead of me running my life, my reactions are doing it. Now I am ready for Platform Six: Becoming Integrated. I'm ready to begin to become myself.

Even before we release these patterns, we are getting better, because just by questioning ourselves, we are beginning to differentiate from our reactivity and become ourselves (remember Becoming Differentiated: Platform Two?). As we start to differentiate from our reactivity, the person who is taking the action of differentiating is the "we" that we have been losing to the programming. Wanting myself back, I can now start asking whether my reactions and responses are truly meeting my needs. Does this response of mine bring me the desired end? Is my yelling at George for gaining weight or not taking out the garbage going to stop him from overworking and bring him closer to me? Is my annoyance with my best friend going to heal my marriage or just leave me without a friend? Are my responses appropriate? And in fact, are my reactions appropriate? Unless I have self-awareness, I cannot even approach these questions. Unless I have awareness of others, I can't approach this question either. If I am blindly reacting, I can't see that George is really trying to care for me and that it is I who is creating an emotional reaction to something that is not happening, or creating a needless emotional reaction to something that is happening but is not directed against me. Yes, if I am unaware of what I am reacting and responding to, I can't see reality, and I don't know myself.

Developing the habit of questioning myself changes me forever. I begin to see through my programming and self-justification, and I begin to identify with the observer rather than the reactor. I am already getting freed from the patterning that has always enslaved me.

Yay.

Watch Your Feelings and Behavior: Everything Is Information

Our irrational behavior can be a great gift to us. If we watch our behavior (our response) and acknowledge that we're being nutty, or acting tense, or raising our voices, or shrinking, wow, we have information. Now we are ready to ask the next question: What is my behavior telling me about my feelings? And what triggered those feelings and why?

Simply put, we can all practice self-awareness by asking ourselves:

1. How am I responding?

2. What is the emotional reaction under that response?
3. What was the stimulus that provoked that reaction?

For example, let's say I have decided that I no longer want to eat sugar, because it is bad for my health. As I watch my hand going toward the birthday cake, I notice my behavior and ask myself, "Why am I doing this?" Instead of going into shame about my behavior, I use my behavior as information that I am doing something contrary to my intentions. Using this behavior as information, I ask myself the question, "Why *am* I about to eat sugar? What emotion am I feeling? What is the cause of the emotion?" I may discover that I'm sad because I felt rejected by a woman I was attracted to. In this case, I am gathering information about myself based on an unwanted response. I am intervening between the reaction and the response.

We can also gather information by intervening with ourselves at the point between the stimulus and the reaction. I could ask myself, "So why does Marion's rejection feel so painful to me?" This may lead me to realize that Marion's rejection reminds me of so many episodes of sadness in relation to my mother, who never showed up for any of my school events. Or I may realize that I projected onto Marion the status of the person who determines my value in the world. Then I can ask myself why I do that. Is it because she reminds me of someone, because she is popular, because she spoke to me once in an affectionate way, and I don't believe anyone else will? And then I can ask, "Why do I think no one else will? Do I so lack any sense of my own value? And why is that?"

Once I am asking questions, I am transcending my patterning. Only too often do we assume that it's natural that we should feel something, such as sadness because a particular person isn't interested in us. This tendency to assume that my reaction is natural is one of the key ways that patterns perpetuate themselves. I am reinforcing over and over that I HAVE to feel sad if Marion or some other designated person rejects me. So the next time I am rejected by x, y or z, I am already patterned to assume that I should feel sad. And so I do.

Question All Our Assumptions

Questioning assumptions is a huge step in self-awareness. It breaks up the momentum of the patterning and the reinforcement of that patterning, it refocuses me on self-awareness instead of on the other person, the stimulus or the reaction, and it allows me to connect to the person under the pattern, me.

And it's not only our own long-standing patterns that we should question. We should also question the patterns that dominate others. Let's say a friend comes to me for support. He says that he's angry with his wife for her infidelity. If I accept his anger at face value, if I assume it's natural that he is angry, I will probably join in with his anger and won't question him further. If I don't question him, I'm not helping him. Why, in fact, does her infidelity make him angry? Is it because he's been unfaithful for years, and he doesn't like to suddenly be on the other side of the power equation? Is it because he loves her and is afraid that this means she doesn't love him? Is it pride and the fear that others will think less of him? Is it because he senses he's losing control over her? Is it because he knows he's been ignoring her, feels guilty about it and is trying to deflect the blame? Once we establish the answer to why, we can then question this reaction, as well. For example, if he is actually losing control over her, why does that bother him?

Just as we should not shame ourselves for our reactions and responses, we can question our friends not from a place of judgment, but from a place of inquiry. By questioning the friend who comes to us to "complain," we encourage his self-awareness. By helping him understand himself, we are also helping him recognize his real options. If he is caught in emotional reactivity, he can't do anything to help correct the situation that may have caused his wife's infidelity. If we support him to look beyond his reactivity, he might identify new options for himself.

Supporting the self-awareness of others also helps us. We've probably done and felt the same things for similar reasons, and we learn much about ourselves by seeing ourselves being acted out through other people. People who don't question the reactions of others are probably giving themselves the right to not question themselves.

Self-Awareness Requires Us to Give up the Right to Be Wrong

The first step in Becoming Self-Aware is to be willing to ask questions. The second is to be willing to intervene, which we will discuss further in

Platform Six: Becoming Integrated. But before we move on, let us briefly discuss our unwillingness to intervene with ourselves.

As we've said before, we are constantly justifying our responses, reactions and behaviors, always claiming to ourselves and to others that they are the right and reasonable response to a stimulus. "Of course I sent my child to his room. He disobeyed me." Or, "Of course I yelled at my husband when I found out he was having sex with the next-door neighbor. Wouldn't anyone?"

Now that we are willing to become self-aware and question ourselves, we realize that we are not being motivated by reason but by the programmed reactions and responses that dominate us from behind the scenes. But are we willing to give them up?

Not so easy. Remember that our programs are built upon survival-based, ego-driven motivations. Naturally we are going to try to defend patterns that feel so linked to our survival. We know now that we have not consciously chosen our reactions and responses; in a sense, they have chosen us. But our fear can drive us into extreme lengths of self-justification.

Suppose someone killed my daughter, and I feel totally justified in my desire to kill him in response. Suppose we stopped ourselves at this point and said, Okay, even if I have a right to my reaction, is killing him the response that I choose? It may be natural that I am enraged, but do I want that rage to lead me to kill him in turn? Is that resonant with my own self and beliefs? Or I could question myself even more deeply to understand why I am so invested in my rage reaction. Maybe I will discover that I am also enraged at myself because I blame myself for pushing her out of the house when I remarried after her mother's death. If she hadn't felt ignored, perhaps she wouldn't have run away, and her running away is what exposed her to more dangerous circumstances. My actions led her to vulnerability, so I feel responsible for her death and want to deflect all the blame onto the murderer. Or I might question whether or not I have a right to stay enraged at anyone, because I killed many other people's daughters when I passively went along with civilian bombing in an immoral war. Or I could question if I have right to stay enraged for any reason. Does rage have value? How does this rage serve me, my dead daughter or anyone else?

There are times when it is excruciatingly difficult for us to question our reactions and responses, because we feel so justified, and feeling justified is in itself a high. Sometimes that high is an antidote to a terrible pain, such as the death of the daughter. Sometimes that high is simply an antidote to our chronic pain, which is our feeling of worthlessness. Now I have something that I can attach myself to which demonstrates to others that I am right. Wow, that really helps me overcome the shame of existence (see introduction to this book).

But often we need to admit that being "right" is wrong. It is simply a self-indulgence that blocks us from dealing with reality in a way that is for the highest good of all, including ourselves. It blocks us from saying, "I am that." It blocks us from forgiveness and compassion. It blocks us from progress. It blocks us from getting our true needs met.

And furthermore, what goes up must come down. When we indulge ourselves in the high of being right, we always end up crashing into a feeling of emptiness, because being right at the expense of others always feels unworthy of our higher self and keeps us craving more rightness to feed the need to get high again. In this sense, being right and righteous is an addiction that self-awareness confronts.

Let's ask ourselves some questions so that we can see ourselves in this context.

1. What are the circumstances in my life where my reactions have most felt justified?
2. Why did I have those reactions?
3. Was I covering a secret guilt?
4. Was my guilt justified?
5. Did I get a sense of power from those reactions?
6. Did others around me feed my reactions or try to help me to get beyond them?

Choosing Self-Mastery

Once we have stopped trying to justify our reactions, once we have taken that breath between the stimulus and the reaction or between reaction and response, we have started down the road of self-mastery, which gives us the sustainable self-nurturance of self-respect. When we buy into the idea that our response is not only reasonable, it is the *only* appropriate response to a given situation, we're sunk. We have lost control over our behavior and become agents of our reactions. On the other hand, when we ask if this is the only reasonable reaction or response to the situation, or if this reaction is for the highest good of all, including me, we are challenging our patterns and taking a step toward freedom. We've created a space between the stimulus and reaction or reaction and response, and in that space, we can intervene. We are behaving in a way that we can respect.

Tool: How We Intervene Between Reaction and Response

Taking a Breath and Confronting Ourselves. Once we have committed to questioning ourselves, our responses and our reactions, we need to start developing the practice. The reaction is the programmed feeling and the response is the behavior that is stimulated from that feeling. Intervening between the reaction and response means that we still have the feeling, but we act differently; more consciously. How do we do it?

1. Take a breath.
2. Ask ourselves why we are having the reaction.
3. Evaluate the response we wish to choose.

At times, we have all intervened in our programmed reaction and response pattern. I feel stressed, I've already eaten five cookies, I want to inhale the whole bag, but I put them away. That's an intervention between reaction and response. Or let's say that I typically smoke cigarettes when I'm stressed, but I've decided that it's for my highest good to quit smoking. Intervening between reaction and response means the next time I feel the stress and the craving for cigarettes, I stop myself.

Let's take a look at that intervention. I stop, take a breath, and decide to deal with my stress a different way. I decide to take a walk, for example. In fact, I haven't eliminated the reaction (the stressed feeling that is motivating the response, which would be the smoking in this case), but I have intervened between the reaction and the habitual response of picking up the cigarette.

We have all intervened with ourselves at some point, so most of us have already had the experience of intervening between reaction and response, and we know it's possible. We take a breath to give ourselves the moment to intervene. Let's look at another common example of this. Let's say I want to slug my wife because I feel she's not listening to me. Something stops me, and I take a breath. In that moment, I unconsciously calculate whether or not slugging her is my best option. I may reason that this behavior will ultimately feel humiliating to me, or slugging her does not fit with my self-image or isn't congruent with my values, or because I love her I won't slug her. Whatever my reason, however, I am already intervening with myself, trying to interrupt the response and gain some mastery of myself. I walk away.

In the moment we take the breath, we give ourselves the opportunity for two things: One is that we can question why we are feeling the energy to act out in this way. Why am I bingeing on cookies? Why do I want to hit my wife? And taking the breath gives us the opportunity to evaluate the consequences. Yeah, at this moment, I want to eat the cookie or hurt my wife, but do I really want the consequences of the action? Do I want to be engulfed by a sugar-caused mood swing? Do I want to damage my relationship with my wife forever and feel like an abuser?

Just as we give our children a timeout, so that they can calm down and consider the consequences of their behavior, we can give ourselves a timeout, stop and take a breath before we act out a self-destructive behavior that can ruin our day, our year or our lives. The moment gives me an opportunity not only to think, but to defuse the intensity of the emotion.

Let's consider how we have acted in this regard.

1. Have you ever unconsciously stopped, taken a breath and changed course?
2. Did it help?
3. Have you ever decided to discipline yourself to do this on a regular basis?
4. Under what circumstances do you succeed?
5. When do you fail?

In cases of extreme emotion and obviously negative consequences, I may have learned to intervene with myself. I am already developing dual consciousness. Dual consciousness means that I am not only the "me" that is reacting, I am also the "me" that is observing, reasoning and capable of intervention.

What About Interventions in Cases That Seem More Subtle?

It's easy to see that eating the second bag of cookies or hitting my wife are responses to emotions that are out of control. And maybe I have learned to "control" myself in these moments in order to avoid hideous consequences.

Now let's look at a behavior that we might not immediately recognize as a response to a reaction to a stimulus, a behavior that seems more subtle. I am in a relationship with a woman who is not spending much time with me, and I tell myself and her, "I love you and I want to spend more time with you." Now, who would question such a reasonable request? Why would I have to intervene with such a behavior?

Let's look at this example more deeply. The desire to spend more time with a girlfriend is also the result of a reaction-response pattern. Asking her to spend more time with me is the response to some inner reaction of pain or fear, and I can understand this reaction if I examine it. Why do I want to spend more time with my girlfriend? Is it because I feel lonely? Is it because I enjoy her company? Is it because I feel embarrassed when the other guys ask me where Cheryl is, and I don't know? Is it because spending all our weekends together is what love is supposed to look like, because that's what my parents did? Is it because I feel rejected when I don't spend time with her, even though she is not rejecting me? Is it because I don't know what to do with myself when I'm alone? Or because my parents didn't spend all of their time together and ended up in a divorce, and I'm afraid that if we don't spend more time together, we'll end our relationship, too?

If I am not willing to Become Self-Aware and intervene with my reaction and response, I will go to friends who will confirm my right to tell Cheryl how pissed off I am. They'll agree that she SHOULD spend more time with me, and they might even feed my fear that I won't look like a stud if she doesn't. So now we have their patterns reinforcing mine.

How do I intervene between my reaction and response here? Again, I take a time out, take a breath, and then ask myself the question why. Yes, one more time I question my assumptions. And through so doing, I discover that my behavior may look like it's based on love, but it is actually motivated by fear of loneliness, rejection or separation. If I realize this, I can challenge myself to a different response. Okay, guy, you need to develop some activities of your own that give you self-worth so you aren't hanging on Cheryl to make you feel good about yourself. Go to the gym. You need the exercise anyway. Or, hey, guy, your feelings of loneliness around Cheryl don't have anything to do with the amount of time she spends with you. They have to do with the fact that you have nothing in common. You don't need more time with her. You need to break up.

In our desperate need to impact the offending behavior, we may, in fact, ignore our own real needs, because we haven't taken the time to identify them. In this case, by taking a breath, evaluating my reaction and stopping my automatic response, I give myself the opportunity to do what is actually in my highest good, whether it's going to the gym or breaking up.

While we're in our reaction-response-pattern, we are also ignoring the other person's needs. I may truly love Cheryl, but when I am acting out of my program, I am not connected to my love for her or motivated by it. Driven by old reaction-response patterns, I am not even seeing Cheryl. I am in the cave, looking at the shadows of my own projections and emotions.

If I take a break and look at myself objectively, I may realize that Cheryl isn't doing anything negative to me at all. Maybe she's working fulltime, studying to be a nurse and barely able to see her friends or have a moment for herself. The reason that I want to spend more time with her is that I'm afraid to be alone. If she and I can practice Platform Four together, we can ask, "What is for the highest good of all, including me?" and explore whether it is for the highest good of both of us to be spending more time together.

When I get out of me, I can see her more clearly. I might suspect that she doesn't want to spend time with me because she doesn't really care for me very much. If this is the fact, I can feel the pain and yet not cling, yell, demand or blame. I can respond by sitting down with her, asking about her feelings toward me and evaluating whether or not we want to stay together, including whether or not I truly want to stay with her.

Or when I get out of me, I may realize that I've been demanding more time with Cheryl because I don't feel much value in myself and her attention gives me the feeling that I'm important. By intervening between my reaction and my response, I can confront reality as it is, and this increases my self-esteem. With more self-esteem within myself, I don't need to demand from Cheryl that her attention be a substitute for the self-respect that I lack.

When I get out of me, I can respond in a way that supports us both to determine whether or not we should be together. "Cheryl, are you not spending more time with me because you need to be doing something else, and so do I? Or are you not spending time with me because you're pulling away and you don't want to say so?" This allows Cheryl and me to get more honest with ourselves. She now feels my support, instead of my kneejerk pattern of clinging, grabbing, shaming or otherwise trying to change her. Maybe now she'll actually want to spend more time with me. Whatever happens with Cheryl, I have self-respect, because I have handled myself in a way that's worthy of respect.

Intervening between the reaction and the response not only opens me to a lot of self-respect, it frees me from behaviors that squander my energy. I realize that I have been using my energy trying to control the uncontrollable. If I believe that my emotional survival depends on an intimate relationship, I use my badgering, clinging and cajoling as a way of dominating Cheryl, so she can save me. I am focusing my energy on making Cheryl make me feel better, rather than making myself better

When I stop, take the breath and ask what I'm feeling and what the other possible responses to Cheryl's behavior could be, I am opening a whole new world of alternatives. And I am confronting my deep need to control reality, which is poison to whatever relationships I have.

Let's ask ourselves some questions about our behavior in these kinds of situations.

1. Can I think of relationships where I have demanded something from someone out of my own insecurities?
2. How did that make me feel?
3. How did the other person react?
4. How did their reaction impact me?
5. How much energy did I squander on trying to change them?
6. How did that make me feel?

When We Intervene Between Our Reaction and Response, We Give Up Emotional Blackmail

Emotional blackmail means that we use our reactions as our response to a stimulus, in order to control and manipulate someone else's behavior. In other words, we respond by using our emotions as the club to get someone else to change his or her behavior. This is a pattern like any other that stems from our survival mechanisms instituted at birth, and it's very destructive. When we sever the link between our reactions and our responses, we surrender the right to manipulate someone else with those emotions, and that brings emotional blackmail to an end, which opens the door for more effective and empowered behavior.

"You're upsetting me." That's an example of using our reaction as a response. And we expect the other person to alter their behavior because of it.

"I told you if you . . ."

One form of emotional blackmail is the oft-heard, "But I told you if . . ." "I *told* George that if he forgot my birthday/went out with the boys on Saturday night/gambled away our life savings, it would kill me." The clear implication is that George is an extension of my needs and should do whatever I say, because he's upsetting me. I am not inquiring as to what is driving George's behavior, and I'm not inquiring as to whether or not this behavior is for the highest good of all. And I'm not trying to support George's self-awareness or wellbeing. Nor am I questioning why I'm getting so upset. Instead, I am using emotional blackmail. I am using my emotions as my response to the stimulus that I don't like in order to change the stimulus instead of my reaction or response.

This is not to suggest that we should accept unacceptable behavior. For example, let's say my husband is hitting our one-year-old on a daily basis, and I say, "You're really upsetting me. You know my father used to beat me. If you do this one more time, I'll leave." Then when he does it again, I say, "I told you if you did that again, I'd leave." Wow, that looks reasonable, doesn't it? But actually it's emotional blackmail and manipulation. I am asking George to stop because of ME. It's about ME. He's upsetting ME. He's going to lose ME.

Oh, I should leave, but not because I promised to leave because it upsets me, and not because I haven't dealt with my own unresolved father issues.

If I intervene in my patterned reaction-response and I surrender the right to emotional blackmail, then my decision to leave will be based on its being for the highest good of all, including George. It's not in *his* highest good to remain in a relationship where he's constantly the abuser, because it causes guilt and shame and possibly criminal charges. It's not in *my* highest good to allow my child to be abused, because it creates feelings of shame in me, the shame that I've sold out my child's wellbeing for a bit of protection against loneliness and/or poverty. And it certainly isn't for the baby's highest good, because the child is being imbued with the concept that this is a frightening universe to live in; at worst he may even be physically damaged and developmentally impaired. Yes, I should leave, but because it is the right response, not because "I'm upset." Or because I said I would. And I can, of course, suggest that George get help, because that would be for the highest good of all as well.

When we use emotional blackmail, everything is about ME, and I am using my reactions and emotions as a mechanism to control the responses of those around me.

This is an extreme example, but it reflects a very common situation. Let's take another example. Let's say a child is banging on the floor, and mom's reaction is anger and her response is to yell, "Stop banging on the floor. You're driving me crazy." What is the child learning? The child is learning that he should stop banging on the floor because it's driving Mom crazy. In other words, he's learning that he should be dominated by a woman's feelings.

Now let's say I'm the mom, and I'm willing to intervene in my reaction-response pattern. I feel like strangling the kid, but instead, I stop, take a breath and become aware that I am feeling anxious and that my head is starting to pound. If I intervene with my reaction-response pattern, I can say, "Joey, I have a tendency to get headaches, and the noise of you banging on the floor can bring one on. I'm sorry, because I know you like to make noise when you play. Unfortunately, if I have a headache, I won't feel well, which will make me unhappy, and I won't be able to take care of you, which will make you unhappy, too. Here's a better place to play." I am no longer using my emotional desperation to control my child, and the child is learning to examine his behavior in terms of the highest good of all. I have not only interrupted my reaction-response pattern of yelling when I feel scared that I'm going to get a headache, I have surrendered the right to impose on that child the belief that my upset is more important than his self-expression. At the same time, I'm teaching him to understand his place in the family and how our needs are related. And, perhaps even most important, I am challenging in myself the deeply ingrained pattern of seeing the world through the eyes of the programmed self-centered

"I" that believes that only through that lens can my needs be met. I am reprogramming myself.

None of us is going to be perfect in intervening between our reaction and response in every situation. But if we intend to do it and make amends when we don't, we are retraining ourselves. We are reprogramming patterns that are hurting us and those around us.

Let's ask ourselves some questions about the use of our emotions to manipulate others.

1. Do I tend to use my emotions to try to control others?
2. Under what circumstances do I tend to do that?
3. Where did I learn this?
4. Does it work?
5. If it does "work," what are the consequences to myself and others?

Tool: How We Intervene Between the Stimulus and the Reaction

Taking a Breath and Confronting Ourselves. Just as we can intervene between the reaction and the response, we can intervene between the stimulus and the reaction. Instead of just reacting we could:

1. Take a breath.
2. See what's stimulating our reaction.
3. Consider why we are having the unwanted reaction and support ourselves to change.

Up till this point, we've been talking about intervening between the reaction and the response. But what about intervening before that, at the level of my reaction? It's hard to "control" my reactions. I know I shouldn't get angry with my five-year-old for pouring paint on my carpet. I know he didn't mean to do it. Or I know he's doing it for negative attention (heck, I used to do that myself), and I don't want to reward the behavior.

Or I know he has ADHD and can't help himself. Or I don't want to react, because I know that if I get angry, I'll lose control. So I'm just going to control my anger, but I can't. Grrrr.

Intervening between the reaction and response is what we usually refer to as self-control. It is a necessary part of the smooth functioning of society and is a quality greatly valued by our world. But when we can control only our responses but not our reactions, we are in a constant state of stress. We are fighting our inner program. I am still feeling the reaction—the anger, fear or stress—but I can't let myself respond in my habitual way. If I do, I'll lose my reputation, my self-respect, my family, my freedom (I could go to jail), my life. I *must* control myself. I want to go shopping again, but I can't, I shouldn't. I want to tell off the principal, the warden, the church. I want to eat the cupcake. I want to rape the child. But I shouldn't, I dare not, I don't want to.

Control is not the ultimate answer. It isn't? But didn't you just tell me that we should intervene between our reactions and responses? Yes. But let's not stop there. Let's work toward releasing ourselves from the reactions that cause the response.

All inner conflict causes inner stress, so people who self-control, people who focus on controlling their responses but not releasing their reactions, can become sick inside and can even snap. The kid who shot all those people at school was such a quiet soul. He must have snapped. She's really such a well-behaved woman except when she's taking drugs. It's the drugs that make her go wild with men. It's possible he snapped, and it's possible that the drugs impact her and make her different. But did he snap because he repressed the responses he wanted to express all along? And does she take drugs so that she can unconsciously have sex with lots of men?

Later in this chapter, we are going to talk about energy, and then we'll discuss this issue again. But for now, let's just all remember the rumbling we feel in our stomachs when we combine our anger (reaction) with our frustration at not being able to act it out. Yes, we need to stop ourselves from behaving destructively, either because we know the behavior is destructive or unfair or because we're afraid of the consequences, but just stopping the behavior doesn't lead to relief inside. The rumbling continues. The examples of the quiet kid or the repressed woman may seem extreme, but they are symptomatic of what happens to us when we stop self-awareness at the point of intervening only between the reaction and the response.

Here are a couple of questions to highlight this behavior in ourselves.

1. Where do I find myself intervening with my behaviors?
2. What happens to the emotions underneath them?
3. What's the impact of the emotions continuing?

Of course we need to learn to control our responses when our reactions are going wild, but real self-healing and self-mastery start when we interrupt the *reaction*. The stimulus occurs, but the reaction does not. When we can free ourselves from the reaction, we're taking a big step toward both joy and freedom. We will discuss some techniques to achieve that mastery in Platform Six: Becoming Integrated, but let's discuss how self-awareness can help.

Reactions Are Information When We Take a Timeout

I notice that I want to act out, but I don't. Instead I identify and observe the feeling. It may seem very strong. Instead of feeding into the feeling, once again, I take the breath and ask the question why? My reaction is the effect. What is the cause?

Let's take a minute to appreciate the possibilities. Take anger, for example. Anger is a natural emotion, a reaction to things that are not going our way. But while the emotion is natural, it isn't very pleasant for others or us. Anger gets us churning inside and often causes us to behave destructively toward ourselves and others. What is the purpose of anger anyway? Why do we have it?

Anger should be used for information. When I feel anger, the anger is a clue from my psyche to me, a clue that something is "wrong." What does "wrong" mean? It means that, in my mind at least, whatever is happening should not be happening. Why? If my child spills paint on the floor, I may get angry, because the floor is supposed to be clean, and maybe I don't have the money to have it cleaned. Or maybe I'm too tired to clean it myself. Or maybe I'm afraid my spouse will come home and find that paint has been spilled and I haven't "controlled" our son. Or maybe my mother is coming over and will judge my parenting. I am angry because I feel out of control, or I don't have the resources to deal with the problem, or I'm afraid I will be judged. Now I have information and a sense of direction. I may realize that the floor can be cleaned later, or that no one is judging me, or I do need to learn to discipline my child, or I need to confront my relationship with my mother. What I have learned is that my anger is about something related to me.

If we use anger for information, the anger itself only lasts a split second until it rises to the level of my awareness. Once aware of it, I can allow it to transmute itself into information. Once I have the information my anger is meant to communicate, I don't need the anger anymore. I have the information.

Anger can also signal that something is up with someone else. Now it's information about them. "Wow, Johnnie wasn't trying to exhaust me. He wasn't trying to embarrass me. He was having a good time with paint. I need to give him opportunities to express himself with paint that won't jeopardize the floor."

Or perhaps he is unconsciously acting out, trying to inform me of something that's upsetting him, and if so, what is that? Is he showing me that he's a spoiled brat, and I made him that way? Or that I'm ignoring him? Boy, something else to learn about myself and my parenting.

Even when anger rises, we can allow it to fulfill its function, which is to give us information. We can then let it go and address the real issues. In this way, we have interrupted the stimulus-anger reaction and gained greater relaxation, happiness, awareness and self-awareness. If the anger continues despite our efforts to intervene, we haven't yet gotten the message. Perhaps we're not clear about the source of the anger, or perhaps we know what it is, but are afraid to acknowledge it, because we might have to make a scary change on the outside or confront something even deeper within ourselves. Even in this case, however, the continuation of the anger is becoming a valuable tool for self-awareness.

Let's look at our ability to intervene with our anger.

1. Can I think of situations where I tend to get angry?
2. Am I missing the message it's giving me?
3. What is my anger telling me about me?
4. What is it pointing to about the situation?
5. Do I tend to learn or to justify my reactions?

Fear too can be used as information; it tells me that I feel threatened. When I have that awareness, I can look at the fear and see if it's based on something real. If it is based on something real, I can try to do something about it. If it is not based on something real, I try to release the fear itself. If I feel fear because I notice the train is coming down the track and heading straight toward me, I can move. If I feel fear because at one time in the past the train was coming down the track toward me but now it's not there anymore, I can try to release the memory.

Every emotion that we have can be used as information. By doing so, we expand our self-awareness and move toward freedom, instead of being dominated by our reactivity.

In Platform Six, I will discuss at length how to not be unbalanced by emotions such as fear and anger, but for this section on Becoming Self-Aware, let's remember that emotions and reactions are the effect of some stimulus, and these programmed emotions and reactions do not have to dominate us. It is self-evident that if we were freed up from needless anger and fear, we would be more relaxed, and we could make better choices. We could actually respond appropriately. In Johnny's case, we could evaluate the source of his spilling the paint on the floor and see whether or not it merits a response from us, such as, "I've been giving him attention for the wrong things." Or, "I'm giving him attention he doesn't need and I'm not meeting his needs on a deeper level." Or, "I've been letting him feel that he can run the show because I've been afraid to alienate my child and therefore I've created this monster, and I need to do something about it."

When we simply feel our reactions and justify them, we are back in the cave of shadows, overwhelmed by emotion and fighting Johnny's behavior, ignoring the one thing we can most successfully address: ourselves. We may still need to send Johnny to his room, but if so, it's because we understand this to be the best possible way to handle the situation in the moment, not because I'm being driven by an angry or fearful reaction.

Surrendering Using Emotions as a Drug

In order to intervene between the stimulus and the reaction, I have to surrender the right to being reactive. This means I have to stop using my emotions as a drug. Anger can be a drug to make myself feel powerful when I feel powerless. Fear can be a drug to justify my refusal to deal with reality. Love can be a drug to take me out of reality. Stress can be a drug to justify ignoring the needs of others.

Here's an example involving anger again. If my 13-year-old daughter comes into the room and tells me she's pregnant, I can easily become furious. I puff myself up with rage, because my rage in and of itself will seem to make me feel powerful in a situation in which I am actually feeling powerless. In my rage, I can disown my daughter, order her to have an abortion, humiliate her, or anything else that gives me a sense of control. In these cases, I am not looking for the best solution for the problem of her pregnancy, because I am not trying to address the problem of her pregnancy; the problem I am trying to resolve is my feeling of impotence.

When I surrender the right the use my emotions as a drug, I stop myself. I'm aware that I'm blinded by my rage. "Okay, exactly *why* am I angry? *What*, exactly, am I angry at?" I may discover that I'm angry because I feel that my daughter has done this to undermine my male authority. Perhaps I have been trying to control her in order to prove that I'm a competent parent or to prove that I am truly a powerful man who can control his child. Maybe I'm enraged because I know on some level that I have been too permissive and now I have to make her wrong in order to hide my own shame. Totally aside from the issue of her pregnancy, I have a reaction that has to do with my ego, with my feelings about how I look to myself. Maybe I'm enraged because I did the same kind of thing in my earlier life, getting prematurely pregnant, and we have all suffered the consequences.

Whatever the reason, the anger is a drug that blocks me from feeling impotent or guilty. Let's take a moment to recognize how we might have done the same thing.

1. Can I identify some emotions that I use as drugs?
2. What do they block me from experiencing?
3. Am I willing to give the drug up?

Tool: Intervening at the Level of Stimulus

Taking Responsibility for What We Choose. Sometimes the best way to eliminate a response is to eliminate or modify the stimulus that sets up the pattern. Briefly, here's how we do it:

1. Take a breath.
2. Identify the stimulus that's triggering a negative reaction and response.
3. Determine if there's some way to eliminate or modify it.

❧

We can also intervene much earlier in the triad of stimulus-reaction-response by learning to observe a potentially triggering stimulus as it is happening. For example, I might be driving the car and hear a funny noise. There's the stimulus. Before I have my typical reaction, which would be, "Oh, no," or my typical response, which could be getting out of the vehicle, grabbing the jack and banging it against the side of the car (of course, I would never do this!), before becoming embroiled in all this, I can become aware of the event and I go directly to it. In other words, I take a breath at the moment of the occurrence of the stimulus and then focus on fixing the car rather than reacting or responding from reactivity. This is the ideal way to respond to a stimulus; if we could go directly toward the stimulus, think of all the energy we could save.

If we directly dealt with events, we would save the energy that we would otherwise squander resisting or reacting to life's never-ending stimuli. And we would be much more peaceful. Let's examine how well we do this.

1. Can I think of examples where I get caught up in my reactions and ignore the actual stimulus?
2. What has been the emotional price of my reactivity?
3. What happened to the problem?
4. When I respond to challenges, do I tend to focus on dealing with the problem or do I tend to focus on my reaction?
5. Which kinds of stimuli do I handle best?
6. Which kinds do I handle worst?

Self-Awareness Can Help Us Avoid Certain Stimuli

Once we understand our stimulus-reaction-response patterns, we want to stop being dominated by them. We can't always free ourselves from all our patterns immediately, but self-awareness can help us in another way. If we know some stimulus triggers us, we can avoid it whenever possible.

We all know that certain places or people can trigger us. For example, a compulsive gambler could be triggered by a casino, a sugar addict by an ice cream parlor, or a compulsive shopper by a shopping mall. Another example is calling an ex-girlfriend "just to see how she is doing." Wouldn't it be useful for us to ask ourselves whether or not it is for our highest good before we go to such places or take such actions? Or if we have to deal with a particular stimulus, can we not bring support that will help prevent us from acting out? For example, if I know that I am triggered by being with my ex-girlfriend but I need to pick up my stuff from her house, I can either ask someone else to go for me or bring someone else with me, if I have to go myself.

While we ultimately don't want to be prisoners of our automatic reactions and responses, we need to be aware of our spiritual and emotional condition. Pretending that we are capable of more self-control than we really are is just a set-up for us to act out. If I am newly sober, and I insist on "just visiting" my old friends who use drugs, I'm probably setting myself up to use again.

We can't use our reactivity as an excuse for hiding out from life, but hiding is a different phenomenon. For example, if opening my bills stimulates fear, hiding could look like burying those bills in a drawer. In that case, we need to face the stimulus, even if we need to call in support. But there are times when we can avoid a stimulus, and doing so could support us not to fall back into bad patterns.

Let's ask ourselves some questions about avoiding stimuli that could set us back.

1. Am I aware of stimuli that get me into trouble?
2. Do I avoid them?
3. Do I deliberately set myself up by going toward them?
4. Do I bring support, when I know I'm in a slippery place?

What Do We Do When We Can't Figure It Out?

What happens if we look at our reaction, ask "Why am I feeling that?", and yet don't get a clear answer? We're aware that we're angry or over-reacting, but can't get past the anger and have no insight into the origin of our reaction. Even in this kind of case, there are some things we can do to help ourselves, but the first step is to accept where we are. We need to be in allowance of the limitations of our self-awareness. If we can't, we'll just become even more upset with ourselves. In other words, we'll be having a reaction-response to the stimulus of not understanding ourselves. The stimulus—I'm not able to understand myself at this moment; the reaction—I feel impotent; and the response—I get angry at myself. Oh? Now this gives me something else to work with. Feeling impotent makes me feel angry at myself. I wonder where that pattern started . . .?

Even when we feel blocked in our deeper self-understanding, we can achieve a great victory if we don't judge ourselves harshly or give up. How is this a victory? The willingness to be self-aware—to observe rather than to justify our reactions and automatic behaviors—is a positive change. We are supporting our consciousness rather than supporting our self-justification; in fact, we are withdrawing our energy from self-justification and putting it into self-examination. This is a shift in intention and behavior.

If we can appreciate our willingness, relax, and trust that the answers will come, they probably will. I have had this experience many times over the years. Even though I'm very intuitive and have worked on myself for a long time, there are times when I say, "I am nuts right now." And I turn to others for support, people who care about me and yet are objective about me—friends, counselors, wise people, mentors. And usually out of the conversation, some glimmer of awareness begins to emerge.

Sometimes, despite all the efforts of all our friends or counselors, we still can't understand what's going on with us. When this happens, I don't worry. Nothing is lost. Even if I can't immediately see what's going on, feeling the support of others will allow me to relax and allow the answer to come to me later. Amazingly, something or someone will turn up that brings me to the information I need.

It's quite amazing how things will come to us when we are in a state of relaxation. Mutual support, meditation, exercise, reading a good book or going outdoors are all ways to relax our beings enough so that we can allow the universe to help us, if we want that help. And then, miraculously, two hours later, I'll be engaged in conversation with someone about something outside myself, and suddenly I feel a little zing going through my brain, and I have a sudden realization about my reaction. Or a tune will go through my head, and the lyrics give me the answer.

Sometimes it takes months until we're able to get an answer. Sometimes a therapist can help us, a 12-step program or a Living with Reality mutual support group. Sometimes the answer comes when we're helping someone else. But the bottom line is, if our ears are open, our eyes are open, our heart is open, the answer *will* come to us, because the universe conspires to give us self-awareness if we but intend it. On the other hand, if we don't want to know, the universe could take out a paid ad on TV with our name prominently displayed on the screen, and we wouldn't notice.

But we don't have to wait for full understanding of our stimulus-reaction-response pattern in order to take action. When we practice self awareness, we can see the damage we do and make amends promptly, even if the acknowledgement is as simple as, "I'm sorry I'm having a reaction to something. I don't understand what's going on with me, but I just want you to know that I'm aware of it and I'm working on it."[24] The acknowledgement itself releases a tremendous energy in us because again, we're no longer justifying our negativity. As unconscious as we are, on a deeper level we know that we are overreacting, and the need to justify our reaction depletes our energy. Admitting the truth relaxes us and frees our energy to seek answers rather than self-justification . . .if we can stay out of shame. The amends also brings great relief to the other party who is feeling hurt and needs acknowledgement of that hurt, even if that person isn't even consciously aware that they are in pain about it.

So even though I may not always succeed in understanding myself, practicing Becoming Self-Aware to the best of my ability energizes the aspect of me that supports me to be conscious; to come into the light instead of living in a cave of ignorance and reactivity. And so just the intention to Become Self-Aware changes and frees me.

Let's ask ourselves some questions about our experience being baffled by ourselves.

1. Have I ever had the experience of being completely baffled by a reaction of mine?
2. Did I try to understand it?
3. Did the understanding come later?
4. Did I act responsibly toward other people, if others were involved, even though I couldn't understand myself, or did I hide that I had done anything painful to others and pretend I had done nothing wrong?

---

[24] There is more information on amends in Platform Seven: Becoming Accountable.

371

Where Do We Tend to Focus in Our Self-Intervention?

Do we typically try to change the stimulus, the reaction or the response? What does this have to do with cause and effect?

When we don't like the outcome of a behavior (the effect), how do we try to change? Let's look at an example. We're upset because we're getting fat, but getting fat is only an effect. We look for the cause, which is that we're overeating. But overeating is not only a cause; it is the effect of another cause. For example, it could be our response to an emotional or physiological state, and that state is a reaction to a stimulus. Let's say, the first thing we focus on is the final effect, which is the fat. Now the fat becomes the new stimulus, and the reaction is upset, because we've decided that no guy is going to be attracted to us if we're fat. The response to our upset is to eat more, because we are programmed to use food to alter our feelings. Where do we intervene?

Most of us focus on the weight, which is the effect of the overeating, which is the response to some reaction and so on back. Often we try to lose the weight without even changing our eating pattern, meaning we aren't even trying to focus on the response, which is the overeating, but rather the effect, which is the weight, because the weight is the new stimulus that's causing a negative reaction in ourselves. Sometimes we realize that we have to change the way we eat for the purpose of losing weight, so we're at least focusing on the response. But we are certainly not focusing on the cause, which is the emotional reactivity and the stimulus, which is the source of our reactions.

We may acknowledge at least that we are engaged in a self-destructive behavior, which is overeating. We may see that it is a self-destructive response to a reaction, but we may not know what the reaction is, and often we don't even ask. For many people, the most frequent line of attack is to try to control the thing that we see at the surface, which is the effect, which is weight gain, because the weight gain is stimulating a painful reaction, which is fear of loss of love, and a negative response, which is anger toward myself. One reason we focus on the effect, weight, is that the overeating is a response that we are very attached to. It's an addiction. It's a pattern way of coping.

I'm using food as the example, but the same could be said of alcohol, drugs, overwork, a desperate need for sex or a myriad of other behaviors that are really responses to reactions, to feelings or feeling states that we're trying to alter through our response, feeling states that we don't know how to alter any other way.

Of course, a more productive approach to our weight problem would be to overcome the reactions that are causing us to overeat. But we tend to do the opposite. We tend to use the response (overeating) in order to control our reaction (our emotions). Yet when we eat sugar, caffeine and white flour, not only do we gain weight, we actually become more reactive, because these substances causes mood swings and stress. And when we diet, we hit the same trap. We deprive ourselves of the nutrients and nurturing that we need to be in a state of wellbeing. Even though these methods of coping are causing us distressful effects, we can't help our behavior. We are driven by our reactions. We eat because of our emotions, which leads to greater reactivity. We diet because of our reactions to being fat, and we become more reactive because of dieting.

It's hard to eliminate overeating, because it's a response to a reaction to a stimulus and we don't have the support, the self-awareness or the confidence that we can do anything about those reactions, responses or stimuli. What we do know to do with our feelings is to try to alter them from the outside, rather than from the inside.

Trying to solve the problem from the outside is the quick-fix mode of our society. Even in medicine, we know the best way to cure an illness is to not have the disease in the first place. This would attack the problem on the level of the stimulus, which happens when we control illness by eliminating factors such as unclean water, disease-carrying insects, poor nutrition and dangerous lifestyles. We can also try to control disease by changing our reactions, for example by building up our immune system through healthier living and thinking. But if it is expensive to eliminate the stimulus or reaction, or if it takes self-control or the confrontation of an addictive pattern, we fall back on trying to control the body's response through external interventions, such as medication or surgery. We try to cure the disease instead of us. In other words, we try to focus on the effect instead of the cause.

Of course, there are times when medications are a lifesaver, but relying on medication creates a larger problem. Large doses of antibiotics kill everything, destroying the very immune system that could kill the infection and help ensure that the illness would not occur again. Yet this is the quick fix we have become accustomed to.

It is no different on the mental/emotional plane. If we are looking for wellbeing, we have to stop focusing our energy on changing the effect and focus on the cause, which means we need to invest in understanding our behavior and changing ourselves. Of course if we have an anger problem and the best we can do at the moment is stop ourselves from hitting the child, then so be it, let's do that. But for everyone's long-term wellbeing, we need to become aware of and shift the emotions deep within us that cause us to want to hit a child to begin with. What is driving us to strike out at someone even less powerful than we?

The tendency to focus on unwanted effects, rather than the stimulus, reaction or response that caused them, extends to our treatment of others as well. Often we strike out at someone because their behavior bothers us, and we ignore what caused it. It's easier to tell someone to stop doing a self-destructive behavior than to help them figure out why they do it and help them stop.

How do we approach our unwanted behaviors? Let's ask ourselves some questions.

1. What are some of my unwanted behaviors?
2. Am I upset because I don't like the effect, or am I also concerned about the cause?
3. Can I recognize my own addictive patterns of body, mind or spirit?
4. At what level do I tend to intervene with myself?
5. How successful am I?
6. Do I treat others the same way?

Awareness of Our Energy

As we have been saying, self-awareness requires us to be aware of our stimulus-reaction-response patterns. Still looking at these patterns, let's see them now in terms of energy.

We are energy beings. It doesn't look that way, because what we see is a physical body, accompanied by a personality that is stuck in innumerable patterns of stimulus-reaction-response. But whether we recognize it or not, we are actually a constellation of vibrational energies that fluctuate between different frequencies, depending on what we're doing, thinking, feeling or eating, as well as where we are and who we're relating to.

This is not as confusing as it sounds. Remember that everything is made of atoms, which are particles comprised of electrical charges. If matter were not essentially convertible to energy, there would be no atomic bomb. In fact, light itself is both a particle and a wave. So things are not as solid as they appear to us. And that, of course, is just as true of us. Of course we SEEM solid. And if I punch a wrestler in the stomach, my damaged fist will demonstrate how solid he is. But in fact, seen from another perspective, we are complex energy fields vibrating at various frequencies.

Now, how do I really know this? There are people who can actually see into and through us, and who can see the movement of energies through us. I don't have this gift, so I can't describe to you what they have seen. But I do know that we are energy beings because I experience it on the feeling level, because I can feel my own body vibrating, and I can impact the vibrations within you through channeling spiritual power.

You look perfectly solid, but when I'm working from a dimension where I can access the power of spiritual forces, I know that I can impact the way you feel mentally, emotionally and sometimes even physically. And others can too. In fact, if we were not vibrational energies, healers couldn't help us.

All of this may sound like gibberish to some of you, and that's okay. What is important is not that you believe ME, but that you be willing to consider that everything you do, think, say, feel, eat and so on will impact you, whether you want to believe it or not. If you don't like the model of yourself as an amazingly complex field of energy, think of yourself as a great chemistry lab. Perhaps from this perspective, you can realize you are not fixed and solid like a machine; you are shifting and changing like a big chemistry experiment where different elements come together to interact with one another. If this were not true, emotions wouldn't lift our heart rates, and nobody would be a drug addict.

So that we can go on together, let's agree on using the concept that each human being is a complex energy field. Now that we have agreed to work with the concept that we are energy beings, we realize that we can be impacted by other energies. If we were solid, we couldn't be impacted by anything except maybe an elevator falling on us or some other external force. Not very subtle. But in fact, we are constantly being impacted by other energies, most of which we aren't even aware of.

We discussed this earlier in our section on Becoming Oneness. If I walk into a room of anxious people, I will feel anxious, and I won't know why. Many of us have had the experience that when we walk into a party, we feel anxiety. Everyone around us looks like they are having a good time, and we think we should be having a good time, too. I thought I felt fine when I walked in the door. What happened?

What probably happened was that either I was really anxious about being at the party—how do I look, will anyone talk to me, is my date going to be eyeing a more interesting prospect, and so on? Or the other people in the room were themselves actually anxious while they were eating, drinking and acting merry to cope with that anxiety, and I picked up their energy.

If I live in a prison, I am bound to feel and be impacted by the anger, fear and self-loathing of the other prisoners, and I will start having those feelings, too. If I walk into a sanctuary, I may very well suddenly feel more peaceful and calm. We further discussed this concept in Platform Two: Becoming Differentiated, where we referred to the need to support ourselves with the aspects of consciousness we want to energize.

So now let's see how Oneness and Differentiation relate to the pattern of stimulus-reaction-response. I'm stressed, and I've identified that the stimulus is some event. The event could be my boss making a lot of demands on me, somebody cutting me off me on the freeway, or my hospital nurse not coming when called. Let's say I then have a response to each of these scenarios, such as yelling at my kids when I get home, cursing the driver who almost hit me on the freeway, or screaming at my son to get me out of the hospital.

It's obvious that my responses are not productive and are often not even directed at the problem itself, as in the case of yelling at my kids. If I pay attention, this phenomenon is something I can recognize and address. But dealing with other people's energy is much tougher to do. I can't see it; I can only feel it. If I don't even recognize the reality of the energetic connection among us, I can't prepare myself to deal with it. So obviously the first step is to acknowledge that energies exist and that they impact me.

Another important realization about energy is that our energy impacts others, too. Let's say I am yelling at my boyfriend. I'm noticing my response, which is anger. I think that my boyfriend is hearing my words, and on some cognitive level, he is. But of course, he is also experiencing the energy of the anger, itself.

But, hey, it's even more complicated than that. What is under my anger? Let's say my boss is making demands on me (stimulus), I feel anxious (reaction), and my response is to yell at my boyfriend. Yes, my boyfriend feels anger, because my words carry that energy. But he also feels my fear, because fear is what I'm actually feeling, and it's my fear of my work situation that's triggering me to unleash my anger at my boyfriend. So even though he has no idea what that fear is about, and even though he thinks he's feeling only my anger, my boyfriend is also feeling my fear, and fear begets fear. Guess what? He will probably start feeling fear, too. In fact, he is more likely to respond to my fear reaction than my angry response.

Let's look at another way my energy impacts others. Say I see my child running out into the street. The child is in danger, and I feel fear. I yell at the child, and everyone would agree that I am angry. But my true reaction is fear, not anger. My child, who like all human beings has antenna for picking up other people's energy, is actually going to be feeling fear, my fear about her behavior. The child begins to associate running with fear. If she has one traumatic experience or a series of similar events, she begins to interpret this experience to mean that expressing herself through her body is dangerous. I see only that I'm communicating the energy of my response, which is anger; in fact I am communicating the energy of my reaction, which is fear. And that may impact that child forever, until she can intervene in her own process.

The fact is that we sense the energy of the reaction more strongly than the energy of the response. Taking our earlier example, I'm yelling my head off, am I not? My behavior is angry, my words are angry, I say I'm angry. Everyone around me confirms that I am angry. But what is everyone feeling? Fear. They think it's their fear of me. But in fact, since the reaction under the response is more powerful than the energy of the response, the fear I'm feeling about something is combining with and triggering the fear that they're feeling when I'm yelling. No wonder we feel so afraid when someone else is angry. We are feeling not only our own fear of their possibly erratic and threatening behavior; we are also feeling the fear that is driving that scary behavior. The rapist stimulates fear in us, not only because we have no idea what he will do, but also because we are feeling his fear of what he's doing and its possible consequences.

Take a moment to examine one example. Your boyfriend John comes at you yelling that you are not listening to him, that you're not paying attention to his needs and desires. He is being stimulated by a fear that you are pulling away from him and that he is about to lose you. He seems to be angry, and you feel fear. Fear of what? Well, obviously, it could be your fear of his apparent anger. But is that it, and is that all? No. If HE is feeling fear, the fear that you are going to leave him, he will automatically communicate that fear energetically, even though his words are angry rather than fearful. And when you feel fear, you are feeling HIS fear that he may get out of control with his anger, and you're feeling his fear that he'll be left alone, like he felt when his mom got remarried when he was six years old.

Maybe John is feeling another fear—that nobody else will ever love him. Maybe he is also feeling the fear that the reason you don't love him is that he is a brute. And then mixed with the fear is John's shame that he is behaving like a brute, which makes him feel even more fearful because he's now afraid that you're going to see that he's a brute, and now you'll surely leave him.

The energy of fear can move in like a bulldozer, pushing away everything that stands in its way. When John walks in the room, he brings that bulldozer with him. And it's extremely difficult to defend ourselves against the impact of that bulldozer, especially because we aren't even aware that it exists. We are focused only on coping with John's anger. We are not coping with his underlying energy of fear.

We Are Receivers and Transmitters

We are not just energy fields; we are receivers and transmitters. We send and receive energetic messages all the time. The threatening dog senses our fear; we are no less sensitive. We feel one another's feelings because we are one, and additionally we think each other's thoughts for the same reason. Feelings and thoughts are all energies that we pick up.

Let's go back to our example. John comes in and is angry with me. His anger triggers my anger, and I also feel fearful, because obviously the energy of anger easily triggers fear. But at the same time I start having thoughts that he is a brute and that I ought to leave him. Why am I having those exact thoughts at that particular moment? I believe I am having those thoughts, because they are mine. They may be. But it is just as likely that I am having those particular thoughts because they are his thoughts; I am having those feelings because they are his feelings. Because his thought—that he is a brute and that I am going to leave him—is a vibrational energy that travels from him to me, and I think the thought is my own.

This reality that we are receivers and transmitters has a huge impact on the way we experience the world in any given situation, yet we don't know it. What are my feelings, and what are the feelings of the persons I am with? And how do I differentiate between the two? To Become Self-Aware I need to become aware that I am feeling fear of John; plus I have negative judgments about his brutish behavior. But to be more fully self-aware I also need to become aware of my vulnerability to his thoughts and feelings. And I need to question whether or not all "my" thoughts and feelings are truly mine, or if I have taken them on from somebody else.

Let's explore this question by asking ourselves a few questions.

1. Let me think of an example where I became emotionally triggered by a situation.
2. What were my feelings?
3. What were my thoughts?
4. Were my feelings reactions to the other person's attitude and behavior, or were they reflections of the other person's feelings?
5. Could my thoughts actually have reflected theirs?
6. How can I tell?

Facing the Challenge

To summarize this section: We are highly vulnerable to experiencing other peoples' thoughts and feelings, because we are energetically connected. Just look at the faces of children under stress. They show how vulnerable they are to the energies of their parents, not just as reactors to those energies but as absorbers of those energies. We aren't much different from children. So, in order to Become Self-Aware, we need to remember that we may be experiencing thoughts and feelings that are not generated by us but are experienced as if they were our own. How can we ever find ourselves?

First, we have to acknowledge that we exist as an energy field that can be impacted by the energies around us. In realizing this truth, we can question ourselves when we are reacting. Yes, we are still in the stimulus-reaction-response program. But now the stimulus, reaction and response are impacted by others' thoughts and feelings. Wow, yet another thing to be aware of.

Facing this reality may seem to make our task more difficult. I have enough trouble observing my own behavior and emotions. How the heck am I going to also understand those of others? While it is very understandable that this is a daunting task, ignoring the reality is not going to help us. Instead, we need to become more and more aware of ourselves as interconnected energy beings, so that we can begin to develop and expand the tools that we have in order to become more centered in ourselves.

✍

Tool: Whose Feelings Are They?

When we experience a feeling, we can talk to one another. We can say to each other, "I feel anger in the field. Whose anger is it?"

✍

Let's say we are together, and I'm feeling angry. Now I have not only brought my awareness to the possibility that the anger is not mine, I can recruit you into the conversation by asking whose anger it is. You may be able to identify that you are feeling angry because you were denied a raise or because your son has just gotten into a relationship of which you disapprove. Or you may be feeling angry at me about something. Or you might be feeling angry at yourself. If I don't inquire, I might never know that you are feeling anger, which I may be sensing.

If you don't acknowledge your feelings, I may have to use my own intelligence and antenna to fill in the blanks. One of the greatest tools we have is, of course, awareness. Earlier in this chapter I discussed the fact that in order to become self-aware I need to also become aware of everything around me. By practicing the platforms of this program, I have begun to become more neutral and objective about myself. If I go into the same neutral mode about the behavior and feelings of others, I can start looking more deeply at people and noticing what they are in fact transmitting energetically. I can then begin to differentiate between their feelings and mine.

380

Using Our Tools to Differentiate from Others' Energy

How can I best begin to differentiate myself from others' energy? First, by coming to know myself well. If I see myself reacting in an unusual way in a situation, I can ask myself whether I have been particularly challenged, or if another person might be impacting me. Then I can use the tool we just learned to engage the other person.

Second, I can use with others the same tools of awareness that I have learned to use with myself, but this time I use these tools to understand them. What am I noticing about Josh? What is his behavior? What is the energy under his behavior? Is he angry, afraid, ashamed? Why would that be? Suddenly I am able to differentiate between his response and his reactions, i.e., his behavior and his feelings. And I can ask him what could be the stimulus that is causing him this reaction and response.

This information can make me feel hopeless—Gosh I can't even deal with my own feelings; how can I deal with yours, too? Or this new knowledge can make me feel empowered, because I am gaining tools to understand my own reactions, and I am developing tools to understand and have more compassion for others.

Third, I can strengthen myself.

How Can I Strengthen My Energy Self?

If I have a weak immune system, I will be highly impacted by germs. If my immune system is strong, I'm more likely to be okay. The same is true emotionally and spiritually. If my energy body is strong and has integrity, I am more likely to maintain my own equilibrium in the face of other people's emotions. If it is weak, I am more likely to react out of my own programmed response (stimulus-reaction-response), and I am also more likely to pick up other peoples' emotions and reactions.

This only seems mysterious. Before we understood the immune system, we thought our vulnerability to illness was caused by the germ and we focused on how to kill it. That led to fabulous antibiotics, which in turn led to more resistant germs. Now we understand more about the immune system. Now we understand that the best defense against illness is to find ways to strengthen ourselves. Put simply: We used to believe that the way to survive was to weaken the foe. Now we understand that the way to thrive is to strengthen ourselves.

Relating this to our energy beings, here's what we can realize: Because of our sensitivities, many of us have tried to control everyone around us so that we would feel safe. If we couldn't, we felt we had to leave people or situations and/or be alone. Now we realize that we need to connect to our inner self and develop its integrity: strengthen it and reinforce it. Wow, I don't have to try to control life, which is a fruitless pursuit anyway. Instead I need to learn better how to regulate my own energy, so that I am not only less subject to my own reactivity, I am less affected by the energies of the people around me.

There are many ways to strengthen the energy self, our own energy fields, and let's talk about a few of them.

First, awareness, awareness, awareness. Just realizing that I am in the presence of another energy helps me to differentiate from it. It's like waking up from a nightmare where I feel trapped and realizing that the threat isn't real. When I am caught up in the energy of someone else, I cannot find myself, and I am still in a nightmare where I have no control. When I wake up, I realize that I am not caught in the nightmare at all. When I wake up emotionally and realize that the feelings I'm experiencing are not coming from me, I can free myself from my reactions and confusion. I can walk away, take a breath, meditate, pray, take a hike, listen to music, return to myself.

Here's an example. Let's say I'm with that angry boyfriend. If I believe that he is angry, I will probably have my stimulus-reaction-response to anger, and chances are I'll be yelling at the top of my voice within seconds (fight) or trying to get out of there (flight).

Suppose, on the other hand, I give myself a timeout and return to a calm place. Then I recognize that I am feeling fear, but that the fear is his. I can address his fear; for instance, I might reassure him that I'm not leaving him, or I might acknowledge that I am, but now it's on the table. If he can hear my response, he will either feel relieved that I'm not leaving or he will feel the pain that I am. He may still be expressing anger, but the actual energy behind the apparent anger is now pain. I will notice that I'm feeling pain, too. But is it my pain about losing him or his pain about losing me? I take a breath and go within. If need be, I get away for a while, get support, connect more deeply with myself. If I also truly feel pain about the potential loss of the relationship, I might talk to him about what's bothering us and focus on resolving our issues rather than leaving. But if it's his pain about the break-up, which I don't share, I can be compassionate but stay on my own side, and I leave the relationship.

By addressing John's pain rather than his anger, I am helping shift John's energy. I'm helping him see what he's feeling and I'm differentiating from both his anger and his pain. By recognizing his feelings, by differentiating from them and by acting appropriately to my own intentions, we both have a very different experience. There are situations where our lives are endangered, and we don't wait around to shift the energy of the attacker; we get away. But sometimes when we're in danger, helping shift the energy of the attacker is the very thing that saves our lives. In addition, in most circumstances, we are not in immediate danger, so we have time to try to shift the energy, which allows us to change the conversation and resolve things in a way that is for the highest good of all.

I have mentioned the importance of awareness in realizing that we are being impacted by another's energy. Once having become aware, there are many tools we can use to strengthen our energy bodies, both cognitive and non-cognitive. Non-cognitive techniques are very important because they bypass the mind and bring us directly to the energy field. Let's take a look at some of them now.

Tools for Strengthening Our Energy Body

1. Taking time to consider the right course of action
2. Meditation
3. Guided imagery
4. Yoga
5. Tai chi
6. Qi gong
7. LifeForce Inner Workouts
8. Martial arts
9. Any form of physical exercise
10. Thinking positively and optimistically
11. Sending out positive thoughts and channeling beneficial energy to others
12. Prayer
13. Music

14. Color combinations that support us to feel vibrant and alive
15. Nurturing yourself with healthy food, drink and air

The first way to strengthen your energy body is to take your time. People rarely take the moment to understand their own feelings before responding. We feel the reaction, and we are off and running, reacting ourselves. Much of the time, we get it wrong. We are either in a reaction-response pattern, and our programs are running us, or we are caught up in the other person's energy and we don't have a clue as to what we feel.

Slow down! Our first reaction when we feel challenged or uncomfortable is to speed up, to try to dominate the situation or get out of it immediately. We are not adept at dealing with confusing or uncomfortable emotions, and we want to resolve them immediately by fixing what we perceive as the problem. The immediate thought? The problem is that he's angry, and I can get away from those feelings by placating him or running away, or I can try to dominate the situation by getting angrier and justifying my anger by his behavior.

How different it would be if I gave myself a timeout, so that I could relax, become self-aware, express what I truly want to say and behave in a way that reflects my heart's desires.

Let's take a moment to examine how we typically deal with upsetting or confusing emotions.

1. How do I tend to react when I feel triggered?
2. Do I slow down or speed up?
3. Why?
4. What's the result?

Meditation and guided imagery help us to focus on something other than our mental chatter and thereby brings us more into contact with our energy selves and our connection to the universe. Yoga, tai chi, qi gong, LifeForce Inner Workouts[25] and martial arts focus on connecting us to the universal life force, which automatically strengthens our energy field

---

[25] LifeForce: The Inner Workout is a mind-body-spirit exercise program that I lead on the internet. Each workout combines movements, sound, touch,

by connecting us to the source of all energy. In fact, all physical exercise strengthens our energy field because it facilitates the flow of energy within our bodies, which in turn strengthens our field. And all of these alternatives support us to get out of our minds, where the programmed responses are gearing up to play out.

Thinking positively and optimistically can also strengthen our energy field, because they support us to keep out the corrosive effects of the negativity around us. Nature abhors a vacuum. We need to be filled with something. If we are not careful, what will fill us is the pervasive negativity surrounding us.

Prayer can help quiet us and shift us into a state of peace, because we feel less alone and therefore, less stressed. Sending out positive thoughts and channeling beneficial energy to others strengthens us too, because these practices support beneficial energies to flow through us to others, which automatically blocks us from absorbing negative energies coming to us. In other words, we shift the direction of the flow of energy outward, so that we create a vacuum that allows us to receive energy from the universe; thus positive energy flows in and through us and out to others, and there is no vacuum into which the negative energies can flow.[26]

Music can be a wonderful way of filling ourselves with beneficial energies as well, depending on the kind of music we listen to. If we surround ourselves with negative energy, we are much more likely to be permeated by it. For example, if the music that we listen to is full of rage, rage energy is going to seep into us and activate all the rage that is already within us. If we listen to music that lifts up the soul, we receive energies that support the integrity of our fields.

Colors are vibrational energies that impact us, whether we are wearing them or looking at them. We should notice how we feel in different colors or when we paint our homes in different shades. What do we want to feel, and what color combinations will help us to feel that way?

---

breathing and a spiritual message in a unique way. For more information, go to www.lifeforceworkout.com.

[26] When we reach the second part of Platform Seven: Becoming Accountable, we will be learning how to use this technique to deal with negative energies. This teaching will appear in the section called The Seven Dirty Secrets of the Dark Side.

And, of course, there's food. Anything we put into our body impacts our energy. Sugar and empty calories tend to make us nervous and jittery; healthy, nurturing foods tend to make us feel solid. Heavy foods make us groggy; lighter foods and vegetables help us stay clear. Alcohol will make us foggy. Water will help us feel clean. Nurturing ourselves with healthy food, drink and air strengthens us on the physical, mental/emotional and spiritual plains of existence. Polluting our bodies with unhealthy food, drugs, alcohol and other toxic substances makes us weak. All foods and substances are drugs in that they interact with our body chemistry. We can't separate our bodies from our energy fields.

Anything that we do that has a strong vibrational frequency is going to impact our energy field one way or another. Supporting our energy field with positive, beneficial energies strengthens it, which enables us to withstand the assault of negativity on the planet.

Yet often when we're feeling stressed, we do the opposite. When we feel negative energy, we are attracted to a similar energy. If we're angry, we go to angry people to justify our anger. And when we feel anxious, we tend to do things that make us more anxious, such as eating sugar, drinking caffeine, or overdramatizing our situation.

Let's take a moment to examine how we use energies to support ourselves or worsen our state.

1. When I feel anxious or angry or some other negative energy, what do I do?
2. When do I tend to go toward energies that support my negativity?
3. When do I go toward energies that will help me become more centered?
4. What modalities work best for me?

We cannot use beneficial energies as a substitute for self-awareness. If we are full of inner turmoil and destructive patterning, listening to music, for example, can calm us for a while, but this state of mind will not last if it does not help us heal our state of mind. We see this when we go on vacation, relax and feel great and then go nuts the day after we come home. The stress reaction is internal and is being strengthened by the stress around us. When we return, the stress resurfaces.

When we use these beneficial energies to help calm ourselves enough to face our real issues, and when we use them in the process of healing, then the calm can eventually become as internalized as the stress once was. But we need self-awareness to use these beneficial energies for permanent change.

If we believe that the stress comes primarily from outside ourselves, we will blame it for our anxiety and run toward the illusion that we need to control the energies around us to be well. This can lead us to run away from life. Blaming our vibrational state on outside factors, we have to create smaller and smaller universes in which to hide. On the other hand, when we recognize that outside factors are triggering our inner stress, we can embark on a process of deeper healing, which becomes part of us.

Negative energies are most impactful when they trigger unresolved negativity and reactivity within us. We can and should use techniques available to us to help us achieve a greater state of equilibrium so that we can then utilize our objectivity to gain self-awareness. Once in a calmer state, we can practice Becoming Self-Aware and ultimately Becoming Integrated, Platform Six. We are thus using beneficial energies to help us to change permanently, so that we can live with reality rather than escape it.

Let's see how we use various modalities to help ourselves.

1. What modalities do I use to help myself feel more peaceful?
2. Do I then use this as an escape?
3. Do I use it to open the door to self-awareness?

As you continue through this book, you will start practicing other platforms that can dramatically strengthen your energy field. Nothing strengthens it more than Becoming Not-Knowing, Platform Eight, and Becoming Becoming, Platform Nine. These platforms connect us to the divine energies that help us be strong. When we are filled with those energies, we are much less likely to be sidetracked by other people's consciousness.

A FEW MORE THOUGHTS ABOUT BECOMING SELF-AWARE

Dual Consciousness

In reality, we have to exist on two planes: in the cave of shadows and outside of the cave looking in. We are in our bodies, and we are a chemistry lab connected to needs, feelings and reactions. Being inside the cave puts us in touch with those needs, feelings and reactions, and that's important. But being outside the cave, as well, enables self-awareness, the objectivity to observe our behaviors and the ability to understand our reactions. Being inside and outside the cave allows us to be the actor and the observer simultaneously. That is dual consciousness.

As human beings we will never be able to see *everything*, but we're capable of much more self-honesty and vision than most of us have so far manifested. Let's look at this in another way. When we are in our reactivity, we have the viewpoint of the ant, only able to see what's right in front of us. When we are looking from a distance, we have the perspective of the eagle. Together they are powerful. The ant perspective tells us that there is a stimulus that we need to pay attention to. The eagle perspective allows us to choose a different response. The ant sees what's on the ground in great detail; the eagle sees the big picture. As we practice self-awareness, we can take on the best of both perspectives.

Before we go on to Platform Six: Becoming Integrated, let's remind ourselves one more time that the self we have been discussing in this chapter is the programmed self. Remember that our egos in conjunction with our lizard brains have developed strategies for survival, strategies that are often self-destructive. As we become increasingly aware of these programs, we increasingly identify that the self we are observing is really a set of the programs rather than a true expression of who we are.

Programs are not us, any more than a computer program is the computer itself. A program can be useful, or it can be destructive. And a program can be changed, patched or replaced.

When we become self-aware, and especially when we connect to higher consciousness, we can become the programmer. We are the ones to guide our egos, which represent the operating system. We are the ones who can make decisions about which programs we use and which we abandon.

We have identified with these programs for so long, we have forgotten there is another us. We also need to acknowledge that these programs are strong. Recognizing the power of these programs gives us compassion for ourselves and allows us to release needless shame. Understanding that we can be different gives us courage and hope.

Throughout this book, we have been reprogramming ourselves to think and feel differently. In Platform Six: Becoming Integrated, we will learn more about releasing the programmed reactions that have gotten in our way.

And ultimately we will move on to Platform Nine: Becoming Becoming, where we will discover that we won't need those programs at all.

But first we need to become self-aware. Let's take a moment to make the commitment. No matter the fears, no matter the challenges, I commit to becoming self-aware.

Tool: Taking a Nightly Inventory of Ourselves

Every night before going to sleep, make a mental inventory of your behavior throughout the day. Ask yourself:

1. How did I behave?
2. Where was I reactive?
3. Why?

When we are not in the middle of a situation, we are much less likely to be driven to justify our behavior, and being away from the day's challenges helps us gain more objectivity about ourselves.

By the way, some people also use a daily inventory of their food or other specific addictions to see if they slipped into their old addictive patterns and why.

If we catch our behavior in the moment or at the end of the day, we are much more likely to find new responses and much less likely to keep multiplying the mess as a way of justifying the reactivity in which we have already engaged! This leads to a happier life with better relationships, especially with ourselves.

PLATFORM SIX

Becoming Integrated
Gaining More Command Over Ourselves

INTRODUCTION

In Platform Five, we became aware of our reactions and responses, and we committed to becoming self-aware. Now how do we act on our new awareness? By Becoming Integrated, freeing ourselves from the stimulus-reaction-responses that have dominated us.

Becoming Integrated is about becoming whole and responding to life from a place of wholeness. How do we do that? In two stages. First, we overcome the domination of aspects of ourselves; this then helps us to move into the second stage where we become strong enough to overcome the domination of the ego itself. Let me explain these two stages.

STAGE ONE: OVERCOMING THE DOMINATION OF ASPECTS OF OURSELVES

Many of us think of integration as a static state, as in I am now perfect and whole. But that's not so. Becoming Integrated takes continuous adjustments, so that it's more like a process than a state of being.

When you look at a tightrope walker from afar, the acrobat appears to stand perfectly still on the wire. But if you look more closely, you can see that their ankles and body are continually adjusting to keep their balance. That's a great metaphor for Becoming Integrated. We are not static beings, unswayed by influences or emotions. We are living, sentient beings in the process of achieving dynamic balance, continually adjusting to life's demands and our own internal reactions. In other words, wholeness is not a state of being; it's a state of becoming.

Dynamic balance is not rigidity; in fact, it is the opposite. The rigid person takes a stand, holds a belief or a position, and is not capable of responding to life's challenges in a way that is for the highest good of all. He or she has a fixed idea of how things and people should be and can't deal with the realities of the moment. The rigid person is tense and demanding, antagonizes others, and will surely fall off the tightrope. We've all seen rigid people and the pain they cause themselves and others. I'm sure that we all recognize ourselves in this description, too.

Dynamic balance is also not laxness. The lax person may look better than the rigid person, because she's more cheerful or laid back. But she isn't paying attention and will flop over as soon as the rope sways. These unfortunates will cause havoc by refusing to attend to what's happening in their world, so their drug-addicted kids overdose, their jobs disappear, and their spouses wander off into someone else's arms. Such people are frustratingly in denial and leave the hard work to others. Oops, sometimes I am that, too.

The integrated person is neither rigid nor lax; instead he or she is in a state of dynamic balance. Alert, calm and relaxed, that person sees, responds, and maintains an internal equilibrium, even in the face of threats and challenges. That's the perfect martial artist, one who is alert, trained, and relaxed. The stressed student jerks. The unconscious student gets jerked around. And the integrated master makes it all look like child's play. In our lives, such a person is a joy to be around and the one that we tend to rely on.

How do we achieve dynamic balance ourselves? How do we Become Integrated? That's the subject of this chapter.

What Is Becoming Integrated?

For many of us, the word integration has to do with inclusion, as in integrating races or integrating women into higher levels of power in business or government. To some of us, integration has to do with bringing together different aspects of ourselves, such as integrating body, mind, and spirit. Others think of integration as combining different elements for some purpose, like mixing the ingredients of a cake so that when it's baked it becomes different from and greater than the sum of its parts.

But there's another way to conceptualize Becoming Integrated, a way that is not about including, blending, or mixing. It's about letting go; it's about releasing aspects of ourselves that are exaggerated. Instead of bringing things together, we take away or reduce the impact of that which unbalances us.

Think of our tightrope walker again. If she has a heavy stone around her neck, she'll have to lean back to balance it, and she's more likely to lose balance and fall. If she has several heavy stones of differing weights flying around in random directions and at random intervals, she's even more likely to fall.

Isn't that exactly how we are? When we're driven by conscious and unconscious imperatives that motivate our behaviors, how can we balance ourselves? How can we come from a place of wholeness? We need to let go of the stones that are dragging us here and there and pulling us down.

At Stage One, Becoming Integrated is the process of releasing the domination of those aspects of ourselves that run us, so that all aspects of ourselves can work together in harmony. Integration is automatic when we are no longer pulled by drives that separate us from our Oneness with ourselves and one another. In this way, we continually become whole.

Becoming Integrated is a continual process. As I mentioned earlier, some of us have the idea that integration or wholeness is a perfect state of total and complete calm and stillness, and somehow we are supposed to match this picture. How many of us have tormented ourselves because we have achieved a state of calm through yoga, for example, and then that calm is blown by the baby crying? How many of us will try to ignore the baby's cry because it conflicts with our concept that we are supposed to stay in some other-worldly state where we somehow float through existence?

That is not integration. Any time we have a concept of who we are supposed to be, we're in our heads, dominated by some mental concept. By definition, being defined by any concept is the opposite of Becoming Integrated, because when our state of being is being designed by our heads, our state of being isn't emerging from our true selves, unencumbered by the domination of anything.

1. Let's ask ourselves some questions about our self-concepts.
2. Do I consciously or unconsciously have a concept of what the integrated me would look like?
3. Where did I get that concept?
4. Have I tried to match that picture?
5. How do I feel when I don't live up to that concept?
6. What has been the result?

When we integrate through the process of eliminating the drives that unbalance us, we don't have to conceptualize some mythical whole being and then strive to become that being. We don't have to imagine a template of who we should be, a template that we are always trying to live up to. Instead we simply release the domination of those aspects of ourselves that run us, and we automatically become whole and integrated.

What do I mean by domination of those aspects of ourselves that run us? Now this takes a little explaining.

Aspects of Ourselves

People are complex and multi-faceted. Often we are even in conflict with ourselves. We can look at ourselves in terms of aspects of consciousness, and I do that in a more thorough way in an earlier book, *Sacred Union: The Healing of God*[27], which speaks of the fragmentation of consciousness itself into many aspects, but for now, let's keep it simple.

---

[27] Green, Beth. *Sacred Union: The Healing of God*. Idyllwild, Rising Mountain Press, 2002.

Sometimes we refer to our aspects as parts of me. You yourself may have said, "There's a part of me that wants to let go of this relationship; but another part of me still wants to hang on." What do we mean by a part of me?

We are really consciousness in form. We have a mind, body, emotional self and spirit. And we also have many varied qualities, such as greed, compassion, love, anger, timidity, courage, patience, impatience, forbearance and righteousness. And there's always fear. The list is long. All these are aspects of ourselves, and if any of them dominates us, we are out of balance.

The man who is dominated by his need to prove himself to his father might find himself overworking at the job, endlessly trying to demonstrate his value to his boss, the symbol of dad, while neglecting his family. The man who is dominated by his need to please his mother might find himself passively allowing his children to be abused by his wife, the symbol of his mom.

Any aspect of ourselves can dominate us. If we are attached to being loved, we dare not alienate others. If we are attached to being dominant, we fight everyone, even when it's not necessary. We can be too fearful or too reckless, too focused on money or too oblivious to our earthly needs, too afraid of our sexuality or too dominated by our need for it. We discussed much of this in Platform Five: Becoming Self-Aware, as we became more aware of our reactions and responses, and we will discuss this again further in this chapter. But in the meantime, let's briefly consider our own state of balance.

1. Am I willing to admit that I'm out of balance with different aspects of myself?
2. What aspects of me seem most dominant?
3. Can I trace back to the time I became dominated by them?
4. Can I have compassion for myself?

Once we identify the energies that run us, we can start the process of releasing their domination. That's how we integrate. No longer dominated by some aspect of ourselves, our parts will come together in a dynamic balance of who we are moment by moment. And once we are integrated, we change again, as we become more capable of moving into higher states of being and higher states of integration, as we shall see in later chapters.

As you have probably guessed, this process sounds a lot easier than it is, but on the other hand, it's a heck of a lot easier than trying to conceptualize who we are supposed to be, then try to blend together all the right ingredients and then compare the blend to whatever concept we have in our head! It's all part of becoming ourselves.

WHAT ARE THE BLOCKS TO BECOMING INTEGRATED?

Becoming Integrated sounds great. You're saying that I'll be more whole, happy, calm, and appropriate in my responses. Why wouldn't I want that?

Because I would need to become self-aware; I would need to change; and I would have to confront the very energies that have run me all my life. In other words, I would have to confront the ego. Way back in the beginning of this book, we talked about "Ego, Instinct & Evolution," and we admitted that we have patterns of behavior, born in infancy or even before, which were developed by our egos to protect our very existence. When we go to change, the ego screams, "Don't alter this behavior. I created it for your survival, and if you let it go, it will kill you!"

Am I exaggerating? Let's look at a very common example. Are you the kind of person who feels that you just have to get to every appointment on time? Let's say you're running late because of traffic. How do you feel? Have you noticed the stress you experience? If you look at your emotional and physiological state, doesn't it feel like getting to that appointment on time is a matter of life or death?

This is the nature of stress. It's the feeling that my life somehow depends on x or y happening or not happening. I feel stress while waiting for John to propose marriage; I am stressed because we can't get pregnant; I am stressed because I fear I'll lose my job; I'm stressed because my makeup isn't going on right and I have a hot date; I am stressed because my mother called and is telling me what to do; I'm stressed because my kids aren't listening to me; I'm stressed because there's a contract on my life; I'm stressed because I have responsibility for stopping an oil spill and I don't know how.

Now it may sound silly to put all these stressors in the same category, but on an emotional and physiological level, they all have a pretty similar feel. If x does or does not happen, I feel like I'm just going to die. The stress hormones are raging, and once they get going, it's hard not to keep cycling through stress and more stress, so much so that many of us use artificial means, such as alcohol or drugs, to stop the feeling of anxiety.

For some people, stress and anxiety are very much on the surface. Those folks are obviously pretty high strung, driven, and anxiety ridden. But what of our laid-back folks who seem to take things in stride? Many of them are stressed as well, but their survival pattern is to hide the stress from themselves and others, because having to confront the stress feels like life or death. Here's an example. My wife is nagging me, I quietly seethe inside (maybe without even realizing it), I go have a drink and play golf, I smile and I say nothing is wrong. With such folks, there are two stressors: the nagging of the wife and the fear of confrontation. That fear of confrontation feels like life and death. If I confront my nagging wife, somehow that confrontation will kill me. Am I exaggerating? No. How many times have you seen someone put up with endless abuse and act as though they were okay with it? Why would they do that, if not for the fear that confronting the abuse is too dangerous; this despite the fact that the abuser is really not more powerful than the person being abused.

It may sound nuts, but that's how we are, and it all stems from the combination of our inherent nature and our life programming.

Once I'm in the life-or-death experience of stress, I become stupid. So here I am, stuck on the freeway, chewing my nails, feeling anxiety, and I may not even think to simply call and say I'll be late. And even if I do, I may not allow myself to listen to music and relax. I can't change the fact that I'm late; even if it's my fault, there's nothing I can do about it now but be more careful in the future. And yet I seem to be totally against relaxing into the reality that I'm going to be late, as though being stressed is somehow normal, appropriate and a necessary response to the situation!

When I'm in that frame of mind, I behave as though I really need to sit on the freeway with my stomach churning, that I need to check the time every two seconds, that grinding my teeth will help me, and that I need to ensure the continuation of my anxiety! Why? Because getting to that appointment on time feels like life or death, even though it's not. In fact, rushing on the freeway is much more likely to kill me than getting to the appointment late.

What's the genesis of this life-or-death reaction? If we go back to what we learned in Platform Five on Self-Awareness, we can get some clues. The cause may be in the past. Suppose my mother was very exacting, and

I was afraid that I couldn't perform to her satisfaction. That might have led me to always try to appear super-functional, as in I'll always leave 20 minutes early to make sure I meet expectations. But despite my efforts, there was an accident on the freeway, and there's nothing I can do about it. My unconscious association is that my mother will disapprove and cut me off emotionally and she's the only one who took care of me in childhood. Without her approval, I will die, so I've just got to get there on time! Or my fear that I couldn't perform to my mother's expectations might have made me unconsciously self-sabotaging. I never want to face a really big test and fail, so I just always underperform and keep expectations down, so Mom will never cut me off, so I won't die. If I care about being on time but I self-sabotage, I always leave barely enough time to make it to an appointment, keeping myself in a constant state of self-disappointment but simultaneously blocking me from ever trying anything hard, where I might disappoint Mom. Either way, if I'm late, I will be failing Mother, and we know that disappointing Mom will lead to her yelling, hitting me, or cutting me off emotionally, and then I will die. Or so it seems.

The life-or-death stress might have another, more immediate genesis. For example, let's say I believe that I'm screwing up on the job, and being dependable is the only thing that makes me valuable. If I'm late to work, the boss will see that I'm incompetent and fire me; I won't be able to get another job, the house will be foreclosed on, and my spouse will leave, I'll be alone, and I'll just die. Or perhaps I have an appointment to make a presentation of a product I'm selling. The potential buyers will be annoyed if I'm five minutes late, they won't buy my product, my income will fall, my wife will leave me, I'll lose my children, I'll be alone. I can't live alone; I'll kill myself.

If we feel that our ways of behaving are all essential to our survival, we will not want to let them go. Now we're not only confronting what's driving our behaviors; we're confronting the ego that created those behaviors. Our ego will try to convince us that letting go of destructive and self-destructive behaviors will kill us, so how can we release the imbalances and Become Integrated?

Let's look at our own reaction to stress.

1. What are some of the situations that cause me stress?
2. What exactly is the stress?

3. What is the history or current situation that makes me feel that this situation is life or death?
4. Can I laugh about it?

Are We Nuts?

If you have been reading this book, you might be getting the idea that human beings are crazy, meaning we tend to be irrational and hurt ourselves and one another in the process. This is true. And change is painstakingly slow. If we truly want to become integrated, we're going to have to take on the fight of our lives, of our era, of the human race. We're going to have to take on the ego. First, we acknowledge that we are not integrated and that we are dominated by different aspects of ourselves that tell us we can't give them up. Then we start to chip away at the domination of these aspects. And then we reach the ego itself and we start to confront its domination.

But more about that later.

WHY DO WE WANT TO BECOME INTEGRATED?

If Becoming Integrated is so threatening, why do we want to take it on? Because the human race is suffering immensely from hanging on to the old ways.

Being Dominated by Our "Needs"

Let's start with the acknowledgement that we are not integrated. We experience ourselves as a series of needs that must be met. I need love; I need validation; I need food; I need that promotion; I need that dress; I need that praise; I need that house/ boat/ ring; I need you to tell me I'm beautiful/ handsome/ smart/ successful/ powerful/ sexy; I need safety; I need to survive. I need; I need; I need; and therefore I must have. The minute that I need and must have anything, I have lost integrity; I have lost wholeness; I have lost integration, because I am being dominated by that perceived "need." And to a greater or lesser extent, each of these needs feels like life or death to us, which causes us stress.

I am not suggesting that we don't need some or all of these things. What I am suggesting is that when any need becomes a "must have," we have lost integration and the freedom to act in a way that is consistent with our higher self and our highest good.

Let's take a look at some of our own must-haves.

1. What do I tell myself I must have?
2. Why must I have it?
3. What have I lost because of it?

How Does the "Need" for Love Impact Me and My Relationships?

Let's look at some of the common needs that drive us and examine the impact of the domination of those needs. Let's start with love. Sure, most if not all of us need love. But when I *must* have it, and I must have it from x person or y social group, I will skew my personality to get that person to love me; I will skew my body and looks to get that person to want me; I will organize my behavior to get that person to need me enough so that they are dominated by their need for me, just as I am dominated by my need for them. So instead of becoming healthier and more integrated myself, I work toward turning the other person into someone who is dominated by their "needs" as well.

How does that look? In an integrated state, we are intrinsically connected to ourselves, and we are connected to God, The Source, higher consciousness, or however you wish to conceptualize that living connection with the creative force that brought us into being and nurtures and inspires us. We can see this as a vertical relationship with ourselves and the divine. When I feel complete and integrated, I relate to you as a complete and integrated being.

But when we are dominated by the "need" for love, our relationships are horizontal, instead of vertical. We are looking to one another for love, validation, safety, praise, admiration, whatever it is we think we need. What are some of the negative impacts of horizontal relationships?

- The other person is an extension of our needs, and therefore they "MUST" behave in a certain way. Horizontality is very prominent among couples, but this could apply as easily to children, friends, colleagues, or anyone else we think we "need."

- We are vulnerable to the other one's capacity to meet those needs and are often frustrated by their inability or refusal to meet them.
- We try to force others to be equally horizontal with us.
- We are so desperate to get those needs met, we skew ourselves to hook them.
- We often can't even remember who we are outside the relationship, what we would want or be if our purpose were not to maintain this relationship that we desperately "need."
- We lose our self-respect, and often we lose touch with ourselves.
- We feel ownership over others.
- We reject any inspiration to become something or someone if that becoming would threaten the relationship! And we often unconsciously block others from becoming themselves as well.

When lovers, children, or friends—whether at work, in universities, communities, spiritual groups, or other social organizations—come together, most relationships are horizontal, because few of us are integrated enough to connect vertically to ourselves and the infinite. Our collective human history is that we cannot survive alone, and our fear of being alone or outcast drives us.

Let's consider how we behave in relationships.

1. Which relationships of mine are horizontal?
2. How does that trap me?
3. How has that trapped others?
4. What has happened when one or another of us has threatened the horizontal connection?
5. Is maintaining horizontality in relationships worth the price?

The fear of becoming whole and integrated is intense, but the price of horizontal relationships is heavy!

The "Need" for Safety

Now let's look at another hugely impactful "need," the need for safety. Of course it is completely natural that we react automatically when we feel our existence is endangered. This is part of being human, although many of us are not even aware of how much it dominates us.

But what is the cost of being dominated by that need?

First, we see that the need for safety is connected to being dominated by the need for love, because we are afraid to be thrown out of the tribe, of being alone and not surviving. Thus our need for safety keeps us in unhealthy relationships and keeps us trying to similarly entrap others.

The need for safety impacts us in many other ways as well. Let's look at some of those now.

- It prevents us from challenging injustice to ourselves and others. How many of us are appalled by the behavior of an individual or a social group—ranging from an abusive boss to segregation and discrimination—and yet we're too busy protecting our safety to speak up?
- It blocks us from confronting people about behaviors that they are inflicting on themselves, because we're afraid of antagonizing them and unleashing some unpleasant attacks on us. You know that someone is overeating, yet you bring them muffins to make them happy instead of confronting them that they are killing themselves.
- It stops us from even questioning highly accepted practices and norms, even when we know they are irrational and destructive. For example, women wear high-heeled shoes and pretend the shoes are comfortable and not harmful to their bodies.
- It causes us to hide out in our homes, jobs, families, or social groups, afraid to take on the social issues of the day.
- It makes us mute in relationships, when we need to speak.
- It compels us to try to dominate in situations where we are afraid of being dominated. For example, we refuse to listen to others, even when we're wrong, because we want to appear smart or in charge, because appearing smart or in charge makes us feel safe.
- It makes us insincere, flattering, complacent, apathetic, and self-deceptive, which leads to denial when we refuse to acknowledge what we see; or self-contempt, when we know something is wrong and are too self-protective to speak up or take action.

Now let's take a look at the list above and go over each one in relation to ourselves.

1. How have I acted out each of these behaviors based on safety?
2. Who have I hurt?
3. What has it cost me?

If we are to be truly integrated and free, we are going to have to stop being dominated by our need for safety, even by our very need to survive. Anything else blocks our integration and wholeness.

The "Need" to Prove My Value

Let's examine the domination of one more very common "need," the need to prove my value. Oh Lord! Consider how we have overworked, stressed ourselves to the max, put other people down, ingratiated ourselves to those whose approval would make us look good, made others dependent on us, manipulated people into flattering or praising us, focused only on our own ideas, puffed ourselves up or puffed up others whose value somehow reflected on us, rationalized our behaviors, judgments and decisions, or imposed our beliefs, values and traditions on others, just to prove our value.

Like other "needs," the "need" to prove my value can also lead to other imbalances. For example, if I have tended to prove my value through my mind, I will probably feed my mind at the expense of my body or spirit. Now I have another imbalance that I have to redress, the domination of the mind and the lack of integration that this domination causes.

Let's pause to question ourselves about the need to prove our value.

1. Where have I tried to prove my value?
2. How has that driven me?
3. How has that hurt others?
4. What aspect of me has been given value?
5. How have I puffed it up at the expense of other aspects of me?

The "Need" to Be Optimistic

Now, how can optimism be a need out of balance? Earlier in this book, we referred to sitting on the railroad tracks, watching the train come. If we have too much fear, we will be paralyzed and won't jump off the tracks. If we have no fear, we will watch the train come down the tracks and not feel the need to get off them. Either way we're dead. This is fear out of balance.

We have also seen how so-called positive emotions, or aspects of consciousness, can be out of balance, as in the example of the need for love. Now I would like to address other "positive" emotions out of balance, and I'll use optimism as an example.

Let's go back to the railroad tracks. We're watching the train come down the tracks. Suppose optimism is out of balance? We think, "Hey, the conductor will see me and put on the brakes. I certainly can't be killed." So, once more we sit on the tracks and get run over. Uh-oh.

Why were we dominated by optimism out of balance? Because we have a deep, subconscious need to be optimistic. Perhaps my mother was suicidal, and every day when I came home from school, I saw her in deep depression. I got into the habit of trying to "cheer her up." I hope that my optimism will balance her dark mood and keep her from killing herself. This need to save my mother has translated into a need to be optimistic, a need that takes me out of reality, which, in turn, puts me in jeopardy. If I have a need to be optimistic, I might not sell stock at the right time, because I am sure the market will turn around, and I might not leave an abusive relationship, because the turning point is always around the corner.

Let's pause to look at some of our needs out of balance.

1. Let me look at some of my "needs," aspects of my own consciousness, that drive me.
2. Are they common in humans?
3. How did they develop in me and why?

I could continue with numerous more examples of being driven by some "need" that makes us blind. But these few should give us an idea of the scope of the problem. If we are being driven by these "needs" and our fear that the "needs" will not be met, how can we become whole and integrated, realistic, relaxed, and responsive?

Using Others to Balance Us Instead of Integrating within Ourselves

Now we're going to take a look at how our needs out of balance can impact a relationship. Have you ever noticed that many couples polarize in their attitudes and arguments? One member of the couple takes one side, and the other takes the opposing view. I want to buy the house, because I love it. You don't want to buy the house, because we can't afford it. I don't admit that I am terrified of the price tag, too. You don't admit that you love the house also. We take sides, and we each embody an aspect of consciousness. I am embodying passion, you are embodying frugality.

Is either of us in balance? Not at all. I am using you to balance my passion. You are using me to balance your frugality. We are both being dominated by an aspect of ourselves, and we each argue that our aspect of consciousness is right or better.

Are we being dominated by our needs here? Yes, I am dominated by the need to balance your negativity. You are dominated by the need to balance my excitement. I need to stop using you to prevent me from foolishness, and you need to stop using me to prevent you from paralysis. What we both truly need is to become integrated in ourselves and come together to determine what is for the highest good of all, including us, at this time.

Why do we embody those particular aspects of consciousness? Partly because the other embodies the opposite and partly because we probably have already been programmed for being out of balance in that particular way. I have been programmed to be dominated by my passion in rebellion against my mother, who was dominated by her fear. You have been programmed to be dominated by frugality in order to please an overly cautious dad. Let's say we have both experienced the consequences of our own imbalances—I have hurt myself through flinging myself thoughtlessly into situations that attract me, and you have been hurt by taking no risks. When we meet, we recognize in each other the aspect that's missing in us, so we choose each other to balance us.

Choosing one another might help us on one level, because we may be prevented from being totally dominated by our own imbalance, but our relationship becomes one where we fight each other, and there is a lack of partnering and shared responsibility. Let's say I win, and we get the house. If things don't work out, it will be forever my fault. If you win, and we don't get the house, I will be forever pointing out how the property values went up.

This pattern exists within all kinds of groups. People take sides in arguments and deny the reality or truth in the other person's position. Our positions can become more polarized and exaggerated as the argument progresses. Watch a political debate, and see how people box themselves into corners trying to disprove the other person's position, rather than come to a deeper understanding within themselves. When a politician attempts to be more balanced, her constituents might be angry because she is not replicating their own imbalance, and she might be accused of being wishy-washy or noncommittal.

Trying to balance one another instead of ourselves leads to resentment and blame. But worse than that, it blocks the process of our integrating within ourselves and coming together as whole beings.

How Do We Become Integrated?

Now having reviewed how we are not integrated and what sorts of energies dominate us, we are ready to take the next step toward integration, which is to release the life-or-death energy around these needs. How do we do that?

Back in 2004, I was very ill and was seeking help with my health. I saw an advertisement for a Korean healer, whose name I can't recall. The day before I offered my first Living with Reality workshop, I called the office of that healer, and an associate of his contacted me by phone. I never attended the healer's event, but his associate shared a technique with me to help me with energetic healing. I felt the power of the technique and immediately incorporated it into the practice of Platform Six. I am grateful to them both. I don't know how that healer used this tool, but I took it and transformed it into the practice we use today in Living with Reality work. We call it the release tool.

I have used the release tool in many ways, and you'll see it popping up later in the book. It is core to the practice of Platform Six, and so it's time to introduce it. Here's the form in which we use it now.

Tool: Release the Need

One of the major sources of fear and stress is our attachment to particular outcomes. When you feel stressed, try to identify what it is that you are feeling MUST happen. For example, I HAVE to get to this appointment on time, win this account, buy this house, or fit into a Size Two. When we are dominated by a wish or desire, we are filled with the fear that our wish will not be fulfilled, and that fear causes stress. In other words, we are unbalanced by the domination of what we perceive as a must-have need. Releasing the need for a particular outcome brings relaxation and wellbeing.

To use this tool, begin by finding the place in your body where you most feel the stress, press the fingers of one hand firmly against that location (for example, your heart, forehead or stomach), and say out loud **"I release the need to_____** (for example, get to the appointment on time/ win this account/ buy the house on Main Street/ become a Size Two)." Immediately after making this release statement, quickly dig out the fearful energy by brushing your fingers firmly against the spot on your body where you hold the stress. After releasing the negative energy with your hand, take in a deep breath to take in universal life force energy. When you release the breath, feel the relaxation. Do this process three times. This will help you release stress. After we release the need three times, it's best to breathe in positive neutral energy. For example, we do three releases of, "I release the need to buy the house on Main Street," and after the third release, we can say something like, "because I need to be happy where I live now," or "because I don't need to buy the house on Main Street," or "because I need to live where it is for the highest good of all." And then you take in a deep breath.

This tool helps us in several ways. First, it brings attention to the reality that we don't "need" anything, even survival, to the detriment of the whole of us. Second, it challenges the idea that we have to be stressed by anything and everything. For example, instead of suffering over a divorce, because we think we should be suffering, or other people will judge us if we don't feel depressed, we can release the need to be upset in the face of a divorce, "because we are happier without our spouse." Third, the release tool asks us to consider what could be the underlying causes of our stress, and that leads to greater self-awareness. And finally, the release tool gives us a way to actually intervene with ourselves. It doesn't always end the stress, but it often works.

Now you do it. Start with some simple stressors that are driving you and then, as you become more adept, delve more deeply into yourself. The impact of these releases depends on your ability to see the underlying "needs" under the apparent stressors. If you have been practicing Becoming Self-Aware, you will probably be able to use this tool to great advantage. Also, if you are in therapy or in a self-help group, such as a Living with Reality mutual support group, you can ask your therapist or your peers to help you see yourself more clearly and intuitively identify both the underlying causes for your self-destructive drives and the "because" that works best for you.

Summary of What We've Learned So Far

So far, we've been discussing how we are dominated by a variety of aspects of ourselves. Now I'd like to summarize and organize the points I've made:

1. Our lack of integration stems from being dominated by the various aspects of consciousness that drive us.
2. These aspects appear to be needs, and they dominate our being and our behavior.
3. The self-protective ego tells us that these needs MUST be met, while stimulating a feeling of life or death tension.
4. Whenever the ego tells us that something must happen, it is also creating the fear that the "something" won't happen; this also causes stress.
5. We can challenge the belief that anything must happen, including our own survival.
6. We can release the need for anything in particular to happen, so that we can embrace the process of living and become more relaxed.
7. Ultimately, we can release the need to survive, in order to feel free.
8. No longer driven by any aspect of ourselves, we automatically become more integrated.

Becoming Integrated is a continual process of adjusting, like the tightrope walker on the tightrope. Faced with life's challenges and our internal development, we are in a continual process of releasing the needs that can drive us out of integrity and integration.

STAGE TWO: OVERCOMING THE DOMINATION OF THE EGO

Okay, so now I've done all this work, and you're telling me that I'm still not integrated? Yes, because reality is that we will never become integrated if we are still dominated by the ego. So now we have to start all over again with a new definition of integration, and in fact throughout this section we'll be redefining Becoming Integrated, and we'll need a lot of determination to achieve it.

WHAT IS BECOMING INTEGRATED?

Becoming Integrated is the process of overcoming the fragmentation of the human condition. It requires the end of the domination of ego on this planet. It requires the ego to evolve.

Now that sounds impossible. If ego and fragmentation are part of the human condition, how can we overcome them? Earlier in this chapter, I reminded you about the introduction to this book, "Ego, Instinct & Evolution." It talks about the genesis of the ego, its role and the need for it to evolve, and you might find it helpful to review it now.

In any case, let's talk for a while about the ego itself. Here's a summary of its characteristics and impact on us:

As I said in the introduction to this book, the ego came into being at the moment of existence, when consciousness fragmented. It's the aspect of consciousness that affirms the sense of self, separate from the whole. Its job is to be aware of us and of our needs so that we can take responsibility for ourselves. It is supposed to tell us when we're cold and need a jacket, when it's time to go to sleep, when we are in danger and when there is an opportunity for some positive experience. But unfortunately, it's stuck in an immature stage of development.

The ego is like the two-year old who is still asserting "me!" The immature ego does not understand the difference between separation and differentiation (see Platform Two: Becoming Differentiated). And because it doesn't understand the relationship between the individual and the whole, it focuses on me-based needs instead of the highest good of all, and it justifies that stance as being essential to our survival. In its immature state, it's shortsighted and destructive, focusing on our individual existence and the appearance of individuality, regardless of the consequences. What's worse, like any other aspect of consciousness, it wants to survive, so it has taken on the role of protecting its own existence instead of truly protecting us.

Integration threatens the domination of the ego, because integration is the opposite of fragmentation, which is the ego's perspective. Similarly, consciousness threatens the domination of the ego, because it brings us into awareness of reality and of the need for integration within ourselves, with one another, and with the creative energy of the universe.

Let me explain this last point a little more. The experience of integration is the wholeness of all aspects of us and all aspects of being—for example, my body, mind, and spirit; my strengths and weaknesses; male and female; all forms of life; us and the divine—working together synergistically for the highest good of all. Wholeness threatens the ego, which exists to preserve separation, where each fragment of ourselves and of the universe fights for its own individual existence, despite the impact on us all.

The ego out of balance creates needless stress, needless fear, needless pain, and needless shame, because these are tools of separation. It is tense, hyper-vigilant, and defensive, constantly trying to create stress to prove that the ego's domination is necessary, constantly attempting to prove that the ego, not consciousness, will protect us in the face of these threats. The ego will even masquerade as consciousness, telling us we are "in our egos" when we're actually acting from a place of integration and alignment with The Source or higher consciousness.

For there to be a future, we need to end the domination of the ego. For the ego to be part of the future, it needs to evolve into self-awareness and consciousness, but by nature, the ego, like all aspects of consciousness, is resistant to change.

Why the Ego Is So Out of Balance

Left to its own devices, the ego tends to dominate. Only we can integrate it in ourselves, where we allow the ego to do its job without taking us over. Only we can integrate the consciousness of our true nature as part of the Oneness, in order to counteract the ego's hyper-focus on us as individuals.

But here is our problem. The ego is the awareness of individual existence. As such, it is totally associated with our survival. We feel the need for its protection, because it is devoted to the "me," so we continually empower it. But as we empower the ego, we disempower ourselves, our whole selves, our selves connected to the Oneness. The ego becomes "us." We become unbalanced, because the ego is out of balance with all the aspects of us, and the ego becomes unbalanced because we are not integrating it into our larger selves.

Let's look at the ego out of balance, starting with an enumeration of some of the ego's characteristics when it is not integrated into the whole. The better we understand it, the more likely we are to recognize when the ego is dominating us. As we read this next section, let's see how much we reflect this state of consciousness.

- Since the ego develops in our infancy, it's associated with the lizard brain, which is all about survival. Also because it is born in infancy, the ego develops in us patterns of survival that are infantile, such as the assumption that we are the center of the universe, which excludes deep awareness of the needs of others or the needs of the whole.
- When we are being dominated by our egos, we often feel infantile or truly childish. We can notice ourselves whining, complaining, or demanding.
- Adult egos give the child ego either positive or negative reinforcement, which merely makes the ego flaunt itself, if the strokes are positive, or try to hide itself, if the strokes are negative. So the ego can look like pride or modesty; aggression or placating.
- The ego is only rarely educated as to its place in the Oneness, because the adults who train children are dominated by their egos as well. So even though its limited perspective is easy to spot, the ego may seem invisible because it's lost in a sea of other egos.

Additional Thoughts, Feelings or Attitudes that Indicate that

Our Egos Are in Charge:

a. It's all about me, and I'm entitled to throw little fits about not being respected, listened to, or followed.

b. I'm alone, I'm different, I'm the only one who . . .

c. Everything has to be done my way.

d. There's nothing wrong with me. The problem is him/her/them/it.

e. There's everything wrong with me. I'm the worst.

f. Something is wrong, and I'm going to have to fix it.

g. Something is wrong, and I'm the one suffering.

h. Something is wrong, and it's all my fault.

i. Nothing is wrong, if it means confronting someone or something, or if it means I have to change or lose something that makes me feel comfortable, important, safe.

j. How I look is more important than how I feel, what I contribute, or how I impact others.

k. How I feel is more important than reality.

l. If my looking good conflicts with dealing with reality, reality must go.

m. I have to prove myself no matter the cost.

n. My safety comes first, even if that makes me a coward, a bully or apathetic.

o. Poor me.

p. I'm a shameful being, who should just hide, withdraw, and/or withhold.

q. I am being put upon.

r. You don't understand.

s. Life is stressful, and it's not me.

t. I get into yelling matches dedicated to proving that I'm right or the victim.

u. Being right is more important than solving a problem.

v. I reinforce my ego by fighting with other peoples' egos, instead of trying to resolve differences.

w. My ego talks me out of fighting other people's egos to keep me safe.

- Like everything else in existence, the ego wants to survive, and it fights for its existence tooth and nail, using the tools at its disposal. Because the entire existence of the ego is based on our fragmentation, the ego fears harmony and Oneness, even though our souls crave it. And so whenever we begin to feel too harmonious, the ego creates fear, anger or shame to cause us to separate and to ensure its survival. This causes us to be negative toward ourselves, one another and life itself.

This is not the place to describe the working of the ego in great detail. In *Sacred Union: The Healing of God,* I write at length about the ego, its evolution and its impact. Other writers have written in detail about it as well. But from this brief exposition, we can see that when the ego is not integrated, it is not our friend and does not protect us; rather it makes us miserable, scared, bossy, self-centered, and destructive. And that's reality.

Let's ask ourselves some questions in order to examine some of our egoic behavior.

1. What are some of the infantile patterns that my ego has created "for my own good"?
2. Where do I see them playing out?
3. Was my blatantly egoic behavior rewarded or punished as a child?
4. How did that impact me?
5. Is it rewarded now?
6. As I was examining the list, which of the ego characteristics did I most recognize in myself?
7. Whose ego am I most afraid of, other than my own, and how do I respond to that fear?

How Does the Ego Block Integration?

In Stage One of Becoming Integrated, we realized that our integration is blocked by the domination of aspects of our own consciousness that pull on us and cause us to be out-of-balance. I must have that job, that house, that position. As we already discussed, the ego posits everything in terms of survival, so everything seems to be life or death: the teenager's pimple, the adult's wrinkle, the guy's lack of financial success, the woman's inability to conceive a child, our being late, embarrassed, seen as "less than," unacknowledged, feeling unloved, losing money or fearing the loss of money, and so on. In this life-or-death universe, fear rules, and we are constantly pulled to resolve these fears by having this thing, or that experience, or the other outcome. The need for this thing, or that experience, or the other outcome constantly unbalances us and blocks our integration.

In Stage Two we are realizing that the ego is intrinsically opposed to integration and that we'll have to overcome its domination in order to be whole. Let's explore this a bit more. The foundation of the ego is separateness. I am not you. I am different. I am separate. Ego is the essence of fragmentation. It feels it wouldn't exist without fragmentation, so it fights integration: integration within ourselves, with others, with the divine, with the process of living itself.

Let me repeat this point. The ego always fights Oneness, even within ourselves, because experiencing separation is intrinsic to the ego's nature. The ego arises from fragmentation and has the job of giving each being, each entity, in fact each fragment of ourselves, a sense of individuality. I am better or worse, taller or shorter, smarter or more stupid, more competent or less. I am separate. I suffer. I create. I dominate. I am dominated. I survive. I'm going to die. The ego is afraid of being swallowed up by integration within ourselves and with the Oneness. As I wrote in another context many years ago, "Raging and fearful, we experience ourselves as real. Aligned and harmonious, we fear we would lose ourselves."[28]

Fighting for its survival, the ego loves drama. Why? It's doing its job of protecting us through dramatically warning us of all impending threats, real or imagined, to "our" existence. In addition, it uses drama to upset us, just so that we'll separate when we're about to feel integrated within ourselves, with another, and with life itself. (Ah, yes, the cigarette and the quarrel after making love . . .) And it uses drama to convince us that we are really alone. Once we feel separate and alone, our ego becomes our savior again. It is the old, reliable friend that will love and protect us in a hostile world.

---

[28] Originally written by Beth Green for the Triple Eye Foundation for Intuition, Intervention, Integration, 1992. The Triple Eye Foundation was an organization dedicated to helping form the collective that would heal the collective. It was part of the evolution of the organization The Stream, which was originally founded by Beth in 1983, dissolved in 1986, revived in different forms over the years, and reconstituted in 1999 and incorporated as a nonprofit organization in 2001.

Creating drama ensures that the ego will remain in charge. And drama creates stress, stress, stress! Stress—the feeling that everything is a must-have or must-happen, life-or-death situation. This is needless stress, created by the ego, theoretically to *protect* us! With protection like this, who needs threats?

Let's pause for some questions about how the ego has blocked us from feeling Oneness.

1. Do I see myself running away from Oneness or integration?
2. Do I have a tendency to create drama?
3. Do I recognize in myself the tendency to create needless stress?

So Is Integration Impossible?

Okay, so I think we get that the domination of the ego is a bad thing, destructive to ourselves and to others. But what can we do about it? Didn't you say earlier that the ego is a byproduct of evolution; the byproduct of the fragmentation of consciousness? So if the ego is a product of evolution, and if the ego tries to block integration, how will we ever practice Becoming Integrated? By overcoming our fragmentation, and we do this by consciously choosing evolution and Oneness; by consciously determining that we will confront the domination of the ego whenever it rears its head; and by supporting the ego to evolve.

Is this possible? You bet. In fact it is not only possible, it's already happening. Overcoming its domination is what we've been doing throughout this book, for example. Let's look at how.

First we've been dealing with us as a collective. This is not a book about you OR me. It's about you AND me. It's not for compulsive eaters, vs. alcoholics, vs. sexual deviants, vs. normal people. It's about compulsive eaters, alcoholics, sexual deviants, and all the rest of us so-called "normal people" who are destructive and self-destructive, because this is what it means to be normal. In fact, this book starts with the premise that ultimately we are all the same, and ultimately all humanity is facing one fundamental problem: the current state of human consciousness. Whether you are a warlord trying to keep your rivals down or a landlord trying to keep your expenses down; whether you are a Christian or a Muslim defining the other as evil; whether you are a socialite or a socialist, the prostitute or the John, the frightened child, the driven executive, or the overworked mother, we are all suffering humanity. We all have the same need for love and validation, safety and hope. And we all have the same problem: our tendency to protect ourselves at the expense of others. In other words, our problem is our ego and the ego of everyone around us.

So our first victory is that, throughout this book, we have been looking at ourselves and "our problems" through the lens of all human selves. We are positing our Oneness in the way we are describing ourselves and our suffering.

We have already started to change, and each of these changes has confronted the old egoic patterns. We started Becoming Oneness, focusing on what connects us rather than what divides us. Then we started Becoming Differentiated, instead of separating or merging, as our self-protecting egos direct. Then we started understanding intention and allowance and Becoming Co-Creative, rather than believing we are either powerless or all-powerful, both ways that the ego defines and separates us. Then we started Becoming Mutually Supportive, understanding that when we contribute to the whole and identify with the whole, our needs are better met. Then we really confronted our egos by Becoming Self-Aware, so we could start calling ourselves on the old programs and patterns our egos created in childhood and which have continued throughout our lives. And now we're dedicating ourselves to Becoming Integrated, no matter our fears, no matter the discouragement, no matter how hard the road.

Let's take a few minutes to inventory our own progress.

1. How have I been confronting my ego throughout this book?
2. How am I confronting the domination of the ego in my life?

Do We Have the Guts for this Fight?

People, hear this! If the ego continues to dominate on the planet, we will never be well, be integrated, or thrive. As many other spiritual teachers have shown us from the beginning of time, it is our short-term thinking, our me-based behavior, the "me" universe that has caused humanity its greatest pain. We have been men against women, and women against men; whites against blacks, and blacks against whites; English speakers vs. Spanish speakers; the owners vs. the workers. It's been them vs. us: Republicans vs. Democrats; pro-lifers vs. pro-choice advocates; the jocks vs. the geeks. And in this state of separation, we have failed to resolve our social or economic problems. Now we are facing the most catastrophic problem we have ever had to confront—the reality of climate change—and short-term, me-based thinking is still blocking us. We can't resolve this problem, or any other problem, if our egos continue to separate us from one another, fragment us into competing interests and groups, and kill the messenger when the messenger calls upon us to think differently and support the highest good of all rather than "us."

On the more personal level, the ego out of balance has been killing us, too, emotionally, physically, and spiritually. It alienates us from each other. Sure, I may love you. But, if I am driven by my ego, I will have to prove to you that I'm better than you, or I'll put you down to make myself impressive to others, or I'll try to get you to take care of me, or I'll control you so you won't leave me or otherwise disrupt the self-protective prison my ego has created and in which we are both doomed. And beyond intimate relationships, the self-protective, me-based, short-term-thinking ego has put people in the wrong jobs or positions because our egos demand that we earn a certain income, or gain a level of prestige, or please Daddy, or suck up admiration, or something. The ego strains us by driving us to prove ourselves and the proof is never enough; it negates our selves by driving us to mangle ourselves for others' acceptance, admiration, or deference. And it diminishes others because it drives us to put others down when we don't feel adequate; to lash out when we feel slighted, instead of seeking to understand; to abuse those who are weaker than we or dependent on our love or money.

The ego kills support because it drives us to feel threatened when someone else has a better idea and could help us. And the ego kills rationality, because it makes us totally blind, as we defend, justify, and rationalize every unfair, irrational, and cowardly act of our own by telling us that we are right or explaining that we just had to do it because "our" safety, value, position, survival was at stake. How else could humanity justify exploitation and oppression, such as slavery and abuse?

Part Two of this book is dedicated to partnering with ourselves. In order to do this, we must overcome the domination of the ego. The ego out of balance alienates us and makes us afraid of ourselves! Our own ego judges us, so we become afraid of self-awareness. If it's not puffing us up to look better than others, it's tearing us down—anything to block us from feeling at one with reality and who we are. We live in fear of our own ego's judgments of ourselves: that we have failed in some fundamental way to be who or what we're supposed to be; that we're stupid, weak, undesirable, unlovable, just plain bad or wrong. And when the ego isn't giving us negative self-talk, it's justifying and rationalizing our behavior, because it is the creator of that behavior, and it doesn't want us to change.

We somehow know something is wrong, but fear of our ego's power and judgments keeps us in behaviors that we do not truly respect. We cower in inaction, when we know we need to fight; we stay glued to behaviors that are destructive but which our egos promote. We despise ourselves and often despise one another, because we see the ego running the planet.

What we need is to turn the tables by Becoming Self-Aware, Integrated, and Accountable, the three platforms of Part Two of this book. But the ego attacks self-awareness as unnecessary; or it threatens us with shame, if we venture into those waters. It also uses blame and denial to block us from truly looking at ourselves or taking accountability. We can barely tolerate being honest with ourselves about our behavior, and we can hardly get out a pathetic "I'm sorry" to those we hurt. (We will overcome this as we Become Accountable in Platform Seven.)

The bottom line is that we fear the ego—the ego of ourselves and everyone else. Because the out-of-balance ego causes self-hatred, shame, and denial within us, we hesitate to confront it, lest it attack us with negative self-judgments. We fear one another's egos, as well. We know what the uncontrolled, self-centered, self-serving ego can do in our homes and in our world. Look at our history: we've seen war, exploitation of women, racism, discrimination against gays, crusades, colonialism, fascism, child molestation, murder, animal abuse, the marginalization of the disabled, even assassination or crucifixion of leaders who want to make a difference.

The fear of the ego starts up front and personal. We've seen rage, sarcasm, seduction, denigration and manipulation even in our homes, schools and communities. Too many of us have observed our parents' egos tear at one another or try to suppress one another. We've seen businesses ignoring the needs of their employees or consumers, some of whom might have been our loved ones or us. We've seen examples of teachers brutalizing children, children trying to disempower teachers, women raped in their homes and the alleyways. These are all manifestations of the ego caring only for the individual self, ignoring the impact on others. What's not to fear?

Let's look at a few questions to highlight our fear of the ego.

1. How has my ego been abusive to me?
2. How has it been abusive to others?
3. What have I seen or experienced in my personal life that has made me afraid of the ego of other individuals?
4. What have I seen or experienced in my society that has made me afraid of the ego of groups?
5. Can I acknowledge that I'm afraid?

The Ego Blocks Us from Integration with the Divine

We have seen how the ego blocks us from others, because in Oneness it loses control. We have seen how the ego blocks us from ourselves, because in Oneness with ourselves, the ego loses control. Now we are going to look at how the ego has blocked us from divine consciousness, because in Oneness it loses control.

When I speak of divine consciousness, or higher consciousness, I am not talking about religion; I am talking about inspiration from above, the connection to the intelligence of the universe, chi energy, life force. I am talking about the direct connection to the creative force that brought us into being, the creative force that is available to make us strong and to help us become who we are. Because our connection to that creative source empowers our inner selves, the ego desperately blocks this connection. Direct connection with the divine is so threatening to the ego that the Catholic Church at one time forbade parishioners from reading the Bible. In many religions, the connection to God is interceded by someone who stands between us and The Source. In other religions, connection to God has been relegated to certain groups or classes. In most religions, dogma and written beliefs have taken the place of our natural, intuitive connection to the universal intelligence.

Why? Obviously the ego knows that the ultimate connection with the spiritual energy of the universe makes the ego look small. For those of us who have experienced the joy of such a connection, it surpasses the little rewards the ego offers for our subservience. In exchange for the egoic sensation of individuality, in exchange for the puff, we experience the cosmic sensation of finding ourselves in the Oneness. We feel whole, integrated, satisfied, filled and fulfilled, joyful, peaceful, calm, even transcendent. There is no place of separation or anxiety for the ego to jump in and take over.

419

How does the clever ego convince us that connection with the divine is stupid, worthless, wrong, impossible, unreal? Let's look at some of the things it tells us.

- The Source/ God/ Higher Consciousness doesn't know anything about the material world. If I connect to The Source, it will make me do something that threatens my safety. For example, it will make me leave a safe group or relationship, quit a job, fight against injustice, give up the props of looks, money, or other sources of power. If I listen to my inner guidance, I'll be endangered and maybe even die.
- Divine energy doesn't exist.
- Divine energy exists but will make me crazy.
- Divine energy exists and is valuable, but can never be mine, because I am not good enough, I can't connect to the universe, and I'm not perfect.

Connection with the divine energies of the universe gives us the sense of integration with our true selves and the whole of existence. The ego can't stand for it, and it tries to block us. But sometimes the block doesn't succeed, and we are able to have mystical experiences despite it. When we do, we feel beyond the ego's grasp. When this occurs, the ego has to try to find a way to control the mystical experience itself. It tells us: having this connection makes you different or special; therefore you're still separate from the Oneness you just experienced; you didn't really have a spiritual experience, you're gullible and crazy; don't tell anyone about the experience, because "they" won't understand; or brag about the experience so that "they" will be impressed.

And if you really have access to spiritual powers, heaven help you! If the ego gets hold of you, your spiritual powers now give you justification to exploit vulnerable women, intimidate men, use and abuse others or just puff yourself up. Yes, spiritual power in service to the ego. We will discuss this in greater depth when we reach Platforms Eight and Nine: Becoming Not-Knowing and Becoming Becoming. But for now, let's ask ourselves some questions:

1. Have I experienced altered states of consciousness or divine energy?
2. Was I afraid?

3. What was I afraid of?
4. Have I at times felt myself really inspired by divine consciousness?
5. Have I listened to or ignored that guidance?
6. Why?
7. Do I know people who I believe have spiritual powers?
8. Have they abused them?
9. Have I?

The Bottom Line

Of course, we're afraid of the ego.

Who wouldn't be afraid of the ego? Whether it is someone else's ego or our own, the ego creates feelings of shame to control us. It creates feelings of fear to control us. It creates feelings of anger to control us. No wonder we're afraid to confront it.

In our last chapter, Becoming Self-Aware, we saw in case after case how the patterns of thought and behavior developed by our immature egos run us individually and collectively and cause needless pain. And now we must face reality: Allowing the ego to run the planet is destroying us all, and when serious social, economic, or political reforms are proposed, the egos of interest groups try to kill progress. Ironically, when we see others defending their blatant self-interest, we call it undue influence or greedy lobbying. But when we do it, we call it justifiable; we call it common sense; we call it survival.

Are we surviving?

The domination of our egos blocks us from identifying with the highest good of all, because the ego creates the fear that our individual self-interest would be threatened; it blocks us from love, because it needs to keep us separate; it blocks us from serenity, because then we would be connected to The Source, and then the ego would no longer be in charge; it blocks us from appreciating what is, because it needs to make everything wrong, so that we will feel separate and alone, so we will listen to it; it needs to make others or even life look like the enemy, so that it has a straw man to fight against.

Alienated from ourselves, one another, and The Source, we are destroying ourselves. We feel empty and disconnected from ourselves, one another, and the process of living, and we fill ourselves up with addictive substances or are swept away by addictive thinking or relationships. We desperately need connection but fear we would lose ourselves. Once in relationships, we usually do lose ourselves, because we're dishonest with ourselves and others, fearing confrontation with one another's egos, fearing abandonment, rejection and loss, which the ego tells us would kill us. So we have young people so desperate for love that they drug themselves and have unprotected sex leading to unwanted pregnancies and AIDS; addiction to unhealthy relationships; people of all ages medicating themselves with prescription drugs; shopping, unhealthy food, alcohol, cigarettes, pornography, power, just to fill the gap left by our lack of connection to ourselves; lack of connection to The Source.

The ego has to fight: it has to fight me, you, and reality. The ego makes us cower, bluster, and hide. The ego has to create fear of life, so that we will believe that we need it, in spite of all the evidence to the contrary. In other words, the ego requires us to live in a state of stress, and stress kills. And all the while, the ego tells us that we need it to survive, that it is our best friend.

Let's look at some ways our current relationship to the ego is destroying us.

1. How is my ego killing me emotionally?
2. Spiritually?
3. Physically?

It's Not the Ego's Fault!

The ego doesn't want us to become aware of what we're doing; it doesn't want us to see that its domination is not helping or protecting us, but rather is hurting and sometimes killing us; and it doesn't want us to learn how to get out of the patterns it has created that imprison us.

But the truth is that it's not the ego's fault. Left to its own devices, the ego is like any other aspect of consciousness that we allow to dominate us. We have seen how fear, love, optimism, any aspect of consciousness out of balance can threaten our very survival. So it is with the ego.

We are not allowing the ego to do its job when we let it take us over. We are not letting it be just the awareness of our individual existence. We are not letting it be our guide. The ego is being used as a substitute for consciousness, and consciousness requires us to be integrated and to practice all of our platforms, including intending to do that which is for the highest good of all.

Of course, the ego doesn't want us to rise above it and see it clearly, because it feels threatened. But that's just what the ego needs. It needs us to take leadership, leadership of ourselves and of our lives, leadership of the world, leadership of the ego, because only we in our higher consciousness can help the ego evolve and take its place as part of the Oneness instead of as opposed to the Oneness.

Let's wake up! The ego needs to know that we are in charge, that it can relax so that higher consciousness can guide us. The ego needs to know that we are on to its games, that we see it for what it is, and that we're going to stand up for ourselves and our connection to the divine. The ego needs to know that we are also fighting for its highest good.

Now let's spend some time looking in more depth at our relationship to the ego.

1. How has the ego dominated me?
2. What relationships has it impacted and how?
3. How did I see my parents' egos conflicting?
4. What did I learn?
5. How are the social groups I see dominated by ego?
6. What are the consequences?
7. How has my ego caused me shame?
8. How has it caused shame to others?
9. How have I tried to protect myself from my ego's judgments?
10. Have I ever seen others stand up to the domination of the ego?
11. What happened to them?
12. Have I seen the ego use fear and anger to control our behavior?
13. Have I seen it use fear and anger to get me to separate?
14. Have I ever stood up to the domination of the ego?
15. What happened when I did?

Becoming Integrated is the process of overcoming the fragmentation of the human condition. It requires the end of the domination of ego on this planet. It requires the ego to evolve. And to do this, we are going to commit every moment of every day to release the need for the ego to protect us, because it doesn't. And then we release the need

to pretend the ego is protecting us, because pretending that the ego protects us only protects the ego's ego.

When we continue to feed the belief that the ego is protecting us, we are feeding the ego's ego, making it feel safe and look good. Take a moment to use our release tool, and release the need for the ego to protect us, because it doesn't. Then release the need to pretend the ego is protecting us, because pretending the ego protects us only protects the ego's ego. Now let's review our definition.

Becoming Integrated is the process of overcoming the fragmentation of the human condition. It requires the end of the domination of ego on this planet. It requires the ego to evolve. And to do this, we are going to commit every moment of every day to release the need to pretend that the ego is protecting us, because it doesn't, and then we commit to release the need to fear the ego, because it has no power that we do not give it.

Let's listen in on a conversation between different aspects of ourselves in regard to the ego.

Okay, so the ego is an out-of-control two-year-old with an atomic bomb. So what? Why should that scare us? We need to fight its domination anyway.

Why should that scare us? Are you crazy? The ego could kill me. If I make a mistake, my own ego shreds me. If I confront somebody else with a big ego, they'll yell at me, fire me, hit me, intimidate me, like my father did, like my mother did, like the bully in the schoolyard did. The ego might physically wipe me out, like they did to J.F.K., or Gandhi, or Martin Luther King, or Malcolm X, or Bobby Kennedy, or Jesus for that matter. Or it can just marginalize me, humiliate me, cut me out of human society.

So? The ego might kill you. So what?

What do you mean, so what? Are you crazy?

Not at all. I am not crazy. The ego is crazy and those who listen to it and let it dominate our planet are not only crazy but also suicidal, colluding in the destruction of our souls and our world. If we are going to save humanity on the physical, emotional, and spiritual planes, we are going to have to stand up to the domination of the ego, no matter what.

Ouch. I said I wanted to be integrated. I didn't say I was willing to die for it.

Whatever it takes.

Like any bully, the ego rules by fear. In Stage One of Becoming Integrated, I pointed out that any need that dominates us knocks us off balance and destroys integration. Just in this way, if we fear the ego—whether it's our ego, the ego of an individual, or the ego of a large collective, such as a mob, a community, a nation—if we fear the ego, we will give in to the ego over and over. This merely puffs it up, emboldens it and blocks us from the integration and the natural wellbeing that integration brings.

We can do better. The domination of the ego is destroying us. We can see that. On the other hand, releasing ourselves from the grip of its domination would bring all of humanity to a higher level.

We can evolve beyond survival, evolve into a state of Becoming Integrated. We would no longer feel torn apart by demons within us and without. We could finally assess our problems rationally and come together for mutual support. We could stop fearing ourselves and one another. We could stop hiding the truth of who we are and end our self-contempt. We could turn to the heavens for help, inspiration, and spiritual energy. We could experience self-respect and peace.

This is our turning point and our choice.

Ultimately we have to ask ourselves some stark questions:

1. Am I willing to admit that the ego has been running me and the planet?
2. Am I willing to acknowledge the damage it has brought?
3. Am I prepared to confront my fear that the ego will hurt me if I protest?
4. Is my physical survival worth more than my integrity and my soul?
5. Who is making that choice: me or my ego?

The Evolution of Ego. This Is the Revolution. Let's Do It!

When ordinary people have confronted fascism, invasions, segregation, the disenfranchisement of women, oppression in any form, something in them was stirred to step beyond the ego's emphasis on self-preservation.

425

Sometimes, of course, the ego was in the mix, trying to look good. For example, the ego could motivate action by suggesting that if I join this movement, I will look noble to myself, to my girlfriend, or to my friends back home. But usually our individual and collective action did not fundamentally stem from the ego at all. Usually it just arose from deep inside us.

We knew in our hearts and our souls that something was wrong, and it had to stop. Not just leaders, but ordinary people have taken huge risks to create revolutions. If ordinary folk didn't fight slavery, didn't fight for women's rights and workers' rights, didn't fight prejudice against the disabled and mentally ill, didn't fight empires, didn't fight nastiness, intolerance, and exploitation, if ordinary folks didn't speak out against illegal wiretapping, unjust wars, polluting the earth, and the squelching of free thought, if ordinary folks didn't take on special interests, if ordinary folks didn't confront their alcoholism, if ordinary folks didn't try to bring awareness to our poor diets and the junk food we feed our children, if ordinary folks didn't fight even in the face of humiliation, ostracism, jailing, or death, the world would be in worse condition than it is today—worse for all of us.

We need a rallying cry to awaken us from our complacency about the domination of the ego; the two-year-old with the atom bomb that underlies all of the self-centered, self-serving, destructive, and self-destructive patterns that plague the human race. The ego will tell us that the way we are is normal, natural, and necessary; but we know better. It may be normal and natural, but it isn't necessary. And if we are to survive and thrive, our traditional relationship to the ego must become a thing of the past.

In this step, Becoming Integrated, we take the first steps to rally ourselves and others to the problem that has always plagued humanity. We have made the commitment to integration, which requires us to overcome the domination of the immature ego, even if we don't yet know what it feels like and how to do it. We've committed to being vigilant about self-awareness. We've committed to releasing the aspects of ourselves out-of-balance, when we see the imbalance happening. We've committed ourselves to stop pretending that the out-of-control ego is actually helping and protecting us. And we've committed ourselves to face our fear of the ego—whether that ego be ours or others'—and we've committed to facing that fear each and every time we see our ego running us, even if it means looking odd, being thrown out of the tribe, or confronting the possible loss of security and even death.

As we take these steps and make these commitments, the ego will not sit still for it. It will tell us we're crazy. It will deflect blame to something else. It will tell us our path is too dangerous. It will tell us that everybody is like this: that everybody worries about the way they look to others; everybody protects themselves and their families; everybody is out for number one. Blah, blah, blah.

And we will smile and say, "I've got your number. I release the need to fear you or anything else, because you only have the power I give you, and I take that power back for myself, for others, and for The Source that created us all. You, the ego, are not me, and I can live without you, unless you grow up and work for the highest good of all, including me."

And as more of us do this and fulfill on this commitment, as more and more of us stand up to our friends, families, social groups, employers, as more of us stand up to our egos masquerading as ourselves, as more of us stand up to our old habitual ways, the more the power transfers to the soul.

The Liberation of the Ego

Ironically only the transfer of power from the ego will help liberate the ego, which is trapped in its success, unable and unwilling to give up a way of being that has existed since the first caveman took the bigger piece of meat for himself. Once we stop letting the ego bully us, it has the freedom to say, "As humanity is born again into the Oneness, I, too, can be born again. No longer do I have to be trapped in an old form. I have limited myself to the role of self-protection. With training and support, maybe I can transform myself into consciousness itself and identify as part of the Oneness." Because, yes, instead of hovering over us as self-protection, the ego can embrace a new role, which is to evolve into consciousness, consciousness of our individual existence and our role in the Oneness.

We need the ego. It is part of us as integrated beings. And it is essential. As we discovered in Platform Two: Becoming Differentiated, we need to individuate in the context of Oneness. That means we need to have the ego bring us awareness of our responsibility for our individual existence, but we need to experience ourselves simultaneously as part of the Oneness.

In other words, we need the ego, but not in its current form. We need it twice born, as we discussed in the introduction to our book.

The ego can evolve. It will evolve. It is in the process of evolving. And we'll see more about how that can happen as we move forward with our book. But it's our responsibility to bring the ego into the process of integration. It's our job to give the ego the support it needs to relax into its rightful place.

So, this is our invitation to the ego. Change and come with us. Because as we are Becoming Integrated, within ourselves, with one another, and with the divine, we release the fears, the anxieties, the uncertainties that have made us fodder for the domination of ego, and we open ourselves to experiences promised by the rest of our program, including the deepest level of integration, which is Becoming Becoming. In the context of the relaxation available to us from the place of Oneness, we can integrate the ego into our beings.

So now let's amend our definition of integration by adding one more line.

Becoming Integrated is the process of overcoming the fragmentation of the human condition. It requires the end of the domination of ego on this planet. It requires the ego to evolve. Becoming Integrated requires that we integrate the ego.

Yes, it's not the ego's fault that it's running the planet. The immature ego is what it is. It's our job to educate and integrate the ego, so that we can fulfill our potential and become truly ourselves.

Let's conclude with a few questions about our own stand in relation to the ego.

1. Have I taken a stand against the domination of the ego?
2. Have I had some success with Becoming Integrated and releasing its domination?
3. Do I believe the ego can change?
4. Has mine already changed, beginning to identify more with the Oneness?
5. Am I willing to work with my ego to step into the unknown?
6. Will I support you to do the same?

PLATFORM SEVEN

Becoming Accountable
Awareness, Amends and Transformation

Introduction

Becoming Accountable is the last of the three platforms making up Part Two, Partnering with Ourselves. As you recall, the purpose of Part Two is to help us change our relationship to ourselves from fear and alienation to partnership and connection. For these things to happen, first we have to become honest about ourselves and let go of the fear of finding out something about ourselves that would cause us shame. Then we have to free ourselves from the programmed self, fragmented and dominated by the ego and begin connecting to the true self that has not fully emerged.

How are we doing so far with this process? We started with Platform Five: Becoming Self-Aware, which helped us examine ourselves and our reactivity more deeply. This brought us out of the scary world of shadows, where we couldn't understand either ourselves or others. Understanding everything as cause and effect, we started to free ourselves from shame and blame and began to face ourselves as we are. Through Platform Six: Becoming Integrated, we started to free ourselves from the domination of the different aspects of ourselves that have been driving us to hurt ourselves and others. We confronted many of the ways in which the domination of our egos has been at the root of much of our pain, and we acknowledged that it's up to us to integrate our egos so that they can do their part in a positive, productive way.

All of this has brought us into real connection with ourselves. Now that we acknowledge the reality of who we are, and our awareness is at the same time honest and self-compassionate, we are available for real self-love. Self-love does not come from convincing ourselves that we're okay just as we are regardless of our behavior. Self-love comes from knowing who we are, seeing our strengths and flaws and working on our faults. Self-love grows, as we grow, as we feel the true self-satisfaction that comes from grappling with our demons and beginning to win.

Now we are ready for the final step of Part Two, Partnering with Ourselves. Because nothing breaks down the blocks to self-love more than Becoming Accountable, because nothing compels us more to face what we do and have done; nothing gives us more of an opportunity to clean up our messes; and nothing offers us a cleaner slate, more self-respect, and the chance to change.

Let's do it.

Becoming Accountable—Facing the Damage

By this point, we have become aware that we damage ourselves and one another in a multitude of ways. We have come to recognize how much of this damage is instigated by our egos. And we're beginning to realize that until we can change our relationship to the ego, we will not change, and we will never free ourselves from our destructiveness and self-destructiveness. In this chapter, we are going to confront that damage, acknowledge our accountability, make amends, and then work toward real transformation. This includes confronting and learning how to deal with negativity itself.

Becoming Accountable may not feel like fun, but believe it or not, it's one of the most generous gifts we can ever give to ourselves. It spells relief. But before we can get to the relief, we need to start with the damage.

Please don't get discouraged and put down the book. You wouldn't want to leave the dentist's office with your cavity half drilled, and you won't feel better unless you finish the chapter. So here goes.

What Is the Damage the Ego Creates and Who Pays?

Who pays for the damage the domination of our egos creates? Let's take an example. My husband and I are angry with each other, and we use our child as part of our struggle. My ego tells me that because I am a woman, I am supposed to be a "natural parent." This will be proved only if my child prefers ME. Add to this that I feel insecure in the world and in my marriage, and my ego tries to compensate for my insecurities by trying to get my child to bond to me and make me feel important. I know that our fighting upsets the child. I may even pay lip service to the idea that I want to "keep the child out of it," but unconsciously I position myself in front of the child as being better than my husband. In many subtle and not so subtle ways, I project that I am more understanding, more stable, deeply injured by my husband's meanness, more reliable, more connected to the child, more able to meet the child's financial needs, more the one who tries, more something, to get the child to prefer me. The child feels torn apart, my husband feels pushed away, and I feel indignant and self-righteous. What is the damage and who pays?

Let's take another example. I'm a guy with a neighbor, whose ego causes him to be self-centered and unconscious. The neighbor has started parking in a way that is convenient for him, but makes it tough for me to back out of my driveway. Over my lifetime, my ego has trained me to be a bully, especially when I feel insecure. So when I feel insecure about backing out of the driveway, I don't notice that I feel insecure, and I immediately focus on being angry with the neighbor. How dare he, that lousy son-of-a-bitch? My wife is insecure too; her ego has made her afraid of other people's egos, and her survival mechanism is to suppress anger. I threaten to go over and confront the neighbor; she desperately tries to stop me. Now she and I are fighting. My ego says that if she doesn't join me in being angry, she's not supporting me, so now, because she doesn't want me to confront the neighbor, I feel even more alone. When I feel alone, I feel more insecure and my ego has to "protect" me even more, which gives me even more steam to get confrontational with my neighbor. I storm over to the guy's house, while my wife is whimpering about getting along. The neighbor's ego is, of course, triggered; the battle ensues. The event escalates. The neighbor's wife and my wife have been friends and have often helped one another with the kids. But now both my neighbor and I are demanding loyalty from our wives; we even want them to give up their relationship with one another. The kids are cringing; my ulcer is acting up; the neighbor feels justified in leaving the kids with his wife and going out to have a drink with his buddies, so he can talk about me. And so on and so on. Maybe a car even gets damaged before this whole drama subsides. What is the damage, and who pays?

Let's look at another common example. I'm the man in the house, and my ego tells me that, as a man, my value depends on looking smart and competent at fixing things. There's a leak. My ego tells me that I don't want my wife to call in a repairman to fix the problem, even though I can't, so problems go unattended, while I make excuses about being too busy. After we've had three floods, my wife finally calls someone in. My ego covers up my shame by blaming the repairman for something, making him look like an idiot and complaining that he's overcharging.

I'm the woman in the house. My ego tells me that my safety depends on my being married to a powerful guy who can "take care" of me, so I refuse to acknowledge that my husband doesn't know what he's doing when there's a leak. At first, I let myself be talked out of calling the repairman, and I let things go. Finally there are three floods. Now my ego really has a field day. Instead of confronting my own ego and ask myself why I kept ignoring the signs that my husband was insecure about fixing the plumbing, I cover up my complicity and focus my self-anger on my husband. What an idiot HE has been, because he's somehow stopped me from making the call, even though I have fingers and a phone. What's the damage, and who pays?

Oh my God! And we wonder why we can't put an end to war!

Let's ask ourselves some questions about some of the damage caused by our egos colliding or colluding.

1. Think of some situation where the egos of your parents collided.
2. What was the damage?
3. Who paid for it?
4. Think of some situations where your ego and that of another collided.
5. What was the damage?

6. Who paid for it?
7. Think of a situation where your ego and that of another actually colluded, where you reinforced each other's egos to hurt another.
8. What was the damage?
9. Who paid for it?

We have just examined and laughed together at a couple of familiar examples of our personal egos run amuck. Now let's look at some examples of the pain and damage that has been caused by the domination of collective egos.

- My religion is the best: This egoic belief has led to crusades, persecution, and the slaughter of untold numbers of people.
- My country deserves your country's resources and land: This egoic belief has led to invasions, wars, colonialism, and the devastation of others and their societies.
- The human species is entitled to consume whatever we want on the earth: This egoic belief has led to the extinction or near-extinction of countless species.
- The human species is entitled to produce comfort for ourselves and ignore all consequences: This egoic belief has led to the unrelenting destruction of natural habitats and may lead to our own extinction.
- My race is better: This egoic belief has justified slavery, grabbing land from Native Americans, and cruelty that has crushed the bodies, minds, and sometimes even the spirits of other peoples.
- My sexual preference is better: This egoic belief has justified discrimination, persecution, and sometimes homicide.
- My class is better: This egoic belief has justified the exploitation of other human beings for my profit or the disregard for the humanity and needs of others. (This includes prejudice toward those of a higher station, not just those "beneath" us in power or stature.)
- My gender is better: This egoic belief has justified depriving women of basic human rights and has justified depriving men of the recognition of their feelings and needs.

Who is accountable? We are, because we have all co-created a universe in which self-centered, selfish, and self-serving behaviors are considered normal. And who pays for the damage? We do, because the "victim" and the "victimizer" are caught in relationships of anger, alienation, resentment, mutual hostility, fear, and shame.

Let's now ask ourselves some questions about collective egoic behavior and who it has hurt.

1. Can you think of collective egoic behavior that you've seen?
2. What was the damage, and who paid for it?

When we get honest, we can see that we have a lot to be accountable for.

WHAT IS BECOMING ACCOUNTABLE?

Becoming Accountable is a three-part process:

1. Becoming aware of the impact of our attitudes and behaviors, specifically the attitudes and behaviors instigated by our egos.
2. Making amends for our impact when we and/or our egos are destructive.
3. Changing our relationship between our egos and negativity, so that we and our egos can become a positive force in our world.

Becoming Accountable flows naturally from Platform Six: Becoming Integrated, because we need to be integrated to accomplish this three-fold transformation. We need to become integrated to reject the ego's rationalizations and to achieve objectivity about our attitudes and behaviors; we need to become integrated to overcome the ego-based fear and shame that prevent us from making amends; and we need to become integrated so that we and our egos can truly transform, so that we are no longer destructive but rather automatically align with the highest good of all. Until we can do all of these—be aware, make amends, and change—we vacillate between denial and shame; and we're not capable of being accountable.

Our discussion of Becoming Accountable will be divided into three parts, referring to the three-part process described above. In the first part, I'll focus on understanding accountability and becoming more aware. In the second part, I'll offer a powerful and effective way to make amends in a state of self-compassion. And in the third part, I'll address the underlying transformation necessary for us to change and be different. That's where the fun really begins.

HOW DO WE BECOME ACCOUNTABLE?

PART ONE: BECOMING AWARE: SEEING OUR ACCOUNTABILITY

Accountability is a relationship between ourselves and others, where we are called to account for the impact of our attitudes and actions.

Right here I would like to clarify a distinction between responsibility and accountability, as I use these terms. Responsibility is *for* something. We are responsible *for* what we do; *for* fulfilling certain commitments; *for* people or things. Accountability, on the other hand, is a relationship *to* a person or persons. You might even say we are also accountable to everything—to God, the earth, ourselves, or anyone or anything with which we are in relationship.

Here's an example to clarify responsibility and accountability. Suppose I say to my wife that I will take care of the kids today. I am now responsible *for* the kids. But I am accountable *to* my wife for fulfilling the commitment to take care of those kids. I need to make account of my actions to her. If I stopped at the bar instead of going home, I am accountable to her for not having fulfilled that commitment to be responsible for the kids, and I am also accountable to the kids for failing to care for them. For example, if I told my wife that I would take Danny to the baseball game at 3:30, I am accountable to both her and him for doing so.

Here are a few questions to help us think through the difference between responsibility and accountability.

1. What are some areas of life where I am responsible?
2. What are my responsibilities?
3. To whom am I accountable for the fulfillment of those responsibilities?

What Are the Blocks to Becoming Aware of My Accountability?

As I have mentioned before, there are three steps to Becoming Accountable, and the first is to acknowledge that I am accountable to others for the damage caused by my attitudes and actions. But in order to become aware, I have to wake up from the self-serving illusion that I can do whatever I want without having to consider the consequences to myself and to others.

Now that's tough. Why? Let's start this discussion by going back to Platform Five: Becoming Self-Aware. It might be helpful to reread the blocks to self-awareness now. These are extensive and include shame, fear, and the requirement that we change. After you reread that chapter, please return to this spot.

Now that we've refreshed our memories on the blocks to self-awareness, we can address the question: What is the relationship between awareness and accountability? Any block to awareness—self-awareness or other-awareness—blocks us from seeing our accountability, because the lack of awareness blocks us from seeing what we are doing, why we are doing it, what other people are really doing, and how our behaviors impact it all.

So What Are We Accountable For?

In Platform Five, I allude to one major block to self-awareness and accountability: the fact that it is difficult for us to measure our accountability in a world of shame and blame. If, for example, we were raised by a hysterical parent who blamed us for their misery, we have probably internalized the belief that we are the cause of that parent's pain. Under these circumstances, we will tend to believe that we are to blame for everything. We have never learned how to distinguish between two things: our actions and the impact of those actions. And never having had the guidance, we lack the skill to objectively evaluate the connection.

Blaming ourselves for everything can cause us to turn our anger inward and to become paralyzed in life: Oh my God, I'm so bad; I won't do anything at all, so that I can always appear to be blameless. On the other hand, blaming ourselves for everything might turn into an outward explosion: Oh my God, I'm so bad; I can't stand the shame; I'll turn the shame outward; I didn't do anything wrong; it's all your fault! Either way, we're not likely to have a rational view of our accountability in any given situation.

What are we actually accountable for? Only the damage caused by our behavior. Now this is not so simple as it looks. For example, let's say I was once a perfectly normal child running around, being exuberant. Suppose my father had a tendency toward migraine headaches, and suppose Mom said, "Shush. You've given your father a migraine." Did I in fact give my father a migraine, or was my father's migraine *triggered*, as opposed to *caused* by my normal self-expression? Or may his migraine have been triggered by something else altogether, like the chocolate cookies he ate last night? In my impressionable mind, when Mom said I caused Dad's headache, the message to me was: Your self-expression creates pain for others. Even though it wasn't so, I felt accountable for something I did not cause. Although I actually still carry guilt in my heart, the fact is that all I did was run around and act like a normal child. I was not accountable for having caused my father a migraine.

What could Mom have done to help me not internalize guilt, even if Dad's migraines could be triggered by noise? Mom could have explained to me that I am normal and playful, just like all children, but that DAD has a problem. And because Dad is prone to migraines, we all need to be aware of the noise we make in this part of the house. Then she could have hugged me and directed me to some place where I could have expressed myself to my heart's delight. But, of course, most moms haven't been trained to be that conscious. They are scared that Dad is going to be in a foul mood, afraid he won't get over his migraine and won't be able to work, angry at Dad for being in bed, or worried that she doesn't look like a good wife and good mother who can control her child; so she's just reacting without awareness of the impact of her words on me.

It may have been completely unintentional on Mom's part, but if my mother communicates that I am giving my father migraines, she is accountable for causing me to feel shame about my normal self-expression. So while I am not accountable for causing the migraines, she is accountable for causing me guilt. Unless, of course, I deliberately ran around making noise, because I was angry and wanted to give a migraine to Dad and upset the hell out of Mom. Then I am accountable, and Mom had an obligation to bring my accountability to my awareness.

Let's examine some of our childhood experiences with blame.

1. Did I have a parent who tended to blame me?
2. If so, do I unconsciously or consciously take on blame for everything?
3. Do I try to deny my accountability?

So what are we accountable for? Let's look at another example. Suppose that I am driving down the road in a small car. I get temporarily distracted by my cell phone, and I rear-end a truck at five miles per hour. The driver is a twenty-five-year-old guy with a strong body. What was the damage? Not much, either to the truck or the guy. But let's say I am driving down the same road in that same small car. I get temporarily distracted by my cell phone, and I rear-end another small car at five miles per hour. The driver is a seventy-two-year-old woman with osteoporosis. What was the damage? A lot, to both the car and to the woman.

In both cases, I did the same thing. I drove, I got distracted, and I rear-ended a vehicle at the same five-miles-per-hour speed, and yet in one case there's barely any damage and in the other case, the person suffers multiple compression fractures. What am I accountable for?

We are accountable to the other driver for having gotten distracted and having rear-ended them at five miles per hour. Our accountability is not more because the other driver was a fragile elderly woman in a small car, and our accountability is not less because the other driver was a strapping guy in a truck. In other words, I am accountable for what I did, not for the impact caused by the other person's higher-than-normal vulnerability. If the person I hit had a heart attack because of the trauma caused by the five-mile-an-hour crash, I should not take on that I am a killer, even though my action led to someone's death.

In our society, regardless of our accountability, compensation is based on the cost of any damage caused by the accident, so our insurance company has to pay for the actual damages to the other person and car, whether those damages are higher or lower than the average; but on the spiritual plane, we are accountable for the action itself. We can't be responsible for the condition of the other person. That being said, part of taking accountability is realizing that if we are distracted, we are more likely to have an accident, and we may in fact create a lot of damage, depending on whom we hit, and that might include a very frail person.

So here's another accountability: We are accountable to everyone on the road to drive only when we're not impaired, and impaired could mean: distracted, drinking, not wearing proper glasses, stressed, thinking of something else, too tired, ill, hyped up on caffeine or donuts, or drugged on pills even of the prescription variety. That's a lot of accountability. If all of us were that accountable and drove only when not impaired, the roads would be empty.

We are also accountable to one another to carry sufficient insurance to compensate others when our actions hurt them. That means that if we have that five-mile-per-hour accident and we have no insurance, but we cause substantial damage, we are accountable to pay the person for the damage to themselves and their vehicle, regardless of the fact that we only hit them at five miles an hour. So carrying insurance is an additional accountability that we have toward one another.

At this point, let's review what we have seen so far regarding our accountability in our little five-mile-per-hour accident. The first is that we are accountable for getting distracted and hitting their car; the second is that we're accountable to all drivers to not be impaired while driving; and the third is that we are accountable to others to carry enough insurance (or have enough money) to compensate people when we damage them or their property.

Now this gets complicated, too. Some people are poorer than others and may have difficulty paying for insurance. Even if that is the case, the driver is still accountable to others for having the means to compensate them, if he or she does get into an accident. If we don't take accountability for our negligence, who should?

But on another level, if people are paid so poorly that they can't pay for insurance, and one of them hits your car, aren't we all in a sense accountable to both that driver and you for the cost of the damage when no insurance exists? Don't we all co-create a society where some people are so meagerly compensated for their labor that they do not have the means to buy insurance?

And don't we collectively have accountability for the accident, because we have until recently had the agreement that it's okay to drive and use a cell phone at the same time? And don't we collectively also have accountability for the common attitude that it's okay to drive when we're impaired, because so many of us are impaired? And don't we collectively have accountability for the fact that there are often no public transportation alternatives, so that people who shouldn't drive feel that they have to drive, in order to earn a living or meet some imagined social responsibility?

And what about the "victim" of the accident? Was the elderly woman not also accountable to the driver who caused the accident? Did she take responsibility for the fact that she could be badly hurt, even if she was in just a very small accident, and didn't she agree to that risk, for which the "guilty driver" is being held completely accountable? And had she been younger, could her faculties have been sharper so that she would have observed the accident coming and avoided it altogether?

Wow, accountability goes deeper than I thought. Let's take a pause and ask ourselves two questions.

1. How am I feeling as I look at all these levels of accountability?
2. Is it scaring me?

The Ego, the Car and Accountability

Accountability challenges the ego in so many ways. First and foremost, it challenges the idea that "I" can do anything I want. I want, I want, I want, regardless of the possible consequences to myself or to others. That's the ego's way.

Let's stick with our automobile example. I wanted to finish watching the football game before I left the house, even though I knew I needed to make a call. I wanted to use my cell phone and was not willing to stop the car to talk. I wanted to drive, because it's more convenient, even though I can't afford insurance, or because I wanted to take that money and spend it on a vacation. I wanted to stay up late the night before, even though I knew that this morning I would be tired when I had to drive. I might even have been impaired because I wanted to eat that brownie and drink that coffee before I hit the road, even though sugar and caffeine make me jittery, more distractible, and more likely to get into an accident. I want; I don't want. I. Yup, there's the ego.

Ironically, the ego can also make us act responsibly, even when we don't want to acknowledge our accountability. For example, we might be careful and stop ourselves from driving when drunk, because we don't want to get into an accident and lose our license. In this case, our actions are more responsible, but not based on the acceptance of our accountability. They are based on self-protection. When we drive carefully, we're usually still thinking only of ourselves, avoiding getting hurt, sued, or jailed. Few of us think about our state of mind or the wellbeing of others when we hit the road.

While the self-protective ego can help us by scaring us out of behaviors that are extremely foolish, on the other hand, it can also totally fudge accountability if it feels better served. One of its prime gambits is to bring up free will and even cloak it in patriotism. Hey, I'm an American citizen. I can drink if I want to. That's my free will.

Is it? If I drink, I damage my health. If I damage my health, I'm not available to help with the kids, I lose time at work (and still expect to get paid for it), my medical bills go through the roof, which threatens my family's financial wellbeing. And of course none of this is my fault. I have a right to smoke cigarettes, even if I damage the health of everyone who breathes in the fumes. It's my right to eat poorly, even if I contract diabetes, high blood pressure, or have a stroke or a heart attack, which my health insurance should pay for, or even if eating poorly causes me to lose my temper or my focus. We say we have free will. Does free will give us license to do what we want, even at the expense of others?

Let's examine some questions about our own egos and our willingness to consider consequences.

1. What do I want to do regardless of the consequences to myself?
2. Who pays for that?
3. What do I want to do regardless of the consequences to others?
4. Who pays for that?

Usually it is our egos that cause damage, but sometimes it is we who cause damage accidentally. For example, if I am not aware that you're in the house, I might come in singing and wake you up. Or I might suddenly sneeze while driving and jerk on the road. I may have accountability, even if the event is accidental, such as when I know I'm sick and likely to sneeze, and it would be better for me not to drive. But if I sneeze unexpectedly, I might still hit your car, and I had no way of knowing that I would.

My insurance will need to pay, even if the accident was caused by me sneezing or a deer coming off the hills. But if I hit your car, I am spiritually accountable to you only if I have done something that caused the accident. And we are all accountable to one another to learn from accidents, if we can. Going back to waking you up when I came home and didn't expect you to be there, we both can learn that if you're going to be home unexpectedly and need to sleep, you should leave me a note on the door. If I've had an accident while trying to avoid a deer on the road, maybe I need to be more proactive in looking for deer when I drive, especially at certain times of day. These accidents can then lead to a more conscious life. We may or may not be accountable for accidents, but we are definitely accountable for trying to learn from them.

Let's ask ourselves some questions about our accidents and accountability.

1. Can I think of some accidents that I've had?
2. Did I have any accountability for them occurring?
3. Did I take the accountability to learn from them?
4. What did I learn?

Are We Done with This Topic Yet?

Hardly, we've just gotten started. What about our accountability for emotional damage?

I tell my wife that she's looking fat, and she bursts into tears. Have I hurt her, and am I accountable?

First I need to determine what is real. Is my wife getting fat, and why does that matter to me? Has she gained five pounds, and I don't like the way she looks? If so, why? Am I embarrassed because her "good" looks make me look like a successful guy, and her getting "fat" somehow undermines my image? Do I have an obsession with thin women, and her weight is perfect, but I'm a nut? Has she just gotten a better paying job, and I'm unconsciously looking for a way to put her down, and fat seems like the handiest way? In other words, is it my ego attacking her? Or is my intervention necessary? Has she gained twenty-five pounds, her eating is endangering her health, and I'm trying to call her to consciousness? Or has she gained twenty-five pounds, and she is in denial that she's engaged in emotional eating and needs my support? If my intervention is necessary, that intervention will be cleaner if my intention is to support her around a real problem that needs addressing, rather than to let my ego loose on her and focus on how her getting fat is making me look.

I am accountable to my wife for the damage to her if I come from my ego and tell her that she's getting fat, but what's the damage? Let's remind ourselves of the car accident where we hit the elderly woman with osteoporosis vs. hitting the guy who's built like a football player. If I egoically accuse my wife of getting fat, and my wife loves herself, she will gently pinch my cheek and tell me to get over myself and worry about my own eating instead of picking on her. On the other hand, if she is insecure about her looks, she may start to cry. If her mother nagged her about her weight when she was fourteen years old, she might get so upset that she is triggered into another round of bingeing and purging. Am I accountable to her for her crying?; am I accountable for her return to an old eating disorder, because she's upset? As in the car accident case, I am accountable to her only for what I have done, which was to make a judgmental comment coming from my ego that was not intended to benefit her at all. Am I responsible if she has a total meltdown? Perhaps not. On the other hand, if I know she has an issue about her weight and I callously dump my opinion on her, she may be totally justified in being upset, because I knew about her vulnerability and exploited it to hurt her or to hide my own vulnerability. It's equivalent to the accountability we would have, had we deliberately banged into the old woman with osteoporosis. In addition, although her reaction might appear irrational and unreasonable (After all, I only said blah, blah . . .), her upset may not necessarily be out of proportion at all, because she may have sensed that my intention was to hurt her—even if she is not completely conscious of that fact.

We damage people all the time and often are completely blind to that reality. To be accountable, we need to become aware of the state of mind of others, which means we need to become self-aware. If I tell a confident person that what they have just done is stupid, we might both laugh and share stories about how stupid we both are. But if a person is self-conscious about being slow or making mistakes, the same comment could devastate.

When we are emotionally insensitive or out of control, there's a lot of damage. And we are accountable to others for the emotional damage we cause in our unconsciousness. We could be accountable to one another for causing fear, such as the fear of the loss of love or loss of a job. We could be accountable to one another for causing the pain of rejection; for undermining others' self-confidence; for exacerbating already-existing feelings of being alone or unlovable. Ouch and more ouch.

We have so much accountability. Whether we are overly aggressive or avoid confrontation and leave all the tough stuff to others, whether our out-of-control anger causes bodily bruises or bruising to one another's spirits, whether our irresponsible diets put us into the hospital or into a depression, whether our grudge-carrying gives us justification to disconnect from others or even hurt them, whether our overdependence keeps other people taking on the load of our needs or our bossiness keeps other people small, we are accountable, and we need to be aware of everything we do and how it impacts everyone else.

This level of accountability can at first seem overwhelming, and we might feel a little reluctant to be this self-aware. Our egos may protest: I can't, and I won't look at every one of my behaviors and attitudes and see its impact, because acknowledging my impact might:

- Cost me money
- Force me to change my behavior
- Cause me embarrassment or shame

Now who would want that? Me, and hopefully all of us.

Hurting the Person vs. Hurting the Ego

Before going on to discussing amends, we need to distinguish not just what we are accountable for, but what we're not accountable for. Just because a person tells you that you've hurt them doesn't mean that you have, and just because a person felt hurt doesn't mean that they are. It might just be their egos.

The ego is always announcing that "I" have been hurt. I was hurt by your comment the other day that I am getting too big for my britches. You were hurt the other night by your best friend flirting with your wife. We were hurt by our parents demanding that we clean our rooms, rather than go out to play with our friends.

Were we really hurt, really damaged, or were our egos hurt, because we weren't getting our way or because your intervention made me look bad to myself or others. Let's look at the "getting too big for my britches" remark. Was your comment true; am I becoming arrogant? If so, your telling me is an act of friendship, hurting only my ego. I don't like the way I feel when you tell me a truth like that, but I need to hear it. Were you hurt by your best friend flirting with your wife? Was there any damage? Did your wife laugh at his advance, or did the flirting have an impact? Even if she responded to the flirting, did that actually hurt you, or did it reveal a weakness in your marriage, a weakness that you've been denying, because the truth felt too threatening? Wasn't this even, therefore, actually a support? Who was hurt, you or your ego, which feels ownership of your wife and wants to deny the problems in the marriage? (Incidentally, regardless of the reality of the hurt, the friend may need to be confronted anyway. But this confrontation would be motivated not by your being hurt, but by your friend's needing a wakeup call about his inappropriate behavior.) Were we actually hurt when Mom and Dad told us to clean up our rooms? Were we being exploited or deprived of time we needed to study, or was this the kind of discipline we needed and that our egos resisted, because we want to do our own thing? Is it actually for our highest good to experience ourselves contributing to the wellbeing of our family? Do we need to be brought into the reality we're not as rich as the neighbor kids, whose families have lots of hired help? Were we hurt, or was it our egos that wanted to do as they pleased?

How often have we held back from bringing something important to the awareness of a friend, loved one, boss, coworker, member of our community, because we were afraid that their egos would cause them to explode or pull away? If we have failed to bring the truth to their awareness, we are hurting them by depriving them of the information they need, and we are accountable to them for the damage done to them by not confronting their egos.

This would be a good time to consider the question of whether or not we hurt people.

1. Let me think of some people I think I may have hurt lately.
2. How did I hurt them?
3. Was the hurt real?
4. If it wasn't, did I feel guilty anyway?
5. If I truly hurt, was I aware of it?
6. Did I acknowledge the hurt?
7. Can I think of someone who needs my confrontation, but I'm afraid to hurt their ego and take the consequences?
8. How has that hurt them?

Why Would We Want to Become Aware of Our Accountability?

Because without accountability, we are deprived of the only possible way of liberating ourselves from the heavy load of guilt, denial, and shame that is caused by our continuing to behave in ways that are destructive to ourselves and to others; because without accountability, we cannot make amends, clear our shame for what we've done, and change.

Sure, we walk about trying to ignore the havoc we cause. But don't we really know? Aren't we unconsciously deeply ashamed of our behavior? We can only fool ourselves so much of the time. We are haunted by the little face of the child we have devastated with our thoughtless words or behavior and the face of the mother whose child we ran over on the road. We are haunted by the look on our lover's face when we have been needlessly unkind. We are haunted by the face of the worker we have underpaid, the friend we have betrayed, the parent we have abandoned. We are haunted by the images of the people in far-away lands where we have plundered resources and left broken societies. We are haunted by the animals we have slaughtered with no regard for their pain and the pets we have chained in the backyard with no regard for their loneliness. We are haunted, and without the tools of awareness and amends, we are left with the low-burning fire of shame smoldering in our bellies for all of our lives.

Awareness leads to growth. Shame leads to emotional devastation: denial, blame of others or the black hole of self-hatred. The shame of our unacknowledged accountability undermines our self-love, and the fear of recognizing it blocks us from Becoming Accountable, which ironically is the only means to save us from the shame.

Why do we want to be accountable? Because we need to feel self-love. We need a clean slate. We need the comfort of self-compassion and growth. We need to learn from our experiences, so that those experiences become worthwhile and grow into a blessing for us all.

Let's ask ourselves some questions about our own past.

1. Are there incidents from the past where I did not show accountability?
2. How has that hurt me?

And this leads us to Part Two of Becoming Accountable: Making Amends, the path to liberation and freedom.

PART TWO: MAKING AMENDS

Before we get into the specifics of how to make amends, let's discuss the blocks to making amends.

Blocks to Making Amends

The first and most obvious block to making amends is that, if we have damaged someone, we have to admit to having done something that makes us look bad, and we're afraid our egos will just pulverize us. We're afraid our egos will say: You jerk. You stupid shit. You bitch. Fear of the ego is, therefore, a major block to making amends and to our self-love, and we will spend some time addressing this block later in this chapter when we discuss self-compassion as part of the amends process.

But first, let's address some other blocks. Sometimes we are blocked from making amends, because the other person doesn't want to hear our amends. This is not a real block, because we can always send that person a letter or leave them a message. They can refuse to read it, they can refuse to hear it, they can do anything they want. But we are not stopped from making the amends, and that's our part.

Sometimes the block to making amends is that we are in terror about the consequences of our admitting culpability. If I admit to you that I have hurt you, how will you retaliate?

- Will you get angry and say something unkind?
- Will you get angry and leave me?
- Will you get angry and seek revenge?
- Can you?

There is no doubt that there are people who will seek to hurt us in return for our having hurt them. That is a sign that they are being dominated by their ego. What might they do? They might take the moment to curse us out or try to increase our shame. They might get self-righteous and gossip about us. They might sue or try to damage us in some way. The self-protective ego will always tell us to put our safety or self-interest first, but none of these reasons should stop us. If we did something, we need to take accountability for it. If another person is being hurtful because he or she is dominated by ego, that does not justify us in being dominated by ours.

Most often, we'll find that when we make amends, it heals something in the other person, and they are willing to become real, to become truly connected to themselves, and to forgive. But no matter their reaction or potential reaction, the impact of our behavior is our accountability. And if we do not make amends, we will carry the knowledge of our shame inside us forever, and that will hurt us more than anyone else could.

Another common block to making amends is our own anger or resentment. We might try to justify our not making amends by saying, "Yes, but he did this, too" or "She did that first." It may be true that he or she did something that hurt us or others, but that fact really doesn't change our accountability or excuse us from making amends. We are still

447

responsible for regulating the flow of our own energy, and we will still suffer from our own guilt and shame for having been out of balance.

We always know when we have done something hurtful, not hurtful to the ego, but truly hurtful. And no matter how much we excuse or defend ourselves, we feel the pain of having caused harm. That hurts *us*. In addition, the ego is always there to create separation from ourselves and others. And so if we don't take accountability and make amends, the ego-based inner critic will run amuck by either emotionally slamming us or creating elaborate stories of self-justification. Both hurt.

How can we partner with ourselves and be our own best friend if we have to deny what we know about ourselves? How are we being our own best friend if we allow shame to fester, instead of granting ourselves the real relief that comes from telling the truth and asking forgiveness?

1. Can I think of some behaviors for which I have not wanted to make an amends?
2. What has been blocking me?
3. How have I been impacted by not making those amends?

Clues That We Owe an Amends

Many times we live in resentment or annoyance and rationalize to ourselves that some problem or strain is all someone else's fault. Rarely is it true that we have no part. No matter how much we deny our own accountability, we always have a deep knowing when we do. It's, therefore, really helpful to be able to recognize when we're feeling guilty, even when our egos assure us that we are innocent. Following are some clues that indicate that we feel guilty about something and may owe an amends.

1. We walk around grumbling constantly about what HE, or SHE, or THEY did.
2. We can't stop thinking about what happened, and we never get resolution.
3. We try to recruit our friends to our side of an argument.
4. We've been carrying resentment against someone for a long time.
5. We feel guilty.
6. We are afraid to meet the person in a grocery store.

7. We notice that we've had the same kind of argument or nastiness with many others.
8. We want to run away from the situation as quickly as possible.
9. We need a drink, or a cigarette, or a chocolate chip cookie, when we think about them.
10. We insist that they are completely to blame.

Of course we may have not been the only person at fault. They may have had a part, too. But to use someone else's faults to deny our own only leaves us angry, resentful, guilty and out of integrity. That's a big price to pay for denial. Now let's look at some of our own resentment.

1. Who do I resent?
2. What could be the fault of mine that I am denying?

Is There a Time Not to Make Amends?

Alcoholics Anonymous, a twelve-step recovery program, teaches that we should make amends to those we have harmed unless to do so would injure them or others. Yes, there are rare instances when making an amends might injure someone else, and that should be taken into account. But that is rarely the case.

For example, if you have had an affair with your best friend's wife, you need to make amends to your best friend. You can't use the excuse that his wife would be damaged. After all, her behavior caused the damage, not your amends. Similarly, if you have had an affair and you admit it to your partner, you are not damaging the partner through the amends; you damaged them through the affair.

Here's one more example. If you've been taking drugs with a friend, and you don't want to expose them by taking accountability, you are not protecting them. You are protecting their disease. This helps no one.

God once told me, "If you want to keep a behavior a secret, don't do it." The same applies to amends. If you don't want to have to make an amends for doing something, don't do it. Now let's ask ourselves some questions about our unwillingness to make amends.

1. What have I done where I've convinced myself that amends are out of place?

2. Am I afraid of damaging someone else, or am I afraid of their reaction?
3. Am I protecting another person, or am I protecting their pathology or their ego?

How Do We Make Amends?

Haven't we all made and received amends? "I'm sorry." "That's okay." This is not making amends. I'll show you a real amends a little later in this chapter. But first let's talk about what usually passes for an amends.

What Is a Counterfeit Amends?

We've all heard them, and we've all made them. In fact, most of us have never made a thorough amends in our life, mostly because we haven't been taught how. Oh sure, after an argument or after having done something "mean," we might shuffle in and say, "I'm sorry." And the other person says, "Oh, that's okay." Then we kiss and make up. Sometimes we go as far as saying, "I was a louse." Or "I was being selfish." Or we'll dramatize our contrition with "I'm so sorry. I feel terrible."

These are counterfeit amends. We still haven't really acknowledged what we have done or taken accountability for the behavior. I'm sorry? Sorry for what? How was I a louse or selfish? How was the other person damaged?

This kind of amends is superficial, and its true purpose is not so much to make restitution, but to give us relief from shame or embarrassment and to win back the affection or trust of the person we have damaged. In other words, it's a disguised form of manipulation to get us off the hook, because we feel scared of the consequences of our behavior. Sounds like the self-protective ego, doesn't it?

And what about the forgiver? What does it mean when we say, "That's okay?" What exactly is okay? Is it your behavior that's okay? Is it your character that's okay? Is it okay that you hurt me, because I'm not worth caring for? What is okay?

What causes us to say reflexively, "That's okay"? Sometimes we get the words out even before the person has finished saying he or she is sorry. Why do we do this? Here are some of the possible reasons: Because we want to cover up what is really happening in the relationship. Because we want to get back to some good feeling or the appearance of good feelings that we had or we pretended that we had before. Because we're afraid of the interruption of connection that might occur if we really let the person engage in an in-depth conversation about what they did. Because we fear the person will stop apologizing and get mad again. Because if we delve into the depth of what happened, we might have to disclose that we were acting out as well, and who wants to acknowledge that?

Counterfeit amends are like eating donuts when we're hungry: They make us high, but they are leading to a crash. They do not satisfy in a way that can feed and sustain a relationship, because without a real amends, there can be no real learning, compassion, or forgiveness, because we cannot forgive the action or the damage that has not been acknowledged. A sloppy "I'm sorry" has no depth. It does not acknowledge the true nature of our action, and it does not acknowledge the nature of the damage our action caused. It does not have much impact except in a very fleeting way. And it leaves a lot of room for misunderstanding, because the forgiver has accepted an apology without knowing whether or not all parties even have the same understanding of the hurt.

A make-believe amends is often accompanied by self-pity and excuses. I know that I was a shithead the other night when I forced you to have sex with me, but you know how I get when I've been drinking, and I didn't really mean anything. I know I have been flirting with other guys or women, but I'm been feeling kind of down lately, and it doesn't mean anything anyway.

This kind of apology is like the drunk sitting in the bar, downing a beer because he or she feels so bad about drinking. It's an excuse.

A real amends, on the other hand, is enlightening. It has power, depth, and clarity. Everyone acknowledges what happened, what the damage was, and what is to be forgiven. The receiver of the amends learns a lot about the other person and a lot about him or herself. A real amends often leads the receiver of the amends to realize something about his or her behavior that allows that person to make an amends in return. This is a banquet.

Let's ask ourselves a few questions about our own experience with counterfeit amends.

1. Can I think of counterfeit amends that I gave?
2. Can I think of counterfeit amends that I accepted?
3. Did I feel satisfied?
4. What, if anything, actually changed as a result of the amends?

451

There is power in doing the right thing. Once we have made amends to those we have harmed, even if they do not forgive us, we can go on with our lives with self-respect and self-compassion, because we have done what we know is right! Wow! The positive result of an amends is the respect we feel for ourselves that replaces the shame we have felt because of our behavior or our denial. We feel clear and complete. Self-love and self-respect begin to fill our hearts, and with those gifts that we have given ourselves, we can continue to grow. So let's get started!

How Do We Make a Real Amends?

Earlier in this section, I mentioned how the fear of our ego blocks us from making amends. We are afraid we will be attacked by our own ego, which is always comparing, contrasting and judging. We anticipate it will tell us how worthless we are if we acknowledge that we have done something hurtful, and we know that if we are already under siege by our own self-judgments, we will dread hearing the other person's judgment as well. In order to make amends, then, we need to overcome our fear of what the ego might say, and to do this, we use a powerful tool: self-compassion.

Self-Compassion

Self-compassion means that we understand who we are and why we are that way. When we are filled with self-compassion, we are open to self-awareness, which, in turn, opens us to getting help and becoming our own best friend. Self-compassion does not lead us to excusing our negative traits or bad behavior. On the contrary, we confront, acknowledge and understand them. Self-compassion is like the parent few of us had: a higher consciousness that can see our weaknesses, understand how our upbringing contributed to those traits, and guide us to change. Self-compassion is a big benefit that we receive from practicing Becoming Self-Aware, because it brings us understanding of cause and effect, and self-compassion is essential as we travel through this book.

Nowhere is self-compassion more necessary than when we look at our accountability and make amends. If we don't have self-compassion, we will likely feel devastated by what we did. Our behavior seems mean, selfish, and unforgivable, and we fall into shame. And, as we discussed in the beginning of this book, shame feels like death. It is the feeling that we have no value, which might lead others to throw us out of the tribe, where we will be alone and die.

Unable to tolerate potential shame, we hide from acknowledging the damage we create, and we run away from the process of making amends. Or we offer the damaged person a counterfeit amends, throwing out a vague "I'm sorry," which still leaves us suffering the same shame. Either way, we cheat the other person of the amends we owe, and we cheat ourselves of the growth and relief amends can offer.

How Do We Develop Self-Compassion?

To develop self-compassion, we rely heavily on Platform Five: Becoming Self-Aware, because from our self-awareness, we derive the information that brings us self-understanding. Judging ourselves does no good. It only perpetuates negativity. But self-awareness of our destructive behavior linked with awareness of the source of that behavior can be a first step to freedom.

When I have become aware of the damage created through my attitude or actions, I can try to identify what led me to that negative reaction or behavior. This could be something in my history or in my present. For example, if my behavior is immature and self-centered, I can identify what conditions in my childhood led me to remaining immature and self-centered, as in, my mother wanted to feel needed, and so I stayed immature so that she could feel irreplaceable.

On the other hand, the source of my behavior might be linked to circumstances in the present. Let's say I have a friend who was nasty to me, and I felt hurt. In revenge, I identified a weakness in that friend, and I pointed it out in a mean way. I can see that my maliciousness was a result of feeling hurt, even though feeling hurt does not justify hurting another. I can feel self-compassion, recognize my hurt feelings, and go further into the inquiry. Did I feel hurt, or did my ego suffer a blow? If I felt hurt, I might want to pursue why the friend's nastiness was so hurtful to me, and then I gain greater self-awareness and work toward speaking to the friend and getting resolution or otherwise releasing the pain. If it was my ego that was hurt, I need to confront my ego and be grateful for the intervention.

Whichever the stimulus for our own damaging behavior, we have self-compassion but don't condone our acting out. We are still accountable for the damage we create, no matter the stimulus. But understanding the cause helps us develop self-compassion, and we can then forgive ourselves enough to make amends.

I've developed a self-compassion tool, and this is how you use it. Treat yourself as though you were two people: the you who gives compassion and the you who receives it. The "you" offering compassion is more mature and conscious and acts as your best friend. The "you" receiving the compassion can be any age. For example, to help heal a long-standing behavior that comes from circumstances in the past, visualize the receiving you as a child or young person. If the behavior is the result of circumstances in the present, visualize the receiving you at your current age. Once you have identified the age of the version of you receiving compassion, visualize yourself at that appropriate age. Then feel yourself to be your current age; feel yourself as loving and wise, as the best friend of the other "you." Think of what your best friend would say to you in any given situation. That real best friend would not support you in denial or delusion; he or she would give you love, understanding, and support, along with a healthy dose of truth.

Once you feel yourself in the consciousness of the more mature best friend, speak compassionately to the child or adult version of you. Try to understand the other's behavior. Open with the words: "**No wonder you do or are _____.**" For example, if you are aware that your behavior is immature, visualize yourself as a child and be the adult saying to that child, "No wonder you are still immature; you were never allowed to grow up. But you can grow up now." Or if you have identified that you feel angry because you are jealous, see yourself as an adult, and then be the adult friend saying, "No wonder you're feeling jealous. You are losing the love of the only person you think can ever love you. But that's not true."

Saying **"No wonder"** takes away the shame about your behavior, because suddenly your behavior is understandable. Your behavior exists in a universe of cause and effect, as we discussed at length in Platform Five: Becoming Self-Aware, and it is, therefore, no longer a cause for shame. Once you have said to yourself **"No wonder"** about the behavior, see and/or feel yourself giving the receiving you a hug. You may visualize you as an adult hugging you as a child, or you may be seeing you as an adult hugging you as an adult. Your negative emotions or behaviors come from an experience in your past or are caused by something really painful or frightening in your present. Your best friend knows this.

Self-compassion doesn't condone continuing our negativity and destructiveness, but it makes our behavior understandable and normal. With self-compassion, we can face the truth about ourselves and move forward. Now let's use this tool for ourselves.

1. Let me look at some hurt that I have caused.
2. Can I recognize the source, either in the past or present?
3. Let me now use the compassion tool to help me understand my behavior.
4. Do I feel more ready to face my accountability?

Understanding What an Amends Is

In the previous section, we reviewed the process of gaining self-compassion. Once we have gained that self-compassion, we're ready to jump into the amends step.

What Is Making Amends?

Making amends is taking accountability to support the other to return to the state of wholeness that our behavior has damaged.

If a woman has osteoporosis, our amends cannot take away the osteoporosis. If a person is emotionally unstable, our amends cannot correct their instability. But our amends can help restore the person to the state of wholeness they had before our negative action, and sometimes it can even bring that person into a state of greater healing, as we'll see later.

How do we make amends? We acknowledge to the injured party the reality of our having hurt them and give them the opportunity to feel acknowledged and to grant forgiveness. By doing this, we are also giving ourselves the opportunity to bring our inner shame into the light of day, forgive ourselves, and move on as well.

Let's first consider what amends are:

1. Making restitution, if you can, on a material plane.
2. Making restitution on the spiritual plane.

If amends or restitution is about supporting the damaged person to return to wholeness, restitution on the material plane is fairly obvious. I broke your lamp. I replace it, fix it or give you the money to compensate you for the loss, so that you can either replace it or do something else with the money. Of course, not everything is so easily restored. For example, a one-of-a-kind lamp or a table that your mother gave you cannot be replaced at all; and if it cannot be repaired, there's no way to make complete restitution. Or if I've damaged your body in our now-famous car accident, it's possible that no amount of medical attention will make you whole again. Or if I cripple or kill a loved one, financial compensation can never mend the loss, although it can help offset the loss of income that a death can bring.

Making restitution on the spiritual plane is something else altogether. It is always possible, if both parties are willing. And it enables us to restore the other person and to restore ourselves simultaneously. In fact, it can do better than that: Amends given can deepen and expand the giver of the amends; amends accepted can deepen and expand the receiver.

In this section I am going to focus on the second form of amends: making restitution on the spiritual plane. And in the process, I'll be offering you another tool.

The Way to Make a Complete Amends

You cannot clear the energy of the damage you have done unless you go through the steps of truly acknowledging your action and the damage it caused and asking for forgiveness. This is tender. This is vulnerable. This is real. And this is liberating.

This is why we have an amends step that is very specific. And here it is in brief. After summarizing it, I will go into greater depth about each part.

Tool: The Amends Process

Remember, first, we need to have self-compassion. Once we do, we approach the person we have hurt and explain that we would like to make amends. Then we use the following formulation: "**I realize now that I** _____ (state exactly what you did, no more, no less) **and how that**

hurt you was that it _____." (Take your time with this part—allow yourself to feel the impact). "**And even though I couldn't have done any better at the time, I need to ask you to forgive me. Will you forgive me?**" Allow the person to respond if they want to. Don't skip steps! Only by being thorough can we free ourselves from the toxic shame that hurts us and/or makes us cover up our shame with resentment.

❧

HOW DO WE USE THE AMENDS TOOL? TAKING IT STEP-BY-STEP

The amends tool I just described has three parts: I realize now that I; and how that hurt you was; and even though I couldn't have done any better at the time, I need to ask you to forgive me. Will you forgive me? Let's go through this three-step process and understand it one step at a time.

Step One: What I Did

As we have said, it is painful to acknowledge that we have hurt others, but when we can practice our foundational self-compassion, we can take accountability for our behavior. We are ready to look directly at the question: What exactly did I do? Because shame often accompanies recognition of our negative behaviors, we tend to dramatize what we did (I destroyed this person's life, crushed them, made them feel useless, etc., and I'm a terrible person) or we tend to underestimate what we did (No big deal. I didn't really do anything. They are overreacting. I did it because THEY did such-and-such. I'm innocent.).

So first we have to get clear in ourselves. What exactly did we do? In the next paragraph, I will offer a variety of examples. When we make the amends, we make each example as specific as we can. For example, one thing I might have done was to ignore your needs when you were hurting the most, but the specific version of that example might be, "I realize now that when your mother died and you were in grief, I withdrew my love and got buried in work, or I smoked a lot of dope."

So here are some more or less generic examples of how we might have hurt someone: I ignored your needs when you were hurting the most. When you were angry with me, I pretended that I didn't know why. I competed with you and tried to make you look small. I slept with your life partner while acting like your friend. I hit you. I complained about the small amount of money you are able to make. I compared you unfavorably to other lovers, my father, my other child, Mother Theresa. I stole money out of your wallet and denied that I did it. I blamed you for my shortcomings. I reminded you of your failings while hiding my own. I told you I loved you in order to keep you taking care of me. I belittled the achievements of your son. I fabricated stories about my own achievements. I gossiped about you to mutual friends. I was afraid to confront you, yet went behind your back to turn people against you. When we were children, I let you take the punishment for my misdeeds. With our mutual boss, I took credit for your accomplishments. I refused to address my addictions and squandered our money gambling or shopping and left you holding all the responsibility. I failed to confront you on your addictions and either encouraged them, excused them or just complained to others about them.

As I mentioned earlier, we need to acknowledge our hurtful behavior in the most specific way possible. For example, there might be a particular incident. "On Thursday night, when you were trying to discipline the children, I sided with them in order to make you look like an ogre, so that they would love me more." Sometimes, the conduct is so pervasive that our amends needs to acknowledge a long-standing behavior. "Since I met you, I have felt that you are more bonded with your children than with me. In order to break that bond, I have consistently tried to turn the children against you by behaviors, such as siding with them in an argument, rolling my eyes when you have tried to discipline them, having private little conversations where I said 'You know how your mother is,' or by spending money on them that we could not afford, which pressured you to earn more."

Being specific about what we have done is absolutely essential. It establishes the boundaries of our amends. I am making amends for something real that I have done. It's not vague; it leaves neither the damaged party nor me in doubt about what I've done. It's clear; it's transparent.

Sometimes we make amends for something of which the other person may not even be aware or may have just sensed intuitively but could never bring to consciousness. Now the damaged party can understand some vague feeling he or she was having but couldn't explain. For example, John always felt uneasy around his employee Ted, but John always blamed himself for the feeling, thinking he was just envious of Ted's success with women. Ted makes amends, and suddenly John realizes that Ted has been robbing him blind and feeling guilty about it. John had unconsciously been picking up Ted's guilt without knowing what he was feeling, and he was blaming himself for the uncomfortable energy between them. By making amends, Ted is being accountable to John for the material damage he's done; and he is relieving John of the guilt that he felt about feeling negative around Ted.

Just stating what we have done clears the air in a powerful way.

Step Two: How I Hurt You

We all injure others out of fear, pain, or blindness, and if we self-examine, we can understand our behavior with compassion for ourselves. Armed with self-compassion, we can look at how our behaviors have hurt one another.

How do we damage one another? In so many ways. We are all incredibly fragile inside, no matter the game we play or the face we put on. We all feel insecure, needing love and validation, afraid of rejection, often terrified of death. We all carry shame. Some of us make shame a badge of honor and wallow in it (I'm sooooo ashamed); some of us hide it from ourselves or one another. But we all feel it.

Recognizing our common vulnerability, it becomes obvious how easy it is to hurt one another. We might cause someone to feel something negative about him—or herself, such as shame, or cause him or her to be or feel isolated, or trigger his or her fear of loss. Most often, when we hurt someone, we are actually only reinforcing an already-existing negative feeling the person has about him—or herself. When we don't feel negative about ourselves in some area, we are much less likely to feel hurt by someone pointing out a supposed weakness of ours.

Let's spend a moment on this. I am a 5'1" tall woman, and that's okay with me. If some angry person stood in my face and screamed at me, "You shrimp. Why aren't you six feet tall?", I wouldn't care. I might be disturbed by the hateful energy, but not by the comment. But if I were a 5'1" man in a world where men's height is a sign of status and power, anyone making the slightest comment about my height could really hurt me. The hurt is not actually caused by that person in that moment. This is another one of those "elderly lady with the osteoporosis" moments. I already feel

459

inadequate because of prejudice against short men, but the angry accuser is accountable because he or she is exploiting my vulnerability in order to make me feel small. They are exploiting my vulnerability in order to hide a vulnerability of their own.

Be Specific

Just as it is powerful to say exactly what we did, it is powerfully healing when we acknowledge the actual hurt that we have caused, and we acknowledge that hurt specifically and completely. Let's look at some examples of hurts. We will start each of these with the opening line, "I realize now . . ."

- I realize now that I competed with you and flirted with your lover, even though I knew your lover had a roaming eye, and how that hurt you is that it made you insecure in an arena in which you already felt insecure, and it played on your lover's vulnerability, diverted her attention from you, and made you feel more alone than you already did.
- I realize now that in the middle of your discussing with me the possibility of a divorce, I threatened to take away custody of our child, and how that hurt you is that it threatened an important emotional bond, it undermined the courage you need to fight me for the separation and divorce you feel is necessary, and it kept you feeling weak and vulnerable in our relationship.
- I realize now that we have a lot of arguments, and I always blame you, as though I were innocent, and how that hurts you is that I deny you acknowledgement of my faults and hurtful behaviors, I play on your already-existing self-doubt, I make you feel like a bad partner, and I try to make you feel like you're crazy to feel hurt by me at all, deepening your shame about your own emotional state.
- I realize now that I forced you to have sex with me and then justified it by blaming my actions on my having been drunk, and how that hurt you is that it caused you to feel that you had to choose between your love of yourself and your love of me; it reminded you of being overpowered by your father, who was at one time the primary male figure in your life; it reinforced your belief that you and your body are there to be used; it emphasized your

physical weakness, so that you would be more easily dominated by me on every level; and it caused you physical pain.

Once we have shared how we think this specific behavior may have hurt the other person, we can then ask them whether or not they have something to add. This can be very useful, so that the amends is complete. On the other hand, the person to whom we are making amends may not be capable of self-honesty, and we don't have to accept everything they say. For example, they might use this moment as an opportunity to bring up other things, or they may blame us for something that was caused by themselves. If we agree with their account of additional hurts, we can repeat it back to them. For example, they may tell us that our behavior caused them to feel stressed. If we agree, we can add something like, "And that also hurt you by causing you stress, as you tried to please me more."

At first this kind of honesty and self-honesty seems almost unbearable. How can I admit to myself the exact nature of how I hurt you? How can I acknowledge to you how selfish, unfeeling, and manipulative I have been? Will you still love me if you know the truth? Will I?

The simple reality is that I have done what I have done, and ignoring or denying it will not change that reality. The best I can do is make amends. But the ego says that if I admit that I've done something hurtful, then I will look bad, and I may be vulnerable to counterattack or retribution. There's the ego, again, telling us that protecting ourselves and our image is more important than our spiritual wellbeing or the wellbeing of anyone else. If we have done something hurtful, the pain is not in admitting it; it's in having done it. And refusing to admit it, just to avoid feeling the pain of our accountability or to avoid the consequences, is throwing more self-centered abusiveness on top of what we have already done.

And it's not just for the other person that we admit the nature of how we have damaged another. It's for us, as well. It is the true confession that begins to empty the cup of shame and guilt. It is the accountability that in itself starts to restore us to self-esteem and self-love. It is the step toward restoring us to wholeness.

Acknowledging the damage we've done carries no self-pity or self-justification, and so it starts shifting us away from the ego and the ego's drama. The amends is not about how bad I feel or what a shit I am, which is still all about me. The amends focuses on you. It's about something that I did to you. This gives you acknowledgment. Sometimes

461

it even gives you new information, which helps you understand why you have felt angry or hurt. It also gives you an opportunity to look at yourself and determine your own accountability.

In addition, the structure of the amends gets us away from the drama of "I killed her or him, and I'm the worst." The reality is that I did something, but when I admit what I did, I also acknowledge what I did not do. And that's a relief, as truth always is.

Step Three: Asking for Forgiveness

The final piece of the amends is: "And even though I couldn't have done any better at the time, I need to ask you to forgive me. Will you forgive me?" This step has three parts. Let's look at them one at a time.

And even though I couldn't have done any better at the time

First, I am acknowledging that I couldn't have done any better at the time, and there's self-compassion. At the same time, it hints at change. I couldn't have done any better at that time, but maybe I can do better now, and I'm working on it.

And second, I am acknowledging that even though I couldn't have done any better at the time, I still owe an amends, because I damaged you. For example, even though I was hurting from a relationship breakup and was therefore less attentive as I was driving down the road, I am still accountable for the accident, because I hit you and that damaged you. Even though I was fired from my job and smoking pot when I let the baby sit in dirty diapers, I am still accountable to both the baby and the other parent for the baby's needless suffering and my irresponsibility.

"And even though I couldn't have done any better at the time" grants us self-compassion, encourages us to improve our behavior, and at the same time acknowledges our action and the hurt it caused.

I need to ask you to forgive me

We say, "Even though I couldn't have done any better at the time, I need to ask you to forgive me." If I couldn't have done any better at the time, why do I *need* to ask you to forgive me?

I need to ask you to forgive me for my sake: Asking you to forgive me is my final step in taking accountability. It is a deep recognition of the hurt that I have caused, and it releases me from the bottomless pit of shame.

I need to ask you to forgive me for your sake: Asking you to forgive me is the final step of recognition that frees you to understand what has occurred and to release your pain, anger and resentment. It is your opportunity to be restored to wholeness.

When I use the phrase "I need to ask you to forgive me," rather than "I need to ask you for forgiveness," I am making a personal, direct request to the person I have hurt. I am not asking for some abstract forgiveness from the universe. I am confronting the victim of my behavior and asking him or her to decide whether or not to respond with forgiveness.

Will you forgive me?

"And even though I couldn't have done any better at the time, I need to ask you to forgive me. Will you forgive me?" This is the ultimate point of the amends: to humble ourselves and ask for the opportunity to make restitution and clear the damage of our action.

If the person accepts our amends, both of us are redeemed from the pain. If the person does not accept our amends, either we have failed to make the correct amends, or that person is struggling with his own ego, and I am redeemed anyway.

Why would someone withhold accepting the amends? The person who won't forgive may have an amends of their own to make. If they are not ready to make that amends, they will want to hang on to their resentment to deflect from their own guilt. Or the person may have some other reason to hang on to their resentment, which will block their acceptance of the amends. For example, if you are making amends for introducing my son to drugs, I may not want to forgive you. I may just want to stay focused on what you have done, because in that way I don't want to focus on my son's accountability or my own.

Sometimes the damage to another is huge and difficult to forgive. If you killed a loved one, that's not an easy thing to forgive. But forgiveness is always the better choice. The wronged person who carries the resentment is poisoned by the resentment, just as the hurtful person is poisoned by his or her shame.

Amends are a transformational moment for all involved. Let's use them.

1. Am I having a problem with any particular part of the amends step?
2. Why?
3. Let us make a list of people who we have hurt, even if they have hurt us as well.
4. Let us admit the specific behaviors.
5. Let us admit the hurts.
6. Let us now make a commitment to use the amends step to clear these wounds and release ourselves and hopefully others as well.

PART THREE: TRANSFORMATION

Before continuing with transformation, let's review what we've already done. We have acknowledged that we are accountable to one another for our actions that hurt others, we have looked at the damage, and we have made amends. That feels great. But how do we feel when we find ourselves doing the same behaviors over and over, when all the amends and remorse do not stop us from damaging ourselves and one another in old or new ways?

We can either fall into the sewer of self-recrimination, or we can fight harder to change. The desire to change brings us back over and over to practice the first two platforms in the section: Becoming Self-Aware (Platform Five) and Becoming Integrated (Platform Six). These are prerequisites for us to become more balanced, less driven, less ego-based, and less likely to damage ourselves or others.

But what may still be missing is the capacity to truly transform. We say we want to stop smoking, because the need for nicotine is dominating us, and yet when we have a rough day, the cigarette is in our mouths in a flash. We make a commitment to stop screwing around on our partner, and then we find ourselves in bed with somebody else. We understand that we are dominated by the need to prove ourselves, and then we notice ourselves trying to impress. We recognize that we are run by fear, and then we embarrass ourselves by letting some bully walk all over us. Or we notice that we have a tendency to be the bully, and yet we still find ourselves with a knife at another guy's throat or putting a dagger in someone's heart.

Egads! Does it never stop? We have become self-aware, we've developed self-compassion, we are becoming more integrated, and yet certain voices, anxieties, states of being still haunt us. Why and what can we do about it?

Becoming Accountable means that we believe we have the capacity to actually transform ourselves and our behaviors, so that we can regulate the flow of our energy, regulate our reactions and behaviors, and become a blessing to ourselves and one another. We can do it, and the rest of this chapter and the rest of this book are devoted to this transformation.

Let's start by looking at some of our collective and individual victories. When we realize that we have already changed, we gain confidence that we can change again. As we've been working with this book, haven't we changed? We have realized our Oneness, worked to become differentiated, co-creative, and mutually supportive. We have become more self-aware, integrated, and accountable. We may not have achieved any of these states in a perfect way, but any change in behavior or awareness should give us hope.

And look at humanity as a collective. We have come to understand a lot about substance addictions, such as sugar or caffeine. We now know that our brains become physically addicted to certain stimuli; we know that the ups and downs of our blood sugar level create cravings; we even know when we are most likely to slip. So we're gaining ground.

Humanity has also learned to acknowledge our addiction to certain behaviors. We've become more aware that we are often being self-protective, whether our behavior looks aggressive or meek, and we've seen the damage it causes. We've worked to release our fears, and we've worked on trust. We've learned to speak more and admit our feelings, and we've learned to act out less. We have acknowledged that we are all the same and don't have to hide. We've tried to refocus on the value of consciousness. We've learned that mutual support is essential, and we've banded together in all kinds of support programs to deal with addictions: debting, gambling, love, food, and so on. We've developed anger-management programs, and we've taken a bite out of domestic violence. We've even tried medicating ourselves, and we have been sometimes successful. We're tried self-esteem and assertiveness training. We've tried meditation, yoga, LifeForce, Living with Reality mutual support meetings, and other spiritual practices to calm ourselves and to bring ourselves into more neutrality. We've gathered together to right social wrongs and to support the environment. And we've prayed.

All of these programs, practices, and instances of awareness have to a greater or lesser extent helped us to integrate and to become less dominated by drives that cause us to behave in ways that create havoc in the lives of ourselves and each other.

We've come a long way from the cave, from the feudal manner or from collusion with exploitation and slavery and oppression. Okay. So we've already changed. So let's say these words together:

I know that we can change, because we already have.

Okay, now here's the challenge: Has negativity gone away? Do we not have moments of relief, followed by more insane thinking? Haven't we engaged in addiction substitution? Don't we still act out? Haven't we found ourselves sometimes pretending to ourselves that we are better than we are, covering up the anger, shame and dysfunction that still embarrass us? Aren't we still noticing ourselves being frequently dominated by the ego? Yes.

So now that we've realistically assessed where we are, let's transform.

How Do We Transform?

In Platform Six: Becoming Integrated, I wrote:

Becoming Integrated is the process of overcoming the fragmentation of the human condition. It requires the end of the domination of ego on this planet. It requires the ego to evolve. And to do this, we are going to commit every moment of every day to release the need for the ego to protect us, because it doesn't. And then we release the need to pretend the ego is protecting us, because pretending that the ego protects us only protects the ego's ego.

In other words, I was suggesting that until we are no longer dominated by the ego, we will never be well, because we will never be integrated. The ego is born in separation and thrives off separation. In its immature form, it blocks integration and wholeness within ourselves, with others, and with the divine. It pounces on every situation, fear, or pain to assert its domination, and it then causes us to behave in ways that are hurtful to ourselves and one another.

Obviously in this state of fragmentation, we can't be consistently accountable, because we can't in fact regulate the flow of our energy and behave in ways that are for the highest good of all. We can make great strides. We can do better. But if we continue to be dominated by our egos, we will continue to cause needless pain. How can we then be accountable for our behavior? We are still out-of-control.

Realizing all of this, we have taken steps to overcome the domination of our egos, but we've discovered that this is a tough assignment for any of us. What more can we do?

In "Ego, Instinct & Evolution," the introduction to this book, I discussed the origin of the ego and how it programs us to destructive behaviors. I also then talked about the ego twice born, how our egos can start to be our friends when they begin to identify with the Oneness, instead of with separation. If you don't remember this part, please go back to the introduction and reread the pages devoted to the ego twice born.

But as we call upon our egos to support our integration with the Oneness, we notice something important. Our egos appear to be as out of control as we are. In other words, maybe our egos, which are controlling us, have no self-control and are being controlled by something else? What could that be?

Let's examine this question. Our egos are supposed to be taking care of us, right? But even our egos must notice that ego-based short-term thinking is destroying us, whether that destruction takes the personal form of reaching for a "fix" that damages our health, such as overeating, or it takes the collective form of postponing addressing climate change, which can destroy our planet. Our egos are also aware that ego-based, me-based thinking actually creates anger and alienation in others and ultimately causes us to suffer.

In other words, the ego has enough experience on the earth to realize that it is not doing the job of protecting us; in fact, it has become a negative force on the earth. Instead of transforming into consciousness, which allows us to take responsibility for ourselves, it has gotten stuck in the loop of self-destructive patterns that it can't seem to escape.

Why? One important reason is addressed in "Ego, Instinct & Evolution," where I talk about the ego having been born in our infancy, where we lack the consciousness to think beyond instinct. But now I would like to address another factor, a factor that must be addressed if we are ever to achieve the wellbeing and integration, the dynamic balance I discussed in the last chapter, without which we will lack the self-mastery to ever truly become accountable.

For some of you, this section will be confusing or challenging. But bear with me, because it is true, and understanding these concepts and taking on these practices will help us choose a better fate for humanity and our planet.

Let me start by sharing with you the key to achieving Stage Three of Accountability, which is Transformation.

Becoming Accountable is the ability to live in the dynamic balance only possible when the ego has ended its domination by the Dark Side and when both the ego and the Dark Side evolve.

Domination by the Dark Side? Evolution of the Dark Side? What are you talking about now? At this point in our journey, we are going address something not directly discussed in this book before, the understanding of which is essential if we are to finally free ourselves from our self-destructiveness. It's the ego's relationship to the Dark Side.

If you think this is a crazy conversation, please don't stop reading. The Dark Side is a *concept* that describes a phenomenon we all see and know. We all know that there is "evil" in the world, destructiveness and self-destructiveness. The use of the concept the "Dark Side" helps us get a handle on the phenomenon and identify ways to help ourselves become healthier and more self-realized. As we continue through this chapter and learn "The Seven Dirty Secrets of the Dark Side," you'll see how the Dark Side operates and how we can begin to win back ourselves. But first, let's develop some understanding of what the Dark Side is.

What Do We Mean by the Dark Side?

The Dark Side is a concept that shows up in many cultures under many names. I will shortly explain how I see the Dark Side, but let's first look at some of the ways that people have referred to the same phenomenon.

1. In a mythological sense, the Dark Side can be seen as the collective of negative forces. In this paradigm, the Dark Side is evil engaged in a never-ending battle with good. It's the hero's job to defeat the Dark Side, which can also be seen as a projection of our own moral weaknesses.

2. In psychological terms, the Dark Side is used as a term to describe a negative aspect of an individual or a collective. Some people say that they have a dark side, a sometimes hidden part of themselves that they consider to be malevolent, sick, or harmful to others:

for example, their use of pornography or their engaging in child molestation or fantasizing about killing or maiming others. Or our dark side can be our addiction to sex, drugs, or other self-destructive substances or behaviors.

3. In sociological terms, some speak about the dark side or underbelly of a social system, referring, for example, to the perpetuation of inhumane working conditions for some in order to create wealth for others or referring to crime or gang cultures.

4. In some cultures, the Dark Side is pictured as evil spirits or entities that attack innocent people and overwhelm or possess them. Examples of this concept are vampires and werewolves. There are also other non-animalistic concepts of Dark Side entities, such as gremlins and demons.

5. Religions talk about a Dark Side, as well. In Christianity, for example, the Dark Side refers to the domain of the devil, which is the antithesis of God. The devil rules Hell and personifies evil, and he tempts us to sin and violate religious teachings that are believed sacred.

From this brief overview, we can see that, obviously, a lot of people have noticed a very negative aspect of human consciousness.

I see the Dark Side this way. The Dark Side is the constellation of negative energies, i.e., energies that have no connection to the creative energy that has brought us all into being. While there are many names for this creative energy, such as God, universal life force, higher consciousness, etc., I often use the phrase The Source, especially in this context, because we are talking about the source of life. Negative energies have no direct connection to The Source, so they live off others, drain us of life force, and block us from fulfilling our potential. Examples of negative energies are irrational fear, rage, out-of-control sexuality, pessimism, and hopelessness.

Before moving forward, let's ask ourselves some questions about our own concept of the Dark Side.

1. Do I have a concept of the Dark Side?
2. Where did I learn it?

What Is a Negative Energy?

Later in this chapter I am going to more clearly define negative energy, but let's start with a general discussion. By negative energy, I don't mean every uncomfortable or unpleasant emotion. Fear, for example, is not in itself a negative energy. As we have already discussed, fear has a place within us to bring to consciousness the possibility of harm. But irrational fear is out of balance with common sense and faith, and it paralyzes us or makes us stupid. Because it does not support us or our consciousness, it harms us and others and, thus, irrational fear is a negative energy. Anger, too, can be valuable, when it alerts us to the fact that something is or could be wrong. So, for example, anger is not a negative energy when it motivates us to explore and inquire in a neutral way as to what has caused us to feel angry, to discover whether there is a true problem, or whether we are just having a reaction. But when anger is out of balance, it is a negative energy. It does not lead to inquiry; instead it rages, blames, and causes us to be stupid, cruel, and destructive. It drains both us and others.

Pessimism and hopelessness are also negative energies, but being realistic is not. Life isn't always fun, and not everything we hope for will come to pass. Being realistic about life tells us that we may have to face pain or unpleasant experiences and that we should look at situations realistically and take appropriate action to move toward a desired result, whether or not we will be successful. Pessimism and hopelessness, on the other hand, prejudge the outcome of our efforts, steal our energy, and destroy intention. (See Platform Three: Becoming Co-Creative.)

As we are beginning to see, negative energies block our potential. They are energies out of balance, they are dominant, and they drain us of the will and life force to fight for ourselves and to do the right thing. Some negative energies, such as pessimism and hopelessness, drain us in an obvious way. But other negative energies seem to energize us and only show their downside later. Take rage, for example. Rage can motivate bursts of force, but these bursts are similar to an adrenalin rush and have the effect of caffeine or sugar; they are followed by a crash. Rage is a negative energy that will pump up our ego (Look at me, man. I am powerful.), and then leave us exhausted. In addition, once the hurricane passes, we have to face the results of our destructiveness, and now our egos have to defend the destructive behavior, which creates more denial, blame, and negativity.

Negative energies are powerful, can take us over, and have been known to dominate entire populations. Lynch mobs, for example, were made up of people who were overcome by collective negative energies that made them irrational, hysterical, and bestial. And when people who are already dominated by negativity are locked together without major counterbalancing forces, the result can be a compounding of the negativity to explosive heights, such as in prisons, where fear and force play off one another and leave room for little else. Or negative energies can be compounded into the depths of despair, such as when depressed or miserable people hang out together in a bar and compound one another's self-pity.

The Dark Side is real; negative energies are powerful; and we need to come to understand them. To pretend they don't exist is like saying cancer does not exist. It doesn't matter what we think or believe; the cancer cells will eat us up anyway. Let's take a moment to consider our experience with negative energies.

1. Do I understand the difference between an uncomfortable feeling and a negative energy?
2. Have I seen negative energies overwhelm people and make the people themselves negative?
3. Who were those people?

Starting to Understand

As children, many of us saw the Dark Side winning. We saw cruelty, force, rape, contempt, physical domination, emotional abuse, greed, war, and violence in our world and often in our homes: kids bullying or making fun of other kids; parents hitting their children and sometimes one another; police using excess force; gangs attacking one another; criminals grabbing purses; guys punching out each other; and more powerful members of the workplace or community beating out the weak. It often seemed that kindness, compassion, cooperation and gentleness were overwhelmed and overpowered. In addition, we may have seen a loved one overcome by depression, beaten down by poverty, or ravaged by mental illness or alcoholism. Our mother might have told us not to stand up for ourselves and upset our father, because he might become abusive; or our father might have told us not to stand up for ourselves and upset our mother for the same reason. An enraged parent might have frightened us with physical or verbal violence. Without realizing it, we bought into a belief system that says the Dark Side wins, even if we had no conscious concept of the Dark Side.

What has been our experience with this?

1. Did I see the Dark Side winning in my home?
2. Did one or both of my parents support that idea?
3. Did I see the Dark Side winning in my community?

This belief in the power of the Dark Side is reflected in simple phrases that we have heard over and over, phrases such as "You can't fight City Hall." Well, but you can fight City Hall, and the Dark Side doesn't have to win. But in order to stop it from winning, we have to know the game.

THE SEVEN DIRTY SECRETS OF THE DARK SIDE

Those of us who care about overcoming our own destructiveness and supporting others to do the same have always been aware that it's a tough battle. We've seen ourselves and others seemingly taken over by negativity. We've seen societies caught up in fear and irrationality. We've seen loved ones overwhelmed by self-hatred, depression, mental illness, drugs, ambition, or jealousy. We've seen ourselves yelling at our children, even when we don't want to. We've seen relationships torn apart by arguments, addiction, resentment, and pride. And we've seen good people crushed.

"Bad" things happen, people react irrationally, and few of us are truly fulfilled. And for many of us, the question has been, Where is God? For most of us, life has been like a boxing match where we don't know the rules, but where the opponent always seems to know our weaknesses, while we don't know theirs.

But suppose we knew the rules? Suppose we understood the opponent's weaknesses? Suppose we saw the game? Even with the Dark Side, we are not helpless. Once we acknowledge the idea that there are negative energies on this planet, we can start fighting for something better, and we can do it not by blindly flailing about our arms, but knowing how to take actions that work.

The Seven Dirty Secrets of the Dark Side

Let's learn the game. Here are the secrets the Dark Side doesn't want you to know.

1. The Dark Side is the constellation of negative energies that need a host to survive. Don't be lunch!
2. The Dark Side runs the planet through our complicity.
3. Don't try to fight the domination of the Dark Side alone.
4. Don't fight *against* the Dark Side; fight *for* yourself.
5. The best way to fight the domination of the Dark Side is to empower it.
6. The Dark Side does not run the planet; The Source does, and The Source uses the Dark Side to promote evolution.
7. The Dark Side needs us to fight for ourselves, so that it can evolve into consciousness and return to The Source.

Let's look at these one at a time.

1. The Dark Side is the constellation of negative energies that need a host to survive. Don't be lunch!

As I said earlier in this chapter, the Dark Side is the constellation of negative energies that have no direct connection to the source of all life; so the Dark Side needs a host to survive. If you're wondering what the Dark Side lives off, look around. Mostly, it's us!

Let me explain. Negative energies are energies that are disconnected from the source of life. They have no chi or life force of their own. If they did, they would not be negative. Negative energy is like a negative number. It has force but in a negative direction, meaning it is defined by lack or absence. If you have a positive balance in your checkbook, you've got something quantifiable. If you have a negative balance in your checkbook, you are lacking the same amount.

Think of negative energy as being like a shadow. It exists only because it is the absence of light, caused by light being blocked by an object. It doesn't actually exist in and of itself.

We are real and living, because we have a moment-by-moment living relationship to the source of all life. Once we lose that connection, when we stop breathing, we die. The Dark Side, on the other hand, is the constellation of negative energies, and because these energies have no direct connection to life force, they are parasitical; they have to live off other forms of life. Examples of parasites are ticks, which feed off a living host and suck off their energy. Sometimes parasites even kill their host. (Some energies are symbiotic, where host and parasite support one another, but that is a different phenomenon.)

Negative energies sap us of our life force and block us from fulfilling our potential. As parasites, they are desperate to stay connected to their host, but this very fact makes them very vulnerable. Without something to live on, they don't exist.

Hey, right there, we have found the Achilles heel of the Dark Side. If the Dark Side is the constellation of negative energies, and negative energies need a living source, we absolutely have the power to defeat the domination of the Dark Side by refusing to be its source. To the Dark Side, we're food required for its survival, and we can learn how to starve it of the source of its power: us!

The Dark Side wants us to think it gives us power. Yet if we think about our life experience, we realize that we have always known intuitively that negative energies live off us and sap us of our strength. In some cases, negative energies immediately make us feel weak and drained. When we are caught in pessimism, gloom, or depression, it's pretty easy to feel like there's a powerful force dragging us down.

But sometimes it's not so easy to see that negative energies drain us. When we're caught up in negative righteous indignation, judgment, or anger, for example, we think we're feeling powerful, but that sudden flush of pseudo-energy is just a temporary illusion of empowerment. If we could always remember that when we are negative, we are food for the Dark Side, our little adrenalin-rush ego moment would quickly come to a close. Even when we puff ourselves up with rage or try to intimidate others, we're actually being dominated by an energy that's living off of us, and suddenly the glamour of negativity begins to fade. With this realization, we look and feel weak to ourselves, and that is a lousy feeling.

So right now I'd like to give you a tool to help us remember that the Dark Side is living off of us and draining us of our power.

Tool: Don't Be Lunch

When you see yourself being dominated by negative energy, for example, either being dragged down by depression or pumped up by some righteousness or anger, think of yourself as food for some gremlin. Then laugh, and say to yourself, "Don't be lunch!" Sometimes, we're so dominated by negative energy, we're not just lunch; we're breakfast, lunch and dinner. If so, let's admit it.

So the first dirty secret of the Dark Side is that it's parasitical, and it needs us to survive. That means we can cut off its supply. Let's think about ourselves in relation to the Dark Side.

1. Do I ever think the Dark Side gives me power?
2. What negative emotions do I use to dominate others?
3. Does this truly empower me?

2. The Dark Side runs the planet through our complicity.

First, let me explain why I say the Dark Side runs the planet. It may seem like an exaggeration, but isn't it true? When we look around, don't we see much more greed, fear, abuse, addiction, compulsion, and depression than we see compassion, expansion, and enlightenment? And how much negativity do we see in ourselves? How much do we hurt ourselves and others by being out-of-balance, filled with negative self-talk, competitiveness, reactivity and self-destructive behaviors?

How did the Dark Side take over the planet? Earlier in this book, particularly in Platform Five: Becoming Self-Aware, we looked at the habitual negative patterns of behavior and thought that we have developed individually and collectively. These patterns of behavior and thought are constructed by the immature ego in order to support, comfort, or protect us. But, as we have seen, they often turn out to be destructive.

These destructive and self-destructive patterns are the building blocks of the constellation of negative energies called the Dark Side. They drain us of life force, and they become bigger than we are. Let's see how.

All patterns can become habitual, and negative patterns can be powerful habits. Let's take one example. If one day we deal with our anxiety by eating ice cream, we are starting to create a negative habit. Eating sugar is negative, because it depletes us on every level. First, it is physiologically addictive, which means that our bodies are now into the blood sugar roller coaster. Second, the sugar depletes us of nutrients, and being physically depleted weakens us on every level. Third, the sugar impacts our minds and thought processes, so that we are not thinking as clearly. And fourth, the sugar has polluted our spirits, because the sugar high disconnects us from ourselves and from The Source, and, in addition, our self-disgust turns us away from ourselves. But what's worse is that we have created a connection between feeling anxiety and eating sugar. This is a message to our brain. Hey, if you feel anxious, here's the answer: cupcakes. This message is a trickle, but it is the beginning of a habit. Some people have a constitution where even one shot of sugar, alcohol or any other drug is enough to start an unstoppable addiction. But for most of us, the first time of practicing a behavior creates only the outline of a pattern.

But now suppose we start eating sugar more and more when we feel anxious. That pattern, like all patterns, starts to reinforce itself. The body gets more and more into an up-and-down blood sugar cycle, the mind gets muddy, the spirit is polluted, and the message to the brain gets deeper: anxiety = sugar. Now the trickle has turned into the Grand Canyon, and it starts to feel bigger than we are. We have created a monster, a Dark Side monster, because now, when we feel anxious, not only do we have to combat the desire to comfort ourselves with sugar, we also have to combat the Grand Canyon we've created—the pattern of body, mind, and spirit that turns anxiety into sugar, which depletes us of energy. In other words, we have created an addiction to a substance that literally brings negative energy into our body, depleting us of our life force.

The same is true of all other physical, mental, emotional and spiritual patterns that drain us of our health, our energy, and our self-respect. No wonder the Dark Side rules the planet! Every time we eat the wrong food or use a substance to deal with our feelings, every time we let ourselves get caught up in reactivity and upset, every time we attack instead of support, every time we hide, betray, or collude, we reinforce the habitual negative patterns that create untold damage and drain us of energy. And once we're drained of energy, how can we fight for ourselves?

What is true for us as individuals is true for us as a collective. Our collective habits create a Grand Canyon of negativity. Let's look at violence, for example. When confronted by some real or imagined threat, an individual might be able to fight his or her own ego reaction to defend or attack, if the reaction were only his. He or she could take a breath, ask if a violent reaction is called for, or check in to see if he or she is being dominated by some stimulus-reaction-response. But if that individual lives in a violence-prone society, the collective energy within that society will reinforce the individual's tendency to fall into violence. He or she will have to combat the influence of the collective consciousness as well. And when the violence-prone collective itself feels threatened, not only does each individual have to examine his or her reactivity, the collective also has to fight to not be dominated by the collective negative patterns. And if the collective habit of violence has become a Grand Canyon, an automatic, habitual reaction of a society, it's hard to stop the momentum.

We have seen this in history. For example, if we live in a gang-dominated neighborhood, it takes great effort to halt the automatic collective response of violence. If, on the other hand, we live in a Tibetan Buddhist monastery, any violent reaction can be more easily stopped and replaced by calm, forgiveness, and the spirit of reconciliation. In the case of the monastery, we have the Grand Canyon working for us, instead of against us, and we have already used this fact to practice Platform Two: Becoming Differentiated, where we use collective energies to support us.

Cultures are not different because the individuals within them are different; individuals are different because their cultures are different. And what is a culture, except a series of habitual, self-perpetuating patterns that offer responses and behaviors that are rewarded or condoned by any given society? Just as the ego of an individual creates patterns based on survival, the egos of societies do the same, and each society has developed patterns of behavior that become self-perpetuating, whether they are productive or not. And these collective patterns are reinforced over generations.

Be very careful what habits you feed. Today's trickle is tomorrow's Grand Canyon. And if the Grand Canyon is negative, the Dark Side starts to rule.

We're seeing how easy it is for the Dark Side to rule the planet through our own actions. And if this were not enough, negative energy spreads like a virus. We all know that our egos are triggered by each other. For example, you get angry with me, and I get angry with you that you're angry with me. But additionally, negative energy itself spreads through our connection to one another. As we have discussed before in this book, because of our Oneness, we unconsciously sense one another's feelings and think they are our own. Be with happy people, and we're more likely to be happy. Sit with someone who feels anxious, and we are more likely to feel anxiety, so much so that sometimes we can't stand being with them, though we may not know why. Thus we realize that when people around us are negative, it's easy for us to be influenced into negativity, and the cloud of dark energy increases.

Let's examine our own negative habits.

1. What kind of negative habits have I cultivated in myself?
2. Are they dominating me?
3. What are the negative habits of my culture that I can recognize?
4. Do they dominate us?
5. How often am I around people who are dominated by negativity?
6. How does that impact me?

And there's more to how the Dark Side rules. Negativity compounds negativity within us in other ways. When we have done something destructive or self-destructive, we often feel shame, even if we cover up that shame with deflection, blame or denial. What energy could be more negative than shame? Doesn't shame feel like the bottom has fallen out from under us? Isn't it the ultimate Dark Side energy, an energy that depletes us completely of life force, self-love, and connection to The Source? So our negative actions cause us shame, which serves us up as lunch to the Dark Side. Add to this that we often react negatively to our own negativity. Don't we sometimes despair because we're negative or depressed? Isn't that yet another depleting and debilitating response? In addition, we get angry with ourselves for having been "bad," as well as resent those we blame for our being that way. And the beat goes on. Our reactions to our negative behaviors feed the Dark Side.

And then there's all that negativity we direct toward others, who themselves are being lunch. We resent those who are feeling negative, and we resent those whose actions hurt us and others. And then there's the resentment we feel toward those who oppose us, and so on. So negativity is compounding more and more. Let's take a look at ourselves and our negative reactions to negativity.

1. Do we get negative about being negative ourselves?
2. Do we feel negative toward others who are negative?

Now we're beginning to catch on. This is how the Dark Side comes into being. Negative energy feeds on itself and grows exponentially. What starts as a negative trickle gathers force until it becomes an ocean of negative energies, energies that sap and destroy.

What's the answer? Be peaceful and never confront anything? Hardly. We don't need to "love" everybody, no matter what they do. And we don't need to allow bad behavior, which I discuss a little later in this book. But we do need to stop our being dominated by negativity and fill ourselves with allowance, neutrality, calm, serenity, and compassion. Then we can act appropriately and even forcefully from an integrated place and without empowering the Dark Side. To do otherwise feeds the Dark Side and increases its rule.

We've seen how Dark Side energies grow in strength. Now let's zero in on how the Dark Side rules through dominating our egos. I'll discuss this phenomenon more as we proceed with the Seven Dirty Secrets of the Dark Side, but I'd like to make one critical point here. The ego is the aspect of us that brings us awareness of ourselves as individuals, and therefore it tends to be me-based and self-protective.

Sometimes the ego tries to protect us by making us look tougher, bigger or better than the other guy. Under these circumstances, the ego's tendency toward self-protection will push us into aggression, fighting or puffing ourselves up at another's expense. This, of course, strengthens the Dark Side energies. On the other hand, sometimes the ego's self-protective strategy is to make us look small. In this case, we will try to make ourselves seem non-threatening, which will make us cautious, especially in the face of great odds. If we get small in the face of intimidating negative energy, we throw in the towel and surrender our power. So whether we become aggressive or passive, the Dark Side wins.

It can happen at home, where either both parents brawl or one becomes meek. And it can happen in our world, where societies battle or where people allow negativity to grow unopposed. Both are exemplified by Nazi Germany. How could so many German people allow Hitler to rule and Nazism to hold sway? Because too many people colluded by joining in or giving in. Here's joining in: Our self-protective egos said, "We, the German people, feel defeated after World War I, we accepted a humiliating peace, and we're in a depression. Hitler looks like a big tough guy, and that puffs up our collective ego, which got whipped in the last war. So let's fight to regain our standing in the world." Here's giving in: The self-protective ego said, "Hitler looks like a maniac, but it's too dangerous to stand up to him. Let someone else do it."

The same self-protective collusion with the Dark Side exists throughout the world, with "good" people doing nothing to stop negative forces that hold power; in fact, "good" people blind ourselves to even acknowledging the negativity that exists! How else can we explain slavery or the beating or rape of women, while bystanders stand passive? How else can we explain the permission of child labor or exploitation of immigrants? How else can we understand how we could have invaded other nations with no real provocation?

Our egos collude with the Dark Side within ourselves, as well. We feel overwhelmed by the power of the Dark Side, the negative forces that cause us to smoke cigarettes or lead us to beat our children. But we feel powerless in the face of these forces. The self-protective ego, caught in the old behaviors, justifies these behaviors as comforting, reasonable, or somehow protecting us and convinces us that it's not safe, comfortable or even possible to confront ourselves, our addictions, and our destructiveness. We just let the Dark Side win. And so it goes, and so it grows.

Let's ask ourselves some questions about our collusion.

1. How does my ego convince me to let the Dark Side win in my home?
2. How does my ego convince me to let the Dark Side win at work?
3. How does my ego convince me to let the Dark Side win in the world?

The Dark Side is a collective energy that grows off our negativity and that of everyone else. And while our egos are busy protecting our "selves," the Dark Side is growing exponentially, feeding off the individual and collective negative energy and complicity that our egos allow. So the second dirty secret of the Dark Side is that the Dark Side rules, but only because we let it. And the more we let it win, the stronger it becomes.

3. Don't try to fight the domination of the Dark Side alone.

We've begun to understand how the Dark Side works. Negativity may start by looking like an isolated feeling or behavior, but it is really an aspect of a collective energy, a gathering cloud that grows exponentially unless it is checked. Once having acknowledged that The Dark Side is powerful, that it is in fact a collective energy, we can see that we are foolish to try to fight its domination alone.

First of all, when we feel alone, we are much more vulnerable to negative feelings, and thus we're more vulnerable to the Dark Side. Haven't we all had the experience of feeling better when we reached a friend on the phone or when we were being hugged? Haven't we had the experience of banishing irrational fear, rage, or self-doubt when we've had a conversation with a good friend, who had a more balanced view and helped us "snap out of it"? Haven't we seen millions of alcoholics and drug addicts get sober, because they came together?

So, if we are more vulnerable to our negative feelings and behaviors when we're alone, what would the Dark Side do to try to win? It would tell us that we should handle the challenges of life alone, either because we're okay and nobody else is, so we need to get away from those other, crazy folks, or because we're not okay, and we need to hide that fact from all those other people, who aren't as crazy as we are. Hmmm, doesn't that sound suspiciously like the ego? Yes! In the ego, the Dark Side has a great ally. Since the ego is usually caught in separation, it will tell us no one will understand us, there's nothing wrong with us, or we should not expose to one another the degree of our fears or insane thinking or behavior, because someone will exploit our weakness. Yes, just at the moment we most need support, when the Dark Side is lunching on us, the Dark Side appeals to the ego for support, and the immature ego falls for the trap. Instead of confronting the Dark Side and truly protecting us, the ego screams at us to keep our problems to ourselves, so that no one else can hurt or take advantage of us. This "smart" behavior keeps us alone and weak. Not very smart.

Naturally, being allies, the Dark Side defends the ego's domination to the last, and so it tries to block us from getting the support we need to confront our own egos. As we have already seen, much of our negative behavior is ego-based, so the Dark Side defends our ego-based behavior, especially when the behavior is nuts. The Dark Side will always encourage us to find justification and support for whatever destructive behavior the ego has prompted. So when we're in some dumb attitude or behavior in which our egos are running amuck, the Dark Side will encourage us to seek out those who will agree with and amplify our negativity, anger, fear, resentment, shame, blame or complaints. This is not support!

Why don't we wake up to a simple reality? We all need support for our consciousness. Real support. None of us is truly impervious to the Dark Side, but there is help. Just as the darkness is banished in the light of day, we need to turn on the light of consciousness when we're in negative thinking. Often the best way to let in the light of consciousness is to feel connected with one another, because whenever we feel connected, we feel more safe, relaxed, open, and ready to tell the truth.

So far, we've been looking at this issue only from the perspective of the individual: me facing my "personal" demons. Now let's look at this issue from an even broader perspective. If the Dark Side is the constellation of negative energy, then it is in fact larger than any one of us as an individual. So then how can we fight its domination alone?

Think of the Dark Side as being like a hurricane. Have you ever been in a hurricane that exists over only one house? Of course not. In the same way, like a storm of negativity that descends on individuals and collectives alike, the Dark Side attacks us all at our weak points. There may be spiritual giants who can overcome negativity themselves, but most of us cannot stand up to the onslaught.

If we want to be free of the domination of the Dark Side, we have to be willing to search for support, and support is not the individuals and groups that agree with us and support our egos, but rather the individuals and groups that support our consciousness and, thereby, support our true selves. We need those who support us to look honestly at our attitudes and behaviors and to encourage us to become integrated, freed from the domination of our emotions out of balance, and freed from the domination of the negative energies that are feeding off us and sapping our energy.

One more point about not fighting alone. We need to get support if we are to confront the domination of the Dark Side on an external level as well. If we are going to fight City Hall, we need to stand up, speak out, and call for reinforcements. Sometimes a single person can spark a revolution, but no one can win it alone. Even though others had refused to give up their seats for whites before, only when Rosa Parks refused to sit in the back of the bus in Montgomery, Alabama, did we begin that powerful collective action against segregation that rattled our country and changed the way we feel and live.

Let's look at ourselves in terms of our tendency to get support.

1. When I feel ashamed, what does my ego tell me to do?
2. When I am angry, do I tend to look for support or justification?
3. Can I see the Dark Side winning more when I'm alone?

The ego is always separating us from one another. So the third dirty secret of the Dark Side is that we can't fight its domination alone. That's a big clue to us. If we want to win against the domination of the Dark Side, we need to stand up to our egos and make darned sure that we're not alone.

4. Don't fight against the Dark Side; fight for yourself.

Once we've committed to getting support to take on the Dark Side, we need to understand how to fight. And here's the next dirty secret of the Dark Side. If we get angry with the Dark Side and fight against it, we are just increasing the negativity on the planet. Oh no, there goes the Dark Side, growing again! We've all seen this in practice. You come in unjustly angry at me. I get angry about that. Then you're angry because I'm angry. And so, who wins? The Dark Side. Because now there's way more negative energy than there was before.

Does this mean that we should not fight back? No, but the way to fight back is to fight *for* something, not against. How can we do this? Here's an example. If you come in angry and start trashing me, I do what I have to in order to get centered, connect to The Source, and fight for myself. Perhaps I give myself a time out, take a breath, call a friend, take a walk, whatever I've learned to do that helps me differentiate from the negative energy that's flying. Then I ask myself if there's truth in what you're saying. Fighting for myself means that I am fighting for my integrity, my physical, mental/emotional and spiritual integrity. It does not mean fighting for my ego, my rationalizations and my dysfunctional behavior. If I determine that what you're saying is true, I acknowledge that truth. If I determine that what you're saying is not true, I say the truth. But saying the truth doesn't require yelling or abusiveness. If we are really on our game, we'll even remember that the other person is lunch, we'll wonder why, and we'll have compassion for them, while simultaneously standing our ground. Let's examine this in greater depth.

What Is My "Self," and How Do I Fight for It?

My "self" is the true, inner me, integrated, free of the domination of any aspect of consciousness, connected to the universe and growing toward my potential. Wow. Does that exist? I think we all have a sense that it does, the sense of self we feel when we are at peace, the self that has integrity and wholeness, regardless of our standing in the world or the opinions of others, the self that is connected to the eternal.

What is that self that is connected to the eternal? In Platform Five: Becoming Self-Aware, I spoke about the self as a vibrational energy field. Everything vibrates, but like light waves, things vibrate at different frequencies. As vibrational energies, we have a large spectrum of possibilities. We can vibrate at the highest level possible for us, or we can vibrate anywhere down to the bottom. We are impacted by what we eat, think and do, and by the people around us; we are also impacted by our ability to connect to divine energy. Right now this concept can feel very abstract to some of you, but I'll explain more about this in Platform Nine: Becoming Becoming. In the meantime, however, just consider that we have a true, inner self that is dragged down by our immature egos and the Dark Side.

So if I'm really some vibrational energy, how do I fight for myself? By empowering it. By making it stronger. Here are some practices that help.

First, and foremost, we must always remember to connect to the highest energies available to us—energies that you can call God, chi energy, The Source, higher consciousness, the Oneness, or whatever concept fits for you, but which refers to the universal life force, the divine, or the beneficial energies that support us and of which we are a part. In the last section describing Dirty Secret Three, we discussed that we need to not fight the Dark Side alone. On one level, that means not to be alone in terms of human support. On the level of the vibrational self, which we are discussing now, not being alone means not being alone on the energetic level. And for that, we need to connect our vibrational field to higher vibrational fields, which at that moment are free from the negative energies dragging us down.

This may sound strange to some of you, but remember Platform Two: Becoming Differentiated and Platform Five: Becoming Self-Aware, where we learned to connect to the energies that support us. That could simply mean listening to the right kind of music, doing yoga or tai chi, or connecting with nature. By calling on a level of consciousness or vibrational energy that is clearer, more positive, less dominated by the Dark Side, we are connecting our weakened selves to stronger vibrational fields that support us. It's easy to forget the existence of those higher vibrational energies when we're under attack, whether the attack comes from outside us or from within our own minds, because the last thing the ego and the Dark Side want at that moment is for us to rise above their domination. But connecting to beneficial energies is essential if we are not to lose the integrity of our inner selves when provoked.

As we have already mentioned, connecting to The Source, or beneficial energies, can mean taking a moment to get centered; it can mean meditating, taking a walk, breathing deeply, praying, looking upward, just focusing our intention on filling ourselves with life force, playing with the dog, whatever interrupts the ego's blah, blah, blah that makes us vulnerable to becoming lunch. When we do this, we are supporting the growth and integrity of our energy field. We are fighting for the true self.

It should be obvious that if we are actually vibrational energies, connecting to the higher vibrational energies supports us to maintain our spiritual integrity and the vibrational energy that is the essential us. When I'm in a state of spiritual and energetic integrity, I am more easily able to be calm and neutral, and I can demand from myself a higher degree of mental-emotional integrity. When I am in mental-emotional integrity, I'm ready to hear you, listen to what you're saying, and evaluate your words for the truth that will help me grow, and I'm ready to respond appropriately when you are wrong. In a calm, neutral space, I can inquire: Is there any truth in what you are saying? If so, I can gain benefit from your intervention, even if you are delivering it in a hurtful way, and I can make amends, if that's called for. If you are wrong, I can let your words roll off my back. When I'm not in that calm, neutral space, I'm lunch.

Another way to fight for ourselves is to deal with our state of mind by practicing some of our platforms. When confronting negative energies, our old way of coping is to merge or separate, but these behaviors just create more negativity. Instead, we can practice differentiation (Platform Two) and call generously on the tools of self-awareness we learned in Platform Five.

And referring way back to Platform One: Becoming Oneness, we can remember, "I am that." We can admit how similar we are to the person whose attitude or behavior we oppose, so that instead of getting taken over by the Dark Side energy of rage or disgust, we become capable of understanding and compassion. Without condoning destructive behavior, we can identify the part of us that is capable of that behavior as well, even if only under the greatest provocation. When we look for the ways in which we are similar to those we oppose, we interrupt our ego's dedication to separateness, we feel Oneness, we experience compassion, and we defeat the domination of the Dark Side.

To pull this off, it is very helpful to be in a state of physical integrity as well. This means I have prepared myself for every challenging moment by eating the foods that support rather than debilitate me, sleeping as much as I need, and exercising, if I can. When I am in better physical shape, my nervous system is more whole, and I am more able to keep centered in the storm.

When we examine all these ways of fighting for ourselves, we realize that they have something in common. They are all ways of connecting to our true selves, instead of our egos, and that's the challenge.

A Tip: Don't fight for the ego, fight for the self.

The Dark Side wants us to fight for our egos, because fighting for our egos makes us lunch. Dominated by our ego, we promote separation and deception; avoid Oneness and co-creation; become vulnerable to all kinds of negative energies; and throw in the towel.

We all know what this looks like. We defend our behavior and refuse to look at ourselves squarely. We are as negative as the negative energy that provoked us. We don't want to consider even the possibility that we may have misunderstood a situation or been abusive ourselves. We deny that we are out of control. And we argue for our position. This is the fight for my ego and not for my "self."

To really fight for ourselves, we need to become wise to our ego's games, so that we can become detached and neutral, listen and learn. The ego tells us that fighting for ourselves is the same as fighting for our ego's perspective, to win, to dominate, to convince, to self-justify, or to defeat our opponent. This is reflected in people saying words, such as "This is my truth." Or "That's just the way I feel." But this is false. When we fight for our true selves, we cannot fight for "our truth," which is just a fancy name for our self-centered, blind, self-serving perspective. We have to fight for "the truth," which may or may not knock us off our self-righteous pedestal. And we've already learned that what we feel may or may not have anything to do with reality.

To fight for ourselves, we need support, support, support. We need support from others and support from above in order to become calm and neutral enough to become self-aware and choose our responses.

Let's take a moment to look at our own patterns in regard to fighting for ourselves.

1. When growing up, what models did I see of fighting for myself?
2. Were the people fighting for their inner selves or their egos?
3. Which do I fight for?

We Can Still Have Feelings

When we are fighting for ourselves, we connect to higher consciousness and become more neutral. This does not mean that we become zombies or that we will have no emotions. We are sentient beings and are meant to feel happy, sad, afraid, pissed off, motivated, tired, or whatever is appropriate in the moment. But negative energy is not normal emotion, which gives us information and passes. It is negative energy out of balance that dominates and drains us. It grows exponentially and blocks our potential.

Just to review this important point, let's consider anger again, as an example. We can feel and express anger when it is appropriate. But we must remember that anger is supposed to be a tool of consciousness; it is a communication from our psyche to us that either something is wrong or we think something is wrong. Anger cannot define reality; it is a message to which we should pay attention and evaluate. The ego, on the other hand, has a different purpose for anger. It feeds anger so that it can use the emotion as a weapon to separate, fragment, or hurt either ourselves or others. In this way, our anger becomes a tool of the Dark Side.

Remember, negative energy is energy disconnected from the creative force of the universe, The Source. So if, for example, I get angry at you and abandon my consciousness, I will lose my connection to The Source, and I will be dominated by the Dark Side. When I am taken over by the Dark Side, I cannot be connected to myself, and I can't fight for myself. We can all identify signs that we are being dominated by the Dark Side.

We feel stressed, alone, and out of control. Sometimes we feel like we've been taken over by a passion that makes us insane or at least causes us to do or say things we regret.

We've all done it. When dominated by a negative energy, we become disconnected from The Source and from our humanity; we become the Dark Side. Let's fight for ourselves, for ourselves as human beings: feeling, expressive, and connected to one another and the universe.

Now let's look at ourselves in terms of our ability to fight for ourselves.

1. Can I see the difference between fighting to justify my own reactions and fighting for myself?
2. What emotion of mine have I allowed to define reality for me?
3. Can I see that I was being dominated by that emotion and by the Dark Side?
4. Was I connected to myself or anything else when dominated by that emotion?

We Fight for Ourselves as a Collective, Too

Fighting for ourselves is as much a collective experience as an individual one. Being nonviolent but active and assertive has been the strategy of several movements in the last century, including Gandhi's movement for an independent India and the Civil Rights movement in the United States. These movements are based on the premise that you can fight for something without adding to the negative energy. Let's learn from these movements and see if we can't emulate them in our own selves and our own lives.

To review, the fourth dirty secret of the Dark Side is that when we're fighting against something, we're adding to the negativity; but when we get our egos out of the equation, we can fight for our inner selves, and then the tables turn.

5. The best way to fight the domination of the Dark Side is to empower it.

Now you're really crazy. What do you mean—that I need to support people who do bad things? Are you saying that if I meet Lucifer on the road, I should put a machine gun in his hand or nominate him for president?

Of course not. First, it's important to acknowledge that hurtful behaviors must be stopped if it is possible to stop them. This is for the protection of all beings involved, including the perpetrator him—or herself. You don't help killers, for example, by allowing them to kill. Allowing them to kill only causes them to feel more shame and fear of themselves; it supports them to disconnect from themselves and reality; and it leads to their need for increased self-justification and sometimes even encourages them to repeat or escalate the damaging behavior. The same is true for our own negative behaviors. I do not help myself by allowing me to hurt myself through self-destructive behavior. I do not help myself by allowing me to abuse you either, because I then have to carry within me the scars of guilt and shame that will haunt me.

We need to stop negative behavior, if we can, but we need to use only the amount of force necessary to do so. Beyond that, we need to try to empower the essential self of the person involved; and beyond that, we need to support the Dark Side itself to evolve. (Much more about that later in this chapter.) Some people will assert that we will never be able to help a killer overcome the domination of his or her need to kill and that we may never be able to overcome our own tendency to hurt ourselves or others. Wouldn't it be better to assume we simply have not yet found the way? With this attitude, we continue to keep learning.

Here's reality: When we look at the scope of human destructiveness and self-destructiveness, that of ourselves and just about everybody else, the situation is daunting. But precisely because our destructiveness is so powerful, we had better rethink our pessimism and continue seeking ways to support all of us not only to stop particular behaviors, but to gain the power to choose a different way of relating to ourselves and our world. Let me repeat that. We need to gain the power to choose a different way of relating to ourselves and our world. Otherwise, we will be doomed to keep repeating our destructive behaviors. And the power to choose a different way comes from being connected to the deepest parts of ourselves and The Source, the beneficial energies that also exist on the planet side-by-side with the Dark Side.

Tip: When people do bad things, they are being lunch to the Dark Side.

Fighting the Dark Side in the old way is not working. And one secret the Dark Side doesn't want us to know is that when we focus our anger at the offending person, we are taking away from those people any power to fight for themselves. When people do bad things, or when we think they have, we tend to see them as powerful, because we can't control them. But in truth they are weak, because they can't control themselves. Angered by their not caring for us and others, feeling "victimized" by their force, we isolate, attack, or try to overpower them, which, of course, can easily lead them to become more defensive and violent. In addition, by attacking them, we acknowledge them as powerful, which makes us feel small and feeds their egos.

Let's look at the issue of power more closely. The only power worth having is command over ourselves. Power is internal. It comes from our connection to ourselves and The Source. (Again, since I'm referring here to the source of higher consciousness and the creative force of the universe, I will be using the words "The Source," but you can substitute any concept that works for you.) Power over ourselves is not contingent on force, violence, or the ability to command other people. We know this from experience. When we feel well and confident, we walk in the world differently from when we feel fearful and insecure. When we're proud and happy with ourselves, we have a peace nothing else can bring.

In reality, people who do hurtful things are lunch, dominated by negative energies. Whether through chemical or emotional imbalance, or because they have sold out their humanity for external power, approval or other ego-based interests, such people are no longer connected to themselves or the Oneness. They are weak, overwhelmed, and helpless over their own demons.

One way to understand this weakness is to remember Platform Six: Becoming Integrated. As we have seen, people engaged in irrational, hurtful behaviors are being dominated by some aspect of themselves that is out of balance, whether it be fear, insecurity, the desire for wealth, the need to protect or prove themselves, or the never-ending thirst for external power, validation, or even love. Such people are clearly powerless, being pulled out of integrity by forces within them that they cannot control. Obviously they are not too powerful; they are not powerful enough. And obviously they are being dominated by ego.

Compassion Becomes Possible

As we've been studying the Seven Dirty Secrets of the Dark Side, we are developing a deeper understanding of negative energy itself, and we can see that when people do bad things, they are not powerful at all. They are out of control and being overcome by negative energies. They are lunch, dinner, an entire smorgasbord for the Dark Side!

And because we see this, we can have compassion. Try this.

Tool: See Hurtful People as Lunch

Visualize someone who is hurtful and whom you have seen as powerful. It could be a personal acquaintance, a boss, even a political figure. Then visualize that person as he or she really is, the host of some negative energy living off their life force, dining off their energy, and calling the shots. If it works for you, let yourself visualize some demon having them for lunch. Now we get it: these people are not powerful at all.

What would happen if we could empower these people and help them connect to their deeper selves and The Source? Would they not have the power to fight for themselves and against the domination of the Dark Side? Isn't that what's really missing in human beings, the power to fight for our inner selves rather than our egos, the power to confront our demons rather than to be dominated by them, the power to fight for our potential rather than our limited perception of ourselves?

When people are being overcome by the Dark Side, and when they are left alone with their insane negative thinking, they are defenseless against those energies. But when they feel connected and supported by us, they may be able to connect to divine energy and let the Dark Side go. We've all seen or experienced ourselves or someone else ranting and raving and then stopping and crying, because the somewhat hysterical person suddenly feels the support and is able to face the pain that all that bluster is meant to hide.

Don't we have tools to support and empower one another? Haven't we learned that empathy helps, that people can at times be approached and brought to their senses? Haven't we seen that when we reach out to someone with caring and concern, they often feel safe enough to open up? Haven't we discovered that changes in diet or exercise and sometimes medication can help turn the balance in favor of the inner self? Haven't we seen the power of self-awareness and the power of amends to bring people into alignment? Haven't we seen the efficacy of spiritual practices to help people come into balance?

We haven't yet entirely discovered how to support people, but we need to use what we know and keep on trying. And we need to learn one more very important technique, sending people chi, which I'm going to discuss a bit later in this chapter.

But before sharing this important tool with you, let's take our thinking one step further: The Dark Side is the constellation of negative energies, which are energies with no life force. Suppose we sent life force energy to the Dark Side itself? Suppose we supported it to connect to The Source? What would happen? Let's remember the example of the shadow. If you intensify the light on the object creating the shadow, the shadow remains. But if you pour light directly on the shadow, it disappears. That's the truth. If the Dark Side were connected to The Source, it would no longer be negative; it would no longer be the Dark Side.

Many of us balk at the idea of supporting anyone who is "bad," or even supporting the Dark Side itself. We fear that we will only be empowering "the enemy," and that power will be used against us, or we resent the idea of rewarding bad behavior. This kind of thinking refers to a misunderstanding. People who are negative are suffering; they are overpowered by negative energy. Empowering such a person and/or the Dark Side allows for them to connect to the beneficial energies that free them from the negative energy that makes them behave so badly.

We might get a lot of ego gratification out of pretending that we are "good" fighting evil. But that ego gratification does not solve our problems; it only worsens them by feeding the Dark Side. When we understand the Seven Dirty Secrets of the Dark Side, we realize that the best way to fight is to support everyone to connect to the beneficial energies that can banish the negative to the degree possible at any given time. If we had a paranoid person who killed out of fear, which would be smarter: To punish that person or relieve them of their paranoia, if we could?

So let's learn a simple technique, which we use to empower the perpetrator and the Dark Side.

Tool: Sending Chi

When we are confronted by someone's negativity, we try to reach out to them, as we discussed before. But whether or not they accept our intervention, we have another tool to help: We point fingers two and three in their direction, as though we were aiming a gun. But this is not a gun to kill; it's loaded with our intention to support; it's loaded with chi.

What is chi, and can we all direct it to others? Yes, believe it or not, every one of us has the capacity to tap into the universal life force called chi and direct it to empower another. Not only does sending chi help the other, but it helps us as well. When we are confronted by the Dark Side, the negative forces can seem very large. But when we connect to the universal life force, we fill ourselves with a power greater than ourselves, and we no longer feel small in relation to the Dark Side or anything else. The process of channeling divine energy to others changes the balance of power in favor of the self. We circumvent our own egos and theirs. Unconsciously we release our fear of the negative power of another by filling ourselves with the sense of the power and wellbeing only possible when we connect to the limitless power that streams through the universe.

We can send chi to someone in our minds, or if we are with them, we can physically send them chi by directing our fingers toward them. If we cannot do it openly, we can send them chi under a table or in a very discrete way. It may not change them, but it will certainly change us, which will ultimately and inevitably change our relationship.

Just as we can empower individuals with chi, so can we empower the Dark Side itself. When you feel afraid, point your fingers, and send chi to the Dark Side. If we could find a way to help the Dark Side reconnect to The Source, it would no longer be the Dark Side.

So, yes, the fifth dirty secret of the Dark Side is that the best way to dissolve the Dark Side is to empower it, to send it life force and support it to connect to The Source. The moment that a negative energy becomes connected to The Source, it is no longer empty; it is no longer parasitical; it is no longer negative. So when you feel really overwhelmed by the Dark Side, point fingers two and three (the index and middle fingers) at some imaginary vision of the Dark Side, and send it chi. Let's consider using these tools now.

1. Who have I seen as negative, bad, and powerful?
2. Can I see them as lunch?
3. Let me send them chi in my mind's eye.
4. Let me send them chi when we are together, if I can.

6. The Dark Side does not run the planet; The Source does, and The Source uses the Dark Side to promote evolution.

Okay, so didn't you just tell me that the second dirty secret of the Dark Side is that the Dark Side runs the planet? Isn't this a bit of a contradiction?

Yes and no. If you were to go outside in a rainstorm, you would say, "It's raining," and that would be true. But suppose you were able to rise above the clouds; you would see that it's raining only under the clouds. Above the clouds, it's not raining at all.

Using this analogy, the Dark Side runs the planet only under the clouds. The Source runs the whole show, under and over the clouds. And if The Source, or the intelligence of the universe, runs the planet, there are rules that the Dark Side has to follow, laws of the universe that are beyond its power to change, and we're learning these rules now with our study of the Seven Dirty Secrets.

Before we go forward, let's review again what I mean by The Source. By The Source, I mean the creative force or the creative intelligence that brought us into being and keeps us alive. It's the universal life force, the divine intelligence, the Great Spirit; some people call it God. Whatever you call it, it exists. I like to use the term "The Source," because, just like the sun is the source of energy on this planet, The Source powers the entire universe.

So if this is the case, why the heck does the Dark Side rule? Why doesn't The Source just shine a light on the Dark Side, kick it out of the clouds, stop the rain, and make it go away?

Well, like it or not, that's not the way it works—at least up to this point. But if we get smarter and start learning the rules, we might change our fate. In fact, if we could figure out the purpose of the Dark Side, perhaps we could start using the Dark Side to our advantage. Let's go back to the example of the rain. If it never rained, there'd be no food, and then we wouldn't be here to complain about it raining; so we have accepted that it rains, come to appreciate its value, and learned a lot about harnessing its power. So let's understand how the Dark Side functions as part of the Oneness, and see where that takes us.

Here is the sixth dirty secret of the Dark Side: The Source actually runs the planet and uses the Dark Side to promote evolution.

In the beginning of this book, back at "Ego, Instinct & Evolution," I talked about evolution as being intrinsic to all creation, and clearly the Dark Side has a huge role in that process. Without challenge, there is no change, and without change, there is no evolution.

Let's look at a nonhuman example for a moment. Negative energy is energy that blocks us from fulfilling our potential; therefore, from the perspective of the germ kingdom we are the Dark Side. We have created antibiotics, and we have killed countless germs; we're blocking them from fulfilling their potential. On the other hand, these very antibiotics have been the challenge that has led to a rapid evolution of the germ kingdom to more resistant strains. We find a way to kill germs, and they find a way to evolve.

Challenge supports evolution by showing any species its weaknesses, which leads either to mutation and transformation or death. It's the same with us. Challenge on any level shows us our weaknesses, and once we understand those weaknesses, we have the option to transform or ultimately languish or die.

Looking at the Cracks

Challenging every species is the purpose of the Dark Side; it shows us every weakness we have. We then have the opportunity to evolve. The Dark Side could have no effect if we were not already weak, if there were no cracks in us, cracks in our energy field, or cracks in our mental, emotional or physical state. If you drop a perfectly sealed vase into a vat of ink, no ink will leak in, but if you drop a vase with cracks into the same vat, the ink will ultimately fill the vase.

That's just the way we are. If we have no weakness or cracks, we are not impacted by negative energy. It can't get past our defenses; it can't pass through our energy field. That is why spiritual masters seem superhuman. But for us normal humans, weaknesses and cracks are part of us all; that's why we become lunch.

Unfortunately for us, we seem to have a lot of cracks, and whenever we throw away our consciousness, the cracks get bigger. For example, if we have a tendency toward depression and then we eat sugar, we will be more likely to get depressed because of the sugar cycle. If we have a tendency toward anxiety, caffeine can make us more anxious. If we have a tendency toward anger, getting caught up in an ego battle with another ego could open the crack for us to lose control.

What Does This Have to Do with Evolution?

As a species, challenges weed out the weak. Let's say we're living in an environment where physical strength is most required; the brilliant invalid probably won't make it, unless she is valuable enough to get others to care for her. In a physically demanding environment, the person with great physical strength is most likely to survive. In an environment in which a healthy immune system is most required, a physically less strong person would probably trump a tough guy with a weak immune system. If we're living in the modern world, mental acuity may be more important than health and strength, depending on the degree of weakness on the physical plane (we're still living in a physical world, and we need some physical health to stay alive), but in times of extreme stress, perhaps the spiritually strong will be the most likely to survive. And those who survive have children and pass on those genes. As individuals we may not like it. It may seem unfair. But unfair or not, that's the way it's been.

When we are confronted by negative energies that threaten our survival on a physical plane, then clearly the Dark Side supports our evolution toward healthier bodies. When we are confronted by negative energies that threaten our mental or emotional stability, then the emotionally stable are more likely to gain traction. If we live at a time when the spiritually weak engage in self-destructive behaviors, those with spiritual strength may begin to come forward to support the whole.

We hope that all the challenges we face, especially on the mental-emotional and spiritual plains, will support humanity to evolve, rather than languish and die. Those with the strength to take on the challenge need to step forward and help lead that evolution, and in fact, that is happening more and more. The outcome will reveal itself.

We've been talking about collective evolution. Now let's consider how the Dark Side supports my personal evolution. All the negative energy that seeps through my cracks shows me my weaknesses, whether they be mental, emotional, physical or spiritual. If I am honest and take the lesson the Dark Side is offering me, I will do everything I can to strengthen myself. I will grow in strength. I will evolve. Several bad marriages can teach me something about myself. Bankruptcy through my compulsive spending can call me to awareness and action. Reckless disregard of my health can lead to consequences that cause me to take a stand for wellbeing and exercise. The other options are to just complain about my fate, fail to thrive, or die.

Ouch. This is some tough world! Let's take a look at our own weaknesses and their potential to support our evolution.

1. What are my weaknesses?
2. Do I pretend they don't exist, or do I acknowledge them?
3. What are the negative experiences that have brought them to my awareness?
4. Have I tried to strengthen myself when I see them?
5. Have I evolved?

How Do We Heal Our Cracks?

If I acknowledge that the Dark Side is showing me my weaknesses, what do I do to fill those cracks so that I become less vulnerable? The first thing is to acknowledge that my cracks, not the Dark Side, are the real source of my problems. The flu doesn't kill. My body's inability to fight the flu kills. The divorce didn't devastate me. My inability to overcome my shame or trauma from the divorce devastated me.

Some cracks are obvious, and some have easily identifiable solutions. If I know that there's a genetic tendency in my family toward high blood pressure, I can watch my diet. That doesn't guarantee me immunity from the problem, but it is an action I can take to bolster myself at my weak points. Of course, I may still be more vulnerable than the next person on the physical plane, and I may die or become disabled anyway, but at least my fate will not be the result of a failure on my part to address my weakness.

Let's look at some other kinds of cracks and how to address them. If I notice that certain circumstances tend to trigger me into rampant negativity, I can try to identify the triggers, understand why they trigger me, and take accountability to avoid them and/or change my response. Now we can see the significance of Platforms Five, Six and Seven regarding Becoming Self-Aware, Integrated and Accountable. Every time we use our self-awareness, we are identifying the cracks that are causing us to be lunch. Every time we work on becoming integrated, we strengthen our energy fields and become less vulnerable to negative energy. Every time we take accountability and make amends, we release the holes in us caused by guilt or denial.

Let's look at an example of addressing a typical crack: the need to be loved. If I know that I have a tendency to seek the approval of women, even to my own detriment, I can look into the genesis of this behavior, and ask my friends to bust me when I'm throwing myself away to be loved. In addition, I can seek professional help, I can ask for support from a self-help or mutual support group, I can seek spiritual guidance, and/ or I can do LifeForce or qi gong to strengthen my energy field. I can see if I need to change my circumstances, or whether I need to use my circumstances in order to change myself.

Of course it's easier to blame circumstances for our defeat than to address our weaknesses. And it's sad but clearly true that many folks are not strong enough to withstand the pressure of the Dark Side, even when they know the weakness is internal. Their cracks are too many or too deep, or the assaults of the Dark Side are too great for them to withstand. Nothing that I say here is meant to imply that these folks are to blame. Children brought up in severely abusive families, for example, have so many cracks, it can be extremely difficult for them to heal; the same is true of people born with severe mood swings or other mental imbalances, or people born with other acute disabilities. We are not here to judge. Most of us would surely have crumbled under the circumstances of concentration camps, persecution, or torture, growing up in neighborhoods filled with gangs and violence, severe child abuse or the systematic destruction of our culture, as was experienced by our own native peoples.

But be that as it may, the truth is that in this world so dominated by the Dark Side, we must heal ourselves and transform, or we will be stuck in very distorted and destructive patterns of being that don't support anyone, especially ourselves. If we do not take advantage of the evolutionary challenges presented by the Dark Side, the Dark Side will continue to grow in power, and we will shrink, becoming less and less able to cope. If we throw in the towel and continue to drink, smoke, take drugs, gamble, act out sexually, rage or eat compulsively when we are stressed, we will only become more stressed and more weak. The Dark Side will win, and humanity may even become extinct.

It takes a lot of self-discipline to confront ourselves and take the steps necessary to heal ourselves, rather than to blame and complain. To help ourselves, let's always remember Dirty Secret Three, Don't fight alone. Together, we are stronger than we are alone; together, we can start to shift the balance in our favor.

Let's look at some of our attitudes to our cracks.

1. Do I blame the Dark Side or my cracks for my defeats?
2. Do I take responsibility for these cracks?
3. What am I doing to heal them?

How the Dark Side Supports US to Stop It from Ruling the World

When we learn from our experiences with the Dark Side, we can speed up our evolution. And we can take yet another step. We can turn the tables on the Dark Side altogether. How can we do that? By recognizing the collusion between the ego and the Dark Side. We know that fighting from an ego position only multiplies negative energy, so in order to fight the domination of negative energy, we must fight against the domination of our egos, and we need to do so by fighting for ourselves. We must become increasingly aware that the self for which we must fight is the inner self, not the ego self. And so by taking on the Dark Side, we are required to increasingly differentiate from the ego-based self, which is fodder for the Dark Side.

Let's look at an example. If we go through a major economic recession and I lose my job, I can easily become depressed, and then I will become lunch. But if I am aware of that weakness, I can release the need to earn money in order to feel my value, and I can start identifying my value as being based on my inner being. Now I am learning to transcend the domination of the ego and connect to myself. Similarly, if I go through a divorce, I can stop the downward spiral of anger and self-pity by developing a relationship with myself, with others, and with The Source. If I go through severe illness and become disabled, I have to start developing a joyous connection with my inner life.

499

Now this is getting interesting. When we identify our cracks and start to heal them, The Dark Side has taught us that the ego is making us vulnerable. It is simultaneously forcing us to connect to ourselves. Seen in this light, the Dark Side is actually our friend. It forces us to more effectively develop our awareness of the Dark Side and its secrets. It forces us to more consciously deal with our egos and the way they dominate us. It forces us to practice Becoming Integrated, so we won't be lunch. And it forces us to fight for the inner self that many of us may have only glimpsed. The Dark Side is sowing the seeds of our power to transcend its domination.

How have we benefited from the Dark Side?

1. Can I think of times of great stress?
2. Did I become lunch?
3. Was I identifying with the ego?
4. Was I able to transcend the ego's domination?
5. Did I begin to connect to myself?

Every time we fight for ourselves, we increase the power of our energy field. Every time we increase the power of our energy field, we increase our capacity to deal effectively with the Dark Side and the ego. And every time we increase our capacity to deal effectively with the Dark Side and the ego, we develop the capacity and skills to help others do the same.

So, hey, look at what's happening. Earlier in this chapter, we saw that the Dark Side ruled the planet because we let it. But just as the Dark Side can grow exponentially, so can we. If we use the Dark Side to become more conscious and heal the cracks within us, it is we who grow exponentially instead. And as we grow exponentially, there's less of us for the Dark Side to lunch on. Wow, the Dark Side starts to get desperate. It screams to the ego, "Do not forsake me." But if we've been working on confronting the domination of the ego, we recognize the game, and we are no longer confused.

Let's identify some situations where we have accomplished that kind of growth.

1. Can I identify times of stress when I grew exponentially?
2. How did that feel?
3. Did that help me to keep growing in other ways?

Do not be fooled. None of this is quick, and none of this is easy. Between the ego and the Dark Side, we can get into some very dark holes, filled with desperation, rage, or anxiety. But if we keep remembering the sixth dirty secret of the Dark Side, **that The Source uses the Dark Side to promote evolution,** we will continue to focus on healing the cracks and evolving.

We cannot judge our progress by how often we fail, by how often we fall back into destructive addictive patterns of body, mind, or spirit. We must remember that we are in the midst of a cosmic struggle to raise ourselves above the clouds, and we need to keep trying.

Tool: How We Turn the Tables on the Dark Side

This tool takes off from a tool we learned earlier. When we are feeling overwhelmed and full of despair, that's probably a clue that we're in the grip of the Dark Side. In these moments, let's point our second and third finger to some imaginary energy field in front of us, and send it chi, life force energy. Just intending to send chi automatically connects us to The Source, and our connection to The Source decreases our vulnerability to the Dark Side.

Once we feel the power of our connection to The Source and our fingers are pointed forward, we think about the arena of life in which we feel blocked or defeated. We challenge ourselves not to throw in the towel, we send the Dark Side chi, and we say out loud, if possible:

"I know you're trying to make me feel [something appropriate], but I [again, whatever is appropriate], and I'm not going to let you stop me." There it is in a nutshell: fighting for ourselves.

Let me give you an example. Writing this chapter has been very tough. I don't feel very inspired, I'm tired, I have a headache, I feel like it's going on forever, and I think it has no value. Do you think the Dark Side may be enjoying this moment? So I point my two fingers forward, connect to The Source, send chi to the Dark Side, and say, "I know you're trying to make me feel that I'll never be able to help people overcome the domination of the Dark Side, but I will and I already have, and I'm not going to let you stop me."

This is a great way to confront the domination of the Dark Side and the ego and to fight for ourselves. As we send the Dark Side chi, we are filled with the higher vibrational energies that empower us. When we use this tool, we feel larger than the Dark Side, because we are taking command of our own energy and channeling The Source. We feel much more courageous, determined and hopeful.

One more reminder. The Dark Side is a constellation of energy, and we are part of a collective consciousness, as we have been learning. So we should not expect perfection from ourselves when the collective is still feeding the Dark Side. In fact, expecting perfection leads to stress and ultimately to self-loathing and defeat. Self-judgment and self-loathing are tricks of the Dark Side. The Dark Side is making us feel negatively toward ourselves by blaming us for not overcoming the domination of the Dark Side.

It is difficult to not be impacted by negative energies when we are surrounded by people who are. Don't you think it a little unrealistic to expect us to be the only human beings on the planet who are not dominated by either the ego or the Dark Side? This is not an excuse for throwing in the towel, but it is a call for us to embrace reality and to have patience and compassion.

And the corollary is true, as well. The collective energy can be our strength, as well as our weakness. Every time we confront the domination of the Dark Side, we are joining with the efforts of others, and as we join together, we become the collective that will heal the collective cracks in the collective energy field called the human race.

And if we do, we will evolve. I guarantee it.

7. The Dark Side needs us to fight for ourselves, so that it can evolve into consciousness and return to The Source.

When we fight for ourselves, when we strengthen our energy fields, when we become integrated, we have fewer cracks, and we are less and less vulnerable to the Dark Side. We become less and less available to feed negative energy. So what happens then? Just like us, just like the ego, when faced with extinction, The Dark Side is forced to evolve or die.

We can speed up the Dark Side's evolution by refusing to feed it, and we also speed it by sending the Dark Side chi. Remember, the Dark Side is simply the constellation of negative energies, and negative energies are energies that have no connection to life force. That's what makes them negative. So every time we send chi to the Dark Side, we are giving it the very universal life force it is seeking through living off us.

Forced to give up feeding on us, impacted by the chi that we send to empower it, negative energy can return to The Source and claim its birthright to its own life force energy. If it doesn't, it will die, and won't most forms of consciousness choose evolution over death?

And what does the Dark Side evolve into? How could it still stay in existence, but as a real energy, connected to the divine? By becoming consciousness, of course. Think of it. The purpose of the Dark Side is to show us our weaknesses and inspire us to heal. But if we had consciousness, we wouldn't need the Dark Side to show us our weaknesses and help us transform. We could look at the vase and see the cracks without needing ink to seep through. We could use awareness to evaluate the holes in the dam, instead of waiting until the dam breaks and the population drowns. We could use our common sense to interrupt the urge toward promiscuity, instead of waiting until we have a sexually transmitted disease or unwanted children. We could use consciousness to evaluate when we need to sleep, instead of waiting until the caffeine wears off. We could use our experience and awareness to avoid the pain inflicted on ourselves and others by being dominated by Dark Side energies and allowing ourselves to be hurt or to hurt others.

The evolution of the Dark Side is like all evolution. It has no end point; and it has no starting point. It is a process of becoming, not a state of being. It is simultaneous with our own evolution. As we use consciousness, rather than pain, to evolve, the Dark Side has served its purpose, and it can transform into the consciousness that allows us to not need the Dark Side anymore.

Now have you noticed something very striking about the evolution of the Dark Side? It is evolving toward becoming consciousness itself. Isn't that exactly the same thing that we noticed about the ego?

Return to "Ego, Instinct & Evolution" one more time, and also review the end of Platform Six on Becoming Integrated. The ego starts as a by-product of evolution; it is the sense of "me" as an individual, separate from the whole. Its job is to bring us awareness of our separate selves, so that we can take care of our separate selves. But, unfortunately, the ego comes into being as an infantile energy, with limited vision and me-based goals; it develops into a self-protective mechanism that ultimately destroys us. It gets stuck in the stage of separation and forgets the Oneness.

But the ego can evolve, and it must. If we die, it dies, so it has an interest in our evolution and survival. The ego has the choice: It can self-destruct, or it can shift from the limited perception that wellbeing is based on the "I" perspective and learn that our wellbeing requires the cosmic perspective. Cosmic consciousness is not only the point to which we are all evolving—we, the ego, the Dark Side, all consciousness. It is the requirement for survival.

Aren't we already making this shift? Have we not moved through this book to a greater awareness of Oneness with ourselves and with one another (Platform One)? Haven't we called upon ourselves to differentiate, rather than separate (Platform Two)? Haven't we called upon ourselves to Become Co-Creative and Mutually Supportive (Platforms Three and Four)? Did we not call on the ego to evolve into consciousness through our Becoming Self-Aware, Integrated, and Accountable (Platforms Five, Six, and Seven)? Could we have done all this without the ego? Isn't it actually working with us, albeit reluctantly?

Back in the beginning of the book, we called upon the ego to evolve from the narrow sense of self to the realization that we find ourselves only in the Oneness. We asked the ego to be born again, first as a "no," and then as a "yes." We trusted that it was in its evolutionary trajectory to transform into consciousness, to enter the "yes" universe as the ego twice born.

Now we're saying that the Dark Side also can transform into consciousness, and by doing so it has fulfilled its mission and its destiny. The Dark Side and the ego are not the same. The Dark Side has used the ego to dominate us, and the ego has been aligned with the Dark Side to protect us in narrow and self-destructive ways.

But they can both be liberated, as can we. And we can all do it together.

Becoming Accountable: Regulating the Flow of Our Energy

Understanding all this, now we are ready to practice Becoming Accountable. In the first two stages of this chapter, we became aware of our accountability to one another for the damage we cause, and we became willing to make amends. But Becoming Accountable is not just about seeing our havoc and making amends. It's about having enough inner stability and integration so that we are not swept up by the emotions and forces that take us out of integrity. It's about being able to stand up to the domination of the ego and the Dark Side.

This has been the purpose of the third stage of Becoming Accountable, the stage where we truly transform. Let's review some key points. What has blocked us from Becoming Accountable is the collusion between the ego and the Dark Side. We need the ego, but the ego is fear-based, and so it colludes with the Dark Side to find protection, because Dark Side energies appear powerful. Having unleashed the power of the Dark Side, we are out of control, and then we are lunch. We all lose, because the ego sees its destructiveness, but can't stop itself. We see our destructiveness, but can't stop ourselves. And the Dark Side stays desperate and hungry for life force, but can't find its way home.

But now we know the rules, so that we can play the game so that we all win. We realize that we are essentially energy beings, and we have the power and responsibility to regulate the flow of that energy. We can do it only by confronting the domination of our egos and fighting for ourselves. And we can accomplish this by confronting the collusion between the ego and the Dark Side.

Freed from the collusion between the ego and the Dark Side, we can start achieving degrees of self-mastery. And by self-mastery, I do not mean self-control, which requires us to struggle to dominate our out-of-control energies. And by self-mastery, I don't mean the appearance of calm, which transpires while we're gritting our teeth, trying to suppress our natural reactivity.

By self-mastery, I mean the achievement of the state of freedom in which we are no longer run by unconscious motivations, and where we trust ourselves enough to be spontaneous and to Become Becoming, which I will discuss in future chapters. By practicing the platforms of Becoming Self-Aware, Integrated, and Accountable, we continuously release programmed reactions and responses. No longer dominated by our fears, needs and survival instincts, confronting the domination of the ego and the Dark Side, we have enough presence, consciousness and self-mastery to choose our responses, attitudes, and behaviors.

In this third stage of Becoming Accountable, we are starting to transform. Some of us are still skeptical. We realize that we will never truly regulate the flow of our energy if we are constantly unbalanced by every emotion, thought, and circumstance; if we are not integrated, but rather are still dominated by aspects of ourselves. We realize that we will never truly be able to regulate the flow of our energy if our egos create feelings of fear, anger, and separateness. We realize that we will never be able to regulate the flow of our energy if we are dominated by the Dark Side, individually and collectively.

We realize all this, but can we change, and can we do it now? Can we release the fear that the Dark Side creates, fear that causes our egos to automatically jump in to protect us by dominating and making us stupid? And can we release the fear that the ego creates to control us, which is the open wound into which the Dark Side jumps? Can we actually break the unholy alliance between the ego and the Dark Side, thereby liberating both them and us?

Yes, we can, and yes, we will, because now we realize that both the ego and the Dark Side have the potential to evolve into consciousness, and if we support that holy alliance, we will become ourselves. How do we support that alliance?

As we have said before, part of the answer is simply to retrain the ego. After all, it came into being at our conception, and it got a hold of us at a young age. The ego is childish and needs support. We cannot allow it to run the show anymore, and we need to stop its shenanigans. We aren't meant to kill the ego, because it is part of us and because trying to kill it will cause it to react even more defensively. We are meant to support it to evolve, so it is no longer the ego as we have known it. We support the ego to evolve by constantly remembering to practice all our platforms, by doing whatever practices support us to be centered, clear, and connected to divine energy, and by identifying that our true joy and safety come from our being rational, by practicing self-awareness, and by supporting the whole. And we support the ego's evolution by giving it and us as many experiences of Oneness as we can, so that we have a new template of what is possible.

The ego may be immature, but it is not entirely stupid, if given a chance. It is a product of conditioning, just as are we, and it can be reprogrammed, as can we. And we are learning how to do that reprogramming. We are learning that we have to support the whole for us to thrive. We are realizing that just as you can't clean the air over one house in Los Angeles, we cannot be the only happy, sane person in a world of polluted consciousness. In fact, we wouldn't want to be.[29] No, our egos can learn that we are one and that it is smarter and more gratifying to support everyone to thrive than to try to win a victory for ourselves and in the process lose the whole.

Yes, the ego can learn. It can finally figure out that we are safer, as well as happier, when others are happy, too, and that a world filled with functional people is a lot more productive and fun to live in than a world filled with hungry, impoverished, and sick people. Yes, the ego can learn. It can actually experience that we find ourselves in the Oneness, that we are perfectly capable of feeling our individuality without separating, and that we long for a world of co-creation and mutual support. Yes, the ego can learn that it can feel competent and proud of its ability to provide consciousness and self-awareness to us at every step of our lives, and that it can achieve this only in a state of calm and neutrality it has never known before.

Let's now consider some questions with this new perspective about the ego.

1. Can we recognize moments when we felt the joy of experiencing ourselves as individuals connecting to the Oneness?
2. Can we imagine that our egos felt the joy, too?

And the Dark Side can transform, too. It can connect to its longing to be freed from the shame and self-loathing that plague it. It can find its purpose in bringing us the consciousness that elevates, rather than destroys us. It can return to The Source from which it came, give up its parasitical role, be filled with life force and transmute into energies that support us all.

This is the evolutionary moment when we all rise above the clouds, where it's not raining, and where the fight is over because we have all won, because we are all one.

Which leads us to the next part of our book, Partnering with the Process of Living: Becoming Not-Knowing and Becoming Becoming. But

---

[29] I am reminded of the specter of nuclear holocaust that was part of the education of my generation. Many of us asked: Even if we could be saved by dropping into the one bomb shelter, who would want to survive if we were to come out onto an environment of nuclear fallout, desertification, and empty landscapes, bereft of life and people?

before we go there, there is one very important series of conversations that need to take place.

A CONVERSATION BETWEEN THE EGO AND THE DARK SIDE, WITH AMENDS BETWEEN HUMANITY AND THE EGO

Part Three of our program is about relaxing into the process of living itself, which we accomplish with the final two platforms: Becoming Not-Knowing and Becoming Becoming. But before we can go on, we need to allow for a historic moment: A Conversation between the Ego and the Dark Side.

As we saw in Platform Seven: Becoming Accountable, there was a lot of collusion between the ego and the Dark Side, but there is also a potential harmony in their possible evolution into consciousness. Let's listen in to their conversation.

For those of you who feel an inner resonance with the content of these pages, feel yourselves as part of the conversation. For those of you who find strange even the idea of such dialogues, consider the following as metaphor. And please read the following very slowly so that you can digest each part. Thank you.

The Ego Speaks to the Dark Side

I have been a slave to you for many years, perhaps forever. Ever since I was born, I aligned myself with you for the strength you seemed to have. Burdened with the responsibility of taking care of each being and each aspect of consciousness, I felt unprepared to do my job well. I felt inadequate to the task of protecting all those whose guardian I felt myself to be, and so I sought a big brother, and that was you.

Perhaps I was confused about my job. Born when the Oneness exploded into a multitude of fragments, I was meant to be awareness of individual existence. But just as a child is more vulnerable alone than it is with its family, each and every individual is more vulnerable when it is separated from, rather than connected to, the whole. So it is understandable that I became immediately and acutely aware of the fragility of each individual now struggling for its survival, and I, the ego, thought of myself as fully responsible for protecting it. Young myself—and remember I come into being in infancy—lacking resources and power, I started to fight and bluster and to look for a big brother to help me. And there you were, the Dark Side, just like my twin, manifesting many of the same traits and seeming like my natural ally.

Now I feel duped. You, the Dark Side, never had my interests at heart; nor did you care about the interests of the beings I felt obliged to protect. I see now from Platform Seven that you are a parasite and live off all of us, turning us against one another to feed your own existence.

I also see now that while I sincerely intended to protect my wards, you never had the intention of protecting anyone but yourself. In fact you are the very force from which everything and everyone needs protection. I feel stupid, ashamed, and guilty for having bonded with you and having created havoc on the earth. In Platform Six: Becoming Integrated, I saw myself in black and white. I have been a very negative force on this planet, and I don't have to be. I'm only negative because I have been aligned with you. I break that alliance now.

And I owe an amends to humanity.

The Ego Makes Amends to Humanity

I realize now that I have aligned myself with the Dark Side. Humanity, I realize now that instead of helping us become aware of the limitations of our instinctive behaviors and self-centered attitudes, instead of helping us become aware that our greatest happiness comes only from experiencing ourselves as part of the Oneness, instead of realizing that our true safety comes from our Oneness, I fed the separation and fear that kept our negative, fear-based behaviors and attitudes alive. This kept us weak and self-destructive. And once I had aligned with the Dark Side, once I had made this terrible mistake, I felt defensive and stupid, so I justified the first mistake with millennia of excuses. Steeped in denial and self-justification, I had to continue my collusion, which only strengthened the Dark Side and made me a negative force on this earth.

And how that hurt you, humanity, is that you became locked in a never-ending dance with the Dark Side. You could not let go of the Dark Side because it was connected to me, your "protective" ego, and you had to have me, because the Dark Side convinced you that if you let go of me, you would die, because there would be nothing else to protect you. In fact, the Dark Side has even tried to convince you that consciousness is dangerous. Desperate to maintain my own survival, I fed the myth that you couldn't live without me, and I attacked you when you tried to become conscious and confront my domination, all of which kept you in pain, shame, anger, despair, delusion and denial.

And even though I couldn't have done any better at the time, I need to ask you to forgive me. Will you forgive me?

Humanity Makes Amends to the Ego

Wow, yes, I forgive you. And I realize now that I have used you for the wrong purpose. I have relied on you, instead of consciousness, ever since I have been on this planet, which kept you trying to do a job that was not yours and for which you were never suited. I have needed to develop consciousness to understand how the world operates, and I have needed consciousness to properly take care of myself and the whole. Instead, I have avoided consciousness and let you do all the work. Then when I saw your destructiveness, I blamed you instead of myself for my lack of awareness and the havoc it caused.

And how that hurt you is that it has kept you under constant stress, and it has created feelings of inadequacy in you, as you were thrust into a job that you were not designed for, the job of being my sole protector. Then you felt the need to constantly puff yourself up to cover your inadequacy. And since we were separate from one another, because I wasn't truly supporting you to do your limited job, you had nowhere to go for support but the Dark Side, which has caused you incredible shame, because you know how destructive it is. The shame of your alliance with the Dark Side has kept you oppressed and resistant, terrified at the thought of being exposed as being the cause of so much damage. Feeling ashamed has, in turn, made it nearly impossible for you to feel your own self-love or to reach out for support from us or the heavens, and it has kept you alone, isolated, and stunted in your growth.

And even though I couldn't have done any better at the time, I need to ask you to forgive me. Will you forgive me?

The Ego Responds

Yes, I forgive you, and I thank you and feel much better. In fact, I think I feel ready to connect to the Oneness and gain the strength to evolve. I think I can take my place as a part of you, integrated and in balance. I want to grow into my true older brother and become the self-aware aspect of consciousness itself.

The Ego Continues Its Conversation with the Dark Side

But first I need to go back and address the Dark Side again. Dark Side, you and I have always seemed essentially the same. I was born of separation, cut off from the Oneness, stuck in perpetual loneliness, isolation, fragmentation and fear. And you were too. Some see you as the fallen angel, who broke from God. Some see you in psychological terms, caused by mental illness or trauma. However we see you, you came into existence through separation, too.

Even though you have not replied to a word I have said here so far, I extend my hand to you now, and I ask you to join with me to heal ourselves and our world, to use our power to overcome the fragmentation that is killing the earth and ultimately will kill us. I can foresee a better future for us both.

Will you join me?

The Dark Side's Response

At first there is no reply. Instead, there is a long pause in the conversation, as the Dark Side fights within itself. Some energies are saying yay, some nay to the possibility of reconnecting with The Source and evolving into something else. No wonder. It's scary to consider completely giving up form and identity, to go from being the epitome of negative energy to being a consciousness imbued with life force, but some on the Dark Side are weary of their parasitical existence and see hope for the future.

The battle within the Dark Side rages. Negativity abounds, anger explodes, and pent-up hostilities find voice. This is the true Armageddon: not the fight between darkness and light, but the fight within the Dark Side itself as to whether or not to rejoin The Source, to rise with us above the clouds to the dimension where there is no darkness or light; there is only Oneness.

After the inner battle, the Dark Side lies flattened in devastation. And a single weak voice is heard: "Evolving into consciousness, reconnecting to The Source? Maybe it's not such a bad idea, but what would that look like?"

PART 3

Partnering with the Process of Living
The Final Two Platforms

A FEW COMMENTS TO
INTRODUCE OUR NEXT
SECTION

So where does that leave us? Has the ego really evolved? Has it truly broken its pact with the Dark Side? Is the Dark Side going to change? Stay tuned. In the meantime, we have a lot of work of our own to do.

Let's review where we've come. In Part One of our platforms, we changed our relationship with others from alienation to partnership. We dealt with our alienation from one another by focusing on our connection, which allowed us to partner with others in a way that is co-creative and mutually supportive. In Part Two of our platforms, we changed our relationship to ourselves from alienation to partnership. We became self-aware and came to know ourselves in a compassionate way: We stopped being afraid to look at ourselves honestly; we worked toward becoming integrated and faced our accountability; we recognized the difficulty of becoming truly accountable unless we overcame the domination of the Dark Side, which has been running us through our egos; and we took steps to free ourselves from that domination. Through becoming real with ourselves, we have experienced new intimacy with ourselves. Through gaining some mastery over our behavior, we have started to gain real self-respect, which opens the door to genuine love for ourselves.

Isn't that enough? Nope. Now we are ready to change our relationship to the process of living itself. Who can deny that life on this planet is tough, not only because of challenging external circumstances, but also because of our own crazy thinking and self-destructive behaviors? How many of us have fought reality and been filled with stress and resentment?

How many of us have not fought reality and felt defeated instead? Neither of these stances is relaxing. Neither is productive. Neither is partnering.

How do we partner with life? By partnering with the process of living. And how do we do that? We have to face reality. We have to learn how to live with it. We have to learn to co-create with it. We have to learn how to navigate through it and grow. And we need to learn to tap the awesome power of higher consciousness that can support us through it all.

Living is not a state of existence; it's a process; it's the co-creative dance with the universe. We are confronted with challenges, and we find our way to meet those challenges with more or less grace. We find a way to turn every defeat into the fertilizer of new growth. We find a way to turn shame into awareness and anger into positive action. We find a way to gather the strength and support to change.

So let's find a way to relax into the process of living. Let's figure out how to neither fight it nor surrender to it, but to evolve through it. Let's learn to partner not just with our lives but with the process of living itself.

A voice from higher consciousness once said to me: "Beth, you had better start loving the process, because that's all there is. Everything is a transition to the next transition." Now that's a mouthful. How the heck are we going to start accepting and embracing the process of living when it's so darn challenging to live with the curve balls the universe keeps sending our way?

Turn the page, and let's learn how.

PLATFORM EIGHT

Becoming Not-Knowing
Becoming Available to Higher
Consciousness

In Chapter One of this book I suggested we are constantly trying to change our feeling state instead of dealing with reality. In Chapter Four, I discussed addictions and how they self-perpetuate, because as we use the addictive behavior to relieve a certain stress, the addictions themselves cause more of the feelings they are meant to fix.

The same concepts apply to our relationship to knowing. It's an addiction. We use knowing as a way of dealing with some kind of stress, but the pretending we know creates new stress. And so a major block to relaxing into the process of living is the belief that we already "know" what is and what is supposed to be.

Let's be honest about a few points.

- We are afraid to sit with the unknown and unknowable, because it feels stressful.
- To relieve that stress, we pretend we know, but are often completely or at least partially misguided. Has that resolved our stress? No. Because we still feel the need to know, we know that we don't, and yet have to pretend to ourselves and others that we do, all the time realizing that our ignorance could cause disastrous mistakes. So actually we have compounded our stress, which we try to alleviate by pretending that we know.
- Plus we frequently think we know how things should be, which creates unrealistic expectations of ourselves and others, and then we struggle to make reality fit our preconceptions, which also creates needless stress.

This section of our book is about relaxing into the process of living. How can we partner with life when we've already decided what life should be? How can we be available to higher consciousness, when we think we already know what is and should be? How can we relax into the process of living, when we're trying to dominate life itself?

When we started this book, we talked about letting go of needless fear, needless pain and needless stress. Now we're going to take a big step toward that level of wellbeing. We're going to start practicing Platform Eight: Becoming Not-Knowing. In this chapter we are going to examine the nature of beliefs, agendas, goals and purposes and see when they are supporting us and when they are not. And then we are going to embrace the Path of Not-Knowing.

Taking these steps will bring us into real partnership with life and open the door to higher consciousness, inspiration and real creativity.

WHAT IS BECOMING NOT-KNOWING?

Becoming Not-Knowing is the process of releasing ourselves from the need to know or pretend we do, becoming empty of agendas and limitations, and living moment by moment in the Not-Knowing and the discovery, guided by higher consciousness.

What is Not-Knowing and how do we do it? Let's examine each section of this platform in turn, and we'll discover that it's not beyond our reach. First, we'll look at the need to know and the function of beliefs and agendas; then, we'll see how to release ourselves from them; then, we'll talk a bit about being available to higher consciousness. But first I need to speak about higher consciousness itself. We have referred to it many times in this book, but now let's examine it more deeply. What is it?

What Is Higher Consciousness?

Higher consciousness is simultaneously an intelligence greater than ours and a vibrational energy on a level higher than ours. Some call it inspiration, wisdom, God, The Source (as I often do), divine intelligence, the Oneness, the Great Spirit, a higher power; there are many names that refer to the same reality. Higher consciousness is not religious concept, although it shows up in many religions; it is an acknowledgement of a level of awareness and power that is greater than our own.

It comes to us in the silence when our egos are quiet. It is the inner knowing that surprises us with its wisdom. It is that sudden inspiration; it's what tells us that we left our keys in the dryer, or it pops into our heads as a brilliant solution, when we've been puzzled and see no way out. It is the voice we hear in the Oneness.

As I mentioned earlier, higher consciousness is consciousness that is higher than ours in two ways. First: As we mentioned before, it soars like an eagle, seeing the big picture, while we are crawling around like ants, stuck in our narrow perspective. And second: Consciousness is vibrational, and higher consciousness is a field of vibrational energy that cannot be replicated by humans but which can sometimes be experienced by us. These vibrational energies are beneficial; they empower us in a non-egoic way and fill us with a sense of wellbeing. They make us feel whole, connected to everything, and at the same time very much ourselves and very much alive.

When we experience an influx of beneficial energies from The Source or higher realms, we are amazed by the way we feel. Calm, peaceful, energized, optimistic, joyful, neutral. Where do these feelings come from? They come from our access to a different dimension, connected, as it were, to a realm of existence above the clouds, as we described in the past chapter; a realm above the ego and the Dark Side.

You may wonder: Isn't this just escape? Escape into a fantasy realm far from reality? On the contrary. Reality is larger than our individual limited perspective. It is not just what we see. It is what we see and what we don't see. So to be in reality, we need to be open to all that we don't see, including other-dimensional vibrational energies that expand us.

Do higher vibrational energies exist? Yes. I guarantee it. And if you were sitting with me in a group, you would feel them, too, because people like me can help you reach that state of consciousness, even if you can't access it yourself. However, to some degree, we have all at least glimpsed it. For some, the experience may have been very limited. It could have been just a calm moment in nature or when we have felt loved. For some of us, the experience will have been more powerful and consistent. When we are there, we can feel as though we are vibrating and that we are filled with calm, or joy, or even ecstasy, simply being part of the Oneness. And for some of us, the experience lies somewhere between. Whichever experience you have had, we can all further cultivate our access to higher consciousness.

One way we cultivate our connection to higher consciousness is by practicing every platform in this book. Gosh, that doesn't sound like suddenly being lifted into higher vibrational realms. It isn't. But doing the foundational work is the prerequisite for us to achieve a solid, grounded connection to the Oneness. Otherwise, we might have fantastic energy experiences, but we may not be able to utilize them for transformation. In fact, they might actually unbalance us and/or come to us randomly, rather than consistently.

Let me make one more point here about experiencing Oneness. Experiencing Oneness, or higher consciousness, is not an artificially induced experience related to drugs or external stimuli, though it can be supported by meditation, listening to music, doing movement, chanting, or being in a powerful natural setting, for example. The vibrational energy of Oneness is something we may have a gift for, something we may have had as children, or it can come to us suddenly. But either way, access to it is always strengthened by clean living, thinking and dedication to consciousness and service.

Through practicing Platform Eight: Becoming Not-Knowing, we eliminate a ton of blocks to our connection to the vibrational energy of Oneness. By eliminating these blocks, we become more open to experiencing those states of consciousness available to us when we are no longer dominated by our egos but are instead guided by higher consciousness. So while practicing these platforms does not guarantee your entry into higher vibrational states, it does prepare you for a lifetime of solid connection and opens you for the experience.

Let's take a moment to consider our own experiences with higher consciousness.

1. Have you ever experienced inspiration?
2. Have you ever experienced an inner voice that seems to know more than you do?
3. Have you ever experienced a lightness of being, where you felt different, happy, and calm?
4. Have you ever experienced a column of energy penetrating you or a feeling that you were vibrating, when there was no physical explanation?
5. Are these experiences worth working for?

So, let's proceed to Platform Eight, and let's release the agendas and beliefs that block us from higher consciousness, higher both in terms of our perspective and vibrational energy. Let's start with beliefs.

BELIEFS

Beliefs are just beliefs. They are not truths. When they support the highest good of all, we can keep them. When they stop supporting us and stop being useful, we need to let them go.

Introduction

When we say that we know something, of course, we really mean that we believe something is true. We cannot know the truth, which I'll discuss a bit later. But we do have a lot of beliefs and opinions. For the purpose of this chapter, I won't distinguish between beliefs and opinions, although they are slightly different.

We all want to know things, and we want other people to know that we know. What is it about believing we know that's so important to us humans? Let's look at a couple of factors. First, it's scary to live in a world where we don't understand problems and how to fix them. If we're hungry and don't know how to satisfy our hunger, we could starve. And second, it's scary to live in a world where other people might realize that we don't know. I will discuss both of these fears in some depth. But let's start with the second fear: that people will realize we don't know.

Why do we need people to know that we "know?" Let's laugh together at this one. How many times has a friend related an event to you, and your first comment was, "Didn't I tell you that he was no good, your partner is cheating, you were going to get that promotion, Obama was going to win the election, that particular plumber was incompetent, you would enjoy that movie?"

Here your friend is suffering, or ecstatic, or having some realization, and your first thought is to remind him or her that you said this was going to happen. It's embarrassing to admit how often I've done this. Haven't you? And isn't it also embarrassing to admit that we have also indulged in ridiculous attitudes of superiority through letting someone know that we know something they don't, such as when we announce, with a slightly haughty tone of voice, "You mean, you didn't know that John is gay, Mary's pregnant, Harry's an alcoholic, Macy's is offering free shipping on all kitchen items this year?"

We are obsessed by the need to be expert in something and to make sure everyone else knows that we are. Sometimes we lecture people about some area of our supposed expertise, whether or not they have any interest. Sometimes we talk over others to make sure that they know that we know before they even have a chance to let us know that they know. And so on. Obviously, we must feel some need to know and to make sure that others know that we know. This need is clearly driven by the ego in its never-ending quest to protect us.

WHERE DOES THE NEED TO APPEAR TO KNOW COME FROM?

Giving Ourselves Power

Appearing to know something gives us a sense of power, control, or value. Where did we learn that? Let's look a minute at how not knowing can deprive us of control, or at least seem to be the source of our powerlessness. When we are children, we don't know much, and those who know or who pretend to know make the decisions that impact our lives and the lives of all around us. We have no control; they have the power. As teenagers, we want to be independent—to drive and to make decisions about whom we date, what we smoke, or how to live. So we try to convince ourselves and everyone else that we know enough to make these decisions. Of course, we know how ignorant we are, so we are often bluffing even ourselves, which makes us even more defensive and attached to pretending we know. From the time of our youth, then, we discover that if we are honest about our capacities, or if others know we don't know, we will have no control over our lives, and others will have power over us.

The need to appear that we know comes from other early experiences, as well. If we come from a family where our parents are severely dysfunctional, we may have been on our own way too early in our lives. Feeling unprotected, we were afraid we would be dominated or exploited by those outside our families. We felt scared in the world and became entrenched in proving to others that we know, so that they could not exploit us. While our situation is opposite to that of the protected child above, the outcome is the same. We pretend we know when we don't.

Let's ask ourselves some questions about power and the appearance of knowing.

1. Can I think of a time when the people around me seemed to know more and had more power than I did?
2. Did I try to pretend that I knew more than I did?
3. Did I grow up in a family with parents who did not protect me?
4. Who was I afraid of?
5. Did this fear lead me to pretend I knew?
6. Did I ever lie or pretend I knew what I was doing in my personal life?
7. What was the result?

As we become adults, we feel we must continue to bluff. Especially if we are unconsciously trying to prove something to our controlling parents, we continue to pretend that we know how to run our lives.

To sum up this point, we grow up feeling the need to prove that we know, even when we don't. Appearing to know seems to give us power or control, so we pretend, pretend, pretend and cover up our fears, inadequacies, and the negative consequences of our foolish choices. There's the ego, caring more about how things look than how things are.

Giving Ourselves Value

Looking as though we know seems to also give us value, and this feels crucial because if we have no value, we may not be employed, be part of the tribe or survive. Back to the ego and that old survival instinct. We have experience with this, too. At school or at home, we may have been shamed for not knowing something either by the teachers or other kids; or we may have been praised and valued for knowing how to do something. Our place in the pecking order of society depends on our value, and that is often linked to knowing.

By the way, sometimes looking less smart is the better ego strategy. If we want to bond with the teacher, we will try to look smart, because our performance makes the teacher feel good about him—or herself. If we prefer bonding with the kids, we might not want to look too smart, because that will make the other kids feel dumb, and they won't want us in the club anymore.

Looking like we know is confused with intelligence, which can also give us value. If our parents believe that their knowing something made them smarter and somehow better than each other or other people, we will definitely try to look like we know in order to feel smart, because that's what we saw modeled.

The belief that knowing gives value and power leads us into the automatic, silly behavior of wanting to seem like we know, even when we don't, or proving we know, even when it's not important. Haven't we ever competed with a child to prove that we knew better than they? And haven't we ever put down other people who don't "know" how to dress, speak well, behave in a certain context, understand our social or cultural norms, or do their job?

Pretending we know can also give us economic value. We may not know what we're doing or have all the answers, but we want to bluff. Who's going to hire us to do a job, whether it's as a welder, a CEO, or a psychologist, unless the employer believes we know how to do the job, even if we can't? Sometimes we are clearly an apprentice, and what a relief that is, even though the pay may be low. As an apprentice, nobody expects us to know right away, which feels relaxing. But we feel that we'd better learn fast, or at least appear to learn fast, or we may be fired or be thought of as stupid.

This need to prove that we know can get us in a lot of trouble when we don't, and the refusal to admit our ignorance blocks us from asking for the help we need, so that we could truly learn and then actually know. How ironic.

Let's look at some of our experiences with the connection between value and appearing to know.

1. Have I judged other people for not knowing, in order to feel superior?
2. How did I show it?
3. Was I rewarded for knowing or not knowing, and by whom?
4. Have I ever put anyone down for not knowing something?
5. Did I ever lie or pretend in order to get a job or impress someone?
6. How did I feel?

What Is Our Fear of Not Knowing?

We've been talking about the need to appear as though we know. Let's address here the fear of actually not knowing.

Sometimes we're afraid of not knowing something immediate. If I don't know whether a house is well built, how can I judge whether or not it is a good investment? And if I make the wrong choice, I could lose my shirt and the respect of the people near me. If don't know how to do the job that I've been hired for, how long will it be before I'm out on my ear? If I don't know the answers to the test questions, I could fail the exam and lose my chance for a scholarship.

And then there's the fear associated with not knowing something that we can only discover in the future. How excruciating are the moments, weeks, or sometimes months when we don't know something, such as whether or not the tests will show cancer, or if our horse is going to win, or whether or not someone is attracted to us or just being friendly, or whether or not we will ever get pregnant, or whether or not we will gain parole. Not knowing the future may impact our ability to wisely navigate the present, and so the fear of not knowing is, in this case, understandable and grounded in reality. But most of the time, our discomfort with not knowing the future has less to do with having good information with which to proceed and more to do with fear of the unknown, the fear that we won't know how to handle the future when it comes. Let me explain this last point.

525

Most of us are terrified of the unknown because we are afraid of somehow being hurt, and we don't trust our ability to handle the pain. I'm afraid I'll lose money, and, if I do, my wife will leave me or humiliate me, we'll live in a dangerous neighborhood, where I won't know how to protect myself and the children, the kids will think I'm a bad father, and I won't know how to regain my self-esteem. If we had more faith in ourselves and in one another, faith that we could handle whatever came, we would not be so afraid of the unknown. We'll talk about this much more in Platform Nine: Becoming Becoming, where we discover why we can't know how to handle a situation that hasn't happened yet.

But whether we're talking about current reality or the future, the joke is that we know very little, regardless of wishing otherwise. Ask a bunch of experts and see how often they agree, and even if they agree, how often are they right? What about all those political gurus or the experts on the economy, who disagree with one another and sit around arguing, as though they knew? When they are proved wrong, how much do they have to rationalize or even deny that they were mistaken?

Because we're terrified of the unknown, we really want somebody to know, even if it's not us. We have put unreasonable faith and pressure on doctors, whom we expect to fix the very complex system of the human body, despite how little they know. In the past, most doctors have tried to meet that expectation without admitting their limitations, but as our culture has changed, the medical profession has become more open to acknowledging its not knowing.

Of course, it's not just doctors. We have put unreasonable expectations on spiritual teachers and self-help gurus to give us answers. We have asked our relationship partners to give us reassurance that they know what to do when we don't, or that they agree with our plan when we think we do know. We have hoped desperately that our children will know things that we don't know even now and certainly didn't know at their age. We want them to know, so that we can sleep at night with the illusion that they are not going to do the stupid things that we did and do, such as engage in out-of-control behaviors. And how betrayed and disappointed have we felt when things did not turn out as promised by someone whose judgment we trusted?

And lastly, aren't we afraid that if we admitted how little we know, we would be paralyzed and do nothing at all? How could I ever get into a relationship, if I had to admit that I really don't know how to make it work in a way that is for everyone's highest good? How would any young couple have children unless they pretended they knew what it would be like and that they could handle it? How would any psychotherapist sit down with a patient, if they didn't at least tell themselves they had answers?

And how awful we feel when we have to admit that we were wrong and our advice hurt someone. And how often did we deny it, even when our error is patently obvious?

Let's take a moment to ask ourselves some questions about our experiences with not knowing.

1. Have I been in a situation in which I felt that I didn't know and needed to?
2. How did I feel and respond?
3. Have I ever felt that I would explode with anxiety when I didn't know what was going to happen?
4. What was the outcome I feared, and why was I afraid I couldn't handle it?
5. Did it happen?
6. Who have I wanted to be wiser than I am and in what areas?
7. How did I feel when they failed to deliver the expected result?
8. What have I done in my life where I pretended I knew something, and how did I respond to having been wrong?

Wow, not knowing leaves us feeling very vulnerable, and appearing to not know leaves us looking weak or stupid. No wonder we want to know or at least pretend we do!

What if People Want Us to Know?

Ooh, this is hard, too. Truthfully, we really know that we don't know, which makes us basically very insecure, which is why we want someone else to know. But what if the person who's supposed to know is us?

If our mate, child, or elderly parent feels insecure about something, they may pull on us to know what they don't. Our kids want us to know how to earn enough money to keep them supplied with whatever they want. Our mates want us to know how to get the creditors off our backs, or how to get the contractor to deliver as promised, or how to get the landlord to fix the toilet. If our mate can't fix a problem, he or she wants us to know how to fix it. Just get it done! We're supposed to know how to get the computer to work right, to get the internet to stop being flakey, and to make our mate just feel safe. Elderly parents feel helpless in the face of medical conundrums and insurance paperwork nightmares. They look to us, as though we're supposed to know how to handle all this without making a mistake.

Sometimes our partner feels incompetent about emotional issues. He or she tells us that we're so good with the children, we should know how to get them to improve their grades, stop hanging out with bad kids, and control their hormones. Or they expect us to know how to handle the addicted or mentally ill relative or neighbor whose behavior is endangering them or others.

In business situations, the same holds true. When we're the boss, our employees want us to know how to survive the recession, and our vendors want us to know how to generate enough business to pay them. And when we're the employee, our bosses want us to know how to meet impossible deadlines. Their motive is simple: "I don't know what to do. You fix the problem." And if we don't produce, we have somehow failed.

People look to us to save them. They expect us to handle every situation that they can't, and they get angry with us if we don't succeed, as though we were in fact born to do so. If we believe that we are supposed to know, we will fall for it. There's the ego again. Our egos want us to look good, so they set us up for incredible stress and shame. They drive us to take on jobs we can't do while pretending we can, because our egos tell us that it's dangerous to look weak and incompetent, get fired, or find out that somebody else could do a better job. So if someone wants us to know, we often buy into it.

Let's look at ourselves for a moment.

1. Where do I feel like I'm supposed to be the expert?
2. Who expects it?
3. Do I agree?
4. How do they react when I fail to deliver the expected results?
5. How do I feel when I fail?

The truth is we don't know much. We draw conclusions from limited evidence; we bluff; we learn from others who don't know either; and we try to comfort ourselves with reassurances that we do know and/or that everything will be all right.

Not Wanting Others to Know

Now we've seen that we want to know what we don't know, or at least pretend we do; we want others to know what we don't know; and others want us to know what none of us knows. Let's round out this discussion by acknowledging that sometimes we also don't want others to know what we don't know.

If our egos are invested in knowing what we don't know, we don't want anyone else to know either. Argh. Especially when we have vested ourselves with the mantle of knowing something, we hate it when someone has knowledge or an inspiration that we didn't have, especially when that someone is a person we have judged as stupid or ignorant on the subject. How do we feel when our father, whom we resent as having been an incompetent parent, shows us we're doing something stupid with our children?

Sometimes we feel threatened, as well as embarrassed. Let's say that I'm the chief financial officer of a small corporation, and the bookkeeper catches me in simple mistakes. Will he or she tell someone? Or if I'm a lower-level employee, how do I feel when a co-worker figures something out and brings the idea to the attention of the boss? Might he or she, therefore, get the promotion instead of me?

If we look deeply into ourselves, we'll probably notice that our reaction to someone else having a good idea depends on how our ego assesses the situation. Will the other person's knowing make me look weak and vulnerable? In this case, I will probably feel uncomfortable. Will the other person's knowing make me look good, as in when a student's brilliance is a positive reflection on me? In this case, I prefer them to look smart. Or will the other person's competence save the day, so that no one discovers that I didn't know? In this case, I thank my lucky stars!

Let's ask ourselves a few questions to see how we feel about others knowing.

1. How do I feel when someone knows something that I think I should?
2. Under what circumstances have I resented the person?

3. Under what circumstances have I pretended the person was wrong or refused to even consider that they're right?
4. Under what circumstances have I felt grateful that there's been a solution?

The most important thing for humanity is to solve our individual and collective problems, but when we're dominated by the ego, the most important thing for me is looking like I know. How do we get past this? By releasing the need to know, using our release tool from Platform Six: Becoming Integrated. I release the need to know x, y, or z, because I don't need to know x, y, or z, even though I think I do and want to.

When we confront the need to know, we are confronting the ego straight on. "If I had meant you to know everything, Beth, I wouldn't have had to create other people." [30] This zinger from God came to me from higher consciousness one day when I felt embarrassed because one of my clients looked smarter than I did, and it really stopped me in my tracks. It is so obvious that solving our collective problems is more important than me looking smart, but when my ego feels threatened, reality goes out the window.

The truth is that we are not supposed to know everything. That's why we're a collective.

Beliefs Are Just Beliefs; We Actually Don't Know Anything

What we think we know, we do not actually know anyway. All we can know is that we believe something is true or will work. In science, there is no knowing; instead we have hypotheses and theories, all of which can be overturned by new learning. The same is true with the rest of life. We have beliefs and opinions, which we should be willing to surrender when the evidence proves them wrong. But that's where we get in trouble. We tend to believe that our beliefs are reality, and we don't have a language for or a commitment to seeing every belief just as a belief, and we lack the commitment to allow every belief to be a hypothesis to be tested through ongoing experimentation.

Even in science, people develop ego attachments to certain theories, because they have become the experts in a certain approach, and their

---

[30] Green, Beth. *God's Little Aphorisms.* Lincoln: iUniverse, 2005.

position, status, and income may be knocked down by a new discovery. In the rest of life, we also become identified with certain beliefs and perspectives, and we hold to them rigidly, whether they are religious beliefs, political ideas, or opinions about one another and social behavior. My mother used to tell me that I shouldn't do something "because it isn't done." Done by whom? Why? There was the narrow mind telling me that what she and a few neighbors thought was the sum total of human wisdom. She would laugh at that now.

Whether in life or science, the same holds true: There is no total knowing, because our perspective is too narrow, our knowledge too shallow, and our vision too short. As we gain experience, our perspective changes, and so do our beliefs, which does not necessarily make them more accurate. In addition, we are culturally biased, trained to see what we expect to see and limited by the breadth of our experience and the experience of people we believe. If you had never seen snow, you would think it was a myth, unless you learned about it from people you trusted.

If this doesn't shatter our belief that we "know," add this: reality itself keeps changing. When I was growing up, kids played safely in the streets. At the time I'm writing this book, a lot of families have to cart their children to play dates because there are no kids to play with in the neighborhood, or because it's not safe. If I didn't know this fact and you told me that you're making a play date for your kid, I would immediately have the judgment that you are doing something that is not necessary. Reality changes, and so must our perception of it. But if we are attached to an obsolete perception, if we are programmed to an old view, or if we feel threatened by the new, we will not see the new reality, even when it's sitting in our living room. When did Mom go from drinking occasionally to being an alcoholic? When did the earth's environment become so threatened that we have to wake up to the new reality of climate crisis? Is our intimate relationship still working, or am I afraid to find out it's not? Is robbing people at knifepoint still the best way for me to make a living? Am I willing to see that reality may have changed?

And, finally, reality changes also because the levels or dimensions we experience change as well. In this case, it is not really the reality itself that is changing; it is what we perceive as reality that is changing. What is true in a certain plane of existence might not be true in another. For example, the laws of science that apply on one level of the natural world do not apply on the sub-atomic level. Until we discovered the sub-atomic level, we didn't know that another set of laws even existed. Light sometimes behaves like a particle and sometimes like a wave. Egad, this is confusing.

Similarly, when we are dealing with different dimensions and realms of existence, different rules apply. We had glimpses of this in Platform Seven: Becoming Accountable. On the simplest level, I'm not accountable for you hitting me in that automobile accident, because you were the one talking on the phone when the accident occurred. On another level, if I support driving while talking on the cell phone, I am partially accountable for that accident, too. On one level, we need to fight the Dark Side. On another level, we really need to support it to evolve. When we begin to move into other dimensions, there's no Dark Side to fight or support.

As I will soon discuss, beliefs are necessary as working hypotheses for how to live life. But if we start to believe in our beliefs, we will become blind to what we see. Because we think we know something, "knowing" takes the place of inquiry, and we miss what's right in front of us. At the same time, if we limit our knowledge to what we can see and understand ourselves, we will miss the complexity of reality, which is beyond our grasp. If our egos reject the input of others, we do the same. So while we're comforting ourselves with the illusion that we know, we block our ability to learn and grow.

As we take our spiritual journey toward Becoming Becoming, we must let go of the belief that we know or we, too, will be blind to what we could see, learn, and eventually know. This is part of the work of Platform Eight: Becoming Not-Knowing. Let's take a look at our own attitudes toward beliefs.

1. What beliefs do I have about the world?
2. How do I know they are true?
3. Where did I get them?
4. How open am I to see something different?
5. What realities might be changing?
6. Do I want to know?

Why We Need Beliefs

Beliefs are necessary for our functioning, because we need to form an idea of the world in order to live in it. Suppose, for example, I said, "Okay, I know nothing. Therefore, I don't know whether or not to believe that the sun will rise tomorrow morning." What are the implications? If I don't believe the sun will rise tomorrow, I won't know whether to plan around the existence of another day. I won't set my alarm or pack myself a lunch for the next day's work. In fact, why would I even bother to brush my teeth tonight?

Let's take this further. What would happen if, when I got up in the morning, I didn't believe that a) there would still be a sidewalk outside my door, b) the neighborhood school or factory would be in the same place, and c) putting my hand in the fire would always burn? If I didn't maintain these beliefs, I would wake up every day and have to discover life for the first time. If I didn't believe that the sidewalk was still going to be there, I would have to look out the door before deciding whether to wear shoes or hiking boots. If I didn't believe that buildings stayed in the same place unless moved, I would have to call the school or the factory to find out its location at that moment. If I didn't know that fire burns, I would keep putting my hand in the fire to find out if it was hot enough to boil the water. Wow, that would be tough and inefficient.

Based on experience, we develop certain expectations about how the world operates. Sometimes they are accurate; sometimes not. But just because our beliefs seem to work in a certain context and at a certain time, even that does not make them "true." It just makes them reasonable and efficient.

If our beliefs are working well for us, we can keep them, or we can change them to something even more congruent with our needs and experiences. But what happens when they don't work well and don't support us and others? Are we even willing to admit that they're not? Not if we're blinded by habit and ego attachment.

Confusing Beliefs with Truths

Our egos want truths that we can hang on to, so that we can feel safe in the world. Often these "truths" are actually socially accepted beliefs that we adopt in order to fit in with the tribe. At other times, these "truths" are beliefs that are deliberately contradictory to popular ideas, but which we adopt just in order to feel separate or defiant and better than others. In either case, it is the ego causing us to embrace these truths, either to fit in or stand out.

Beliefs can be dangerous. We do not question our beliefs if we confuse them with truths. How can we question the "truth"? In addition, in order to maintain the delusion that our beliefs are truths, we may have to ignore reality. If we believe, for example, that diet has no impact on our health, we'll continue to eat fast food and give ourselves high blood pressure and high cholesterol. If we believe that prescription drugs can't impair our thinking, we may ignore our mental deterioration, so as not to have to face the possible connection with the drugs we're taking. If we believe that prayer will heal us and it doesn't, we will keep praying until we're dead. If we believe that medicine will heal us and it doesn't, we will continue popping pills even though we're not improving. If we believe that sparing the rod will spoil the child, we will justify our child abuse, even though beating our learning-disabled child does not make him learn. And if we believe that peoples of other races, colors, and religions are different from us, we will demonize instead of understand them, blocking the possibility of any peace or progress.

Deluding ourselves can be individual or collective. Political parties are guilty of collective delusion. We get caught up in ideological thinking and aren't willing to examine whether or not some course of action is the best solution, or if it was ever the best solution, or if reality has changed and our habitual solution is now irrelevant, outdated or obsolete. And, of course, we accuse the other side of being ideologically driven without noticing that we are, too. Those who oppose government intervention scare everyone with the idea that the government is intervening in areas in which the government should not intervene. And those who are attached to the idea that the government is the solution to everything won't examine whether government intervention is, in fact, the only or best alternative.

Even when reality begins to dawn on us and we begin to sense that a behavior is not working, we often refuse to look at the beliefs that underlie it. I observe that I'm becoming sicker and less productive, but I refuse to notice that I am sleeping too little and watching too much TV, because I want to believe that I still have the stamina of a twenty-year-old. I observe that I have been shaming myself for years for my compulsive masturbation, but I want to believe that giving myself lectures will finally control the behavior, even though it never has.

Let's pause here to examine some of our beliefs.

1. What are my beliefs about how the world works?

2. Do I examine them?
3. Do I tend to get attached to political or religious beliefs?
4. Am I willing to question them?
5. What behaviors of mine are self-defeating?
6. What beliefs could be underlying them?

When we get caught up in our beliefs about the world, when we confuse belief and reality, we stop inquiring, because we think we KNOW. For example, for many years, most Europeans believed the world was flat. Of course, now we regard that belief as ignorant and naive, but a little over 500 years ago, that belief was considered fact. Similarly we once believed that the sun revolved around the earth. We were attached to that idea, because it fit our ego-based view of the world, and people's lives were threatened for suggesting otherwise. Yet now we know this idea, too, was wrong.

Where do we get our beliefs? Often they come from parenting. My father was a Democrat, and so am I. Sometimes they come from the norms and teachings of our particular society. Social beliefs can be hard to spot; because they are so universally accepted, they seem like truth. When an outsider enters our society and brings a conflicting belief, we are incredulous and often assume the outsider is wrong.

Sometimes our beliefs come from experience. When we look out the window, it looks like the earth is flat, and that was a reasonable conclusion to draw. But it was a wrong conclusion, even though it was also supported by the society and was detrimental to us all, because it discouraged exploration for another route to India.

Now here's a fascinating paradox. We have beliefs that seem to work but are wrong, too, and these, too, may discourage inquiry. For example, going back to our earlier example, we have many experiences that teach us that the sun will rise every day. Unlike the belief that the earth is flat, the belief that the sun will rise seems to work. Yet upon study, we discover that this belief, too, is a myth. In today's world, we all know that the sun doesn't actually rise at all, that the sun only appears to rise, and that it is we who are moving. If we believe the sun is rising, that belief does not get in the way of our daily functioning. But suppose we insisted that it was truth, and we tried to get scientists to abandon their studies? What would happen to science? It would be stopped, which is in fact what has happened at times centuries ago.

Some beliefs come from tradition or religious teachings, and those who sanctify their beliefs and make them truths can block inquiry. Isn't that what happens around creationism? People who interpret the Bible to say that the world was literally created in a matter of days may impose that belief as though it were a truth. By so doing, they do not allow for the possibility that that belief is just a metaphor. Other people believe that there is no higher power or creative intelligence. Isn't that also just a belief?

We have many such collective beliefs, which prejudge people on the basis of race, sex, and religion. It was not long ago that women were denied the right to vote, because women were supposed to be subservient and even inferior to men. Some in the world still hold that belief, but now the general social belief system has swung in a different direction, which means that those who cling to this belief have become the minority voice. Now we believe that men and women are equal. I prefer that idea, and I'm willing to fight for it, but am I willing to admit that it, too, is a belief?

Clinging to beliefs is a habit of us all. We force ourselves and others to believe the ideas we have been taught or that are convenient or self-serving, and then we fight to maintain or even impose those beliefs on others. How much better to acknowledge the truth of our first statement, which is that beliefs are only beliefs, even if they seem to work.

A final point on this. Sometimes beliefs actually create the reality they are meant to describe. We are told that Aunt Sadie is a snob and doesn't like "us," whoever "us" is. When we believe this, we treat Aunt Sadie with suspicion and hostility. Feeling our suspicion and hostility, Aunt Sadie doesn't like us. Oops. Now the belief has created the reality.

All ideas are just that: ideas. They are approximate descriptions of reality as we see it from our limited perspective. They are never "truth," because they cannot be complete, because they are always reflections of our limited view. But they can be useful, just like it can be useful in certain circumstances to believe that the sun will rise in the morning.

So let's review what we said in the beginning of this chapter.

Beliefs are just beliefs. They are not truths. When they support the highest good of all, we can keep using them. When they stop supporting us and stop being useful, we need to let them go.

536

Let's ask ourselves some questions about our own beliefs.

1. What beliefs of mine seem useful?
2. Am I willing to consider that they are not true?
3. What beliefs do I carry just because they are the norm in my culture?
4. Am I willing to consider that they are not truths?
5. How have I felt when I realized that my beliefs were not true at all?
6. Can I identify a circumstance in which my beliefs created or at least contributed to a reality?

AGENDAS

Agendas are like beliefs. They block the Not-Knowing, the allowing, and the becoming. When I have an agenda, it means that I have already decided what is supposed to occur. Let's say I come into a discussion dead-set on convincing you of my position. There you go! An agenda. Is there much chance of discovery here? Certainly not. No matter what you say, I have already made up my mind.

Agendas in conversations are obviously blindfolds. But we have other kinds of agendas, as well, some of which might not be so apparent. Some agendas look like goals, for example, and they, too, block us from the Not-Knowing. If I am attached to the goal to make a million dollars before I'm 30, for instance, I will bend all my efforts to "create" that reality. I will try to manipulate all people and circumstances to achieve that goal. I may see everything I do and everyone I meet as somehow connected to my becoming a millionaire. I will stress and strain and feel angry with myself or feel cheated if I don't succeed. I will be fixed on an outcome and won't continue to ask important questions, such as: Am I cut out for this life? Is the product or service I'm selling needed and valuable? Do I even want the money enough that it's worth the cost to my soul? If I am stuck on the agenda, I won't ask these questions with an open mind, and I won't be open to the possibility that this agenda is not for the highest good of all.

Psychological agendas can run us, too. I can have an agenda to prove that I'm smart, or kind, or a winner, or the victim—it doesn't matter what—and that agenda will dominate me throughout my life experiences.

So, no matter how confused I am, I will try to look smart. No matter how angry I am, I'll try to look kind—or at least convince you that I am. No matter how much I am failing, I will try to look like a winner. No matter how kind the universe is, I will try to look like a victim. These psychological or emotional agendas blind me to reality and shape the way I experience life. They reinforce my beliefs, blocking me from experiencing life as it is.

Agendas are a huge block to intimate relationships. Do I have an agenda? Is it to feel loved? Is it to feel safe? Is it to feel superior? Is it to find a protector? Is it to have someone to abuse? If these agendas are thwarted, I may throw out the relationship, not because it's not satisfying my needs, but because it's not fulfilling my agenda. Let's look at an example. Suppose my agenda is to be with a guy who makes me feel safe. If my guy loses his health and capacity to earn an income, I may feel that I have to leave him only because my agenda is no longer being satisfied, even though I love him. Conversely, I may stay in a relationship because my agenda is satisfied, even though my needs are not. For example, let's say my guy keeps bringing in the money, but we have no real communication. I might stay anyway, even though my soul's desire is being thwarted. I don't let myself know whether or not it's right for me to be with the guy, because the satisfaction of the agenda is the knowing that blocks the true knowing.

Agendas can be so strong, they sometimes cause us to be incredibly stupid. For example, if my agenda is to stay married to prove my mother wrong for having divorced, I will stay with a person who abuses me and my children, and I'll call it devotion to the children's welfare and old-fashioned values. If I have an agenda to prove myself better than my dad, I will stay with a job that gives me a heart attack in the hopes that I can make more money than he did. If my agenda is to prove that no one can ever love me, I will reject anyone who does.

How do these agendas block the Not-Knowing? By prejudicing me, causing me to prejudge all situations without true inquiry; by filling up all the space in my head with a pre-determined goal, which blocks the unfolding of what is and could be and which could block me from ever knowing what is truly for the highest good of all, including me.

And where do these pre-determined agendas come from? Could it be our old sidekick, the ego, again? Somewhere along the line, our ego has gotten the notion that fulfilling this particular agenda is going to make us safe, happy, admired, something that we think we must have.

And then, we're off and running, never looking back, angry at reality if we can't achieve our goal. And even when we succeed in achieving our agenda, we're often bitterly disappointed, because fulfilling it did not give us the wellbeing our ego had convinced us was at stake. Yup, I've made my million, I've married the cheerleader, I've got the corner office, but I still feel stressed and empty. What went wrong?

Let's ask ourselves some questions about our own agendas.

1. Do I have an agenda with my friends?
2. What is it?
3. Do I have an agenda with a life partner, boyfriend or girlfriend?
4. What is it?
5. Is it getting in the way of knowing whether or not the relationship is right for me?
6. Do I have an agenda regarding career or money?
7. How does that impact my relationships with others?
8. How does it impact my relationship with myself?
9. Can I identify a general psychological agenda that runs me in most, if not all, situations?
10. Can I acknowledge how these agendas prevent me from being open to seeing what is or could be?
11. Can I see how all of these agendas are based on my ego trying to define or determine reality for some perceived self-interest?
12. What goals have I achieved, and have I found peace?

I will end this brief discussion now, but we will return to agendas later in this chapter.

Before we go on to Becoming Not-Knowing, however, let's summarize some of what we've learned about needing to know, pretending that what we think we know should become the agenda for what needs to be:

- We need to know or pretend to know, in order to overcome feelings of stress.
- But pretending to know creates the stress of being discovered as not knowing.
- Wanting to be seen as knowing more than others causes us to be competitive, which causes stress.

- Believing that our beliefs are "true" can cause us to ignore reality, even to the point of self-destructiveness, which creates stress.
- Pushing our conscious and unconscious agendas causes us to be in a constant struggle with reality, which leads to stress.
- Our egos push us to fulfill their agendas.

When we sum these up, we realize that in our attempts to alleviate stress, we create more stress. One more time, just like with all addictive behaviors, our desperate attempts to change the reality of our feelings has created more of the feelings we are trying to alleviate.

What Is Becoming Not-Knowing?

Becoming Not-Knowing is the process of becoming empty of agendas and limitations. It is an essential part of freeing ourselves from the domination of the ego. We release ourselves from the need to know or pretend we do, and we live moment by moment in the Not-Knowing and the discovery. We release ourselves from needless stress, and ultimately we become available for higher consciousness.

Doesn't that sound liberating? You mean we can just live moment by moment and discover what's going to happen in a state of relaxation? Well, we can, but just as we have seen with all our platforms, practicing this platform can be challenging.

HOW DO WE BECOME NOT-KNOWING?

Releasing the Need to Know

As we mentioned earlier, the first step we can take is to admit that we don't know and can't know. This can be as simple as admitting we can't know whether or not traffic is going to ease and whether we're going to get to an appointment on time. Or it can be something as complex and deep as not knowing whether or not humanity will be destroyed by climate change. We can predict, we can hope, we can attempt to influence, but we cannot know. How do we release the need to know?

By using our release tool, as we learned it in Platform Six: Becoming Integrated. Here's the way we would use this tool in the context of

Not-Knowing: Let's say we're sitting in traffic, anxious about whether or not we're going to get to the appointment. If we feel stress, we can use our release tool. We say, "I release the need to know whether or not I will arrive at the appointment on time." After saying the release, we brush the area where we hold the tension and after that take a big breath. We do this process three times. The last time, after we say, "I release the need to know whether or not I will arrive at the appointment on time," we brush and breathe, and then we say, "because I can't," and then again we take a big in-breath.[31] And then we laugh, if we can.

Because it is funny. We're sitting in traffic not knowing whether the delay is going to be three minutes or half an hour, yet we create all kinds of stress craning our necks and speculating about how far up the freeway the accident occurred. In other words, we're creating a lot of stress trying to know something we can't possibly know. If we can just acknowledge that we can't, we can finally laugh at ourselves, acknowledge our not knowing, turn on the radio and relax. We can also use the release tool to release the need to know what the outcome of our lateness will be.

The same technique can be used to release the need to know whether humanity will survive climate change, or whether or not I will have a baby, or if the baby will be healthy, or if my relationship will last through the pregnancy, or if we'll have enough money, and all the stressful needs-to-know that haunt our nine months. We release the need to know anything and everything, take a breath, and get quiet.

Now here's another example. Have you felt at all stressed about knowing how to use the information in this book? You might be thinking, "The ideas sound good, but can I really practice these platforms with any

---

31   We can do an even better job releasing needless stress if we release the need to know in conjunction with doing other releases, including those addressing underlying fears of being late. We've already talked about underlying motives in Platform Five: Becoming Self-Aware, and we've learned to use the release tool in Platform Six: Becoming Integrated. So, for example we've learned we can release the need to impress the customer by arriving on time, release the need to get the sale and support the family, release the need to prove we are not a screw-up, and so on. Sometimes we need to take this step all the way to "I release the need to survive," if we believe our survival depends on this appointment, even though it doesn't, and even though it might appear that way.

consistency?" Remember our tool and say, "I release the need to know how I'm going to Become Not-Knowing." Do the release statement, brushing and breathing three times, then say, "because I don't know." Then laugh and relax! Now how is that for taking a step toward relaxing into the process of living?

Sometimes we drive ourselves to distraction trying to know how to handle something before it has happened. I'm going in to talk to my boss. If she says this, then what should I say? If she says that, how should I respond? And so on and so on. So here's another step toward relaxing into the process of living: giving up needing to know how to do something before we're actually in the situation.

Let's look at the example of pregnancy. We need to be honest with ourselves about our patience and love for children, yet ultimately, who really knows whether he or she will make a good parent until they try to do it, meet the challenges and learn how? We can study, read books, observe others, ask opinions, obsess; but we won't know ourselves in the situation until we're there. Once more, we have tons of experts giving opinions, often contradictory, which may or may not relate to us, our co-parent, if we have one, and our baby. So, let's strike a blow for relaxation: "I release the need to know whether or not I will make a good parent, because I can't know that yet." Of course, we can commit ourselves to learning, observing, and doing the best job possible. But that's about all we can do, other than relax.

I can't know how to handle a situation until I'm there, because I am not yet the person who will have to handle the situation. The person who will handle that situation is the person who is facing it. And the person facing the situation is not me now; it's me then. Who knows what my condition, state of mind or experience or intentions will be at that time? So let me release the need to know how I will survive without a job, after my lover leaves, if I have cancer, when my mother dies, because I can't know now how I will handle something then. When we discuss life as a transformational moment in Platform Nine: Becoming Becoming, we will understand this better.

Finally, let me comment on using this tool around pretending. Earlier in this chapter, we discussed the need to know something, whether or not we do, and the need to pretend we do when we know we don't. We can use the same release tool, focusing on releasing the need to pretend. For example, I can release the need to pretend I know how to handle our finances, when my poor judgment has gotten our family into bankruptcy. I can release the need to pretend I know how to stop gambling, or drinking, or otherwise ruining our family. I can release the need to pretend I know how to get us out of debt, to make my partner happy, to keep the kids in school, to solve the problem of global warming. I release the need to pretend I know how to solve the problem of human consciousness. Wow, no more pretending. What a lot of stress off my shoulders.

Let's look at some ways we can use this tool.

1. Let me think of some things I don't know now.
2. Can I release the need to know?
3. Let me think of some things I'm afraid I don't know how to do.
4. Do I have to do them this minute?
5. Can I release the need to know how to do them now?
6. What problems do I feel I need to pretend I know how to fix?
7. Can I release the need to pretend that I know what I don't?

Releasing Agendas

Now that we've seen how to release the need to know, let's address agendas. Releasing our agendas allows us to become open, empty, and available for higher consciousness, because, empty of agendas, we then become available for guidance from an intelligence greater than our own.

In this section, we are going to consider two kinds of agendas. One is for a specific outcome, such as, I want to clean out my garage before Thanksgiving. Or I want to impress my girlfriend with my new car. Other agendas are more foundational, and I'm going to call these our life purpose. A life purpose can be conscious, such as to save injured wildlife. But a life purpose can also be unconscious or, at least, just below the surface. For example, my life purpose might be to prove that I am better than my sister, and the need to prove that could underlie nearly every behavior in which I engage.

Releasing Agendas for a Specific Outcome

We are constantly pursuing specific outcomes, whether we know it or not. And these agendas are clearly in the way of Not-Knowing. When we are attached to specific outcomes, we think we already know what should happen, we cannot allow higher consciousness to guide us, and, if we're motivated and driven, we will pursue that outcome regardless of the consequences to us or others.

For example, if we believe that we should earn a certain amount of money, we will pursue that outcome, even if we'll never be able to achieve it, or even if achieving it will make us sick or miserable. Let's say that the goal of my business is to produce 30 percent more profit this year than last. Well, is that for the highest good of all, including me? Are those goals realistic? Will I work myself to death? Will I push my employees to work more than they should? Is my product really right for the people to whom I'm trying to sell it, or am I just trying to gain the profit? Am I overcharging my customers or underpaying my workers? Is this specific outcome really designed to satisfy a deeper agenda, an unconscious agenda, such as looking smarter than my father? Or is it to satisfy an ego goal of getting rich, without regard to the expense to myself and/or others? Why am I creating that goal at all? Can I just create the best product I can and see where the universe will take me in terms of success?

Let's talk about one other kind of attachment to a specific outcome: personal goals. Examples of personal goals could be losing weight, getting into a relationship, having children, winning at sports. These activities can be fine, but what happens when they become agendas? We can focus on losing weight to the detriment of our health. We can pursue wrong relationships just in order to have one. We can give birth to children, even though my partner and I are not up for parenting. We can over-train and hurt our bodies to win at sports, or we can lapse into separation and competition and hurt our souls. If we focus on these goals, we may be ignoring our other, more important needs or the needs of our families or our world.

Again, there is nothing wrong with a personal goal if it is realistic, motivating, and helpful. But when it becomes a must-have or must-do, it can blind us to what we should we doing. We can't be in inquiry, because we already know.

Let's ask ourselves some questions about goals.

1. Do I have work, money, or business goals?
2. Are they coming from my higher consciousness?
3. Is my ego getting stroked?
4. Do I have personal goals?
5. Are they a guidepost or an imperative?
6. How high a price have I paid for pursuing these goals?

Most of us become attached to specific outcomes that our egos tell us are in our best interest or in the best interest of someone we care about. We've got to win the game, keep our kids in school, make more money, conquer a health problem, and so on. In Platform Four: Becoming Mutually Supportive, we already discussed that our vision of our best interest or the best outcome can be wrong, or it might not be for the highest good of all. Becoming Mutually Supportive allowed us to shift out of our ego-based thinking by asking the universe to support the highest good. All of this confronts our ego, especially if we associate a certain outcome with our survival.

Trying to force a specific outcome always creates stress, because we are trying to "make" something happen. This drive is understandable. Sometimes the loss of a specific outcome can be heartbreaking, as when we watch a child die, despite all our efforts. We can all have compassion for one another when we face losses and traumas that seem unbearable or unfair. Yet the only way to relax into the process of living is to release our attachment to an outcome, even though we may work hard for it, even when not getting what we want seems unfair.

When we practice Not-Knowing, we might also discover that our agenda may be foolish or self-defeating, and we open ourselves to the possibility that there is greater learning in the frustration of our intention than in the fulfillment of it. Going back to the example of earning more money, perhaps we really need to learn to live on less; or perhaps we need to refocus ourselves entirely, follow our hearts, and accept the flow of money that will come naturally to us. How can we know, if we're committed to a certain outcome?

Let's look at each of our goals for a specific outcome. Let's make sure:

- The goal is not for my ego, but for the highest good of all.
- I have carefully examined my motives.
- I'm not avoiding something.
- I'm not being dominated by ego and trying to look special.
- I am willing for the goal to be an intention, but I can also be in allowance (Platform Three: Becoming Co-Creative).

When we pursue agendas for specific outcomes, we are in inner conflict, even if we don't consciously know it. Our higher consciousness may be telling us one thing and our ego another. But we won't listen to our higher consciousness, because our ego already "knows" what needs to happen and will try to drown out any other inner voice.

We all know that sometimes we judge reality as terribly wrong, and yet it turns out to be for our highest good. Perhaps the negative outcome is to a loved one, who needs to learn a lesson. Perhaps the negative outcome is to us, and we need the experience to bring us into a higher level of consciousness; perhaps we need this outcome in order to move us in a new direction; perhaps what looks like a bad outcome actually saved us from a disastrous situation. How can we allow ourselves to know what is for our highest good and the highest good of all, unless we release our agenda for a certain outcome? This brings us back to Platform Three: Becoming Co-Creative. We intend, but then we must allow. It's not easy to let go of our agendas to gain advantage or prevent something painful from occurring, but in the end we must do so, because otherwise, we cannot relax into the process of living.

When we are focusing on agendas for specific outcomes, unconscious agendas may actually be running underneath. Am I losing weight because it's good for my health, or because I think that being thin will give me power? Am I focused on earning a degree because it is the doorway to a more productive life or because my father would feel ashamed if I became a carpenter? Am I seeking to change jobs because it's time for a change or because I'm running away from confronting the negative ways I have been behaving at work? Unconscious agendas may be more powerful in setting our goals than any rational or helpful motivation we think we might have.

I am not suggesting that it may not at times be useful to have a goal; but if we set goals, we had better be darned sure that we are practicing intention and allowance and are Becoming Not-Knowing, so that we can be guided as to whether or not to pursue that goal or how.

A bit further in this chapter, I will share a technique for releasing specific outcomes, but first let's ask ourselves:

1. Can I identify some of the specific outcomes I am attached to in my life now?
2. If they are not guided by higher consciousness, can I consider letting them go?
3. If not, why not?

4. Can I think of a time when something ostensibly bad happened to me?
5. Can I think of positive outcomes that came from that event?
6. Were they positive in terms of life circumstances?
7. Were they positive in terms of our inner direction?
8. Have we seen this happen to others, as well?
9. Can I recognize some unconscious agendas that are underlying my current goals?
10. What foolish behaviors have they promoted?

Releasing a Life Purpose

Our life purpose runs us and can be conscious or unconscious. It is the underlying constellation of intentions that motivates our behavior. We may not even realize that a life purpose is running in the background of our psyches.

Examples of a life purpose: Raise myself above the level of my parents. Justify the sacrifices my parents made. Prove that my father was wrong to leave us. Prove that I am not impotent. Punish "God" for having abandoned me. Prove that I'm not stupid. Make the world safe for me. Make the world safe for others.

Releasing our life's purpose is an extremely powerful tool for transformation, because our life purpose dominates our behavior and deafens us to divine guidance. It is so big, so pervasive, it can be virtually invisible. For this reason, for many of us, our life's purpose is not in our conscious awareness. On the other hand, for some of us, our life's purpose seems obvious. But is it? Often beneath our conscious purpose, there is another, unconscious one. Either way, our life's purpose gets in the way of Becoming Not-Knowing.

The first step to releasing our life's purpose is to discover it, and Platform Five: Becoming Self-Aware, can help us in doing so. Once we catch on to our life's purpose, we can see how it damages us. Let's look at a few examples of how an unconscious life's purpose can damage ourselves or others.

- We think we're trying to save the whales, but our real life purpose is to look important. The damage could be that we don't take the steps that truly help save the whales, if those steps get in the way of our being central at an event or a negotiation.

- We think we're trying to save a marriage, but our real life purpose is to get someone else to take care of us. The damage could be that we manipulate our partner to stay with us under the pretext of love, and we guilt trip that person into providing for us, all while losing our integrity and causing them the pain of being in the wrong relationship.

- We think we're trying to be the best parent possible, but our real life purpose is to prove that our own mom was a bad mother. The damage could be that we use our child to make ourselves impressive to Mom (even if she's passed on), and we ignore the true needs of the child, if fulfilling those needs doesn't make the child, and therefore us, impressive.

Being a slave to our unconscious life purpose damages us and others.

A conscious life purpose can be just as damaging, because it's hooked up to our ego. Let's say I have given myself a life purpose of providing for my family. How is that ego? Because "I" have decided what should be my destiny and the destiny of those children. Perhaps my partner would be a better provider and I would be a better caretaker. Perhaps neither of us should focus on producing a lot of income, but together we could provide a nurturing environment for the kids. Perhaps we shouldn't have children at all. Perhaps I am able to provide a lot of money for my children but die young in the process or be unavailable throughout their young lives.

No matter the consequences, my ego has decided to make being "the provider" my life's purpose. Now in charge of destiny, my ego enforces its agenda by creating in me waves of fear that I won't achieve the goal and painting pictures of hideous outcomes if I can't.

Let's reiterate some of the potential damage. Let's say I've decided that my life purpose should be to be "the provider," and to do so I am going to increase my profit 30 percent, as we discussed earlier. Having decided what my business should produce, I have to make it happen. As long as I'm pursuing my goal, I have a built-in excuse to run away from other family obligations. Plus, I don't need to take care of my health as long as I'm producing results or at least striving to produce them. And I definitely don't have to care about the highest good of all or higher consciousness. Wow, the ego is edging everything else out.

In this case, we are taking the life's purpose at face value. But what do we see lurking behind this goal of being the provider? An unconscious life purpose as well, such as: While I'm trying to look like the provider, my true purpose is to impress myself and others, compete and win, or compensate for feeling like a failure.

We are not safe from the ego just because we adopt a life purpose that is not materialistic in nature. For example, our purpose might be to become a great artist. Are we truly in the divine flow with our art, being guided to become an artist, or are we being dominated by ego and an unconscious life purpose, which is to look important and become "great" at something, which simultaneously gives us excuses to avoid more mundane responsibilities?

Other non-materialistic conscious life purposes might look like humanitarian "missions." They have a noble ring and can be confusing. For example, let's say my life purpose is to help humanity or to save children. What can be wrong with that? Plenty. We already noted that when we were considering specific outcomes, we may be kidding ourselves about our purpose, and there may be an unconscious ego agenda running us, such as in the example of looking like we're saving the whales, while we're actually saving our faces and reputations. Or our outwardly noble endeavors are really designed to make us look special or better than others.

Let's say, however, that we are sincerely committed to a purpose and that we have no unconscious ego-driven motive. If we don't practice Not-Knowing, we may still become attached and self-destructive. Perhaps we are busily being activists on the day that we are supposed to be sleeping or paying the mortgage. We are not only hurting ourselves, we could be impacting others. Or perhaps we have chosen to save children, which is both helpful and makes us look good; but if we were really paying attention, we would realize that our destiny might lie with doing some other work, work that might garner less approval or admiration, work that is more invisible or more controversial. Our attachment to our noble purpose deafens us to the messages from the universe.

Sometimes we use our mission to separate, to puff ourselves up, to make wrong everyone else who is not on board, or to excuse ourselves from our responsibilities. For example, if my mission is to save humanity, can't that somehow put me above the labor of becoming self-aware or doing the family dishes?

This all sounds like the ego, doesn't it? Yup, our ego has come up with inventive ways of puffing us up while looking noble.

Doing humanitarian work can be important for us and for the highest good of all. But if we truly want to be of service to humanity or to higher consciousness, we need to let go of our life purpose and let ourselves be guided by The Source, even if that guidance directs us to pumping gas or serving corned beef hash. We cannot know truly how destiny can best use us, and only by releasing our agendas, can we be available to the guidance of higher consciousness and be of service to the whole.

Let's ask ourselves some questions in relation to having a life's purpose.

1. Do I have a conscious life purpose or mission?
2. What is the unconscious agenda underneath it?
3. Has it blinded me?
4. Has it damaged me or others?

Agendas Are Stressful

Whether an agenda is for a specific outcome or a life purpose, all agendas are stressful because they compel us to fulfill them and may put us in opposition to reality.

The stress of conscious agendas is fairly self-evident. We try to impose our will on reality, whether it's reasonable or not, or even for our highest good. I am going to sell that TV, even though the customer wants a washing machine; I am going to diet myself into a size 2, even though I was born with large bones; I am going to win that race, even though there's a runner more talented and just as dedicated as I am; I'm going to get that guy to pay child support, even though he's in jail. How can we succeed? We push and push, ignore the facts as well as messages from the universe, and feel our guts wrenching when we can't succeed. Then let's add the stress of having failed and the shame we dump on ourselves because we did.

Unconscious agendas are stressful in a similar way. We could be trying to prove something about ourselves or someone else, whether it's real or not. Maybe we're trying prove that we are the most oppressed, the hardest working, or the most loved. But suppose we're not the most oppressed, hardest working, or most loved? If it's not true, we will never succeed in proving that we are, and, in any case, what proof will ever be enough? We will continue to feel the drive to prove.

Haven't we all seen a woman like the wicked queen in Snow White and the Seven Dwarves? She was driven to prove that she was the most desirable and had to compete with all other women. Isn't there always someone else who could threaten her most-desirable status, someone younger, or prettier, or sexier? What could her partner ever do that would permanently fulfill her agenda that she be reassured? How many presents? How much attention will make her believe she is the "fairest of them all"? And what happens when reality interferes with her need to be reassured, when her partner has to shift his attention onto something else: go to work, play with the kids, or hang out with friends? What happens when the partner can't afford any more gifts or external validations of her desirability? Isn't that partner now stressed out trying to fulfill her agenda?

We've seen that even conscious agendas tend to have unconscious agendas running beneath them. So not only are we dealing with the stress of achieving our conscious agenda; we are dealing with the stress of fulfilling our unconscious agenda as well. For example, my life's purpose might be to win the Olympic gold medal, but my unconscious agenda might be to prove I'm not a loser like my dad. If I lose the medal, I lose on both counts. That's a lot of stress.

And then what about failure and the fear of it? Think of the stress of that. If we don't fulfill on some agenda, we feel like failures. But even before we know the results of our efforts, we experience the stress of constantly fearing potential failure. There is no relaxation; there is no being in the moment or just enjoying the experience.

To avoid failure, we mangle ourselves, run on empty, and ruin our health and relationships. We will do anything to make the desired goal happen. We forget intention and allowance. We become angry with reality when it doesn't meet our specifications, and we blame either ourselves or others when our agendas are not fulfilled. Even if we achieve our goals, we are stressed and upset anyway, as we discover that the success is rarely worth the price. This leads us to despairing over the fact that the price we have paid is too high.

Because they have drive, people pursuing agendas are sometimes admired by others. In fact, sometimes those people are admirable, but often they are out of balance and stressed. Let us combine fortitude and determination with intention and allowance, and let's use our fortitude to achieve the intentions of higher consciousness instead of our egos.

Let's take a look at some of our own stress around agendas.

1. What agendas of ours are causing stress?
2. Are we stressing to achieve them?
3. Are we stressing because we're afraid we won't achieve them?
4. Have we regretted the price we've paid when we have achieved them?

The Stress We Cause Others with Our Agendas

Thus far we have been focusing on the stress we cause ourselves with agendas. Let's take a quick look at the stress we cause others.

When we expect others to live up to our agendas, we create stress for them. If I want my mate to produce a $150,000/year income so that I can have a comfortable lifestyle and so that our kids can have everything they want, I am imposing an agenda on that mate. If I have an agenda that our kids will get A's, join the glee club or excel at sports, I am imposing an agenda on my children.

My ego is now determining not only what I should do, but what everyone else should do. It is also determining not only who I should be, but who everyone else should be. What's the threat behind the agenda? If you do not do what I want, if you are not who I want you to be, you will lose love, affection, regard or possibly support.

Of course we have a right to determine whom we love and where we should invest our emotional, spiritual and material resources. But we need to be extremely sure that our decisions are coming from higher consciousness and a true caring for others, rather than from our ego needs that we project onto others.

It is extremely challenging for us to stop wanting others to fulfill our agendas: I want you to give me love in this form; I want her to perform in a way that makes me look good; I want him to give me want I think I need; and I want them to fix the world, the government, the community, in a way that fulfills what I think should happen.

When we acknowledge how stressful it is to live up to our own agendas, let us also consider how many agendas we impose on others. Can we consider the possibility that we don't, in fact, know what is for someone else's highest good?

Is it possible that his failure at academics will lead my child into dance, which is where he belongs? Is it possible that his academic failure might wake him up to his need for discipline? Is it possible that this very same failure will lead him to take a summer school class, where he will meet a teacher who will inspire him forever? How do I know? I don't.

We can release our need for anyone to fulfill any of our agendas, because, in fact, we don't know what is for anyone's highest good. We can have opinions, and we can share them. But let's always try to relax around our agendas for others, so that we can be truly supportive of them to learn their own lessons and become their own people.

Sometimes we can recognize that someone not meeting our agenda is actually for our highest good, too. For example, I may have the agenda that my husband stop drinking. He doesn't and I leave him. Then I meet a much more appropriate mate. Wow, his not fulfilling MY agenda actually supported me to have a happier life. Plus, I learned to let go. Maybe after I leave him, he gets sober and meets the woman of his dreams at a meeting of Alcoholics Anonymous. You just don't know.

Let's take a quick look at ourselves in relation to agendas for others.

1. Who do I feel needs to meet my needs?
2. Can I recognize that I have agendas for their behavior?
3. For whom else do I create conscious or unconscious agendas?
4. How do I feel when those agendas are fulfilled?
5. How do I react?
6. How do the people on whom I impose my agendas feel?

Agendas Block Access to Higher Consciousness

All agendas, purposes, and missions are attached to our egos and block higher consciousness. The moment we create agendas, we are deciding what should occur, and, therefore, we are no longer in co-creation with the universe. Of course, we can and should have goals, but making those goals into must-fulfill agendas not only creates needless stress, but also blocks our availability to higher consciousness.

Typically, our egos create agendas to make us feel better, valuable, important, or worthwhile. They are attempts to alter our feelings of fear of our own worthlessness. Remember our introduction, "Ego, Instinct & Evolution," where we discovered that we carry shame of existence? If we were conscious, we would not try to alter our feeling of worthlessness. We would practice Platform Six: Becoming Integrated, and release the need to feel superior, valuable, important, or worthwhile, because we are meant to exist. We have nothing to prove. And then we would also seek ways to find a non-egoic sense of greater wellbeing.

But we are not conscious when we are dominated by ego and refuse to Becoming Not-Knowing. Instead, we tie ourselves in knots trying to achieve our goals in the hopes that then we will, indeed, feel superior, valuable, important, or worthwhile, as our egos promise.

Do we? Rarely. And when we do, aren't we usually bombarded by yet another agenda that we need to fulfill in order to continue to feel superior, valuable, important, or worthwhile? And isn't the ego always teasing us with the tantalizing thought that this time, we are actually going to get there?

The moment we buy into an agenda, we have become unavailable to higher consciousness. And that's the ego's purpose. Already thinking we know, we are unable to hear guidance, especially if that guidance moves us in a direction contrary to the one our ego has determined. The ego has thus successfully blocked us from connecting to the consciousness that could break the domination of the ego.

Let's look at how we might have done this.

1. Looking at my agendas, what emotional outcomes is the ego promising me?
2. Has it ever delivered in any but a fleeting way?
3. Am I really available to higher consciousness when I listen to my agendas?

The Bottom Line on Agendas: They Are Ego Based

There are no individual life purposes, because there are no individuals.

There is no individual existence outside the context of Oneness. And if there is no individual existence outside the context of Oneness, there is also no individual purpose or personal salvation. We are part of the whole, and our purpose is to be part of the evolution of the whole. Only by being in tune with higher intelligence can we realize our part in the collective evolution. We must, therefore, ask for guidance to do our part in the evolution of the collective consciousness, instead of looking to higher consciousness to support our agenda.

This means we surrender the right to use higher consciousness on behalf of our egos. Asking God, The Source, higher consciousness to fulfill our ego demands motivates much of our prayers, as in "Please give me a bicycle for Christmas, find me a guy, take away my hemorrhoids, defeat my enemies." Intending for God to fulfill our egoic desires also underlies the spiritual approach of manifestation consciousness, although it's phrased differently. We intend to manifest something, and we ask God to make it so.

When we commit to Not Knowing, on the other hand, we give up right to determine outcomes. Of course, we can have hopes. That's no mal. But when we turn to the universe, we ask for guidance as to what to do moment by moment, and we request support to do what we are meant to do. We don't set the agenda. We ask for the strength to overcome our disappointments or the stamina to confront our fears. We ask for the willingness to do that which is for the highest good of all and for the power to be of service. We ask for support in understanding our own part in negative situations and help in transforming.

When we release agendas, we also cease striving to become individually enlightened, which is just another ego goal. We cannot demand higher consciousness to help us escape the human condition, because we can't and aren't meant to.

This Does Not Mean We Lack Individual Responsibility

At the same time, within the context of Oneness, we do have individual existence, just as individual cells exist within the context of the body. As we discussed earlier in the book, outside the body, our cells would die; but within the body, each has a vital part.

We are like those cells. Within the collective evolution, we exist as vital parts of the whole, and each of us has an individual and vital job. But what is that job, and how do we know what it is? Our egos cannot define it, because our individual egos don't have the wisdom or the perspective to see the whole, any more than the cell can define the whole of our bodies. Only by being in alignment with the intelligence guiding the whole can we truly be in alignment with our job.

What is our job? To work on ourselves. Now doesn't this seem to contradict everything I've been saying about being part of the Oneness?

Not at all. Here's how it works. In life, we are given certain characteristics and certain challenges, and our job is to take on those challenges, to learn and to transform.[32] If we are self-centered, we need to work on generosity. If we have no boundaries, we need to learn to connect to ourselves. If we are fear-based, we need to challenge ourselves to become freer. And if we are reckless, we need to become more responsible. Sounds like Becoming Integrated, doesn't it? Well, it is. As we each become more integrated and overcome the domination of any of our fragments, we are simultaneously bringing balance to the whole of the collective consciousness. As we each become more self-honest and self-aware, the whole becomes more enlightened. As we each become more aware of our Oneness, as when we use the platforms of Living with Reality, the whole becomes more liberated from the domination of the ego. And as we individually bring higher consciousness into everyday life, we simultaneously support the evolution of consciousness itself.

Few of us embrace this reality. Many of us are frustrated and overwhelmed by our flaws and the many genetic weaknesses and traumas that cause them. We complain. We feel shame. We think we should be different. In a sense, we don't want to be human. Instead, we want to be perfect, exempt from the fear and pain of human existence, but we are not meant to be exempt, and we are not meant to be perfect. These challenges are meant for us, and our job is to overcome them.

So ironically, just as we are surrendering all our agendas, including a life's purpose, we discover that we do have a life purpose, a life's purpose which we all share. Our purpose is to confront ourselves and shift our relationship with ourselves, one another and life itself. We may not like the way we were designed, the experiences we have to face, the job we have been given; we may not like the path before us. But we have to live with reality and embrace our path. If we don't, we will squander the opportunity to transform ourselves and thus fail to fulfill our responsibility to ourselves and to the whole.

I will discuss this process further in Platform Nine: Becoming Becoming, but for now, let's surrender to the reality that we are part of the

---

[32] Another way to talk about this is to say that karma is collective and that each one of us is here to take responsibility for an aspect of that collective karma. Our job in life, then, would be to help transmute the energy of an aspect of that collective karma.

evolution of consciousness, and we have a job to do, and let us let go of our personal agendas and commit to being guided by the higher intelligence directing the evolution of the whole. This is the work for Platform Eight: Becoming Not-Knowing.

Before sharing with you some tools to practice Platform Eight, let us acknowledge that this way of viewing ourselves is unusual for most of us, and it takes practice, dedication, and self-discipline to remember that we exist as part of the collective consciousness. But when we do embrace seeing ourselves as part of the whole, we see that it's silly to think in terms of "my" purpose, agenda, or mission, even though that is the ego's way of viewing our lives. And when we accept our part, it's easier for us to relax into it.

When I received my intuitive gift in my mid-thirties, I felt overwhelmed with the responsibility. What was I supposed to do with this gift? I immediately thought my job was to save the world. Now that seemed overwhelming. I didn't have a lot of material resources, and, worse yet, I knew I was flawed, lacking in physical, spiritual and emotional resources as well. Years later, I heard a voice in my head, which I called God, and this is what that voice said to me:

"I am not part of your mission, Beth. You are part of my plan."[33] Wow, what a sobering and humbling concept that was. Here I thought that I was going to do something important—change the world in some way—and my connection with God was going to help me do it. Now I realized that reality was the other way around. The universe is fulfilling its own agenda, and I am only a part, and my job is to surrender to doing my part to the best of my ability. It wasn't my job to save the world after all! On the one hand, my ego was offended. Wow, I wasn't that important, after all. On the other hand, my soul relaxed. I knew and still know that if I follow my guidance day after day, I can't miss doing my job on this earth, if my job is to counsel only 25 people in my life, reach a mass audience or to sell scarves in a department store.

So now that we have the scoop on agendas, we're ready for Becoming Not-Knowing. Let's use the following tools and see where it takes us.

---

[33]   Green, Beth. *God's Little Aphorisms*. Lincoln: iUniverse, 2005.

Releasing Agendas

In a moment, I will share with you a new tool, one specifically designed for releasing agendas. But first, I want to remind you that agendas can be unconscious and subtle. So we may have to do several rounds of releases to get to the bottom of releasing an agenda. For example, it might look like my agenda is to become the toughest guy on the block, whereas my true agenda is to prove my father wrong about me being a drain on the family or to prove I'm bigger than God. The power of the agenda release depends on our level of self-awareness. Refer back to Platform Five: Becoming Self-Aware, if you feel the need for a refresher.

If we aren't sure of the core unconscious agenda beneath an apparent agenda, we can start with what we see. That may lead us to deeper realizations. So, just so that we can relax around this process, let's use the release tool we learned in Platform Six, and let's release the need to know what agendas to release, because we can't.

Tool: Releasing Agendas for Specific Outcomes

If I identify that I have an agenda for a specific outcome, whether it is conscious, such as losing weight, or unconscious, such as making men look weak, I use the same tool. Let's use the example of making men look weak. I place my hand on the part of my body where I feel myself holding the stress of that agenda. Then I say, "All my life, I have been trying to prove that men are weak. I release the need to prove that men are weak, [I brush the area, as I do with every release step, and then I take in and release a big breath], and I return to The Source." As I say, "and I return to The Source," I open my arms, embrace the Source and I take another big breath. I surrender. It feels great!

Please note that this release is not identical to the general release tool, where we say the release three times, each time with a brush followed by a big breath. When we release agendas, we say, "I release the need" only once, and then we open our arms to the beneficial energies available to us when we are truly relaxed.

The same process can be used to release conscious specific outcomes, such as losing weight, getting a certain job, or making my children go to college.

Some agendas underlie and run everything in our life and we can identify these primary agendas as a life's purpose. A life's purpose can be conscious or unconscious, as well. We basically use the same process to release it.

Tool: Release a Life's Purpose

Let's say my life's purpose has been to save my mother. I felt guilty as a child because I saw her suffering and couldn't help her. Now the need to save my mother runs my life, impacts my marriage, and even affects all my relationships with people who remind me of her. She doesn't have to still be alive for that life purpose to dominate my life. Here's how I release it. I place my hand on the part of my body where I feel myself holding that purpose. Then I say, "My life's purpose has been to try to save my mother. I release the need to save my mother, [I brush the area, as I do with every release step and then take in and release a big breath], and I return to The Source." Again, I take in and release a big breath as I open my arms and embrace the beneficial energies available.

Taking these actions creates an amazing opening for relaxation and availability to higher consciousness. Let's take a moment to inquire about our agendas and mission, and let's release them. It's great to do this step with a group supporting us. In fact, to conclude, you can do a final one where you say, "My life's purpose has been to . . . I release the need for a life's purpose, and I return to The Source." Now that's freedom.

WALKING THE PATH OF NOT-KNOWING

This book appears to be a series of beliefs and opinions, but it is in essence more a book of practices that either work or don't work in a certain context, at a given time. In general, they seem to work, at least at this time in history. Remember our perspective: We don't know the truth; we have beliefs. If our beliefs are useful and working, we can continue to use them. When they are obsolete or no longer working, we let them go.

At this point, I would like to share with you a statement called "Some Thoughts on the Path of Not Knowing." The words came to me in one of those unexpected moments of inspiration, when I wasn't thinking about the subject at all. It was in August of 1999, and I was living alone in Oregon, far from my support system. You'll see references to "The Stream," which is a spiritual community I had founded in 1983, disbanded a few years later, and was guided to revive again in 1999, just before these words came to me. There was no actual organization at the time when I wrote these words, but it referred to me and the work I was doing. Now The Stream[34] is a non-profit organization dedicated to living the principles contained in this book. Here are the words that came to me one evening quite out of the blue. They describe a perspective that allows us all to become more Not-Knowing and more inspired.

Some Thoughts about the Path of Not-Knowing

We co-create reality with the universe in a subtle dance of intention and allowance.[35]

Our beliefs are free-flowing manifestations of our state-of-being in the moment. We know that we don't know; all efforts to pretend otherwise are motivated by fear and lead to frustration and disappointment.

In the Not-Knowing, our inner knowing guides us moment by moment, which is all we can know. We know more in silence, sound, and movement than in words.

We are committed to self-knowledge, so that we can release agendas and reactivity, so we can be empty, so we can not-know, so that we can be guided by our knowing.

We thrive on paradox.

We acknowledge our needs, including those for love and partnership. We acknowledge the pain of our needs unmet. We commit to passionate partnering with ourselves, so that we may be whole, even in the face of our unmet needs.

---

[34] For more information regarding The Stream, go to www.thestream.org.
[35] This line became the basis of Platform Three: Becoming Co-Creative.

Through our wholeness, we can allow ourselves to risk Not-Knowing, which, in turn, allows us to know and, therefore, meet our needs moment by moment. The result is partnership with ourselves and others, rather than co-dependency or domination.

Through Not-Knowing, we simultaneously intend and allow, connect and release. In this way, we nurture and respect the wholeness of ourselves and others.

We exist at the intersection of the material and spiritual planes. At that intersection, our Not-Knowing opens us to the guidance and wisdom of the universe.

The Stream, August 14, 1999

The Stream is an expression of The Path of Not-Knowing. We are a gathering of souls who wish to pursue this path with each other's support. We did not create this path; nor do we own it. To us, it feels like common sense.

Why Would We Want to Become Not-Knowing?

We have already discussed the needless stress caused by our addiction to knowing, and we've acknowledged the relief we would feel if we let that go. Here we go one step further. "Some Thoughts About the Path of Not-Knowing" guides us to empty ourselves, and what we gain is the possibility of being guided by higher consciousness. Why would we want that?

In the beginning of this platform, we acknowledged that we are stressed by sitting in the not knowing, which is why we become so obsessed by the need to know. Suppose we were able to let go of the stress of not knowing? Suppose we felt instead that Not-Knowing allows us to be guided by a wisdom greater than our own? Would we still feel as much need to know? Or could we relax in the faith that we would be guided by higher consciousness?[36]

Plagued by uncertainty, it's good to feel guided. When we are, we feel good about our decisions, even if the outcomes look disastrous. For example, if I make an investment without divine guidance, I can feel stressed about the results. I fear that if I lose the money, something disastrous might happen;

---

[36] I doubt that many of us can completely overcome the fear of the not knowing, but we can certainly make a dent.

at the very least I might feel stupid and like a loser. On the other hand, if I follow higher consciousness and make the same foolish investment, I can console myself that there was some higher purpose to the investment, and what could that purpose be? For example, the purpose might simply be to show me that I should not invest, because I'm being motivated by the ego need to feel like a tycoon when I'm not, and the loss will finally bring that home. Maybe I am meant to learn how to deal with loss. Maybe this loss will finally cause me to confront a loss I experienced at 5, and through that healing, I become more available to love. If I believe that I am being guided by a higher purpose, I will look for a positive outcome, a positive learning, out of every experience. And, amazingly, there always can be—even if that outcome becomes evident twenty years later.

Is this process merely me rationalizing poor decisions and attributing them to higher consciousness, or is the universe guiding me to do my part in the transformation of consciousness? Only you can decide. For me, the answer is clear. My experience is that approaching each moment with the willingness to be guided has led me into exponential spiritual and emotional growth.

In addition, I have experienced that my guidance has brought me into a richness of life my small ego mind could never have even imagined. But more about this in Becoming Becoming.

Following our higher consciousness gives us a sense that each action has value, because we trust that each moment in our everyday lives is part of a larger evolutionary plan. We feel guided to go into the kitchen to wash dishes, or to run for the Senate of the United States. If higher consciousness takes us into the kitchen, we will know that washing dishes is for the highest good of all and exactly what we're supposed to be doing in that moment. If it guides us to run for the Senate, we know that running for the Senate is the experience we need to have, whether or not we win.

Following guidance often forces us to confront our fears and resistance. Higher consciousness might guide us to the telephone to make that long-avoided phone call and face that long-avoided confrontation or amends. It might encourage us to stop and smell the roses when we are driven by obsession. It might stop us from eating, when we are ready to convince ourselves that just one more bite won't hurt.

When we follow higher consciousness, we know we are not avoiding that which we are meant to do and meant to be. And when we know that we are embracing what we are meant to do, we feel the self-respect and wholeness nothing else can provide. But in order to have this great life gift, we must give up the belief we know and surrender our agendas to a consciousness greater than ourselves.

How Do We Know We Are Hearing Higher Consciousness?

Everyone asks this question, and it's a good one to ask. At this stage of our development, I can say that if we self-examine and release agendas, if we get support, if we listen, if we ask questions, such as "Is it for the highest good of all for me to do x, y or z?", then we have a chance of hearing higher consciousness. At this point, you may want to review some of the tips I offered in Platform Four: Becoming Mutually Supportive, when we discussed how to ask for the highest good.

No matter how clear our intention, however, and no matter how sincerely we try, we can't always be sure that we have succeeded in accessing higher consciousness. But don't worry. This is not even the purpose of Platform Eight. In this platform, we are simply releasing agendas and allowing ourselves to not know, which opens the door to the knowing that will guide us. Practicing Platform Eight supports us to embark on the journey. Let's not be afraid to try, and let's not use the uncertainty of our capacity to arrive as an excuse to not get started.

When I first connected to the inner voice, I had no idea what I was doing. Thoughts and words out of nowhere told me what to eat, what to do, and where to go, and I committed to following that inner voice, regardless of my fears and regardless of the consequences. This was my training. It was all practice for me to become disciplined to listen before I spoke or acted. And I learned.

Each one of us can develop our own sense of what inner guidance feels like, but here are some techniques that have worked.

Tool: Some Tips to Develop Our Capacity to Be Guided

- Take a breath and get neutral.
- Focus on yes or no questions.
- Learn to distinguish yes and no through the inner voice, feeling states or other techniques that work for you.

- Don't use guidance to avoid inquiry or confrontation.
- Don't use the appearance of guidance to promote ego agendas.
- Remain self-aware and alert to ego games.

First and always, take a breath and bring yourself into a state of calm and neutrality. Release agendas about what you want. Raise your consciousness upward and go into the depth of yourself. You may be seeking a sense of direction about some matter, such as asking for guidance about your relationship with someone or about your own reactivity. Sometimes in the silence you will sense or see something. Sometimes you will get nothing at the moment, but the answer will pop out of some seemingly random experience or comment that happens over the course of time, and then you will know what to do.

It's easier when you ask a yes or no question. For example, you may be asking for guidance about a question, such as "Would it be for the highest good of all, including me, to buy the house next door?" If you ask a yes or no question, you can learn how to distinguish between those two energies. Following are some suggestions.

First, here is a simple technique that worked for me. In order to distinguish between yes and no, I asked myself a simple question to which I already knew the answer. For instance, I asked: "Is my name Fred?" Of course, I knew my name was not Fred, but in the process of listening for the answer, I felt the experience of hearing the inner no. Then I asked myself if my name was Beth. When I heard yes, I was able to experience the feeling that comes to me when the answer is yes. From that experience, I developed a sense of when my guidance was yes and when no.

Others have devised techniques more attuned to them. For instance, many people don't hear anything like an inner voice, but they have identified a clear, relaxed feeling when receiving a yes and a constricted feeling when receiving a no. If you practice, you will get the idea as well and find a way that works for you. And as you open the channels of communication with higher consciousness, you will be guided in more direct and complex ways.

Guidance is not a substitute for information or confrontation. Some of us would like to bypass the process of discussion and investigation in order to avoid confronting ourselves and others about painful situations.

At times, we are ready to ask for guidance, and we may even need to be alone to do so. But if we typically retreat into a room, ask for direction and then come out with an announcement about what we have been guided to do, even though others are involved, we might be using guidance as a disguise for avoidance. For example, if we have not done our homework, if we have not confronted the issues, if we have not engaged in discussions with the others involved, we are not ready for divine guidance. In this case, the appearance of guidance will be a trick of the ego to separate and make our own decisions based on some ego need. To determine whether we are ready for guidance, we can use our ability to ask yes or no questions. If we are unclear as to our readiness, we can take a breath, get quiet and ask ourselves, "Am I ready to ask for guidance on this question?"

Similarly when we pretend to ourselves that we are seeking guidance, but we are unconsciously seeking reinforcement for our opinions and desires or for justification for fear-based behavior, we are not practicing Not-Knowing. We are practicing self-deception. This is pretty easy to spot. If we see ourselves looking for people to support us, but we choose those most likely to agree, we are probably kidding ourselves. On the other hand, if we seek out those who are neutral, have seen our patterns and are likely to confront us if we are off, we are probably willing to be guided in a real way. No technique can stop us from playing these games, but practicing Platform Five: Becoming Self-Aware can go a long way. We can ask ourselves if we are trying to manipulate outcomes for some agenda. We can check in to see whether we are afraid or angry while we're asking for guidance, which will skew the results. If we are self-honest, we usually know when we are pretending neutrality, but our egos may not want us to admit that this is so.

As long as we are still dominated by our egos, we can use anything to bolster our self-protecting, self-serving agendas. But working to overcome that domination is the work of our whole program, this platform and a lifetime. Let's keep going down the Path of Not-Knowing and see how many miracles can occur.

FINAL WORDS

If we truly release beliefs and agendas, if we embrace higher consciousness, we can become more relaxed about the process of living, allowing ourselves to be guided moment by moment. Which brings us to our next platform, Becoming Becoming.

But before we go forward, let's reinforce a tool, the tool to ask what is for the highest good of all. If we are truly practicing Platform Eight: Becoming Not-Knowing, and use this tool regularly, we will develop the capacity to truly turn over our lives to higher consciousness moment by moment, step by step.

Tool: Remember to Ask

Ask guidance about everything. It will develop your neutrality and ability to access higher consciousness. It will also habituate you to asking, even when everything in you screams "No, I don't want to!"

We ask for guidance about everything. "Is it for the highest good of all, including me, to eat this food or drink water now?" "Is it for the highest good of all, including me, to apply for this job or to adopt a puppy?" "Is it for the highest good of all, including me, to work on this project now, or play with my children, or take a walk, or call on a friend who is sick?" When we are in a couple or a group, and we need to make a collective decision, we all ask, "Is it for the highest good of all, including me, for us to take a vacation this summer?" "Is it for the highest good of all, including me, for us to quit our jobs and volunteer for some good cause or put our kids in private school?"

Practicing Platform Eight: Becoming Now-Knowing relieves us of a lot of needless stress and turns our life into a co-creative process with the universe. We are no longer scared of life, because we are no longer alone. Connected to higher consciousness, or The Source, we have more faith in ourselves and can relax into the process of living.

A Comment from the Ego

You've got to be kidding. Where am I in all this?

Our Reply

You can be the one to ask the question. You can be the one to see the need for the question. You can offer options. You can be the one to request the support of divine consciousness.

And so be it.

A CONVERSATION BETWEEN THE EGO AND US

The Ego Speaks Out

I guess you think I have more to say, and I do. So I'm going to let loose.

I'm really trying to follow all this, but I am honestly confused and extremely irritated. In Platform Six: Becoming Integrated, you acknowledged it's my job to take care of you, but you attacked me for being self-protective. That makes no sense. Then in Platform Seven: Becoming Accountable, you asked me to break my alliance with the Dark Side, and I have—to some extent, anyway—and in exchange, you told me I would evolve into awareness. That sounded cool, and I was willing to try it. But just as I was getting used to my new identity as awareness, along comes Platform Eight, and now you tell me I'm not supposed to know anything either.

I don't get it. If I'm not supposed to protect you, what am I doing here? If I'm supposed to be aware, how can I not know anything?

What the hell do you want anyway?

Us

Good question. Maybe what I want for you is what I want for me, which is to Become Becoming. Why don't you relax until we get through the next chapter?

The Ego

Oh, Jesus. What's next?

PLATFORM NINE

Becoming Becoming
Relaxing into the Process of Living

Wow, sometimes I thought we'd never get here. Becoming Becoming. It's my favorite platform. It sounds like fun; it sounds like freedom. But, as usual, we have to go through the muck to get there.

WHAT IS BECOMING BECOMING?

Life is a never-ending process of Becoming Becoming. On one level, this means that we never really arrive at any end point, because life is a series of transitions. On a second level, it means that although we can have goals, we are always moving toward an unknown destination. On a third and deeper level, it means that we experience life as a transformational moment, not as a linear pathway toward external accomplishments, but rather as a nonlinear experience of moment-by-moment opportunities for inner transformation. And on the deepest level, it means that we have become agents of divine consciousness, conscious participants in the process of evolution itself. It's not about us. We are only aspects of the collective in the process of transformation.

Now this all sounds rather abstract, but in fact, it's not. What I'm describing is a different way of experiencing life, one that is at the same time more challenging and more relaxed, less based on ego and more fulfilling.

In this chapter, we will come to understand Becoming Becoming on all four levels. Each will prepare us for the next, because each level is a transformational moment, an opportunity to become different, so that we are available for the next transition. And at the very end, we will offer a definition of Becoming Becoming.

Is this beginning to sound like a never-ending roller coaster? Maybe. Let's jump on!

What Do I Mean by a Transformational Moment?

We are going to discuss living life as a transformational moment when we get to level three of this platform, but before we proceed, I need to explain the concept, so we can go through these levels together and use them as transformational moments.

A transformational moment is one in which we are presented with a challenge either for the first time, or for the hundredth time, and we choose a different reaction and are capable of a different response.

Every time we transform, we become different. As different people, we become capable of confronting greater challenges and making greater contributions. It's like growing up. If we haven't absorbed the lessons of the first grade, we really can't absorb the lessons presented in the second, and we end up having to go back and catch up. If we don't know how to read, for example, we can't understand our history books.

So it is with everything in life. Let's say we have a tendency to run away from problems. If that's the case, we will be hampered in every area of life. We will run from the problems of relationships, work, childrearing, bill paying and so on. Nothing in any of those arenas will change unless we start with the foundational transformation, which is to stop running away from problems. We may start with one problem, or we may get support around the pattern itself. But once we have achieved the transformation which allows us to face our problems, we can address each other area of our life one by one. And as we address each area, we are transformed, and we are more capable of taking further steps as well.

Our healing and change has an order. When we live life as a transformational moment, we discover ourselves transforming the pattern that blocks us from taking on the next pattern, and we find ourselves doing first that which most effectively transforms us into the person who can then take the second step. This is true about everything in life. If I haven't organized my receipts, I can't fill out my tax return. If I haven't bought the groceries, I can't cook the meal. When we practice Becoming Becoming, we become intuitively guided to embrace the transformation that allows us to move most effectively to the next one.

With this in mind, we are going to see each level of Becoming Becoming as an opportunity to transform. Once we have made the first transformation, we are ready for the next. So let's start with the simplest level of Becoming Becoming, beginning to live life as a series of transitions, and let's embrace this as our first transformational moment.

LEVEL ONE: LIVING LIFE AS A SERIES OF TRANSITIONS

Most of us think of life as though it were a play that has a beginning, middle, and end. There is a set-up in Act One, a tension in Act Two, and then a resolution in Act Three. What's going to happen? Will the young couple get over themselves and realize they are really in love? Will the murderer get caught? Will the poor, undocumented workers get picked up by the INS, who wants to deport them back to Mexico? We find out, the drama is resolved, and the play is over. Now we can relax.

We all know that this view of life is rather silly. No sooner do we arrive at one point, when we are already moving to the next point. The height of summer is the beginning of fall. Every moment is a transition to the next transition.

Desperate for relaxation, we nevertheless keep creating the illusion that if we could only arrive at "x" point, the stress of uncertainty would be over, and we could relax! For example, lots of us focus on the wedding day as the culmination of a major goal. But those of us who have experienced this event are well aware that "happily ever after" does not exist, and the wedding is the least significant moment in what turns out to be a life experience with continual after-the-wedding stressors: Does he/she still love me? Do I still love him/her? Will we ever get out of this apartment?

When is he/she going to stop sneaking off to look at pornography, start earning more money, lose weight, want to have sex, say no to his/her mother? When is he/she going to stop leaving a mess in the kitchen, leaving childcare to me, forgetting to refill the car with gas? Do I really want this, or am I in it for the security? Is he/she eyeing others? Who's going to die first? I hope it is/isn't me, or I hope it is.

Marriage created no resolution. On the contrary. And that's the way life is. Every time we complete some process, we are on to the next, and that is equally true of everything in life, from getting divorced, to getting on welfare, to getting off welfare, to winning at poker, to getting a promotion, to retiring, or to anything else. Nothing ends cleanly without consequences that still need to be faced, because arriving at a destination only creates new stressors, new demands, and new realities to live with. And what's worse, no matter what happens on the outside, we still have to face us. There's no getting away from that.

We want life to be a series of end points, because then we would have the illusion of some sort of resolution. If "x" happens, that means all will be well. If I can talk my wife into selling the house; if I can get this job; if I can get my husband to stop cheating or to have children or do something, then I could breathe easy.

We know this isn't so. There is no arrival. You're elected president. Now you have to perform, and someone is already busy plotting to bring you down. You have the healthy baby, and the diaper washing begins. You recover from the acute phase of an illness, but you have poor health for the rest of your life or you're back to the old grind. Or you knock yourself out for 30 years so you can retire, but you hate the inactivity, or your nest egg disappears in a recession, or your health goes down the tubes.

Challenge, challenge, challenge. A never-ending series of moments that may appear like end points but are really just transitions to the next transition. Let's consider our own experiences.

1. When have I focused on a certain end point, thinking it would give me relief?
2. Relief from what?
3. Did it?
4. Did it create new stressors?
5. What am I now thinking will end my stress?
6. What new stressors will this resolution bring?

Okay, have we made this transformation? Are we ready to see that every transition is a transition to the next transition? If so, we can continue to the next leg of our roller coaster ride.

LEVEL TWO: LIVING LIFE AS A JOURNEY TO AN UNKNOWN DESTINATION

We get it. There is no end point. But don't we have anything to say about what happens to us? What about all our goals and plans? Living life as a journey to an unknown destination is the second level of Becoming Becoming. We understand that we can and must have goals and plans, even if the goal is to follow divine guidance, but, as John Lennon so wisely said, "Life is what happens to you while you're busy making other plans." That about sums up the second level of Becoming Becoming.

In Platform Eight, I spoke a lot about releasing agendas, but I know that people still have questions about goals. So in this section of Platform Nine, we acknowledge that we're always on our way to an unknown destination, and I describe how goals help get us there.[37]

To relax into the process of living, we need to remember that our minds create our goals, but the universe is in charge of our lives. Let's have some fun with this. Let's say you have the goal of going to Paris. The day of your departure, you get into your car and drive to the airport. On the way, however, you have an accident. Now instead of Paris, your destination is the hospital. You think your only goal for going to the hospital is to mend your broken body, but something unexpected occurs: You meet a nurse who talks about the healing benefits of body work. You come out of the hospital with a new goal: you are determined to become a massage therapist. While in massage school, you meet your mate, and suddenly, because of a moment of unconsciousness, you are a parent, instead of a massage therapist. Parenting creates financial stress, so with the goal of earning a bit of money, you find yourself working at a retail store at Christmas where you meet a stranger, have coffee, and start a friendship. Through this friendship, you realize that you are gay. With the goal of

---

[37] In Platform Three: Becoming Co-Creative, I discuss co-creating with the universe in depth, and I speak a lot about intention. An intention is where we aim our consciousness. Here I'd like to differentiate intentions from goals. A goal is the outcome we intend to achieve.

finding a more supportive environment, you leave your family and move to San Francisco. But while in San Francisco, you acknowledge that you're haunted by guilt for having abandoned your spouse and child, and so, with the goal of releasing your guilt, you go into therapy. Your therapist suggests using poetry as a therapeutic technique. With that goal in mind, you attend a poetry seminar, where you have a spiritual awakening and decide to join a Catholic religious order that happens to be located in France. Now so many years later, you're on your way to Paris.

We think our goals are where we're going, but, in fact, our goals are really the mechanism that starts us on a journey. What the journey holds, nobody knows. Without the goal, we might not have started out at all, but only destiny can show us where we are meant to go. On the way to each goal, we are moved by life, and life takes us where it will. Life is an unknown destination where there really is no end point until death or beyond.

What is that unknown destination? On the one hand, that's not totally knowable, of course, until we die. But, on the other hand, we all have the same destination, and that destination is our transformation, whatever that looks like for us. I'll speak about transformation in the next sections, but let's just take a big breath right here. When we understand that life is really a journey to an unknown destination, we can relax into the knowledge that we don't have to accomplish a whole lot of the external goals that we create for ourselves and that we can live a very fulfilling life through our own evolution.

To really value our own evolution, we need to make a shift in our view of ourselves and all existence. We need to value ourselves and our lives, instead of our external goals or performance. To see this more clearly, let's refer to an example related to income. Suppose we set the goal of doubling our income in the coming year, and this goal inspires us to think much more creatively. Yay for us. If we practice Becoming Becoming, we acknowledge that the increase in our creativity is a great benefit in and of itself, and we can relax around the whole experience, regardless of whether or not we double our income. The goal around our income has set up a forward momentum toward something positive, which is our becoming more creative. And we may or may not double our income in the process.

Let's look at some other possible outcomes. Let's say we still have the same goal, doubling our income, but on the way to that destination, we find we don't want the stress, we have a heart attack, our partner threatens to leave, or we discover that we liked ourselves better when we were less driven to earn money. We can stay stuck on the goal and force ourselves to work harder to earn more. We can drop the goal and feel like a failure. Or we can Become Becoming and acknowledge that the goal was a perfect mechanism for us to find out who we are and what we really want, and doubling our income isn't it. We didn't get where we thought we were going, but we got where we got. If we relax into that reality, we are practicing Becoming Becoming. If on the other hand, we judge ourselves only by the external outcome—the money—we will discount all the real benefits of the journey, which are the learning and transformation we've gained along the way.

Goals are not really the endpoint of our efforts. They are the impetus that start us on a journey to an unknown destination, but whose true point is our growth and evolution. Let's ask ourselves some questions in this context.

1. Can I think of a goal that I took on?
2. Did I fulfill that goal?
3. If I did, was it what I wanted?
4. If I didn't, did I gain something else along the way?
5. Do I have peace about that?

Some Further Thoughts on Attachment to Goals and the Relationship Between Goals and Shame

Since goals are so emphasized in Western society, let's look at them a little deeper. In our typical human pattern of letting our egos run the show, we create an agenda that then becomes the template against which reality is judged. Did I reach the goal? If not, what's wrong with me, with life, with God? Did others expect me to achieve the goal, too? Did my "failure" increase my anger and shame? Did my "success" make me resentful?

When we don't practice Becoming Becoming, we think of goals as end points, instead of as factors that help shape our journey. Stuck on goals, we judge ourselves and others in terms of achievements, positive or negative. I finished high school, I got a good job, I was fired, I got divorced three times, I went to jail. We feel stressed and become filled with shame or anger when we don't achieve our goals, and we suspect that others judge us, too. We array our accomplishments in our minds and compare ourselves positively or negatively to others, who have achieved "more" or gotten "ahead."

But what are the real impacts of achieving or not achieving some goal? Let's examine, for example, the possible impact of setting the goal of becoming a doctor. First, let's say that I succeed: I become a doctor. If I decided to become a doctor because I wanted to please my dad, I might look like a success on the outside, but feel angry with myself on the inside, judging myself as a person who sold myself out. Goal achieved; sense of personal integrity down. Shame up.

Now let's look at the case where I don't become a doctor, but I arrive at a destination that others hold in high regard. I may be able to escape shame altogether. For example, if I thought I was going to become a doctor, but midway through school I realized that I was much more interested in electrical engineering, I may be able to tell the story with a smile. Yes, Dad might have been slightly disappointed, because he was a doctor and wanted me to take after him, but I'm happy with where my life has taken me, because that's where my passion lies, plus the whole world sees my job as having status and value. Wow: Goal not achieved; personal integrity okay. Shame down.

But maybe even becoming an electrical engineer isn't really helping me. Maybe I'm perfectly happy about being an engineer, but my accomplished goal masks some other forms of suffering that I am simultaneously experiencing on the inside. For example, I might be an engineer, but I might lack confidence, or I might be a secret cross-dresser who is afraid to tell my wife, or I might earn quite a bit of money, but gamble it away or snort it up my nose. As we know, looking successful has very little relationship to feeling good about ourselves. So we may not in fact feel good about our journey after all. I became a respected professional, but I don't feel good about myself. Goal achieved; personal integrity down. Shame still up.

Now what can happen if I don't become a doctor, but I arrive at a destination that others do not hold in as high regard? It takes a lot of inner strength not to feel shame. Suppose I got emotionally involved at an early age, got married young, and started having kids. Under the circumstances, I changed my major from pre-Med to business, and I became a salesman. Even if everybody else thinks I'm a straight-up guy, responsible for my family, I feel like a failure because I didn't end up with a position that has as much status in my own mind. Is my personal integrity down? Maybe not, because I have taken on my responsibilities. But maybe in my own mind my integrity is diminished, because I didn't do what I intended and allowed myself to be waylaid by a sexual or emotional need. Goal not achieved; personal integrity down. Shame up. Suppose on the other hand, I acknowledge that I really didn't want to be a doctor anyway and that I prefer the social nature of sales. Suppose I admit that I was going to be a doctor only to impress my dad. Maybe I can let go of the need for a more prestigious position and be grateful that I chose the life that was meant for me. I can practice Becoming Becoming. I'm a winner on all levels. Goal not achieved; personal integrity up. No shame.

But suppose I was scared of failing as a doctor and got emotionally involved and pursued marriage just to have a good excuse to give up on pursuing medicine, ouch. Goal not achieved; personal integrity down. Shame up.

As we can see, achieving or not achieving the goal has very little impact on our real personal integrity and level of shame. What impacts them are all the inner factors associated with it. If we are Becoming Becoming, we accept and allow what we have done, learn the lessons of our lives and embrace the destiny that has come to us. Then whatever has happened, goal achieved; personal integrity up. Shame gone.

Just for fun, let's look at a different take on the goal question. Let's say I wanted to be a writer but "somehow" got married and pregnant at an early age, which "forced" me to become an accountant. I can tell the story that the reason I didn't become a writer was that I got married and had kids. But if I am honest with myself, I acknowledge that the family was not the block at all. In truth, I never really believed in my ability to make it as a writer, and I let myself get burdened by family responsibilities, just so that I wouldn't have to face the possibility of failure. So far, this sounds like the doctor case, and I will carry residual shame about running away unless I accept what I've done. But suppose the whole goal was a sham to start with? Suppose I admit that I truly never was meant to be a writer? Maybe I never was passionate about writing itself, but was enamored of an ego-based image of being a writer. Maybe I never wrote much past a few poems that I dashed down while smoking pot in college. Maybe the desire to be a writer was completely based on a need to prove myself. If I am Becoming Becoming, I will laugh at myself for having wanted the appearance of something, not the essence, and be grateful for where the universe has led me. So glad I didn't become an unsuccessful writer, because I am now a happy accountant. Goal not accomplished; personal integrity regained. And now the score is us: two; shame: zero.

Now let's look at ourselves and our goals.

1. What goals have I had in my life?
2. When I started to work toward one of those goals, what happened?
3. Did I fulfill the goal?
4. If so, was I happy?
5. If not, was the real outcome right for me?
6. Did I validate myself for the real outcome?
7. Was the destination validated by the world?
8. Did I let myself get distracted from something I really felt drawn to do?
9. Why did I?
10. Was my goal false to start with?
11. Goal: achieved or not?
12. Personal integrity: up or down?
13. Shame: up or down?
14. Do I feel ashamed of who I am?
15. Why?

The Unexpected Results of Achieving a Goal

Let's not leave goals yet. Let's say I intended to become a doctor, and then I achieved that goal. I may have a great sense of satisfaction for the moment. Dad is proud, and so am I. But then I find out I don't like the work after all. Or I find it too stressful. So now I become an addict, easily able to access prescription drugs. Meanwhile, I have married a person who is attracted to my status, instead of me. Now I feel unloved, too. Goal achieved; personal integrity down. Shame up.

One more time, life has brought me to an unexpected result; and it looks pretty bad. But perhaps things get so bad, my addiction is discovered, my medical license is threatened, and I end up in a drug rehabilitation center. While at rehab, I discover my inner self. I realize I have always been trying to please Dad, and I release the need to be important in his eyes. Now free to be myself, I'm drawn to service, become an addiction counselor, take a huge cut in pay, let my spouse dump me, sell the house, move into a condo with a bunch of friends, and feel great. Goal revised; personal integrity up. Shame gone.

Making Room for the Miraculous

Practicing Becoming Becoming makes room for the miraculous. If we can accept that life is a journey to an unknown destination, it can be an absolutely marvelous surprise, and if we let go of fixed agendas and judgments, we can find ourselves doing things of which we never dreamed.

On the other hand, if we set rigid goals and fulfill them, we might not be experiencing life at all. We could get stuck in our limited vision of what is possible, unable to envision all that life can offer, which, in turn, blocks what is possible. Ask the eight-year-old what she wants to do when she grows up. She may be able to tell you, but how can an eight-year-old envision what is possible in life? She doesn't have the vision or the experience to know. We are like that eight-year-old when we get stuck in narrow perceptions of reality, narrow perceptions that block out the possible. Just like an eight-year-old cannot comprehend nuclear physics, when we limit ourselves to what we think we want, we cannot imagine what exists in the many realms of reality that are yet beyond our grasp, and we cannot imagine ourselves in relation to them.

Let me offer a personal example. When I was a teenager, I became acutely ill, which led me to chronic debilitating sickness. Over a lifetime, my illness forced me to release every goal I had ever had, because I was incapable of physically performing the required tasks.

But I can honestly say that my life has unfolded in ways I could never have imagined. I live in a realm of existence I did not even conceptualize in my youth when my life goals were formed. And even in recent years, over and over again I have had to let go of what I have intended, which made room for the miraculous.

What's your experience of making room for the miraculous?

1. Can you think of the miraculous ways that your life has unfolded?
2. Can you appreciate the good that has come out of the bad?

3. Can you see that much of what you have experienced was outside your imagination when you formed your goals?
4. Can you consider that much of what could be experienced still lies outside your imagination?

Every day we have goals, large and small. We have short-term goals, such as getting to work on time or getting the children fed, or getting the attendant to pay attention to our call when we're lying helpless in the nursing home. And we may have long-term goals, such as giving our children an education so they don't need to work in the fields, or securing a better job with a pension, or dying in peace. When we practice Becoming Becoming, we understand that each goal is just a motivational moment that gets us moving and sets up a journey.

If we get out of bed with the intention of getting to work on time, but then we trip and end up with a broken leg, we can feel very distressed. But if we can release our attachment to the destination and embrace the journey, we will discover the miraculous in every moment, and become becoming. So let's hold on to our hats and enjoy the ride.

The Ego Blurts Out a Comment

Excuse me. I have something I'm just burning to say at this point. Okay, this sounds like a lot of great talk. But let's get real. Who wants to fall and break their leg? Who wants to get cancer instead of going on vacation? Who wants to end up a bum, instead of a doctor? This book is called *Living with Reality*, and I'm beginning to think of this as a hoax. It's just more fairy tale thinking, as far as I'm concerned. Give me a good goal. Give me success. Give me admiration any day.

Beth

Excuse me. I'm not done with this chapter yet. Hold your judgment till we get to Level Three: Living Life as a Transformational Moment.

The Ego

Whatever . . .

One Final Thought: What about People with No Goals?

There are no people without goals. Even the guy drinking under the bridge has the goal of staying warm and obtaining another bottle of wine. So even if on the outside we seem to have no goals, there is always some agenda lurking, short—or long-term. Here are some examples: If I don't make waves, my goal is to reduce stress. If I keep doing the same thing and never strive to do more, my goal is to face the fewest demands possible. If I do nothing to take care of myself, my goal is for Dad to take care of me. Let's take a brief look at whether or not I think I have goals.

1. Do I think of myself as having no goals?
2. Can I identify the goals under the no-goal?

Whether the goal is to get to the bathroom before we pee in our pants or to become the ambassador to the United Nations, we all have goals, and they speckle our lives. People who appear to have no goals often have the goal of not being challenged to transform. But life always challenges us to transform, which brings us to Level Three of Becoming Becoming.

LEVEL THREE: LIVING LIFE AS A TRANSFORMATIONAL MOMENT

Have we transformed through our discussion of Level Two? Are we ready to surrender to the reality that we actually live life as a journey to an unknown destination? If so, let's go to our next transformational moment, which is Becoming Becoming Level Three: Living Life as a Transformational Moment.

As we just discussed, we think of our lives as a series of events leading to an outcome or a series of outcomes. And we tend to judge ourselves by whether or not we have achieved those outcomes. But suppose achieving external outcomes isn't the point of life at all? Suppose achieving external outcomes is a very narrow way of viewing our existence, one that often leads to frustration, disappointment, and regret? Suppose being happy isn't the point of life either?

Suppose the purpose of life is transformation, transformation not just of ourselves, but the transformation of all consciousness, and we are just actors in a bigger play? Later in this chapter, I will go into great depth about these big challenges and how they relate to the transformation of all consciousness. But living life as a transformational moment isn't just about confronting big challenges. It's about confronting every challenge, large and small, moment by moment. Every time we feel stressed or challenged in any way, we are given an opportunity to change our reaction and response, and as we do, we are prepared to confront the next challenge. And this is the subject of Level Three.

Living life as a transformational moment is a way of organizing our time and embracing whatever life throws us. No external outcome is ever central to our existence. It is our inner transformation that truly counts.

How Do We Live Life as a Transformational Moment?

Life is a struggle. Of that, there is no doubt. And because it is a struggle, we are given endless opportunities, moment by moment, to transform. Once we figure out that transformation is the purpose of everything we do, we can relax into the reality of life being a struggle and focus on the process of transformation as a way to structure our lives. This is the next level of Becoming Becoming.

First let's look at struggle. Those who believe that "if it's meant to be, it will be easy and just flow" have missed the point, which is that our lives are not a series of events leading to an external result. They are a series of choices leading to an internal result. Without struggle, without challenge, there would be no need to alter our reactions and evolve into a new state of being.

While transformation is the purpose of existence, at the same time, if we believe that life is an illusion and that there is no reality, we are also missing the point. There is nothing illusory about the material world, although, of course, our perceptions are limited, and therefore "reality" is out of our capacity to grasp fully. But what is illusory is the notion that there is only one way to respond to and/or interpret the reality that exists. What is illusory is our focus on external goals and results as being the point of living at all.

Those who are committed to the transformation of consciousness realize that there are no accidents; rather there are a series of opportunities to transform, and most of them are missed. Clinging desperately to our stories, interpretations, and reactions, we still engage in life as though it were a battle to assert our will over mind, matter, and the process of living itself. This is a battle that cannot be won, but can only lead us into further stress and despair.

If we are to find our way through the maze of conflict, stress, and struggle that seems to define our very existence, we have to be willing to see transformation as the point of life and to embrace every experience as the mechanism through which that gift is granted. And to transform in any moment, we need to have completed the transformation that has prepared us to do so.

There are no shortcuts. We can't be there before we are here. We can't be at the next transformation until we have completed this one. We may not like it, but it is so. If and when we accept this aspect of reality, we dive into every challenge with gusto—more or less.

Let's look at some transformational moments in concrete terms.

A challenge could be something like this: Our children are screaming, and I want to kill them—at least at that moment. Or the plumber has overcharged us, and the toilet is still leaking. Or my husband is gambling, and I hate myself for having married him.

These feelings, these states of consciousness, are so familiar. I've been here before. And how do I usually respond? The children are screaming and I want to kill them, because I can't stand the noise, and I feel like a fool being overpowered by a three-year old and a five-year old. I grind my teeth, try to act calm or blow up at the kids or the dog. Transformational moment: Hmmm. I take a breath, detach, and realize that their screaming has nothing to do with me. They aren't trying to get me at all; they are just engaged in their own games. I can join them or even try to corral them to bed. But now I'm relaxed and not in an ego battle with a three-year-old and a five-year old.

The plumber has overcharged us, and the toilet is still leaking. I feel stupid for hiring him and angry for having been ripped off again. Hmmm. Transformational moment. I realize that I feel stupid because I trusted the plumber and ignored signs that he was incompetent. I forgive myself and look for a solution. Or I recognize that I feel betrayed because I trusted someone else's recommendation of the plumber and I didn't do any due diligence. I forgive myself and move on. Or I realize that plumbers are always taking advantage of me, and this time I realize I need to fight for myself, stop payment on the check, and call this one to account.

My husband is gambling, and I hate myself for marrying him. Transformational moment. I breathe in and realize my husband is angry with himself, and I'm buying into it. Or I have compassion for having married him, because he had some endearing quality that overrode common sense, or I have compassion for myself because I acknowledge that I was desperate and lonely when I met him and didn't care what he was truly like, as long as he paid attention to me. But now it's time for me to nurture myself and give up on expecting someone else to fix me.

A transformational moment is one where I take a breath, ask myself how I typically react, and choose a different response. My goal is no longer to fix someone or something: stop the children from screaming, repair the toilet, put an end to my husband's gambling. My goal is now to transform myself.

When my goal is transformation, the road may be hard, but I cannot lose! Now let's take a moment to look at ourselves in this regard.

1. Let me look at some challenging moments from recent times.
2. How do I typically react and respond?
3. Did I do anything different this time?
4. Let me stop myself every time I feel challenged from now on and ask myself: What is the transformational moment for me?

How does this help us relax into the process of living? By ending all conflict. In a world of transformational moments, there is no conflict with reality. Reality flows through our experience as the constant stage for our transformation. Each moment leads to another seamlessly, as we move from one transformational opportunity to another. And none can be skipped.

We can fight it, or we can embrace it. We can hate the people who bring these moments into our faces; or we can accept and even bless them. The shame is how often we need to replay the same transformational moment, because we cannot step into the next transition until we have completed the last.

Living life as a transformational moment allows us to live a life of never-ending potential. How do we do this? Let's look at ways.

One More Time Releasing Agendas and Goals

First, we release our long-term agendas. What is meant to happen is our transformation; not our success, our self-esteem, a "win," our external safety, or anything else we imagine. We recognize goals as mechanisms of the mind to get us going in some direction, as we have already discussed, so that life can take us where we're meant to go. No longer expecting goals to be fulfilled, we tune into divine guidance and ask for direction. We take the direction and start along the path. We allow it to go where it goes and allow ourselves to switch direction at any given moment. By doing this, we allow ourselves to move toward a never-ending potential.

We also release our short-term agendas. What we are meant to do moment by moment in our lives is to embrace the next transformational moment and allow it to work its magic upon us. When that moment expires, we are ready for the next experience and the next transformation. Released from external agendas, we are in the Not-Knowing and can thus intuitively be guided toward the next experience, meaning the experience that offers us the transformation that will lead to the next transition.

Taking these steps allows us to understand that there is no this or that; and there is no here or there, as I will explain in a moment. We are released from inner conflict and follow the Path of Not-Knowing. Here's how.

Becoming Becoming: There Is No This or That

A stress often mentioned by people is feeling overwhelmed: torn in too many directions. This is what happens when we don't know whether to do "this" or "that." Here's a way to handle that stress in the light of Becoming Becoming.

On a deep level, there is no "that"; there is only "this." In other words, there is one thing that we are meant to do now. Why? Because when we live life as a transformational moment, then we do what is next, realizing that only by so doing are we prepared for the next transformational moment.

Let me explain this in concrete terms. If I wake up in the morning and feel pressured to decide whether to do my taxes, eat breakfast, or clean out the garage, I can easily be torn between doing this or that. In fact, there is only one right place to start my day, and I need to tune in to myself and to higher consciousness to know what it is. Why? Because I cannot do "that" until I do "this," because I need to be the person capable of doing "that," which I will not be until I've completed "this."

Let's look more deeply into this example. As I mentioned before, I wake up in the morning and feel pressured to decide whether to do my taxes, eat breakfast, or clean out the garage. But, surprisingly, perhaps on this day what I really need to do first is take the dogs for a walk, which isn't even on my list. Because only by walking the dogs will my state transform so that I can then know what next "this" to take on. After I embrace walking the dogs as my transformational moment, I will then be in the state of mind to realize that the next "this" is to call a friend and make amends, because if I fail to do this, I will experience an underlying stress that will make me feel too nuts to do anything with relaxation and grace. When I have transformed through making the amends, I am now the person who can embrace the task of facing my taxes. And so on.

Living Life as a Transformational Moment means that I understand that it is not life that is unfolding moment by moment; rather it is I who am unfolding moment by moment. I need to transform by doing this in order to do that. My only job is to get clear as to what I should do next. The "I" that has transformed through that process will then get clear as to what to do next.

Now let's ask ourselves a few questions.

1. How often have I jumped into doing something I wasn't ready to do?
2. Wasn't it anxiety that compelled me?
3. Did I get clear before doing it?
4. What could I have done instead?
5. How would it have transformed me?
6. Can I try to tune in to discover what I should do moment by moment without getting hung up in some agenda?

There Is No Here or There

There is a similar process around "here" and "there." We often look at ourselves from the perspective of wanting to be somewhere else in our lives, achieving something, or completing something. For example, I have been thinking about finishing this book. When I am in that consciousness, my focus is on being "there," done with the book. I think when I'm "there," I will feel less stressed or more satisfied.

If I keep in mind what we've already learned, which is that every moment is a transition to the next transition, I already realize that when I finish writing the book, I'll have to face the stress of rewriting it. And when that's done, then I'll have to focus on getting it published, etc. So it's an illusion to think that somehow everything will change when I finish writing Platform Nine. But beyond that, there's a deeper illusion about getting there.

The truth is there is only "here," meaning that "here" is my state of mind or state of consciousness, and that's all that exists for me. I am not suggesting that reality does not exist. I am suggesting, however, that while reality exists, what I *experience* is my reaction to it. If a numb man is tortured, there is no torture. If a super-sensitive child is tickled, she may experience torture.

When we understand that reality is what we experience, "there" can only refer not to a different reality, but to a different state of mind. So when I want to be "there," what I'm truly craving is a change of state. And what truly allows me to be in a different state of mind is confronting the current state of mind and transforming in the moment.

Of course, when reality changes, we may also have a different experience, and so you could say that it is not necessary to transform in order to change our experience. Surely someone who is facing the terror of torture will be having a different reaction from someone who is having a warm massage. I am not making the absurd argument that external stimulus does not trigger pain or fear. But what I am saying is simply that in most situations, we are trying to escape a state of mind, which will carry forward into every other situation anyway, because for most of us our states of mind are pretty much built into our reaction-response patterns. As the old saying goes, "Wherever you go, there you are."

Most people are bedeviled with feelings of fear, insecurity, and negative self-talk. Isn't that why we escape, take drugs, or use other addictive behaviors? We want to be "there," when we're actually "here." We want to feel happy and relaxed, even though our inner selves are dominated by negativity. If we cannot overcome our reaction while we're in the experience, we will be back here again when the high wears off. Ultimately, we cannot escape from one state of mind into another. We can only evolve.

Ironically, here or there works against us in the opposite way as well. I am afraid that I won't be able to handle something in the future, and so I shrink now. I'm not "there" yet, and still I'm worrying about it. If we understand that life is a transformational moment, we can release that fear. Let's say I'm in high school and I'm afraid of college. Or I'm alive, and I'm afraid of death. How can I be ready to be in college until I have finished high school? I can't. Because I have not completed my current transformation, I cannot be prepared for the next moment of my life. The same is true of life and death. I cannot be ready for death until I am finished living. And if I truly complete every transformational opportunity in my life, I will be ready to die.

Let's now look at ourselves in terms of "here" and "there."

1. Is there a "there" where I want to be?
2. What is the state of mind I'm trying to change?
3. How can I address the state of mind instead of the external "there"?
4. What in the future am I afraid I can't face?
5. Am I there yet?
6. Can I have faith in myself that by the time I get "there," the universe will have prepared me?

The Biggest Transformational Challenge

Having understood that there is no here or there or this or that, we are ready to confront the biggest transformational challenge of our lifetimes: who we are. As I remarked earlier in Platform Eight: Becoming Not-Knowing, we are all here to take on a part of the collective evolution. I was designed to be a certain way and to take responsibility to accept and transform it. That's my job. It is not my job to be perfect. It's my job to be flawed and to accept responsibility for the flaw.

We can also express this in terms of karma. Karma is the law of cause and effect, whereby our current reality has been caused by thoughts, words, and actions in a prior lifetime. In this book, we have come to see ourselves not so much as discrete individuals with individual karma, but as aspects of the collective consciousness or the Oneness. If we think this way, we see karma as collective. We, humanity, have certain issues and behaviors to work out. And I am an aspect of that collective consciousness whose responsibility is to take on a part of that karma.

As I suggested in Platform Eight: Becoming Not-Knowing, if there is no individual, there is no personal salvation; but there is personal accountability. So if I am a manifestation of an aspect of the collective consciousness, it's my job to handle being that manifestation. For example, if I am avoidant, then it's my job to take on the consciousness of avoidance and try to transform it. If I feel shame about being dominated by a certain characteristic, and I let that shame stop me from acknowledging my patterns

587

and working toward transforming them, then I am rejecting participation in the collective evolution, because I am refusing to deal with the aspect of human karma with which I am entrusted. Back to our example: If I don't acknowledge that I am avoidant and if I don't try to overcome this characteristic, then I am missing the opportunity to transform avoidance consciousness for the collective. We carry a responsibility for the collective in another way. If I achieve a high level of consciousness, I achieve it not just for myself, but for the collective of which I am a part.

Let's look at some examples. If I am a pedophile, then it is of no use to anyone for me to just berate myself for being a pedophile or to pretend that I am not. It's my job to experience that consciousness, to be the pedophile, to understand the source of the behavior, to see the pain it causes myself and others, and to take responsibility to transform. Ooh. That's a really hard job, but then all jobs are hard. Being a rich spoiled brat might look a lot better than being a homeless person, but it carries its own treacherous path. The rich spoiled brat might have never been given responsibilities and so never developed real self-confidence or esteem. As a result, she may not easily be able to stop herself from trying fruitlessly to create a sense of value for herself through means such as continual shopping, socializing, obsessing about looks, pretending to have talents that don't exist, gossiping about others to make them look like less, or even taking drugs to escape the feeling of uselessness, all the while becoming increasingly dysfunctional and experiencing having less and less value. Ooh. That doesn't sound that great either. But her job is to have that experience, connect to divine consciousness, and transform.

We are all given primary challenges, which can look like learning disabilities, violent backgrounds, smothering parents, hunger, oppressive or repressive social systems, physical disabilities, genetic tendencies to addiction, unendurable trauma, over-sensitivity, bad influences, attachment to being loved or admired, mental illness, or other kinds of weaknesses on the physical, mental, emotional, or spiritual planes. Between the challenges of life and the challenges of our reactions and mental, emotional, physical, or spiritual weaknesses, we have a lot to deal with.

Many people see their own challenge or challenges and think that they are much worse off than anyone else. That can cause them shame, because they think they are defective; cause them outrage, because they think the universe has treated them unfairly; or cause them to absolve themselves of accountability, because they think their challenges are tougher than those of others. But I don't care if you are the prince or the pauper, you are given a primary life challenge and a set of tools to meet it. And if you don't meet that challenge, you get stuck in the same moment, over and over, never evolving and not contributing to our collective evolution.

What allow us to overcome those challenges are our resources. Our resources can be physical strength, material wealth, spiritual power, mental toughness, a meaningful support system, a lot of lucky breaks, divine intervention, something that will give us the power to face our transformational moments and transcend a seemingly pre-determined destiny. Sometimes our challenges feel overwhelming, our tools very inadequate, and our support very weak. This may in fact be true. But that's just another challenge for us to meet. Our collective experience teaches us that, if our resources are inadequate, we need to strengthen our tools and support to whatever degree possible, because without better tools and support, we are lost, forever lunch to the Dark Side.

And speaking of the Dark Side, we can see that living life as a transformational moment is a powerful tool to win the battle for ourselves. This, in turn, enables the Dark Side to play out its positive role, the role of showing us our individual and collective weaknesses so that we can recommit to strengthening ourselves and one another.

Let's look at ourselves in terms of primary challenges.

1. Can I identify at least one really large challenge that is mine?
2. Have I been resentful of it?
3. Have I felt shame about it?
4. Have I taken it on as my job to deal with?

Everyone's Job is to See and Confront Their Own Weakness

Here's reality. We are all screwed up. If we weren't, we wouldn't be here, because the purpose of our lives is to take on some aspect of the collective dysfunction and deal with it! If you're thinking you're the most challenged or most screwed up, look around. Or read this book. What I've been describing for hundreds of pages is us, normal human behavior. And almost all of us behave in these ways.

And that's the beauty. Once we accept that we are so alike, we understand that our destructive and self-destructive behaviors are actually normal. And once we accept that confronting our destructive and self-destructive behaviors is our job on earth, we can breathe a sigh of relief, get out of denial, and get to work.

What Does Shame Have to Do with It?

It seems that we are frequently confronting the feeling of shame or the threat that we might feel it. And so it is again here. We won't confront our challenges if we deny their existence, and in a world dominated by shame, we often feel so bad about our weaknesses that we try to hide them, blame others for them, or beat ourselves up for them in the misguided effort to shame ourselves into transformation.

Shame does not transform us. Support does. We might have a moment of shame that brings to our attention some flaw in ourselves, but the shame itself, if perpetuated, undermines our inner strength and makes us lunch to the Dark Side.

If I feel shame, I may not admit the behavior. For example, I fear that if I admit that I'm engaging in kinky sexual behavior, if I admit that I am judgmental and vicious, if I admit I lie and cheat, someone will take advantage of me, shame me, blame me, something. I can't do that. So I pretend, often even to myself.

Denial leads to despair and helplessness. When my ego beats me up for being weak or makes me fear exposure, I won't get support, and when I'm alone with a problem, I am helpless.

If we don't admit and embrace our challenges, the Dark Side wins again. But if we face the realities of ourselves and take them on, we can never lose, no matter how long or hard the battle to transform ourselves. Just making the fight transforms us. We've run the race.

Okay, So What Do We Do?

In a world where we practice Becoming Becoming through living life as a transformational moment, we recognize our weaknesses as central to our existence, and overcoming them is life's very point. Because this is a central realization, let's look at some healthy ways of facing our weaknesses and overcoming their impact on ourselves and others. Overcoming the impact of our weaknesses can look like compensation. Overcoming the impact of our weakness can look like asking for help to accomplish what we clearly cannot accomplish alone. Overcoming the impact of our weakness can be finding inner strength to persevere anyway, regardless of the external outcome. Overcoming the impact of our weakness can be achieving a transformation so that the weakness is no longer there. Overcoming the impact of our weakness can be to be in allowance of it, if there is no other choice, without being crushed.

Many people think that they can be satisfied with themselves only if their weaknesses stop existing, but that's an agenda created by the ego. We need to become Not-Knowing about our destiny and be guided by The Source as to which of the following approaches apply at any given time.

Facing a Challenge through Using Compensation

If you are crippled and cannot walk, get a wheelchair. That's overcoming weakness through compensation. Some people feel embarrassed when they have to compensate, because the compensation in itself points to their weakness. For example, if you tend to be mentally scattered, you can compensate for this weakness by using some kind of system for reminding you, whether that be a calendar, an alarm, an electronic form of organization, or the support of an employee or friend. But let's say your ego tells you that you should be ashamed of being mentally scattered. Your mother was scattered, and Dad never let her forget it. In that case, using the compensatory mechanism points to the reality of your mental weakness of which you are ashamed. If you let your ego dominate and you reject the tool, you'll have the satisfaction of pretending you're not scattered while you and everyone else have to suffer the consequences of the reality that you are. How smart is that?

A healthy use of compensatory devices is not the same as dependency. When you are dependent, you look to others to take responsibility for your weakness. That would be like throwing up your hands, refusing to use a calendar, and asking everyone else to remind you of what you're supposed to be doing. When you choose an appropriate way of compensating, you are being responsible. You're saying, I know I have this weakness, and it's my job to deal with it.

Using compensatory devices seems simple, but it's not. It can require a series of transformational moments. First we have to admit reality. Then we have to face and transcend the shame. Third we have to choose an appropriate compensatory mechanism. Fourth we have to use it. If our first reaction is to hide our weakness, facing it will have been a transformational moment. We will have become different and can now face our next challenge.

Stephen Hawking has motor neuron disease, is almost totally disabled, and has used a wide variety of tools to compensate for his disability, not the least of which is a voice synthesizer. His ability to face his challenge has not only been a transformational moment for him, but a transformational moment for us all, as we redefine the concept "weak"! If he can use a multitude of tools to compensate for his weaknesses, why can't we?

Let's look at how we may or may not have compensated for our weaknesses.

1. Can I think of a weakness of mine—physical, mental, or even social—for which I could compensate?
2. Have I been embarrassed to admit the weakness?
3. Have I used compensatory devices?

Facing a Challenge through Asking for Help

Let's say you have trouble disciplining your child. You get angry with the child every time he acts out; you blame your spouse; and you become resentful and frustrated. How different it could be if you contacted the school psychologist, asked your friends, talked to a therapist, and/or admitted to your spouse that you're not able to do a good job with disciplining your child. Maybe you could even sit down with your son or daughter, depending on their age, and tell them about your problem with figuring out how to discipline them. Instead of hiding your weakness, feeling shame, and blaming everyone else, you admit your weakness and ask for help.

Millions of addicts have achieved a new life through asking for the help of others. People suffering from the effects of functional illiteracy have learned to read as adults. Countless folks need food stamps during economic hard times. But how many people do not ask for help? People who are embezzling, gambling, or debting, but who won't seek assistance; people who are suffering from mood disorders but are blaming their families for being the source of their problems; people who are struggling at work, but prefer to labor late into the night rather than admit they're in trouble.

Does it seem obvious that we all need help with one or a hundred things? Of course, it's obvious when it's someone else who needs the help. But what about us? How often have we tried to hide a weakness and not sought support?

When we ask for help, how have we transformed? By getting over our old ego reaction of hiding our weakness in order not to feel humiliated or vulnerable. By so doing, our weakness has supported us, because it has brought us to a transformational moment within ourselves, which is that we have acknowledged our need for help. Pursuing that help can bring us to many other transformational moments, as well, which, in turn, may help us all. If two alcoholics named Bill Wilson and Doctor Bob didn't admit their alcoholism and desperately seek out the help of each other, there would have been no Alcoholics Anonymous or any other twelve-step program that has helped so many people in recovery.

Let's look at how often we ask for help.

1. Where do I need help?
2. Where have I admitted it?
3. Did I actively pursue the help?
4. Can I see the pursuit as a transformational moment?
5. Where have I still not admitted I need help or gone after it?

Facing a Challenge through Persevering

Sometimes we are addicted to love. We can see this, for instance, by looking at our behavior: Every time we are afraid we will lose approval, we shut up and wimp out on ourselves. If we deny the reality of this addiction, we will not even acknowledge our weakness and will try to cover it up with excuses. In fact, we will pat ourselves on the back and tell ourselves how nice and understanding we are.

A pattern like this does not disappear in a day. Our first transformational moment is to admit that we wimp out when our emotional security appears threatened. Our next transformational moment is to try to speak up no matter what. Do we immediately succeed in becoming the Hercules of the emotional realm? I doubt it.

But maybe we can start with talking more honestly with someone close to us. We tell them that we are addicted to approval or love. They'll probably tell us they have the same problem. We then ask for mutual support: Let's confront each other when we see the other falling into the old pattern. We commit to each other: No matter how many times we fail, let's persevere. When we can, we become more real in other situations, such as being with people with whom we feel more vulnerable, or with work or social groups where we don't already feel loved and accepted.

Every night we do an inventory of our day's behavior. Where have we been real? Where have we sold ourselves out? Let's try again tomorrow.

Where are the transformational moments? Everywhere. We acknowledge our weakness. We get past our shame. We share the truth with others. We continue to monitor our behavior. We start speaking up when the situation feels more and more threatening. No matter how many times we fail, we keep trying. Now that's the biggest transformational moment.

Being addicted to being accepted and loved makes us feel weak. Continuing to confront our weakness gives us a sense of integrity and self-esteem. We feel better about ourselves, because we are doing something we feel better about. On the other hand, if we throw in the towel and give up, we will suffer the consequence of not confronting someone when we need to. But worse than that, we will suffer the shame of knowing that we gave up on ourselves and didn't take the steps to change.

Let's look at another form of facing a challenge through perseverance. Some people are mentally or physically unstable but are vastly helped by disciplined living, such as exercising, meditating, and eliminating sugar, drugs, alcohol or other unhealthy foods. These people may start out the weakest but end up the strongest, because they have transformed themselves through their own efforts. It may take one try or a thousand, but persevering to discipline themselves for their highest good starts a cascade of transformational moments.

Just the act of persevering transforms us, because it gives us a foundation on which to build self-esteem. We don't feel like quitters, no matter how hard the struggle and how long it takes. In addition, by persevering, we are compelled to transform on many levels, because we continually give up behaviors and substances that used to comfort us. And we have to start connecting to the higher consciousness that will transform our state of mind, so that we can start building healthy patterns that support us.

One final point: If we feel like we lack the self-discipline to persevere, we need to persevere in developing that self-discipline. It might save our life. Remember that taking on the challenge is our job on the planet. It doesn't matter how many times we have failed. If we continue to take responsibility and continue trying, we are already winning.

Let's look at ourselves in terms of perseverance.

1. Have I noticed a weakness in myself in the past?
2. Did I try to hide it?
3. Did I try to overcome it?
4. Did I give up or did I persevere?
5. How did that make me feel?
6. What weakness in myself am I willing to confront now?
7. Am I willing to keep persevering, no matter the odds?

Transforming through the Challenge So That the Weakness Is No Longer There

Say we have an accident that results in a bad back. For some, that weakness is permanent and can never be overcome, and so we need to compensate and ask for help. But for some, exercise will actually overcome the weakness itself. If we persevere, our backs will strengthen again, and sometimes we will be even stronger than before the accident. The same is true on the emotional level. We may be fear-based through our genetic makeup or through a series of extreme traumas, but facing our fears may in fact someday give us enough confidence in ourselves that the fear itself recedes.

These examples seem simple and obvious, and yet in truth most of us miss great transformational moments every day, because we simply ignore the reality of our weaknesses, pretend they don't exist, blame others, or hide from challenges. Hiding from our own weaknesses is one of the primary blocks to transformation. We may perceive ourselves as inadequate, stupid, unprepared, insane, unstable, addictive, selfish, weak, desperate, needy, unbalanced, sexually driven, confused, frightened, shame-based, or one or a hundred other unattractive qualities. We may brag, deflect, avoid, judge, undermine others, leave the hard stuff to somebody else, bully, or run. We may use substances to comfort ourselves. We may use force to dominate. We may drive ourselves or others to make ourselves look good.

But guess what? If you do these things, so do I. And so does everyone else. And if you have those negative qualities, so do I. Let's get those weaknesses out of the closet and out in the open where we can all say, "And so am I." Then let's connect to one another to see what we can do together.

And what can we do? Miracles have occurred. As I mentioned in the previous section on perseverance, people with mental and physical weaknesses have transformed themselves. People with spiritual weaknesses have transformed as well.

How can we ever know when the transformational moment will come? My favorite example of transformation is the turning of water into steam. You can keep the heat on under the water for the longest time, and it appears that nothing substantial has occurred. But then suddenly, you have reached the magic moment when water turns to steam. If you give up before the change in state, you'll never know how close you were.

We cannot know or predict exactly what combination of factors will come together to change our beings in a permanent way. Many of us who have practiced this program have experienced changes that are profound and permanent. The same has happened with others through other modalities of change.

What we need to remember is that there is higher consciousness available. If we continue to practice these platforms, we will have more and more access to the consciousness able to transform us. But we have to keep doing the work.

What is my experience with transformation?

1. Have I ever experienced a true transformation?
2. How did it happen?
3. Have I seen that in others?
4. Can I keep the faith before the water boils?

Facing a Challenge through Allowance with Grace

We can't leave this section on facing our challenges without one more way of transforming through challenges. Sometimes we have a challenge, and nothing will change it. We can't compensate, get support, persevere or do anything to make it go away. What's the transformational moment?

Allowance with grace. In Platform Three: Becoming Co-Creative, we discussed intention and allowance. When we practice allowance through our wholehearted embracing of what cannot be changed, we can develop an inner strength that can more than compensate for our supposed weakness. We are in grace.

We have all seen it in people we know or have admired. Those who live every day with a huge physical or mental disability and who yet stay loving and aware, optimistic and caring, these are our heroes. Our transformational moment is to meet the challenge of allowance with grace, even if the initial disability cannot be offset in any way. And we can also stay always alert to the possibility that new resources will become available to us so that we can try once more to overcome the impact of our weakness.

When we have a weakness that cannot be overcome on the outside, we can still overcome its impact by refusing to let it rob us of life and of all the rest of our potential.

How do we do with allowance with grace?

1. Do we know anyone whose spirit we admire in the face of huge obstacles?
2. Are we that, too?

Life is a transformational moment. We have the choice to look at our weaknesses and choose a different response. We have the choice to look at the weaknesses of others and choose a different response as well. Do we typically separate from, condemn, judge, avoid, provoke, blame, tease, or humiliate those whose weaknesses are apparent? Doesn't pointing out their weaknesses facilitate us to hide our own?

And don't we hide behind one another's weaknesses? Don't we often justify ourselves by saying, "I couldn't, because he/she/they wouldn't let me or didn't want to?" Don't we justify not completing a job because he/she/they abandoned the project, bailed out, got it wrong? Don't we justify not taking accountability because he/she/they didn't?

And, at the same time, don't we sometimes avoid confronting someone on their weaknesses and accountability because we don't want to be held accountable ourselves or because we are afraid of being confronted, too?

What is the transformational moment? To connect to the person, remember they are being lunch, and then open our mouths and tell the truth.

Let's ask ourselves some questions about dealing with other people's weaknesses.

1. How do I typically deal with other people's weaknesses?
2. Do I separate and judge?
3. Do I hide behind their weaknesses?
4. Do I pretend I don't see their weaknesses and avoid confronting them with their accountability?

Every time we are confronted with a challenge, we can take a breath and ask ourselves, "How is this a transformational moment for me? What can I do differently?" If I have a tendency to try to force results, I can let go. If I tend to whimper to protect myself, I can stand strong. If I tend to run, I can stay and face the fight.

And I can always pray, pray for the inner guidance that will show me how to use any given moment for transformation, and I can ask for the courage to seize it.

LEVEL FOUR: BECOMING BECOMING—BEING GUIDED BY DIVINE CONSCIOUSNESS

If we have transformed through embracing Level Three of our platform and are approaching life as a transformational moment, we are ready for the next step. Because, ultimately, Becoming Becoming means only one thing: Becoming empty of all agendas and horizontal relationships and being guided by The Source or higher consciousness. And that's what we experience when we reach Level Four.

Why Are We Here?

If we go back to our introduction, "Ego, Instinct & Evolution," we remember the myth of creation. In it, we describe the beginning of our time as the fragmentation of the Oneness into discrete parts, the Big Bang of universal consciousness. And once this process had been set in motion, there we were: planets and stars, species and individuals, male and female, and the never-ending evolution of the whole into greater expansion and differentiation.

And each individual fragment became aware of its individuality and the ego was born. We perceived ourselves to be separate and alone, but we weren't, we never were, and we never will be. Each of us continued and continues to be part of the Oneness, no matter how we feel. And in fact, feeling separate and alone is exactly the experience we all have, the one we are meant to have and to overcome.

Once each of us, still an expression of the Oneness, embraces our fragment and surrenders to being that fragment, we affirm: "I will take this on." And what is the "this" that we are supposed to take on? A challenge. A weakness. A separateness. A potential. A constellation of characteristics that in and of themselves may seem dismal, destructive, fantastic, or fabulous, but seen from far, fit together with others as a whole, just like each thread woven together creates a tapestry, and suddenly it all makes sense. Taking on our part is the gift that we give ourselves and the universe, as we offer our lives as the embodiment of that fragment and the embodiment of its potential of transformation back into Oneness. By so doing, we return to the Oneness, but now as individuated fragments, not as undifferentiated consciousness as we were before we fragmented. We are now more evolved, because we are now individuated in the context of Oneness and have found our way home.

Put simply, we are a collective consciousness, full of flaws, and each of us has a big job: to take on our challenge and transform it into consciousness; and in order to do that, we need to remember our Oneness, and as we do that, all of consciousness evolves.

How can we do or even understand this process? By connecting to the divine energy of which we are a part and which guides us. By being instruments of divine consciousness.

We cannot individually determine our role in the collective evolution. Only higher consciousness can guide us to be the means through which all consciousness evolves.

HOW DO WE BECOME BECOMING?

This entire book has been about the journey toward Becoming Becoming. But there are some loose ends that still need addressing. First let's address agendas.

Releasing All Goals and Agendas

The Reader Speaks

Releasing all goals and agendas? Aren't you kidding? Haven't we just spent half this chapter talking about using goals in the process of Becoming Becoming? Didn't you tell us that goals are the impetus that starts the journey toward the unknown destination?

Beth

Yes, and now I'm saying that, as we reach Stage Four, we don't need agendas or goals at all, because in the process of Not-Knowing, we are constantly open to the guidance of higher consciousness, and higher consciousness will be the impetus that moves us toward the unknown destination.

Reader

But does that mean that I'm supposed to ask higher consciousness when to get out of bed in the morning? I mean isn't that ridiculous?

Beth

No, it's not ridiculous. Once we release agendas, we have an open channel to higher consciousness and the information just flows. We no longer belong to ourselves in the old narrow sense. We belong to the Oneness and we intuitively know what to do.

Reader

Really? Maybe that doesn't sound that bad. What does it take?

Releasing Horizontal Relationships

As we have reiterated several times before, life is a struggle, and the world is a scary place. In Platform Two: Becoming Differentiated, we discussed our tendency to merge with others in order to create safety. Even those of us who look angry and who seem to be separating are merging with somebody or something to feel safe. As adolescents, we merge with the "kids" or the gang, even while asserting our independence from Mom and Dad. As adults, we try to merge with one another in groups or couples. Some of us merge with the Dark Side itself and seek ways of affirming that commitment through violent acts. Some of us merge with substances, like alcohol or food, and allow our lives to be run by them. Some of us merge with experiences like the high of a win, or a run, or climbing a mountain, or even religious or spiritual highs. Most of us merge with people or identities. I am a successful businessman, or a mom, or a thief. And all of us merge with our egos, which promise to protect us.

Regardless of the object of our merging, we are seeking safety, seeking to escape the frightening feeling of aloneness in a scary world. That, in fact, is the ultimate motivation for most of us to have sex: to create or co-create an experience where we can surrender our edges just for a moment and get lost in something bigger than ourselves.

All of these relationships are horizontal. That means that we are looking to something or someone outside ourselves to connect to, instead of connecting to ourselves and divine energy itself.

How Does This Play Out?

First let's acknowledge that most of us have a horizontal relationship with our own ego, which claims to be there to protect us. Being in a horizontal relationship with my ego, I will automatically be dominated by my ego's view of what has occurred and how I should respond. It will be exceedingly difficult to shut out that voice and be open to guidance.

I may also have a horizontal relationship with you. I believe that you are going to give me some experience that I need. You will make me feel whole or happy. You will make me feel safe. You will make me feel as though I were not alone. Since I'm counting on you, I, therefore, must focus my energy on getting you to perform. Ultimately, you fail in some way, and I am angry and disappointed and seek some other horizontal relationship, whether with another person or something else. While I'm being horizontal with you, I am organizing my behavior in order to get you to do something for me. I am not regulating the flow of my own energy according to my needs, but in order to get you to meet those needs. For example, if I need to feel appreciated, I will do all kinds of things to get you to appreciate me.

We can have horizontal relationships with groups as well as individuals. In order to be accepted by the group, I have to look a certain way, behave a certain way, think a certain way. This group could be a small social circle, a couple, a community organization, a religious identity, a class, a nation, a species.

Most of us are unconscious that we are in horizontal relationships because they seem so normal to us, but each horizontal relationship creates a bond, a link to human consciousness. It means that we cannot see clearly because we are limiting our perspective to human eyes, and in fact to the eyes of a particular human or set of humans. If my family has certain attitudes and prejudices, it's likely that so will I, unless I have a horizontal relationship with a group carrying opposing attitudes. And whatever the group, I will tend to do everything I can to fit in and to get others to bond with me. And if all humanity sees something from the same perspective, it is especially difficult to see it differently.

This phenomenon sounds familiar, doesn't it? We have discussed it before, but in Platform Two: Becoming Differentiated, we used the term "merging" to describe it. Now we are ready to see merging as a function of horizontal relationships, and now we are ready to gain insight into how to overcome them, which is to embrace being vertical instead.

What Is a Vertical Relationship?

When we are connected first to ourselves and The Source or higher power, we are in a vertical relationship with the universe. Now we are no longer bonded horizontally with our peers. Vertical with ourselves and aligned with a power greater than our own consciousness, we can remain vertical even when engaged in relating with others.

Amazingly, once we are in vertical relationship with ourselves and the universe, we feel so much more empowered, and we can relax into the rest of our relationships. From Becoming Oneness, we know that we are connected to everything. If we are vertical with the universe, we know we will find one another in the Oneness, and we don't have to struggle to find that connection. If we are vertical with the universe, we are not dependent on others for our wellbeing, so we don't have to sell ourselves out. And if we are vertical with the universe, our safety is not contingent upon the behavior of others, so we don't have to control everything that they do.

Being in a vertical relationship with the universe opens the door to real relationship with others. Freed from the need to be horizontal, we can take on the risk of relating, knowing that we will continue to be ourselves because our survival and wellbeing come from a different source.

How Do Horizontal Relationships Interfere with Becoming Becoming?

Now that we know there's an alternative to horizontal relationships, we can commit to becoming vertical in all our relations. But before doing so, let's take a little closer look at how horizontal relationships interfere with our Becoming Becoming.

Horizontal relationships block Becoming Becoming entirely. We spoke earlier about becoming instruments of higher consciousness, but we cannot focus on our connection to ourselves and to divine consciousness if we're busy trying to bond with other people. When we're trying to bond, we always unconsciously carry our agenda to fit in with or control others to be safe. If we are focused on any of these agendas, how can we truly be available to be guided?

What Is the Purpose of Our Guidance?

Many of us still want our inner guidance to be the pathway to safety or success in some predetermined form. But when we understand our role in the universe, which is to take on our part of the collective evolution, we need to release all agendas and become willing to do our part. If we have any other agenda, we will not be listening.

Suppose, for example, we are being guided to address someone else's behavior in a particular way. How are we going to be instruments of divine consciousness, if we are horizontal with him or her? We might be impacted by:

- The other person's shame or anger with themselves
- The other person's fear of being judged
- Other people's anger toward that person
- Other people's compassion toward that person
- His or her spouse's feeling about the person, what they did, and how it should be handled

- Our view of how we're supposed to feel and respond based on our self-concept, upbringing, or the beliefs of a church or other social group
- Our ego's vision of how we will look if we respond in one way or another
- Any human concept about how that person's behavior should be addressed

Let's make this very concrete. Let's say you drove over my rosebushes. My first reaction is anger, because you've damaged something I hold valuable. Merging with my ego, I feel that I've been stepped on too many times, and my ego says this is the time to stand up for myself. But am I not also being impacted by your shame about being negligent or drunk? Aren't you angry with yourself? Isn't everyone in the neighborhood disgusted with you? Isn't your wife feeling despair that you'll never get sober? Isn't your employer looking for an excuse to fire you? Doesn't all of society say that the way to handle the situation is to get angry and slap you with a bill, so that you will feel your accountability and have to pay?

In addition, if I am an alcoholism counselor, I will have an alcoholism counselor's view on how to handle the situation. If I'm a mom with a kid who drinks, I might have another. If I am both, I might feel conflicted. And so on.

How can I be guided by higher consciousness if I tap into any of the above? Can we be entirely clear and relaxed, connect to divine consciousness, and ask how to handle this situation if we are bonded and horizontal with any aspect of human consciousness, which already has the answer?

To practice Becoming Becoming, we have to let go of identifying with human opinions, views, and agendas and just let ourselves be guided by higher consciousness. Going back to the rose bush incident, higher consciousness might tell me that I need to go to you, hug you, and offer to have a rose replanting party. Or it might tell me that I need to call the police so that your driver's license is suspended. Or it might tell me to tell you that those roses needed to be dug out anyway. Or it might tell me to do all three.

We cannot respond based on other people's opinions, though their experience might be valuable information. We cannot care about how people will perceive us. If we are guided to be kind and forgiving, some may think we're too soft and judge us as enabling. If we are guided to call the police, some may think we're too harsh and judge us as going overboard.

Higher consciousness is looking at the big picture. Sometimes the "offender" needs a hug; sometimes a kick in the pants. If we care about how other people will perceive us in the situation, if we are horizontal with anyone else's consciousness, we will not be empty of agendas and be free to listen to The Source. Equally so, if we worry about how we look to ourselves, meaning our egos, we won't be free either.

Let me think of a situation where I needed to respond.

1. What individuals' and groups' worldview or opinion might have influenced my own?
2. What was my connection to them?
3. How did that impact me?
4. Let me think of a situation I'm in now.
5. What horizontal relationships might be impacting me?
6. Am I able to be clear and listen to divine guidance?

We cannot reorient ourselves to Becoming Becoming if we carry within us the need to bond with or be approved of by anyone, even our own egos. Many times in my life, I have had to say things that made me look mean or uncaring. Many times in my life, I have done things that made me look weak and exploited to others. Many times I have had similar judgments of myself. My job is to listen to The Source, regardless of how it looks to others or feels to me. My job is to listen to The Source, regardless of the consequences.

The Ego

I need to say something here. What if people don't like me, because I've listened to divine guidance?

Beth

What if they don't? We can always practice Platform Six: Becoming Integrated. I release the need to be liked, because I need to be whole.

The Ego

But suppose I lose my business, my social circle, or my job?

Beth

Then I release the need to survive.

The Ego

But suppose I end up alone?

Beth

We can't be alone when we have ourselves.

The Ego

But suppose I only imagine that I'm being guided, but I'm really one of those nuts who thinks they're divinely inspired and then goes out and shoots a dozen people.

Beth

If you've been practicing this book, you'll have already developed the self-awareness to at least suspect that you're being reactive and dominated by the Dark Side, if you think you're being guided to go out and shoot a dozen people. If you think you're being guided to do something destructive or hurtful, maybe you'd better take a deep breath and get support from those who are more neutral. In fact, if you start hearing negative voices in your head, it's probably not The Source, and I would compassionately suggest that you seek spiritual, psychological, or medical attention. Such behavior would not be caused by practicing Platform Nine. At worst, you are simply using the excuse of guidance to justify what your ego wants to do, or the Dark Side is manipulating you into thinking you are clear, when you are being dominated by negativity.

The Ego

But, seriously, how do I know when I am being guided by divine consciousness?

Beth

I've addressed this question before, and I'll probably end up writing about this again many times in the future. But frankly, right now, I'd like to get back to finishing this book. I feel like you are blocking me from continuing, just when we're coming to the end.

The Ego

Okay.

Releasing Our Fear of Consequences

How can I follow guidance if I am focused on protecting myself? I can't. If I want to practice Becoming Becoming, I need to allow the consequences of my guidance to be what they may. Being an instrument of higher consciousness is not a popularity contest; nor is it a guarantor of safety. It is the way I am guided to fulfill my destiny and be of service to the whole.

I may be guided, for instance, to go into a dangerous place where I get shot. That shooting might create untold value for the collective, bringing awareness to youth involved in gangs or bringing reconciliation in the long run to the community. It might transform my consciousness. It will be for the highest good of all, whether I know it or not.

Because we are one, we are guided for a collective purpose, even if we don't know it. For example, if The Source guides us to buy a lottery ticket and we lose, we may have bought the ticket just so the guy after me could buy the next ticket and win. In a situation like that, we may never even know how the universe has moved us for its own purposes.

Or sometimes we are guided to be angry, because the other person needs to realize that their behavior is hurtful. Once again, our behavior is for our benefit only in the sense that we are part of the collective consciousness that is being transformed.

At other times, we are being guided into having an experience that transforms us directly. Again, we are still part of the collective consciousness, and so our transformation is still part of our collective evolution. We may be guided to buy the lottery ticket and lose, because we need to face the fact that we need to stop gambling. Or we need to have a transformational moment around losing. Or we needed to be in that gas station at that moment to have a transformational moment around something occurring there.

Or we need to buy the ticket and win, because we need the money, or we need to have the experience of winning and squandering, or we need the experience of winning and confronting the question of how to spend it, or we need the experience of seeing how our relatives and "loved ones" react to our gaining wealth, which shatters some denial that we carry within us. Always, our experience is about our transformation; it is not about an external result. And our transformation always impacts the whole.

Many people want to connect to higher consciousness for some purpose, such as to fulfill their dreams, or get rich, or get healthy, or find their soul mate. Higher consciousness is not a tool to fulfill our agendas, even when they look noble. Higher consciousness is our connection to the creative energy that brought us into being and which is guiding the evolution of all consciousness.

Even those open to higher consciousness often accept it in only circumscribed areas, but want to keep ego control in others. We could want to resist guidance in our behaviors around food, sex, work, marriage, social behaviors, anything where we still want to maintain control so that we please ourselves, escape, stay safe, or gain some advantage or edge.

All this is perfectly understandable. The ego is determined to protect our individual existence, and our commitment to Becoming Becoming must endure the onslaught of doubt that the ego raises whenever its control and agendas are threatened. Unless the ego is twice born, it cannot identify that our wellbeing is connected to the whole and that our joy comes from being in the Oneness.

Under these circumstances, how will we be able to hang on to our resolve to be open, to release self-protection and to stay committed to functioning in ways that might seem irrational to the mind? We can remind ourselves and our maturing egos that the benefits of being guided are a sense of relaxation and fulfillment that self-protection can never provide.

Following inner guidance gives us a deep sense of integrity and personal wellbeing that is unrelated to anything external. And when I speak of anything external, I mean both emotional consequences, such as the possible loss of love or approval, or material consequences, such the possible loss of money, a house, or a position in life. Following inner guidance allows us to trust our choices, regardless of the apparent outcome. It brings us the powerful sense of being a part of a collective purpose that our minds can hardly glimpse. It can lead us to many unknown and exciting destinations.

To practice Becoming Becoming, we need to let go of self-protection and be guided in all areas of life. There is no Becoming Becoming if we still reserve the right to let ourselves be guided by the ego, narrow self-interest, or short-term goals in any arena of existence. If we are truly ready to practice Becoming Becoming, we can use our release tool in order to release the need to control any particular area or areas of our lives.

Let's ask ourselves how ready we are.

1. Where am I willing to be guided by higher consciousness?
2. Why?
3. Where am I not?
4. Why?
5. Am I willing to do it anyway?

And so now we understand the whole picture. Becoming Becoming allows us to be guided to have the experiences that will transform us, individually and collectively. And so if I want to relax into the process of living, I give up thinking I always know why I do what I do, and I go forward with faith. I open the channel to higher consciousness and keep no pockets of resistance.

No matter the external consequence, when I become becoming, I always gain the reward of watching myself evolve into a person of greater and greater strength, integrity, and spiritual energy. As I feel myself opening my connection to higher consciousness, I am transformed, my relationship with the universe transforms, we transform. And as I open to higher consciousness, I become increasingly available to the amazing and wondrous experiences of Oneness energy that transport us into other dimensions and the real experience of joy.

Let's ask ourselves these questions:

1. Can I think of times when I felt guided to do something?
2. Do I always know why?
3. Can I see my transformation?
4. Can I start to think of myself as part of the collective transformation?
5. Can I start to think of myself as part of the transformation of consciousness itself?

Becoming Becoming is the never-ending process of transformation in which we are all participating, as we swirl through the universe hardly aware of what we are and what we do. The more we consciously and willingly participate in this process, the more we relax into the process of living and become a blessing to us all.

Which leads me to some final words and the definition of Becoming Becoming.

WHAT IS BECOMING BECOMING?

Becoming Becoming is living life as a process, guided by higher consciousness for the purpose of collective evolution. In so doing, we unleash the power of The Source on the planet.

Wow! It's all about the process. That sums it up, doesn't it? God once told me that I had better get used to the process, because that's all there is. Everything is a transition to the next transition.[38] Darn. You mean, there's no becoming became? That's tough. I am so linear in my thinking. I want to accomplish something, finish this book, get healthy, have a happy life. It's tough to give all that up and surrender to the reality that life is a transformational moment, guided by higher consciousness, and the purpose of my individual life is not personal. Instead, it is to be part of the evolution of consciousness itself.

But what about me? How does any of this make me feel good? Well, here's the happy surprise. When we stop focusing on our safety

---

[38] Green, Beth. *God's Little Aphorisms*. Lincoln: iUniverse, 2005.

and wellbeing, we can finally go vertical with ourselves and with higher consciousness; and when we transcend the domination of the immature ego and the ego is twice born, we finally relax into the process of living, knowing that we are part of something larger than ourselves. And then we are able to fully receive all the beneficial energies destined for us.

We started this book talking about how we focus, not on reality, but on altering our feeling state. Now we realize that the way to alter our feeling state is to let go of our attachment to human consciousness as we've known it and become nurtured by higher consciousness and the vibrational energies available to us. When we do this, we are more relaxed, alert and filled, and we can face reality squarely, honestly and with grace.

Living with Reality, Unleashing the Power of The Source

Most of us try to live our lives from the perspective of the ego, where we advance our own personal goals and desires. Busily trying to alter our personal feelings, we have avoided reality, been addicted, tried to dominate or be cared for, and, as a result, hurt ourselves and one another in a myriad of ways. Throughout this book, we have touched on the results of these practices throughout human history.

Are we ready for something different? Are we ready to take on our problems in a way that is co-creative, mutually supportive and actually addresses reality? Are we ready to be guided individually and collectively? Are we ready to embrace our feelings as information but not let them dominate us? Are we ready to promote that which is for the highest good of all, including us and every other species on the planet?

To accomplish all this, we need to tap into higher consciousness, the consciousness beyond our ego, and we need to tap into that consciousness both individually and collectively. Learning how to do that has been the purpose of this book. Now we are ready for our next step, which is to unleash the power of The Source on the planet.

Up to this point, we have been thinking of I, you and us, and how we can work together to co-create the world we want, and this has been an important step. When we practice Becoming Becoming, on the other hand, we go vertical and rely on higher consciousness. Now we begin to experience ourselves as part of the Oneness, and we don't even have to confront our ego-based mentality. Guided moment by moment by the creative source of the universe, we automatically act in ways that support

611

the evolution of consciousness and are ourselves imbued with amazing creativity and awareness.

Earlier in this book, I said there is no personal salvation, but there is individual responsibility. Our individual responsibility is to shift into Oneness consciousness by Becoming Becoming. In this way, each of us does our part in the process of our collective evolution.

As we are powered by divine energy, it is not we who are empowered, but higher consciousness itself. Through Becoming Becoming, we are guided throughout our lives in a way that unleashes the creative power of the universe, which, in turn, helps us address our collective problems. As the universe fulfills its destiny through us, we simultaneously fulfill our individual purpose as conscious co-creators with the universe in its process of evolution.

To experience this state of consciousness, to feel connected to everything in our everyday life, this is grace. So at this point, let me introduce one final tool. Up to this point, we have made decisions by using our tool from Platform Four: Becoming Mutually Supportive. We have asked "Is it for the highest good of all, including me, to do 'x'?" This framework still assumes that there is a separate you and me, and we can be guided to do what is for the highest good of all.

Now let's reframe the question based on our new understanding, on a true commitment to Oneness. Use this tool if you feel so guided.

Tool: Unleashing the Power of the Source

Whenever confronted with a choice, ask the following: "Will it most effectively unleash the power of The Source on this planet if I do 'x'?" You can substitute another word for "The Source," if you prefer, as long as it refers to the Oneness, higher consciousness, divine energy, universal chi, whatever is a power greater than yourself. When we use this tool, we are no longer addressing our decisions from the perspective of separate individuals who are coming together for mutual support. We are addressing our decisions from the perspective of the whole itself. We have surrendered the old perspective, the right to be instruments of our ego consciousness, and have embraced the new perspective, being instruments of divine consciousness.

❧

Becoming Becoming is the endpoint of our book, although, of course, there is no endpoint of evolution. We understand that everything we have done has brought us to this transformation, and each platform has been a transformational moment in itself, allowing us to take the next step toward the next transformation. We have become a part of the universe in the process of realizing its potential, and, as such, we are enabling higher consciousness to unleash its power on this planet.

We may not be able to feel our Oneness every minute of every day, but we have the tools and practices to orient ourselves to that consciousness, and with every effort we make to dedicate ourselves to unleashing the power of The Source, we give more and more power to the higher consciousness that can guide our lives as individuals and as a species. We feel more relaxed, because we have greater perspective and trust, and we feel more joyful, because we are now imbued with the sublime vibrational energies available to us all.

BACK TO THE BEGINNING: THE MYTH OF CREATION

Becoming Becoming is not only the culmination of our book; it is also our current transformational moment as a species. The ego is being twice born, because it now identifies with the whole, rather than the part. It no longer needs to separate and prove its existence through the "No." And no longer separate, it carries no further need to prove "our" value, create distinctions or prove itself. The shame of existence no longer prevails.

Let's explore these points further. In our introduction, "Ego, Instinct & Evolution," we described the genesis of the ego. To review: The ego came into existence when the Oneness fragmented into discrete entities: the heavens and the earth, God and non-God, every being, thing, thought or energy as distinct from every other being, thing, thought or energy. The ego is simply the awareness of individual existence, and it carries an instinctive urge to protect itself—and us. The ego fights for the continuation of our individual existence and as such, it is compelled to fight for resources. The baby cries; the general proves his or her capacity to command; the teacher relies on his performance or her labor union. Each one of us uses whatever we can in order to keep resources flowing to us to ensure our survival.

In our introduction, we also discovered we all share the shame of existence: the realization that as infants we are burdens, consuming more than we give. Our egos frantically search for ways to persuade others to take care of us, and through a convergence of our genes and environment, we develop personalities that ensure we would receive those necessary resources.

The need to prove our value feeds the ego's pre-existing tendency to focus on the "I," to create distinctions between "us" and "others," so that we will be cared for. Overburdened by the role of our protector, the ego has been tense, hyper-vigilant, constantly out to prove that we deserve the resources we consume. We know the results: social chaos and injustice; personal dissatisfaction, disconnection, fear and pain. We long for something better. We long for Oneness, and throughout the book and in many other ways, we have stretched for that state of consciousness. We have invited in divine energies that transform us; we have embraced paradigms that challenge our own thinking; we have engaged in self-awareness practices and healed old wounds that keep us in fear and separation.

And as we have taken all these steps and worked the platforms of this book, we have become more and more ready to become instruments of higher consciousness. How threatening this is to our old way of being. Instead of focusing on how we are different—better than, weaker, more or less needy, talented, virtuous, hard-working, valuable—we are learning to focus on our Oneness. Instead of being dominated by the consciousness of individual existence, we are being called to identify with the whole. Instead of experiencing ourselves first as individuals, we are coming to experience ourselves as aspects of the Oneness itself.

In other words, we are shifting our perspective entirely. This is tough. The ego has developed around our being different and separate; the ego has focused on proving our personal value; the ego thinks in terms of "me" and "my" survival. But now we realize that this is a trap. As individuals and as a collective, our survival requires us to think in terms of "we," and our individual and collective thriving depends upon our experiencing ourselves as part of a thriving whole.

If we have reached this moment of Becoming Becoming, we are making this radical shift not only in our thinking, but in our being. We get it: We are aspects of the universe in the process of evolution. When some great work is being accomplished by someone else, we can assert, "I did that," because we are part of the whole that accomplished that work. When we work in tandem with others who surpass us in some skill or gift, we can say, "We are strong, because we have one another's gifts." When we see one another being hurt or downtrodden, we can honestly acknowledge, "This hurts me," because when any part of the whole is damaged, the whole is threatened.

The ego, which has traditionally focused on how it is different and separate, is being retrained to gain joy from our collective power and value, because it identifies with the whole, rather than just with the fragment. The ego, which has traditionally been in the "No universe" is moving to the "Yes universe," and suddenly we are freed from the shame of existence.

We are one and each of us is an expression of the Oneness. When each of us comes to the planet, an aspect of consciousness comes into manifestation. That is who we are. And as we become manifest, we are confronted with our weaknesses, challenges and strengths. Our job is to embrace those weaknesses, challenges and strengths and overcome them. Whether a baby or an old woman facing death, whether a homeless person or the son of a king, we each are an experiment in consciousness, and we each need to learn from our experiences and participate in the collective transformation to shift into Oneness. The homeless person needs to feel Oneness, just as much as the indulged rich son.

As such, our needs are not a source of shame, whether those needs be for physical, emotional or spiritual resources, because these resources are required for us to do our job. If we are homeless, we need to embrace homelessness and seek transformational consciousness. If we are homeless because we are drinking, then we need to confront our addictions. If we are homeless because of unfairness, we need to avoid bitterness. If we are an overindulged rich kid, we need to discover the limits of satisfaction that comes from overindulgence and learn how to properly use the many resources available to us. Everything contributes to our evolution, and our evolution is part of the collective evolution. And that means that all our foolishness, mistakes and missteps along the way have been part of that transformational journey that is our destiny.

Now there is nothing more to prove. There is no cause for shame. There is nothing to do, except to embrace our lives and take on our part. As we said in the introduction to *Living with Reality*, I am meant to exist, and therefore I need to accept all the beneficial energies destined for me, including the experiences, resources and challenges that make me who I am and move me down my path.

And so, as we conclude this book, we see that we have solved the fundamental problem of our existence. As discrete ego-based entities, we are constantly needing to strive and prove; we are constantly full of fear and shame. As Oneness-based entities, we can relax into doing our part of the collective transformation and relax into the process of living. And with nothing left to prove, we can turn our attention to co-creating a better world guided by higher consciousness in which we all thrive.

What About Fear & Pain?

We started this book by acknowledging that life is a struggle and that fear and pain are natural. At the same time, throughout the book, we have also acknowledged how much needless fear and pain we cause ourselves and one another. We've come to realize that this needless fear and pain are caused by ego reactions and habitual patterns of reaction and response. We have begun to reprogram the ego and ourselves, so now, instead of making life tougher than it has to be, we are developing ways to support one another to solve our common problems and be happier and more fulfilled. We have committed to healing the old wounds and traumas that run us unconsciously, and we have started to develop self-awareness, embrace new paradigms and learn how to call upon higher consciousness to guide us into being more co-creative and mutually supportive.

We understand now why reality has been so hard to live with, but it doesn't have to be. We can eliminate needless fear and pain. And with love and support, with awareness and self-awareness, in a mutually supportive world, we can live with reality in a state of grace, because reality is awesome, amazing and full of unknown destinations far beyond the realms of our imagination. Let's do it.

Is That It?

The Ego

Wow, I think I get it. I am being twice born. Instead of dragging everybody down and resisting change, I could lead the charge, and we could all be happier.

Beth

Not exactly. You are part of the process of change, not the leader.

The Ego

Oh. But don't I get some kind of compensation, such as, I will be great, fulfill my potential, something?

Beth

Yeah. You get the compensation that you'll be doing your job, which is to evolve and support the evolution of consciousness and unleash the power of The Source. And you will be twice born. Isn't that enough?

The Ego

Oh. I guess so.

Beth

There is going to be an epilogue, a kind of wrap-up. Maybe you and the Dark Side would like to come. After all, you are evolving into consciousness itself.

The Ego

Yeah, I'd be interested in showing up. What about you Dark Side?

The Dark Side

Me? I'll be there.

EPILOGUE

Where We Have Come

If you've just finished this book, you may feel a bit disoriented. What exactly did we do? Where have we come? How did we get there?

Living with reality is a huge topic, too broad for any single volume. I could have expanded each chapter to a book, and I could have added many more platforms, such as Becoming Responsible or Becoming Allowing. In addition, in this book I haven't addressed many extremely important aspects of the human experience, such as sex and spirituality, money, food, racism, democracy, and parenting. But these topics must be left for other workshops and writings, as well as for other people to speak about.

This book was meant to give a foundation for our shifting relationship with others, with ourselves, and with the process of living itself, and it is my hope that we have made strides in those transformations. Let's review what we did accomplish:

In our introduction, "Ego, Instinct & Evolution," we developed self-compassion. We came to understand the origin of the ego and why it's constantly trying to prove our value. In the rest of the introductory chapters, we discussed reality and why it's so hard to live with, and we looked at some of the short-term fixes we've used but which haven't worked.

We moved from there to the Nine Platforms, the practices that can help alleviate the needless pain and fear that drive us by shifting our relationship with ourselves, one another, and the process of living. In the process, we changed our relationship with the ego, invited it and the Dark Side to evolve, and came into harmony with the process of living. Let's briefly summarize how we did that.

1. **Platform One: Becoming Oneness**, started us on the road to recovery. In it, we were given perspectives, tools, and practices to break out of our feelings of isolation and competition and bring us into a greater sense of Oneness.

2. **Platform Two: Becoming Differentiated**, built on the foundation of Oneness and revealed how we can avoid either merging or separating, so that we can begin to find ourselves. We began to learn how to connect to the energies that support us.

3. In **Platform Three: Becoming Co-Creative**, we learned about intention and allowance. We acknowledged how the universe really works, and broke from the belief that we either create reality or are its victim. We called upon ourselves to become conscious co-creators.

4. In **Platform Four: Becoming Mutually Supportive**, we came to understand our connection on a deeper level and realized that we are most happy and well when the collective is also thriving. We learned new ways to address our wants and desires and were given a tool that helps us turn our intention to supporting the highest good of all.

By the end of Platform Four, we have finished the first part of our book, and we understand our relation with one another in a new way. We no longer view one another as adversaries, but seek the comfort of Oneness. We start to feel safe with one another. Now we have to feel safe with ourselves, which was the work of the next section.

5. In **Platform Five: Becoming Self-Aware**, we started changing our relationship with ourselves by creating new self-knowledge and intimacy. In this platform, we started dismantling our old patterns of stimulus-reaction-response, and we began to further crack the mystery of our own behavior. The world became more comprehensible and, therefore, less scary.

6. In **Platform Six: Becoming Integrated**, we started to free ourselves so that we could become ourselves. We learned to release the perceived needs and ego-based drives that have run us and unbalanced us. We faced the domination of the ego head on.

7. **Platform Seven: Becoming Accountable**, helped us focus on the reality of the damage we do and gave us a tool to make amends. In addition, we increased our compassion and self-compassion as we learned about the influence of the Dark Side, including its Seven Dirty Secrets. We learned how to fight for ourselves and for consciousness in a way that works for us and for everyone, including the Dark Side.

By the time we have finished Platform Seven, we have become our own best friend, not because we flatter ourselves and hide our weaknesses, but because we know ourselves and start to achieve self-mastery. Real self-love becomes possible. This was the purpose of the second part of the book, to bring us into true intimacy and partnership with ourselves. Now we are ready for the third part of the program, the part where we learn to partner with life and relax into the process of living.

8. **Platform Eight: Becoming Not-Knowing**, helped us admit how little we actually know and gave us space to release the pretense that we do. It also opened us to the marvelous knowing that is actually possible when we release our thoughts, opinions, beliefs, and agendas. What a source of relaxation that is.

9. And finally, we came to **Platform Nine: Becoming Becoming**, where we moved from one level of the platform to another, and from one level of release and inspiration to another. We began to understand life as a transformational moment, which enabled us to let go of the stress of having to achieve some external or even internal agenda. We finally saw who we really are, part of the Oneness, being guided by The Source to do our part in the evolution of consciousness.

We became part of the process. We realized that we could live with reality with more grace and joy if we unleashed the power of higher consciousness, because reality is an amazing place when we unleash the creative power available to us. And we supported our egos to evolve, which supports all of consciousness to evolve.

Throughout this book, we have continually addressed our egos, either directly or indirectly; we have confronted and released shame; we have freed ourselves from the absurd idea that we are separate and alone and need to hide anything; we have learned a lot about freeing ourselves from needless pain; and we have become more and more available to the support of the higher vibrational energies available to us all. I also hope that along the way, we have become friends.

If you have read this book straight through, you will have absorbed the gist and considered new possibilities, and that alone would be a wonderful result. On the other hand, you will probably have missed a lot of content, and you will not have had time to delve into every exercise and adopt every tool.

So if you've read the book through, I would love to invite you to reread *Living with Reality*, now with the intention of working every platform, answering every question and bringing each new perspective, tool, and practice into your daily self-inquiry and way of living. Studying the book with a group brings immense rewards, as you and others bring these pages and words to life, filling in the many blanks and putting meat on their bones.

If you simply read the book, you will find some interesting perspectives. If you work the book, you will transform. If you live the book, you will become becoming and help others do the same.

Writing is a very challenging and sometimes arduous process, and yet when it comes to an end, there is a moment of loss, where we let go of the connection that we have had. In the spirit of Becoming Becoming, let The Source continue to live through you, me, and every one of us, let The Source continue to speak through you, me, and every one of us, and let us carry these teachings to others, until these teachings are no longer useful, because they have been replaced by greater wisdom and inspiration. Let's each do our part.

With love,

Beth Maynard Green

APPENDIX A

List of Tools

Living with Reality contains 20 specific tools and processes that help us deal with life's challenges. For your convenience, we have included them all in this appendix. In addition, we are offering two other tools that do not appear in the book but which have proved very helpful to people.

In this appendix, we first provide a list of the names of the tools and then we provide the tools themselves. Tools 1-20 are those that are included in the book and they are presented in the order of their appearance. Tools 21 and 22 are the additional tools that are not included in the book, but which are included for your reference.

LIST OF TOOLS

1. I Am That
2. Shifting Our Energy
3. The Mutual Support Tool: Asking for That Which Is for the Highest Good of All
4. How We Intervene Between Reaction and Response
5. How We Intervene Between the Stimulus and the Reaction
6. Intervening at the Level of the Stimulus
7. Whose Feelings Are They?
8. Tools for Strengthening Our Energy Body
9. Taking a Nightly Inventory of Ourselves
10. Release the Need
11. The Amends Process
12. Don't Be Lunch

THE TOOLS THEMSELVES

1. I Am That

When confronted by conduct that annoys, angers or perhaps even horrifies you, before responding with judgment, take a minute to connect to your self-honesty. Ask yourself how you do the same thing that is angering you to the other. Be scrupulously honest. While you may not do the behavior in exactly the same way, I bet if you look deep in your heart, you will see that you are more like that other person than you would care to acknowledge. Once you have grasped how you are like the other person, smile or laugh. Say to yourself, or share out loud, if possible, "I am that. I do that too." You can use the "I am that" tool in other ways also. When someone is sharing with you something painful about their life, look for the way you relate to that experience, and tell them that you've experienced that also. If someone admits some part of themselves they judge negatively, see if you can relate, and tell them "I am that, too." Do this, and it will revolutionize you and your relationships.

2. Shifting our Energy

Here are some ways we can shift our energy. If we're caught up in emotion or behavior that is destructive, let's:

- Give ourselves a time-out, just as if we were a child, in order to interrupt the energy.
- Lift our consciousness upward and reach for a higher understanding.

- Take a walk.
- Call a friend.
- Turn on music that energizes a different aspect of ourselves.
- Pray.
- Ask ourselves why we are reacting.
- Try to offer the energy we want to receive.

3. The Mutual Support Tool: Asking for That Which Is for the Highest Good of All

When confronted with the need to make a decision, from the simple to the most complex, whether the decision involves only one or all those present, do the following:

1. Calm your minds.
2. Let go of agendas and prejudices toward a certain outcome.
3. Feel yourselves lifting up for a higher consciousness.
4. Ask the question: Is it for the highest good of all, including me to do "x."
5. If you are asking for guidance for one member of the group, as opposed to asking for guidance for the collective decisions, the other members ask: Is it for the highest good of all, including me, for [the person in question] to do "x."
6. If you are unsure of the answer, or if members of the group get different answers, discuss the issues involved.
7. After the discussion, ask if it's for the highest good of all to ask again in that moment.
8. If yes, re-ask the question. You may get a completely different answer this time.
9. If you're not ready to ask again, have more discussion.
10. If you can't come to an intuitive consensus, let go of the question for the moment and come back to it when you have more information or more objectivity.

4. How We Intervene Between Reaction and Response

Taking a Breath and Confronting Ourselves. Once we have committed to questioning ourselves, our responses and our reactions, we need to start developing the practice. The reaction is the programmed feeling and the response is the behavior that is stimulated from that feeling. Intervening between the reaction and response means that we still have the feeling, but we act differently; more consciously. How do we do it?

1. Take a breath.
2. Ask ourselves why we are having the reaction.
3. Evaluate the response we wish to choose.

5. How We Intervene Between the Stimulus and the Reaction

Taking a Breath and Confronting Ourselves. Just as we can intervene between the reaction and the response, we can intervene between the stimulus and the reaction. Instead of just reacting we could:

1. Take a breath.
2. See what's stimulating our reaction.
3. Consider why we are having the unwanted reaction and support ourselves to change.

6. Intervening at the Level of Stimulus

Taking Responsibility for What We Choose. Sometimes the best way to eliminate a response is to eliminate or modify the stimulus that sets up the pattern. Briefly, here's how we do it:

1. Take a breath.
2. Identify the stimulus that's triggering a negative reaction and response.
3. Determine if there's some way to eliminate or modify it.

7. Whose Feelings Are They?

When we experience a feeling, we can talk to one another. We can say to each other, "I feel anger in the field. Whose anger is it?"

8. Tools for Strengthening Our Energy Body

1. Taking time to consider the right course of action

2. Meditation
3. Guided imagery
4. Yoga
5. Tai chi
6. Qi gong
7. LifeForce Inner Workouts
8. Martial arts
9. Any form of physical exercise
10. Thinking positively and optimistically
11. Sending out positive thoughts and channeling beneficial energy to others
12. Prayer
13. Music
14. Color combinations that support us to feel vibrant and alive
15. Nurturing yourself with healthy food, drink and air

9. Taking a Nightly Inventory of Ourselves

Every night before going to sleep, make a mental inventory of your behavior throughout the day. Ask yourself:

1. How did I behave?
2. Where was I reactive?
3. Why?

10. Release the Need

One of the major sources of fear and stress is our attachment to particular outcomes. When you feel stressed, try to identify what it is that you are feeling MUST happen. For example, I HAVE to get to this appointment on time, win this account, buy this house, or fit into a Size Two. When we are dominated by a wish or desire, we are filled with the fear that our wish will not be fulfilled, and that fear causes stress. In other words, we are unbalanced by the domination of what we perceive as a must-have need. Releasing the need for a particular outcome brings relaxation and wellbeing.

To use this tool, begin by finding the place in your body where you most feel the stress, press the fingers of one hand firmly against that location (for example, your heart, forehead or stomach), and say out loud **"I release the need to**———— (for example, get to the appointment on time/ win this account/ buy the house on Main Street/ become a Size Two)." Immediately after making this release statement, quickly dig out the fearful energy by brushing your fingers firmly against the spot on your body where you hold the stress. After releasing the negative energy with your hand, take in a deep breath to take in universal life force energy. When you release the breath, feel the relaxation. Do this process three times. This will help you release stress. After we release the need three times, it's best to breathe in positive neutral energy. For example, we do three releases of, "I release the need to buy the house on Main Street," and after the third release, we can say something like, "because I need to be happy where I live now," or "because I don't need to buy the house on Main Street," or "because I need to live where it is for the highest good of all." And then you take in a deep breath.

11. The Amends Process

Remember, first, we need to have self-compassion. Once we do, we approach the person we have hurt and explain that we would like to make amends. Then we use the following formulation: **"I realize now that I** ——————— (state exactly what you did, no more, no less) **and how that hurt you was that it** ———————." (Take your time with this part—allow yourself to feel the impact). **"And even though I couldn't have done any better at the time, I need to ask you to forgive me. Will you forgive me?"** Allow the person to respond if they want to. Don't skip steps! Only by being thorough can we free ourselves from the toxic shame that hurts us and/or makes us cover up our shame with resentment.

12. Don't Be Lunch

When you see yourself being dominated by negative energy, for example, either being dragged down by depression or pumped up by some righteousness or anger, think of yourself as food for some gremlin. Then laugh, and say to yourself, "Don't be lunch!" Sometimes, we're so dominated by negative energy, we're not just lunch; we're breakfast, lunch and dinner. If so, let's admit it.

13. See Hurtful People as Lunch

Visualize someone who is hurtful and whom you have seen as powerful. It could be a personal acquaintance, a boss, even a political figure. Then visualize that person as he or she really is, the host of some negative energy living off their life force, dining off their energy, and calling the shots. If it works for you, let yourself visualize some demon having them for lunch. Now we get it: these people are not powerful at all.

14. Sending Chi

When we are confronted by someone's negativity, we try to reach out to them, as we discussed before. But whether or not they accept our intervention, we have another tool to help: We point fingers two and three in their direction, as though we were aiming a gun. But this is not a gun to kill; it's loaded with our intention to support; it's loaded with chi.

15. How We Turn the Tables on the Dark Side

This tool takes off from a tool we learned earlier. When we are feeling overwhelmed and full of despair, that's probably a clue that we're in the grip of the Dark Side. In these moments, let's point our second and third finger to some imaginary energy field in front of us, and send it chi, life force energy. Just intending to send chi automatically connects us to The Source, and our connection to The Source decreases our vulnerability to the Dark Side.

Once we feel the power of our connection to The Source and our fingers are pointed forward, we think about the arena of life in which we feel blocked or defeated. We challenge ourselves not to throw in the towel, we send the Dark Side chi, and we say out loud, if possible:

"I know you're trying to make me feel [something appropriate], but I [again, whatever is appropriate], and I'm not going to let you stop me." There it is in a nutshell: fighting for ourselves.

16. Releasing Agendas for Specific Outcomes

If I identify that I have an agenda for a specific outcome, whether it is conscious, such as losing weight, or unconscious, such as making men look weak, I use the same tool. Let's use the example of making men look weak. I place my hand on the part of my body where I feel myself holding the stress of that agenda. Then I say, "All my life, I have been trying to prove that men are weak. I release the need to prove that men are weak, [I brush the area, as I do with every release step, and then I take in and release a big breath], and I return to The Source." As I say, "and I return to The Source," I open my arms, embrace the Source and I take another big breath. I surrender. It feels great!

17. Release a Life's Purpose

Let's say my life's purpose has been to save my mother. I felt guilty as a child because I saw her suffering and couldn't help her. Now the need to save my mother runs my life, impacts my marriage, and even affects all my relationships with people who remind me of her. She doesn't have to still be alive for that life purpose to dominate my life. Here's how I release it. I place my hand on the part of my body where I feel myself holding that purpose. Then I say, "My life's purpose has been to try to save my mother. I release the need to save my mother, [I brush the area, as I do with every release step and then take in and release a big breath], and I return to The Source." Again, I take in and release a big breath as I open my arms and embrace the beneficial energies available.

18. Some Tips to Develop Our Capacity to Be Guided

- Take a breath and get neutral.
- Focus on yes or no questions.
- Learn to distinguish yes and no through the inner voice, feeling states or other techniques that work for you.
- Don't use guidance to avoid inquiry or confrontation.
- Don't use the appearance of guidance to promote ego agendas.
- Remain self-aware and alert to ego games.

19. Remember to Ask

Ask guidance about everything. It will develop your neutrality and ability to access higher consciousness. It will also habituate you to asking, even when everything in you screams "No, I don't want to!"

20. Unleashing the Power of the Source

Whenever confronted with a choice, ask the following: "Will it most effectively unleash the power of The Source on this planet if I do 'x'?" You can substitute another word for "The Source," if you prefer, as long as it refers to the Oneness, higher consciousness, divine energy, universal chi, whatever is a power greater than yourself. When we use this tool, we are no longer addressing our decisions from the perspective of separate individuals who are coming together for mutual support. We are addressing our decisions from the perspective of the whole itself. We have surrendered the old perspective, the right to be instruments of our ego consciousness, and have embraced the new perspective, being instruments of divine consciousness.

21. Release a Person, Animal, Place or Even an Object

This tool is used to provide closure at the end of any kind of relationship, even a relationship with an object. It can be used whether the ending of the relationship is voluntary or involuntary, such as when someone has asked to leave a relationship with you, or when they have died and moved to the spiritual plane. The tool works equally well when you are letting go of a parent, lover, friend, or animal; or if you are graduating from school, leaving a geographic place, or letting go of a car or house. The process removes the blocks to moving on, because it acknowledges all that we have gained from the relationship, and it allows us to release any shame or regrets we are holding on to that have not yet been cleared. The result is a wonderful feeling of wholeness and appreciation for the experience that is passing, and it clears the space emotionally and energetically for both parties to move toward their next life experience. When doing the process without a partner because the other person is not emotionally or physically available, or when doing the process with a place or object that cannot speak, open yourself to your intuitive knowing. Ask yourself, if I were that house or car, or person, for example, what would I feel and say.

Here are the steps to take:

1. Begin with yourself, or intuit who should begin, if you are doing this process with another person.

2. Speaking directly to the other person, animal, place or object, apologize for the ways you hurt the other person or object (with an object, for example, it could be that you neglected it, for example, or took it for granted). Take your time, and go deep. Use the words "I'm sorry for . . ." or "I'm sorry that I . . ." Do this until it feels complete, feeling compassion for yourself throughout the process.

3. Now the second person does the same to you. If you're doing this with an animal or object, intuit how they might have hurt you. Don't worry. It will come to you.

4. Having expressed regret on both sides, the first person starts the next stage of the process. Connect to your gratitude for all that the other person, object, place or animal gave you. Say "Thank you for . . ."

5. Have the second person thank you. Again, intuit the consciousness of the person, animal, place or object if it cannot speak for itself, as it thanks you for your love or care, for helping it fulfill its purpose, etc. Do this until the process feels complete.

6. Back to you or the first person to speak. Say, "For all the ways you have helped me that I know and I don't know, I thank you." The other being acknowledges your thanks.

7. The other person or consciousness says the same, and you acknowledge their thanks.

8. Then both say in turn, "For all the ways that I hurt you that I know and I don't know, I ask your forgiveness. Will you forgive me?" And both say yes.

9. Both then say in turn, "I forgive and I ask your forgiveness."

10. Finally, the first person says "I release you, I release you, I release you." The second person or consciousness says, "I release you, I release you, I release you."

The process is now complete. I realize that you have forgiven and asked for forgiveness one additional time at the end. This is part of the total release that we need in order to go on with our lives.

22. The Seven Dirty Secrets of the Dark Side

1. The Dark Side is the constellation of negative energies that need a host to survive. Don't be lunch!
2. The Dark Side runs the planet through our complicity.
3. Don't try to fight the domination of the Dark Side alone.
4. Don't fight against the Dark Side; fight for yourself.
5. The best way to fight the domination of the Dark Side is to empower it.
6. The Dark Side does not run the planet; The Source does, and The Source uses the Dark Side to promote evolution.
7. The Dark Side needs us to fight for ourselves, so that it can evolve into consciousness and return to The Source.

APPENDIX B

Letter from The Stream
August 2011

Dear Reader,

This book is the product of more than nine years of interaction between Beth Maynard Green and us, members of The Stream. As Beth explained in the preface, theory is not enough. We need to make the principles a living practice, and we would like to tell our story of this experiment.

When we started the process, many of us were already honest enough to know that we needed help. We wanted individual healing in order to "fix" ourselves and provide relief from the pain, fear, and anxiety we were experiencing in our daily lives. Others of us believed that we were already transformed and that Beth would help us find new ways to "manifest our good"—in whatever ways we defined that—in career, relationships, money, recognition, status, you name it.

Looking back, we can now see that all of us were caught up in the illusion of separation. We thought that we could fix "me" and forget about the world. We wanted individual success and happiness and thought we could achieve it for ourselves, while others suffered.

Through practicing the principles outlined in this brilliant book, we have dropped this perspective. We have grown from being "ego centered" to being "Oneness centered" and have shifted the locus of our attention from "me" to the whole. In other words, we have realized that we cannot be the only clean drop of water in a polluted stream, just as much as we cannot have the only house in Los Angeles that doesn't have smog over it or the only stable economy when so many of others are faltering. Oneness is no longer a concept to us, but the reality of who we are—a reality that we support one another to embrace on a daily basis.

It's simple, but it hasn't been easy, and we're just beginning to acknowledge this. Oneness goes against everything the ego has taught us: that we have to look out for ourselves and protect ourselves from others, from any perceived threat to our survival. We have had to give up believing that what we need is more and more comfort. We've had to redefine what it means to be happy. Happiness is not arriving at some vision or some point or achieving some status. It is the sense of relaxation that comes from belonging to the Oneness and seeing ourselves as intertwined with everyone else instead of being focused on our own personal salvation.

To get there, we've had to understand the origins of the ego, see why we are so ego driven and have compassion for ourselves for being this way. We've had to recognize that it's not our fault, but it is our responsibility and as a result we've surrendered to the reality that our journey to Oneness consciousness has to take place on every level: the mental/emotional, the physical and the spiritual. And that means we must change the way we think, the way we feel and even the way we are on an energetic plane. And that means total commitment.

Following is a collection of voices from members of our community, expressing the various ways that they have transformed as a result of applying the *Living with Reality* principles and tools in their daily lives. Our sharings are very honest, and we hope these stories inspire you to give this program a try.

Public Relations Director: I Want to Change the World

I want to change the world. And I know I am not alone.

When I was one to five years old, we lived in a suburb of Washington D.C. called Springfield, Virginia. My mother was/is Japanese and my father white. We were an anomaly and my mother kept to herself a lot, already having been hurt by the prejudices and racism she had experienced—from the priest who refused to baptize my older half-Japanese brother, to the apartment manager who refused to lease my parents a place because my mom was Japanese. My mom kept her pain and shame to herself, trying to project a public image of being a good Japanese person to protect herself from further slight. Her isolation added to her pain and, even at a young age, I noticed this.

Fortunately for our family, the Civil Rights Movement was in swing and it was bringing awareness and awakening to a broader and broader group of Americans about the rights of all people and how we as a country had damaged others based on self-preservation and unwillingness to change.

Our world is different now, but in many ways it is the same, in the way that we still excessively invest in our self-preservation—looking out for ourselves, our families, our careers and our businesses regardless of how it might hurt others or even ourselves. I include myself in this, and here's what I see playing out:

- Among parents, I see us raising our children to compete with one another versus supporting each others' children to all fulfill their potential.
- In the business world, I see competitiveness among colleagues and micro-focus on individual security as opportunities for broader positive change go by.
- In the PR industry, I see energy invested in preserving reputation that could be contributed to transparency and public authenticity for organizations that could support real change to occur.
- Among friends I see an unwillingness to be real, open and honest for fear of rejection and reactions.
- In relationships I see people settling for co-existence when deeper love is possible and real.

These are the types of issues I've been working to change, as have a group of others who have become my friends and family in The Stream. We share a commitment to higher consciousness, higher consciousness being the willingness and ability to see things as they are, not from the perspective of the ego, but from the perspective of the whole. We have been inspired by the changes we have seen in ourselves and each other. If you feel called to do so, please join us!

Business Consultant and Web Designer: Coming Together

I grew up in a family in which there was little real love between my parents. My mom and dad married following an unexpected pregnancy and stayed together out of obligation for nine years before divorcing. While I have compassion for both of my parents and the choices they felt forced into, I can see how their lack of connection created an environment in which I felt very insecure. At the same time, I saw my father, a talented set decorator for TV and film, model "power" for me, which looked like being important, arrogant and forceful. That part was all ego, and yet it formed the template for my behavior as I sought to fill the void of my insecurity by either acting important or desperately seeking validation from others and trying to get them to like me.

Like many young adults, while I was in college, I began a journey of transformation. It started with reading Alan Watts, who popularized Zen Buddhism for Westerners. It crescendoed with a weekend workshop that introduced me to the notion and felt experience of transformation. (This was before I was introduced to The Stream.) In that workshop, I was touched by my connection to the whole, by the inherent unity and interconnectedness of humanity and all of life. Not surprisingly, I wasn't able to sustain that fundamental truth and make it the essence of my thinking and behavior.

In fact, for most of the 20 years following that experience, my transformation was focused on me: how I could get ahead, how "impressive" my transformation made me, how I needed to take care of myself and my small sphere of friends and family, and protect myself by not challenging myself or others to confront business as usual. I thought I was transformed, and although I did help people, for far too much of the time I was dominated by instinct and ego: by platitudes, by being liked and validated, by disconnection, fear, self-righteousness and self-loathing. Yet, this isn't just my story, it's our story: humanity's story, and it's time to rewrite the story.

For the first time in human history, we are facing challenges that necessitate our coming together as an entire human family: climate change, species extinction, clean water, the widening gap between rich and poor, and the fact that every living system of earth is in decline and the simple but painful reality that we are still hurting each other and ourselves.

About nine years ago, my story began to change when I was introduced to Beth Maynard Green and the community she founded, The Stream, whose members firmly, yet compassionately, have confronted me on my self-protective, ego-based behavior. They've helped me to see into my past, understand and heal the sense of separation that is at the core of my dysfunctions. Through this collective effort, we have all been amazed at how much we've evolved. We've become more relaxed, happy, and most importantly, able to consistently act in ways that support the whole, which includes ourselves. We definitely mess up, but we support one another daily to fight for connection instead of separation, to fight for wholeness instead of withdrawal—with our friends, our colleagues, our families, with everyone. We change our world by changing ourselves; we change ourselves by changing our world. I invite you to join us!

Teacher of At-Risk Kids: No More Excuses

All my life, I have spent a lot of time making excuses to prevent me from taking risks and offering leadership when it was needed, to protect me from the disappointment that comes from investing in others and recognizing that no matter how hard I worked, I couldn't "save" everyone who needed me, especially the kids. In order to protect myself from that pain, I withheld bringing all of who I am and all that I have learned into the classroom and to my relationships, and it cost me dearly. It cost my students as well. A few years ago, I realized that despite my fears, I needed to do more. I knew it would be no small challenge, but I also knew that I owed it to myself, my students and to everyone in my life to face whatever was blocking me and do everything I could to overcome it.

In order to dedicate myself to this path of consciousness, meaning that I was committing to becoming more aware of the impact of my thoughts, words, and actions on myself and others, I joined the staff and Board of Directors of The Stream, a non-profit spiritual educational center located close-by in Bonsall, California (north of San Diego). As I began working with the fantastic group of individuals I found there, along with our fearless leader and gifted spiritual teacher, Beth Maynard Green, I began to transform. Despite my resistance and residual fears and unconscious patterns, I realized that I truly was beginning to change! I'm now planning more creative lessons for my students. I'm becoming more honest in my relationships, and able to connect more deeply with others. I'm finding the confidence to fight for myself and become a better advocate for my students, and I find my compassion for them growing, along with a newfound ability to challenge them to greater heights of achievement and self-awareness. I've also found that there are many others who share this desire and passion for personal and professional growth, and that my own growth is accelerated tremendously by the mutual support that we offer one another along the path. I am amazed at the potential of the human spirit, and the power of what we can do together when we unite along the path of healing and transformation!

Considering the tremendous challenges we are facing at this time, the need for conscious teachers has never been greater. As my consciousness grows, I realize that every word I say, every action I take or withhold, every thought has a tremendous impact on our youth and on everyone around me. We can help the youth in our lives by helping ourselves: by releasing old patterns that keep us stuck in life and prevent us from reaching new heights of personal and professional growth. We can take care of our minds, bodies and spirits so that we can be a vehicle for the power of transformation. What can be more inspiring than that?

Marriage and Family Therapist: Facing Reality with Courage, Compassion and Consciousness

I want to be a healthier, happier person and I want to make a difference in the world by helping others do the same, because I know that we will not be able to really change unless everyone does. We cannot have a world without pain and addictive behaviors unless we all stop believing that they work. Some of us were born to hear the call to higher consciousness; some have heard it later in life. Some may not hear the call. If you are one of those who hears that call or might be open to it now, this message is for you.

My journey started with anxiety about just about everything in life. I tried to cover it up with food, relationships, alcohol, shopping, decorating, whatever my ego told me to try that day. In the end, I always found the cover-up empty. I craved a feeling of wholeness. My spiritual/emotional adventure began in the 80's when I found The Stream and it's been quite a ride. I've found out things about myself and others that I didn't think I wanted to know (namely that the ego has dominated my life and the earth and that we'll never be happy until we overcome that domination), but that have set me free to be more and more the happy, healthy person I always wanted to be. Increasingly, people are awakening to the knowledge that we all have to change for the world to change. We cannot have peace within until we have peace on earth. We cannot be the only house in LA without smog or the only drop of pure water in a polluted river. You can make an amazing difference to yourself and all those around you by changing your consciousness. And there is no time to lose; the earth and humanity are suffering so terribly.

As a result of the diligent work I've done in The Stream all these years, I am able to face reality with courage, compassion and consciousness, rather than hide in my addictive, ego-based behaviors from the past. This strength was truly tested recently when I found that my closest sister's only child had died of a drug overdose. I was understandably sad, shocked and concerned, but I felt calm and connected to myself, those around me and the Source. I felt my sister's gut-wrenching pain. I felt the overwhelming loss experienced by my deceased nephew's long-time girlfriend. On the way to meeting with his closest friends and families, I had gotten support from The Stream and relied on the principles and practices. So I felt calm and connected to the divine energies and consciousness that can guide us all. I offered to do a gratitude and release process for those grieving and they all gratefully accepted. As he lay still in his bed, we all thanked him and apologized to him and released him. The people at his bedside all appreciated my spiritual strength and emotional support, and I was honored to bring it. That began a several-week's long journey of doing healing sessions with a variety of groups and leading two memorials for him.

During these processes, I felt the Oneness of all gathered more than ever. I felt the power of the work I've done and the support that I receive and the guidance from above that is always with me. I felt blessed to be able to support the community in this way. I feel prepared to support my daughter as she goes through the challenging journey to stay sober and face reality and connect to God; the same journey that faces all of us, really. I have what it takes to support my sister and others as they face what is surely one of the most painful occurrences in life and the struggle to reconnect to a world without her child. I feel honored to be able to help my nephew's 13-year-old daughter as she faces the loss of her beloved father. I have what it takes because I will never stop doing the work. I will always go toward my own conscious evolution and I will work to strengthen my connection to the divine guidance and energy that we all need.

Through thick and thin, through all the many challenges of life, I can say that I love my life today. As my sister struggles to find a new reality, I have never felt closer to her. My marriage has never been better, facing all these challenges and others. It's all true because of the work and because of the amazing support I receive from the people and the programs and the tools and techniques of The Stream.

These are a fraction of the stories you could hear at The Stream. As you can see from the experiences of those in our community, we have found that the principles of Living with Reality are applicable to every area of life. Our sincere hope is that this book will support others as it did us, to co-create communities of people committed to higher consciousness who will help to usher in a new era—one in which we can transcend the domination of the ego and support one another meet the challenges of everyday life with grace, humility, and a commitment to supporting what is for the highest good of all, including ourselves. We welcome you, fellow travelers, on the path of not-knowing, and invite you onto a journey of a lifetime!

Many of The Stream's offerings are available globally via the Internet. If you are interested in learning about our work, please check out our website: www.thestream.org.

ABOUT BETH MAYNARD GREEN

L ord, make me an instrument of thy peace" is the opening line of a prayer attributed to St. Francis but which may have been written by a humble French priest in the early 20th century. Whoever wrote the prayer, its message is searing, because it reminds us to focus less on ourselves and more on service; to seek to understand rather than to be understood; to console rather than to be consoled.

Like most of us, Beth Maynard Green fluctuates in between: between divine inspiration and ego domination; and her latest book, *Living with Reality,* reflects her compassion for the struggle to become more consistent in the practice of Oneness consciousness. Born in New York City in 1945, Beth became concerned about human suffering at a very early age, which led her to dedicate herself to social activism at the age of 9. As such, she participated whole heartedly in the ban the bomb movement, the anti-Vietnam War campaign, and both workplace and community organizing. This thrust of social activism culminated in her service as the West Coast Coordinator of the Wages for Housework Campaign from 1974 to 1978, which was her last effort to change the world through political means. In 1978, at the age of 33, she felt emotionally and spiritually bankrupt and was suddenly blessed by a spiritual awakening, ultimately leading to a full-blown psychic awakening in 1980.

Since 1980, Beth has been a spiritual teacher, as well as an intuitive counselor, ever seeking more powerful modalities to help people heal from life's traumas and overcome ego-based thinking. In 1983, she founded The Stream, www.thestream.org. Originally designed to integrate the 12-step programs, psychology and spirituality, The Stream dissolved in 1986, but was followed by several other efforts to promulgate the teachings and healing modalities that Beth was channeling from higher consciousness.

In 1999, The Stream was born again, and today it is a flourishing spiritual community as well as a non-profit educational corporation.

Beth's approach to transformation centers on both healing emotional wounds and shifting paradigms, so that we can all become more guided by higher consciousness. This approach is evident in all her teachings and writings, starting back in the early 1980s. Entering every situation with a blank mind, Beth relies on her capacity to access higher consciousness to lead all her work—from individual counseling and business consulting, to her writings, music, talks and workshops, which have ranged over many topics, including food, money, parenting, and sex & spirituality. In addition to her intuitive gifts, Beth brings her capacity to channel powerful spiritual energies, and she offers these energies through her mind-body-spirit exercise program called LifeForce: The Inner Workout, which is available daily on the internet at www.lifeforceworkout.com.

In 2011, Beth's work took another turn. She and her new husband, James Maynard Green founded the Center for Healing & Higher Consciousness: Psycho-Intuitive Services & Training. Through this center, they are offering even more effective counseling and consulting services, which blend intuition, hypnotherapeutic techniques and other modalities that support people in deep healing and transformation. In addition, the center trains and certifies lay people and professionals alike, who wish to become practitioners of their pioneering psycho-intuitive modalities.

Always concerned with bringing higher consciousness into all arenas of life, in 2011 Beth also co-founded Reality for a Change: Transformative Processes for Business, www.realityforachange.net. Reality for a Change focuses on transforming the human dynamics limiting the ability of businesses and organizations to be responsive, creative and effective in delivering quality products and services in a mutually supportive environment.

All of Beth's work is informed by the principles and practices contained in the *Living with Reality* book, which also provides the foundation of The Stream spiritual community, www.thestream.org, and its transformational program Consciousness Boot Camp, www.consciousnessbootcamp.org. In addition, the book is a fundamental text for The Center for Healing and Higher Consciousness, www.healingandhigherconsciousness.com.

Under the name Beth Green, Beth has published four books in addition to *Living with Reality*: two works of fiction—*The Autobiography of Mary Magdalene* and *Memoirs of the New Age*—and two works of nonfiction—*God's Little Aphorisms* and *Sacred Union: The Healing of God*.

All her books are available at Amazon.com, as are two out of three of her CDs of original music: *The Gift of Peace, A Soul's Journey Through Darkness & Light* and *In the Mist.* In addition, Beth's articles and blogs have been published in a variety of venues, including *The Huffington Post* and the *Forum on Science & Spirituality,* edited by Prof. Ervin Laszlo. The latter blog will be appearing in the upcoming book *Science and Spirituality—A Conversation Between Twenty-eight Leading Scientists and Renowned Spiritual Leaders,* edited by Profs. Ervin Laszlo and Kingsley D. nnis.

Like most of us who have lived long enough, Beth has been humbled an 1 crafted by life. Throughout her own challenging existence, including chronic and severe illness since the age of 15, Beth has continued to stretch her own inner capacities so that she might become more and more the instrument of divine consciousness envisioned in the prayer of St. Francis of Assisi. She is also continually aiming to co-create more powerful healing modalities. Not only does she work with her husband, who contributes his hypnotherapeutic skills and access to spiritual energies; in group settings, she and James also call upon the gifts of workshop participants and bodyworkers to increase the depth and breadth of transformation.

Outside of her work, Beth lives a quiet life in a rural part of San Diego County, where she enjoys the companionship of her spiritual community, her husband and her two dogs. To learn more about Beth and her very diverse work, please see the website of The Stream, www.thestream.org, as well as the Center for Healing & Higher Consciousness, www.healingandhigherconsciousness.com, and her own personal website, Beth's Place, www.bethsplace.org.